AF527797

Systems of Rural Settlements in Developing Countries

Systems of Rural Settlements in Developing Countries

R.B.MANDAL

CONCEPT PUBLISHING COMPANY NEW DELHI-110059

ISBN 81-7022-203-6

First Published 1989

Ram Bahadur **Mandal** (*b*. 1948.   )

Published by
Ashok Kumar MIttal
Concept Publishing Company
A/15-16, Commercial Block, Mohan Garden
NEW DELHI-110059 (India)

Lasertypeset by
Microtech Advance Printing System (Pvt) Ltd.
H-13, Bali Nagar, New Delhi-110015

Printed by
D.B. Offset Works
B-218, Naraina Ind. Area
New Delhi-110028

PREFACE

The grouping and arrangement of houses in rural area is known as the rural settlement. In the field of geography rural settlement study comes under Human geography. It explains cultural phenomena, economic development and environmental accountability of rural ecological conditions available for human living.

In developing countries the systems of rural settlements are quite different in comparison with urban settlements and the situations available in developed countries. In this book the main thrust is on analysing the origin & evolution of rural urban linkages, national settlement system, satellite villages, village viability assessment, resettlement schemes along with the regional conditions available in Tangania, India, Israil, Pakistan, Zambia, Cuba and others.

This book has been designed to be acceptable to geographers in particular and the social scientists in general, and hence quantitative cum descriptive approaches have been adopted towards analysing the spatial concepts of rural settlements. I hope specialists, students and general readers will like it as a basic text on rural development & planning.

The author expresses obligations to the valuable suggestions of Professor T.G. Jorden, Chairman of North Texas University and retired Professor K.H. Stone of the University of Georgia, U.S.A. I am grateful to Dr. P.S. Maro and Dr. Allan Armstrong both of the Department of Geography, University of dar-es Salaam for their criticisms and suggestions along with Dr. B. Thakur of the University of Delhi and Dr. V.N.P. Sinha of Patna University who are my real source of inspiration in goading the destiny of this book.

I never forget the help redered by my respectable teacher and supervisor of this work Prof. L.N. Ram and Prof. P. Dayal of Patna University. In the field of computations and data programming the help rendered by Dr. S.D. Sharma of Rajendra Agricultural University are highly commendable. Constructive criticisms and suggestions are invited for further modification of this work.

Ram Bahadur Mandal

September
24.9.1988.

Department of Geography
R.D. & D.J. College
Munger-811201
Bihar, India.

CONTENTS

LIST OF TABLES

LIST OF FIGURES

ONE

NATURE OF RURAL SETTLEMENT GEOGRAPHY

The studies of rural and urban settlements are two areas that constitute the discipline of Settlement Geography which itself is a recent branch of Human Geography. Settlement geography is a study of the form of the cultural landscape.[1] It is a science of systematic inquiry of occupancy features distributed over space with differentiation in relation to man. The minutest detail of the distribution of population manifests itself in the form of grouping of houses scattered at places and agglomerated at others. Siedlungs Geographie[2] is a German word that represents the concept of settlement geography and the cultural landscape developed by man in the process of occupancy. Doxiadis[3], the architect of the capital city of Islamabad in Pakistan, used the Greek word *Ekistics* which again means the science of settlement.

Rural settlement, as man's living and functional space, dots the countryside since prehistoric times and forms an integral part of the human life. A rural settlement, as the point of origin and primary residence of human society, is the linking thread and life blood of all geographical studies. Therefore, the consideration of settlement runs like a thread through almost the whole fabric of geographic thought.[4]

Many European and other scholars have contributed substantially to this branch of geographical knowledge. Ritter(1779 - 1859) was the pioneer of the geographical study of rural settlement. But the history of systematic study of rural settlement goes back to the twenties of the present century when scholars like Paul Vidal de la Blache, Aurousseau, Ahlmann, Demangeon, Brunhes and others started laying foundations of the branches of settlement geography. The appointment of the Commission on Types of Rural Habitation[5] under the auspices of the International Geographical Union, however, is a iandmark in making definite beginnings in the study of rural settlement geography. Its first report published in 1928 aroused much interest among geographers.[6] But the science of human settlement still continues to be in an experimental stage. Despite numerous studies made in many parts of the world, no general law has been formulated so far which can be universally applicable and is 'comparable to the principles of location in industrial geography and nationalism in political geography.[7] Besides, geographical, the economic, and social conditions obtaining in India are very different from those found in Europe and America. The present study, therefore, may open up new avenues for the study of settlements under Indian conditions and may also indicate a few principles applicable, if not universally, at least to the geographical conditions obtaining in developing countries of the world.

Definitions:

Settlement is the topographic expression of the grouping and arrangement of two fundamental elements houses and highways - Brunhes.[8]

Settlements refer to the grouping of peoples and houses into hamlets, villages, towns and cities - Dicken and Pitts.[9]

Rural settlement is the spatial differentiation of the grouping of houses and highways in rural areas where social cohesion and cultural ties are strengthened according to the needs of the society and mankind - R.B. Mandal.[10]

Settlements of the rural areas is a sign of extensive use of land, or it may be an extension of the city resulting from the development of the commuter train and the private motor car - Wibberley.[11]

Settlement is defined as the place where one person or more

dwells regularly, or the act of establishing a permanent residence - K.H.Stone.[12]

Generally rural settlements are studied in terms of their location, site, situation, dispersion, form, function, size and hierarchy. An example will illustrate all these terms. Settlement M is located at the confluence of two rivers, the site consists of the flood plains of the rivers and high terraces of the foothills and the settlement is situated along the southern side of national way. It is a compact settlement with clustered houses amidst agricultural tract. The form is square with streets crossing at right angles as grid-iron pattern, the function is to collect farm products from the surrounding area, the size of the settlement is small just 400 persons spread over two hectares of land in 100 family groupings or households. In terms of hierarchy, it is a lower order village of 30th rank in the Block or Ward administrative unit.

The rural settlements had a millenial tradition of aiding each other and working together. No dogmatic stalinist mass collectivization ruined the rural structure.[13] But recently in many countries, the rapid population growth has further aggravated the problems of poverty, unemployment and inequality in rural and urban areas. In India, the main focus of development is widely accepted especially on meeting the basic human needs of the entire population, rather than on providing western levels of consumption to a privileged minority, rural inhabitants.

It is essential to define ecology and ecosystem. According to Webster New International Dictionary, 1950, ecology is biologically defined as the "natural relationship between organisms and their environment", which conforms with an early definition of ecology by Hackel in 1886. Later on, developed the new school of thought which emphasized the importance of man the dominant organism within the ecological system and thus the terms 'social ecology' and 'human ecology' developed. In the present context of rural settlement study, ecology will be used to consider as the reciprocal relations between man and environment.

The term 'ecosystem' was first of all introduced by Tansley (1935)[14] to mean the system resulting from the integration of all living and non-living factors of an environment. Here ecosystem is considered as a functional unit consisting not only of man but also the system of society within an environment of specific areas. It is a structural unit therefore, an ecosystem varies in size like a village, a block, a district and a physical regional unit.

AIMS OF HUMAN SETTLEMENTS

Aristotle described that 'happiness and safety are the main aims of cities and other human settlements'.[15] But it is difficult to identify happiness and physical safety besides safeguards from exploitation and fear. These two words of 'happiness and safety' have a direct help in planning. One way of measuring happiness may be 'the quantity of satisfaction felt by man, as seen in his different aspects'.[16] According to Doxiadis a frame for measuring human happiness may be in terms of his body, mind, sense, intelligence and soul. It should be based on the 'interplay of man and environment which is a dynamic balance, a balance which he can reach without endangering the happiness of others'.[17] Hence, the sole aim of settlement planning should be the welfare of mankind and the development of people and the society beginning from the grass root level. In terms of good human settlements, the future provision should satisfy the housing needs without adversely affecting the relationship between man and nature or without disturbing the legitimate interest of other social groups. In case this standard is accepted as norms of analysis and decision making, then the investigators role is to determine the biological needs of man, such as clean air, water and food; his psychological needs i.e., satisfaction, contentment, prestige, privacy, choice, freedom and security of life and property, besides interactions with other development and cultural phenomena.

Nowadays besides accepting above norms, the others are **scientific** i.e. the standards of settlement designed in a systematic way; cultural i.e., **cultural** feasibility and requirements and **social** i.e., improvement in the quality of life of downtrodden masses of the society. In practice these three dimensions should be amalgamated so that the standards become a balanced cognition of scientific, cultural and social principles, suitable to the place, time, culture, economy and technological advancement of the society. The standard should be such which is 'scientifically desirable, culturally feasible and socially acceptable'.[18]

The objective of this study is to highlight the spatial organization of rural settlements and service centres in the Bihar Plain and some other regions of the world in its totality and suggest some measures for its planning, particularly with a view to checking the present situation of haphazard natural growth to allow utilization of available limited amount of natural resources. In brief following are the objectives of this study:

(a) Maintenance of social equality, security and increase of protected living space;

(b) Provision of habitable residential houses to each family and estimation of its shortage;

(c) Best possible utilization of available limited resources of land and infrastructure facilities;

(d) Provision of a decent living to the ever-increasing population based on fixed and finite limited resources;

(e) Safety from the rigours of climatic hazards and communicable diseases;

(f) Increasing the accessibility, approachability and provision of highways and service facilities through growth points, growth centres and growth poles in a systematic manner.

Significance of Study

Most of the settlement planning studies undertaken in the past have been concerned with the economics of urbanization and its related problems. Rural settlement planning has long been a neglected branch of the subject. Only recently a need for such studies has been increasingly apparent in response to three major trends. Firstly, the demand for raw materials and consumer goods by large modern urban centres as central places has impinged increasingly on rural and sub-urban zones. Consequently, an imperative need has been felt in changing both the socio-economic life of the rural population and also the pattern of land utilization. In such a situation, it is essential for our general well-being that the modifications which will take place in rural areas should be guided rationally. Secondly, there has emerged a growing demand for residential houses along with the provision of adequate transport facility. This needs to be based on the changing technology in agricultural sector, so that this may ensure the economic viability of our rural settlements in future. This is perhaps the more urgent problem in Third World Countries. Thirdly, in many rural areas, on smaller settlement site, the rudimentary houses have been built in such a congested manner, that the eradication of these rural slums by shifting houses from the central site to the peripheral zone of settlement or near farming site is necessary in addition to remodelling and reconstructing houses on central site of the village.

In planning and spatial organization of rural settlements, a number of authors have recently stressed purely locational relationships of rural settlements, working on the premises that the spatial distribution of human activity reflects an ordered adjustment to the factor of distance, that locational decisions are generally taken so as to minimise movements, and that all locations are endowed with a degree of accessibility but some locations are more accessible than others. This happens due to the varying locations of land, water, building materials and fuel in space which exert varying pulls on the location of settlements, distorting a theoretically regular distribution of settlements in a planned way.

DYNAMICS OF RURAL SETTLEMENT LOCATION AND FUNCTIONING

With the assumption of ubiqutous availability of plain land for the location of settlement, water and clean air, following are the dynamics of rural settlements which constrained at any place by the systems of agriculture, livestock rearing, congregation of people, number of houses, modes of highways and market factors under the process of feedback mechanism (Fig.1.1).

1. **Agriculture** :

The growth and development of agriculture guides the functional activities, and is the income base for rural settlements. On the other hand, types and patterns of rural settlements determine the mode of agriculture. Agriculture provides food to the livestock and people living in rural and urban areas. On the other hand, population and livestock help in cultivating the land for the production of food crops. Market centres provide fertilizer and high yielding variety of seeds to the agriculture sector whereas agriculture provides raw materials to the market oriented industrial centres.

2. **Livestock**: Livestock and human being in conjunction together give rise to pastoral settlements and skin roofed huts or tents in both hot and cold deserts of the world. On the other hand, rural settlements provide place of safety to the livestock. Livestock supplies protein to human being whereas people serve as rancher to the livestock.

3. **Population**: Population as the greatest resource activises all the resources of the rural settlement system. Population is the creator of houses, and on the other hand houses provide safety from environmental hazards to people. Rural settlement is the mainstay of people whereas population determines the size of rural settlements.

4. **Houses**: It is an essential component for rural settlement, whereas rural settlements provide proper siting conditions for houses. Highways provide frontage for the location of houses besides determine the morphological characteristics of rural settlements in conjuction with the houses.

5. **Highways**: Highways provide linkage of one settlement with the other whereas settlements provide nodes for route network to the highways. Highways give trade routes to the market, but the size and income base of the market decide the intensity of flow of goods, people and traffic on a particular route.

6. **Market**: Market supplies consumer goods to the rural settlements in the surrounding zone of influence, whereas rural settlements in conjunction with population and agriculture provide labour force, food and raw materials for industries to the market.

FIELD OF STUDY

Rural settlement means the totality of human community in rural areas with all the social, material, organizational, spiritual and cultural elements that sustain a community. These elements may be spelt out in terms of physical requirements for housing, work, energy supply, transport, communication, water availability and sanitation; services for education, health protection and welfare; systems of territorial organization, government, law, economic management and cultural facilities for art, recreation, leisure etc., with factors like the growing population, increasing migration from rural to urban areas, demand of habitations for rehabilitation of displaced persons, etc., widens the scope of rural settlements and requires an integrated approach for their solution.

Permanent settlement is a distinct phase of civilized life. The nomadic and semi-nomadic people of early prehistoric times led an unsettled life. They depended for their livelihood on hunting and fishing etc., wherein permanent settlement was unthinkable. The change in the pattern of life from that of constant wandering to one with permanent agriculture on a fixed piece of land marks the origin of the settled life. The character and pattern of settlements in any region are very intimately linked with the organization and practice of agriculture, its historic evolution and the cultural advancement of people inhabiting it.

Habitations, like any other cultural trait, evolve through both time and space. They, inevitably, carry within themselves some hidden and apparent characteristic elements of their times and areas. Hence, they provide us with one of the most readily available forms of synthesis, the temporally changing patterns of the inter-regional and intra-regional character of the cultural landscape. As settlements have an enormous range of variations in terms of their attributes and they also vary along with physical and cultural elements of particular areas, all of them can be closely integrated to give character to diverse areas.

While natural resources and economic development are integral parts of the establishment and growth of settlements, other associated factors are elements of cultural geography, cultural history, culture processes, culture ecology and culture area as well as locally significant factors like typology, distribution, variation, integration and area characterization.[19] The study of settlements has great significance, especially in the field of analytical study of the distributional pattern of population, with special reference to size and spacing of rural settlements.[20]

Settlement geography, deals with the facilities built in the process of human occupance of land. Their nature and distribution are related on the one hand to the mode of living and on the other to such physical factors as water supply, slopes, forests, and marshy lands. The external form of the settlements reflects the architectural styles of the time, culture and region in which they evolved. Their distributional pattern is distinguishable in the landscape. Once created they may outlive both the architectural style of their time and the function for which they are originally designed. For these reasons, they reflect changes in human occupance of the land and may also exhibit relict expressions of the past cultural landscape.

A settlement is an organized colony of human beings, including the buildings in which they live or work and the tracks or streets over which their movements take place.[21]The centre of interest in settlement geography is the built-up structure and its relation to the environment. In the beginning, these settlement features bear simpler forms and relationship with the environment but with the growth of civilization and technical knowledge, the degree of variability in their size and the complexity of their relationship becomes overwhelmingly greater.

Generally, individual buildings and other facilities are grouped in permanent clusters at nodal points in a settlement. These groups range from a simple cluster of farm house to most complex cultural organisms. Thus settlement geography includes not only the buildings grouped around agricultural fields, but also the temporary camp of the nomadic herder, running the scale from hamlet to village, to town, to city, to metropolis and to ecumonopolis of total world urbanization.

Geographers consider rural settlement as a man-made habitat on the rural landscape, based on primary occupations such as agriculture, forestry, mining, fishing, hunting, etc. which flourish on local resources. They examine the settlement features such as buildings and their architectural styles, roads, and lanes in order to distinguish new categories and patterns and determine their functional relationships. Thus the size, spacing, form and functions of rural settlements and their origin are essentials of the subject matter. Their regional variations are mostly dependent on the sequential growth of their morphology and the social and economic structure of the society they represent and serve.

Geographers study settlement units and their distributional patterns for analysing the sequence of change in the cultural landscape. The character and layout of buildings, roads and fields and their arrangement for business, worship and recreation varies according to the merit of place and time on the one hand and tradition, technical knowledge and necessity on the other.

Buildings and transport routes form the fixed elements of landscape and they continue as relict features even after the way of living, they represent, is changed. In the Bihar Plain, India several ancient temples have been converted into mosques on the same foundations. New towns have come up on the ruins of the old ones or in their close proximity. Rebuilding of old sites was common during the Muslim period, and even in the British period civil-lines and cantonments were sometimes developed as twins to the older Indian settlements. The ruins of rural settlements of the past still survive as mounds even in the centre of new settlements, often bearing the same name. Such settlement sites in a region exhibit the nature and pattern of the ancient settlements and show details of the lines of migration of certain ethnic groups. One reason why the old and the new settlements are found closely associated is the lack of higher building sites in plain lands subject to recurrent floods. The newer settlements naturally tend to gravitate towards the high level ground selected by the earlier settlers perhaps for the identical considerations.

The functional analysis of settlements has added new significance to the modern social, economic, political layout and organisations. Functions performed by different elements of the settlement impart distinctive shape and form to it. They also affect spatial distribution of land use inside the settlement. The Indian village as a self-sufficient unit may be distinguished in different cases by the spire of the temple located centrally or by the house of the landlord or by the central block of residents belonging to the higher castes, surrounded by the peripheral circle of agricultural labourers and artisans. In different economic and cultural regions, the grouping of buildings around the cultivable lands takes place according to the needs of the area. The community has its distinctive religious sites: temples, mosques and churches, educational and recreational institutions and other features according to the needs and tradition of local people. The analysis of functions also covers the broad land use patterns, nature of occupational structure and other aspects related to institutional framework of a settlement.

Thus the functional analysis of rural settlements made no emphasis. In any programme of rural development it is of paramount importance to know the distributional pattern and type of services, the number and functional inter-relationships of the service areas, the occupational structure of people and the functional segregation of land use in various settlements. The study of functional aspects, however, is of recent origin.

The problem of an economist is to analyse the vacant/marginal or submarginal lands to determine the possibilities of their economic utilization. Similarly, a geographer approaches the pioneer fringe to know the potentiality of new settlements. "The pioneer fringe is a laboratory of exceptional scientific work because there human intelligence is pitted against extreme or unusual environmental conditions".[22] These conditions may have applied to the earlier settlers in Bihar Plain. Today, however, the region is extremely amenable to human occupance owing to its warm – humid climate and fertile alluvial land. It is densely settled, although most of the area is rural and the clusters have not developed into large towns. Bowman has remarked that 'city geography is at one end of the scale of settlement, pioneering at the other.[23] The growth of cities has not been possible owing to economic backwardness of rural areas. The region under study falls between these two extremes.

CONCEPTS OF RURAL SETTLEMENT GEOGRAPHY

The concepts of settlement geography include the spatial arrangement of houses in relation to transportation lines, industrial locations, agricultural operations, utilization of land, ranching of cattle, technical know-how through educational institutions, defence from thieves and hazards of climate, etc., all for the welfare of human society. These are directed towards understanding the variable traits of settlements, the causes of their location, consequences and above all, their interactions with physical and cultural parameters. Settlement study is, therefore, multi-disciplinary in nature where geographers study the spatial arrangement of habitation, sociologists focus attention on social groups, economists study its optimum location for economic gains, while planners' interest centres round the best environmental conditions in it.

The concepts of settlement study are basically related to the following:

(a) The use of natural resources i.e., environment, soil, space, time, energy, goods, techniques, money, information and other resources for the best location and distribution of human habitation over earth surface;

(b) The colonization, spread and competition, density, change and growth of settlements depend upon the economic conditions, history of land occupancy and availability of food in any region;

(c) The settlement attributes as the addition of clan settlements, types, morphology, materials of wall and roof, facilities of professional services available and the transformation of rural settlements into urban settlements play an important role in the growth and development of rural settlements themselves;

(d) Settlements on a particular place and time provide an opportunity to make the best use of available resources for the construction of houses, production of food, shelter from the rigours of climate and defence from thieves and wild beasts, and

(e) Planned development of rural settlement is necessary for regional economic development and welfare of people.

The settlement evolved with the use of resources available locally according to the sources of information of a person and the society. The concept of evolution of rural settlement also includes the colonization, spread and competition of different clan groups in the process of origin and growth of rural settlements. Generally, settlement originated on higher level ground amidst fertile agricultural areas, where water supply was plentiful and life could be secure. In this way, the rural settlements originated with the emergence of permanent agriculture. The infighting of plundering hordes, migration of clan groups and the succession of one political power after the other, during historic times, led to the evolution of settlements of varied nature with respect to monumental designs, architectural style of the time, place names, territorial organization and the union of clan groups into rural settlements.

The concepts of density and distribution of population are correlated and their studies are not possible in isolation. The high density of settlements has depended upon agricultural prosperity and suitability of the region for human settlements since historic times. On the other hand, distribution of settlement may indicate the agglomeration or dispersion of settlements in a particular ecological condition. This gives an idea of types of rural settlements in which the compact, semi-compact, semi-sprinkled and sprinkled settlement forms are generally observed in a regional analysis of Indian rural settlements.

The concepts of size and spacing of rural settlements are again correlated and inter-dependent upon each other. In areas with large size settlements, their spacing is abnormally high while in areas with small settlements the spacing is very close, except for the hilly, forested and flood affected areas.

The concepts of patterns and process of village morphology include the measurement of shape of rural settlements variant from the circle, identification of external shape of settlements from a bird's-eye view and internal layout of streets and lanes.

In the concept of house types, the regional variation of houses in relation to the material of wall, roof, construction method, architectural style, cost involved and placings of courtyard, inner verandah, eavesline, female apartment and male apartment are important aspects of consideration. The density of houses, occupancy rate, and demand and shortage of houses are also the subject matter of this study.

The concept of regional patterns of rural settlements includes the regional conditions of their density, as also residential houses, settlement types and other elements of settlements in totality.

The concept of rural service centre includes the primary, secondary and tertiary service centres. The concepts of rurban centres, centres of trade and commerce and central place hierarchy all come under the category of service centres. The centres which provide goods and services to their zone of influence are known as service centres: The functions which are performed by a centre for the hinterland are known as central functions, while the functions centred in urban areas are called nodal functions.

The concept of hierarchy of service centres ranges from a roadside settlement to a megalopolis, fabroblast and sacroma settlements. A roadside settlement is an isolated house of a motel or a petrol pump station or an eating place for passers by. In India, roadside settlement is a common feature especially a betel shop. A hamlet is larger than a roadside settlement and this includes some residential houses besides commercial establishments. A village is larger than a hamlet with varied functions of agriculture, residence, craftmenship and commerce.

A town is a settlement with marked tertiary functions, daily retail market, large population size, development of educational institutions, industries, hospital, telephone exchange, wholesale market, etc. When a town has reached the stage of 100,000 population that is known as a city. When several industrial cities coalesce physically and economically, even if they are politically independent they are known as conurbation.

The term metropolis is applied to such a city which has a population of 10,00,000. This is also known as a millionaire city. When several conurbations and metropolises coalesce the term megalopolis is applied to such a contiguous urban area. Such a megalopolis is discernible on the eastern sea coast of United States.

The fabroblast and sacroma settlement terminologies are generally applied to the highly congested and overcrowded urban places. Similarly, growth centres and growth poles are applied in India to developing service centres like small towns and developed service centres like State capitals respectively.

Locational decisions are generally taken in recent times, on the basis of locational relationship of rural settlements which reflect an ordered adjustment to the factor of distance. The concept of rural settlement system may be seen as an adjustment to a combination of physical, biological and cultural inputs, so that a change in inputs may be expected to lead to a readjustment within the system. When the chronological relationship of different grades of settlements is applied with certain logical principle, it is called system analysis. A system generally works with the process of feedback mechanism, whether be it a close or open system. In 1976 R.L Singh has given a call to social scientists to find out 'national settlement system' for Indian settlements.

There are some common concepts in settlement geography which have linked the rural and the urban settlements together in a single unifying bond. The separation of rural from urban studies may be permissible in geographical work, but it should not stand as a barrier between the two. For example, it is not possible to analyse the service centres purely as a rural phenomenon; they should preferably be studied in close association with the urban studies. One effect of such studies is the central place analysis, an important concept in settlement geography devised by Christaller in 1933.[24] The geometric figures drawn up by him, as well as by several other geographers recently, give expression to the theoretical spacing of central places of different ranks in an area of evenly distributed rural settlements. For such studies, therefore, it is essential to exceed the realm of rural settlement geography in order to appreciate and to do justice to the subject.

RELATIONSHIP TO OTHER BRANCHES OF GEOGRAPHY

The subject of rural settlements is associated with that of regional economy, particularly in the fields of land-utilization, and transport network. In land utilization, settlements are included in the category of land not available for cultivation. The spatial arrangement of habitations has a vital bearing on the existing patterns and the future planning of better land use. The relationship between transport network and settlements can be considered as the cause and effect of each other. This relationship is increasing with the slow change in subsistence economy due to regional inter-dependence and market location. The increasing volume of both freight and passenger traffic results in considerable changes in the settlement network, particularly, in its systematic hierarchy.

Rural settlements are also related to population geography, both in its historical and functional perspectives. The settlement site is pivotal to all branches of geography, because the house is a fundamental concept in human geography. It is the link between man and the land, and serves not only as a shelter or a place of residence, but also as a place of work. A settlement is a fixed element of the cultural landscape, while population is a mobile element on it. Geography is primarily concerned with the distribution and spatial patterns of these phenomena. The settlement map of any region gives the most meaningful picture of population distribution for at least a considerable part of the earth's surface.

Settlements and historical geography are genetically similar in their approach. The study of the evolution of settlements is profitable in determining their origin and development of morphology. Whatever interpretation a geographer may give of the present form or pattern, it must be considered in terms of the processes at work which generated them. Historical geography should be studied in terms of the changes and past distribution of settlements. The significance of place names in examining historical geography is, therefore, obvious as they help to identify various groups of settlers and their culture in the past.

The study of settlements as a permanent element of the landscape is most important for the purpose of terrain evaluation in military geography. Settlement features are also included in tactical and strategic studies of modern warfare as expressed in road patterns and their focal points.

Highways are the fundamental concepts in settlement geography which provide a common link with other branches of geography. As a matter of fact, the study of transportation cuts across all fields of human geography. A settlement can be visualised as an arrangement of houses and highways, but the link between settlements is provided by transport routes. Any change in the modes of transport, has an influence over the settlement pattern of an area. In regions having ancient civilized culture, the patterns of transport routes are often guided by the location of settlements. These patterns have been constantly changing from the days of bullock carts to jet planes, and have, in turn, influenced the morphology and the character of settlements they serve.

Rural settlements are primarily agricultural in character. Hence, settlements are intimately related with field patterns, and any change in land use pattern would affect the settlement pattern. Similarly, the regional distribution of rural settlements has some relationship with the regional distribution of crop combination and agricultural practices. Agricultural geography, on the other hand, would be incomplete if it did not take into consideration settlements as focal points for the marketing of agricultural produce as well as a source of labour for all agricultural operations.

Rural settlement geography, thus has a number of aspects related to human geography and includes a large number of topics such as house types, patterns, morphology, functions, spatial distribution, and rural-urban relationships, which must all be examined thoroughly in order to appreciate and understand this vast and distinct subject.

Settlement geography thrived on methods developed in economics, biology, mathematics, statistics and social sciences. A settlement geographer need to be a combination of historian, cartographer, artist, market researcher, sociologist and statistician. His work is to assess building, streets, inhabitants, functions performed by community, mapping, correlation and interpretation of comparative studies, etc.

In the present study a systematic approach has been applied and a balanced geographical account of the rural settlements in Bihar Plain and other parts of the globe have been developed on a firm statistical base. Certain specific rural-urban relationships have been determined and the complex settlement unit has been broken down to its formal or basic geographical units. While a large number of techniques have been applied to the preparation of maps and diagrams, the choropleth and isopleth techniques are the ones most frequently used. Several maps have been drawn to illustrate the results of various statistical techniques applied to analyse and properly interpret the available data.

The data has been collected from a number of sources and include both published literature, census data, unpublished data from official sources, field investigation and statistical analysis of relevant data. An attempt has been made to analyse and interpret this data scientifically and objectively by applying suitable statistical and cartographic techniques. The hierarchical and functional studies of the rural settlements made on the basis of theoretical models should be useful in regional planning and rural development.

METHODS OF STUDY

The trends of rural settlements growth and development is a result of the ecological system as interrelated with other social systems like political, cultural and spatial structures in the area under study totality approach has been adopted by tracing the socio-ecological patterns emerging due to the development of village at different periods from historic upto the present, besides highlighting the methodological development. For understanding these processes the author applied a modified version of Moss's[25] three strategic levels of study of the functional variables in time and space: the reconnaissance level, the regional appraisal level, and the project level.

1. **The National Level**: At this stage the national settlement policies have a definite impact on the location and siting of human settlements in the study area both during the colonial and post-colonial periods. At this level, the information is available on both physical and cultural environments besides social systems which affect the growth and development of rural settlements.

2. **The Regional Appraisal Level**: At this level the information is

available about population, settlements, houses besides environmental conditions and economic development.

3. **The Village Level**: At village level, field study is necessary to determine the changing character of ecosystems of the village as the base for development. This consists of the understanding about the evolution and change in agricultural systems within the village because it is affected by the political and cultural change. At this level village maps, cadastral sheets and aerial photographs are more useful in conducting the survey.

Besides these three levels of inquiry there are various other methods[26] which can be adopted to analyse the growth and development of rural settlements in any area.

Experimental Method

Modern science is considered as experimental. In social science, the investigator seldom goes to observe consequences of a particular phenomena. He performs the function which he observes as the chain of interactions from purposive action to experiences others. In case the experiences appear relevant to the problem with which he is concerned only then experimental inquiry makes it a purposeful research.

Historical Method: As human experience is a temporal moving process, all evidence with testing force is historical. It is not only relevant to the past but the present event can be identically similar to any other past event in all respects. The past events provide the only possible experimental reliable evidence, in case the relevant and irrelevant elements are differentiated. Further-more, history does not start and stop in the past, but past experience reaches up to become the moving present in which problems are felt and solutions are applied.

Analogical Method: No method is more universally exercised than analogy. It is generally compared with other more scientific methods. In case, it is more expertly used than other methods of learning from experience may be more frequently used rather than to any inherent limitation of the method. It is said that all sciences are analogical since any purposive action controlled by intelligence is controlled by what has been learned from past experiences in nearly comparable circumstances. A careful analogy is inherent in research.

Logical Method: The logic comprises a method and standard of conceptual reasoning. Hence logical method refers to a part of full inquiry. It handles concepts whose operations are a part and continuing aspect of every inquiry, and they are instrumental in devising tests.

Statistical Method: The statistical techniques enjoyed a great favour among social scientists. They believe that statistical devices are their primary inheritance from the natural sciences. In this book it is more helpful in terms of its functional role in the full range of inquiry.

Statistical method includes sampling design, model building, cost-benefit analysis, correlation, regression, multi-variate analysis, principal component analysis, etc. Settlements are generally chosen on the basis of random, systematic, clustered, multi-stage and purposive sampling. In model building graphical and deterministic models are generally used in settlement geography.

THE UNITED NATIONS AND HUMAN SETTLEMENTS

The first international programme in the field of human settlements had been formulated by the United Nations Reconstruction and Rehabilitation Agency in 1944, but the United Nations Organization was established in 1945, when the responsibility of this sector was vested in the Economic and Social Council (ECOSOC). In the year 1962 a special ECOSOC Committee on 'housing, building and planning' was established. After a long gap in 1977 the United Nations General Assembly decided on new institutional arrangements for international cooperation in the field of human settlements, after amalgamating the former centre for housing, building, and planning, the Habitat and Human Settlements Foundation, and some other institutions.

The functions of United Nations Commission on Human Settlements (UNCHS or Habitat), with headquarters at Nairobi, Kenya, are to serve as a focal point for action, co-ordination and evaluation of human settlements activities in the United Nations System. It also assists the commission on Human Settlements in Coordinating human settlements activities in the United Nations System, and to review and assess their effectiveness.

The Habitat Centre at Nairobi carries out an integrated research, technical cooperation and information programme structured into the following eight sub-programmes: settlement policies and strategies; settlement planning; shelter and community services ; development of the indigenous construction sector; low-cost infrastructure for human settlements; land use; mobilization of finance for human settlements development, and institutions for settlement management. In 1985, UNCHS has convened eighth session of the commission on "planning and management of human settlements, with emphasis on small and intermediate towns and local growth points".

INTERNATIONAL YEAR OF SHELTER FOR THE HOMELESS (1987)

The General Assembly of the United Nations proclaimed 1987 as the International year of shelter for the Homeless (IYSH) with the help of governments and non-governmental organisations (NGO's) to achieve this objective. It is essential as the problem of shelter is increasing for the World Community and it affects the daily lives of hundreds of millions of people who suffer from inhuman housing and living conditions.

The problem of providing low income group with adequate shelter and basic services has been easily solved in industrialized countries. But in the Third World it is of such intensity and dimensions that it deserves a much higher priority on the international agenda. The magnitude of the problem can be illustrated by the fact that in most large cities in the Third World 40 per cent or more population live in slums or squatter settlements. Due to the lack of safe drinking water, sanitation and other facilities, living conditions in the rural areas are usually not so congenial for human living. Altogether it is estimated that more than one billion (1,000,000,000) people in the Third World are deprived of the basic right to adequate shelter.[27]

HABITAT INTERNATIONAL COUNCIL

Habitat International Council (HIC) is the successor of the committee which organized the non-governmental Habitat forum on the occasion of the United Nations Conference on human settlements in Vancouver, 1976. Its present board consists of the representatives of the following organizations:-

1. Afro-Asian Housing Organization;
2. Australian Institute of Urban Studies;
3. Commonwealth Human Ecology Council;
4. Housing Research and Development Unit, University of Nairobi;
5. International Council of Building Research and Documentation;
6. International Cooperative Alliance;
7. International Institute for Environment and Development;
8. International New Towns Association;
9. International Real Estate Federation;
10. International Rural Housing Association;
11. International Union of Architects
12. International Union of Local Authorities;
13. Mazingira Institute;
14. Postgraduate Centre for Human Settlements, Katholieke Universitiet Leuven;
15. Town and Country Planning Association; and
16. United Towns Organization.

The activities of the Habitat International Council are as follows:

It promotes and exchanges the ideas on housing, land and other human settlement problems, policies, and activities among non-governmental organizations and United Nations bodies. It also stimulates public awareness for increased support regarding human settlement programmes through contribution of research papers, holding international conferences, and by publishing NGO News.

SINA NEWSLETTER

Settlement Information Network in Africa, (SINA) Mazingira Institute, Kenya publishes bi-annual newsletter about the activities of scientists and the governments of Africa regarding their actions and reactions concerning human settlements. Under its auspices various seminars, symposiums and training camps have been organised on self-help basis for the better arrangement of settlements, alleviate housing shortage, improvement in sanitation beside sites and service schemes, and community participation. In 1982 'Shelter-Afrique' has been established in Nairobi by 23 African countries with the hope to assist member governments through financial and technical support, to formulate and implement housing policies to benefit appropriate target groups.

REFERENCES

1. T.G. Jordan: "On the Nature of Settlement Geography", *Professional Geographer*, Vol. XVIII; 1966, pp. 26 - 28.
2. R.L. Singh and K.N. Singh (Edt.): *Readings in Rural Settlement Geography;* National Geographical Society of India; Varanasi, 1975, p. VII.
3. C.A. Doxiadis: "The Future of Human Settlements" in Tiselius, A. and Nillson, S. (Edt.): *The Place of Value in a World of Facts,* Almquist and Wiksell, Stockholm; 1969, pp. 307 - 338.
4. C.F. Kohn: "Settlement Geography," in P.E. James: *American Geography, Inventory and Prospects,* University of Syracuse, 1959, pp. 125 - 139.
5. A.B. Mukurjee: "Spacing of Rural Settlements in Rajasthan",*Geographical Outlook,* Vol. 7, 1970, p. 2.
6. J.M. Houston: *A Social Geography of Europe:* London, 1953, p.30.
7. C.F. Kohn: *op. cit.*, p. 125.
8. J. Brunhes: *Human Geography,* Rand McNally & Co., New York, 1952, p. 152.
9. Dicken and Pitts: *Introduction to Cultural Geography;* pp. 317-321.
10. R.B. Mandal; *Planned Development of Rural Settlements;* Concept Publishing Company, New Delhi, 198,1 p. 2.
11. G.P. Wibberley: "Rural Activities and Rural Settlements", Mimeographed Paper presented at the Town and Country Planning Associations Conference, London; February, 1972; p. 2.
12. K.H. Stone: "The Development of a Focus for the Geography of Settlement", *Economic Geography,* Vol. 41, 19[illegible], p. 348.
13. Sarat Aziz: Rural Development Learning from China; The MacMillan Press Ltd., London, 1978, pp.1-5.
14. H. Ellenberg: *Integrated Experimental Ecology;* 1935, p.2.
15. A. Doxiadis; Ekistics, *An Introduction to the Science of Human Settlements,* Hutchinson, London , 1968, p.50.
16. *Ibid.*
17. *Ibid.*
18. F. Hendricks and M. Macnair; 'Concepts of Environmental Quality Standards Based on Life Styles, *Ekistics,* Vol.30; 1970, pp. 139 - 144.
19. G.S. Gosal: "Geography of Rural Settlements" in *a Survey of Research in Geography;* Indian Council of Social Science Research, New Delhi, 1972,

pp.188 - 202.

20. A.B. Mukerjee: *Op. cit.*,pp.1 - 19.
21. R.L. Singh: "Meaning, Objectives and Scope of Settlement Geography", *The National Geographical Journal of India,* Vol. 7, 1961, pp. 11 - 2o.
22. I. Bowman: "Settlement" in *The Geography in the Twentieth Century;* Second Edition, 1953, p.266.
23. *Ibid.*
24. W. Christaller: *Central Places in Southern Germany,* translated by C.W. Baskin, New Jersey, Prentice Hall; 1966.
25. R.P. Moss: "Land Use, Vegetation and Soil Factors in South-West Nigeria", *Pacific View point:* Vol. 9, No. 2; September, 1968.
26. Leonard A. Salter: *A Critical Review of Research in Land Economics;* The University of Wisconsin Press; Madison, 1967, pp. 70-74.
27. *NGO News on Human Settlements* (Non-Governmental Organizations) No. 2; 1984, pp. 1-4.

Fig. 1.1

Dynamics of Rural Settlement Location and Functioning through the Processes of Feedback Mechanism

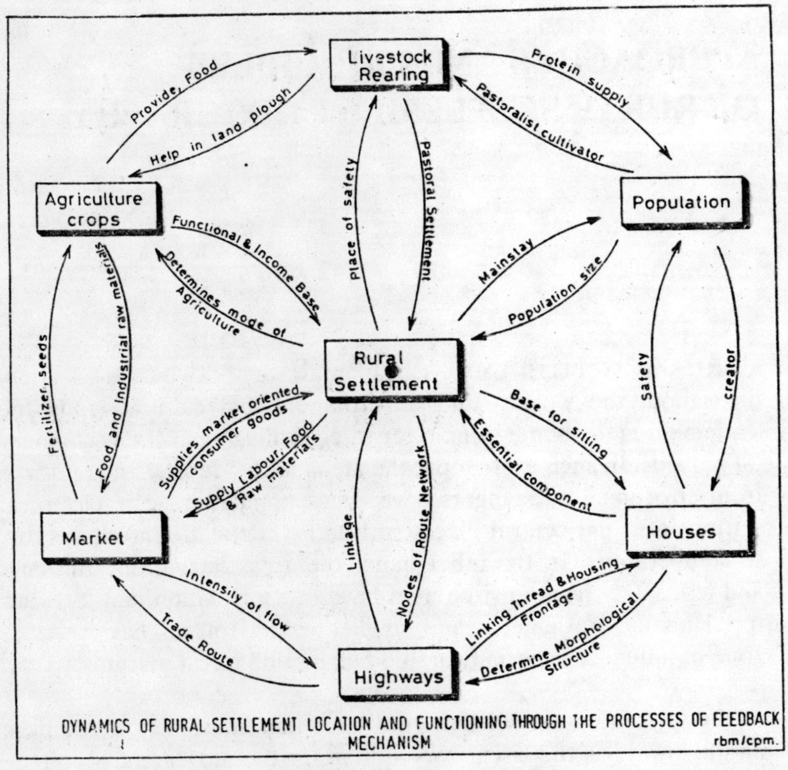

TWO

APPROACHES AND PRINCIPLES OF RURAL SETTLEMENT GEOGRAPHY

RURAL SETTLEMENT is the mainstay of human society throughout the world. Built environment and cultural landscape settlement is the home of man for safeguarding against environmental hazards. In such a situation, the areas having fertile land and free from environmental dangers have dense population, compact rural settlements, and central places with more confined hinterlands due to competition. On the other hand, the areas having infertile land and less safety from environment have low population density, scattered human settlements and smaller central places having wider zone of influence especially in flood plains and forest margins.

In any settlement whether rural or urban house acts as the flesh and highways as the circulatory system for the movement of human being. In this way, the study of rural settlement as the place of residence, concentration of services, nodes of transportation lines on growth points, growth centres and growth poles and their integral part houses in spatial integrated planning should be considered pivotal in any scheme of regional development and planning.

The location and functions of human habitation on the earth surface are the outcome of human behaviour in a particular geographical environment in relation to current needs of the society. Wherever the location of houses is systematic on beautiful sites and protective space it increases the accessibility and efficiency of work performance, and releases valuable *bariland* for the production of fruits, vegetables and food crops. In case where growth and development are haphazard it decreases human effort, and accessibility and makes living uncomfortable and leads to *insanitary* and vice of the underworld. Hence systematic living is the sign of good environmental conditions, whereas the zig-zag fashion of roads and congested huddled houses are indications of environmental pollution, unscientific living and the development of slums.

Rural development is a highly complex socio-economic process which must take place over an extended time period. Rural development must aim at helping the entire population, not merely agricultural producers; the integration process must focus on a minimum number of factors in order to meet major needs; and rural development projects must make provision for, and encourage, the development of local institutions rather than relying on government institutions.

The Asian Institute of Technology (A.I.T.) in Bangkok, Thailand, explained in the plan of operations for its new division: "the human settlements approach focuses on the spatial units of society - its regions, cities, villages and communities - as the appropriate units for the implementation of social and economic development. This approach aims at reaching all people, particularly those now being neglected, and bring them into the orbit of improvement and advancement".

The program itself is already in progress. It has three main goals: (1) educating high-quality manpower for human settlement planning, development, management and education; (2) research on human settlements in the Asia region; and (3) dissemination of information.

Both ideographic and nomothetic approaches are generally utilized in rural settlement studies. In recent years most of the studies are directed towards quantitative approaches, which are mere tools to explain the complicated problems of spatial analysis in geography. The approaches of settlement geography are mainly concerned with the growth and distribution of settlements, functional classification and hierarchy of settlements, types, patterns, spatial diffusion and development of rural and urban centres; measures of centrality and nodality, settlement planning, problems of settlement growth, model building etc.

Rural settlement studies generally make use of the following approaches:

(a) Retrogressive approach;
(b) Retrospective approach;
(c) Prospective approach;
(d) Environmental approach;
(e) Case study approach;
(f) Regional approach;
(g) System analysis approach;
(h) Interdisciplinary approach; and
(i) Principle approach.

In retrogressive approach the interest centres round the past and it also considers such aspects of the present pattern of rural settlement which throws light on earlier conditions. The retrospective approach probes the present, and the past is considered for the understanding of the future. The prospective approach concerns with the future, but the past and the present are considered as relict features of adjustment with future probable needs.

Environmental approach comprises factors like topographic conditions, forest cover, climatic conditions, availability of water, food, employment, technical abilities of people, agricultural prosperity, mineral exploitation and the development of industries. All these factors have profound effect on the types, patterns, growth and dispersal of rural settlements in a particular locality. O ly the sum of the conditions as emerged from the association of above mentioned variables can be said to be particular level of effect in developing a definite character of settlements growth, functions, spatial diffusion, concentration, dispersal and housing conditions at a specific place and time.

Case study is an approach of detailed analysis of selected few representatives from the vast field of research, even then it should be analysed in such a way as to offer evidence of relationships which may be helpful in decision making.

The settlements are generally selected in random, systematic, clustered or nested sampling basis. The emphasis is given on a particular settlement from different geographical points of view. It also establishes as to when, where, why and how a habitat has evolved and is still continuing on a particular place.

In regional approach, the country may be divided into settlement regions. The regional study approach to settlement is influenced not by political boundaries but by physical factors. In this approach, the repetition of the same study for different units in not possible. For instance, the geographical areas along the equator may constitute separate nations but the regional conditions on the equator are the same everywhere and so are the living conditions in this region.

The system analysis approach takes stock of the process of feedback mechanism, open system, closed system and the corollaries of systems and sub-systems studied for different levels of settlements in different time and space.

Under interdisciplinary approach, the methods used in other branches of geography or in allied sciences are applied to settlement geography for studying various problems, e.g., the same methods, which are generally used in functional classification of settlements, are applied to crop combination. So far as the principle approach is concerned the application of the theory of central place can be applied in any region with some positive result.

Applications of paradigms, systems analysis and probability theory are currently changing the geographer's attitude towards rural settlement studies. In a system of steady state, it is not necessary to study history of settlements in order to understand its form and the process going on. Such an approach does not fit into the traditional triology of form, function and genesis treated as the approaches to geographical knowledge of rural settlements.

The contributions of European scholars to the knowledge of rural settlement geography are old and original but these could not be synthesized into a specialized branch of geographical knowledge, being much varied in character from country to country and from region to region. The study of urban centres caught the fancy of

European geographers as this was a developing subject and also was much easy to study and analyse. Hence, the advancement of urban geography constitutes the bulk of studies in settlement geography.

In geographical etymology, settlement is a multi-meaning term. It is defined as 'the place, where one person or more dwells regularly, or the act of establishing a permanent residence'.[1] The first meaning has been adopted for the purposes of this study. A full-fledged subject of settlement geography came to be developed around this meaning through the studies of the French and German geographers in the 19th century. The German geographer, Carl Ritter's works during the late XVIII and early XIX centuries are considered to be constituting the base of settlement geography. His settlement studies are mainly related to the various phenomena and processes resulting from complex man-land relationship.[2] It is apparent from the bibliography of Freidrich Ratzel that many early contributions on settlements were made by German geographers who examined mainly two aspects of house types and urban centres. In 1895, Meitzen[3] considered the form of European settlements and laid emphasis on the morphology of rural settlements. The same trend was followed by Beresford.[4] Schluter in 1899 considered things in a wider context of the location, size and growth of settlements and their relationship with the nature. He was the pioneer in identifying the relationship of settlement geography with cultural geography. Wagener, emphasized the importance of dwellings in settlement geography. His studies strengthened the view that the land, used by the inhabitants of the dwellings, formed part of the settlement.

During the last few decades, settlement in German geography has come to be recognised as temporary and permanent or as rural and urban. According to Schwarz 'rural settlement geography includes the study of man's use of plants and animals to procure food and clothing of an economic area larger than the dwellings and of direct relationship between the economic area and the dwellings'.[5] Vidal de la Blache was an early French settlement geographer, whose voluminous studies enriched the field of human geography. Demangeon made studies of field ownership, cultivation, building materials, house types and the distribution of towns, rural settlements and human dwellings. The credit of spinning up the basic idea of settlement geography goes to the authoritative work of P.E. James and others.[6] Lefevre of Belgium had made some notable contributions between 1921 - 1964 to the study of patterns of rural settlements. Aurousseau[7] conceived of settlements as the 'arrangement of dwellings'. I.G. Grano undertook pioneer studies in Finish settlement regions and his works are characterised by analyses of the form and location of rural dwellings, hamlets and settlements.

Binus noted that it is quite necessary to continue research on rural settling process than ever before, because now the settlements are becoming more numerous and more complex in form due to the increasing trends of population. Some new rural settling and resettling activities are going on.[8] But Bowman[9] noted that the world's lands which are physically best suited are largely occupied more than 30 years ago. Hence, careful inventories and plans are needed to insure permanent new settlement as well as the efficient use of human labour force, time and money in the process of settling.[10] One such area is the World's high latitudes e.g. Northern America or Norman and Scandinavian States including Finland or Norden. In all these areas the advance and retreat of settlements are continuing since long.[11] These areas of Norman and Norden are physically and culturally diverse and the investigations done for one area and settling process cannot be blindly applied to the other area, but it can significantly be delineated in almost the entire northern lands,[12] and perhaps throughout the world, on the basis of small-scale and large-scale considerations of the isolation of settlers.[13]

Since the publication of the first report of the Commission on Types of Rural Settlements by the International Geographical Union in 1928, considerable work has been done in this area. Matui,[14] a Japanese geographer, did valuable pioneering work on quantitative rural settlement geography in 1932. Yonekura[15], another Japanese geographer, has made very noteworthy and original contributions comprising about seventy research papers and more than nine books upto 1975. This huge quantum of research is directly or indirectly related to the cultural heritage and rural settlements of Japan in particular, and Asia and India in general.

In June, 1983 the Commission on National Settlement Systems of the International Geographical Union held discussions in Leipzig about the impact of national policies on settlement systems, growth and change in the settlement system of the German Democratic Republic, international linkages and national settlement systems, as well as theoretical and methodological aspects of research on national settlement systems.[16]

In spite of urban and industrial development recent increase in rural population accounts for a large share of total population in East Central Europe. This has drawn the attention of Velchev,[17] who studied the rural population of Bulgaria in the Post War years. Besides the study of origin and spatial structure of rural settlements nowadays more and more studies are coming up regarding the functions, layout and field patterns.[18] The specific character of Hungarian settlements is reflected in the emphasis on agricultural towns and dispersed settlements which had developed when the plains depopulated during the Turkish invasion, and later on resettled.[19]These days, the study of rural settlements in relation to the physical environment is rare.[20] On the other hand, a growing body of literature represents a more applied type of approach. It is found mainly among studies of the dispersion of rural settlements and possibilities of ways to rearrange them.[21]Similarly a practical aspect has been covered regarding the accessibility of rural settlements[22] in a Czech study. Like urban geography functional classification of rural settlements is also found in Czechoslovakia and Hungary.[23] There are also studies of transitional settlements, whose role is increasing in East Central Europe.[24]One category consists of studies describing different aspects of rural settlements of a particular area, which are especially popular in Romania and Yugoslavia.[25]In Romania, place names are studied within the geography of settlements.[26] In most of the other countries, toponym has developed as a separate discipline, although sometimes closely connected with geographical analysis.

A review by Kosinski[27] describes the geographical studies of population and settlements in Bulgaria, Czechoslovakia, the German Democratic Republic, Hungary, Poland, Romania and Yugoslavia, and discussed the theoretical research followed by description of structure and changes of population, settlement network and the review of rural and urban settlements.

The value of aerial photographs to archaeological investigation has been well established in many parts of the world, but their value for the analysis of modern rural and urban settlements has also been established.[28] As for example Kohn (1951) utilized both field observation and photo interpretation techniques in the study of rural settlements in Wisconsin dairy area, North Dokota spring wheat area and Washington irrigated areas.[29]Tator (1951)[30] has written about Indian village sites on the Mississippi delta: "the flatness of the delta terrain, along with the factor of subsidence, make difficult the location of old sites, particularly on the ground. Careful study of large-scale aerial photographs; with detailed analysis of contrasts of tone and shape of soil and vegetation patterns is required."

In Britain after 1940 quite a large number of studies about rural settlements have appeared by geographers and other social scientists. Arensberg and Kimball (1940) published *Family and Community in Ireland,* which shows how closely - knit a group of small farmers can be in their kinship, political, social and economic life. J.M.Mogey (1947) in his book *Rural Life in Northern Ireland* gave an account of rural life in Northern Ireland since 1700's and gives contemporary study of fourty-four inhabited houses of a village. A.D. Rees (1950) in his book *Life in a Welsh countryside,* highlighted that the family and kinship groups were woven directly into the culture without the mediation of community. Williams's (1963) in his book *A West country Village : Ashworthy,* describes a 'truly rural 'community in a part of South Devon which has experienced outward migration since long.

C.J. Galphin,[31] the American rural sociologist, published his work on the rural communities of Wisconsin in 1915 and he formulated a new concept of 'rurban community'. The classical concept of central place by Jefferson and Christaller[32] was developed further by Ullman (1941)[33], and Dickinson (1947)[34], Brush (1953)[35], Berry and Garrison (1958)[36] and Beavon and Mabin 1975.[37]. Beavon and Mabin derived a full set of discrete market areas for any sized region. Their study was based on Losch system and also included solutions of mathematical equations as put forward by Losch.

K.H. Stone, another leading American geographer, in his various studies on rural settlements emphasized that the 'settling, stability and abandoning of rural settlements' are important aspects of rural settlement geography.[38] According to him Rittter's approaches to rural settlement geography were confusing and to remove the confusion he gave a more specific definition of rural settlement geography as 'the description and analysis of the distribution of buildings by which people attach themselves to the land for the purposes of primary production.[39] Jordan found Stone's view narrower. According to him the concept of cultural landscape is a multitudinous concept comprising settlement morphology, vertical arrangements and dimensions of houses, horizontal arrangements of the houses and of distribution of buildings, the floor plans of houses, the patterns of fences and fields,and the material components of houses.[40] Bowman[41]has studied the pioneer fringe of rural settlements. Edgar Kant's study is also very significant as he has represented the density of rural habitations in several ways following the methods of different investigators.[42]

Hillman's[43] work on Community Organization and Planning is important but his approach is mainly sociological. The key note of Jacobsen's[44] sociological study is that a scientific way of investigation in rural settlement geography is possible. Chisholm[45] has paid greater attention in showing the relationship between land use and rural settlements. Doxiadis[46] has endeavoured to develop an independent science to study human settlements to be known as Ekistics. Learmonth[47] has published a number of studies on rural settlements with special reference to the Asian and Indian cultures. F.S. Hudson's[48] work is mainly directed towards the basic ideas of rural and urban settlements.

Attempts have also been made at the investigation of the mathematical and theoretical aspects of rural settlement geography. J.C. Hudson[49] in his location theory has spaced the existence of three phases of colonization, spread, and competition in the settling process and the continuity of the settling process is the continuation of the three phases in a cyclic order. According to Grossman's[50] theory, African societies have two fundamental characteristics. Firstly, each clan and each cultural unit has its own method of spatial organization; secondly, the communities have control over matters relating to land tenure and land allocation. Bylund[51] presented his ideas of settlement diffusion through deterministic models, for the Lapland area in Sweden. Morrill[52] has developed probabilistic models taking one from the stochastic processes and random numbers. Curry[53] applied random processes to the making of settlement patterns with varying degrees of industrial specialization. Meining[54] had distinguished three major zones of core, domain and sphere of Mormon influence inside the settlement. Landing[55] has prepared a simulation model in the real occupance patterning of a group of people. Bjorklund[56] has emphasized the role of religio-cultural decisions in the settling process of an area.

HIROSHIMA SCHOOL OF SETTLEMENT GEOGRAPHY

This school is founded by Jiro Yonekura and later on advanced under the leadership of Hiroshi Ishida. The project entitled "the changing Rural Scene of India and Japan" is sponsored by Japanese Government. R.L. Singh has studied about the Japanese rural settlements in 1971. R.P. Singh (1974) has studied about the transformation of rural landscape in Japan. Applying the nomothetic approach Ishida has studied the field patterns and morphological structure of the Indian village, and has proposed some diagrammatic models of the village and field patterns in the Ganga Plain with special reference to the Middle Ganga Valley. He has developed the concept of Indian Village as the living fossil of the village community(1972)[57]. In the context of delimiting regional personality Ishida and his colleagues have contributed substantially to the depiction of rural landscape in the Punjab through sample village studies.

ISRAELI SCHOOL OF SETTLEMENT GEOGRAPHY

Under the leadership of Moshe Brawer, during four years (1972 - 1976), a new direction of studies concerning rural settlements has received a significant place. In 1974, Tel Aviv geographers have completed their project on **Model of Settlements in Developing Countries** under the guidance of Ktatzman and S. Pohoryles (1974). It also reviews case studies of existing models of agricultural settlements in Iran, Zambia, Nigeria, the Ivory Coast, Peru and Mexico.

VARANASI SCHOOL OF SETTLEMENT GEOGRAPHY

Under the leadership of R.L. Singh, K.N. Singh and Rana P.B. Singh, the founders of the school, scholars have paid their attention to analyse various dimensions of rural settlements through various approaches.

Dholri village (Singh, 1971)[58] is an attempt to sketch in microcosm the various aspects of a large agrarian and fruit growing settlement in the fertile Ganga - Yamuna doab. **Rural Settlements in Monsoon Asia** (Singh, 1972)[59] presents an integrated picture of the various contributions made by researchers in the field of rural settlements in Monsoon Asia, as discussed in the two symposia - Varanasi and Tokyo. It contains a comprehensive introduction divided into two parts, covering the historico-cultural background , physical features and some aspects of economic activities. **Rajput clan Settlements in Varanasi District** (Singh,1975)[60] attempts to trace and reconstruct the cultural landscape developed by the aboriginal people during the pre-Rajput period (about 12th century A.D.) as well as to delineate the impact of Rajput clans on the process of their transformation. **Readings in Rural Settlement Geography** (Singh, et. al; 1975)[61] contains the articles of theoretical, methodological and research orientation, which are arranged into five sections, i.e., approaches and methodology, theory and model, spatial distributional pattern, histogenesis and evolution, and morphology and pattern formation. **The National Geographical Journal of India** (Singh, 1975)[62] deals with rural settlement analysis, agrarian system dynamics in Tamil Nadu (India), pattern and process in frontier farm settlement, spatio-temporal diffusion of clan settlements, accessibility and cultural areas in rural U.P. (India), aerial photography and mapping of settlements, nearest dwelling distance analysis, rural planning system, and space articulation in Indian village. **Geographic Dimensions of Rural Settlement** (Singh, 1976)[63] represents the work carried out by geographers in diverse areas of rural settlement geography with various approaches and methodology, and provide some basis of model building, theoretical insights and generalizations. **Clan settlements in the Saran Plain** (1977)[64] studied eight villages to establish the validity of caste theory. **Approaches to Abandoned Settlements Geography Review and Bibliography** (Eidt, 1977)[65] is designed to provide a general introduction to abandoned settlement analysis within interdisciplinary approach, along with a detailed bibliography. In another book **Approaches to Rural Settlement Geography Conceptual Framework and Bibliography** (Singh,1977)[66] an attempt has been made to set out the common elements of approaches as well as the fundamental characteristics and basis of rural settlement geography, which organize the conceptual framework of the discipline. **Men, Culture and Settlement** (Eidt, 1977)[67] is a compendium of essays written by geographers of various countries, on the topic agro-ecological set up of different environs of the world.

The Indian geographers have made liberal use of the ideas of the western geographers. But this trend has resulted into anomalies as the conditions in the Western World are often entirely different from those prevailing in India. It is in recent years only that the study of different aspects of rural settlement geography has acquired some importance in India. Despande[68] has studied **Settlement Types of Bombay Karnatak** with special reference to population size of the villages. S.M. Ali[69] has discussed rural settlement types, patterns, locations, sites and house types of the Ghaggar plain in relation to population distribution. Ahmad[70] has discussed rural settlement types of Uttar Pradesh. He has also analysed village patterns in zones of compact and fragmented types of settlements, and their regional distribution.[71] Buschman[72] has examined various aspects of rural settlements. R.L. Singh[73] has elaborated the meaning, objectives and scope of rural settlement geography. He has also traced the evolution of settlements in the Middle Ganga valley from prehistoric to modern times and distinguished compact, semi-compact, fragmented and sprinkled types of settlements.[74] A.B. Mukerjee[75] has discussed the type, size and spacing of rural settlements with special reference to the areas of Punjab, Rajasthan, Andhra Pradesh and Uttar Pradesh.

Lahiri[76] has studied the settlements of Ajoy valley. He has also traced the cycle of growth of settlements through successive stages of youth, maturity and old age. Bhattacharya[77] has examined the effects of caste factor on types of rural settlements in Western Uttar Pradesh, where the inhabitants prefer to live close together in large agglomerated habitations. R.L. Singh[78] in an another study of the typical rural dwellings in the **umland** of Varanasi found that the rural house was well adapted to the physical and cultural environment of the region.

R.L. Singh[79] has analysed various aspects of rural settlement geography with special reference to Uttar Pradesh. Sinha[80] has discussed houses and house types of Chotanagpur Plateau in Bihar.

R.B. Singh[81] has studied rural settlement types, their distribution and future trends in Varanasi district of Uttar Pradesh. The functional studies have started appearing very recently.[82]

So far as the advancement of existing knowledge and available resources for the study of rural settlements are concerned several symposia have been organized in recent years. The I.G.U. Commission held a symposium in 1971 at Varanasi and its proceedings were published as Rural Settlements in Monsoon Asia[83] in 1972. R.L. Singh has also organized other symposia on rural settlements e.g., at Palmerston North, New Zealand in 1974, Symposium on Rural Settlements in Monsoon Lands in 1975 at Varanasi and Pre-Congress Symposium at Tashkent in 1976. Indian Institute of Technology, Kharagpur (India) organised a symposium on 'Rural Community Development' in 1976. The theme of the symposium was multi-disciplinary approach for integrated rural development. The Department of Botany at the University of Rajasthan also organised a symposium on the problems of human settlements and multi-disciplinary approach for integrated rural and urban development.

R.K. Mukerjee[84] published his well known work, *Man and His Habitation* in 1968. R.C. Sharma[85] published his doctoral work entitled *Settlement Geography of Indian Desert* in 1972. Ayodhya Prasad[86] published his post-doctoral work entitled *Chotanagpur: Geography of Rural Settlements* in 1973. V.N.P. Sinha[87] published his Ph. D. Thesis entitled *Settlement Geography of Chotanagpur Plateau* in 1976. Thakur[88] published his paper on *The types of rural settlements in North Bihar*, and this is the only study undertaken on North Bihar as the predecessor of this specific region.

In 1975, the 'Commission on Rural Settlements in Monsoon Lands' considered the following approaches of rural settlement study as details of the three approaches discussed above:[89]

(a) Historical development of the methodology of settlement analysis;
(b) Relation to history, anthropology, agriculture, economics and other social sciences;
(c) Field survey and first hand observation and collection of data;
(d) Census records and maps, historical records and documents,

toponyms, etc.;

(e) Data analysis, mapping and computer programming;

(f) Conceptual framework, concept of ecumene, position, form, structure, distribution, growth, hierarchy, linkages, types, patterns, etc.;

(g) Characteristics, and elements of rural settlements and inter-relationship among them - theoretical, organic as well as behavioural approach;

(h) Development of paradigms, hypothesis, etc.; and

(i) Methodological approach - empirical, statistical etc.

In order to analyse abandoned settlements R.C. Eidt (1975)[90] has utilized the techniques micro separation, pollen analysis, carbon 14 dating and sequential soil phosphate fractionation which are generally used by archaeologists and physical scientists. B.P. Birch (1975)[91] after considering the deterministic models of diffusion of settlements of Bylund and Hudson, highlighted the three stages of colonization, spread and competition in the location of frontier farm settlement.

R.S. Mann (1974)[92] while delineating the neglect of rural settlement study in India highlighted that rural settlement study should consider: (1) the physical and cultural factors in the origin of the nucleus of settlements, (ii) reactions of the nucleus, through its functional and morphological development, i.e. the impact of historical events; (iii) the life and organization of the contemporary settlement; and (iv) interrelations with the environs. B.J. Murton (1973)[93] examined the village settlement processes in Salem district of Tamil Nadu from historical and spatial perspectives. Har Prasad (1975)[94] analysed settlement as the product of interaction among space utilization activities, spatial social processes and socio-economic amenities and services operating over the landscape in relation to Dun region, U.P. Rana P.B. Singh (1975)[95] highlighted the concept of rural settlements as revealed in ancient literature in terms of the structure and articulation system both of which are governed by religio-ritual and secular norms. R.C. Tiwari (1973)[96] discussed the theories of rural settlement study and suggested that geographers should engage in identifying patterns and trends of rural settlement development and formulate related principles based on rural environs. N.N. Bhattacharya (1974)[97] discussed about five patterns of rural settlement in the Brahmaputra valley.

Rabindranath Bhattacharya (1975)[98] studied the settlement patterns of deltaic West Bengal in relation to the physiography and agricultural land. B.S. Negi (1973)[99] analysed the types and patterns of rural settlements and house types in Uttarkhand area of U.P. and investigated a clear cut distinction between hilly and plain area settlements. V.K. Srivastava and Ivon Richards (1975)[100] presented analytical study of spatial distribution of rural settlements by using nearest-neighbour technique to identify the pattern of settlements at the Tehsil level. H. Yadav (1973)[101] gave an account of the distribution of rural settlements, population and house types in Goa. S.L. Duggal and H.S. Malik (1974)[102] investigated the structure of agricultural markets in Haryana. V.K. Srivastava and I. Richards (1978)[103] discussed the evolution of rural settlements in Meerut district with the help of models of spatial diffusion during different periods and presented their own model of settlement evolution in the study area. N.D. Bhattacharya (1978)[104] studied about human settlements in the changing courses of Padma river of West Bengal. R.B Mandal (1977)[105] analysed the effect of the completion of the Kosi Project on rural settlements in the flood plains of Kosi. Further, he examined the relationship between types of settlements and dispersion index with special reference to ecological condition and associated problems of flood in the Kosi basin. Rana P.B. Singh and K. Majumdar (1978)[106] analysed the pattern of rural settlements of Eastern Gujarat on the basis of size, spacing and distribution of villages. G.S. Bisht (1978)[107] as a case study of Chatripur analysed the community morphology, house types, socio-economic structure and the spatio functional organization of the village. Lallan Singh (1978)[108] analysed the socio-spatial structure of villages in Patna district, Bihar through the religio-ritual and secular-dominance models. M.M. Jana and K. Bagchi (1978)[109] discussed the hierarchy of settlements in the lower Silabati Basin on the basis of centrality scores of existing functions in 382 villages and 2 towns. A.B. Mukerjee (1976)[110] applied the multiple collinear diffusion models and some elements of the dominant clan to explain the patterns of rural settlements in the Chandigarh Siwalik hills. A. Noble (1977)[111] studied about the migration and settlement patterns of the herding communities of the Nilgiri district of Tamil Nadu. S. Panchadhyayi (1976)[112] concluded that the distribution and density of settlements are significantly going to be affected due to the development of commerce. S.R. Roy (1977)[113] analysed the pattern of rural settlements in Bhojpur district, Bihar and suggested fieldwork for better planning of rural settlements both at micro and macro levels. Lallan Singh (1977)[114] traces the evolution of rural settlements in Patna district, Bihar and found three stages of settlement growth through colonization, dispersion and consolidation. L.K.P. Singh (1976)[115] identified four types of rural settlements in the Son Valley Plain. He observed that distribution, size and shape of settlements are largely governed by the physical and cultural factors. J. Sen and R. Bhattacharya (1977)[116]analysed the growth and decline, in a changing ecology and economy of some of the settlements along the Ajoy river valley in West Bengal. K.K Khatu (1969)[117] highlighted the various transitional stages in rural settlements and agricultural landscape in India. Further he emphasised that the transformation programme for a particular rural area harmonises with the trends and requirements of a region.

PRINCIPLES OF SETTLEMENT FORMATION

Geographers have studied rural settlements at different levels. At the lowest level, they have been interested in the characteristics and qualities of structures, such as farmsteads, fences, fields, houses and highways. Considering these aspects, Doxiadis[118]has classified settlements into four component parts, i.e., homogenous part (residential houses); central part (court-yard or chauk)' circulatory part (highways) and special part (tolas besides bigger settlement). At another level geographers have been concerned with the functional interrelationships of these structures that give rise to contrasting and dynamic character in rural settlements. In the beginning, rural settlement geographers were concerned with the 'form, function and genesis' like the core concept of 'structure, process and stage' in geomorphology.

The principles of rural settlement formation that emerge out of these two studies are:[119]

(a) Maximization of potential contact;
(b) Minimization of effort;
(c) Optimization of man's protective space;
(d) Optimization of the quality of man's relationship with the environment;

(e) Optimization of the synthesis of all the above principles.

The first principle is the maximization of man's potential contact with natural elements, cultural elements and the people. The principle of minimization of effort in the location of rural settlement helps inhabitants in achieving man's actual and potential contact according to the general principle of least effort. For example, in both the compact and dispersed settlement patterns, the principle of economy of movement in farming operations lies there. The farmers desire to minimize the distance they need to travel to the site of labour, or the distance which they need to herd livestock, to move farm implements and also for gathering crops. In the farming system it may be wise to locate compact settlement in between three fields in order to minimize the movement of men, farm implements and animals.

The third principle in the location of rural settlement is the optimization of man's protective space. For example, higher level ground for settlement site is needed to avoid menace of vulnerable diseases, etc. Protection is needed from inclement weather. These are some of the prime determinants of the optimization of man's protective space in the establishment of a settlement, whether it is permanent or temporary, a single house or a group of houses.

The fourth principle is the optimization of the quality of man's relationship with the environment. It is said that nature dictates human living but man endeavours to make life worth living by modifying the environment, for example, by constructing houses, by harnessing natural resources like water, minerals, food, construction of reservoir, river embankments, transport and communication channels, etc. Even in adverse environmental conditions man tries to optimise the relationship with the environment for his living.

The fifth principle is the optimization of the synthesis of all the above principles. In reality, the rural settlement system may be seen as an adjustment of a mixture of physical, economic, cultural and biological factors in the environment at a particular place and at a particular time. Much also depends on man's abilities to create a synthesis. Besides these, the type of economy and distribution and territorial organization also help in determining the character and form of settlement.

CONSTRUCTING HYPOTHESIS

Hypothesis is a statement of expected relationship between events. In geographical investigation, hypothesis often are statements about expected associations in space between two or more phenomena. It is quite clear that there must be a logical basis for any such association. Hence, the rationalization of hypothesis requires knowledge of the phenomena and of their relationships with one another. Hypothesis should be constructed in such a way that it may be either accepted or rejected on the basis of some kind of test. In geographical analysis the most common kind of test is that of visual correlation, in which maps of the phenomenon dealt within the hypothesis are compared.

Procedure for Hypotheses Formulation:

With the help of independent variable hypothesis can be formulated which would explain at least the regional variations of motor accidents, using the data available. Different hypotheses can be separated into groups, each of which would highlight one central theme. Only those hypotheses are considered best which can be tested. Some of the hypotheses formulated and the basic rationale for each are as follows:

1. Spatial variation in motor accident is associated with spatial variation in total population. It seems logical that where there were more people the motor accidents would be more, and where there were fewer people there would be fewer such accidents.

2. Spatial variation in motor accidents is associated with spatial variation in proportion of population living in urban areas. It seems logical that in urban areas due to congestion, with more people, more cars, more intersection of roads and traffic hazards favours more motor accidents.

3. Spatial variation in motor accidents is associated with spatial variation in the proportion of population of age 65 and over. The

rationale for this hypothesis was that older people tended to have relatively slow reactions to situations encountered in traffic, which may be instrumental in bringing about accidents.

4. Spatial variation in motor accidents is associated with spatial variation in per-capita liquor sales. The reasoning is, areas having high rates of liquor consumption would very likely to have high incidence of motor accidents.

Hypothesis can be formulated with various purposes in mind and on the strength and quantum of the available data. The hypothesis will tend to prevent the research from wandering all over a series of closely related phenomena by pin pointing on one or two specific situations of research. This conceptualization of research process may be descriptive, provisional, vaguely felt, or explanatory in nature. Errors in the hypothesis may be due to side issues or representation of faulty picture of the real world situation.

Hypothesis may also be designed for remedial action that existing research will continue in future or not. Such hypotheses should logically flow from the previous ones. The investigation which stops hypothesis testing from finding relationship between variables would only be superfluous. Thus with the help of personal ingenuity, hypothesis should be so formulated that they may provide specific direction to the later phases of study. These hypothesis will need to be worked over, revised, combined, and rephrased until they form a hypothetical statement of the relationships, found to exist in the real world situation.

The preceding discussion has enabled us to draw some tentative hypotheses which are dealt in the following paragraph:

Statement of Hypothesis:

1. The availability of higher ground sites less threatened by recurrence of floods on the river banks and the accessibility through roads are the main determinants of the spread of siting of rural settlements. The intensity of rural settlement siting has been mostly determined by the route network, occupational diversity and the exploitation of natural resources.

2. The number of satellite villages are inversely related with the intensity of flood and the scattering of cultivated land in the village.

3. Types and patterns of rural settlements are the outcome of topographic features of the land, climatic conditions and the available field pattern.

4. The typology and intensity of rural dwellings are governed by the population size of rural settlements.

5. Besides agriculture, the functions and functional organization of rural settlements are governed by the number of occupational castes residing in the village.

6. The population size and the spacing of rural settlements are guided by the intensity of flood and the development of agriculture.

7. The regional patterns of rural settlements are the outcome of physical environment, types of agricultural activities developed besides the density of houses, rural settlements and population.

8. Rural and urban settlements are interlinked in terms of hinterland organization, consumer behaviour pattern and the service capacity of central places.

9. The integrated rural development is possible, in case planning would be accomplished of all the sectors and for all the people of the society in relation to the behavioural processes of local people.

Testing the Hypothesis: An Example

Statements of expected spatial association of variables in geography usually are tested by means of visual correlation of maps. This kind of test is done by comparing maps of the dependent and independent variables in order to see whether the map of the independent variable is similar to the map of the dependent variable or not. If it is, the hypothesis is accepted; if not, it is rejected as an "explainer" of the dependent variable.

The Investigation of real world situation and the theoretical ideas suggest that the distribution of population in the Bihar Plain should have close relationship with the distribution of villages in 1971. The problem can be restated by the hypothesis that the distribution of population (dependent variable) in different districts is dependent upon the distribution of village (independent variable). This simple relationship is illustrated in a scatter diagram (Fig.2.1), with the dependent variable on the Y axis and the independent on the horizontal. To know the distribution and magnitude of one variable with the other, comparisons may be made so that their correspondence can be estimated.

TABLE 2.1 **Districtwise Population and Distribution of Village**

District	No. of village in '000's (1971) (X)	Population in millions (1971) (Y)	XY	X^2	Y^2
Patna	2	3	6	4	9
Gaya	6	4	24	36	16
Shahabad	5	4	20	25	16
Saran	4	4	16	16	16
Champaran	3	3	9	99	9
Muzaffarpur	4	5	20	16	25
Darbhanga	3	5	15	9	25
Munger	3	3	9	9	9
Bhagalpur	2	2	4	4	4
Saharsa	1	2	2	1	4
Purnea	4	4	16	16	16
Total	37	39	141	145	149

Based on the above table the product moment correlation coefficient has been calculated as:

$$r = \frac{\sum xy - \frac{\sum x \sum y}{N}}{\sqrt{\left(\sum x^2 - \frac{(\sum x)^2}{N}\right)\left(\sum y^2 - \frac{(\sum y)^2}{N}\right)}}$$

Approaches and Principles

where r = Pearsonian correlation coefficient,

Σx = Sum of all values of independent variables,
Σx^2 = Sum of squares of all independent variables,
Σy = Sum of all values of dependent variables,
Σy^2 = Sum of squares of all dependent variables;
Σxy = Sum of products of all x and y values, and
N = Number of units.

$$r = \frac{141 - \frac{(37 \times 39)}{11}}{\sqrt{\left(145 - \frac{(37)^2}{11}\right)\left(149 - \frac{(39)^2}{11}\right)}}$$

$$= \frac{10}{\sqrt{231}} = \frac{10}{15} = 0.66(r)$$

we get the value of product Moment Correlation Coefficient as r = 0.66. This shows that the relationship is very close. The result has been tested by student 't' test by the formula.

$$t = \sqrt{\frac{r^2(n-2)}{1-r^2}} = \sqrt{\frac{.4356(11-2)}{1-.4356}}$$

$$= \sqrt{\frac{3.9204}{.5644}} = \sqrt{7.00} = 2.64$$

H_o = According to null hypothesis (H_o) there is no correlation between the distribution of villages and population in different districts of the Bihar Plain in 1971.

H_1 = According to alternative hypothesis (H_1) there is correlation between the distribution of villages and population in different districts of the Bihar Plain in 1971.

Table value of 't' at 5 per cent level of significance and df 9 is 2.282, whereas calculated value of t is = 2.64.

Since the calculated value of 't' is greater than the table value at 5 per cent level of significance and degree of freedom 9, therefore, null hypothesis is rejected in favour of alternative hypothesis that there is correlation between the distribution of villages and population in the Bihar Plain in 1971.

REFERENCES

1. K.H. Stone: "The Development of a Focus for the Geography of Settlement", *Economic Geography,* Vol. 41, 1965, p. 348.
2. A.R.H. Baker: "The Geography of Rural Settlements", in Cooke and Johnson (Edt.): *Trends in Geography,* Oxford Pergamon,1968, p. 123.
3. A.Meitzen: *Stedlung and Agrarwesen der westgermonn and ostgermanen der Berlin,* 1895.
4. N.W. Beresford : *The Lost Villages of England;* London, 1954.
5. K.H. Stone: *op. cit.*
6. P.E. James, C.F. Jones and A.K. Wright: *American Geography Inventory and Prospect;* University of Syracuse, 1959, pp.125-139.
7. M.Aurousseau: "The Arrangement of Rural Populatioqn", *Geographical Review,* Vol. 10, 1920, p. 223.
8. B.O. Binns; *Land Settlement for Agriculture;* FAO Development Paper No. 9, Rome, 1951.
9. I Bowman; "The Scientific Study of Settlement", *Geographical Review,* Vol. XVI; 1926, pp. 647-653.
10. "Report of the Director on Land Settlement", *International Committees for European Migration;* Geneva, Mimeographed, 1956.
11. K.H. Stone: "Swedish Fringes of Settlement", *Annals of the Association of American Geographers;* Vol. LII; 1962, pp. 373-393.
12. K.H. Stone: "Geographic Aspects of Planning for New Rural Settling in the Free World's Northern Lands" in *Problems and Trends in American Geography* (Edt. S.B. Cohen); Basic Books inc. New York; 1967; pp. 221 - 238.
13. K.J. Pelzer; "Pioneer Settlement in the Asiatic Tropics", *Studies in Land Utilization and Agricultural Colonization in Southeastern Asia;* American Geographical Society ; New York, 1945.
14. Isamu Matui: "Statistical Study of the Distribution of Scattered Villages in Two Regions of the Tonami Plain, Toyama Perfecture", *Japanese Journal of Geology and Geography;* Vol. 9, 1932, pp. 251-66.
15. R.L. Singh (Edt.): Rural Settlements in Monsoon Asia; *The National Geographical Society of India* ; Varanasi, 1972, p. 13.
16. F. Grimm (Edt.); Wissenschaftliche Mitteilungen 10; *The National Settlement System* V; Leipzig,1983, p.5.
17. I. Velchev; "The Territorial and Structural Changes in Bulgaria's rural population in 1946-1965"; *Izvestia na Bulgarsko Geografsko Druzhestvo;* Vol. 7, 1967, pp. 109-126.

18a. B. Milojevic; "Types of Villages and Village Houses in Yugoslavia"; *Professional Geographer;* Vol. 5, 1953, pp.13-17.

18b. S.Golachowski, "Old Pattern And New Models Of Villages", *(Zasopismo Goegraficzne,* Vol. 35, 1964, pp.371-386.

19. E. Tajti, "Changes in the Development of Dispersed Settlements And Their Population In The Danube-Tisza Interstream Area", *Foldrajzi Ertesito,* Vol.

5, 1966, pp. 71-80.

20. Z. Laznicka, "A Contribution to the Characteristics of Our Settlements From The Point Of View Of Slopes And Morphological Conditions", *Sbornik*, Vol. 67, 1962, pp. 285-302

21a. M.K. Zalcska; "On the Types of Networks of Rural Settlements and Their Transformations",*Przeglad Geograficzny*, Vol. 37, 1965, pp. 455-480.

b. E. Petri, "The Elimination of Farmstead Settlements in Hungary and Its Geographical Problems", *Vestnik Moskovskogo Universiteta Seriia 5, Geografiia*, Vol.22, 1967, pp. 91-98.

c. I. Sandru; "A contribution in Applied Geography concerning Rural Settlements in Romania",*Analole*,Vol. 12, 1966,pp. 215--219

d. C. Votrubec, "On the Changes in Settlement Structure", *Sbornik*, Vol.68, 1963, pp. 81-83.

e. K.Kovacs, "Demographic Questions of Agricultural Settlements", *Foldrajzi Ertesito*, Vol. 15, 1966, pp. 97-111.

22. I. Vleek, "Transportation Links Between Rural Settlements and Service Centres", *Sbornik*, Vol. 69, 1964, pp. 200 - 12

23a. P. Beluszky; "A Classification of Rural Settlements in Hungary", *Foldrojzi Ertesito*, Vol. 14, 1965, pp. 149-63.

b. Z. Laznicka, "Functional Classification of Rural Settlements in Southern Moravia", *Zpravy O Vedecke Chinnosti, Ceskoslovenska akademie ved Geograficky Ustav*, Vol. 6, 1967, pp. 47-61.

c. K. Ivanicka; A. Zelenska and J. Mladeck, "The Functional Types of Rural Settlements in Slovakia", *Geographica, Vol.* 6, 1966, pp. 51-92.

24. M. Chilczuk; "Functions and Dynamics of Transitional Type Settlements in Poland", *Geographica Polonica*,Vol. 2, 1964, pp. 133-138.

25. M. Sic; "Contribution to the Better Understanding of the Characteristics and Development of Agricultural Settlements in the Middle Posavina in Croatia", *Geografski Glasnik*, Vol. 27, 1965,pp. 149-192.

26. I Conea; "Problems and Scientific Tasks of our Toponymie", *Seria Geografie;* Vol. 12, 1965, pp. 179-86

27. L.A. Kosinski; "Geography of Population and Settlements in East Central Europe", *Annals of the Association of American Geographers*, Vol. 61, No. 3, 1971, pp.599-615.

28. G.A Storkes: "The Aerial Photograph: A Key to the Cultural Landscape", *Journal of Geography*, Vol. 49, 1950, pp. 32-40.

29. C.F. Kohn: "The Use of Aerial Photographs in the Geographical Analysis of Rural Settlements", *Photogrammetric Engineering;* Vol. 17: 1951, pp. 759-71.

30. B.A. Tator; "Some Applications of Aerial Photographs to Geographic Studies in the Coastal Gulf Region",*Photogrammetric Engineering;* Vol. 17; 1951, pp. 716-725.

31. C.J. Galpin: *The Social Anatomy of an Agricultural Community;* University of Wisconsin; Agriculture Experiment Station Bulletin; No. 34, 1915.

32. W.Christaller: *Central Places in Southern Germany*, translated by C.W. Baskin, New Jersey, Prentice Hall, 1966.

33. E.L. Ullman: "A Theory of Location for Cities": *American Journal of Sociology*, Vol. 46, 1941, pp. 853-864.

34. R.E. Dickinson: *City Region and Regionalism;* London, 1956,

35. J.E. Brush: "The Urban Hierarchy in Europe", *Geographical Review*, Vol. 43, 1953, pp. 414-416.

36. B.J.L. Berry and W.L. Garrison: "The Functional Bases of the Central Place Hierarchy", *Economic Geography*,, Vol.34, 1958, pp. 145-154.

37. K.S.O. Beavon and A.S. Mabin: "The Losch System of Market Areas Derivation and Extension",*Geographical Analysis, 1975.*
38. K.H. Stone: *Op. cit.,* p. 374
39. *Ibid,* p. 347.
40. T.G. Jordan: "On the Nature of Settlement Geography", *Professional Geographer,* Vol. XVIII; 1966, p. 27.
41. I. Bowman: *The Pioneer Fringe;* American Geographical Society, Special Publication No. 13, New York,1931.
42. E. Kant: "Some Notes on the Representation of the Density of Rural Habitations", *Indian Geographical Journal,* Vol. 30, 1955, pp. 1-8.
43. A. Hillman: *Community Organization and Planning;* MacMillan; New York, 1950.
44. C. Jacobsen: "Modernity in Traditional Villages", *Rural Sociology, Vol.* 38, 1973, pp. 283-95.
45. M. Chisholm: *Rural Settlement and Land Use,* Hutchinson, London, 1962.
46. C.A. Doxiadis: "Ekistics, the Science of Human Settlements", *Science,* 170; No. 3956, pp. 393-404.
47. A.T.A. Learmonth and A.M. Learmonth: "Aspects of Village Life in Indo-Pakistan", *Geography,* Vol. 40,1955.
48. F.S. Hudson: *A Geography of Settlement,* Macdonald and Evans, London, 1970.
49. J.C. Hudson: "A Location Theory for Rural Settlement", *Annals of the Association of American Geographers,* Vol. 59, 1969, pp. 365-81.
50. D. Grossman: "Do We have a Theory for Settlement Geography-The Case of Iboland", *Professional Geographer,* Vol. 23, 1971, pp. 197-203.
51. E. Bylund : "Theoretical Considerations Regarding the Distribution of Settlements in Inner North Sweden", *Geografisca Annaler,* Vol. 42, 1960, pp. 225.31.
52. R.L. Morrill: "The Development and Spatial Distribution of Towns in Sweden, an historical predictive approach", *Annals of the Association of American Geographers,* Vol. 53, 1963, pp. 1-14.
53. L. Curry: "Random Spatial Economy: an exploration in settlement theory", *Annals of the Association of American Geographers,* Vol. 54, 1964, pp. 138-46.
54. D.W. Meining: "The Mormon Culture Region : Strategies and Patterns in the Geography of the American West," *Annals of the Association of American Geographers,* Vol. 55, 1965, pp. 191-200.
55. J.E. Landing : "Geographic Models of Old order Amish Settlement," *Professional Geographer,* Vol. 21, 1969, pp. 238-43.
56. E.M. Bjorklund: "Ideology and Culture Exemplified in South western Michigan", *Annals of the Association of American Geographers,* Vol. 54, 1964, pp. 227-41.
57. H. Ishida : " Introducing Professor Jiro Yonekura", in *Rural Settlements in Monsoon Asia,* (Edt.) R.L. Singh, The National Geographical Society of India, Varanasi, 1972, pp. 3-15.
58. S.P. Singh : *Dholri Village;* The National Geographical Society of India, Varanasi, 1971.
59. R.L. Singh (ed.): *Rural Settlements in Monsoon Asia;* The National Geographical Society of India; Varanasi, 1975, p.13.
60. R.B. Singh: *Rajput clan Settlements in Varanasi District;* The National Geographical Society of India; Varanasi, 1975.
61. R.L. Singh and K.N. Singh (edts.) : *Readings in Rural Settlement Geography;* The National Geographical Society of India; Varanasi, 1975.

62. R.L. Singh (edt.): Special Issue of Rural Settlements. *The National Geographical Journal of India,* Vol. XXI; Part 3 & 4, 1975.
63. R.L. Singh et al. : *Geographic Dimensions of Rural Settlements;* The National Geographical Society of India, Varanasi, 1976.
64. Rana P.B. Singh : *Clan Settlements in the Saran Plain;* The National Geographical Society of India; Varanasi, 1976.
65. R.C. Eidt: *"Approaches to Abandoned Settlement Geography Review and Bibliography"*, The National Geographical Society of India, Varanasi, 1977.
66. R.L. singh, et.al: *Approaches to Rural Settlement Geography, Conceptual Framework and Bibliography*; The National Geographical Society of India; Varanasi, 1977.
67. R.C. Eidt (edt.): *Men, culture and Settlement,* Kalyani Publishers, New Delhi, 1977, p.9.
68. C.D. Despande: "Settlement Types of Bombay *Karnatak", Indian Geographical Journal,* Vol. XVII, 1942, pp. 115-131.
69. S.M. Ali: "Population and Settlement in the Ghaggar Plain", *Indian Geographical Journal,* Vol. XVII, 1942, pp. 157-182.
70. E. Ahmad : "Rural Settlement Types in Uttar Pradesh", *Annals of the Association of American Geographers,* Vol. XLII, 1952, p. 229.
71. E. Ahmad: "Indian Village Patterns", *Geographical Outlook,* Vol. 3, 1962, pp. 5-15.
72. K.H. Buschman: "Settlements and Habitations in India, Parts I and II", *Geographical Review of India,* Vol. 16, 1954, No. 3, p;. 19-40 and in No. 4, pp. 13-18.
73. R.L. Singh: "Meaning, Objectives and Scope of Settlement Geography", in R.L. Singh and K.N. Singh, (Ed.): *Readings in Rural Settlement Geography,* The National Geographical society of India, Varanasi, 1975, pp. 4-11.
74. R.L. Singh : "Evolution of Settlements in the Middle Ganga Valley", The *National Geographical Journal of India,* Vol. 1, 1955, pp. 69-115.
75. A.B. Mukerjee: "Spacing of Rural Settlements in Andhra Pradesh", *Geographical Outlook,* Vol. 6, 1969, p.1.
76. R. Lahiri : "Settlement Type is Ajoy Baraker Basin", *Calcutta Geographical Review,* Vol. 12, No. 4, 1950,.
77. A.N. Bhattacharya: "Effect of Tribal and Caste Factor on Rural Settlement in U.P.", *Indian Geographical Journal,* Vol. 31, 1956, pp. 94-104.
78. R.L. Singh: Typical Rural Dwelling in the Umland of Banaras". *The National Geographical Journal of India*, Vol. III, 1957, p.52.
79. L.R. Singh: The Terai Region of U.P.: *A Study in Human Geography,* Allahabad, 1965, p.37.
80. V.N.P. Sinha: "Houses and House Types of the Chota Nagpur Plateau", *Geographical Knowledge,* Vol.2, 1969, p. 91.
81. R.B. Singh: "Rural Settlement Types and their Distributions", *The National Geographical Journal of India,* Vol. XV, Part 2, 1969.
82. K.N. Singh: "Spatial Pattern of Central Places in the Middle Ganga Valley, India", *The National Geographical Journal of India,* Vol. 12, 1966, pp.218-226.
83. R.L. Singh (Ed.): *Rural Settlements in Monsoon Asia,* The National Geographical Society of India, Varanasi, 1972.
84. R.K. Mukerjee: Man and His Habitation: *A Study in Social Ecology Bombay,* Popular Prakashan, 1968.
85. R.C. Sharma: *Settlement Geography of the Indian Desert,* Rajesh Publications, New Delhi, 1972.

86. A. Prasad: Chota Nagpur: *Geography of the Rural Settlements,* Ranchi University, Ranchi, 1973.

87. V.N.P. Sinha: *Settlement Geography of Chota Nagpur Plateau,* Rajesh Publications, New Delhi, 1976.

88. B. Thakur: "Types of Rural Settlements in North Bihar", *Transactions of the Council of Indian Geographers,* Vol.5, 1968, pp.157-63.

89. I.G.U. Commission on Rural Settlements in Monsoon Lands (1972-76), News Letter, Banaras Hindu University, Department of Geography, 1975; pp.7-11.

90. Robert C. Eidt: "Towards a Unified Methodology in Abandoned Settlement Analysis: Contributions from Geography and Archaeology", *The National Geographical Journal of India;* Vol. XXI; Nos. 3 & 4, 1975, pp. 135-150.

91. B.P. Birch: "Pattern and Process in Frontier Farm Settlement ", *The National Geographical Journal of India,* Vol. XXI; Nos.l, 3 & 4; 1975, pp. 166-171.

92. R.S. Mann: "Meaning, Aim and Future of Rural Settlement Geography, with Reference to India; *Indian Geographical Journal;* Vol. XLIX; No. 2, 1974; pp. 53-66.

93. B.J. Murton: "Some Propositions on the Spread of Village Settlement in Interior Tamil Nadu Before 1750 AD", *Indian Geographical Journal,* Vol. XLVIII; No. 2, 1973, pp. 56-64.

94. Har Prasad: "Evolution, Growth and Distribution of Settlements in Dehra Dun; *Indian Gegraphical Journal*; Vol. L; No. 2, 1975. pp. 1-9.

95. Rana P.B. Singh: "Indian Village: It Concepts, Structure and Articulation Pattern", *Geographical View Point,* Vol. V; Nos. 1 & 2, 1975, pp. 40-43.

96. R.C. Tiwari: "An Appraisal of Location Theories for Rural Settlements", *National Geographer;* Vol. VIII; 1973, pp. 77-83.

97. N.N. Bhattacharya: "Rural Settlements in the Brahmaputra Valley: A Geographical Analysis"; *Journal of North East India Geographical Society;* Vol. VI, Nos. 1 & 2, 1974, pp. 15-19.

98. R. Bhattacharya: "Settlement Pattern in Deltaic West Bengal", *Geographical Review of India,* Vol. XXXVII; No. 4, 1975, pp. 305-309.

99. B.S. Negi: "Rural Settlements in Uttarakhand Division of Uttar Pradesh; *Geographical Observer;* Vol. IX; 1973, pp. 43-50.

100. V.K. Srivastava & Ivon Richards: "Spatial Distribution of Rural Settlements: An Analytical Study", *Uttar Bharat Bhugol Patrika,* Vol. XI; No. 2, 1975, pp. 54-64.

101. H. Yadav; "Rural Settlements in Goa", *Uttar Bharat Bhugol Patrika;* Vol. IX; No. 2, 1973, pp. 82-92.

102. S.L. Duggal & H.S. Malik: "A Classification of Agricultural Markets in Haryana", *Geographical Observer,* Vol. X; 1974, pp. 73-78.

103. V.K. Srivastava & Ivon Richards: "Evolution of Settlements in the Upper Ganga Yamuna Doabs: A Case Study of Meerut District", *Geographical Observer,* Vol. XIV; 1978, pp. 24-29.

104. N.D. Bhattacharya: "Changing Courses of the Padma and Human Settlements", *The National Geographical Journal of India;* Vol. XXIV; Nos. 1 & 2; 1978, pp. 62-76.

105. R.B. Mandal: "Ecology of Rural Settlements in the Kosi Basin", *Indian Geographical Studies;* Bulletin 8, 1977, pp. 45-50.

106. Rana P.B. Singh and K. Mazumdar: "Spatial Analysis of Rural Settlements in an Indian Environment, Case of Eastern Gujarat Region", *Geographical Review of India;* Vol. XL; No. 2, 1978, pp. 108-112.

107. G.S. Bisht: "Settlement Morphogenesis and Spatial Functional Organization of Village Chatripur", *Geographical Review of India,* Vol. XL; No 3; 1978, pp. 244-250.
108. Lallan Singh: "Spatial Relationship and Morphological Structure of Rural Settlements in Patna District", *Deccan Geographer;* Vol. XVI; No. 1, 1978, pp. 406-416.
109. M.M. Jana & K. Bagchi: "Hierarchy of Settlements in Lower Silabati Basin", *Geographical Review of India*; Vol. XL; No. 4, 1978, pp. 386-399.
110. A.B. Mukerjee: "Rural Settlements in the Chandigarh Siwalik Hills: An Application of Multiple Colinear Model; *Deccan Geographer;* Vol. XIV; No. 2, 1976, pp. 105-134.
111. A. Noble: "Settlement Patterns and Migrations Among Nilgiri Herders, South India", *Journal of Tropical Geography,* Vol. XLIV; 1977, pp. 57-70.
112. S. Panchadhyayi: "Economic Activities and Rural Settlement Patterns of Subernarekha Kaliaghai Interfluve" *Geographical Review of India;* Vol. XXXVIII; No. 4, 1976, pp. 408-412.
113. S.R. Roy: "Patterns of Rural Settlements in Shahabad, Bihar", *Uttar Bharat Bhugol Patrika*; Vol. XIII, Nos. 1-2; 1977, pp. 67-75.
114. Lallan Singh: Evolution of Rural Settlements in Patna District (Bihar) *National Geographer;* Vol. XII; No. 2, 1977, pp. 173-185.
115. L.K.P. Singh: "Rural Settlements in Son Valley Plain in Bihar", *Indian Geographical Studies*; Bulletin 6, 1976, pp. 40-45.
116. J. Sen and R. Bhattacharya: "A Study of Settlements Along the Ajoy Valley", *Geographical Review of India;* Vol. XXXIX; No. 2; 1977, pp. 146-155.
117. K.K. Khatu: "Significance of the Study of Rural Settlements in Their Transitional Stages", *Indian Geographical Journal;* Vol. XLIV; Nos. 3-4, 1969, pp.52-63.
118. C.A. Doxiadis: "The Future of Human Settlements" in A. Tiselius and S. Nilson (Edt.): *Place of Value in a World of Facts;* Stockholm, Almquist and Wiksell, 1969, pp. 307-338.
119. *Ibid.*

Fig. 2.1

Bihar Plain : Relationship between Rural Settlements and Rural Population (1971)

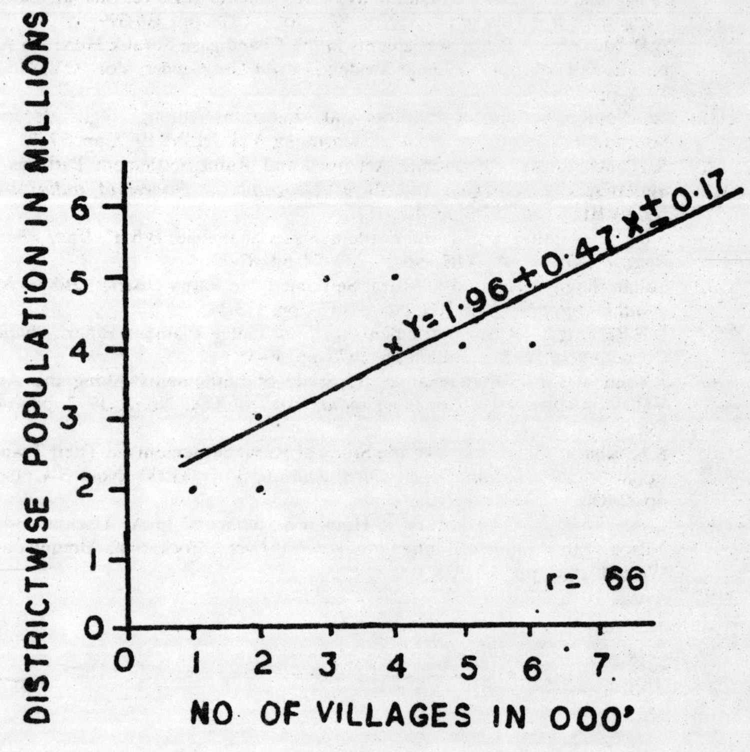

THREE

MODELS IN RURAL SETTLEMENT GEOGRAPHY

A MODEL is a simplified representation of the real World situation.[1] It is also called an analogy, an ideal, a representation, a description, an abstraction, a generalization, a frame of reference, a programme of research, an explanation of how a system works, a theory and a demonstration in the process of simplification of complex situations to a diagrammatic or mathematical form. A model building is understood to be a nomothetic approach in geography which explains the complex perception of any spatial distribution in a logical and the simplest possible systematic manner. The purpose of this chapter is to show the models used in settlement geography and the modes of their formulation. Any consideration of model building in settlement geography should be able to account for the following questions:

(a) What should be the approach of settlement model building?

(b) What should be the methods of settlement model building?

(c) Why the models should be built?

(d) What is the level of model building in settlement geography?

(e) How the models for settlements should be classified?

Regularities in Models of Settlements

Generally most of the models of rural settlement location and structure are measurable in terms of spatial arrangement and human behaviour. This has been established on the following six premises[2] which implied in most of the models of settlement geography.

1. **The Spatial distribution of human activity reflects an ordered adjustment to the factor of distance:**

According to Watson 'geography is a discipline in distance'. In case all the space is filled by houses without any areal differentiation, that would be geographic. At the first glance, the spatial regularities may not be clear enough but "there is more order in the world than appears at first sight is not discovered till order is looked for". For example, in movement models-time taken in travel, transport costs and kinds of road surface are more important factors to consider than linear distance. Non-linear models are related with distance decay function e.g. density distance, income-distance and land value distance to reveal regularities in the distribution of these items within settlements.

2. **Locational decisions are taken to minimise the frictional effects of distance:**

This concept is known as the 'principle of least – effort' or the 'law of minimum effort' which suggests that events reach their goal by the shortest path. In the models of rural settlements, the minimization of movement is fundamental to an understanding of the location of rural settlements.

3. **All locations are endowed with a degree of accessibility but some locations are more accessible than others:**

Accessibility denotes the 'ease of getting to a place'. Hence it is a locational quality of settlements. Relatively one place may be more accessible than others with a particular mode of transport. On the other hand, it indicates nearness to some functions or locations. In reality, it is a concept of movement minimization in terms of costs involved and overcoming a distance.

4. **There is a tendency for human activities to agglomerate to take advantage of scale of economies:**

It denotes the savings in operational costs by concentrating various activities in close proximity of central site of the settlement, e.g. the distance of farms and tethering ground, the nearness of tethering ground to grain storage, place of livestock tethering ground and place of water to wash them and allow them to quench thirst. Residential houses in a village may be considered as agglomerations and distance to the place of work farm as scale of economies.

5. **The organization of human activity is essentially hierarchical in character:**

The places which are more accessible appear to be the sites of larger agglomerations. The sites which are larger in population size are the places of higher order goods and services, whereas in smaller settlements lower order goods and services are found, such as central place hierarchy.

6. **Human occupance is focal in character:**

This concept highlights the functional region or the zone of influence of a place. The bigger service centres have larger zone of influence and in smaller centres it is very small. Hence the least-cost effort, accessibility, scale of economies in agglomerations and hierarchical ordering of settlements are linked together to form a system of settlements in space.

TYPES AND FORMATION OF MODELS

Content-wise the model may be classified into the following types:

(a) An iconic model is a three dimensional representation of a real world situation, and the globe is a very succinct example of this model;

(b) In analog model, one phenomenon is represented by another;

(c) In symbolic model, the situation is represented by mathematical symbols or diagrammatic representation;
(d) Theoretical model deals with concepts only.

Form-wise the model can be classified into the following types:

(a) Descriptive model presents a description of the reality;
(b) Normative model is obtainable under certain defined and controlled conditions. Deterministic and stochastic models are examples of normative models;
(c) Static model concentrates on equilibrium structural features;
(d) Dynamic model concentrates on processes and functions through time.

In model building, it is necessary to have complete and thorough information about the real world situation for which the model is going to be constructed. A cyclic and logical arrangement of important facts is also necessary so that a feedback mechanism naturally emerges from the model.

W. Christaller developed diagrammatic models for central places in 1933. In the school atlases he observed a typical settlement phenomenon in the fact that smaller towns constitute the surrounding zone of influence of a big city and these smaller towns are located in a circular pattern. As a first step in model building he tried to join the smaller towns by a circle. Thus contiguous circles were formed in the surrounding areas of big towns. In most cases only six towns surround the big city and a fraction of area left unserved in between these circles. As a second step he tried to join all the small towns hexagonally according to degrees of similarities noticeable in functions. This hexagonal linkage of points also covered the fractional area left unserved in between circles previously, and ultimately a hierarchical hexagonal net of centres from higher to lower level was formed.

For a real world situation, only a distorted shape of the hexagon is obtainable. This is due to the differentiation of environmental factors distributed over space. On account of this, Christaller postulated isotropic landscape feature which is conducive to a hexagonal arrangement of towns and central places. In this way, the central place model as a theoretical distribution of market centres was formulated.

MODELS APPLIED IN SETTLEMENT GEOGRAPHY

Settlement geography includes both rural and urban settlements. The models in these areas are simplified ones and they are really an abstraction from reality. Conceptual model is a 'web of reality' in image while deterministic model is based on the classic mathematical notion of direct cause and effect relationship, consisting of a set of logical mathematical argument.[3] Stochastic models which are based on probability instead of mathematical certainty are obviously more early to investigate relating to human geography, rather than physical geography. With the help of analog natural model Bunge[4] has compared the shift of highways with the shift of rivers and has applied the mathematics of crystallography to central place theory in considering the growth and shrinkage of market areas as similar to the patterns associated with two-dimensional crystals. Garrison has developed an icecap analogy of city growth[5] just like law of allometric growth of living beings. In rural settlement geography Bylund has given deterministic models which make certain assumptions about the nature of new colonization through time.[6] In Morrill's[7] probabilistic model the growth of settlement patterns is simulated by random processes which are in turn restricted by the operation of certain rules based on empirical observations of colonization process. The formulation of deterministic and stochastic models is not different. The deterministic gravity formulation can be related to several existing stochastic models of human interaction which itself can be transformed into a model of that type.[8] Typically, these interaction models consider two sets of probabilities, one set specifying the number of opportunities already reached and accepted by a trip-maker, and the second set specifying the proportion of trip makers going beyond a certain distance to reach an acceptable opportunity.

The probabilities in some cell-counting models can be interpreted in essentially the same manner. For example, Medvedkov[9] has employed the entropy concept of information theory as a technique for quantifying the agreement between empirical and theoretical settlement distributions. He has, further, suggested that Christaller's hexagonal central place pattern be regarded as the signal, and the random element be attributed to deviations from the isotropic conditions. Medvedkov viewed the spatial distribution of places as result of a set of regulated accidents in which randomness has affected the outcome from the otherwise deterministic central place theory. A similar approach has been adopted by Dacey[10] who felt that urban places as points are dislocated by institutional factors from their theoretical position on the hexagonal lattice. A variant of the cell-counting technique was used to verify that the distribution of places in almost homogeneous areas follows a double poison distribution, although the locations in inhomogeneous areas are better described by a double negative binomial. These and other distribution functions have recently been discussed by Olsson.[11] Hudson[12] has used them in analysing the rural settlements while Roger[13] has used them in studying the shops within cities. Subsequently, Harvey[14] analysed the cell count in detail in diffusion studies showing a way in which time and space could also be treated in the same model.

K.N. Singh[15] presented a simulative structural model which shows the evolution of basic rural territorial and settlement pattern in a small region of eastern Uttar Pradesh. His semi-deterministic formulations are based on four sets of valid assumptions. He has schematised the process of spatial diffusion within five time periods. In time period I (generation 1 through 3), the clan centre is established in the occupance territory and grows through generations one through three by natural growth as well as by immigrational accretion. With increase in population and consequent need for more agricultural land new villages are established around the clan centre. In time period II (generations 4 through 6) the clan area is subdivided into tappas and tappa centres were established beyond the core area by the prospective young families of the viable clan centre. In time period III (generations 7 through 9) the existing nuclei of settlements grow into units of different sizes. In time period IV (generations 10 through 12) new population movements take place within the occupance area and a few new tappas were established by the families of the core area. In time period V (generations 13 through 15), the growth of population continues, remaining patches and narrow strips of forest land are taken under settlement and a few new tappas appear in the clan territory. Thus, within the above five time periods through 15 generations or about 350-400 years, the entire occupance area of the clan is occupied. The pargana and tappa centres as well as many villages and hamlets have also proliferated on the landscape. A new model has been devised by the author to express the unstable character of spatial organisation of central places and this has been developed as 'the Dynamic Theory of Central Place Location'.

The beginning of settlement by the first settler had taken place in ancient times in the forest environment, when there were no transport routes at all. Later on, the beginning of second settlement in the neighbourhood might have given rise to one way connection of transport linkage. This may be known as K = 1. Further, in addition to the original point the growth of two centres provided two directional connection of transport routes as K = 2. Similarly, three centres gave three directional linkages as K = 3, four directions as K = 4, five directions as K = 5 and six directions in a hexagon as K = 6 for the densest packing of centres of the same order (Fig. 3.1).

But with the increase in number of centres in a triangle or in a hexagon, the K value will increase upto a very high figure. This will help in finding out the problem areas for infrastructural planning of services in relation to the location of first ranking central place of the region. This model also believes in the hierarchy of central places according to the increasing K value for a particular point in a equilateral triangle. This may be analysed with the number of transport route connections in between the settlements of hinterland and from the original central place. This will automatically give high K value for the centres treated as original point in the centre of the zone of influence of different central places. In this way, the model also satisfied the conditions of hierarchy of central places, keeping in view the consumers of different rural settlements which visit a central place.[16]

An another 'ecological model for spatial development' has been formulated by the author in 1974 after considering the growth of administrative and religious centres in ancient period, transport nodes in medieval period and industrial establishments in modern period. These have led to a corresponding change in the size and spacing of central places during different periods (Fig.3.2). According to this model the central places in ancient period were few and far between having small population. After the growth of roads and railways and faster modes of travelling, the distance between them was reduced. In between the growth of small administrative centres of ancient period and industrial centres of recent times, are the centres of transport nodes having medium sized population. In spacing also, transport nodes are in between the higher spacing and lower population size of the ancient period and the lower spacing and higher population size of the present (Fig. 3.2).

Hiroshi Ishida presented several diagrammatic models[17] while delineating overseas comparison of the location of rural settlements in relation to field pattern in the Middle Ganga Valley (Fig.3.3).

In the village territorial structure of Varanasi district in Uttar Pradesh the zonal arrangement is as follows: (Fig. 3.3)

> *bara* (immediately adjacent to the housing site), *goind* (intermediate land around the village, that is land between the *bara* and the *palo*) and *palo* (outlying unmanured land around the village beyond the inner and intermediate zones and is least productive). *Gauchar* (village common pasture) and fallow lie generally in the *palo*. *Bara* means enclosure including male houses (*ghar*) as opposed to *ghar* (female house). Sex segregation is not so distinct in western U.P. and Haryana as in the Punjab though the male house is in many cases separated from the female house within the enclosure. Apart from this, the outer fringe of settlement is also called **bara**. Around this **bara** a ditch was dug or a wall was constructed against invaders. An old village is still encircled by the remnants of a ditch or a wall today. Many are encircled by a passage.[18]

W.B. Morgan[19] while presenting his paper on expansion of settlements in Iboland, argues briefly, "that the degree of nucleation in northern Ibo settlements is conditioned mainly by the stage of growth that has been attained. The transition is from highly dispersed settlements in the early "colonization stage" to nucleated, well defined "towns" in the later, "continuous settlement" in the eventual disintegration stage in which settlements grow towards each other until they fill in all the spaces between them and produce a continuous belt of uninterrupted settlement.[20] However, Morgan made it clear that owing to cultural and ecological differentiation, this model is useful only for describing process in northeastern Ibo culture area. The restricted use of this model is due to the fact that (a) each clan and cultural unit has its own method of spatial organization, and (b) the community has control over matters relating to land tenure and land allocation.

D. Grossman[21] while dealing with settlement pattern of the Nike Clan in northern Iboland noticed the following features of settlements which are still under colonization:

A. The settlement pattern is unusually symmetric in its broad outline. There is some resemblance between the Nike settlement pattern and Bylund's "Model D" which emerges according to him, in areas where some physical or human barrier to expansion exists on side.

B. Under conditions of colonization, we would expect closer areas to be settled earlier than more remote areas. Here, however, frontier areas are settled while more accessible localities are left unused.[22]

According to Grossman both these features are intentionally coined rather than random growth and they make sense only if the composition and history of the Nike Clan are understood.

Hagerstrand[23] presents a four stage model for the passage of innovation waves for the dispersal of settlements. In the first stage, origin and evolution of initial agglomeration has been considered. In the second stage, diffusion is marked by centrifugal effect and creation of new centres in distant areas. In the third stage of condensing process, equal relative increase in the size of all locations is contemplated while in the saturation stage asymptotic increase towards maximum dispersal has been analysed.

Bylund[24] has presented a four stage diffusion model of settlements in Inner North Sweden. This is an important contribution for dispersal process. The only difference among his four stage models is in the number and size of settlements increase and the location of parent settlements. His A and B models assume spread from a coastal location while C and D from inland location (Fig.3.4). In formulating this model, he assumes that (a) the physical conditions of the land are similar in all directions and (b) further area will not be occupied until those close to the 'Parent settlements' have been occupied.

The processes governing the development of new settlements to create a spatial pattern have been the subject of numerous historical studies. In many cases special factors, such as the land policy in USA and the homestead acts, the political and religious pressures involved in colonization in Eastern Europe during the late Middle Ages, political decision making in Russian colonization schemes, make it almost impossible to set up theoretical models of settlement development. One interesting study of Bylund (1960) is the settlement process in Lappland. The problem that Bylund set out to explain was the failure of the colonizers to locate on the best lands before bringing poorer lands into cultivation. A model was developed which contained three major features (Fig. 3.4). The colonizers, it was assumed, wished to minimize distance between their new settlement and (a) their parent settlement, (b) a church, and (c) an available communication link. Using arbitrary values over a grid of equal sized cells Bylund simulated the spread of settlement around an initial set of settlements and drew attention to the broad similarity between the simulated map and an actual map of dispersion of settlement in the area. This very simple deterministic model indicates how formal models of the colonization process might be developed to some advantage.

Hudson after adopting principles operative in biological sciences proposed general laws of changes in rural settlement distribution over time. He postulated that the patterns of human mobility are arranged at random, a kin to the random dispersal of plant species. The spatial distribution of rural settlement usually passes through three stages of 'colonization', 'spread', and 'competition' as these patterns are observed in plant growth. Hudson does not subscribe to preplanned settlement distribution excepting that "the existence of highly regular settlement distribution in carefully planned colonies is no more interesting than the regular spacing of plants produced by a mechanical planter. This is the theory of spatial competition in natural vegetation".[25]

Cross-examining Hudson's observations, D. Grossman argues that human settlement pattern and expansion even in the under-developed economy are more similar to the planting of a mechanical planter than the growth of natural vegetation.[26] Thus, free competition in the spread of settlement rarely occurs and when it does, it is a matter of specific cultural values of the people rather than normal human behaviour. Grossman felt that the laws of rural settlements are meaningless outside the specific cultural and technological context in which the settlement is located.

Doxiadis[27] has developed a four stage model which can be applied to the composite individual settlement of all sizes in a territory as well as in its constituent parts (Fig.3.5). Hypothetically any settlement consists of four parts: (a) homogeneous part, (b) central part, (c) circulatory part, and (d) special part. These parts are subject to change but they always present in a living settlement or ekistic unit.

Model of Alpha and Beta Technologies in Settlement Analysis

Alpha is clearly the organization of the modern state, exemplified by the airline network emanating from the capital city; the Beta is a structure that consists of many smaller units, less related or even unrelated.[28] (Fig. 3.6).

By and large the picture given by the table is simply this: strengthen the local basis of the beta unit by reviving traditional techniques and introducing new ones, compatible with the beta structure; weaken the alpha structure above all by recentralizing its periphery and distributing sites of production and consumption more equitably in society - not decentralizing but multi-centralizing society.

Concretely there are at least three ways in which the alpha and beta systems can be integrated:

functionally, in space and overtime.

Sector	Alpha Technologies	Beta Technologies
Shelter	Curtail international housing business.	Try to restore local house building patterns of local materials.
	Make houses and habitats less centre-Periphery dominated; transfer more work to homes.	Collectivize ground that can be used for housing.
Environment	Recycling, cleaning up technology.	Local control and more dependence on smaller economic cycles.

Model of Rural Settlements in Relation to Land Management:

The main problem of the arid zone of Sahel in Africa is the management of grazing lands under marginal and fluctuating climatic conditions in a certain social, economic and cultural context. Considering these points in view Gabriel Boudet[29], a french scientist in grazingland management has suggested an outline of land management scheme which would involve a change from migratory to sedentary cattle farming. This model would be applicable in areas where conditions were favourable for fodder production and water supplies were adequate. It is related with a careful study of the carrying capacity of area concerned and would involve some 700 head of cattle representing the combined herds of 70 families or a total of about 350 persons.

The area to be managed would centre on a deep well along with the rural settlement which would provide a source of water during the dry season. A village to house herdsmen families would be situated up to 500 metres from the well. The dry season pasture would consist of an area of some 31,500 hectares forming a circle of land within 10 kilometres radius around the well (Fig. 3.7).

On outerside of the circumference of this circle would be a ring of land, some three kilometres wide, which would serve as grazing land for the rainy season. Spaced out at regular intervals in this area, would be a series of 10 "guzzlers", or artificial ponds, capable of holding sufficient water between major spells of rain to provide for the needs of 700 head of cattle (1/10th of the total herd) for about

15 days. Round each "guzzlers" would be an 840 hectares grazing area.

In the dry season each herding unit of 700 cattle would be brought inside the 'dry season circle' but would remain towards the outer edge of the circle. Each day the cattle would go to be watered at the central well near settlement, being driven along narrow well defined paths in order to avoid trampling the pasture land. Later, the herds would move again up to five kilometres of the well, thus reducing the distance to be covered to obtain water during the period of greatest heat. But this scheme needs cooperation of peasants to adopt new habits and control of herds.

For the rural settlements of West Africa two rural settlement models have been presented by Udo in 1963, and Prothero in 1972.

Udo's Model: In one of the theoretical statements on rural settlements Udo (1963)[30] claimed that compact settlements characterize the periphery of human land occupation, whereas the dispersed dwellings represent the more developed centre. Udo found the compact settlement to be historically tied to collective agricultural practices, and to a system of defence. Both features are identified as frontier (periphery) phenomena that breakdown with peace, population expansion and consolidation of man's control over the land. Changes then take place in the agricultural system where block farming by the entire compound gives way to individual farming on separate plots. Land scarcity arises through population expansion, and places a premium on the occupation of plots: the best proof of one's claim to land is to settle on it. Along with such changes there is a shift from rotation of bush and forest fallow as the entire compound moves to annual cropping in permanent settlements. As the idea claimed by this model near the northern border areas of Champaran and Madhubani.compact rural settlements are found whereas in the peaceful areas of dense population in Saran, Siwan and Vaishali districts semi-sprinkled settlements are found in Bihar Plain.

Prothero's Model:

Prothero (1972)[31] accepted the ideas of Udo with some qualifications to support Boserup's concept of population. He suggested a model of population-land relationships which involves a continuum of changing phases:

(a) from extensive and unsettled to fixed and intensive modes of land exploitation,
(b) from virgin land to total use of all cultivable land,
(c) from low population density to high density,
(d) from shifting cultivation to rotation cultivation, semi-permanent and finally permanent cultivation, with the gradual introduction of manuring techniques.
(e) from communal land rights to individual land rights, and
(f) from non-permanent (migratory) settlement to permanent settlement and;
(g) from nucleated villages to dispersed settlement.

A Model of village Socio-Economic System During and After Colonial Period in Tarime District: Tanzania

At each village level in Tarime district in Tanzania, the socio-economic system had developed two categories of settlements structure, the upper social structure and the lower social structure (Fig. 3.8).

1. The Upper Social Structure or Family: A

The upper social structure consists of rich cattle owners at each village who occupy larger tribal land for cultivation. The rich farmers or pro-Kulaks, are few in number but most of them own more than 200 herd of cattle. Since the dowry to girl party which the boy has to pay, varies from twenty to fifty cows, the rich men were able to get married to more wives and got more children. With a big family, the labour force of the proto-kulak was enough to increase agricultural production. The rich people who can afford to increase agricultural production had ploughs, tractors, bicycles and lorries for transportation.

2. **The Lower Social System or Family:B**

Consists mostly of poor peasants who own less cattle, (below 100), which come from various rich cattle owners in group A. The families in group B only take care of these cattle given to them by the proto-kulaks. The poor farmers are allowed to use the milk and blood from the cows and for ploughing if he has a plough. Whenever the rich farmer wants his cattle back he is free to take them back. The offsprings of the cattle also belong to the owner, the proto-kulak. If a cattle or its offspring dies, the meat and skin or the money obtained from the sale of the meat and skin is returned to the owner. The poor peasant in the social systems also profit from the animal manure he obtains from the cattle. Having lower man-power and wives and children he could only cultivate a smaller amount of land and obtain less surplus. Some of the families in group B are able to mobilize enough capital from their activities and buy cattle of their own. If he diligently used his cattle savings, then B can rise to the A group and become A_2, A_3, and so on, as there are also B families to support through "Kusagarya System".

Both the upper and lower social systems operate with inter relationship within a village ecosystem. Between the families of each of the two subsystems of the village ecosystem there is an exchange of services and goods which maintains the structure. The aim of each family is to advance its social and economic status within the system. Competition between the families made the families of A sub-system to maintain their status, although some of them were forced to go back to B sub-system. The A social group also maintained a higher political and cultural status in the village. The B families depended on A family for material help and innovations, but the B families also depended among themselves for communal activities such as cultivation, grazing and building known as 'saga'.

The impact of villagization to ecology has been not only due to the change in settlements but also the change in land-use-vegetation system as affected by the increase in mechanisation and communal land tenure. With these changes some private farms have also been put into production. Recently, due to increase in population density in many areas people have disturbed the ecological balance in terms of stopping the regeneration of bush and woodland.

Model of Zande Settlement Scheme in Sudan

Most of the models of settlements in Africa were formulated without evaluating the efficiency of such a design. They simply stressed the need for cooperation and access to works and services. They were designed as centralized homesteads with small food-production plots in the backside. "One of the earlier models for the clustered village homesteads would front on three roads or paths - the largest of which would be a focus for scheme services (Fig. 3.9)"[32]. This H-plan is a sort of linear settlement form which does not give a coherent view of village structure because the necessary service facilities which should be given to the village are lacking, and hence the settlement pattern eventually reverted to the sprinkled form. Rural settlements developed on H plan are found in Rukwa Region of Tanzania.

Model for Internal Structure of Tanzania Resettlement Scheme

A model for Tanzanian rural resettlement was designed to provide various services such as school, dispensary, shops and staff quarters in the centre besides three residential sections where settlers built homes and cultivate some crops in one acre of land. Fields for cash crops have been given near the periphery of the settlement and the same may be allocated to individuals or as communal farm according to an overall farm plan[33] (Fig. 3.10). In Tanzania this type of model cooperative villages has been activated in order to create planned compact rural settlements (Ujamaa villages) which are the resettled homesteads of farmers who were earlier living in scattered dwellings. This can help in communal organization of agricultural and industrial production, planned arrangement of houses, boosting marketing, trade, water supply, transportation, education and health services for integrated regional economic development.

A Simulation Model for Rural Settlements

Once the author observed with skin deep eye the roots and various parts of a tree on the slope of observation hill Dares Salaam and came to realise the similarities between the location and growth of a human settlement with that of a tree. This can be seen in the following points:-

Points in case of a Tree	Points in case of a Village
1. A tree always develops with trunks, branches and leaves.	1. Similarly a village always developed with roads, main thorough fare, footpaths and houses.
2. One can always observe vertical and horizontal expansion in a tree.	2. Similarly one can always observe a vertical growth and horizontal expansion in a village.
3. For the proper development of a tree there is a need of fertile land, availability of water and protective space.	3. The proper development of a village also needs fertile productive land, availability of water and protective space.
4. Wherever trees are closely located on the earth surface the development of roots, trunks along with heights and breadth do not seem to be proper.	4. Similarly wherever settlements are closely developed in such a situation due to their close competition their growth and development are found to be constrained.
5. For a proper growth, tree wants proper location on a commanding and favourable site.	5. Similarly a settlement is always in need of a proper location on a commanding and favourable site.
6. In case of haphazard growth of trees we call them increased entropy. But for the systematic growth of trees we are planting the tree in a garden in a systematic manner or we are doing afforestation for forest planning.	6. Similarly, in case of haphazard growth of settlements we call them increased entropy. But for the systematic growth of settlements we are following the path of fresh planning on a new site.
7. Tree is a shelter for man created by the nature as a natural feature.	7. Settlements provide shelter for man created by human being as a cultural feature.

8. Recently due to increasing cultural influence of man on vegetation the trees are dwindling.	8. Due to reckless destruction of forests by man and the hapazard growth of settlements the environmental pollution is increasing.
9. Nowadays trees are the shelter of birds, wild lives and poor fellows in different parts of the globe and it is known as plant kingdom.	9. On the other hand, villages are the mainstay of rural folk and the centre for primary occupation throughout the world.
10. Tree gets its food from the land in the presence of sun-rays and the air.	10. On the other hand, the construction of houses in the village and the food for human being are possible only with the proper development of tree, and for this fact the cycle seems to be incomplete in the desert environment, because high temperature restricts plant growth.
11. There are different stages of the growth and development of a tree.	11. Similarly, there are different stages in the growth and development of a rural settle -ment.
12. Trees are of different types and patterns.	12. Similarly, rural settlements are of different types and patterns.
13. Trees are performing different functions in spatio-temporal dimensions.	13. Similarly rural settlements are performing various functions in spatio-temporal dimensions.
14. Breakout of fire is generally found in the forest (*Dawanal*).	14. Similarly, breakout of fire is a common feature in rural settlements.

15. There are some parasitic (*banjhi*)branches in a tree.	15. Similarly there are some squatter settlements found even in rural areas.
16. The trees having perfect development of roots on the ground are found to be high and thick.	16. For the sound growth of the village, the development of transportation lines are highly needed.
17. Besides root, the development of a tree is dependent upon the variety of seeds, fertility of the land, siting conditions, climatic conditions and locational desirability.	17. For the growth and development of rural settlements besides transportation linkage the technical abilities of people, income potential, industrial potential, siting and climatic conditions are some of the other points which should be considered.
18. Some trees bear no fruit, while others give sweet fruits in bulk.	18. Similarly, some settlements are found to be uninhabited due to flood, war, cultural and political factors while in others varieties of inhabitants are residing.
19. It has been found that the birth and death of trees take place in different time and space.	19. Similarly, the beginning and the end of settlements are variously found on the earth surface.
20. The diffusion of tree is going on with the dispersal of seed from the ripen and dry fruits in accordance with the prevailing wind and in a forced manner taken away by the men and birds.	20 Similarly, the diffusion of settlements takes place with the migration of population and diffusion of houses from the congested old village either voluntarily or forcibly according to socio-political norms.

21. It has been found that water-logging and desertification act as the constraints for the development of a healthy tree.	21. Similarly flood, waterlogging and desert environment act as constraints for the growth and development of human settlements.
22. Tree gives us shadow and shelter since olden days.	22. Similarly settlement saves us from the rigours of climatic since prehistoric times.
23. It has been considered that trees are the natural wealth of the human society.	23. Similarly, settlements are the man made wealth of the human society.

24. In case the plantation of trees and the planning of settlement are done together side by side then to a large extent it will help in checking the environmental pollution and maintaining the 'ecological balance'.

25. In between trees and settlements the process of feedback mechanism is continuously working (Fig. 3.11).

26. Tree gives protection from natural hazards to both human being as well as settlements.

Model of settlement Pattern in the North-East Polder, Netherland

In rural settlement planning of the North-East Polder an attempt has been made in which a central settlement has been established at the inter-section of roads with smaller service centres surrounding it (Fig. 3.12). Finally a decision has been made to build ten villages for a population of 1000 to 2000 each and the central settlement at Emmeloord with a population of 10,000. Later on it has been found that the growth of central settlement is fast growing while the population of the surrounding rural settlements is either declining[34] or in some cases stable.

REFERENCES

1. R.J. Chorley and P. Haggett: *Physical and Information Models in Geography;* Methuen, London, 1970, p.22.
2. B.J. Garner: "Models of Urban Geography and Settlement Location", in R.J. Chorley and P. Haggett (edt.) *Models in Geography;* Methuen & Co. Ltd.; London, 1967, pp.304 - 305.
3. C.H. Coombs, H. Raifa and R.M. Thral: "Some Views on Mathematical Models and Measurement Theory", in R.M. Thral, etc., *Decision Process,* New York, John Wiley, 1954, pp.25-26.
4. W. Bunge: "Theoretical Geography", *Land Studies in Geography,* Series - C. No. 1, 1962, pp. 7-13.
5. W.L. Garrison: *Lecture delivered at Regional Science Seminar,* University of California, Berkeley, 1962.
6. E. Bylund: "Theoretical Considerations Regarding the Distribution of Settlement in Inner North Sweden", *Geografiska Annaler,* Vol. 42, 1962, pp. 225-231.
7. R.L. Morrill: "Simulation of Central Place Patterns Over Time", *Lund Studies in Geography,* Series B. No. 24, 1962, pp. 109-120.
8. G. Olsson: "Central Place Theory, Spatial Interaction. and Stochastic Process", *Papers, Regional Science Association,* Vol. XVII, 1966, pp. 13-45.
9. Y. Medvedkov: "The Regular Component in Settlement Pattern Shown on a Map", *Soviet Geography,* Vol. 8, 1967, pp. 150-168.
10. M.F. Dacey: "A Probability Model for Central Place Locations". *Annals of the Association of American Geographers,* Vol. 56, 1966, pp. 549-68.
11. W.K.D. Davis: *The Conceptual Revolution in Geography,* University of London Press, 1972, p. 358.
12. J.G. Hudson: *Theoretical Settlement Location, (Unpublished* Doctoral Dissertation) University of Iowa, Department of Geography, 1967.
13. Andrei Rogers: "A Markovian Policy Model of Inter-regional Migration", Papers, *Regional Science Association,* Vol. 17, 1966, pp. 205-224.
14. D. Harvey: "Geographic Processes and the Analysis of Point Patterns: Testing Models of Diffusion by Quadrat Sampling", Transactions and Papers, Institute of British Geographers, No. 40, 1966, pp. 81-85.
15. K.N. Singh: "The Territorial Basis of Medieval Town and Village Settlement in Eastern Uttar Pradesh, India", *Annals of the Association of American Geographers,* Vol. 58, 1968, pp. 203-220.
16. R.B. Mandal: *Planned Development of Rural Settlements,* Concept Publishing Company, New Delhi, 1981.
17. H. Ishida: "Village and Field Pattern in the Middle Ganga Plain: A Diagrammatic Model and Some Overseas Comparisons", in R.L. Singh (ed.): *Rural Settlements in Monsoon Asia,* The National Geographical Society of India, Varanasi, 1972, pp. 173-74.
18. *Ibid.*
19. W.B. Morgan: "The Grassland Towns of the Eastern Region of Nigeria", Transactions and Paper, Institute of British Geographers, No. 23, 1957, pp. 213-224.
20. D. Grossman: "Do We have a Theory for Settlement Geography? The Case of Iboland", *Professional Geographer,* Vol. 23, 1971, pp. 197-203.
21. *Ibid.*
22. *Ibid.*
23. T. Hagerstrand: "The Propagation of Innovation Weaves", *Lund Studies in Geography,* Series B, Geography, No. 4, 1952.

24. E. Bylund: "Theoretical Considerations Regarding the Distribution of Settlement in Inner North Sweden", *Geografisca Annaler,* Vol. 42, 1960, pp. 225-231.
25. J.C. Hudson: "A Location Theory for Rural Settlement", *Annals of the Association of American Geographers,* Vol. 59, 1970, pp. 365-381.
26. D. Grossman: *op. cit.*
27. C.A. Doxiadis: "The Future of Human Settlements", in a Tiselius and S. Nilssa (ed.): *Place of Value in a World of Facts,* Stockholm, Almquist and Wilksell, 1969, pp. 307-338.
28. Johan Galtung: "Choice of Technologies - Choice of structures", *African Environment,* Vol.III, No. 3-4; pp. 49-50.
29. H. Brabyn: "The Drama of 6000 kilometers of Africa's Sahel", *Unesco Courier,* April, 1975, pp. 5-9
30. R.K. Udo: "Patterns of Population Distribution and Settlement in Eastern Nigeria", *Nigerian Geographical Journal,* Vol. VI, 1963, pp. 73 - 88.
31. R.M. Prothero: *People and Land in Africa South of the Sahara,* Oxford University Press, London, 1972, p. 332.
32. C.C. Reining: "The Zande Scheme: Northwestern University Press, *Evanston,* 1966, p. 105.
33. S. Watts: "The South Busoga Settlement Scheme", Occasional Papers; *Syracuse University Program of East African Studies,* No. 17, 1966.
34. I.R. Meyer and R.J. Huggett: *Settlements,* Harper and Row Publishers, London, 1979, P.48.

Fig. 3.1

A Model of Transport Network Evolution

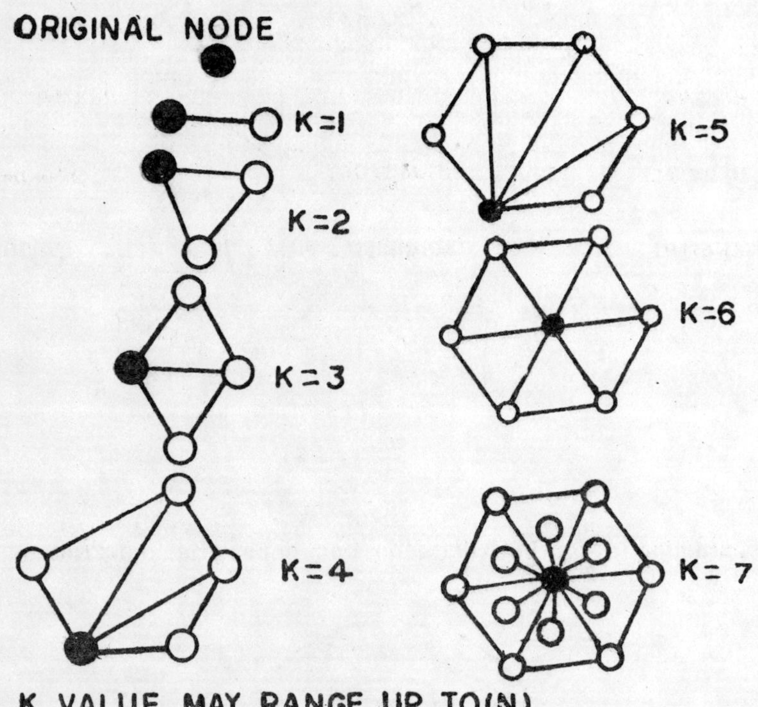

Fig. 3.2

Model for Spacing of Settlements

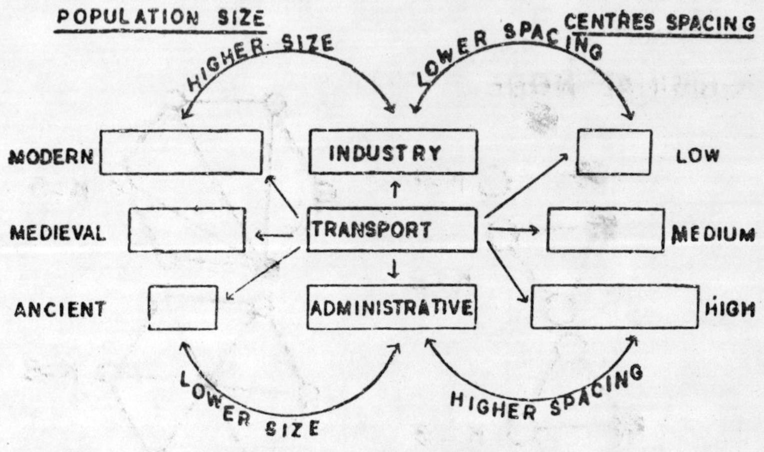

Fig. 3.3

Diagrammatic Model of Village Territory in Eastern Uttar Pradesh

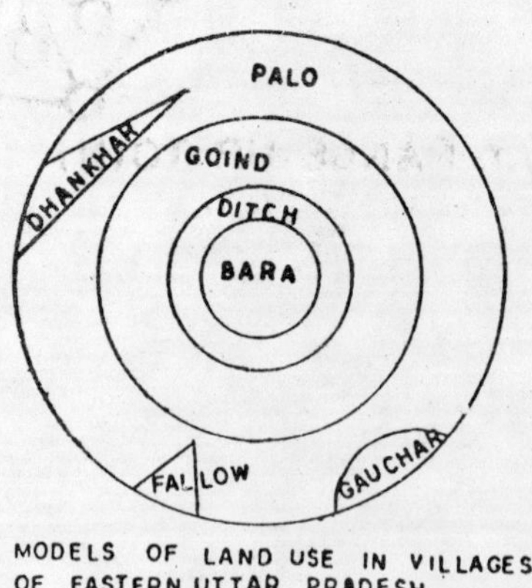

Fig. 3.4

Models of Settlement Diffusion

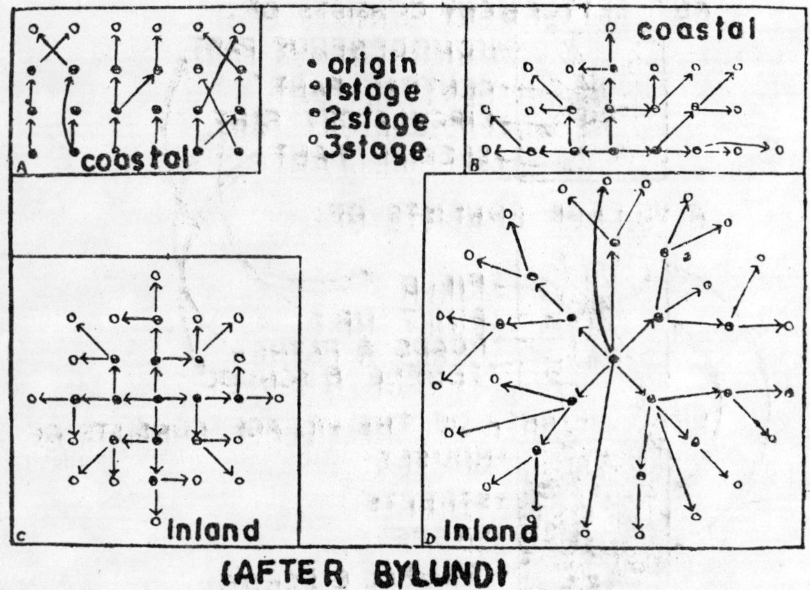

Fig. 3.5

Models for the Parts of Settlements

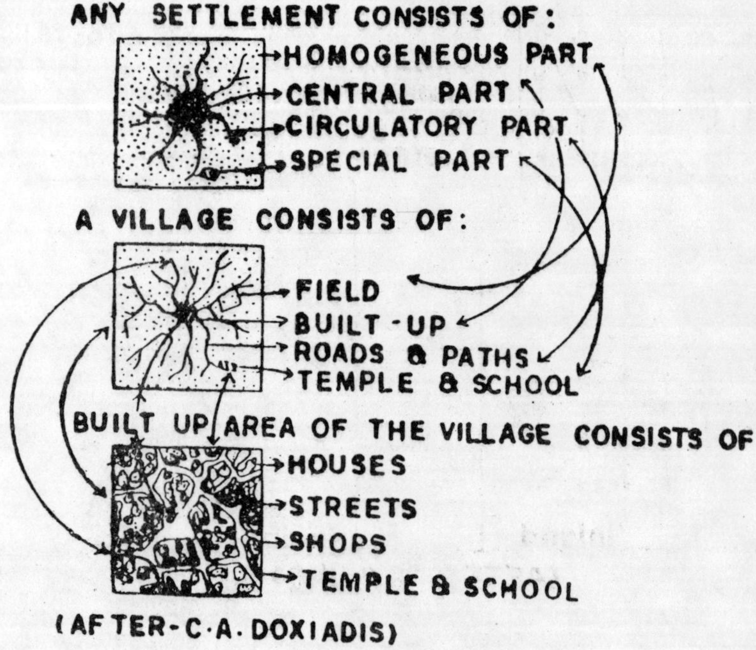

Fig. 3.6

Alpha and Beta Model of Rural Settlement Growth after : Bugnicourt

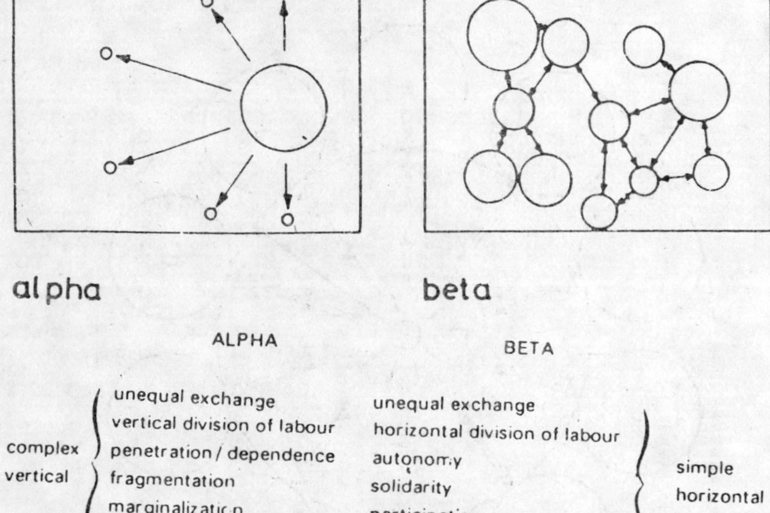

Fig. 3.7

Model for Location of Rural Settlement and Land Management Scheme by Gabriel Boudet

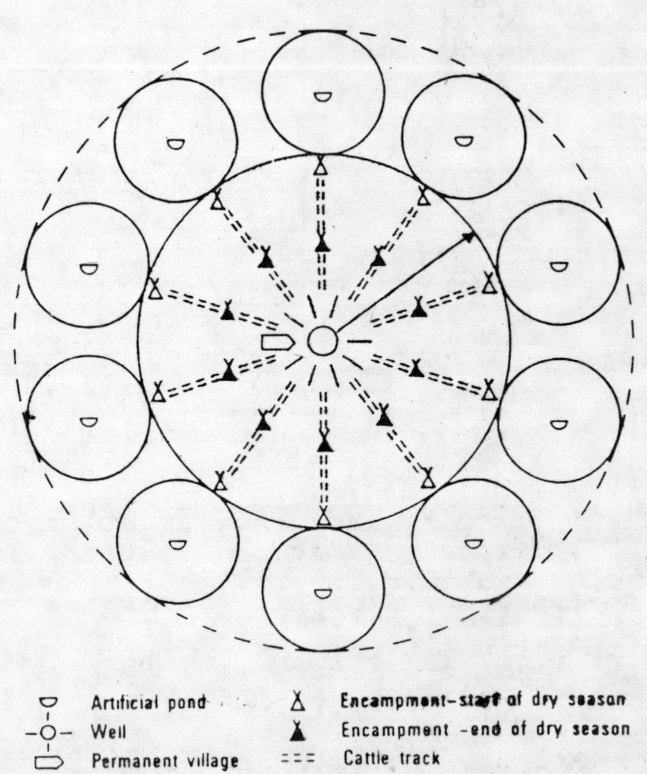

Fig. 3.8

Model for the Socio-Economic Structure of Rural Settlements in Tarime District, Tanzania

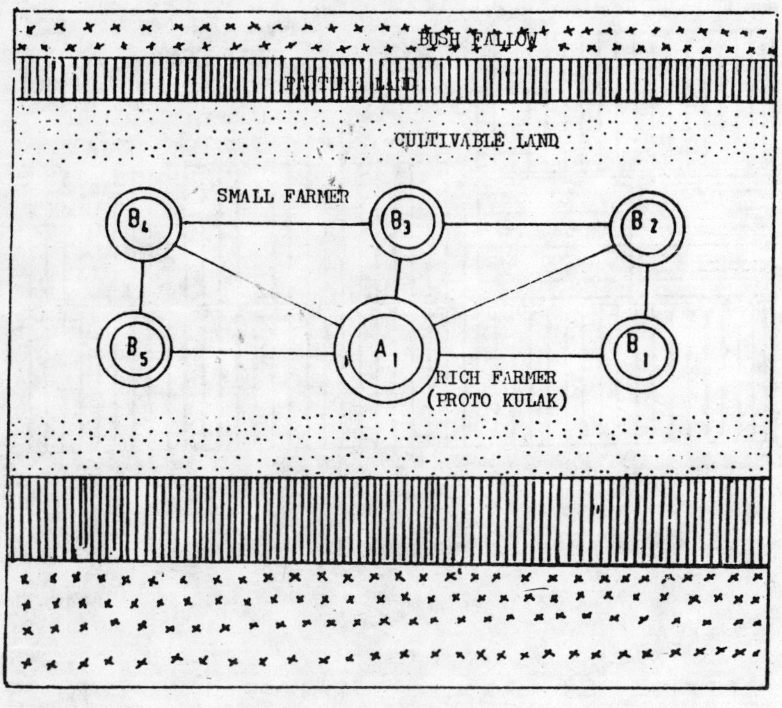

Fig.3.9.
Model of Rural Settlement Zande, Sudan

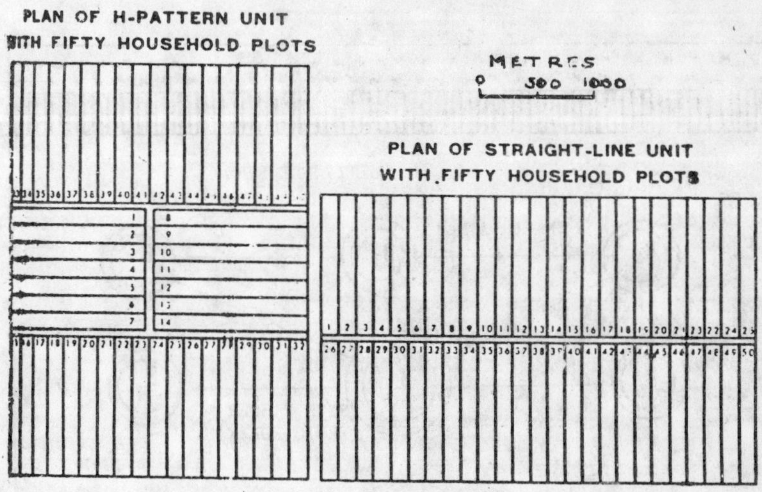

Source : Redrawn from Reining (1966 : 105)

Fig. 3.10
Model for the Establishment of Rural Settlements in Tanznia (After-S. Watts, 1966)

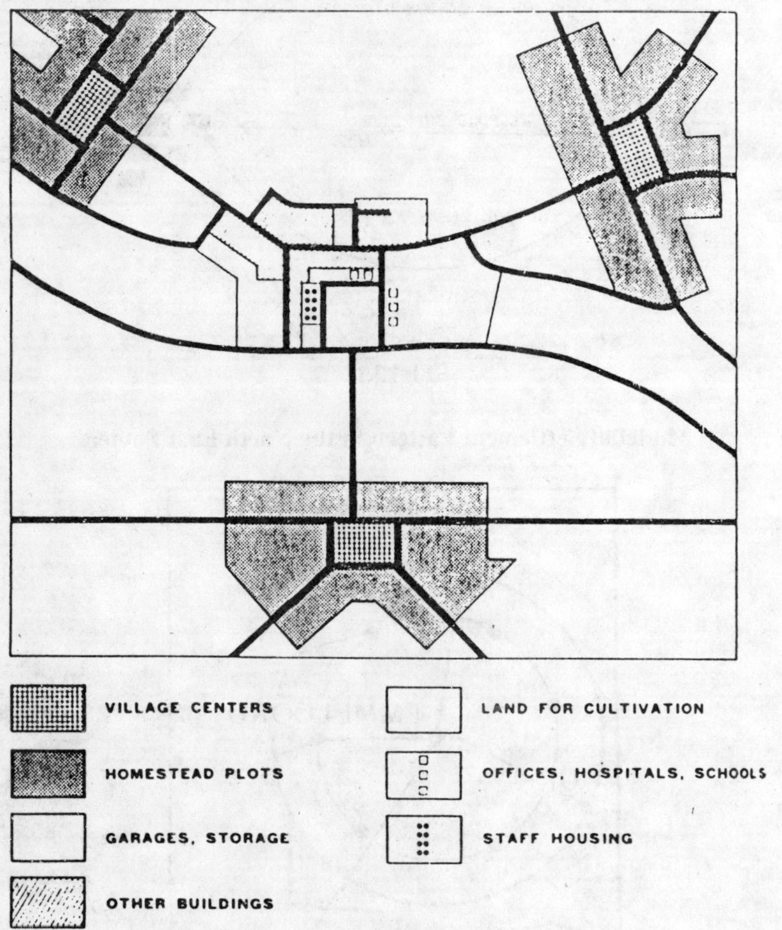

Fig. 3.11

Process of Feedback Mechanism between Tree and Rural Settlements

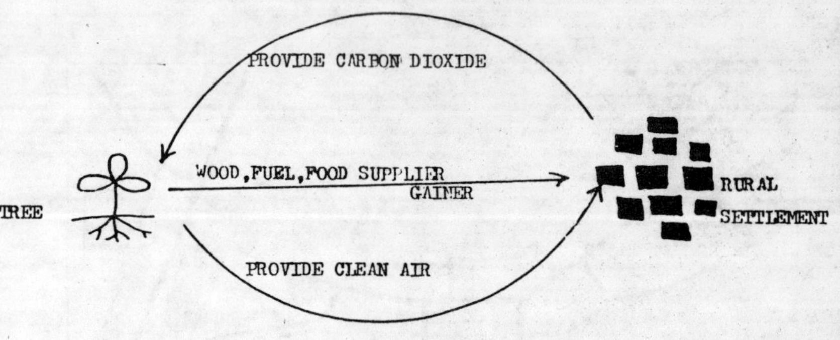

Fig. 3.12

Model of Settlement Pattern in the North East Polder

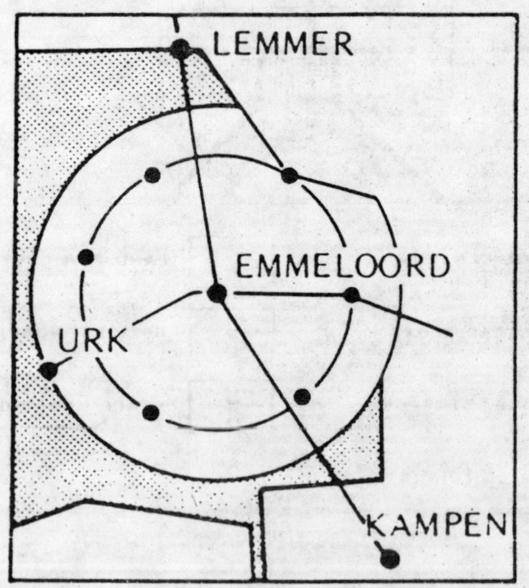

Source : The Zuider Zee Guide (1975)

FOUR

APPLIED QUANTITATIVE METHODS OF RURAL SETTLEMENT GEOGRAPHY

SHELTER is the most important need of man in rural areas, where the irresistible hazards of the climate and the scorching sun do impart uninterrupted discomfiture to human life. Rural settlement is the only area in human geography where we may really search and try to locate the genesis of settlement geography. Rural settlement is the outcome of the combination of several physical and cultural factors and these are expressed here with different quantitative methods.[1]

There are two sets of variables which have a bearing on the settlement types in rural areas. These variables may be termed as agglomerating and deglomerating factors. These parameters are both physical and cultural and lead to compact and dispersed settlements according to the relative influence of the centrifugal and the centripetal forces.

In most countries of the world two methods of rural settlement classification have generally been used, (a) personal observation and (b) quantitative methods for determining the types of rural settlements. The significance of some of these quantitative methods for measuring the indices of agglomeration and dispersion have been discussed in this chapter.

In 1909, Woiekof[2] devised a formula as:

$$K = \frac{P}{H}$$

where K is the index, P is the number of inhabitants and H is the number of inhabited places. This, however, gives merely the average population size of rural settlements, irrespective of settlement dispersion. In the same way in 1924 Kristofferson[3] classified the rural settlements below 50 metres spacing as dispersed and more than 50 metres as compact. In 1926 Lefevre[4] used the number of houses per square kilometre grouped into classes of 1-10, 11-25, 26-50, 51-100, 101-250, 251-500, 500-1000, and 1000+as the basis of classification and dispersion of settlement types. But this method only gives the density classes of houses, and not the types of settlements.

In 1931, the French scientist Bernhard[5] devised another formula,

$$K = \frac{S \times M}{N^2}$$

where K is the index of concentration, S is the total number of houses, M is the area and N is the number of settlements. This formula, however, does not distinguish closely between the settlement variations and K can be identical in value with very different patterns.

Another successful formula for measuring dispersion is that of Demangeon[6] developed in 1933. He expressed the settlement pattern as

$$K = \frac{E \times N}{T}$$

where K is the co-efficient required, E is the population of the commune except for that of the chief nucleated settlement, N is the number of isolated settlements, and T is the total population.

In 1934, Zierhoffer[7] devised another formula on the assumption that the degree of dispersion of settlements will increase with the corresponding increase of area per dwelling and the degree of dispersion can be represented as

$$R = \frac{P \times S}{d} \times K$$

where R is the degree of dispersion, P is the average area per dwelling, S is the number of house groups in commune, d is the total number of inhabitants and the constant K is 0.005. This method, however, does not give sufficient contrast to the value of R in intermediate categories between complete dispersion and absolute nucleation.

In 1938, Pawlowski[8] while studying the concentration of settlements derived the following formulae:

$$C = \frac{A}{AS} \text{ and } MC = \frac{AS}{S},$$

where C is index of concentration, A is 25 sq. km and represents area occupied by settlements; Mc is mean index of concentration, S is number of settlements. Debouverie[9] in 1943 tried to relate regional variations of settlements with the standard concept of concentration. His formula is as follows:

$$K = \frac{X \times L}{H},$$

where K is the index of concentration, X is the minimum number of dwellings per settlement, L is the number of settlement units and H is the total number of dwellings in the commune. This formula is useful in distinguishing types of nucleation.

In 1950, Kant[10] presented an indigenous formula to measure the concentration of settlements more precisely. The formula is as follows:

$$X = \frac{1}{M}\sqrt{\frac{A}{D}},$$

where X is the relative interval between two settlements, $\frac{1}{M}$ is map scale; A is the area; D is the density of habitations.

Based on Demangeon's formula, Houston[11] devised another method in 1953.

$$K = \frac{S \times N}{T - E},$$

where K is the index of dispersion, S is the area of commune, N is the number of isolated settlements, T is the total population and E is the population of commune minus its chief place or urban centres.

In 1957, Tanioka[12] devised a new formula to measure the index of dispersion of rural settlements. The formula is as follows:

$$M = \frac{S \times T}{S \times N},$$

where M is index of dispersion, S is area of map sheet (1/50,000 scale), T is per cent of land cultivated, S is average agriculture area worked per family, N is average number of rural houses per village.

In 1962, K.H. Stone[13] devised a formula to measure the continuous and discontinuous settlements in any region. The measure developed by him is as follows:

R or FZ = Nh + Nr,

where R is measure of continuous or discontinuous settlement, FZ is *fringe zone* in discontinuous settlement region, Nh is pattern of permanent residences within 5 kms long 1-6 major directions from any one permanent residence, Nr is number (1-4) of inter-regional and local routes of transport within 16 to 40 kms of each permanent residence.

In 1964, S. Inouye[14] devised a measure of dispersion of rural settlements on the basis of 50 metres of spacing. In this measure isolated means less than 3 houses within 50 metres of each other, concentrated means more than half of the houses in a village distributed into one group within 50 metres range, condensed means more than half of the houses in a village centralized into one core.

In 1969, R.B. Singh[15], expressed the following formula to measure the compactness and dispersal of rural settlements.

$$Hn = Vn \quad = Compact$$

$$Hn = Vn + 1 \; to \; Vn \times 2 = Semicompact$$

$$Hn = Vn \times 2 + 1 \; to \; \frac{OUn \times 2}{3} = Hamletted$$

$$Hn = \frac{OUn \times 2 + 1}{3} \; to \; OUn = Dispersed$$

where Hn represents the number of hamlets, Vn is the number of villages in an administrative unit and OUn is the number of occupance units in the same area. In 1972, Mandal[16] devised the following measure of dispersal of rural settlements.

1 = Average Population Size of Tola/Average Spacing of Tola

where 1 is index of dispersal. Index of dispersal values grouped according to mediau and quartile values (the highest value shows the agglomeration while the lowest shows the dispersal).

In 1973, A. Prasad[17] while studying the rural settlements of Chotanagpur Plateau devised a formula of descriptive nature after considering the *deviation from standard index.* Ten highly compact villages from the adjoining parts of Gaya district have been selected. On the basis of village maps of the concerned settlements, the actual built up area in each case is reduced to the percentage of the total area within the homestead boundary. The average percentage of the ten villages has been taken. This average is expected as the standard index of agglomeration for Chotanagpur as a whole. To determine the agglomeration quotient similar percentage value for any other cluster is divided by the standard index and is then multiplied by 100. If it is 100, the cluster has the highest degree of agglomeration and compactness. If it is more than 100, the agglomeration is of exceptionally high order. The quotient under 100 indicates a decrease in agglomeration tendency and a corresponding increase in deglomeration tendency. Fifty is the critical value. As the quotient declines below 50, the settlements are to be classed as dispersed. Dispersal can be easily determined by subtracting the agglomeration quotient from 100. The remainder is dispersal quotient for a cluster.

In 1977, Mandal[18], while studying the *Planned Development of Rural Settlements in North Bihar* devised a measure of dispersal index to determine types of rural settlements. The formula is as follows:

$$\text{Dispersal Index} = \frac{\text{Total Rural Population of an Anchal} \times \text{Number of Tolas in an Anchal}}{(\text{Total Rural Area})^2}$$

To determine the validity of this formula, the relationship between the rural area of *anchals* in thousand square kilometres and the number of *tolas* multiplied by rural population of an *anchal* were plotted along the X axis and Y axis respectively. Both axes were on logarithmic scale and data was plotted for all the 241 *anchals* of North Bihar (Fig. 4.1.). For this set of data, the product moment coefficient of correlation value comes to r = 0.56 and regression value of Y = Log 10.33 + Log 0.14X. Fig.4.1 shows the types of rural settlements in which upper part of the dispersion graph represents compact - rural settlements, middle part semi-compact, and the lower semi-sprinkled. The breakpoints have been achieved with the **anchalwise** ranking of dispersion index. The dispersion index 478 is a breakpoint in between compact and semi-compact and semi-sprinkled. One may get these values after dividing 1000,000 the base value of Y axis with 2090 in case of 478, and again dividing 1000,000 with 3400 in case of 294. These two give the lines of equal distribution of the density of dispersal index.

The density of habitations (d) is the ratio of two quantities - C and A, the number of habitations (C) belonging to a given area (A):

$$d = C/A$$

In order to prepare map the density value should be arranged serially either on the basis of Quartile, Octile or Standard deviation. Other methods of grouping can also be used.

METHODS FOR MEASURING SPACING OF SETTLEMENTS

Geography is a discipline in distance. Thus the spacing of rural settlements is largely governed by their size. Large rural settlements would be widely spaced, while smaller settlements would be closely spaced.[19] These spatial patterns are constantly changing in time and space which resulted in an increase in the size of centres and reduction in their spacing. There are methods which may be employed in measuring the spacing of settlements.

METHOD 1

Walenty Winid, a Polish geographer, assumed that settlements are ordinarily placed at the intersection points of a rectangular grid, and the best figure to use for inter-settlement distance is equal to the square root of the area divided by the number of settlements within that area.[20]

$$D = \sqrt{\frac{A}{N}}$$

Where D is average distance between settlements, A is the total area of the region under study, N is the number of settlements

METHOD II

According to Barnes and Robinson[21], if the number of settlements and the area of the region are known, we can determine the approximate distance between each under its nearest neighbour and would be under conditions of an even spatial distribution. It can be computed by a simple formula,

$$Hd = 1.11\sqrt{\frac{A}{N}},$$

where Hd is the hypothetical distance, A is the area of the region, N is the number of settlements, 1.11 is the constant value. In this formula A/N indicates the average area that belongs to a settlement. In representing this area by a hexagon, the distance D of a settlement from its six neighbours, is equal to twice the height of equilateral triangle obtained by linking the corners of the hexagon to its centre. The area of the hexagon is[22]

$$A/N = \frac{1}{2}\sqrt{3.D^2}$$

Consequently

$$D = \sqrt{\frac{2A}{n\sqrt{3}}} = 1.11\sqrt{\frac{A}{N}},$$

METHOD III

In 1944, Mather[23] devised a formula to measure the spacing of settlements. The formula is as follows

$$D = 1.07\sqrt{\frac{A}{N}}$$

where D is average distance of a settlement to its six nearest neighbours, A is the total area of study and N is the number of settlements.

The verification about the correctness of Barnes-Robinson and Mather methods was presented by Rana P.B. Singh.[24] He endeavoured to solve this disputable method in this way:

If in Fig. 4.2, A and B are the two points, then AB will be their interpoint distance. Take first the ΔADC (right angled at C).

$$Total \quad area \quad of \quad \Delta ADC = \left(\frac{AC.DC}{2}\right)$$

(MATHER'S METHOD) SPACING -	(ROBINSON'S METHOD) SPACING -
$1.0746d^{-1/2}$	$1.11d^{-1/2}$

Let AD = X,

and it is known that AC = $\frac{\sqrt{3}}{2}$X and

DC = $\frac{X}{2}$; and AB, the required inter-village

distance (D) = $\sqrt{3X}$.

$$Total\ area\ of\ \Delta ADC = \frac{\sqrt{3}}{2} X \frac{x}{2}, \cdot \frac{1}{2} = \frac{\sqrt{3}}{8} x^2$$

The area of the hexagon should correspond to the average are of a village i.e.; A/N;

$$\therefore\ 3\frac{\sqrt{3}}{2} . x^2 = A/N$$

or

$$3x^2 = A/N . \frac{2}{\sqrt{3}}$$

$$= \frac{2A}{\sqrt{3N}} \text{ or } 1.1547\left(\frac{A}{N}\right)$$

$$\therefore \sqrt{3x^2} = \sqrt{1.1547} . \sqrt{A/N}$$

$$\sqrt{3x} = 1.0746\sqrt{A/N}$$

Thus it is proved that inter-village distances in hexagonal arrangement will be 1.0746√A/N not 1.11 √A/N as formulated by Robinson and Barnes", and 1.1284 √A/N by Mukerji.

As these measures present overlapped area, so they are wrong in their propositions (Fig.4.3).

METHOD IV

Like Robinson and Barnes, A.B. Mukerji[25] assumes that the average area of village will be a circle πr^2. So the transformation as of average village area into circle, result in the theoretical distance between two villages. According to him, area of the village will be πr^2

$$Now,\ if\ \pi r^2 = \frac{A}{N} ; r^2 = \frac{A}{N x \pi}$$

or

$$r = 2\sqrt{A/N\pi}$$

Thus the inter-village distance

$$(D) = 2\sqrt{A/N\pi} = 1.1284\sqrt{A/N}$$

In this method empty space is left in between three circles, so this method is also not suitable for measuring inter-village distance. Thus, it is apparent that the theoretical spacing between settlements will be $1.0746\sqrt{A/N}$

not $1.11\sqrt{A/N}$; nor $1.1284\sqrt{A/N}$

Finally the formula used by A.B. Mukerji for the computation of spacing in kms of rural settlements in an *anchal* or *taluka* is as follows[25]:

$$S = 2x\sqrt{\frac{A}{N \times \pi}}$$

where S is spacing in kms, A is the rural area of an *anchal* and N is the number of rural settlements.

METHOD V

In the given co-ordinates of any two points on a plane, the distance between them can be easily computed by using the Pythagoras Theorem. This question can be generalized to measure distances between points in n dimensional space for given coordinates and is as follows[26]:

$$dij\sqrt{\sum_{z=1}^{n}(Xiz - Xjz)^2}$$

where dij is the distance between points i and j in a space of n dimensions with Xiz and Xjz being measures along the zth co-ordinate. This is the simplest distance measure and has been used by Berry in 1961.

METHOD VI

If (x_1, y_1, z_1) and (x_2, y_2, z_2) be the rectangular coordinates of two points P_1, P_2 respectively and O is the origin points then[27]:

$$\overrightarrow{OP}_1 = x_1 i + y_1 j + z_1 K$$

$$\overrightarrow{OP}_2 = x_2 i + y_2 j \div z_2 K$$

$$\therefore \overrightarrow{P_1 P_2} = \overrightarrow{OP_2} - \overrightarrow{OP_1} = (x_2 - x_1)i + (y_2 - y_1)j + (z_2 - z_1)K$$

$$Hence \quad P_1P_2 |\overrightarrow{P_1P_2}| = \sqrt{(x_2 - x_1)^2 + (y_2 - y_1)^2 + (z_2 - z_1)^2}$$

This will give the distance between the points P_1, P_2.

METHOD VII

In 1901, Bannerman used the following formula for calculating the distance between each village:[28]

$$2\sqrt{\frac{(\cos 30^\circ)}{3}} \times \sqrt{\left(\frac{Area}{No.\ of\ villages\ and\ Towns}\right)}$$

$$2\sqrt{\left(\frac{.86603}{3}\right)} \times \sqrt{\left(\frac{50\,km^2}{10}\right)}$$

$$2\sqrt{.28867} \times \sqrt{5}$$

= .338 x 2.23

= 0.75 kilometres average inter village distance.

METHOD VIII

According to Clark and Evans, the nearest neighbour scale can be referred to as an R_n scale, and the individual R_n value can be calculated as follows[29]:

$$Rn = \frac{\bar{r}A}{\bar{r}E}, \quad Where \ \bar{r}A = \frac{\sum r}{N}$$ or the mean of the series of

distances to nearest-neighbours r n being the distance from each point to its nearest-neighbour (actual) and

$$\bar{r}E = \frac{1}{2\sqrt{P}} \quad \text{or} \quad \bar{r}E = \frac{1}{2\sqrt{\frac{N}{A}}}$$

Where the expected mean distance ($\bar{r}E$) to the nearest neighbour in an infinitely large random distribution of density P (E meaning expecte d) and P = $\frac{\text{No. of settlement}}{\text{Total area}}$

The R_n value should range between 0.2.1491 meaning maximum dispersal at the end, with unity (1.00) indicating the presence of a random observed distribution, while the values near O indicate clustering of settlements. This index of Rn value can be correlated with variance (V) for further testing, which can be calculated with the help of following formula[30]:

$$V = (4 - \pi/4\, d\pi)$$

In the case the $\bar{r}E$ value is larger than the V, the distribution is termed regular; when the V is larger than $\bar{r}E$, it is termed clustered and the term random is applied to the case when V and rE are equal, i.e., the variance mean ratio is one.

The test of the significance of rE was made about the hypothesis of randomness on the basis of standard error ($\sigma\bar{r}E$)[31] which is as follows:

$$\sigma \bar{r} E = \frac{0.26136}{\sqrt{(nd)}}$$

Where n is number of total villages in the areal unit and d represents density of villages per square kilometre.

In the nearest neighbour analysis, the differences between the observed and expected frequencies were analysed by a Chi-square test. Chi-square test was used because it was assumed that the distances are not normally distributed. Thompson[32] has provided a suitable procedure of chi-square test and it has been reviewed by King.[33] The values of chi-square are given by[34]:

$$2\pi d^{1/2} \sum_{i=1}^{n} rij$$

Where n is the number of points in the pattern, d is the observed density, rij is the order-nearest-neighbour distance for i and is distributed as chi-square with n-2 degree of freedom.

The index of standard variate of normal curve (C) can be calculated as:

$$C = (\bar{r}O - \bar{r}E)/O\bar{r}E$$

Where $\bar{r}O$ is observed value and $\bar{r}E$ is expected. The upper and lower ranges of random matching at the 95% probability will be computed with the help of $O\bar{r}E$

$$i.e. = \frac{(2\sigma\bar{r}E \pm \bar{r}E)}{\bar{r}E}$$

The application of these tests has been made by Rana P.B. Singh in his paper related to distribution of rural settlements.

METHOD IX

King suggested formula for calculating the R value in nearest neighbour analysis is as follows[35]:

TABLE 4.1: **Results of Nearest Neighbour Measures**

Class of Urban Places	No. of urban places	Density per sq. mile	Average observed distance in miles $\bar{r}A$	Average Expected distance im miles $\bar{r}E$
Hamlets	59	0.0127	4.881	4.442
Villages	93	0.0200	3.487	3.538
Towns	37	0.0079	5.931	5.609
Cities	14	0.0030	10.407	9.119

Contd. Table 4.1

Class of Urban Places	Pattern Statistics R	Chi-square (X^2)	Degree of freedom	Significant
Hamlets	1.098	194.484	118.0	Yes
Villages	1.126	314.393	186.0	Yes
Towns	1.057	117.363	74.0	Yes
Cities	1.141	47.934	28.0	Yes

Source: B. Thakur, Indian Geographical Studies, 1973.

$$Rn = 2d\sqrt{\frac{N}{A}}$$

Where d is the average observed distances between each point and its nearest neighbour, N is the number of points and A is the area under study.

METHOD X

In 1967, Birch had applied nearest neighbour measures in Mid-west of U.S.A.[36] The formula is as follows:

$$R_1 = \frac{\bar{r}A}{(A/N)^{-1/2}}$$

Where R_1 is index of randomness of regularity or agglomeration of farmsteads, $\bar{r}A$ is the observed mean distance between each point and its nearest neighbour, A is the area, and N is the number of rural settlements.

METHOD XI

In 1975 a modification in nearest neighbour technique has been presented by Pinder and Witherick.[37] According to him nearest neighbour analysis is generally used in two-dimensional point patterns. No exploration has been done for distribution of points along a line. The method presented by Evans and Dacey is simple but its result is misleading especially when the number of points in the pattern is low.

In the normal analysis of nearest-neighbour by Clark and Evans method, the formula for predicting the average distance between randomly distributed nearest-neighbour ($\bar{r}E$) is as follows:

$$0.5\sqrt{(a/n)}$$

Where a is the area studied and n is the number of points. This method has been designed to fit in two dimensional patterns.

In order to predict the mean nearest neighbour distances in a unidimensional situation, the average distance between randomly distributed linear nearest neighbours (L$\bar{r}$E) may be derived from the following formula:

$$L\bar{r}E = 0.5\left(\frac{L}{n-1}\right)$$

Where L is the line length and n is the number of points. This is the first stage of this linear nearest neighbour technique. This indicates that the predicted random average is half the mean distance that would separate the points if they were distributed with regularity throughout the line.

TABLE 4.2 : **Comparison of Predicted and Eeperimental Values of L $\bar{r}$E**

No. of points per Pattern	Predicted mean 0.5 (L/n - 1)	Experimental mean	Predicted Mean Less Experimental Mean
10	55.56	55.89	-0.33
20	26.32	26.62	-0.30
30	17.24	17.57	-0.33
40	12.82	12.74	0.08
50	10.20	10.21	-0.01
60	8.48	8.34	0.14
70	7.25	7.12	0.13
80	6.33	6.23	0.10
90	5.62	5.59	0.13
100	5.05	5.04	0.01

Source: After Pinder and Witherick, Geography, 1975.

In this table, for a linc of 100 units comparison of predicted and computer generated experimental values of L $\bar{r}$ E have been given. This provides extremely close correspondence between the two sets of means as given in the second and the third columns, and further emphasis is put forward by the last column, where the discrepancies between the predicted and experimental means are presented.

Further, linear nearest neighbour statistic (L R n) can be defined as:

$$\frac{\bar{D}obs}{L\bar{r}E} \text{ or } \frac{\bar{D}obs}{0.5(L/(n-1))}$$

Where Dobs is average observed distance between nearest neighbours, L is length of the line studied, n is the number of settlements. In case L R n value is 1.00 suggests random situation. Less than 1.00 values are indicative of clustering while more than 1.00 shows the presence of some regularity.

In a perfect regular situation LRn equals 2.00 and this is half the observed mean distance between settlements.

METHOD XII

ORDER NEAREST NEIGHBOUR ANALYSIS

Dacey has given the formal derivation of poisson Probability law for two dimensional random point process. He assumed that those neighbours whose distance is greater than the parent point-distance from the boundary of the map, the number and distance of such neighbours should be ignored from the study. The formula through which the mean observed distance upto four neighbours can be calculated is as follows[38]:

$$\bar{r}j = \frac{1}{N} \sum_{i=1}^{n} rij$$

Where n is the number of points in the area, rj is the mean distance from i to any other point, i is any point, and rij is the distance between i and jth nearest point.

Dacey has generalised these concepts of order distances to nearest neighbour to handle the description of pattern in multi-dimensional space. The non-standardized mean value of distance of urban places in Bihar upto four neighbours is given below:

TABLE 4.3 : **Order Distance Statistics for Urban Places in Bihar, 1971 (Miles)**

Order j	n	$\sum_{i=1}^{n} rij$	rj
1	163	1361.00	8.35
2	143	1693.75	11.84
3	133	1894.50	14.24
4	127	1997.75	15.83

The above observed mean distances can be used in comparison with the hypothetical estimated distance for pattern interpretation.

METHOD XIII

REGIONAL METHOD OF NEAREST NEIGHBOUR ANALYSIS

Dacey and Tung has put forward alternative approach to the description of point patterns which is known as regional method. They divided the map around each point into six K equal sectors. The distances from the central point to six neighbours in each sector are measured and 'these observed distances are used to classify the regions in some systematic fashion and a separate mean is obtained for each kind of region'.[39] The formula used is as follows:

$$\bar{r}ik = \frac{\left(\sum_{i=1}^{k} \bar{r}ik\right)}{n}$$

Where i is the central point, 1 is the set of n points for which the measurements are made, n is the number of point in a region.

He again assumed that those neighbours whose distance is greater than the parent point distance from the boundary of the map than the number and distance of such neighbours can be deleted.

METHOD XIV

BACHI'S STANDARD DISTANCE STATISTICS

Bachi's standard distance is a measure of the dispersion of a set of points in respect of two right angled axes. It may be expressed as:

$$dij = \{ (xi - xj)^2 + (yi - yj)^2) \} 1/2$$

Where x and y are two coordinates, and dij is the standard distance.

The above formula will give us distance between two points in Euclidian Space (Fig. 4.4). For the n set of points. n^2 of these distances can be calculated, so that the distance between the two points is itself included and every standard distance is measured twice, once for i and secondly for j.

Bachi's Standard Distance Measure between two Points

For this set of n^2 distance, Bachi suggested the mean quadratic distance, as:

$$D = \left[\left(\frac{\sum_{i=1}^{n} \sum_{j=1}^{n} dij^2}{n^2} \right) \right]^{1/2}$$

Then, the mean centre of the distribution have the coordination as:

$$\bar{x} = \frac{\left(\sum_{j=1}^{n} xi \right)}{n}, \quad \text{and} \quad \bar{y} = \frac{\left(\sum_{i=1}^{n} yi \right)}{n}$$

$$then \quad D = \frac{\left(2 \sum_{i=1}^{n} d^2 ic \right)^{1/2}}{n}$$

Where dic is the distance from point i to the mean centre

$$C = \{ (xi - \dot{x})^2 + (yi - y)^2 \}1/2$$

then the standard distance is[40]:

$$d = \left[\frac{\sum_{i=1}^{n} d^2 ic}{n} \right]$$

Further "Bachi notes that the square of distance (d^2) for the entire area is equal to the sum of a 'within-regions' squared distance (d^2_b)".[41] and 'between - regions' squared distance (d^2_6)".[41]
Then $d^2 = d^2w + d^2_b$

$$= \frac{\sum_{j=1}^{k} \sum_{i=1}^{nj} [(xij - \bar{x}j)^2 + (yij - \bar{y}j)^2]}{n} + \frac{\sum_{j=1}^{k} nj[(\bar{x}j - \bar{x})^2 + (\bar{y}j - \bar{y})^2]}{n}$$

Where (xij,yij) are the coordinates of the ith point in the jth region

($\bar{x}$,$\bar{y}$) is the regional mean centre,
($\bar{x}$,$\bar{y}$) is the mean centre for the whole distribution-
(d^2b/d^2)is the ratio which provides a crude measure of significance of the regional divisions. Ratio I is the maximum differentiation.

Where O shows the same mean centre as exists in the total pattern.

METHOD XV
COMPUTER FUNCTION TO MEASURE ARC DISTANCES

The calculation of the arc distance comes from spherical trigonometry. It assumes that the earth is a sphere. The necessary formula for determining the arc distance between points A and B is given by Robinson. The formula is as follows[42]:

Cos d = (Sin a Sin b) + (Cos a. Cosb. Cos P)
here d = arc distance between A and B.
a = latitude of A,
b = latitude of B,
P = degrees of longitude between A and B.

Using this formula to calculate distances has proved satisfactory. Accuracy has been good (calculated distances between cities on opposite sides of the Pacific have varied only a few miles from distances quoted by air lines) and seems to be limited more by point measurement than by computer rounding errors or the off spherical shape of the earth".[43]

If all settlements are equally spaced over a region, a uniform distribution is obtained. This distance (δ) is obtained by the relation,

$$\delta = \sqrt{\frac{A}{N}}$$

Where A is the total area, and N is the number of settlements. The degree of concentration (DC) of settlements (nc) is given by

$$DC = \frac{\delta}{S},$$

Where S is the average separation between settlements. The quality nCS^2 is designated as the derived area (ac) of the concentration. We get a level of concentration (LC) expressed in the form

$$LC = \left(\frac{\delta}{S}\right)\frac{nc}{N} = Dc^2\frac{nc}{N}$$

It should be noted that any quantity of LC in fact represents a set of values with varying δ and nc; hence its designation is 'level'. A number of concentrations in a region can be grouped together to form agglomerations. If the distance (As) between two contiguous concentrations is less than or equal to, the sum of the average separations of settlement, within the concentrations, thus the concentration can be grouped to form an agglomeration. Two contiguous concentrations are brought together under an agglomeration if

$As \leq S_1 + S_2$,

where S_1, and S_2 refer to the average separations of settlements in concentrations. To demarcate the dispersion group, the distance relevant to dispersion (s) is derived as follows:

$$\Delta = \sqrt{\frac{A - \sum ac}{N - NC}}$$

Where N is total number of settlements, NC is the number of concentrated settlements, and ?ac is the sum of the areas of all concentrations. As in the case of concentration, the degree of dispersion.

$$\text{Dd} = \frac{C}{\Delta},$$

Where C is the average separation in a dispersion group. The area of dispersion,

$$\text{ad} = \text{nd}C^2$$

Where nd represents the number of settlements involved in the dispersion group. The level of dispersion,

$$Ld = \left(\frac{c}{\Delta}\right)^2 \frac{nd}{N} = Dd = \frac{nd}{N}$$

The change in any settlement is generally introduced by transport linkage. Inversely in this formula the rate of transportation is determined by the change in a settlement. The formula is as follows[44]:

$$Rn = \frac{Dn}{Tn}$$

Where Rn = rate of transportation
Dn = degree of transportation
Tn = time unit of transition in a settlement

$$\therefore Tn = \frac{Dn}{Rn}$$ Dn →Length of phase of development; Rn →Rate of transformation in nth phase.

$$\therefore T = \sum \frac{D}{R}$$

$$T = \sum_{n-1}^{n} \frac{Dn}{Rn}$$

Where T is the time required for attaining total development through transformation.

To express the change in number of lower order central places mathematically, the average rate of change can be calculated with the help of the formula[45]:

$$b = \frac{Pn - Po}{n}$$

and the arithmatic approximation to an average rate is given by:

$$r = \frac{b}{\frac{1}{2}(Po + Pn)} \times 100$$

Where, Po is the initial number of centres, Pn is the number of centres at the end of the period (n year), n is the time in years, and b is the annual amount of change.

In a geometric series, the frequency distribution increases or decreases at the same rate over each unit of time, e.g. each year. If this constant rate of change is represented by r and the initial number is represented by Po, then after n years the final frequency of central places is given by:

$Pn = Po\ (1 + r)\ n$

with the observed data that is available, we get

$$1 + r = n\sqrt{\frac{Pn}{Po}}$$

$$\text{or} \quad \log(1 + r) = \frac{\log Pn - \log Po}{n}$$

$$\frac{\log\left(\frac{Pn}{Po}\right)}{n}$$

$= \frac{1}{5}[(\log 342 - \log 239)] = \frac{1}{5}[(2.53403 - 2.37840)]$
$= 0.03112$ Taking antilog I + r = 0.10748
$\therefore r = .10748$ i.e., the rate of change is 10.75 per cent per annum.

REGIONAL PECULIARITIES IN THE DYNAMICS OF RURAL SETTLEMENTS

The visual evaluation of the degree of change in settling patterns may be supplemented by an objective measure of the magnitude of change in the form of the sum of deviations of the 1980 distribution curve from the 1969 curve. For this purpose use was made of the simple index Kr (the coefficient of redistribution of population among size classes during the study period). If the distribution of population by size classes did not change, then Kr = O; the index will increase with the scale of structural changes in the network of places. The co-efficient can be calculated as follows[46]:

$$Kr = \sqrt{\sum_{P=1}^{n} (P_{70} - P_{59})^2}$$

Where n is the number of size classes, P_{70} is the percentage of 1980 rural population living in places of particular size class; P_{59} the same for the 1969 rural population.

The formula applied for size of the rural settlements is as follows:

$$S = \frac{P}{N}$$

Where S is the average size of population per village, P is the rural population of the anchal, and N is the number of villages in the anchal.

Another possibility is as follow:

$$S = \frac{\text{Number of Houses in an Anchal}}{\text{Number of Settlements in an Anchal}}$$

Information may be collected from Census returns.

MEASUREMENT OF SHAPE OF RURAL SETTLEMENTS

METHOD I

In order to determine the shape, a circle with its circumference touching the two extreme points of settlement was drawn. Now the pattern seems to be obvious in its geometrical perspective in comparison with the circle. The formula for the measurement of this is:[47]

$$MC = \frac{100 \times Aa}{\pi 2r^2}$$

Where MC is the measure of circularity in shape; Aa is the actual area contained in the settlements and πr^2 is the area of circle of settlement = A.

METHOD II

The shape of settlements can also be measured with Simmon's measure. He devised a method based upon area of a settlement and its outer boundary. The measure is defined as the ratio of the sum of distances of all settlements arranged in a regular network within the boundary of the residential area of a settlement to its centre. The formula for measuring shape is as follows[48]:

$$S = \frac{\sum_{i=1}^{n} Ri}{\sum_{i=1}^{n} ri}$$

Where Ri is the distance for the settlement area, and ri is the area for the circle. Here for a given settlement with given centre and boundary; S is a function of n type of network of settlements.

METHOD III

According to Boyce and Clark, the formula for measuring the outer boundary of a settlement is as follows[49]:

$$S = \sum_{i=1}^{n} \left| \frac{Ri}{\sum_{i=1}^{n} Ri} . 100 \quad \frac{100}{n} \right|$$

Where S is the measure and the Ri (i = 1, 2.....n) are the lengths of radial lines measured from the settlement centre to the boundary along equally spaced radii.

METHOD IV

The shape of rural settlement is theoretically circular at its peripheries for the distance between the central point and the edge of the territory is always shorter and quicker in space and time in comparison with any other geometrical shape of the settlement. But circles either overlap or leave gaps between them. The hexagonal pattern of rural settlements, therefore, is the ideal shape as it approximates the shape of a circle. Settlements in the area are neither equally spaced nor have equal size. The distance that should actually exist among settlements in a particular region with homogeneous character throughout, has been called as 'mean actual distance' (Da). It has derived from the following equation.[50]

$$Da = \frac{\sum Ps_1 + Ps_2 + Ps_3 + \ldots\ldots Ps_n}{\sum N}$$

Where Ps stands for the distance of possible straight line joining the different villages and 'N' stands for total number of lines joining n villages. In case the same number of settlements are supposed to be arranged on a hexagonal pattern in the same region occupying the same area, their inter-distance, as it is called Hypothetical Distance (Dh), is derived from the following equation[51]:

$$Dh = \sqrt{\frac{\sum A_1 + A_2 + A_3 + \ldots\ldots + A_n}{\sum N}}$$

Where 'A' denotes the area of settlements upto nth number in Km^2 and N stands for the number of settlements.

In case Da equals Dh, there is a likelihood of equi-spaced normal settlement pattern. If Da is more than Dh, there will be a tendency towards dispersed pattern and if Da is less than Dh, the settlements will adopt a concentrated pattern. Hence, the above mentioned technique will help in determining the spacing, regularity and type of settlements in the study area. Now Dh being the ideal distance, is supposed to be 100% and the regularity index (Ir) is derived from the following equation:

$$I_r = 100 - \frac{Da \times 100}{Dh}$$

The indices derived out of this formula will be either positive or negative. The negative indices will suggest concentration while the positive, dispersion.

The smaller urban settlements or the larger villages have been described variously as rurban settlements. A rurban centre is essentially a focus of activities and is marked by commercial, industrial, administrative and cultural institutions. Centres, having at least three out of the 9 central functions (viz., education, medical, communication, finance, transport, administrative, trade, recreation and percentage of workers engaged in tertiary occupations) have been considered as rurban centres. Classification of rurban centres on this basis from the list of villages is easy, but a problem arises in the selection of rurban centres from the list of towns. Both towns and cities have functions of a higher order as compared to the rural, which creates confusion. In the selection of rurban centres from the list of towns, the following formula may be used.[52]

$$Rl = PC \times \frac{tw \times 100}{TW}$$

Where Rl = Rurban index

PC = Total Population of the centre

tw = workers engaged in tertiary occupations in that centre, and

TW = Total number of workers in that centre.

After calculating the value of Rl by giving proper weighting to above mentioned 9 functions for all towns, the mean was determined. On accepting the mean as the line of demarcation, all towns having an Rl less than mean were classified as rurban centres.

MEAN CENTRE OF RURAL SETTLEMENTS

Using the idea of 'mean centres of population' of Hart,[53]

D.K.Singh and others have written a paper on 'rural settlements of Orissa' which deals with the mean centre of rural settlements. Their idea about this method is as follows:[54]

Rural settlement types and patterns give the simplest description of arrangement of settlements according to the physiography, drainage, transport and communication system. But this, would not help in assessing the grouping of settlements around the centrally located rural settlements which might help in representing the mean centre of settlements for the State as a whole in order to act as the point of diffusion for rural development innovations.

This mean centre over space is a "centre of gravity of a point, at which objects on a weightless surface will balance".

For the rural settlements of Bagamoyo district, Tanzania a demonstration of the calculation of mean centre and standard distance of Robert Bachi (1942) is presented here.

In case of Fig.4.5 the whole map has been divided into various cells at equal interval. Then X axis has given the name horizontal tier (xi) and Y axis vertical tier (yi). These tiers have been marked with odd numbers (1, 3, 5, 7, 9, etc.) which are known as tier numbers. Then points (P) have been counted in different tiers (Table 4.4).

TABLE 4.4 : **Data Matrices for Spatial Mean Centre of Rural Settlements in Bagamoyo District, Tanzania**

X Axis Horizontal Tier			Y Axis Vertical Tier		
Xi	Pi	Xi.Pi	Yi	Pi	Yi.Pi
1	12	12	1	1	1
3	22	66	3	4	12
5	11	55	5	11	55
7	14	98	7	19	133
9	9	81	9	11	99
11	0	0	11	9	99
-	-	-	13	8	104
-	-	-	15	5	75
Σ	68	316	Σ	68	578

Horizontal Tier Moment $\bar{x}c = \frac{\sum(XiPi)}{\sum Pi} = \frac{316}{68} = 4.64$

Vertical Tier Moment $\bar{y}c = \frac{\sum(YiPi)}{\sum Pi} = \frac{578}{68} = 8.50z$

With the help of horizontal and vertical tier moments fulcra point could be located on the map (See Fig. 4.5), which is the spatial mean centre of settlement distribution, around which the rural settlements are equally distributed in the region.

Standard Distance

Based on the value of above tier number and $\bar{X}$ C and $\bar{Y}$ C standard distance of rural settlements for Bagamoyo district could be calculated with the help of following formula:

$$SD = \sqrt{\frac{\sum[Pi(xi - \bar{x}c)_2]}{\sum P;} + \frac{\sum[Pi(Yi - \bar{Y}C)^2]}{\sum Pi}}$$

Where Xi and Yi are horizontal and vertical tier values.
$\bar{X}$ C and $\bar{Y}$ C horizontal and vertical coordinate values
Σ Pi is the total number of rural settlements.

Xi	($\bar{X}$ C)	(Xi-$\bar{X}$ C)	(Xi-$\bar{X}$ C)^2	Pi	Pi(Xi-$\bar{X}$ C)^2
1	4.64	-3.64	13.25	12	159.00
3	4.64	-1.64	2.69	22	59.18
5	4.64	+0.36	0.13	11	1.43
7	4.64	+2.36	5.57	14	77.98
9	4.64	+4.36	19.01	9	171.09
11	4.64	+6.36	40.45	0	0
				68	468.68

$$= \frac{\sum[Pi(Xi - \bar{x}C)^2]}{\sum Pi} + \frac{468.68}{68} = 6.89$$

Yi	$\bar{Y}C$	$Yi-\bar{Y}C$	$(Yi-\bar{Y}C)^2$	Pi	$Pi(Yi-\bar{Y}C)^2$
1	8.50	-7.50	56.25	1	56.25
3	8.50	-5.50	30.25	4	121.00
5	8.50	-3.50	12.25	11	134.75
7	8.50	-1.50	2.25	19	42.75
9	8.50	+0.50	0.25	11	2.75
11	8.50	+2.50	6.25	9	56.25
13	8.50	+4.50	20.25	8	162.00
15	8.50	+6.50	42.25	5	211.25
				Σ68	787.00

$$+\frac{\sum[\text{Pi } (Yi-YC)^2]}{\sum \text{Pi}} = \frac{787.00}{68} = 11.57$$

$$= \sqrt{6.89 + 11.57}$$

$$= \sqrt{18.46} = 4.27\,kms.$$

Method of Key Settlement Selection in Rural Areas

Accessibility to employment was one of the criteria measured as part of the key settlement selection procedure in rural areas (Warwickshire country Council, 1973). An index was interpolated from the formula.[55]

$$Ai = \sum_j \frac{Oj}{DijCj}$$

Where

- Ai = Job accessibility of settlement i,
- Oj = number of jobs in employment area j,
- Di_j = travel cost from settlement i to employment area j,
- C_j = Competition for jobs in employment area j from all other settlements.

One criticism of this index is that it does not take into account the sufficiency of local jobs, but this factor does not greatly detract from the overall pattern of employment accessibility.

Housing problems & Demand

1. The housing problem can be expressed by the identity.[56]

   N.C = Y

   where N stands for the number of housing units required, C is the cost of each unit, and Y is the total expenditure.

2. The total demand for housing in a year (i + 1) can be presented in the following equation:

$$H = \frac{Pi\ (1 = Gm)}{1} + \frac{Pi\ (1 + Gm)}{A} + \frac{S}{L} + \left(\frac{Psi}{A} \times \frac{1}{N}\right) + \left(\frac{Pi - Psi}{A} - \frac{S \times R}{2}\right)$$

Where Pi is the total urban population,

Gn is the natural growth rate of the urban population in percentage in yeari.

Gm is the rate of immigration into the towns in per cent of town population.

A is the average number of persons in a household.

S is the stock of regular or acceptable houses.

L is the average life of a house in years.

Psi is the total urban population living in sub-standard housing in year i.

N is the number of years in which overcrowding and sub-standard houses are to be removed.

R is the average number of rooms in the regular housing stock, and

H is the total requirement for housing in year i + 1.

Chi - Square (X^2) Test

The X^2 test is a measure of association i.e. the degree to which two or more groups of data are related to one another. It is an useful test, since the variables need not be quantified beyond their expression in a number of categories; i.e. it can be used with ordinal and even nominal data. This also helps in testing the null and research hypothesis that the observed results do not differ or differ significantly from those which are to be expected by chance.[57]

The hypothesis, that the environmental factors are also responsible for the pattern variation of settlements, is tested by Chi-square analysis[58] (Table 4.5). The calculated value (13.07) of Chi-square is greater than the tabulated value (11.07) for 5 degree of freedom but significant only at 5 per cent level and poses a weak challenge to our hypothesis. It may be inferred that the physical factors are not so strong, though important, as to influence the pattern of settlements to a great extent in the study area, but the nearness to urban centre has exerted a stronger influence to the pattern of settlement distribution. The formula for **Chi-square** test is as follows:

$$\text{Chi-square} = \frac{(D - E)^2}{E}$$

where E stands for expected number of settlements, D stands for number of settlements.

The degree of freedom: n-1 = 6 - 1 = 5.
The Table 4.5 as given will clarify the calculation of Chi-square test.

TABLE 4.5 : **Chi-Square Test**

Sl. No.	Factors affecting rural settlements	Observed number of settle-ments (D)	Expected number of settle-ments (E)278/6= 46.33	$(D-E)^2$	$\frac{(D-E)^2}{E}$
1.	Plains	48	46	4	0.80
2.	Hills	56	46	100	2.10
3.	Ravines	38	46	64	1.40
4.	Shrubby	58	46	144	3.10
5.	Reserved Forests	49	46	9	0.19
6.	Around Urban Centres	29	46	289	6.20
	Total Observations	278	276	610	13.07

Thus, it can be said that most of the statistics used in rural settlement geography are concerned with the formulation of types of rural settlements, spacing of settlements along with the density, size and functional hierarchy. Only some of the methods which are simpler in relation to others are presented here for the students of geography, sociology, anthropology, economics and statistics.

REFERENCES

1. J. Brunhes : *Human Geography*, Rand McNally, New York, 1952, p. 152
2. A. Woiekof : "Le groupement de la population rurale an Russie", *Annales de Geographie*, Vol. 18, 1909, pp. 13-23.
3. A. Kristofferson : *Landskapsleildens foran dringar i norra och ostra delen av Fars Harad*, Lund, 1924, p. 141.
4. M.A. Lefevre : *L-Habitat Rural en Belgique, Liege,* 1926, p.114.
5. J. Bernhard : "Une Formule Pour la Cartographic de l'Habitat rural avec Application au Department de Youne", *Comptes Rendu*, 1931, Vol. III, pp.108-117.
6. A Demongeon : "Une Carte de l'Habitat," *Annales de Geographie* Vol. 42. 1933, pp. 225-232.
7. A Zierhoffer : "Sur Une Formule Servant a Exprimer la Dispersion et la concentration Absolve de l'Habitat Rural," *Comptes Rendu*, 1934. Vol. III, pp. 410-415.
8. S. Pawlowski : 'Encore Une Methode de Representation Cartographique Generle de l'Habitat Rural", *Comptes Rendu*, 1938, Vol. 2, pp. 129-30.
9. A.H. Debouverie : "Pour la Cartographie de l'Habitat Belgique", *Bulletin, Societe Belge de Etudes Geographeques*, Vol. 13, 1943, pp. 146-196.
10. E. Kant : Quelque Problems Concernaut la Representation de la Densite des Habitations Rurales, *Lund Studies in Geography,* Series B, No. 2, 1950, pp. 1-9.

11. J.M. Houston : *A Social Geography of Europe,* London, 1961, p. 83.
12. T. Tanioka : "Differenciation Regional des Types de l'Habitat au Japan," in *Proceedings of the International Geographical Union Conference*, Tokyo, 1957, pp. 503-512.
13. K.H. Stone : "Swedish Fringes of Settlement," *Annals of the Association of American Geographers*, Vol. 52, 1962, p. 374.
14. S. Inouye : "Settlement Measurement in Japan, in *Abstracts of Papers, XX International Geographical Congress*, London, 1964, p. 308.
15. R.B. Singh : "Rural Settlement Types and their Distribution", *The National Geographical Journal of India*, Vol. XV, 1969, p. 100.
16. R.B. Mandal : *Geography of Rural Settlements in Bihar Plain* Unpublished Ph.D. Thesis. Patna University, Department of Geography, 1972, p. 148.
17. A. Prasad : Chota Nagpur : *Geography of Rural Settlements*, Ranchi University, 1973, pp. 314-315.
18. R.B. Mandal : *Planned Development of Rural Settlement*; Concept Publishing Company, New Delhi, 1981, p. 241.
19. P. Haggett : *Locational Analysis in Human Geography*, London, Edward Arnold, 1966, p. 107-13.
20. J.A. Barnes and A.H. Robinson: "A New Method for the Representation of Dispersed Rural Population," *Geographical Review*, Vol. 30, 1940.
21. G.T. Trewartha: "The Unincorporated Hamlet : One Element of the American Settlement Fabric," *Annals of the Association of American Geographers*, Vol. 33, 1943, pp. 32-81.
22. Edgar Kant : "Some Notes on the Representation of the Density of Rural Habitations," *The Indian Geographical Journal*, Vol. 30, 1955, pp. 1.8
23. E.C. Mather : "A Linear-Distance Map of Farm Population in the US," *Annals of the Association of American Geographers,* Vol. 34, 1944, pp. 173-80.
24. R.B. Singh : "Pattern Analysis of Rural Settlement Distribution and Their Types in Saran Plain : A Quantitative Approach," *National Geographical Journal of India*, Vol. 20, 1974, p.126.
25. A.B. Mukerjee : "Spacing of Rural Settlements in Andhra Pradesh : A Spatial Interpretation," *Geographical Outlook,* Vol. VI. 1969, p. 3.
26. C. Board Etc, (Ed) : *Progress in Geography,* , Edward Arnold, London, Vol. 2, 1970. p. 14.
27. R.S. Lall and A.N. Mehra : *A Text Book of Vector Analysis*, Lucknow, Prkashan Kendra, 1965, p. 14.
28. A.D. Bannerman : Census of India, 1901, part 1, Lucknow Government Press, 1902, Quoted by R.C. Sharma : *Settlement Geography of India Desert,* Kumar Brothers, New Delhi, 1972, p. 107.
29. P.J. Clark and F.C. Evans: Distance to Nearest Neighbour as a Measure of Spatial Relationships on Population," *Ecology* Vol. 35, 1954, pp. 445-453.
30. M.F. Dacey : "Order Distance in an inhomogeneous random point pattern," *Canadian Geographer*, Vol. 9, 1965, pp. 141-153.
31. P.J. Clark and F.C. Evans *: op.cit.*
32. H.R. Tompson : "Distribution of Distance to nth Neighbour in a Population of Randomly Distributed Individuals," *Ecology*, Vol. 37, 1956, pp. 391-94.
33. L.J. Ring : *Statistical Analysis in Geography*, New Jersey, Prentice Hall, 1969.
34. B. Thakur : "Nearest Neighbour Analysis as a Measure of Urban Place Patterns," *Indian Geographical Studies*, No. 1, 1973, p. 66.
35. Peter Ambrose : *Analytical Human Geography,* Longmans, London, 1969, p. 119.
36. B.P. Birch : "The Mesurent of Dispersed Patterns of Settlements," *Tijdschrift voor Economische en Social Geographie*, Vol. 58, 1967, pp. 68-75.

37. D.A. Pinder and M.E. Witherick : "A Modification of Nearest Neighbour Analysis for Use in Linear Situations," *Geography*, Vol. 60, No. 266, 1975, pp. 16-23.
38. L.J. King : *op.cit.* p. 89.
39. M.F. Dacey and T. Tung : "The Identification of Randomness in Point Patterns," *Journal of Regional Science Association*, Vol. 4, 1962, p. 85.
40. R. Bachi : "Standard Distance Measures and Related Methods for Spatial Analysis," Papers *Regional Science Association*, Vol. 10, pp. 83-102.
41. L.J. King : *op.cit.*, pp. 92-93.
42. A.H. Robinson : *Elements of Cartography*, (Ed.2) Jon. Wiley, New York, 1964, pp. 16-23.
43. W.J. Craig : "A Useful Computer Function to of Measure Distance," *Professional Geographer*, Vol. XXIII, 1931, pp. 157-158.
44. K.K. Khatu : "Significance of the Study of Rural Settlements in their Transitional Stages," *Indian Geographical Journal*, Vol. XI, IV; No. 3-4, 1969, pp. 52-63 (61).
45. R.B. Mandal : Planned Development of Rural Settlements, *op.cit.*
46. S.A. Kovalav: "Regional Peculiarities in the Dynamics of Rural Settlement in the USSR (1952-70)", *Soviet Geography*, Vol. XV, 1974, p. 5.
47. Jack P. Gibbs : *Urban Research Method,* New Delhi, 1966, p. 101.
48. B.J.L. Berry, et al : "Urban Population Sensities : Structure and Change", *Geographical Review*, Vol. 53, 1963, pp. 389-405.
49. R.B. Boyce and W.A.V. Clark : "The Concept of Shope in Geography", *Geographical Review*, Vol. 54, 1954, pp. 561-62.
50. I. Singh and V.K. Asthana : "Spatial Distribution of Rural Settlements in the Foothill zone of Haryana", *Paper presented at Varanasi Symposium*, December, 1975, pp. 3-4.
51. L.J. King, *Op. cit;* p. 103.
52. R.B. Mandal : "Rurban Centres in Bihar Plain", *Indian Geographical Studies*, Vol. No. 1, 1973, p. 16.
53. J.F. Hart : "Central Tendency in Areal Distribution," *Economic Geography*, Vol. 30, 1954, pp. 48-49.
54. D.K. Singh, B. Routray and S. Jena : "Spatial Analysis of Rural Settlement Pattern in Orissa," *Paper Presented at Varanasi Symposium*, December, 1975, pp. 5-6.
55. Paul Cloke : Key Settlements in Rural Areas, *Warwickshire country Council*, 1973, p. 133.
56. M.A. Bieneteld : "A Long Term Housing Policy for Tanazania, *Economic Research Bureau*, Paper No. 70. 9, UDSM, 1970.
57. F.J. Monkhouse and H.R. Wilkinson : Maps and Diagrams; Methuen & Co. Ltd; London, 1973, p. 503.
58. C.R. Pathak and R.K. Dhabai : "Rural Settlement Structure of Mewar Rajasthan", I.I.T. Kharagpur, Silver Jubilee Symposium on Rural Community Development, April, 1976.

Fig. 4.1

North Bihar : Types of Rural Settlements

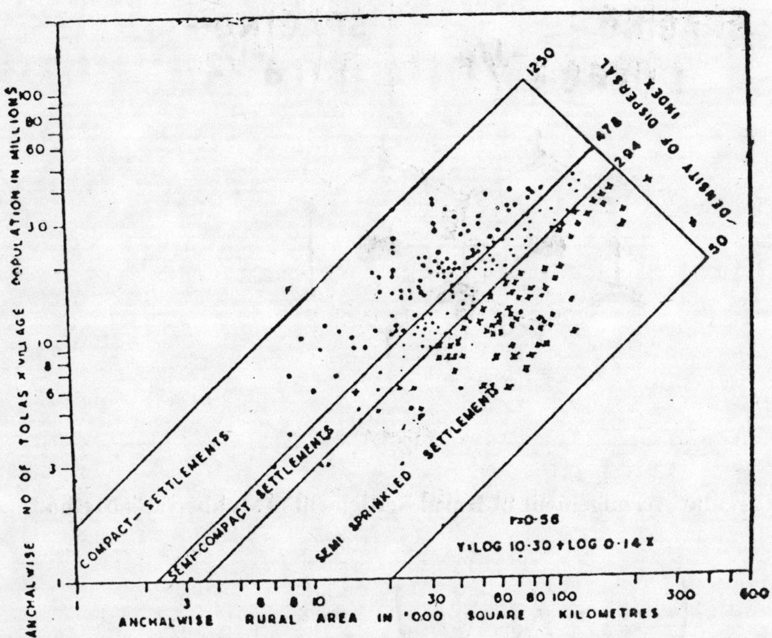

Fig.4.2

Hexagonal Arrangement of Rural Settlements

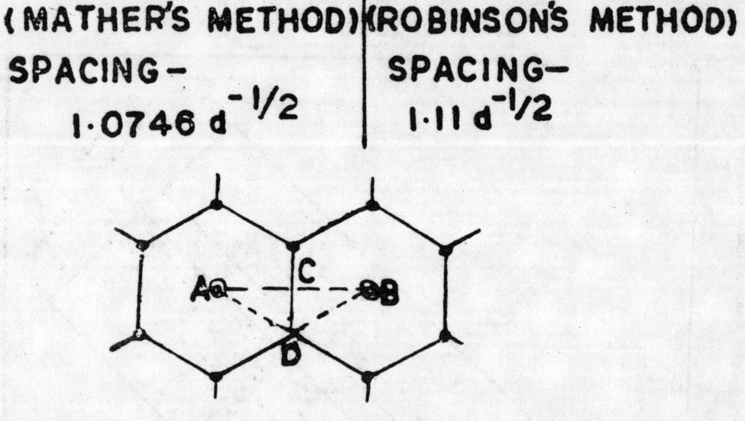

Fig.4.3.

Circular Arrangement of Rural Settlements (Mukherjee's Method)

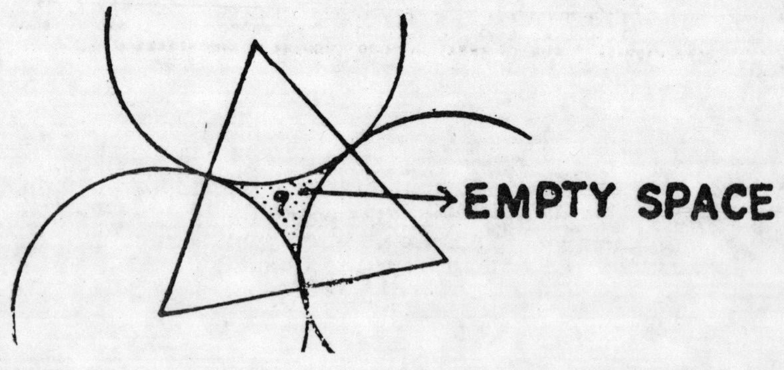

Fig. 4.4

Bachi's Standard Distance Measure between two Points

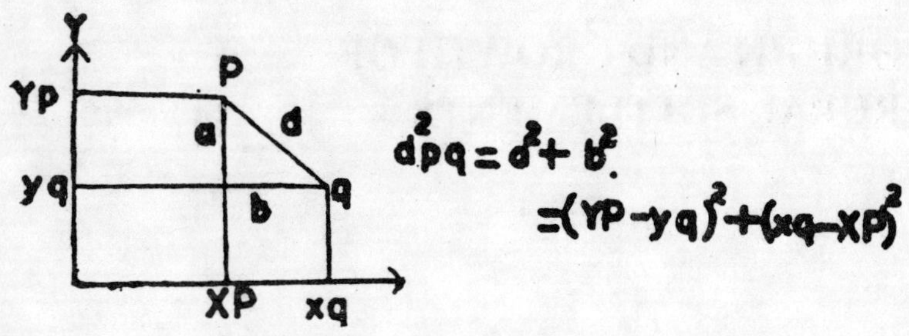

Fig. 4.5

Location of Mean Centre of Rural Settlements in Bagamoyo District, Tanzania (1985)

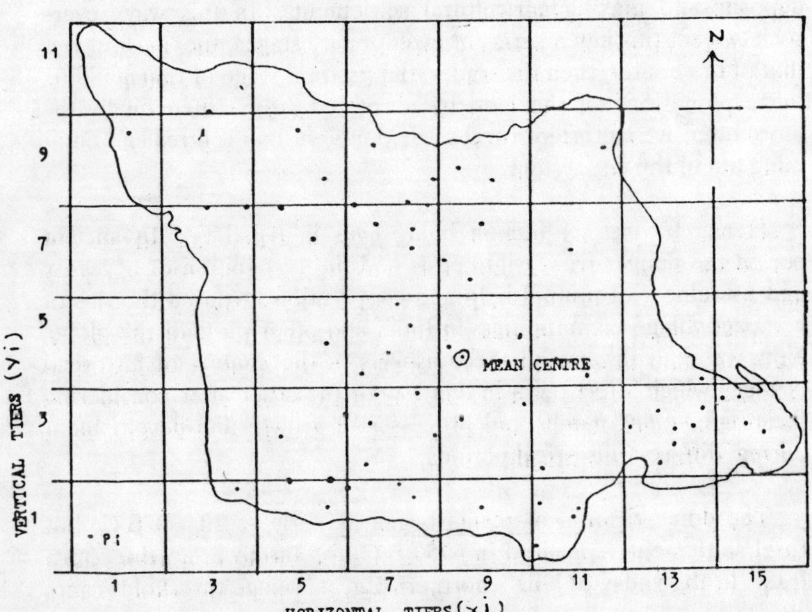

FIVE

ORIGIN AND GROWTH OF RURAL SETTLEMENTS

The evolutionary history of human settlements can be interpreted in terms of the migration of people into a sparsely populated area. The people of Indian and European origin slowly advanced into the interior of continents of North and South America; subduing the indigenous Red Indians and Yahgan Indians, exploiting mineral deposits and making agricultural settlements. In this way, every society went through a series of evolutionary stages; the earliest was that of the hunter, then the trader, the pastoral stage of ranchers life, the exploitation of the land by unrotated crops, then finally the more intensive culture of rural settlements, rurban centres and humming life of the city system.

Hence by instinct human being lives in tribal tie. In ancient period the danger from wild beasts and the recognition of necessity and usefulness of mutual help and cooperation favoured the rise of compact village communities in India and other parts of the globe. Now we shall discuss all these aspects in the context of historical changes which affect them in one way or the other after considering the origin, place names and processes of growth and development during different historical periods.

The domestication of plants began as early as 10,000 B.C. but rural settlements appeared in 6750 B.C. for Jarmo in north-eastern Iraq. In the valley of Nile - northern Egypt "village threshold" came into being in 5000 B.C.; in Atlantic Europe about 4000 B.C.; in India about 2500 B.C.; in West Africa about 1500 B.C. and in Meso-America about 3000 B.C. In almost all areas whereever agricultural development effectively replaced earlier hunting and collecting patterns village life firmly established.

The evolution and history of rural settlements in Bihar Plain should be systematically analysed with the dawn of civilization. Excavations have revealed relics and evidences of its glorious past. The temple of Bodh Gaya, the monasteries and universities of Nalanda, Odantpuri, and Vikramshila; the cyclopean Walls of Rajgir[1], the remains of Kumhrar, Vaishali, Chirand and Lauriya Nandangarh; the splendid tombs of Yahya shah Maneri and Daulat Shah; the mausoleum of Sher Shah at Sasaram and many other historical remains bear witness to the spread of civilization and growth of rural settlements in this region.

The dogmatic effects of different historical periods on rural settlements have brought about changes in their own way. As a rural settlement is primarily an agricultural workshop, any change in the agricultural landscape is bound to radiate modifications in the character and distribution of settlements. The shape and arrangement are often in conformity with the nature of work and agricultural techniques. The evolution of rural settlements can be traced back to the earliest organised settlement of men in the region. But the first settlers have hardly left any actual record of their habitation. The relics of the implements used by them at some places can be helpful in forming rudimentary ideas of their lives. Hence the evolution of settlement in the region can be discussed mainly with reference to the historical periods.

A careful inquiry into the origin of rural settlement is necessary because the present structure and character of a rural settlement can hardly be comprehended without knowing the complex cultural background which began with its origin[2]. The process of early settling led to the union of families into villages. The fields once cleared laboriously were to be kept cleared. This demarcation of fields from habitation developed a sense of integrated community life comprising several families[3]. The idea of collective security and defence against different kinds of adverse and inclement forces further strengthened the process of cohesion among families

The settling of men in the clearings of dense forests may be regarded as the precursor of rural settlements. These inhabitants were constantly exposed to the hazards of life and belongings from the plundering hordes of tribes and also from wild animals. The instinct to combat the danger from surrounding tribes and the need of collectivity and cooperation in the construction of building, village wells and tanks for irrigation etc, brought people closer and closer. When the country was organised by petty chiefs, the need for meeting the needs of these chiefs and their local agents was pressing and such needs also provided incentive to unite. In areas where wandering tribes had settled down, the mere tribal instinct of association induced stimulus to form compact settlements[4].

These settlements originated on relatively high sites amid fertile agricultural areas where water supply was plentiful and life could be secure. They were, however, unplanned villages with poor transport facilities. For this reason, they were often close to river courses. Thus rural settlements emerged with the emergence of permanent agriculture.

The process of division of labour between different classes of inhabitants according to their capabilities led to the division of the village on the basis of *Varnas* which in the beginning were merely the professions followed by different people. Thus came into existence the professional settlements as distinct from the ones inhabited by general agricultural communities. Beyond the fringe areas of the central settlement, satellite settlements or sub-villages locally called *tolas* came to be occupied wholly by members of one group having the same profession. For example, Bahadurpur is a village on the south-eastern side of Laheriasarai town which is wholly inhabited by people of *Thatheri* caste. In the countryside away from urban influence, professional villages existed which provided agricultural tools and implements to the farmers of the neighbouring villages. As the time went by the *Varnas* got stabilized into castes, the caste system bred intolerance of people of different castes towards one another. The lower caste people gradually came to be settled in separate *tolas*, leading to the origin of cluster and hamlets type of settlements. *Chamar Toli* on the southern side of the main Parwana settlement in Rusera Block of samastipur district is an example of this type of settlement.

Another cause leading to the origin of new villages, used to be the royal decree by which the King ordered the establishment of new village settlements on new sites or on old ruins, either in an irregular fashion or on a planned basis. The Muslim rulers founded a number of settlements but more commonly they merely changed the names of existing settlements.

Wherever in rural areas the land is suitable having adequate water supply, relatively higher and slopy ground free from floods, and a fertile agricultural land surrounding this site, settlements such as a hamlet or a village attracted to it. The origin of several villages in Bihar Plain is due to this reason. These factors also determine the morphometric development of rural settlements in the region.

In ancient times settlements also originated around an *ashrama*, or the centre of learning at the abode of a hermit. The folk tradition tells that Chirand in Chapra district grew around the hermitage of *Chayavan Rishi.* Numerous other rural settlements have also originated around centres of religious importance or temples or mosques. In the Buddhist period, settlements originated due to clan migration. These clans migrated from several clan centres[5], such as the Sakyas from Patna, the Videhas from Mithila, the Lichhavis from Vaishali, the Jyatri from Kundapura (near Vaishali), the Mallas from Pawa (near Rajgir), the Moriyas from Piplivana (areas of Champaran).

Two other settlements Kundapura and Vinayagrama are also stated to be in the neighbourhood of Vaishali. Beyond Kundapura lay in the suburb of Kollaga or modern Kalhua which appears to have been principally inhabited by Kshatriyas of the Jyatri clan, to which belonged Vardhamana Mahavira[6]. The rural settlements related to the hermitage of Buddhist monks are Buddhiagarhi, Buddhmaghat and Buddhauli in Saharsa district, Tetrawan, Begampur and Telhara in Patna district, and Areraj and Kesaria in Champaran district. Muslim rulers also established numerous settlements such as Bakhtiarpur by Bakhtiar Khilji, Sasaram by Sher Shah, Muzaffarpur by Muzaffar Khan etc. Yet others are Phulwarisharif, Biharsharif,

Sultanganj, Bibiganj, Noorsarai, Mirganj, Islampur and Khodabandpur.

During recent period, the caste factor has given rise to most of the villages in Bihar. Initially the persons of one caste settled at a place. Others of the same caste soon migrated to that place and a village grew around the original settlement. The significance of names like *Brahman toli*, *Kurmi Toli*, *Chamar Toli* and *Guar Toli* are fairly indicative of this fact.

Thousands of villages grew up along the network of the communication system. The opening of railway stations and creation of cross roads give rise to new hamlet, which developed with the advancement of time and needs of the inhabitants. Shops were attracted to such centres and they gradually developed into rural trading centres. Shivaji Nagar settlement in Rusera Block of Darbhanga, which is fast developing into an important urban centre, is an example of this type.

Rivers are effective barriers in the land routes and tracts. Ferry crossings came to be established on such points. Here a village or hamlet frequently came into existence. North Bihar Plain is a land of rivers and water-ways and there are numerous ferry points or *ghats* like Akharaghat, Bariahighat, Kolhuaghat, Khararighat, Hayaghat, etc. which have distinctive settlements.

Quite a number of rural settlements have come into existence or are under development in recent years due to population pressure in the main settlement, leading to partition of joint families and overcrowding of houses. There are a number of settlements like Baghauni Kothi and Bhadulia in Beheri Block and Gairba in Rusera Block of Samastipur district, which owe their origin to such factors.

Due to the devastations by floods and the resultant damage of habitation along river banks, new settlements have developed in areas and are now protected from floods by newly constructed dams. Lalpur and Ghibahi settlement on the bank of river Baghmati in Rusera Block of Samastipur district are examples of this fact. Besides these two, there are several other settlements on the banks of the river Kosi and the Ganga which have come into existence due to resettlement. Purnea and Saharsa districts have numerous villages developed due to resettlement, because the Kosi river has shifted its course 114 kilometres west within 214 years[7].

Rural settlements of political origin are also common in Bihar Plain. Since times immemorial, kings or *zamindars* or local chiefs built settlements on defensible sites, usually along river banks or on strategic hill areas. They built forts or walled settlements on commanding sites. They also created settlements for revenue collections. Around such settlements gathered the warriors, the followers of the chiefs and farmers because these settlements had the advantage of defence, availability of water and trade facilities.

During the last two decades the Block Development Offices, the educational institutions like the colleges and the high schools as well as weekly village markets have attracted some shops and thus new settlements are gradually taking roots at such centres.

PLACE NAMES OF RURAL SETTLEMENTS

An analysis of the names of rural settlements is interesting because it gives suggestions and hints about the origin of villages as embedded in local legend, history, mythology, ecology and epic stories. The study of place names is of great help in the present analysis as the names bear identifiable associations with the physical and cultural characteristics of the region, and serve as a basic source of information about geographical surroundings. Brunhes thinks of place names as fossils of Human Geography[8]. A knowledge of the regional language of any area is helpful in finding out the real significance of place names. An examination of prefix and suffix[9] of the names is essential to reveal the past associations and affiliations of settlements. Though such analysis is complex, it provides some clues to the early human habitats of the area concerned[10]. The linguistic elements in the rural areas also give clear evidence regarding the movement of people, area of their colonization and their relations to earlier and subsequent groups. They also help in indicating the period of their establishment as well as the reason for their nomenclature.

In a large number of instances, the place names are connected with the natural features like a forest, a tree, a river, a mountain, a tank or character of the soil, or slope of the land, etc. The character of land is often signified by a suffix or prefix in the place name e.g. *tanr* or *dih* (upland), *pahari* (hill), *Khoh* (cave skirts of the hills), *pokhar* or *tal* (tank), *bandh* (embankment), *Chaur* (marshy land shaving low relief), *daha* (water affected areas), *diara* (sandy land in the riparian tract), etc. Settlements having such additions to their names invariably indicate the influence of site on their origin. The name of any village ending with *chaur* indicates that the village has low-land areas suitable for pastures and paddy cultivation in its vicinity. A group of village ending with *daha* indicates that the region is susceptible to floods. There are place names such as Bandarjhula, Bhoulmari and Gidarganj in Bhagalpur district, which suggest that the wild animals were found in the region. In the same way, names such as Bandar Kala Pahar and Banspahari, suggest that the former village originated in an area infested with monkeys while the latter grew near a bamboo grove on a hillock.

Villages sometimes bear the name of a deity, or a chief, or a king or other patrons of the region. There are numerous place names based on population size, such as, those ending with *kalan*, *khurd* and *buzurg*, (a large sized village). Some place names are based on trades, occupations and are known by the suffix *ganj*. Village names are based on religion. Names like Mohammadpur and Khodabandpur have their affiliations with the Muslim religion whereas names like Sitakund, Ramnagar, Kusheswar Asthan and Ghanshyampur come from the Hindu religion. Rajnagar, is a centre associated with cultural features and was built by the Darbhanga Raj. Lakshman Nagar, Hanuman Nagar, Ram Nagar, Kanta (Weighing Scales), and Susta found in Gaighatti *Anchal* of Muzaffarpur district, are the villages having a cultural tinge in their names. There are legends behind all these villages which suggest their association with the marriage of Lord Rama and Sita. It is said that when the marriage party left Awadh for Janakpur, the places where Hanuman, Lakshman and Rama waited with their parties were named as Hanuman Nagar, Lakshman Nagar and Ram Nagar respectively. Similarly the place where the food grains were weighed came to be known as Kanta (weighing scales), where the marriage party took rest, got the name of Susta. All the villages are of Aryan times. In this way, there are thousands of villages in Bihar Plain, which tell their own stories. Another example of cultural impact are the villages ending with the suffix *Wan* (the woods) for example, Tetrawan, Punawan, and Jhawan in Bihar and Noorsarai Anchals of Nalanda district.

Bihar as the craddle of Buddhism and Jainism saw the rise and fall of many monasteries or *viharas*, such as Nalanda and Odantapuri. All these *viharas* were destroyed during the Muslim period. The Muslims gave the name Biharsharif to Odantapuri and the name 'Bihar' was given to the entire state in the 12th Century A.D.[11] Similarly, the name Purnea is said to have been derived from *Purain* or the lotus flower, found in abundance in the channels of the Kosi and Mahananda rivers in the past.[12] The name Champaran is a corruption of *Champaranya*, i.e., the forest of Champa trees.[13]

The Name Mithila came into existence wher a prince emerged from the *Churu* (Pot) and was named Mithi[14], who succeeded his father as a king. His country came to be known after him as Mithila. It is also said that Nimi whose death was due to a curse was rightly called *Videha*, and his successors have been known as *Videha*[15] in Mithila. There is much difference of opinion about the derivation of the name Tirhut and the modern name of Mithila. It is corruption of *Tirabhukti*, which in Sanskrit means people residing on the river banks. This would truly describe the modern Tirhut with its numerous rivers.

It is said that the tappa Duho-suho is called after the two wives of Raja Uttampada, Du Rani and Su Rani. The village Pawapuri in Biharsharif subdivision of Nalanda district five kilometres north of Giriak is a corruption of Pabapuri, i.e. the pure and the sinless. It is a sacred place of the Jains. Lord Mahavira left his mortal coils at this place. The name Rajgir[16] (Rajgriha, or the royal residence) in Nalanda district was given when the Saisunaka kings made the place their capital. The name Shahabad (royal city) came into existence when Emperor Babar stationed his camp in Arrah in 1529 and established his dominion over Bihar. The village Shergarh in Shahabad is ruined hill fort built by Shersah Suri. Muzaffarpur district takes its name after its chief Muzaffar Khan, a revenue officer under the Mughals. About 65% of the villages have names of Mohammadan origin and about 26% names bear the suffix 'pur'.

The name Darbhanga has been derived from *'Duarebhanga'* or Dar-i-Bengal meaning the gate of Bengal[17]. Balirajgarh is a village in Madhubni district containing the ruins of a fort known as the *garh* of Raja Bal. The name Motihari means a necklace of pearls, and is suggestive of the pretty lake surrounding it. The name Bhainsalotan in Champaran district suggests a place where the buffaloes wallow, and is apparently derived from the fact that the place used to be the haunt of wild buffaloes of the Terai region[18]. The name of the village Bawangarhi in Bettiah subdivision literally means fifty two forts. Sitakund village in Motihari subdivision also contains the remains of an ancient fort. There is a holy tank inside the fort and Sita is said to have used this tank.

The name Saran is a corruption of Saranga-aranya or the deer forest. It was said that Sringi Rishi had his abode at Singhai, a few kilometres east of Chapra, in the midst of a dense forest abound with deer. Chirand, lying 10 kilometres east of Chapra in Saran district is said to have originated about 2000 B.C. around the *ashram* of Chyawan Rishi. Munger is a corruption of the name of the Monger which is the name of Mudgala Rishi in Prakrit. There is a village Sitakund in Munger subdivision containing a hot spring. According to the legend, Sita bathed here after her *agnipariksha,* i.e. walking through fire to prove her chastity when in the captivity of Ravana. A village in Munger district is named after Ram Bahadur Singh, a local chief around 1900. The estate is known as Bahadura and the village as Bahadur[19]. Similarly Patna, the name of the capital of the state, has changed several times from Patligram (Patali village), in ancient times to Kusumpur, Puspapur, Patliputra, Azimabad, etc.

Similarly, Bhagalpur was formerly known as Champa when it was the capital of Anga Kingdom in the ancient period. Karangarh in the nearby lands takes it name after the fort built by king Karna which occupied part of the site of ancient Champanagara around 1400 B.C.[20]. The chief town Saharsa is named after a village Saharsa settled three kilometres away from the railway station and is obviously a corruption of the word *Saharsa*(thousand). Some settlements in Saharsa district were associated with the names of the Pala rulers and it was through this district that the Palas could establish contact with Nepal.

TABLE 5.1 : **No. of Occurrence of Some Prefixes and Suffixes in Place Names of the Bihar Plain**

Prefix or Suffix	Districts										
	Patna	Gaya	Shahabad	Sasaram	Cham-paran	Muzaff-arpur	Darbh-anga	Munger	Bhag-alpur	Saharsa	Purnea
Pur	738	1228	1245	1125	363	1092	756	1197	762	207	669
Chak	122	213	85	141	-	61	146	287	199	5	38
Nagar	9	-	6	10	17	29	38	30	-	28	64
Khurd	5	65	56	73	19	36	8	13	18	-	16
Buzrug	6	19	7	20	-	37	10	8	9	-	-
Kalan	5	46	65	61	16	7	-	10	7	-	10
Ganj	10	17	14	10	-	4	6	-	-	-	44
Patti	1	-	31	54	3	58	108	-	-	57	7
Dih	16	74	112	16	22	17	15	189	110	-	2
Arazi	1	14	6	18	-	-	22	92	120	16	29
Milki	16	2	3	-	-	-	7	-	54	45	309
Chapra	1	-	6	129	29	54	-	-	-	-	-

Source : Counted from the District Census Handbook 1961 for all districts mentioned above.

Gaya, as mentioned in the Bhagwatpuran, was the name of a king, who dwelt on the place in Treta Yuga[21]. Most of the settlements in this district were established by the Muslim rulers and therefore, many place names are of Mohammadan origin, for example, Imamganj, Nabi Nagar, Aurangabad, Daud Nagar, Arwal, Jehanabad, Makhdumpur, Khidirsarai, Warsaliganj, Wazirganj, Hisua, Fatehpur, etc.

The suffix sarai (a tavern or an inn) indicates that in ancient period people used to proceed on long journeys. For example, people from North Bihar went on pilgrimage to Deoghar in Santal Pargana and to Bodh Gaya as they do even today. Similarly, people travelled along the Grand Trunk Road, spanning the country from Peshawar in west Pakistan to Calcutta in the eastern region of India. Thus settlements sprang up around the inns along the travelling routes, and have now developed into urban settlements of today. Such place names bear the suffix sarai. For example Lakhisarai, Begusarai, Dalsinghsarai and Laheriasarai are en route to Deoghar; and Ekangarsarai and Khidirsarai are en route to Bodh Gaya.

The place name Shikarpur in Champaran district indicates that it was a centre for the hunting of wild animals. The name Sherghatti in Gaya district reveals that tigers roamed in abundance in this valley. Similarly, the name Siwan came into existence because it is the *Siwana* (boundary) separating Bihar and Uttar Pradesh.

According to the above table the suffix *pur* (habitat) is widely distributed all over the region. The suffix *chak* (large area) and *dih* (upland) predominate in South Bihar Plain. *Nagar* (large-settlement) and *patti* (smaller settlement) on the other hand are associated mainly with the North Bihar Plain. *Khurd*(small) and *Buzurg* or *Kalan* (large) are also widely distributed in the entire region, except in the district of Saharsa. But these are more important in Gaya, Bhojpur and Saran district. The suffix *ganj* is also recurrently in use in Purnea, Gaya, Bhojpur, Patna and Saran districts. Such settlements are trading centres, for example, Paliganj in Patna, Warsaliganj in Gaya, Bikramganj in Bhojpur, Revelganj, Maharajganj and Gopalganj in Saran; Forbesganj and Kishanganj in Purnea, etc.

The abundance of *dih* or upland settlements in South Bihar Plain indicates that settlements are situated on higher land since historical times. They have formed due to neo-tectonic earth movements. In contrast, the absence of this suffix in North Bihar is suggestive of the heavy rainfall and the shifting courses of the river that have eroded away the *dih* lands. Settlements are now located a little farther away from the river banks. But some like Naulagarh in Munger district and Havidih in Darbhanga district still retain their tradition of ancient days. *Chapra* is an important name in Saran, Champaran and Muzaffarpur districts. *Milki* is another name very common in Purnea, Bhagalpur and Saharsa districts. *Patti* is the same as *milki* but is common only in Saran, Muzaffarpur and Darbhanga districts. Thus it may be observed that the study of place names would be vital to any study of cultural history of the region under study[22].

THE PREHISTORIC SETTLEMENTS 20,000 B.C.-2,500B.C.

The period includes the following four divisions:

(a) The Early Stone Age,
(b) The New Stone Age,
(c) The Age of Metals, and
(d) The Copper Age.

Long before the arrival of man, the Bihar Plain must have been covered with forests and swampy vegetation. The *Atharva Veda* contains copious references to the *Vratyas*, who according to some historians were the Pre-Aryan inhabitants of Magadha[23]. During the early stone age they lived on the fruits of the *jungles* and their hunting. They had to wage a constant war against dangerous beasts. Fire might have been discovered by the friction of sticks with sticks or stones with stones. They had no permanent abodes and led a wandering life. Followed on heels the New Stone Age and during this period man learnt to live in caves. Many such caves have been discovered with floors littered with ashes, charcoal, bones and pieces of crude pottery. For example, the ancient site of *Asura* habitation near Gaya is named after a demon called Gaya, where seven rockcut caves are still to be seen in the Barabar hills, 26 kilometres north of Gaya[24]. During both the periods of the stone age Bihar Plain was covered with dense forests. It was difficult even for primitive men to live there. Human habitations were, therefore, confined to the fringe of the forest regions. Gradually men migrated from the south and later from the west and made clearings and settlements. The traces of Neolithic culture (2500 B.C.)[25] probably covered nearly 10 kilometres at Chirand[26] east of Chapra. The remains of Rishi Chyawan's hermitage have been found in excavations here.

It appears that fifteen thousand years ago the men in the Bihar Plain were still in the Paleolithic stage. Civilization as based on agriculture and metal dates back to less than 10,000 years[27]. Prior to 'aryanisation' most parts were occupied by the aboriginals (Proto-Indices or Proto-Australoids) and the Mediterranean Armenoid people, the latest of whom were Dravidian speaking people. In early Sanskrit texts they have been described as Nisadas, Bhararas and Savaras. The associations of these ancient people particularly the *bhars* are found in the names of settlements like Bharapura, Bhaur, Bharairam, Bharagama, Bharau, etc. in Darbhanga district. *Soeries* in South Bihar Plain, *Tharus* in North-Western Champaran, and *Cheros* in Shahabad districts are the tribal folks found in the region. Shahabad formed at a later date the meeting ground of the two greatest prehistoric people viz., the mediterranean-Armenoid and the *Munda* speaking people. Here, Bhojpur village nearly three kilometres north of Dumraon is named after Raja Bhoj of Ujjain. It has been speculated that Raja Bhoj invaded the district of Shahabad and subdued the aboriginal cheros. The settlement of prehistoric period are Uttar, Deviasthan, Jagat, Benipatti, Uchhaitha, Bhitha-Bhagwanpur, Bahera, Bhagirathpur and Tarapatti in Darbhanga district; Kumhrar (Patna) and Rajgir[28] in Patna district; Gaya and Gopalpur in Gaya district; Buxar[29] in Bhojpur; Chirand in Saran district and Karanpur and Dharhara in Saharasa district which were built by Raja Karan in 3000 B.C.[30]

Thus it appears that the Aryans had nothing to do with the original village settlements of the Middle Ganga Valley[31]. The Plain was inhabited by a few tribals often separated from one another by broad rivers and impenetrable forests. This circumstantial factor, later on, encouraged the growth of independent republics like Vaishali[32], Videha, Magadha, Karusha, and Anga. It is on such foundations that the Aryan settlers with superior power and intellect erected their own cultural structures and establishments based on metal.

ARYAN SETTLEMENTS 2500 B.C.–600 B.C.

According to the Upanishads, the Ramayana, the Mahabharata, the Puranas and other numerous old records, the Bihar Plain was inhabited by a mixture of races before the advent of the Aryans. Among them were the primitive Tharus, Kikatas, Kanvas, Bhars, Cheros, Koles and the Munda speaking people. These people were ranked low in Aryan society and were called Dasyu and slaves. They were the descendents of the prehistoric inhabitants of the region. Above them were the more advanced Koles (Australoids) and the civilized Dravidians, who had made the land habitable by the cutting and burning down of the forests. The whole region between the Himalayas and the Vindhaya mountains extending from sea to sea on the east and the west has been given the name of *Aryavarta* the country of the Aryans. The date of the Indo-Aryan movement is generally placed between 2500 B.C.and 600 B.C. during which they advanced from the Kuru Panchala country to the country of the Videha[33] (North Bihar).

In the beginning the village community of the Aryans was largely based on the Dravidian village institutions[34]. The Vedic Aryans lived in villages but as a natural consequence of the growth of territorial kingdoms in the Epic Age, many village settlements developed into large towns and capital cities, e.g. Vaishali in North Bihar Plain and Anga and Rajgir in Sough Bihar Plain. Since the historical evidence of the settlement of the various early Aryan tribes is not available it may be considered that among the tribes who settled in different parts of the region were the Janakas of Videha and Vaisalakas north of Patna at Vaishali. The Anus of the Punjab had sent their families to the east during the period when the Haihayas were ravaging the *Doab*. They established themselves in East Bihar and created the principality of Anga[35].

The society of the Aryans was based on the family (Kula). The families were grouped into cultivators, warriors, priests, sages and artisans. These groups were also noticeable in original inhabitants the Dravidians and the pre-Dravidians. There was constant friction between the Aryans and the non- Aryans and the people lived in fortified village. The detailed regulations for planned and fortified types of rural settlements are prescribed in the 'Mansara

Shilpashastra'[36]. According to Havell and R.L. Singh, the Aryans lived in eight types of planned villages, Dandaka, Sarvatobhadra, Nandyavarta, Padmaka, Swastika, Prastara, Karmuka and Chaturmukha[37]. (Fig. 5.1). Locationwise these villages are rectangular or square in type and are similar in essentials. Each village is surrounded by a wall and a ditch for defence purposes. There were generally four gates in the middle of the four sides, thus dividing the village into four quarters. The centre of the village was generally occupied by a temple, or a tank or a public hall. The four quarters were further subdivided by straight streets, inhabited on the basis of the *Varnas* and professions. The best quarters were generally occupied by the Brahmins and the Kshatriyas.

Mithila is a part of the territory in which the Videhas settled on their migration from north-west India. Agni (Vaiswanara, the god of fire) accompanied the *Videhas* on their march towards east from the bank of the Saraswati. The true historical account of Mithila goes back to 1500 B.C.[38] when the Satpatha -Brahmana is assumed to have been given its final shape. At Mithila, the capital of Videha, the Janakas maintained for some time a magnificent court which was thronged with brave men. But later the dynasty was overthrown and the Videha became a republic. The most notable sites of Aryan period in North Bihar are Malaul, Bisaul, Pandaul, Kamtaul, Kakraul and Ahiari in Darbnhanga district; Kanakpur and Mahadeokal in Purnea district; Mehsi and Biratpur in Saharsa district; Dharampur, Deokuli, Sitamarhi, Pandaul and Punarua in Muzaffarpur district; Sitakund in Champaran district; and Lichhichak, Donbuzurg, Revelganj and Chapra in Saran district. The village Ahiari, 24 kilometres south-east of Kamtaul in Darbhanga district, was the abode of the Gautam Rishi, whose consort Ahilya was s celebrated beauty of her times[39]. Sitamarhi is said to have been the birth place of Sita.

Vaishali became the headquarters of the Lichhavis, who are known to have been the first in the world to establish a republic. The kingdom was known as *Vijita-Desa*, a conquered country. Its mention in ancient literature occurs in the Puranas which speak of Manu's family[40]. It consisted of eight small republics namely Bharg, Anga, Angutarai, Kanjangal, south-west of Suhya, western part of Pundra, Alkap and Pipli Kanan[41], in North and South Bihar Plains. As a result Mithila came to be aryanised earlier than the Magadha[42].

At this time Magadha continued to be efficiently governed by the Barhadrathas dynasty which claimed to have descended from Kuru. The greatest king Jarasandha of this dynasty was killed by the Pandavas. But the Bharatha war did not shake the power of Barhadrathas, and under them Magadha became one of the most important kingdoms of Northern India. The Aryan settlements of South Bihar Plain are Sarodag, Neorus, Jhorpa, Suggikhoh and Ram Dih in Bhojpur district; Sarea, Bhelawar, Deoghara, Kurkihar, Rasulpur and Barana in Gaya district; Mai, Gokulpur, Kushar and Ghorkatora in Patna district; Belgudar, Nonag and Sitakund in Monghyr district and Karna Dih in Bhagalpur district. In Bhojpur district, Bakri Gram near Arrah was an Aryan settlement which derived its name from Bakasur, who seems to have lived in 1800 B.C. Similarly Masarh village near Karisoth was an Aryan settlement because this was the living place of the Banasur in the Vedic Age[43].

The Age of Aryan settlements lasted from around 2500 B.C. to about 600 B.C.[44]. During the 2000 years, the Aryans colonized Northern India, conquerred its original tribal inhabitants, established kingdoms and spread their language and culture all over the Bihar Plain. The Aryans also developed a number of arts and industries. They lived in houses, and constructed dwellings of clay, bamboo and thatch for the commoners, and of bricks for the rich. Timber and metals[45] were used in the construction of doorways and pillars. There were six types of human habitations in the Aryan times[46].

(a) Ghosa or Gopa (cattle rancher),
(b) Pali (a small barbarian settlement),
(c) Durga (fort),
(d) Grama (village),
(e) Kharwat or pattana (town), and
(f) Nagar (city).

Thus, the Vedic Aryan lived in village[47] (Grama) which was the fundamental unit of administration and had its own head called the Gramini[48]. Whether these villages were close to each other or were scattered far and wide is not known, but there were village paths, which connected each other and hence were termed as Manglavithi[49] (the path of blessings).7

The rural settlements of Aryan period were identified by the generic name *dih*, and had considerable land around them. The village consisted of several joint families. The rural community or territory based on the decimal system existed in groups of 10, 20, 100 and 1000 villages. The rulers of each groups were called *Dasgramini*, *Pinstipa*, *Satgramini*, and *Adhipatti* respectively[50].

Sonepur across the Ganga from Patna is one of the religious centre of this period, where the battle between *Gaja* (the elephant) and *Graha* (the crocodile) had taken place and Lord Vishnu had to appear to protect Gaja. At present there is a temple of Lord Vishnu at this place. Ami, nearly 22 kilometres east of Chapra is another mythological centre where King Daksha held an Yagya, and Sati, consort of Lord Siva sacrificed herself in the sacred fire. In Purnea district the river Mahananda traditionally makes the farthest eastern limit of the extension of the Aryan influence[51].

SETTLEMENTS OF THE BUDHIST PERIOD 600 B.C.–A.D. 700

During the times of Lord Budha (550 B.C.), the Bihar Plain was covered by a number of republics comprising well organised village communities[52] from Chota Nagpur Scarp Belt in the south to the Terai of Nepal in the north. On the basis of ancient relics scattered all over the region, it is possible to conclude that the region was inhabited and cultivated by a civilized people whose stupas, mounds and special architectural features still attest to their greatness and grandeur in the past. The Bihar Plain being the ampitheatre of Budhism gave rise to thousands of rural settlements. Records particularly make mention of those around the towns of Rajgir and Biharsharif.

About 540 B.C. king Bimbisara founded the Magadha empire and strengthened his position by matrimonial alliances with the royal family of Kosal and the Lichchavi clan of Vaishali. He extended the frontiers of Magadha by the annexation of Anga (Bhagalpur and Munger districts) and built a settlement of Rajgriha at the base of the hill, crowned by the ancient fort of Jarasandha. His son Kaniska Ajatsatru is called Vaidehiputra in the Budhist literature. Budhism flourished under the imperial patronage of Ashoka. Lord Buddha visited Rajgir frequently. Other centres where Budhist sites have been found are Revelganj, Dewti, Gopalpur and Amarpur in Saran district; Kesariya, Uren, Lauriya Nandangarh and Sagardesh (Motihari) in Champaran and numerous villages around Vaishali in Muzaffarpur district. Various sites in Saharsa district now completely eroded and destroyed by the Kosi, viz. Bitarpur, Budhigarhi, Budhmaghat, Budhauli, Pithahi and Mathani were also associated with Budhism.

After some time the village Palibothra (Patliputra) was made the capital of Magadha and was strengthened with fortification. The archaeological excavations at village Kumhrar[53] in Patna have brought to light the structural elegance of the buildings, halls and drainage system of ancient architecture in Magadha. In South Bihar Plain all the rural settlements with *awan* suffix are considered to be the settlements of Budhist period, e.g. as Mahiawan, Dahiawan, Tetrawan, Jhawan, Punawan, etc. Village Ghosrawan[54] in Biharsharif subdivision is the site of an old Budhist settlement whose remains are marked by several mounds. In Munger district, Budhist relics are to be found at Rajouna and Hussainganj near Lakhisarai and at Uren near Kajra[55]. In South Bihar Plain the Budhist settlements are also found around Rajgriha, Biharsharif, Kako (Gaya), Kumhrar (Patna), Bodh Gaya, etc.

Allied to the Lichchavis were the Jyatrikas, whose capital was at Kundagrama adjacent to Vaishali[56]. According to Smith the Lichchavis were hillmen of the Mongolian type akin to the Tibetans[57]. All the Budhist settlements in Champaran district were probably situated along the imperial road from Patliputra the capital of Ashoka, to Kusinagara, the scene of Budha's death. This road is believed to have passed through Basarh (Vaishali), Kesariya, Lauriya, Aroraj, Bettiah, Chankigarh, Rampurwa[58] and the Bikhnathori-pass[59]. Twenty one kilometres south of Motihari, Sagardesh or Sagra's castle and Budhna Pokhar are also sites of Budhist settlements.

Lord Mahavira, the 24th Jain Tirthankar and a contemporary of Lord Budha was born at Basokund village in Muzaffarpur district in 599 B.C. and he spent his early years at a monastery at Vaishali.

Later he spent about 42 years wandering in Bihar Plain including Vaishali and Rajgir. He had a large number of followers, but since Jainism did not get royal patronage, it left little impact upon the cultural life of the people of the region. Lord Mahavira attained *Nirvana* at Pawapuri east of Biharsharif in Nalanda district.

The settlements of this period were mostly in the form of compact villages and the houses were so closely built that any conflagration could engulf and endanger the whole village[60]. The smallest unit of the settlement was the *griha* (the house), the habitation of a joint family (the kula). The houses were built mostly of mud, called *wattle* and *daub*[61].The village consisted of 30 to 1000 families. The entire village was enclosed by a hedge but the individual holdings abided by the open field system as prevalent in the Vedic age. The centre of the village at the intersection of two main village streets was earmarked as a meeting place for the meeting of the council of elders, who administered the local affairs. A banyan or *peepal* tree planted on a mound sufficed for the assembly hall, except where the village was a large one and could afford a pillared *mandapam* or pavalion of wood brick or stone during Magadha rule[64]. The village superintendent remained under the direct supervision of the King during Magadha rule[63].

The word *gama* frequently used today means a hamlet or a temporary settlement. Vinaya writers have defined a *gama* which may consist of one to four *kutis*[64]. The term *kuti* is normally translated as a hut, usually made of stick, grass and clay. However, *kuti* when mentioned as a *gama* cannot be single cabin or a little hut. A *gama* of one *kuti* (*eka kuti ko gama*) then, would probably refer to a hamlet or a large farm house, perhaps surrounded by a few smaller buildings in which the dependents and servants of the family dwelt. Most likely, this and the *gamas* of two to four *kutis* were dispersed settlements in the forests, outlying woodlands, hilly tracks and mountainous areas which surrounded the rich plains of the Gangetic valley. They were inhabited by *Bhikshus*, some of whom have been described as forest dwellers and others specially referred to as staying in the forest *kutis*[65].

In the sphere of common activities, the two terms *gama* and *nigama* are often mentioned together. But the size of a *nigama* seems to be somewhere between that of a *gama* and that of a *nagara* or *rajdhani*. The term *nigama* has been variously rendered as a market town, a town or a township. In the Vedic literature we have no equivalent term for *nigama*, which probably corresponds to the Sanskrit term *Mahagama*, which is found in the contemporary sutra literature[66]. If we take *gamas* as settlement of kinship-groups or occupational and professional groups, the *nigama* should be taken as a *gama* composed of members of various groups, more or less integrated. The *nigama*, therefore, should be considered as a large and complex *gama*, a bigger economic unit.

He has described a well-evolved system of military fortifications for village communities in the Bihar Plain. The examples may still be seen in the relics of the fortifications of old Rajgriha, Patliputra, Vaishali, and Lauria Nandangarh.

SETTLEMENTS OF THE POST-BUDDHIST PERIOD A.D. 700-A.D. 1200

During this period, Biharsharif as the provincial capital of Magadha, and Nalanda as the educational and religious centre were the most important places of influence. The inhabitants were wealthy and prosperous. The towns and villages were located close together[68]. However, the records of history after A.D. 657 the ascendancy of the Pala dynasty A.D. 600-A.D. to 1200 are not available. The universities at Odantapuri in Biharsharif and Vikramshila in Bhagalpur were established during the period[69] of Pala dynasty[70].

Bihar had to face a series of invasions in the seventh and eight centuries A.D. Sasanka of Gauda, Maukharis of Kanauj, Harsavardhan of Thaneswar, and the Tibetans successively established their authority over parts of Bihar. Early in the 8th century, Adityasena of the later Gupta dynasty of Magadha drove out the Tibetans, and having brought Patna and Bhagalpur divisions under his rule, waged wars successfully against the Maukharis of Uttar Pradesh and the rulers of Assam. But after the death of Adityasena and his three successors, Bihar Plain again fell a prey to the invasions of Yasovarman of Kanauj and also of the Kashmir kings, Lalit Aditya and Jayapada. Thereafter, the Bihar Plain became the greatest centre of learning in the whole of India and famous scholars from various parts of the world came to study at the universities of Nalanda, Vikramshila and Odantapuri. The region suffered from political disintegration and instability again from the middle of the eleventh century. In the century preceding the Turko-Afghan invasion, Mithila fell to the armies of Bengal. Gaya, Bhagalpur and Shahabad came to be ruled by petty independent chiefs. Patna and Munger survived as the sole remnants of the Pala Empire.

Thus with the downfall of Budhism and Jainism and disappearance of the rural republics by the end of the fifth century[71], the bulk of the region became once more sparsely populated and overgrown with *jungles* and woodlands. In the absence of stable administration, settlements must have suffered a decline.

In Mohania Block of Bhojpur district, the remains of a Budhist temple in the village Akhorhi are said to be about a thousand years old. There are inscriptions about Lord Budha on the stone walls. The temple was demolished during the reign of the Mughal Emperor Aurangzeb. In Fatepur Block of Gaya district Jaipur and Pahsi are two settlements of this period with the temples of Lord Shiva and Lord Budha. In Noorsarai Block of Patna district, the village Ajaipur is believed to be the seat of King Ajaipal of the Pala dynasty. The village has ruins of an old tank and an old mound. Some inscribed stone images believed to be of A.D. 500 have also been found there[71]. Kurkihar is the site of a famous Budhist monastery of Pala period. In the year A.D. 816 King Gopal ruled South Bihar Plain and made the town of Bihar his capital. His descendents were Budhists and a number of Budhist remains of their times A.D. 815-1200 are still existent.

The other settlements of post-Budhist period are Udaipur, Pirpainty and Tilaundha in Bhagalpur district; Indpe, Bardih, Naulagarh, Kharagpur, Mahsaur in Munger district of South Bihar Plain. In North Bihar Plain, the settlements of this period are Paikdara in Purnea district; Bhelwa in Saharsa district; Rudrapur and Kaspur in Darbhanga district; Nanpur and Pratap-Tandi in Muzaffarpur district; Dighwara, Kachnar and Kusaundhi in Saran district; Bhainsalotan, Bhawanipur and Darubari in Champaran district. Garhodih, Devandadih, Kopagarh, Burwadih, Ghaskhan-Ka Garh, etc. are settlements of the Pala period in Saharsa district[72].

SETTLEMENTS OF THE MUSLIM PERIOD A.D. 1200–A.D. 1400

With the arrival of Mohammadans, the region faced remarkable changes in its settlements. After A.D. 1193 Mohammad-bin-Bakhtiar Khilji invaded Bihar. The monasteries and the universities of Odantpuri, Nalanda and Vikramsila were ruthlessly ransacked and the monks slain. He forced Budhism to disappear from its birth place. But the Muslim hold on South Bihar was never extensive[73]. The most notable example of the encroachment on sites of Hindu worship by the Muslims is the conversion of hot springs of Sringi-Rishikund into Makhdumkund at Rajgir and the transformation of the miracle working Budha, into a Muslim saint, Makhdum Sahib. the Muslims also changed many place names as well as established new settlements. In the vicinity of Panchkosi in and around the village of Mahisi are the famous villages of Sahi-houl, Ekamma, Bijalpur, Rajoura, Rampur, etc, which formed mulgrama of the various mulas introduced by Harsimhadeva[74]. The monuments at Khanjarpur built in the 16th century by Ibrahim Hussain Khan, the mosque at Bhikhanpur built in the 15th century by Bandugi Sah Nakuam, and the mosques at Quazichak and at Colgong are important places in Bhagalpur district.

The modern subdivisions of Hajipur and Samastipur (originally Shamsuddinpur) were founded by Haji Shamsuddin Ilyas of Bengal. During Muslim period Gaya was named as Ilahibad. Most of the settlements in this district were established by the Muslim rulers and that's why there are place names like Imamganj, Nabinagar, Aurangabad, Daudnagar, Arwal, Jehanabad, Makhdumpur, Khidirsarai, Warsaliganj, Wazirganj, Hisua, Fatehpur, etc. Rural settlements of the Muslim period in South Bihar Plain are Islampur, Mera, Barara, Fatwah and Bakhtiarpur in Patna district; Hussainabad, Sheikhpura, Kajra, Simri-Bakhtiarpur, Pirpahari, Amarpur, Maulanagar, Pachnan and Sadipur in Munger district; Bibiganj, Karam Nagar and Harbhoj in Bhojpur district.

In the North Bihar Plain, Nanyadeva retained complete independence in Mithila till A.D. 1324, when Mohammad-bin Tuglak defeated Hari Singh. During the Muslim period, Saran was connected with the fortunes of the Hathwa family, whose headquarter was at Husepur. Siwan and Manjhi were fortified seats of the turbulent Muslim freebooters, while Manjha, Parsa, Mirjapur, Paterha and Chirand were the headquarters of the powerful Hindu chieftains. Bahera, Havidih, Harsimhapur, Sibaisinhpur, Deokuli, Kamsar, Narayana Dih, Padhuma, Sahit, Garh-Sisai, Bishnupur, Nawada, Bhatpura and Raghopur in Darbhanga district are settlements of this period. The village Shiva-Singhpur derives its name from Shiva Singh, the Raja of Mithila in the 14th century.

In Muzaffarpur district, more than half of the place names are of Mohammadan origin. For example, village Lalgarh derives its name from the ruins of a fortress ascribed to Lal-Khan. It is possible, however, that many settlements existed since ages and only their names were changed during the Muslim rule.

SETTLEMENTS OF THE MUGHAL PERIOD A.D. 1401–A.D. 1750

A struggle between the Afghans and the Mughals took place in the 15th century A.D. in Bihar. In 1541, Shershah transferred the capital of Bihar from Biharsharif to Patna, where he built an exceptionally strong fort. In A.D. 1574 Akbar had to fight against the Afghan princes and the Hindu chieftains of Bihar[75]. He captured Patna and Hajipur and drove the Afghans upto Barh. Raja Todarmal and the newly appointed Governor of Bihar, Munim Khan captured Surajgarh, Munger, Bhagalpur and Colgong and the Hindu Rajas of Kharagpur and Gidhaur were made to pay tribute. However, greater difficulty had to be encountered in suppressing the revolt of Raja Gajan Sahi and the chiefs of Bhojpur, Behea and Jagdishpur. The strong fort of Rohtas could be occupied only after the subjugation of the Rajput chief.

During Mughal period, the administrative units were divided into *mahals* or *parganas* subdivided into *tappas* and *turfs*[76]. Some clan areas were typically named after the number of villages included in them such as *Athgawan* (8 villages) and *Chaubisi* (24 villages). The course of rivers, patches of forests, woodlands or wastelands formed boundaries between villages and more commonly between clan areas of different local chiefs. Shershah built the Grand Trunk Road, which passed through Gaya and Shahabad districts in South Bihar

Plain, and *sarai* or inns were built at numerous places, such as Laheriasarai, Dalsinghsarai and Begusarai in North Bihar and Lakhisarai, Ekangarsarai and Khidirsarai in South Bihar. The district of Muzaffarpur takes its name after its chief town founded by Muzaffar Khan a revenue officer, under the Mughals. The village Sursand has the ruins of a fortress, known as Sursandgarh, constructed during the Mughal period by King Sursen. Bakar a rural settlement in Muzaffarpur district has a 300 years old brick memorial to Bakar Mian after whom the village is named. The village Shergarh in Shahabad district has a ruined hill fort built by Shershah Suri. Tavernier[77] visited Rohtasgarh, Bhabua, Sasaram, Buxar, Aurangabad, Akbarpur, Sherghatti, Gaya, Nawada, Tajpur, Hajipur, Rusera, Darbhanga, Dalsinghsarai, Chapra, Dinapur, Arrah, Biharsharif, Jamui, Supaul, Purnea, Araria, Karhagolaghat, Lakhisarai, Munger, Siwan, Motihari, Sitamarhi, Muzaffarpur, Jagdishpur, Chenari, etc. in the Bihar Plain during A.D. 1670-1689. He has mentioned that Aurangabad was a place where Aurangzeb won the battle against Shuja, the Governor of Bihar.

Langain, Kujha, Mohanpur, Rangaon, Dhouni, Dhoi, Madho Rampur, Kurudih, Samastipur, Sojaur, Pachkathia, Khaira, Amarpur, and Benhara are settlements of this period, in Bhagalpur district. Amarpur was founded by Shah Umar,Vazir of Shuja while Benhara was the headquarters of Mughal Emperor Shahjahan in Bhagalpur district. The village Deoraj in Gaya district belonged to one of the oldest families of Bihar in the 15th century A.D. Daudnagar in Gaya district was founded by Daud Khan, the Governor of Bihar under Aurangzeb. Darauli, Mahmada Garh, Phaur, Sheikhpura, Baghauni, Parauli, Saghar-Sultanpur, Sultanpur Khurd, Asuri-Kalan, etc. in Saran district, Jandaha and Manikchak in Muzaffarpur district; Jalalpur and Pir Mokani in Purnea district; Hamidpur and Gamharia in Saharsa district; Pateshwa and Jhar-Mahul in Champaran district; Bakhri, Safiabad and Mansurchak in Munger district, Akbarpur, Daudnagar and Ismailpur in Gaya district and Pingi and Monda (200 years old Memorial to a Muslim pir) in Darbhanga district are important settlements which had their origin during this period.

SETTLEMENTS OF THE BRITISH PERIOD A.D. 1751 - 1947

During the late Mughal and early British periods, Buchanan travelled widely over the region. He entered Bihpur[78] in 1811 and passed through Phulout, Alamnagar, Mahinathnagar and Chautham. He has mentioned that a number of powerful chiefs held sway over several areas, such as the rulers of Tekari in central Gaya, Kamgar and Naudar Khanin Narhat and Sami in the east, Siris and Kutunlea in the west and Ramgarh in the south. Prior to this the region was under the trade influence of the Dutch and the Portuguese. There were several centres of their trade such as Patna, Sonepur, Chapra, Revelganj and Motihari. But as soon as the British occupied this territory in the 18th Century, the rural areas underwent significant changes in settlements. Several roads were constructed to connect important places for convenience in administration. The area was subdivided into administrative units such as division, district, subdivision and revenue thanas. They also constructed hospitals, dakbungalows, public schools, circuit houses, district and local boards, and railways. The trade developed with the establishment of law and order. Remarkable changes were brought about in the nature of dwellings. The British organised permanent settlements and dwellings by restricting shifting cultivation. Around early 20th century the village boundaries were demarcated with flagstones.

The department of revenue administration prepared detailed large scale maps of rural settlements, showing individual agricultural plots, inhabited sites, roads, water-bodies, forests, etc. The village life became peaceful. Settlements grew in size and importance depending upon the fertility of land, freedom from floods, facilities for irrigation and above all, the relative nodality of particular centres. The most important factor of nodality was a railway station preferably with a highway connecting it to the country side, for example, Bihta in Patna district or Katihar in Katihar district. In areas where there were no railways, cross roads or highways or bridge sites became important, for example, Banka, Darbhanga, Saharsa, Muzaffarpur and Barauni as bridge site towns. With the take over of river borne trade by the railways, river ports like Revelganj, Hajipur and Mokameh declined in importance.

Established by the British, there were 25 indigo concerns in

Darbhanga and Muzaffarpur districts in 1800[79]. These were Daudpur, Saraiya, Dholi, Atnar, Shahpur, Kanti, Motipur, Deoria, Bhowrah, Muhammadpur, Belsar, Pipraghat, Dalsinghsarai, Jitwarpur, Tewara, Kamataul, Chitwara, Pupri and Shápurundi. The village Bara in Champaran district had an indigo factory in 1813 near Chakia railway station and village Lalsaraiya 8 kilometres from Sugauli railway station. Chautarwa and Madanpur (16 kilometres north-west of Bagaha in Champaran district) were other settlements of the British period.

A number of *Kothis* (settlements), for example, Daulatpur Kothi, Ilmasnagar Kothi, Hathauri Kothi, Baghauni Kothi and Jitwarpur Kothi in Darbhanga district and many others were established by the British for the ease of administration and indigo cultivation in the region. With the decline of indigo industry in the 20th century, all these centres declined except where there were trade or administrative convenience. The highest density of rural settlements in Bihar Plain was to be found in the fertile plains of Patna and Saran districts according to 1901 Census. The subdivisions of highest density of rural settlements per square kilometre were Dinapur 1.13, Gopalganj 1.06, Bihar 1.02, Chapra 0.80 and Barh 0.78. The lowest figure was for Jamui 0.30, Munger 0.32 and Madhepura 0.25. While the first two subdivisions have rugged terrain with low fertility of soil, Madhepura lies in the flood belt of the river Kosi.

SETTLEMENTS FROM A.D. 1947 ONWARDS

After independence, settlements show a general tendency of dispersal, because the fear of freebooters and foreigners has ended and the inhabitants feel greater freedom and security. Primary schools, rural health centres, *Panchayat Bhawans* (village council house), milan mandir (community centre), libraries and many other public buildings have rapidly changed the rural landscape. According to 1961 Census, the villages were closely settled in plains and their distribution was mainly dependent upon the agricultural prosperity of the region. Many administrative changes have also been brought about. Saharsa, a subdistrict, hitherto, was constituted into a full-fledged district, comprising Supaul and Madhepura subdivisions, in 1954. An area of 1876.17 square kilometres comprising the police station of Golpokhar and portions of Thakurganj and Karandighi in

Purnea district was transferred to West Bengal with the reorganisation of states in 1956[80].

The growth of many villages into towns and towns into cities led to a very remarkable change in settlement pattern. For example Rajgir, Rajauli, Warsaliganj, Gopalganj, Mirganj, Sugauli Bazar, Raxaul Bazar, Shikarpur, Bagaha, Chakia, Lauthaha, Kesaria, Mahnar, Dumra, Dalsingsarai, Barahiya, Jhajha and Kharagpur were all classified as rural settlements in 1941 Census, but with the growth of population and tertiary occupational activities, they were declared towns from 1951 census onwards. Similarly Bakhtiarpur, Bodhgaya, Bikramganj, Maharajganj, Barauni, Banka, Sultanganj, Naugachhia, Supaul, Saharsa, Madhepura, Murliganj, Birpur and Nirmali which were treated as rural settlements in 1951 Census, were categorised as towns in 1961 Census. Many towns grew into cities, for example Gaya (1941), Bhagalpur (1951), Darbhanga (1961), Muzaffarpur (1961), Munger (1971) and Biharsharif (1971) increased their population to over 100,000 for the first time in the years noted against their names.

Besides the outgrowth of the older settlement, several new settlements cropped up on account of economic development and also the construction of the highways, for example, Baheri, Bahera, Jhanjharpur and Jainagar in Darbhanga district; Raghunathpur, Bikramganj, Jagdishpur and Kudra in Shahabad district; Pundarakh, Barh, Bakhtiarpur and Mokameh in Patna district; Banka on the highways in Bhagalpur district and Katihar in Purnea district as an important railway junction. So far as the evolution of newer settlements are concerned, Dulha, Pithaunjhia, Anantpur, Muktapur and Thalwara originated in recent years around railway stations in North Bihar. Several settlements grew up or came into existence in the vicinity of industrial establishments or development projects, for example, Birpur in Saharsa district is headquarters of the Kosi project, Barauni in Munger district has witnessed settlement growth on account of the fertilizer project and oil refinery located there, and Kanti and Colgong associated with the super thermal power projects (1980).

The process of urban expansion has assimilated or rather absorbed several rural settlements. For example, the growth of Birpur in Saharsa district absorbed Basantpur and Hanuman Nagar,

Bakhtiarpur absorbed Hakikatpur, Bulan-Buzurg and Modhopur and Kasba Bazar absorbed Phulwari, Jawanpur, Marancha-Ujiarpur and Dogacch, etc. Thus all towns and cities have a number of constituent villages absorbed or merged within the perimeter of the urban territory. Sometimes the outgrowth of settlements is not due to any natural process, but is the result of expansion of trade activity or the development of transport routes, for example, Kako in Gaya district. Growth of settlements due to development of irrigation or industries and the establishment of block development offices and educational or medical institutions, etc. has led to the evolution of *tolas* (hamlets). This is a process of dispersal which has become quite noticeable in recent years.

TABLE 5.2 : **Showing Change in the Number of Totals (Hamlets)**

Name of the District	Total no. of tolas in 1957	Total no.of tolas in 1965	Difference
Patna	4704	5132	+428
Gaya	11330	11543	+213
Shahabad	6018	6030	+12
Saran	6841	6952	+111
Champaran	6245	5382	-363
Muzaffarpur	5689	5847	+158
Darbhanga	6180	6241	+61
Bhagalpur	4096	4247	+151
Monghyr	5298	5344	+46
Purnea	8335	8656	+321
Saharsa	2527	3035	+503

Source : All India Second Educational Survey, Bihar, Govt. of Bihar, Department of Education, December, 1965.

This table shows that the number of rural habitations are increasing very rapidly in the region, except in Champaran district where the construction of canals and irrigation dams have led to the destruction of several small hamlets which have amalgamated with larger settlements.

Another change in settlement patterns is the more rapid development of brick built houses as compared to the mud, thatch and tile-roofed houses in the region. This is more noticeable in the prosperous areas such as in Patna, Gaya and Saran districts. During the medieval period, the size and number of villages continued to grow. But because there were frequent political changes, it is not possible to conclude that there was a steady growth. The Muslim rulers built a number of settlements, but they fought amongst themselves and there was political instability.

The first survey and settlement operations in the Bihar Plain were conducted between 1890 and 1920. Complete land records for the entire permanently settled area were prepared. Cadastral maps for each plot in every basic unit called the revenue village were drawn in which the broad land use like settlements, communication lines, water bodies and orchards or forests were also shown. Since then there has been no change in the total number of revenue villages in rural areas although numerous new hamlets have sprung up and many old revenue villages have been included within the municipal borders of the over growing towns. According to 1981 Census, the present size of rural settlements varies from 5 to 25000 persons. Their morphological growth, however is still purely unplanned in character.

DENSITY OF RURAL SETTLEMENTS

Bihar Plain is one of the most densely settled parts of India. The high density of population, particularly in the central and northern parts, has led to an equally high density of rural settlements in these areas. In contrast, settlements are thinly distributed in the hilly areas along the southern border of the region.

The density of rural settlement has been calculated by taking the revenue *mauza* which is the smallest administrative unit into consideration. The area of each *anchal* has been divided by the number of revenue *mauza* it contained, to give the density of villages per sq. kilometre. Each of these *mauza* may comprise one or more settlement units or *tolas*. These, however, cannot be considered in the absence of population data and the exact number of *tolas* in existence. These have not been provided in the Census.

There are 395 *anchals* in the region under study and the density of rural settlements in them ranges between 0.08 and 1.29 per square kilometre. The mean of these is 0.44 and the Standard Deviation is 0.09.

$$\sigma = i\sqrt{\frac{\sum fx^2}{N} - C^2}$$

where σ = Standard Deviation
i = is the class interval
Σfx^2 = is the sum of the squared deviation in units of class interval. taken from the assumed mean
N = Number of *anchals*
C^2 = is the squared correction in units of class interval

On the basis of Standard Deviation, the total range of settlement density has been divided into eight groups as follows:

Groups	Range	Value
I	Over M+3σ	0.71
II	Over M+2σ	0.71 to 0.63
III	Over M+1σ	0.63 to 0.54
IV	+1σ to Mean	0.54 to 0.44
V	Mean to-1σ	0.44 to 0.35
VI	Under M-1σ	0.35 to 0.25
VII	Under M-2σ	0.25 to 0.16
VIII	Under M-3σ	0.16

The above groups have been shown in Fig. 5.2 with the help of choropleth technique and clearly bring out the areas of relative density.

Anchals, falling in the first group, are concentrated on either banks of the river Ganga in the districts of Saran, southern Muzaffarpur, eastern Patna and parts of Gaya and Bhagalpur districts. The highest density of over 0.81 i.e. M+4σ is to be found in the *anchals* of Gurua and Kutumba *anchals* of Gaya district; Amnauri, Guthani, Uchkagaon, Bijaipur, Bhorey, Katia and Kuchaikot *anchals* of Saran district; Mehsi *anchals* of Champaran district; Mahua, Jamdaha, Vaishali, Hajipur and Bidupur *anchals* of Muzaffarpur district and Jagdishpur and Rajaun *anchals* of Bhagalpur district. These *anchals* are areas of high fertility. They are also free from floods. They also have better transport facilities on account of relatively higher level of land.

In contrast, the regions of lowest density are the flood affected areas of Purnea, Saharsa, Khagaria and eastern Darbhanga districts, where elevated sites for building settlements are few and far between. Another patch of low density is along the Terai Belt in North Muzaffarpur and Champaran district where the soil and drainage conditions are also unfavourable. The third zone runs along the southern border of the region particularly in the hilly areas of Vindhya Plateau and Chotanagpur Scarps. The lowest density of less than 0.16 i.e. under M - 3σ is to be found in the following *anchals*.

Flood affected		**Hilly and Rugged**	
Districts	Anchals	Districts	Anchals
Patna	Mokameh	Shahabad	Rohtas
	-	-	Nauhatta
	-	-	Adhaura
Champaran	Madhubani, Thakrahan		
Darbhanga	Jainagar		
Munger	Khagaria, Alauli		
-	Beldaur		
Bhagalpur	Gopalpur, Bihpur		
-	Naugachhia		
Saharsa	Singheshwar asthan		
-	Chausa		
Purnea	Narpatganj, Barari		

The very low settlement densities of 0.11 and less per sq. kilometre in Mokameh, Madhubani, Thakrahan, Gopalpur and Chausa *anchals* are the direct result of regular annual inundation of these areas. These *anchals* suffer from waterlogging in the monsoon season and the land becomes marshy for several months after the water drains out. Mokameh is locally known as the *tal* or lake area. Madhubani and Thakrahan fall in the flood plains of the Gandak river and are predominated by swamps locally called *Chaurs.* Gopalpur is affected by the floods of the Ganga.

The comparatively low density in Rohtas and Adhaura *anchals* of Rohtas are due to the forested and rocky nature of the land. The scarcity of water and lack of fertility in the soil which render them unfit for human habitation.

REFERENCES

1. Bihar, Department of Public Relations: *Facts and Figures about Bihar*, Patna, 1958,p.1.
2. E. Ahmad: *Geographical Essays on India*, Patna, 1954, p.33.
3. B.H. Baden-Powell : *The Indian Village Community*, London, 1987, p.51
4. B.H. Baden-Powell: *Land System of British India*, Vol. 1, London, 1892,p.108.
5. T.W. Rhys, Davids: *Buddhist India*, Calcutta, 1959(Reprint edition)p.11.
6. Hariranjan and Jamadar Kumar Ghosal: *Buddhism and Vaishali*, Patna, 1957, p.1.
7. Satish Chandra Singh : "Changes in the Course of the Kosi," *The National Geographical Journal of India*, Vol. XVI, 1970,p.265.
8. J. Bruhnes: *Geographic Humaine de la France*, Vol. I. Paris, 1920.p.239.
9. C.M.S. Ramchandra Chattiyar : "Place Names in North Arcot District, *Indian Geographical Journal*, Vol. XVIII, 1943, p.67.
10. V.S.Agarawala, : "Geographical Data in Panini" *Indian Historical Quarterly*, Vol. XXIX, 1953, pp.1-3.
11. P. Dayal: "The Bihar Plain - a Regional Study," *Transactions of the Indian Council of Geographers*, Vol.5, 1968, p.1.
12. Census of India, 1961: *District Census Handbook*, Purnea, p.1.
13. L.S.S. O'Malley : *Bengal District Gazetteer Champaran District*, Calcutta, 1907, p.1.
14. Shyam Narayan Singh: *History of Tirhut*, Calcutta, 1922, p.3.
15. *Ibid;* p.4.
16. Such urban settlements of today were rural settlements at the time of their origin, hence it is necessary to consider them in the study of place names of rural settlements.
17. Mahendra Prasad Verma : *Bihar Directory*, Patna, 1954, pp. 9-47.
18. L.S.S. O'Malley : *Bengal District Gazetteer Champaran*, Calcutta, 1907, pp.171 and 182.
19. L.S.S. O'Malley: *Bengal District Gazetteer, Monghyr*, Calcutta, 1909,p.49.
20. Census of India, 1961 : *District Census Handbook, Bhagalpur*, by S.D. Prasad, Patna, 1965,p.1.
21. Mahendra Prasad Verma : *op.cit.*
22. B.C.N. Rao : "A Study of Place Names in the Anantapur District", *Journal, Madras Geographical Association*, Vol. 10, 1935, pp. 22-43.
23. Bihar, Department of Public Relations : *Facts and figures about Bihar*, Patna, 1956.
24. James Fergusson : "Bihar Caves", in *History of Architecture*, London, 1867,pp.482-83.
25. "Neolithic Culture Found at Chirand", *Indian Nation*, May 1970, p.5.
26. Chandrashekhar Singh : *"Chirand" Bihar Samachar*, 1971, p.26.
27. Radhakamal Mukherjee: *The Changing Face of Bengal*, Calcutta, 1938,pp.233-34.
28. Anant Prasad Banerjee, Shastri: *Asura India*, Patna, 1926, p.71.
29. Chitta Ranjan Prasad Sinha : "Buxar in Archaeological perspectives", *Journal, Bihar Research Society*, Vol. XLIX, 1963, P.107.
30. Census of India, 1961: *District Census Handbook*, Saharsa, by S.D. Parasad, p.52.
31. B.H. Baden-Powell: *op.cit.,* p.42.
32. Anant Prasad Banerjee Shastri: *op.cit., p.96.*

33. Mukheriee, L. : *History of India: Hindu Period*, Calcutta, 1968, p.28.
34. Ibid,p.18.
35. Tarachand: *Short History of Indian People*, Calcutta, 1934,p.36.
36. A.B. Havel: *Ancient and Medieval Architecture of India*, London, 1985,p.7.
37. R.L. Singh : "Evolution of Settlements in the Middle Ganga Valley"*National Geographical Journal of India*, Vol.1, 1956,p.77.
38. "Mithila-Mihir", Patna 24 November 1968,p.26.
39. L.S.S. O'Malley: *Bengal District Gazetteer Dharbhanga*, Calcutta, 1903,p.141.
40. U. Thakur : *History of Mithila*, Darbhanga, Mithila Institute, 1956,p.115.
41. Ramrijhan Rasalpuri: "Kumhrar", *Bihar Samachar*, October 1, 1967,p.8.
42. J.N. Samaddar: "Aryan Settlement", in *The Glories of Magadha*, Patna, 1927,p.2.
43. Bishnu Shankar: *Welcome Address to the 20th Sub-School Inspector Conference Arrah*, 26th June, 1971,p.1.
44. Tarachand: *op. cit.*, p.41.
45. *Ibid,*p.44.
46. R.L.Singh : *op. cit.,* p.73.
47. Praphullachandra Basu: "The Village Community", in *Ind, Aryan Policy*, Allahabad, 1919,p.21.
48. Radhakamal Mukerjee : *op. cit.,* pp. 140-43.
49. A.B. Haveli: "Communication during Aryan Period and Mauryan Period", in *History of Aryan Rule In India*, London, 1920,p.72.
50. E.W. Hopkins: "Posision of the Ruling Caste in Ancient India", *Journal, American Oriental Society*, Vol.13, 1888,p.84.
51. *Imperial Gazetteer of India, Bengal*, Vol.II, Calcutta, 1909,p.182.
52. R.K. Choudhary : "Early History of Vaishali", in *Vaishali Vishesank,* 1960,p.7.
53. Ramrijhan Rasalpuri: *op.cit.,* p.8.
54. Manoranjan Ghosh: *The Patliputra*, Patna Law Press, 1919,p.5.
55. L.S.S. O'Malley: Bengal District Gazetteer, *op.cit.*p.49.
56. Ghosal, Hariranjan and Jamadar Kumar: *op.cit.*
57. L. Mukerjee : *op.cit.,* p.59.
58. Anant Prasad Banerjee Shastri: *Early Inscriptions of Bihar and Orissa*, Patna, 1927, p.114.
59. L.S.S. O'Malley : *Bengal District Guzetteer*, Champaran, *op. cit.* p.85.
60. Radhakumud Mukerjee : *Hindu Civilisation*, Calcutta, 1950, pp.296-97.
61. *Ibid,* p.199.
62. A.B. Havel. Ancient Medieval Architecture of India, *op.cit.*p.11.
63. R. Fricks: *The Social Organism in North East India in Budhas* Time, Translated from German by S.K. Maitra, Calcutta, 1920 p.160.
64. *Vinaya*, III: p.46; or *Dharma Pada* 1, p.3B; where a gama of eight Kutis is mentioned atha kutiko gama.
65. *Indian Antiquity,* Ed. by G.V. Deva Asthali: Vol.1, 1964, pp.219-253.
66. I.B. Harner: "Middle Length Savings II", p.30 and Choudhary, Ram Gopal, *India of Vedic Kalpa Sutra,* p.150.
67. Nagendra Nath: "Kautilya Kalim Gramya Byabastha," *Bihar Samachar,* No. 12, November 1968,p.15.
68. S. Beal: *Budhist Record of the Western World*, Calcutta, 1884, p.62.
69. L. Mukerjee: *op.cit.,* p.213.
70. K.P. Jaiswal: *Hindu Polity*, Calcutta, 1934, p.165.
71. Census of India, 1961: *District Census Handbook*, Patna, by S.D. Prasad, p.ixv.

72. B.S. Verma: "Archaeological Remains of Mithila," *Journal of Bihar Research Society*, Vol. XLVIII, 1962,P.95.
73. P.C. Roy Choudhary: *Bihar District Gazetteers*, Gaya, Patna, 1957,p.34.
74. P.C. Roy Choudhary: *Gazetteer of India*, Bihar, Saharsa District, Patna, 1965, p.31.
75. S.R. Sharma: *Akbar the Great*. New Delhi, 1952,p.47.
76. Ibid; p.42.
77. V. Ball: *Travels in India by Jean Baptiste Tavernier*. Vol. 1, London, 1889, p.115.
78. *Ibid;* p.115.
79. P.C. Roy Choudhary: *Bihar District Gazetteers:* Darbhanga, Patna, 1964, p. 43.
80. *Census of India,* 1961: Vol. IV, *Bihar*, Part IIA, by D.S. Prasad, Patna, 1963, p. 9.

Fig. 5.1

Aryan Settlements

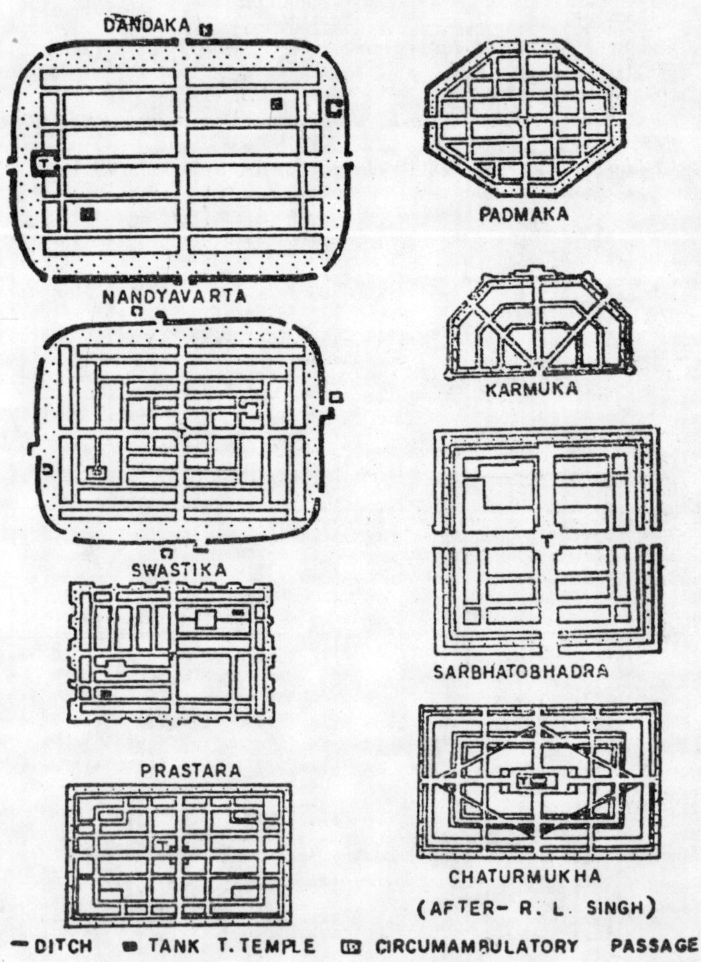

Fig. 5.2

Bihar Plain : Density of Rural Settlements

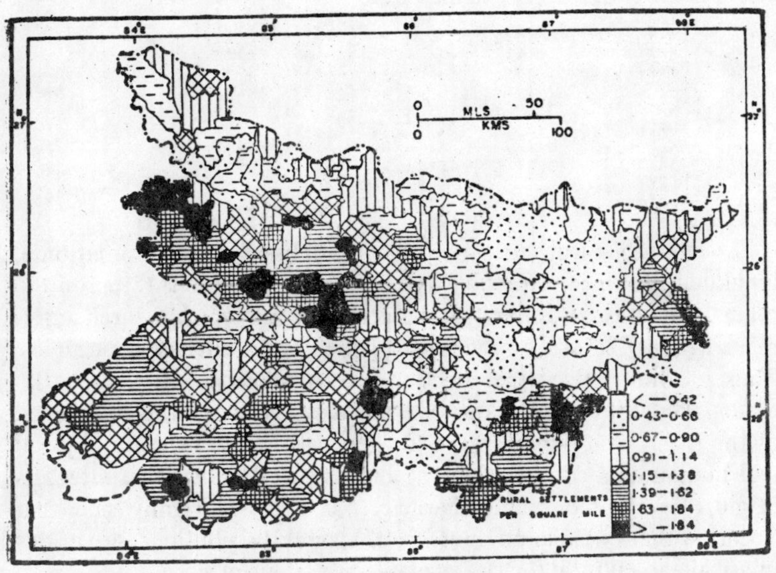

SIX

LOCATION AND SITING OF RURAL SETTLEMENTS

Location of rural settlements can be defined in terms of latitude, longitude, distance, direction and ecological conditions. Site, on the other hand may be defined as the ground upon which a rural settlement actually stands or the tract of the earth's surface it occupies. Thus location guides the function and significance of rural settlements, while the morphology of a particular settlement is influenced by the site. Location embraces the general conditions, both physical and human of a rural settlement and its surroundings that affect its origin, development and character. It is, thus rightly said that "location theory explains the laws of spatial distribution"[1] of various physical and cultural factors available at various places.

According to Preston E. James we identify things geographical because they deal with location - and with the succession of settlements or other items that occupy space. To Paul Vidal de la Blache, the whole of geography lay in the idea of 'place'. Geographically, the first question of all is 'where'?[2]

Hence locational attributes are characteristics of man and earth which are associated with a particular location. E.W. Soja (1971) emphasized that "the difference from place to place, is relative as well as absolute location, and in terms of other features such as climate, economy, language, wealth and culture-shape the nature and intensity of relationships between people and between the locations they occupy".[3]

The spatial pattern of locational attributes may have a great influence on spatial interactions and spatial organization of human behaviour and settlements. Similarities in certain types of locational attributes of settlements, industries, language, culture and the level of education may facilitate interactions. Differences in the locational attributes between place stimulate interactions due to complementarity. For example, differences in resources of two areas mean there is a potential for mutual trade beneficial to both areas.

In order to understand the current spatial organization and in planning for future changes, information on locational characteristics of a settlement is valuable.

The majority of people in the entire world live in groups as village communities. In primitive societies, a self supporting group of people settles and sets up a village at a spot where food, water, fuel and building materials are all at hand, though in some cases defence, religious and behavioural factors were more important in the location of village site. Slowly with the evolution of social norms and rising exchange of goods with the trade and economic development play an over-riding role in the siting of settlements.[4]

The classification of settlements according to the suitability of site/location assists in highlighting the various kinds of geographical advantages which led to the origin and growth of rural settlements.[5] In most cases more than two advantageous factors operate in conjunction to determine a settlements location.

Classification of Rural Settlements By Locational Origin

1. At the confluence of rivers.
2. At a bend in river.
3. Where a river has cut a gap through a range of hills.
4. At a fording point.
5. Where a river enters or leaves a gorge.
6. Where a narrow river valley broadens out into a plain.
7. Where a river enters or leaves a lake.
8. Where a loop in a river provides a defensible position espe-

cially in case the loop encloses an elevated area.

9. Where an island in a river affords a defensible site or an easy crossing place.
10. At the head of ocean navigation or at the head of river navigation
11. At the lowest bridging point. This may be understood in the light of man's former capabilities. The lowest point at which a bridge could be built. This also may be the head of navigation.
12. At or near the spring line where permeable and impermeable rocks meet. Numerous examples of spring line villages are found in Kent and Sussex in England.
13. At the centre of an area of fertile lowland.
14. Where land routes converge e.g. nodal village.
15. On 'islands' of permanently dry land having marshy ground in the surrounding areas. These are known as 'dry point' settlements. In case most settlement seeks water then the same may be called 'wet-point' settlements.
16. Where a path of coastal plain occurs in the side of a mountain.
17. On the shore of an indentation in the coastline which provides a sheltered anchorage.
18. Religious places, tourist spots, bus stops, educational institutions, hydro-power-stations and mining centres.

Factors Affecting Location of Settlements

Two basic factors physical and cultural, affect the location of rural settlements.

Definition of Location:-

The location of rural settlements is always decided in response to variety of influences. In the territorial organisation of any group of people, settlements are placed as advantageously as possible in relation to physical features of the landscape. They need well drained land, protected spots, commandable position, adequate transportation and communication links, perennial sources of water and availability of fuel close to the working places and agricultural fields. The subsistent peasants of Brazil generally establish their homesteads in or very close to the centre of cropping fields. The Baltic fisherman's house site is located close to his boat-house on the shore. Millions of people in South-East Asia live on artificial mounds amidst the flat and inundated rice fields. Wherever natural landscape conditions are not suitable, artificial foundations for house sites are generally built. The Neolithic lake dwellers of central Europe constructed their houses on piles, buildings movable causeways over the water. The early inhabitants of northwest Europe made dykes and mounds and built houses on these higher surfaces; whereas both peasants of the mediterranean and migrants to Los Angeles made terraces on hill sides on which to construct their houses.

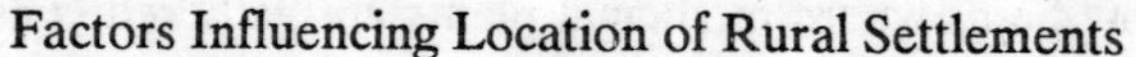

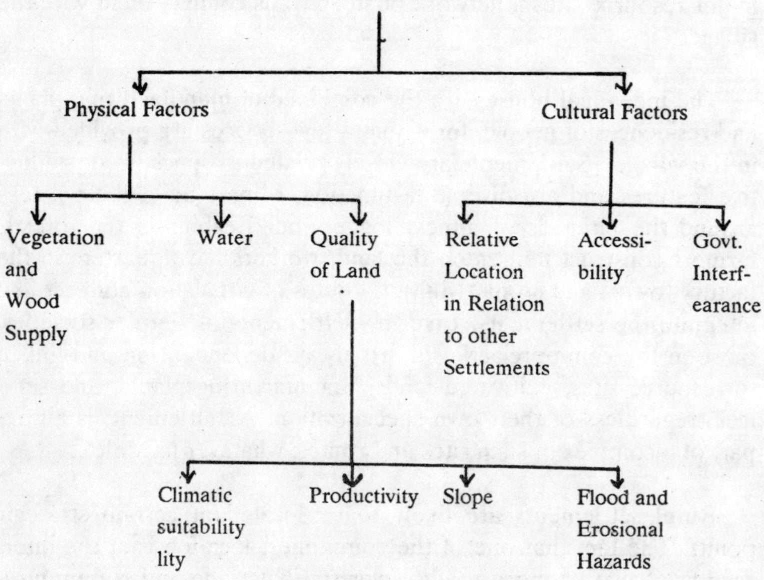

The location of a rural settlement may also be dictated by the availability of sunshine. In the valleys of the Alps in Europe and on the southern slope of Siwalik Himalaya, the maximum amount of sunshine is received by a settlement on the south facing slopes, as the settlements on the other side of the valley receive sunshine for only a few hours even in summer.

The rural settlements whether it is a hut in a lonely forest or large village of thousands of people is so situated that the means of livelihood are available to its people, and they have the facility to secure goods and services for consumption. A peasant family needs to reside in close proximity to its fields, drinking water well or spring, and to fuel wood. Hence each and every settlement needs to be accessible to appropriate resources. For an Indian village in Maxico these facilities may be organized well over a distance of 100 kilometres, and the whole complex may be a miniature universe. The cornfields near the village, the pine forests where the kindling and torches are cut, the grassy glades where roofing material is secured, the hardwood forests from which come building materials for the construction of house, the springs, the clay pits for pottery, and the old fallow fields where medicinal plants are gathered constitute the major resource sites a network of steep trails connect them with the village.

The individual houses are the combined of manufacturing plants and residences of people, for whom a few services are provided with in the village . Settlements are closely related to specialized productive features and are diverse in function. Miners build their shacks around the pitheads of mines; loggers build cabins in the forests; farmers construct houses on the land, workers have quarters in the factory towns, and so on. Multiple routes of circulation connect and integrate the settlements. Like the settlements of simpler societies, those in the commercial world are always dependent on and linked to resource sites, cultivated lands, manufacturing plants, and services, regardless of their own specialization. A settlement "is always part of a complex of such sites and routes, whatever its scale".[6]

Rural settlements are likely to be located at certain strategic points. The fact that one of the commonest location is at the intersection of two or more roads, suggests that trade and communication play an important role in the grouping of houses to form villages. Quite often, a settlement develops at a point where it can take advantage of the introduction of new form of transportation. A settlement is also likely to be established at a point of meander of a stream where there may probably be a bridge or a ferry.

In hilly and mountainous land rural settlements are often located with respect to slopes. For example, a hamlet or a village may be originally established on a hill top for reasons of defence and then maintained the same site even after the need for defence has been obviated.

During ancient times many villages in northern India were located on river embankments, because the migratory people who came from drier west of the Punjab and Uttar Pradesh were obssesed with water and hence they settled on river embankments.

Nowadays villages are also located as suburban village, industrial village, dormitory village, tourist village and vacation villages outside the large urban and industrial concentration. Hence the locational decisions on rural settlements may be very many according to the physical and cultural conditions.

For example, in Kharsam village of Samastipur district, India both physical and cultural factors exert a definite impact on its location. Here the vegetation is semi-deciduous which provides various types of wood for fuel, furniture and building materials; drinking water is available from 5 masonry wells and 5 tubewells. For washing livestock, the Kareh river flows throughout the year just 100 meters south of the village. The village site is on highland above the flood level which has been further artificially raised by the villagers on the plots of their own house. The agricultural land of the surrounding area is productive as the loamy sand enables three crops per year to be grown. It is a plain area of even surface free from flood hazard since the village is protected by a five metres high dyke on both sides of the river Kareh.

As regards cultural factors Kharsam is accessible by boat through river Kareh upto far-flung places in the south-east and north-west of the village and the flood proctection dyke is so wide along the river course that it serves the purpose of a highway (Fig. 6.1). One unmetalled road passes through the village south to north, and at a distance of one kilometre north linking this village with Darbhanga-Kusheswar Asthan metalled road. Hence this village is quite accessible from all directions. There is no government interference in case of Kharsam, India as we see in Tanzania where the government has been persuading the peasants to live in compact Ujamaa villages on selected sites. So far as the relative location is concerned the village Kharsam is located in the centre of several villages all at a distance of one kilometre such as in the north Sripur and parsa; in the West Sarhila and Boran, in the south Parwana and Mahdeva and in the east Banda, Jankinagar and Majrahia villages.

Another example is the Keneba village located at about 160 km. from Bathurst in Gambia, West Africa. Its main source of communication with the outside world is via the River Gambia and its tributaries, but even after the construction of a road that passes within about twenty kilometres, the village remained isolated and showed little interest in the resources, values, and customs of outsiders. The people mainly subsist by cultivating land around the village. They are muslims who have incorporated aspects of local beliefs, and the men are polygamous.

The village is located in a clearing in the wooded sevanah that is characteristic of this part of Gambia. People live in mud walled houses with thatch or corrugated iron sheets as roof. Numerous pathways develop to the fields where cultivation takes place, but these are periodically abandoned as the patterns of land use change.[7]

Game for Rural Settlement Location

It is known to us that location of rural settlements depends on many interacting factors, besides the technological know how of peasants. In order to learn the location of rural settlements the students should be given the information sheet and the map. The aim of the student may be to build up a settlement pattern, a route network and a regional environmental organization on the map provided (Fig.6.2). This is one kilometre equal to one centimetre map where settlements of having 500 population each should be located following the general pattern of rural settlements as found in the topographical sheets.

Extension of the Game :-

This game may be expanded by dividing the map into different cells and considering the factors such as geological variations, the presence of rivers, marshes, highlands, and putting weight to the negative and positive variables, and the selection of settlement site in cells having positive mark only according to random number allocation or phase wise settling.

Information Sheet:-

The establishment of most of the permanent rural settlements in North Bihar, India took place in the sixteenth and seventeenth centuries. The rural settlements generally established with clusters of houses with arable lands around. Most of the agricultural implements were primitive. Lands near big rivers were mostly lowlying marshy ground.

The settlers of North Bihar had several needs, and sites of their settling must be chosen very carefully, for most of them have survived over 350 years to the present day. In order of importance their needs were as follows:[8]

1. Access to a constant supply of drinking water.
2. Access to cultivable land so that time may not waste in travel.
3. Avoid marshy ground because that was unfit for raising crops and establishing houses.
4. Access to fuel wood and transportation lines is essential.

In order to have these requirements fulfilled, settlements spread 1 kilometre apart in the best conditions, and more than that in adverse circumstances.

Workout The following:

1. Mark suitable sites for 8 groups of rural settlements.
2. Mark highways path to connect the settlement groups.
3. Show the village surroundings with equal share as cultivable land, pastures and mango orchards.

Site of Rural Settlements

The most common site is the flood plain of a stream where the land is level, easily raised above the flood level and has ready access to water. If the site is subject to frequent floods, a part of the settlement may be shifted to the higher ground. Hillside sites offer some difficulties in construction of houses but may be preferred as it may be safe from floods and having better drainage. If the function of a settlement changes, the choice of the site may also change. The Hopi Indian settlements of the U.S.A. occupied sites on the top of Mesas for defence purposes, but since defence is no longer necessary and due to cultural preferment and the lure of modernity, the Hopis have moved down to the adjacent plains. The sites with large facilities for livestock farming have given vivid examples of radical transformations in their settlement structure as a result of structural changes in agriculture.

The consideration of site in settlement study is significant because during the ancient period, each community depended almost entirely on its own resources. In such a situation a riverside site, which provided fresh water for drinking and fertile alluvial soils in which food could be grown, was usually chosen in preference to others. Defence was also necessary which caused many settlements to grow up on incised meanders or on low hills, where rivers were shallow enough to be forded, where bridges could be built at the cross-points of highways where business may be profitable, congregation of more and more people possible and bus depot can be established.

According to Bourne "an association of sites constitutes a distinct region" and the regional boundary is marked by the appearance of new types of site. He defined site as 'an area which appears for all practical purposes to provide throughout its extent similar local conditions as to climate, physiography, geology, and soil..."[9] This concept of sites and association of sites forming regions is essentially geographical, whether one thinks in terms of 'areal differentiation' or environmental approach. But the knowledge of environment is never perfect as Mitchell says:[10] "The first settler in a place must often have made false starts and sometimes settled down permanently on a less good site even with a better site nearby, like a picnic party trying first this then that side of a bay, first one side of a hedge then the other, and in the end putting up with such that is not ideal rather than move yet once again".

The concept of site may also be detected in the studies of Garnett on isolation and relief in mountainous regions. The concept of site and of regions which are site associations provide one method of sub-dividing settlement area. Many, though not all, of the French Pays are regions of this type. Such regions have some element of generic quality: a dissected plateau is always a rough land.

This is because the nucleated rural settlement, once established, tends to draw some unity in different parts of the contrasted countryside which serves it and which it serves; it acts as a focus for common living. In much higher degree, however, they are specific depending for many of their features upon climate and cultural impress. The same site would not be generated even upon the same morphological basis by either an equatorial or a Mediterranean climate. Different cultures and economies will develop similar site groups differently.

FACTORS AFFECTING RURAL SETTLEMENT SITING

The siting of villages depends partly on the behavioural patterns of the community, the location of existing villages, and the physical constraints of the environment. Prior to the specialization of villages, they were sited where the essential resources such as water, fuel and fertile plain land were available although primitive technology and physical barriers were there.

There are two sets of factors which affect settlement siting in rural areas e.g. physical and cultural (Fig. 6.3).

1. **Physical factors influencing settlement sites during ancient times:**

(a) **Water seeking**: forest village, valley village, contact point village, scarp belt or spring line settlements in Peninsular India.

(b) **Water Shunning**: contact line village on the fringe of marshy and flooded areas of Saharsa and Purnea in North Bihar, fall lines of the eastern side of foothills of Appalachian mountain in U.S.A. and the eastern and western sea coasts of Peninsular India.

(c) **All Settlements seeking**: Level land, fertile soil, favourable climate, elevated site and physically good land for settlement.

2. **Economic and cultural Influences predominating the more modern siting of rural settlements:**

(a) **Nodal Points**: cross roads, ferry points, rail-road stations, bus depot, and smaller retail or business centres.
(b) **View Points**: school, college, temple, church, mosque, dak-bungalow, hospital, block development office, adult literacy centres, conference centres, and places of tourist interests.
(c) **Social traditions**: religious, caste, clan and communal groupings and tribal affiliations leading to economic and cultural influences in the rural society.

Site is the topographical detail of the immediate environs on which village stands. It guides the internal morphological characteristics of the settlement. Thus, the site, the land on which the houses and other structures of the settlement are built along with location are the second main focus of rural settlement study.

Among physical features the slope of a small hillock, a level terrace of gravel just above the flood-plain of a river, a slopy ground with a spring, supply of drinking water, a patch of suitable land for cultivation and pasture, and a foot path providing access to food-grain wholesale centre are considered as suitable site for settlement siting. Hence, in case the village has fertile land and drinking water available, the current siting of the village may continue without any disturbance.

In North Bihar, India changes in the site of rural settlements occur in response to large scale alleviation, meandering of rivers and excessive floods resulting in the destruction of settlements, cultural features and crops, and the development of waterlogging, marshy lands, formation of alluvial fans, cones and intercones, due to unequal deposition of sand bodies and sheet wash erosion. These are some of the geomorphic aspects which have an overriding importance for a geographer to study about the siting of rural settlements.

The siting requirements of fishing village may be different i.e., an inlet sheltered from storms and gales, safe from pirates, besides an access to fishing grounds. Mining and quarrying villages grow up very close to the pit-head but transport linkage upto the nearest market is quite necessary. Industrial villages are found as residential colony very close to the industry. Sea resort villages are found near the broad sandy beach, or a narrow raised beach, at a fjord head, and where a river and creek reaches the sea such as Kunduchi village north of Dar es Salaam, Tanzania.

Valley villages are found especially in Chhotanagpur plateau, Vale of Kashmir, Valley of Kangra and Kulu in Himalaya, Valley of Rhone in Alps, because the valley sites are usually well provided with flat land, fertile tract, high water level and it becomes easy to make transportation lines. In the Pennine hills of northern England swiftly flowing rivers provided good siting conditions for wool manufacturing in numerous villages. Similarly on the lower slopes of Kilimanjaro (up to 2000m) due to the availability of perennial spring water and the absence of both the bitter cold of higher areas and the hot malarial climate of the plain, settlements cling like beehive on mountain slopes and valleys of various heights.

In order to avoid flood hazard rural settlements cling to the river embankments in a linear fashion in the flood plains of the Kosi, the Ganga, the Mahananda, the Brahmaputra and the Hwangho of China.

There are many spring line villages in England. They have the dual advantage of access to permanent water supply and nearness to different kinds of agricultural land. "Wet point" settlements in the Sahara desert are examples of rural settlements sited according to similar considerations.

In Germany "dry-point" rural settlements are found on artificial high mounds locally known as *terpen* especially in the provinces of Friesland and Zealand as they are liable to inundation. England has also dry point villages in the Trent Valley, Vale of York, Plain of Glastonbury and in the Vale of Pickering e.g. Ayton, Rillington and Hovingham.[11]

In south-eastern Austria villages on mountain slopes are common such as Riegersburg. The level land is used for crops and pastures; the steep slopes are occupied by the village with an ancient castle crowning the highest portion of the hill.

Selection of Rural Settlement Site

The selection of rural settlement site matters much to peasants than pastoralists because in farming the intended use of land is more intensive, selective and the expected occupation is much longer. The selection of a site requires a clear cut understanding that whether the settlement be regarded as a self-sufficient one or it has to participate in commercial cum industrial and modern cooperative farming. The idea of Chisholm in settlement location in an agricultural subsistence economy is as follows[12] (Fig. 6.4.):

In the majority of cases the need for water and arable land weigh strongly as influences upon site choice, and the grazing often gets discounted. Building materials are needed sporadically and they are themselves influenced by location. Although fuel is frequently needed but in arable land it is fulfilled by dried stems of crops and dried cowdung, whereas in plateau and forested lands the dense vegetation cover is a good alternative.

Thus, there are no intricate rules of site selection; one place is as good as another, and the village mounds are often not their own creation, but the dumping ground of the rubbish of past generations.[13] But any discontinuity and break in the imperceptible slope, produces linear settlement patterns on the margins of abandoned river courses. Quite often such sites are the only dry points during the rainy season and only water-points in the hot weather.[14] In Maharashtra, India water points are favoured sites for the establishment of rural settlements; tanks other than village ponds are few, but the lavas include good acquifers, and wells in the valleys are usually reliable.

On a rocky surface, the required structure of settlement site should be examined in close connection with the underlying rock formations, their resistance to erosion and suitability for foundation should be carefully examined. In plain land of alluvial formation the underlying horizontal and vertical layers are composed of soft soils of clay, loam and sand. But sometimes the presence of nodular reefs in these layers impart to the site an extraordinary stability especially if the settlement is located on a river bank. In some cases, the site may be an alluvium covered ridge e.g. the slopes of Kilimanjaro, the coastal tracts of India and the Delhi ridge. The natural drainage of the settlement is largely dependent on the natural landscape, hence before planning settlement the depth and variations in water table of rivers and lakes should be examined. In settlement, the soil-profile obtained by boring should be examined because in some sites weak soils are not suitable for high structures while others may have resistant strong soils. The presence of any dominant feature should also be examined because that has a great impact on the morphology of the settlement.

The factors determining the choice of habitable site have been widely studied by geographers. In the Casamance region of south Senegal, the rear of the village extends into the forest while the front faces the river.

In hot arid regions, the scarcely available water is a major organizing factor. As for example, among the Bushmen of Kalahari desert of South Africa, water collection and storage fosters tight bonds between members of hunting tribes. In areas experiencing relatively high rainfall, the problem of the non-availability of drinking water during the dry season remains unsolved. For example, in northern Togo during the dry season, villagers are forced to fetch drinking water at great distance. It is also important that the available water should not be polluted. For example in Baoule Country of Ivory Coast, numerous villages are without water wells, and hence the inhabitants obtain water supplies from water holes. Although this water is sweet and tasty but it is unhygienic for drinking purposes. With the depletion of drain during few months of dry season causes outbreak of various diseases in most of the villages such as amoebiasis, filariasis and Guinea worms which debilitate many adults. Hence amongst environmental factors, water is one of the most decisive for the creation and survival of the social and economic activities of human settlements.

An Interfluve Settlement Site Theory

R.K. Udo while studying the patterns of population distribution and settlements in Eastern Nigeria,[15] Africa emphasized the marked tendency of concentration of rural settlements on the watersheds (Fig. 6.5). While commenting on Ngwa settlements in Aba Division,

Morgan observes that this tendency seems to be a common Nigerian phenomenon.[16] Now the people are avoiding settlement sites, on hill tops due to the problems of land cultivation as in Bende Division and also avoid valley bottoms which are liable to flood or provide mosquito breeding grounds.

For the Ibo people of Nigeria, Smith observed that "the interior eastern Ibo show a reluctance to live in close proximity to a large river or stream, even though they depend upon it for water......"[17]. Similarly, in relation to the Owerri-Onitsha down lands, Grove points out that "the bulk of the population here is concentrated on non-riverine areas." Water supply has not been of first importance in the selection of settlement sites, that free drainage and ease of movement both of which are favoured on the uplands with open grass plains, seem to be the important factors."[18] Some of these quotations indicate that the interfluve is the principal topographical feature controlling the location of rural settlements in Eastern Nigeria.

The defensibility of site which was an important factor for the location of rural settlements in the past, helps to explain the selection of interfluve settlement sites. Besides avoiding the river valleys for safety from raiders, the interfluves afford defensive sites. The persistence of interfluve sites even today is due to the growing tendency towards fixed settlements after independence. Sometimes such sites are found away from the coast, the main reason appears to be economic considerations of keeping near the place of work i.e., agricultural fields. Both agricultural farms and the oil palm groves are the two main sources of income in the region which are situated on interfluves and the household requirements of water is partly met from the rains (March to October), and catch pit take care of the short dry spells. There is only a seasonal need of fetching water from the stream. These are some of the factors which indicate that interfluve is the principal topographical feature controlling the location of rural settlements in eastern Nigeria.

Influence of Site on Settlement Pattern

The siting conditions of rural settlements in different parts of the continent of Africa can be used to illustrate the influence of site on settlement pattern.

Malawi: In Malawi villages are small having twenty to thirty huts. All huts are occupied by the family members of one group. Generally they keep the number of huts small so that all the cultivated fields must lie close to the settlement site. In some areas of the Lilongwe Plain, the villages during ancient periods were situated near spring at the foot of valleys, while the plateau surfaces were used both for cattle grazing and shifting cultivation. But later on due to fear of war, people established their villages on rock outcrops and hill tops for the purpose of defence, but now such villages are again relocated near springs and water sites.

Ghana: In the Southern Ashanti District of Ghana, the effect of cash crop farming on settlement distribution, and the need for villages to be near transportation lines can be observed as influential siting conditions. It is an area of dense population where although villages are small but located very close to each other, small towns have developed as collecting centres of cocoa and other agricultural products. These rural settlements are sited along the main roads while outlying agricultural fields are linked to the market by foot-path.

Gambia: In Gambia, the rural settlement sites are influenced by landscape features and commercial interests. In river courses in areas of incised meanders and swampy land, rural settlements are sited on the high plateau above river bluffs or ultimate point of the reach of flood water. In areas of the mid-valley of the Gambia river each village is surrounded by small patches of vegetation. Small settlements have developed near the river's edge, where goods from down stream and groundnut exports are handled for trade (Fig. 6.6).

Kenya: In the Kenya Highlands cultivation methods of the Kikuyu led to an open settlement pattern with the thick forests providing protection. The growth of population resulted in few villages but gave rise to many scattered homesteads. Between 1952-1960, the colonial authorities forced the Kikuyu to live in concentrated large rural settlements surrounded by defensive walls. Each village contained 1500 huts. In most cases villages were sited on top of broad ridges(Fig.6.6).

Zimbabwe: In Mashonaland of Southern Zimbabwe, villages are small and cultivated fields lie close by, often abutting on to those of a neighbouring village. The rural settlements extend on both sides of the unmetalled road, and the larger the village population the greater the extent of the village. The form of rural settlement is elongated and villages tend to be fairly close together, but in north-eastern Zimbabwe, the creation of compact 'protected villages' has obliterated the former patterns.

Nigeria: On the Jos Plateau of Central Nigera, rural settlements were built on secluded spots hidden by rocky ridges, dense bushes and cactus thickets. Huts were constructed close together on higher rocks so that early warning may be given, enabling the villagers to return quickly to their homes. Thus the rural settlements are of clustered form but well spaced from one another. But now in peaceful time scattered settlements have also developed.

Zanzibar: In Zanzibar Island of Tanzania, villages are situated at the foot of a coral ridge. On lower slopes along the line of springs and relatively deep soil cover the rural settlements are sited in a linear form. Mostly settlements avoid the coastal plains due to floods and insects but isolated fishing hamlets are found here and there. In Zanzibar and Pemba, the physical environment favours elongated patterns of rural settlements.

Upgrading Site of Rural Settlements

In order to make rural settlements a better place to live and work comfortably, the environmental modification of a rural area is necessary which should be based on the expressed need of peasants after discarding the earlier development due to oversimplification and strict adaptation to local conditions in favour of varied modern technological choices. At village level the specific cultural characteristics and the problems and prospects of various groups of people are of decisive importance.

Bugnicourt (1981)[19] presented an example of a locality in Toucouleur country of the Senegal river valley, where like most of the Third World countries peasants have many problems including excessive deforestation, water runoff and soil erosion, an inadequate control of flood water, undeveloped and un-levelled undulating lands in dry areas and conflicts over the crossing of cattle herds with regard to the village, and an insufficient protection against the danger of fires spreading to the proximity of neighbourhoods. In addition villagers face the lack of drinking water, malnutrition for certain categories of population, grain storage losses, the arduousness of the daily pounding of maize, millet, sorghum and wheat by women, etc.... with regard to both the area cultivated and inhabited. Hence one of the salient features is the total dependence on human labour and the absence of machines.

In case the present underdeveloped condition would not be allowed to continue an upgradation of siting should be ascertained with firm determination to maintain cultural values of development in relation to the aforesaid problems. Tree planting and protective tree belts would be an initial kind of response. Use might also be made of the cactus both to divide off sections of the village agricultural holdings and to contribute to livestock feed during periods of drought. *Marigots* should be developed and levelled just like the water sector, using simple technique of making dykes of packed earth. In the dry season wells driven by donkeys would permit the irrigation of gardens and standing crops in the fields.

In the village some new sources for the production of energy may be tapped such as windmill, solar energy so that it can energise millet mills, provide lighting for schools and youth houses where homework, meeting and recreational activities could be organized. A drinking water well may also be planned which would give water to both people and livestock besides helping the mills to run. The village school should have large buildings so that it can provide space, for the television antennae which would permit access to quality training for various category of labourers in the village. The school should not be isolated from the village as most of the services done by the students would consist of development and production activities besides reading of books.

Houses may continue to be constructed of traditional materials but roofing should be waterproof, ventilation improved and walls should be rebuilt according to the capacity of the individual's resources. Each house should have a latrine. The backyard should allow for a compost ditch for cow dung, house waste and green leaves necessary to boost agricultural output in the fields. When these schemes are making headway, solutions to other problems may be sought (Fig.6.7).

A case study of a village can give a better idea of these developments targeted according to people's aptitude and the input of additional skills. On the one hand the reflection of traditional knowledge, the identification of causes and consequences, the improvement of means of expression considered an increase in the group's ability to understand its own problems and the required possible solutions lead to a broadening of rural community's organizational capacity. This would also help peasants in acquiring the technical know how of new measuring tools, thought of action, explanations of environmental problems and linking it with traditionally known concepts of combined technology aiming both at understanding and use of modern techniques.

The diffusion of some of these innovations may be possible through village meetings, group discussion, short training programmes involving few peasants for learning specific practices because an individual decision is crucial for the upgradation of village site, rural development and enhancing the educational, industrial and agricultural production for the social justice of rural poor 'the contact planner'.

Location and siting are primary aspects of rural settlements but their proper selection or upgrading is vital both for resource development and the living conditions of their residents. Location and siting guides the importance, function, layouts, production patterns, beauty of local sceneries besides socio-economic development of inhabitants. The villages developed in forests, deserts and hilly areas cannot be as prosperous as those in plain areas. Patterns of road linkage, intensity of disaster, level of environmental hazards, water supply, potential trade and commerce, and the level of personal income all depend on location and siting of settlements. The resettlement experience, approaches and measures taken provide guidelines to others in similar situations, and also raise issues of strategic importance in planning and implementing resettlement and development programmes.

REFERENCES

1. J.C. Hudson: "A Location Theory for Rural Settlements", *Annals of the Association of American Geographers,* Vol. 59, No.2, 1969. p.366.
2. P.E. James: *All Possible World*, Prentice Hall, 1969, pp.459-460.
3. E.W. Soja: "The Political Organization of Space", Commission on College Geography, Resource Paper No.8, *Association of American Geographers,* 1971, p.3.
4. I.R. Meyer and R.J. Huggett: *Settlements*, Harper and Row Publishers, London, 1970, p.10.
5. H.R. Cain: *Human and Economic Geography*; Longmans, London, 1963, pp.353-355.
6. Philip Wagner: *The Human Use of the Earth*; The Free Press, New York, 1960, pp.149-151.
7. D.F. Owen: *Man's Environmental Predicament*; Oxford University Press, London, 1973, pp.36-37.
8. C.A. Joseph: "Settlement Game", in *New Directions in Geography Teaching* (Ed. R. Walford); Longman, 1973, pp.18-20.
9. S.W. Wooldridge and W.G. East: *The Spirit and Purpose of Geography*, Hutchinson University Library, London, 1963, p.150.
10. J.B. Mitchell: *Historical Geography*, English Universities Press, London, 1954, pp. 84-85.
11. F.S. Hudson: *A Geography of Settlements*; Macdonald and Evans, London, 1970, p.45.
12. M. Chisholm: *Rural Settlement and Land Use*; Hutchinson University Library, London, 1973.
13. O.H.K. Spate: *India and Pakistan*: Methuen & Co. Ltd.; London, 1964, p.172.
14. E.G.H. obby: "Settlement Patterns in Malaysia", *Geographical Review;* Vol. XXXII; 1942.
15. R.K. Udo: "Patterns of Population Distribution and Settlement in Eastern Nigeria", *Journal of the Geographical Association of Nigeria;* Vol. 6, No.2, 1964, pp.85-87.
16. W.B. Morgan: "Farming Practice in South-Eastern Nigeria", *Geographical Journal,* Vol.121, 1955, p.321.
17. S.R. Smith: *The Ibo People*; Unpublished Ph. D. Thesis, University of London, 1929, Vol.I, p.160.
18. A.T. Grove: Land Use and Soil Conservation in Parts of Onitsha and Owerri Provinces', *Geological Survey of Nigeria,* Bulletin No. 21, 1975, p.22.
19. Jacques BugniCourt: "Needs of the Peasant Community and Combined Technologies: *An Example", African Environment,* Vol. III, No.3-4, 1981, pp.339-343.

Fig.6.1

Factors Controlling Location of Village Kharsam, India

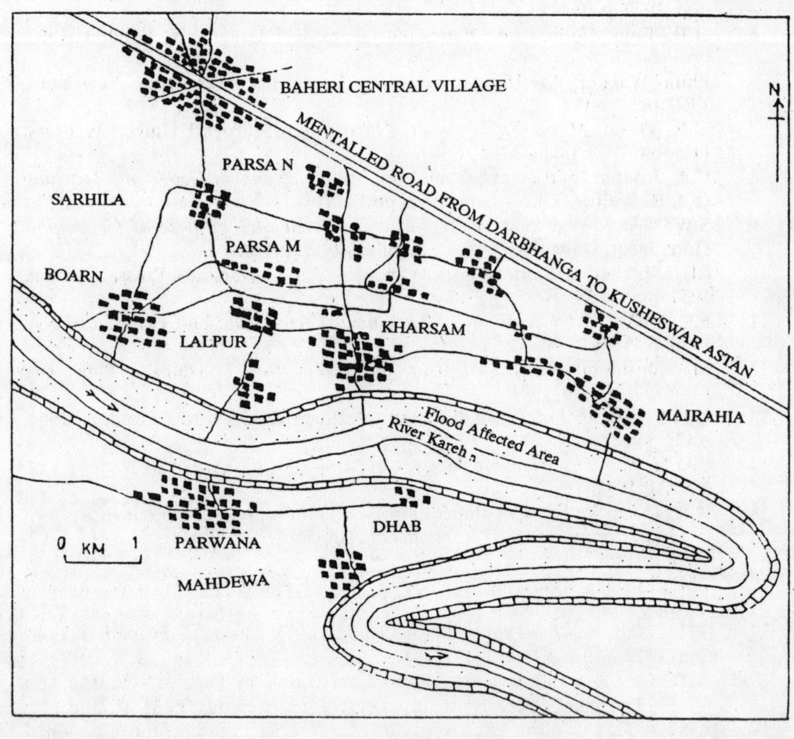

Fig. 6.2

Hypothetical Map for the Rural Settlement Game of North Bihar

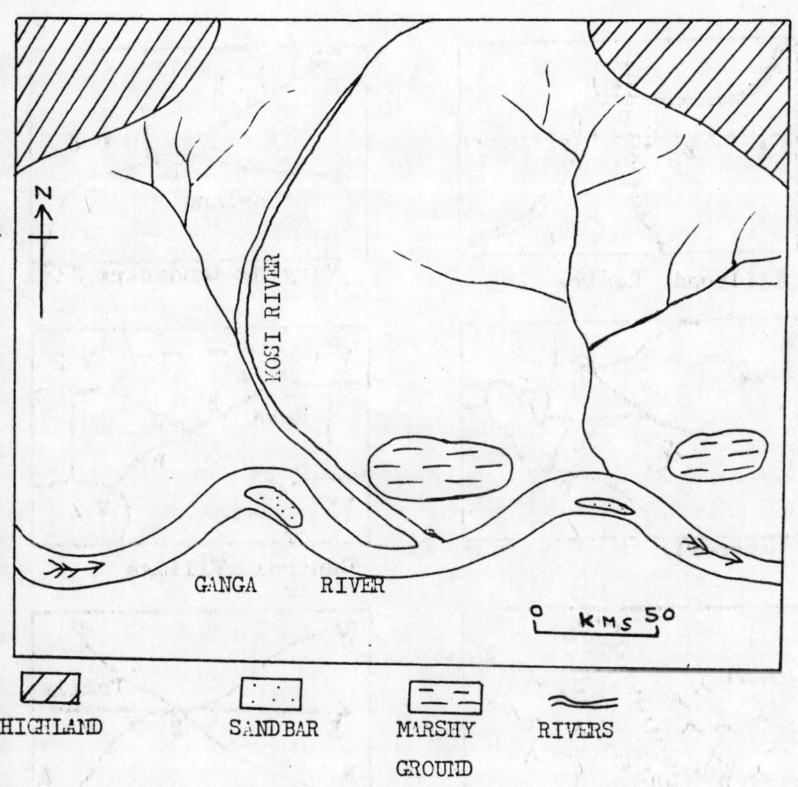

Fig. 6.3

Effect of Physical and Cultural Factors on Rural Settlement Sites

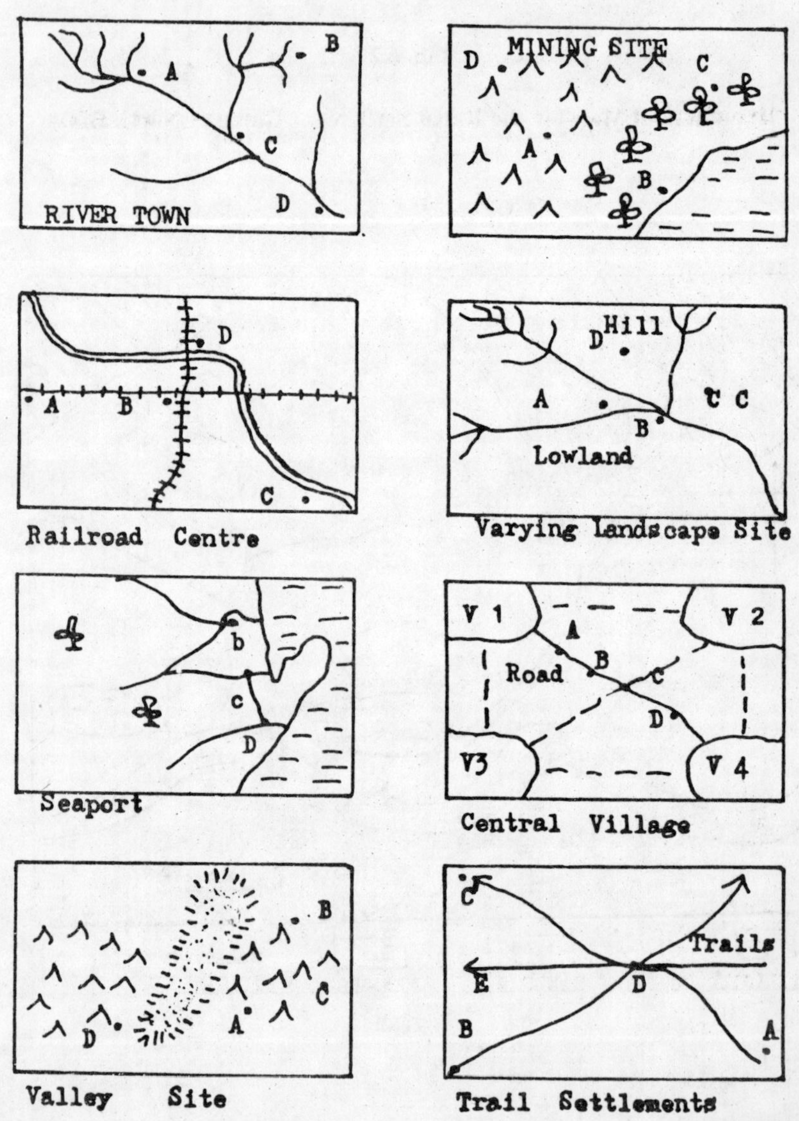

Fig. 6.4.

Rural Settlement Location in Agriculturl Economy by Chisholm

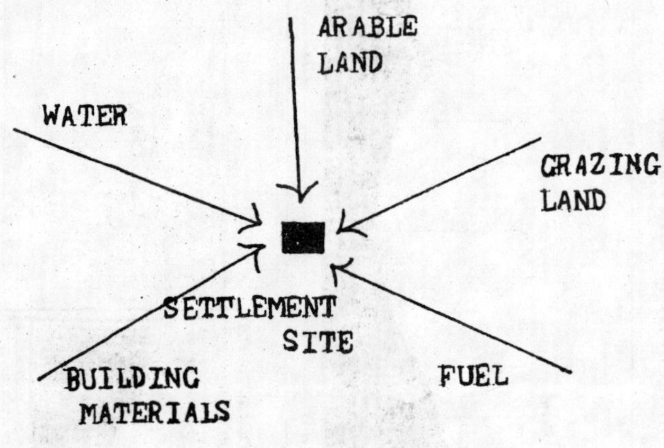

Fig. 6.5

Interfluvial Location of Village Lugoba, Tanzania, 1983 (After-Fennia, 1983)

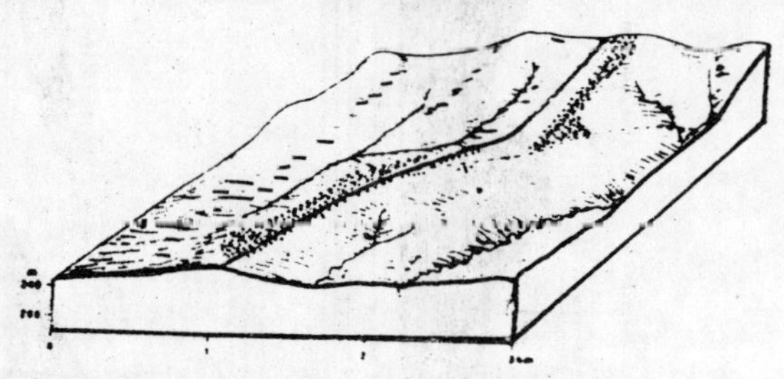

Fig. 6.6

Physical Influences on Village Sitingi in Kenya and Zambia

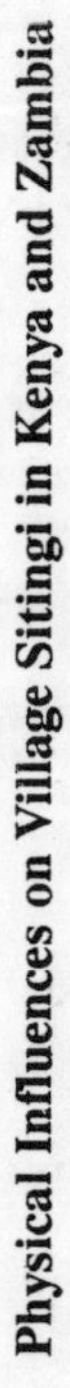

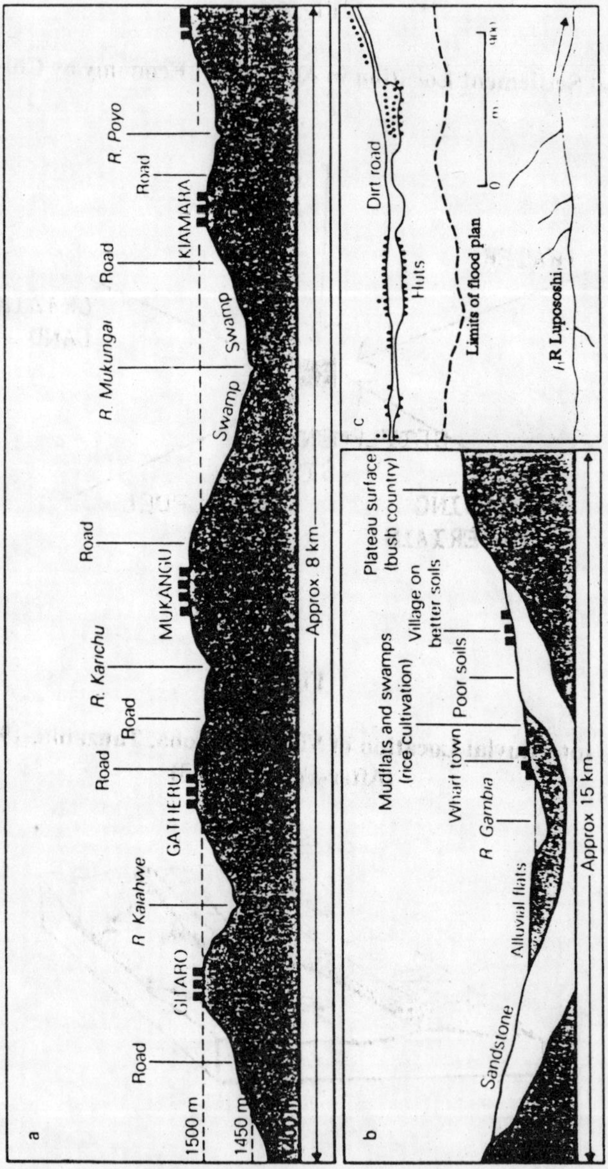

Source : J. M. Pritchard, 1979

Fig. 6.7

A Model for Village Site Upgradation of Toucouleur
After;- Bugnicourt

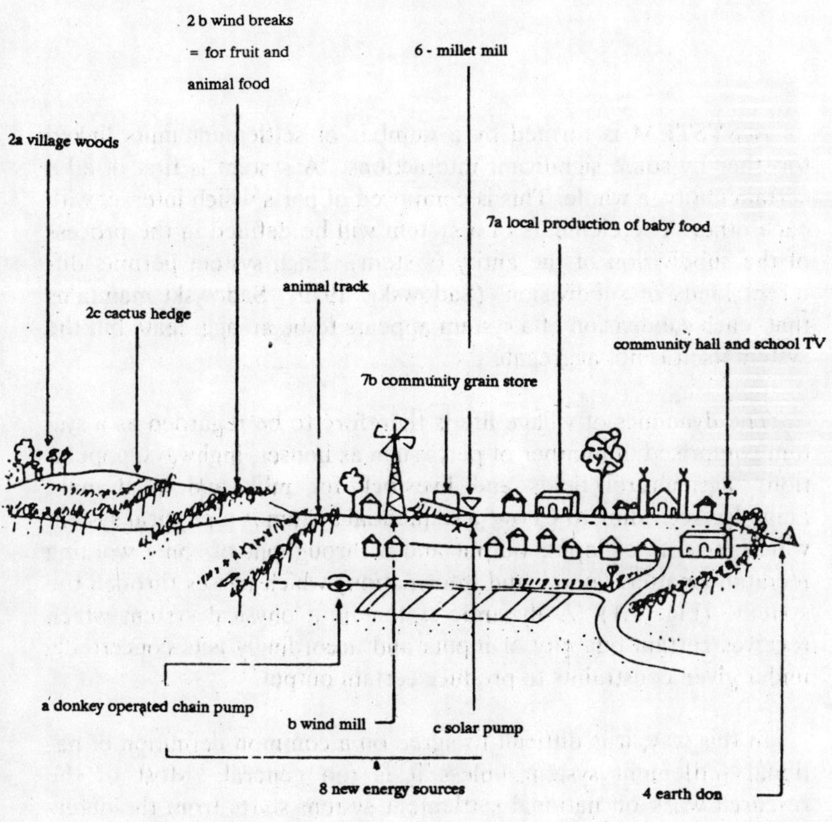

SEVEN

THE NATIONAL SETTLEMENT SYSTEM

A SYSTEM is formed by a number of settlement units linked together by some significant interactions. "A system is first of all a certain entity, a whole. This is composed of parts which interact with each other. The elements of a system will be defined in the process of the subdivision of the entity (system). Each system permits different kinds of subdivision" (Sadowski, 1979). Sadowski maintains that "each subdivision of a system appears to be an aggregate but the system itself is not aggregate".[1]

The dynamics of village life is therefore to be regarded as a system comprised of number of parts such as houses, highways, population, agricultural fields and livestock for milk and as draught animals. According to Chow[2] a sequential system is a physical system which consists of input, output and a throughput of some working medium (matter, energy and information) which passes through the system. (Fig. 7.1). A dynamic system is a physical system which receives certain quantity of inputs and accordingly acts concertedly under given constraints to produce certain output.

In this way, it is difficult to agree on a common definition of national settlement system unless it is too general. Most of the research work on national settlement system starts from the determination of single settlement and of certain relations between settlements which are considered to be significant. In reality, these approaches treat aggregate of settlement units but no systems.

Systems analysis may be considered in a hierarchical sense, since the output from one system may be an input to another. As for example, an attempt to develop operations models of settlements should be based on linking together sub-models of land use, transport, etc. each sub-model being in itself a system (McLoughlin, 1969).[3]

Hence by definition in case the working of the system is independent of the output produced the system is regarded as being open. In case its operation depends upon the feedback of all or parts of the output the system is regarded as closed. The location, growth and development of rural settlement depend upon agricultural produce, livestock wealth, population, houses, highways and nearness to the market, and all of them are linked closely by their respective output and hence the rural settlement system is a closed one in the sense that the output of these systems will have a substantial effect upon the balance of the system. But in geographical studies, all systems are open in some degree, that is, there is transfer of either mass or energy or both, across the system's boundaries. In case the component parts of a system itself has the qualities of a system, it may be regarded as a subsystem or as a separate system depending upon the objective of research. As for example within a national settlement system villages, towns, cities and metropolises may be regarded as subsystems but independently they are sub-systems in its own right.

The commission on National Settlement Systems of the International Geographical Union discussed the impact of national policies on settlement systems, growth and change in the settlement system of different countries of the World, besides international linkages and theoretical cum methodological aspects of research on national settlement systems in Leipzig, June, 1983. Such IGU conference has been organized in August 1984 at Pisa, Italy. In all these conferences there were two basic assumptions: human settlement embraces all the settlement units of a nation, and secondly it is useful to treat them as a system.

"Such systems are both open and dynamic, i.e. changing in space and time, although preserving their basic identity. This implies that their definition in specific cases involves the identification of component units, of their mutual interactions (i.e. of the functional structure of the system and of the relation of the whole system to its environment (including linkages with other settlement systems....) changes, the development of a system in space and time, may involve its individual units, sub-systems, interactions and environmental relationship... National states currently represent the most fully developed and crystallized political and economic entities (regions) which tend to generate specific settlement systems of their own".[4]

Components of the Settlement System

The national settlement system can be viewed spatially from village upto the highest order settlement of national capital in terms of linkages, interactions, spatial arrangement, hierarchy and functional relations. According to the requirements of inhabitant and importance of the functions, the whole settlement system may be divided into different groups. Those components which are urgently required by the inhabitants of a settlement and can be managed easily are generally found to be located close to the settlement as urgent and local components, and those which are rarely required and can be managed on high costs come under regional and external components (Fig. 7.2).

A list of various components of a rural settlement is as follows:

1. **Urgent Components** : Fertile land for agricultural crops, livestock wealth, population, houses, highways and water sites are immediately required for the location of a rural settlement, and all these are both internally and externally related with the process of feedback mechanism.

2. **Local Components** : The local components are mainly labour relations, marriage relations, village market, primary and middle schools, oilman, *purohit* (man who helps in worshiping), barber, trade relations, carpenter, *panchayat* (local court) relations, carpenter, black smith, gold smith, dyers, fisherman, butchery and bangle sellers are more important. All these functions are locally arranged for a rural settlement, but all of them are internally and externally related with the process of feedback mechanism, and help in the growth and development of national settlement system.

3. **Regional Components** : The variables which serve a wider region are known as regional components. They include the location of a high school or college, state boring for irrigation, dispensary, temple, mosque and church, block development office, bus stand, fire brigade, railway station, police station, land registry office, deisel station, veterinary hospital, rural cooperative bank, wholesale grain market and religious fair. All these are inter-related with the process of feedback mechanism both from the higher and lower order function in judging the national settlement system.

4. **External Components** : External components are bigger installations such as national parks, high court, hospital, high order religious places, big fair, heavy industries, provincial capital, air port, health resorts, mining and quarrying centres, museum, ports, district offices, commuter relations, higher education, national capital, national banks, specialized training centres, divisional offices, big commercial centres, besides international relations. All these functional establishments are interrelated in space and have definite social-political, cultural and economic impact in the growth and development of national settlement system.

According to Haggett (1972) the proposition for types of system in relation to various components is as follows:

"Relations between individual components are built up by statistical association to produce positive or negative bonds. Changes in the level of one component cause associated changes in other components. Such systems vary in the number of components, the strength of the links between them, and the arrangement of the links into positive or negative feedback links".[5]

Origin and Growth of Settlement System

All villages grew in spatio-temporal dimensions, thereby consolidating the existing network of rural settlements. During the post independence period rural development took place within the context of democratic socialism, which gave an enormous up-start to rural settlements and eliminated all characteristics of an economic periphery. In almost all Third World Countries the problems of rural development were increasing due to constant migration of people from rural area into the rapidly growing urban places, but even then it has failed to splinter the national systems of rural settlements. Since thousand years back several kings and administrators came to rule the country-side and gone but the system of rural settlements remain unchanged. In recent years settlement policy has been increasingly concerned to reduce the trend towards concentration and to preserve the living standard of population, also to a larger extent in its decentralised distribution. This requires the national economy to be geared to intensify all processes including building resources in the country.

As the modernization of production sectors have priority, this has given impulses for the construction of dwellings in many small settlements. Rural settlement planning has the task of controlling this process in such a way that new construction does not encourage rural-urban dichotomy which is unwarrantable with regard to the future. In case the modernization of building appears to be justified, in all settlements new construction must be pursued because this can only guarantee the high standard of living conditions.

With the organization of agriculture on community basis, it is important to ensure that the location of key managerial and production functions coincide with that of focal points of settlements which are responsible to serve as infrastructural institutions.

Social, economic and spatial framework of human settlements which act as the functional space of human being serve the purposes of settled agricultural communities, as well as the people engaged in trade and commerce in urban centres. "The spatial form of this organizational framework manifests as a system of settlements in a hierarchy, starting with the small village and encompassing the market town, the trading centre, the large city and the metropolitan complex. These settlements or 'nodes' as they are called, act as vehicles in space through which the organizational framework functions effectively. Functional hierarchy and grouping have also led to the development of settlements of different sizes, nature and character".[6]

In different historical periods various types of socio-economic organizations existed under different economic and political systems. These development and decay of civilizations could be correlated, in order to judge the effective or ineffective socio-economic organizational structure of societies of various historical periods.

During ancient period in forest economy the population size of the settlements was small, they were located far away from one another and 'might is right' was the rule of law. Secondly, when people started taming animals they were more and more pastoralists. During this period the population size of settlements increased and inter-spacing decreased. Again agricultural economy has helped in sustaining a large number of population under reduced spacing of settlements. Nowadays with the growth and development of industrial economy more and more people can get the support for their lives even if the settlements are close together (Fig. 7.3).

During different phases of the growth and development of settlements a certain amount of duplication and overlapping of functions between settlements located close to each other was inevitable which arose competition among them. During ancient period the cities of Venice, Geneva, Torino and Marseilles were of this kind. In modern times such examples are the cities on the eastern sea-board of USA-Boston, Philadelphia, New York and Baltimore - which are less complementary and more competitive due to mal-distribution of functions and wasteful duplication of effort among them.[7]

Third World Countries today with their scarce resources can ill afford to go through such a "trial and error" process and allow a wasteful duplication of effort and resources. Due to our urgent social needs, the developing countries today have to leap-frog some parts of the evolutionary processes, and make up the back-logs in their economic and social infrastructure over a comparatively short time, e.g. in Tanzania due to planned economy the duplication of effort is not found in any settlement system out of three : Mwanza, Arusha - Moshi - Tanga - Tabora, and Dar es Salaam. In the process of growth and development they are trying to develop interdependent, well-knit and complementary economic and social settlement systems which may well serve the present as well as the future needs of the rural communities in their hinterland.

The task is essentially to organise the physical components of the various developmental processes in space in such a compatible combination that it leads to the maximization of efficiency of the whole system. In an unguided system, each single purpose system like marketing, industries, postal services, medical institutions, etc. would tend to locate themselves in random places. But in the economy of planned settlement systems, however, the nodal points of the compatible systems are made to coincide at various levels so that certain economies of scale as well as of concentration would accrue to the economic activities in those centres as interrelated and synchronised system.

Hagerstrand[8] suggests that there may be close connection between the hierarchy of "mean information fields and the hierarchy of towns within the system of central places". According to Hagerstrand "the leading cities within a country should give impulses first of all to towns next in rank. The further spread is then heavily regulated by distance friction; strong ties of the major towns with the capital over a rather long distance occur; the local influence is exerted on lower order centres closer by. "Similarly, the process of trickling down takes place through a network of intermediate and subsidiary growth centres and growth points in a hierarchy of national settlement system (Table 7.1).

It is clear that the settlement system is not just an outcome of human adjustment with the environment of a particular geographical space, but it is a main participant in the development process of a nation. The settlement system has not only key role to play especially in setting the goals on a right path but it also determines the intensity of highways linkage, opportunities for better living and the exploitation of land resources, besides a deciding factor or constraints for future development. For this fact, the United Nations (1976: 4-6) in the Vancouver Habitat Conference considered human settlement as an instrument and object of development and recommended that "it is the responsibility of the government to prepare spatial strategy plans and adopt human settlement policies to guide the socio-economic development efforts. Such policies must be an essential component of an overall development strategy, linking and harmonizing them with policies on industrialization, agriculture, and cultural preservation, so that each supports the other in a progressive improvement in well being of all mankind"[9]. It is true because a settlement system evolves under the spatial strategies of social, political and economic environments of a particular region which affect its form and direction of growth.

The current settlement systems of most of the developing countries reflect the cultural heritage, colonization patterns, local resource development and the present socio-economic and demographic policies of the government. In this way, on the basis of environmental quality or ecological conditions, the settlement system may be classified into various subsystems:

(a) Urban Settlement sub-system,
(b) Rural Settlement Sub-System,
(c) Administrative Settlement sub-system,
(d) Religious Settlement Sub-System,
(e) Educational Settlement Sub-System, and
(f) Industrial Settlement Sub-System.

Although settlement gives an integrated view of the above components, which form different settlement sub-systems but hierarchical linkage interactions of all of them is the best example that how various settlement sub-systems are working in configuration together in India and in various other parts of the world (Table 7.1).

In our national settlement system all cities form their own sub-system and they are characterised by the specific functions and relationship within that sub-system and rest of the settlement system.

Table 7.1: Hierarchy of National Settlement System

Serial No.	Level of Settlement System	Example	Population (1981)	Level of Administration/Characteristics
1.	A Household	Budhan	7	Family
2.	Caste or clan Grouping	Chamartoli	180	Clan Group
3.	Satellite Village	Lalpur	300	Ward
4.	Village	Kharsam	900	Village
5.	Large village	Semra Labedaha	27000	Panchayat
6.	Small Town	Chanpatia	15000	Block Development

7.	Town	Rosera	25000	Sub-divisional Head quarter
8.	Major Town	Bettiah	60000	District Head quarter
9.	City	Muzaffarpur	500000	Divisional Head-quarter
10.	Megalocephalis	Patna	800000	State Capital, Bihar
11.	Metropolitan Centre	Delhi	6200000	National Capital, India
12.	Conurbation	Calcutta	8900000	Brick, mortar contiguity of cities
13.	Megalopolis	North Eastern USA	80000000	Urban agglomeration of conurbations.
14.	Tyranopolis	Continental Level		Biggest urbanization of continental or national level
15.	Ecumonopolis	World Urbanization		World as urban community
16.	Nekropolis	Dead city or Ghost city	Hiroshima in II World War	It can be achieved at any stage of settlements growth

Source: R.B. Mandal - Planned Development of Rural Settlements,1975.
* Megolocapbalis is necessarily multi-functional in nature.

The politico-administrative functions of settlements in India clearly derive from the pattern of administration. India has 22 states, 9 centrally ruled states, 500 districts, 2000 urban settlements and 800,000 rural settlements in 1987. All these various levels of settlements serve as political, social and administrative centres since times immemorial

In the hypothetical scheme of the three tiers of national settlement system, the first category is the macro-structure of national settlement system, second is the meso-structure of regional settlement system, and third is the micro-structure of rural settlement system at local level.

Similarly, Fig. 7.4 shows the linkages and hierarchical ordering of national settlement system in India based on the scheme of the political-administrative territory and function of settlements. From village up to the national capital level, the economic growth and politico-administrative dimensions are increasing, and that is considered here as the main determining factor of forming different levels of settlement systems on national scale.

Functional Aspects of Small National Settlement System

The population size of national settlement systems varies in spatio-temporal dimensions. Hence for different size of settlement systems the approaches of research may vary. For a small size of settlements detailed analysis is possible along with the testing of certain theories in depth. As such within a small size of settlement system the organizing factors originating in the demands of the settlement system might be weaker than those originating from an external factor. In building a small national settlement system the physical environment is a better guiding factor in comparison with large settlement. In this way, the results of small settlement system are too locality oriented and hence mostly unsuitable for wider application. Nowadays, in most countries of the world theoretical studies of central places and gravity models are more commonly in use in demarcating theoretically new functional subsystems. Even then the boundaries follow waterdivides, lakes, rivers, mountains and marginal areas in between two centres of population concentration, and the choice of problems is getting deviated from the set path especially in a small national settlement system due to these physical obstructions.

The provision of infrastructural institutions and access to them are among the central questions determining further population development in all sparsely populated spaces in Europe. Even if in our country economic losses are accepted as the price we have to pay to ensure the supply of consumer goods and services to that part of the population which lives in disperse settlements, no national economy can afford such a thing as a mass phenomenon. But if, as it occurs increasingly, economic or functional minimum requirements are not met in the running of certain institutions, the living conditions in some settlements are in danger of not keeping pace with the rising expectations of people.

The size of settlements is not the sole factor in determining the level of their facilities. Such factors as the position relative to larger centres and to main roads, the function for other settlements or the division of functions within a certain group or a system of settlements are also important. Thus the structure of settlement systems proves to be an essential determining factor for the quality of individual settlement. For example, settlements within the system of rurban centres, besides having disadvantages of splintering, suffer from being far away from centres which offer a great variety of services and facilities. As such centres of high rank are important for the working and living conditions of the population in all parts of the regions, the formerly closed rurban settlement systems have opened up to a considerable extent as a result of modern development.

The general task is to facilitate the *imminent* positive consequences of urbanization to develop in all settlements. In many decisive fields this process has led to the extensive assimilation of working and living conditions in the country to urban standards (A.V. Kanel, 1983)[10]. Occasionally, the availability of facilities and institutions of social infrastructure in the country is more favourable than in towns. On the other hand, in view of the specific conditions of production, a complete equalization of patterns of living is not desirable.

Internal Organization of Settlement System

Various sub-systems of socio-economic space are certainly affected by the arrangement of the settlement structure e.g. size and functions. The settlement sub-system as the territorially most universal component of the socio-economic space is modelled strongly by processes and the structure of industry, services and agriculture as more specialized sub-systems. Therefore, the study of settlement should deal with the problems related to transport, recreation, industry and agriculture.

The relations of one settlement with the other may be defined by commuting to work, movement of people to service facilities, movement for recreation purposes and economic cooperation.

Hence, the interrelations of settlement structure in relation to man may be subdivided into:[11]

(a) linkages and flows proceeding from a greater number of settlements to a lesser number of higher order settlements.
(b) Linkages characterised by spatial dispersion.

Although commuting affects a small group of people in the surrounding area of industrial city but the trip is more regular. For example, labourers are coming daily from rural areas to work in the Jamalpur Railway Workshop in Bihar as commuters from Kajra in the West, Sultanganj in the east and Munger in the north. The daily flow of labourers is 4000 from each direction.

The trip to obtain certain service facilities from rural tc urban settlements is known as consumer behaviour pattern. According to the range of goods or services, consumer behaviour pattern for different size of firms and the quality of goods are found to be different for various categories of settlement networks. The recreational trip may be a picnic spot, summer resort, site of hot spring, navigation, mountaineering, horse riding or attraction of cinema or theatre centre of urban places. Economic cooperation from one rural settlement to others may be cooperation in performing agricultural works, irrigation, defence from floods, making a road on self-help basis or cooperation in food processing and wood works. Besides these, among social relations marriage migration and caste or clan affiliations are more strong ties in the internal organization of rural settlement system.

In terms of structure, a village is considered as a component of the whole settlement system both in spatial and functional sense. Hence a settlement system could be local, regional, national and international as they pass through different stages of growth and development (Table 7.1).

Network Analysis of Settlement System

Studies dealing with the total settlement network, including both rural and urban centres, are mainly concerned with settlement systems, central places, types of communities, and ranking of settlements. In the early postwar years there was some critical discussion of Christaller's central place theory, especially in East Germany, and several studies were published. Recently, central places have again attracted the attention of scholars, especially in Germany and Hungary.[12] In Czechoslovakia centrality was investigated in connection with the reform of administrative divisions, and the desire to concentrate investment in administrative centres.[13] In Poland, a study based on Germany was published by Kania. According to her findings the settlement network in part of Silesia should be adjusted according to central place theory, and she reconstructed the map of villages selected by Nazi regional planners for development as prospective regional planners.[14] Classification of communities based upon social, demographic and economic criteria have been popular in Germany, and published in Yugoslavia.[15] In Poland, the rank-size rule was applied by Kania to all the settlements of a region.[16] Zagozdzon studies the spatial links and grouping of settlements, their patterns and components, and suggested a typology of the existing complexes[17] of settlement system.

The analysis of linkages of rural settlement system represents a interaction between each place in the system with every other place. Hence, it may be useful to apply graph theoretical constructs in order to explain the degree of connectivity of the system, and the structure of linkage patterns. Further, graph theory or matrix algebra can help in the identification of settlement hierarchy and in isolating areas poor or rich in settlement growth. The dynamics of the settlement system can also be examined if the same matrix algebra applied for successive census periods. For Fig. 7.5 the graph theoretic matrix is as follows:

Table 7.2a : C_1 Matrix

	1	2	3	4	5	6	7	8	9
1	0	1	1	1	1	1	1	0	0
2	1	0	1	0	0	0	1	1	1
3	1	1	0	1	0	0	0	0	0
4	1	0	1	0	1	0	0	0	0
5	1	0	0	1	0	1	0	0	0
6	1	0	0	0	1	0	1	0	0
7	1	1	0	0	0	1	0	0	0
8	0	1	0	0	0	0	0	0	0
9	0	1	0	0	0	0	0	0	0

Table 7.2b : C_2 Matrix

	1	2	3	4	5	6	7	8	9
1	6	2	2	2	2	2	2	1	1
2	2	5	1	2	1	2	1	0	0
3	2	1	3	1	2	1	2	1	1

4	2	2	1	3	1	2	1	0	0
5	2	1	2	1	3	1	2	0	0
6	2	2	1	2	1	3	1	0	0
7	2	1	2	1	2	1	3	1	1
8	1	0	1	0	0	0	1	1	1
9	1	0	1	0	0	0	1	1	1

$C_2 = C_1 \times C_1$

Table 7.2c : C_3 Matrix

	1	2	3	4	5	6	7	8	9
1	12	12	10	10	10	10	10	2	2
2	12	4	9	4	6	4	9	5	5
3	10	9	4	7	4	6	4	1	1
4	10	4	7	4	7	4	6	2	2
5	10	6	4	7	4	7	4	1	1
6	10	4	6	4	7	4	7	2	2
7	10	9	4	6	4	7	4	1	1
8	2	5	1	2	1	2	1	0	0
9	2	5	1	2	1	2	1	0	0

$C_3 = C_1 \times C_1 \times C_1$ or $C_1 \times C_2$

Table 7.2d : T_d Matrix

	1	2	3	4	5	6	7	8	9	Total
1	18	15	13	13	13	13	13	3	3	104
2	15	9	11	6	7	6	11	6	6	77
3	13	11	7	9	6	7	6	2	2	63
4	13	6	9	7	9	6	7	2	2	61
5	13	7	6	9	7	9	6	1	1	59
6	13	6	7	6	9	7	9	2	2	[illegible]
7	13	11	6	7	6	9	7	2	2	63
8	3	6	2	2	1	2	2	1	1	20
9	3	6	2	2	1	2	2	1	1	20
Total	104	77	63	61	59	61	63	20	20	528

$T_d = C_1 + C_2 + C_3$

Row or column total gives measure of accessibility of individual node.

According to Td matrix Table 7.2d the most accessible point is 1 followed by 2nd, 3rd and 7th. Node number 8th and 9th are least accessible in comparison with others. It means the nucleus point in this system is node one. Almost all nodes may be hierarchically arranged in this system according to the transport linkage or the row total of Td matrix.

The degree of connectivity can be measured with the gamma index as:

$$r = \frac{2e}{v(v-1)} = \frac{2 \times 14}{9(9-1)} = \frac{28}{72} = 39\%$$

where e is number of edges and v is vertices. Here the degree of connectivity is 39 per cent. The percentage of gamma index has a direct relationship with levels of economic development of a particular settlement system.

City-Hinterland Relations and the Settlement System

The efficiency of settlement systems depends to a large extent on their centres and particularly the bigger urban core which plays an essential part in the development of the productive forces. It includes the size, infrastructure and dynamics of a centre, and therefore its influence, attractiveness and diffusion of innovation patterns are determined by the entire settlement structure of a region. The studies about urban and hinterland relations conducted in India have brought to light considerable regional differences between rural areas and other parts of the country, particularly with regard to the distribution, functions, infrastructure and accessibility of efficient centres.

Viewing at the settlements upto city level in the macro-structure of the settlement network in connection with strategic settlement structure, planning shows that they lag behind expectations as their distribution is not so equal as to make it possible for everyone living in their hinterlands to reach them in one hour travel time which is justifiable.[18]

On the basis of rural settlement data, the changing degree of urbanization from city to the zone of influence could be measured on the basis of density of population, sex ratio, literacy rate, non-agricultural workers, and people engaged in trade and commerce. Fig. 7.6 shows that schematic map of city hinterland relationships of the systems of settlements in India. A description of different sectors of the schematic map is as follows:

1. Inner wards of the city,
2. Sub-urban wards of the city,
3. Sub-urban belt,
4. Sub-urban ribbon
5. Secondary roads sector, and
6. Interstitial villages.

In India due to the practice to annex territory surrounding the urban settlement, the "outermost sections of the city contain an interesting mixture of old village centres, government and private housing projects, scattered private housing, improvised village type housing of refugee and in migrants, scattered industrial and commercial developments, and patches of agricultural land, usually referred to as 'undeveloped land'.[19] The inner wards developed mainly due to legislative annexation practice.

Modelling of Settlement Systems By G. Kind

Amos 2 Model: It means targets for partial models aimed at optimizing the settlement structure. It is the outcome of work done in the Dresden Technical University, GDR and improved on the work done by B. Malisz on the Threshold Theory.[20]

- The smallest unit of calculation is the settlement.

- The calculations regarding the technological infrastructure are conducted for route networks.
- Commuting to work and to service facilities is included as a cost factor, and the time spent for these purposes is minimized.

- As the internal feature of the model, the population distribution causing least expenditure in terms of the national economy is determined.

- The structure of the model makes it possible to include non-quantifiable factors.

- Calculations are made for a number of variants as regards the population of the settlement system. The results have been summarized to give expenditure functions of the settlement system for changes in distribution and for an increase in the total number of inhabitants (Fig. 7.7)

The target function of the model is as follows:

$$Km = \min \sum_{i} \left\{ \sum_{j} \frac{Pij}{bj} \left[w_j(x_j) + a_{ij} b_j + \mathrm{Min}(a_{jd} + V_d) + \mathrm{Min}(a_{jr} + v_r) + \sum (a_{js} + r_s) \right] \right\}$$

Indices:

where m is a variant which consists of the number of workers and the distribution of working places within a settlement system.

i is the settlement as the site of working places.

j is the settlement as the site of housing.

d is shopping and service centre of low hierarchical order.

r is shopping and service centre of more important hierarchical order.

s is recreational area.

Symbols:

Km is the total costs of the variant m.

P_{ij} is the number of working places in the settlement i.

P_i is $\Sigma_j P_{ij}$ the number of working places in the settlement i.

P_j is $\dfrac{\sum_j P_{ij}}{b_j}$ the number of inhabitants of settlement j.

b_j is the degree of employment in the $w_j(X_j)$ is value of the cost function of settlement j for a number of inhabitants.

a_{ij} is per capita costs of transport between the place of work and residence.

a_{jd} is per capita costs for transport between the place of residence and shopping and service centres of low hierarchical order.

a_{jr} is per capita costs for transport between the place of residence and shopping and service centres of more important hierarchical order.

a_{js} is per capita costs for transport between the place of residence and recreational areas.

v_d, v_r, v_s are values of the cost functions of shopping and service centres of different hierarchical orders and recreational areas.

The problem can be solved with the functional relations between people having in a settlement system. These can be represented as a graph and transformed into a directed network. An approximate solution is possible if this is delineated as an optimal path problem.

With the help of a graph (Fig. 7.7) G Kind has shown the application of Amos 2 model for an agricultural district. The initial point of intersection gives the expenditure for the reproduction of the infrastructure and for commuting, if the jobs and the inhabitants remain in the same locations as in 1981. The second variant starts from the distribution of jobs in 1981 and gives the optimal distribution of the inhabitants for this situation. All the other variants prosuppose a drop in the number of these employed in agriculture and different degrees of growth in the number of those employed in industry in different locations. After considering all variants as a basis the 'most favourable' expenditure function can be determined for the district. Hence it is possible to take into account the conditions of development of the distribution planning and the distribution of productive forces. G.Kind claimed that he has conducted several experiments successfully with the Amos 2 model.

Hierarchy of Rural Settlements in India

In India four grades of rural settlements can be distinguished.[21] At the lowest hierarchical level are tiny hamlets of below 200 people on inferior quality of land, and as such satellite settlements are found in inferior environmental conditions, as such no one is economically sound. These rural settlements are made up of inhabitants mostly from only one caste, and by profession. They may be farmers, shepherds, carpenters, cobblers and black smiths. They have few artisans and depend on larger centres for supporting services. Due to their poverty the hamlets are of little importance to the larger villages nearby and are generally ignored by the Block Development officials. They have little social life, few ceremonies, no theatres, and no fairs, but now with the beginning of green revolution the situations are changing.

Rural settlements having 200 to 1000 persons are of second grade. In such settlements inhabitants of various castes are found who provide various supporting services for themselves, such as ranching, combination of crops, cleaning of clothes, shoe making, basket weaving and oil crushing, etc. But basically most of them are peasants and they have their own arrangement of entertainment along with elaborate ceremonials. In the rural settlements of this category one resourceful family may be the central figure for the whole community.

Medium sized rural settlements of the third grade having a population of 1000 to 4000 people, may be the residence of several big landowners, middle class peasants as well as labourers. Such villages are self-sufficient with multi-caste people. Such settlements are also focus of attention for government officials, besides a high school, mosque, temple and a family planning centre.

The fourth grade rural settlements have a population from 5,000 to 30,000, and are as much central place for other neighbouring settlements as themselves. Such villages generate their own wealth by agricultural operations and market mechanism and they are base for village level worker (VLW) with jurisdiction over small villages in the surrounding area. In fact, the large rural settlements include a number of hamlets and satellite settlements for administrative purposes. Such settlement often has a high school, college, rural bank, post office and some retail shops for the hinterland.

REFERENCES

1. W. Sadowski: "Methodology of Science and Systematic Cogitation" in *Gesellchaftswissen Chaften,* Moscow, 17, 1979, pp. 106 - 125.
2. V.T. Chow: "Systems Approach in Hydrology and Water Resources", *The Progress of Hydrology, University of Illinois, Urbana,* Vol. 1, 1969, pp. 490 - 509.
3. J.B. McLoughlin: *Urban and Regional Planning: A Systems Approach,* Faber, 1969.
4. Guidelines for the contents of individual national reports on settlement systems; in *Geographia Polonica,* Warsaw, Vol. 39, 1978, pp. 235 - 240.
5. P. Haggett: *Geography: A Modern Synthesis* - Harper and Row, 1972, p. 44.
6. C.S. Chandrasekhra, et. al: "The Role of Growth Foci in Regional Development Strategy", in *Urban Systems and Rural Development,* Part I(edt. R.P. Misra et al), University of Mysore, 1972, pp. 36 - 70.
7. *Ibid.*
8. T. Hagerstrand: "The Propagation of Innovation Waves", *Lund Studies in Geography,* Series B, Human Geography, No. 4, 1932.
9. United Nations: *Report of Habitat:* U.N. Conference on Human Settlements, New York, 1976.
10. A.V. Kanel: "Development of Settlement Systems in Rural Regions of the GDR", in *Geographia Polonica,* Vol. 44, 1981, pp. 123 - 131.
11. M. Macka et al: "Selected Aspects of the Internal Organization of a settlement System", *Geographia Polonica,* Vol. 44, 1981, pp. 65 - 88.
12. F. Boros: "The Association Between the Size of Settlement and the Supplying Function", *Foldrajzi Ertesito,* Vol. 16, 1967, pp. 239 - 250.
13. F. Culik: "The Structure of Settlements in CSSR and the Possibility of Selecting Appropriate Centres", *Acta Geological,* Vol, 6, 1966, pp. 303 - 318.
14. C. Kania: "The Problem of Central Places in the former Regierunsbezirk Oppeln", *Materialy i Studia Opolskie,* Vol. 4, 1963, pp. 95 - 99.
15. V. Duric: "An Economic Geographical Classification of Communes in Serbia", *Zbornik Radova;* Vol. 13, 1966, pp. 93 - 108.
16. C. Kania, "Method of Analysis rank - and size' on the example of the Voivodship of Opole", *Czasopismo Geograficzene,* Vol. 37, 1966, pp. 311 - 323.
17. A. Zagozdzon, "Problems of Settlement Complexes", *Czasopismo Geograficzne,* Vol. 35, 1964, pp. 387 - 398.
18. A.V. Kanel: 1981, *op. cit.*
19. R.A. Ellefsen: "City Hinterland Relationships in India", *India's Urban Future* (Edt. Roy Turner), University of California Press, Berkeley, 1962, pp. 94 - 116.
20. Gerold Kind: "Modelling of Settlement Systems for Regional Planning", *Geographia Polonica,* Vol. 44, 1981, pp. 33 - 43.
21. R.A. Harper and T.H. Schmudde: Between Two Worlds: *An Introduction to Geography:* Houghton Mifflin Company, Boston, 1978, p. 27.

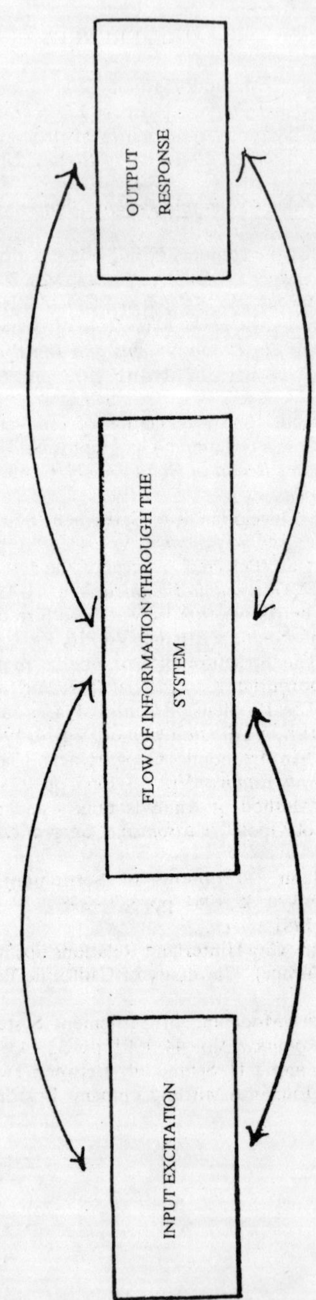

Fig. 7.1

Diagrammatic Representation of a Sequential System

Fig. 7.2

Dimensions of National Settlement System

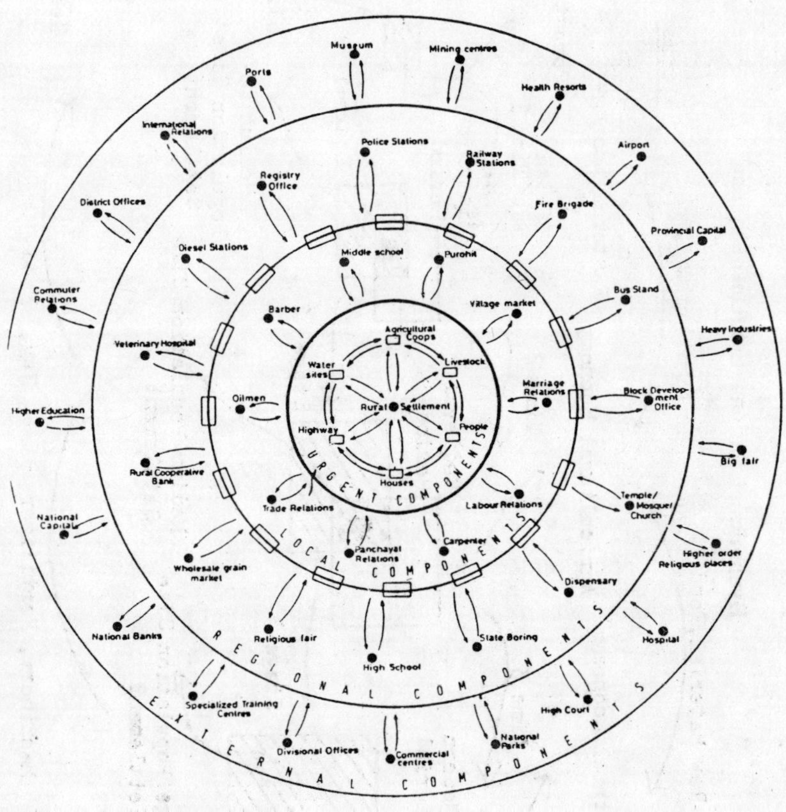

Fig. 7.3

Dynamics of National Settlement System

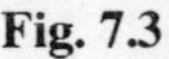
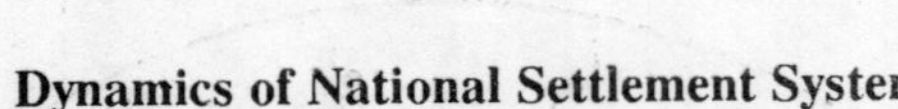

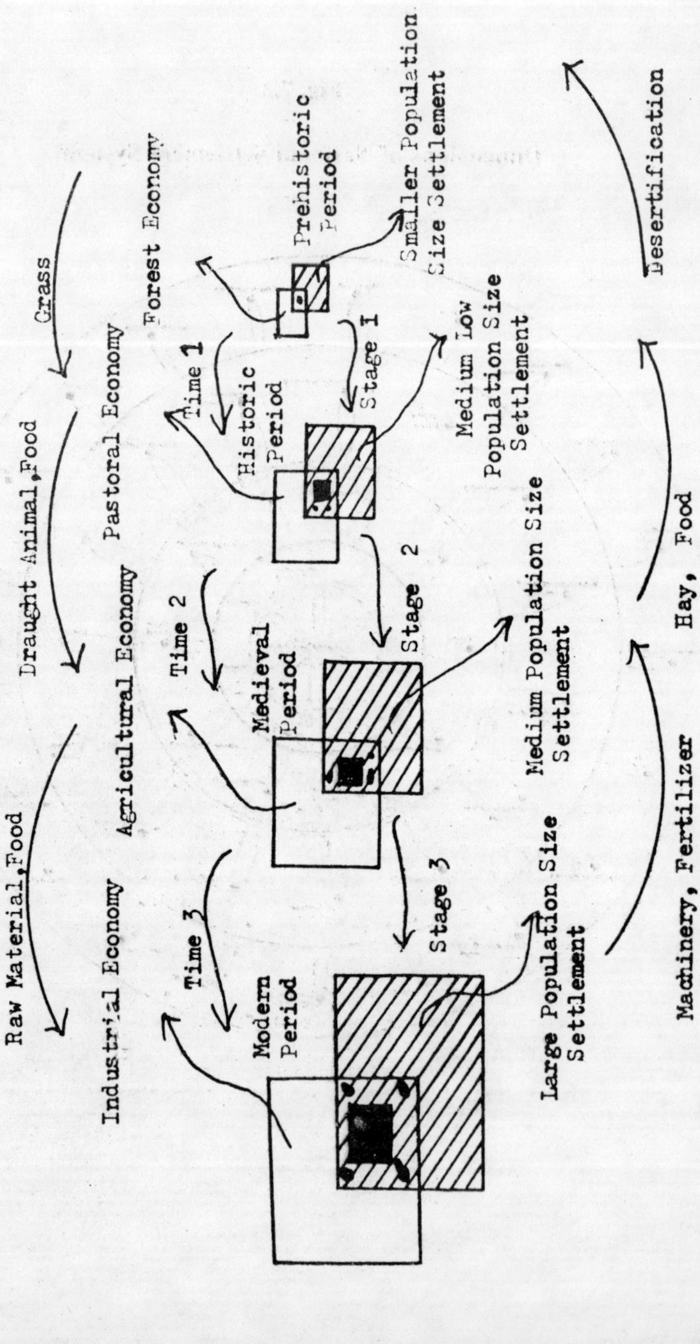

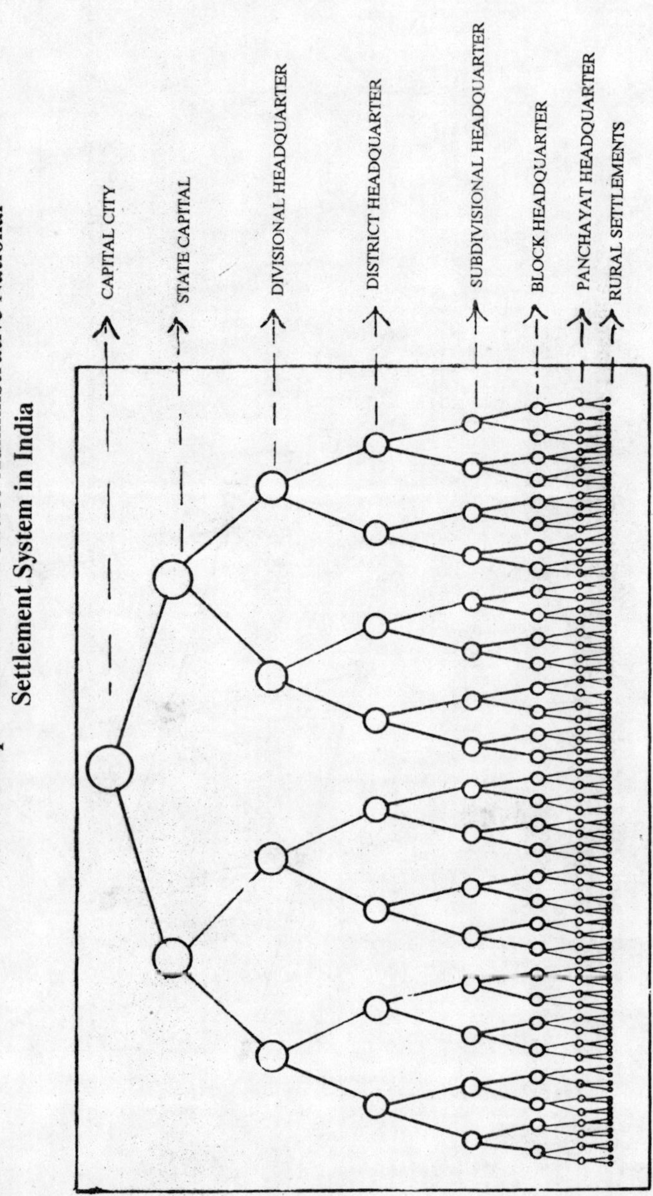

Fig. 7.4

Schematic Representation of Politico-Administrative National Settlement System in India

Fig. 7.5

Settlements Nodes with Transport Linkage

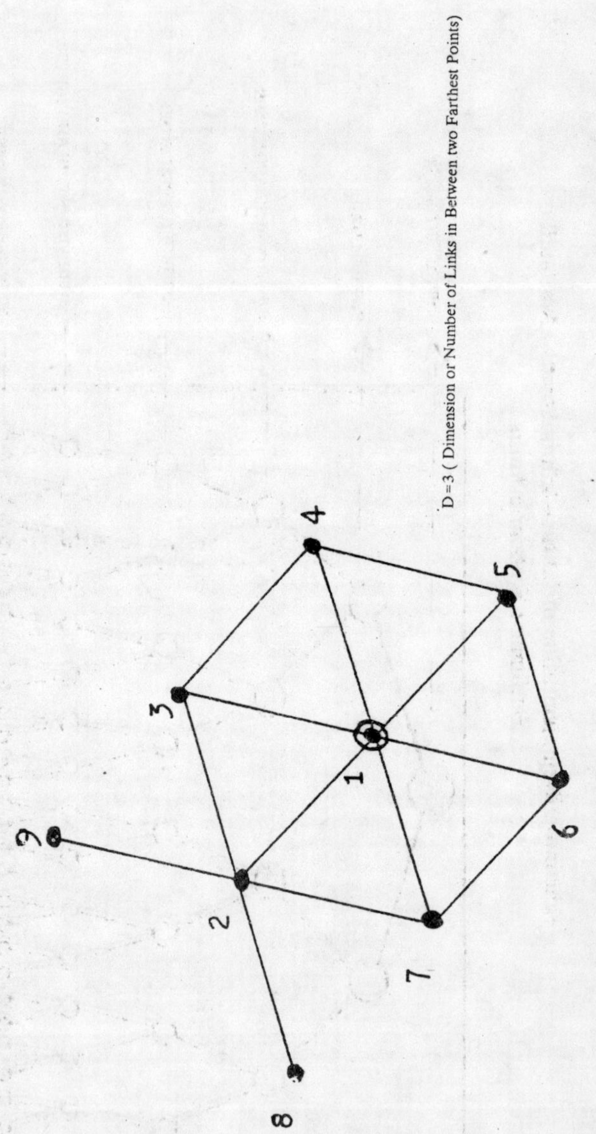

D=3 (Dimension or Number of Links in Between two Farthest Points)

Fig. 7.6

Schematic Representation of Indian City and its Hinterland

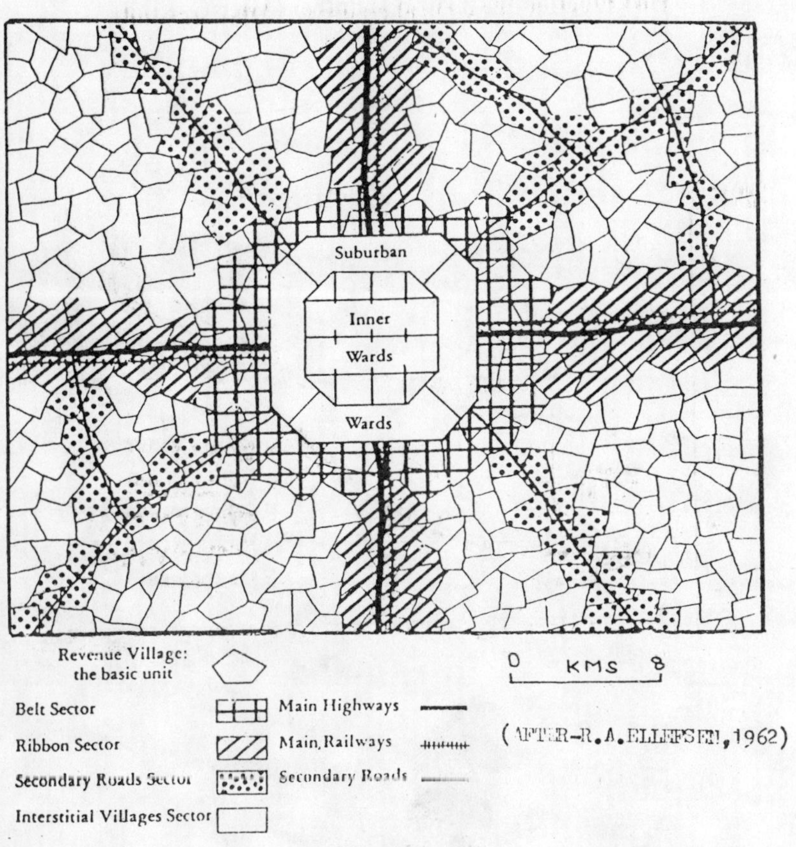

(AFTER-R.A.ELLEFSEN, 1962)

Fig. 7.7

Applications of AMOS 2 Model for an Agricultural District (real cost function for a rural country) (After G. Kind)

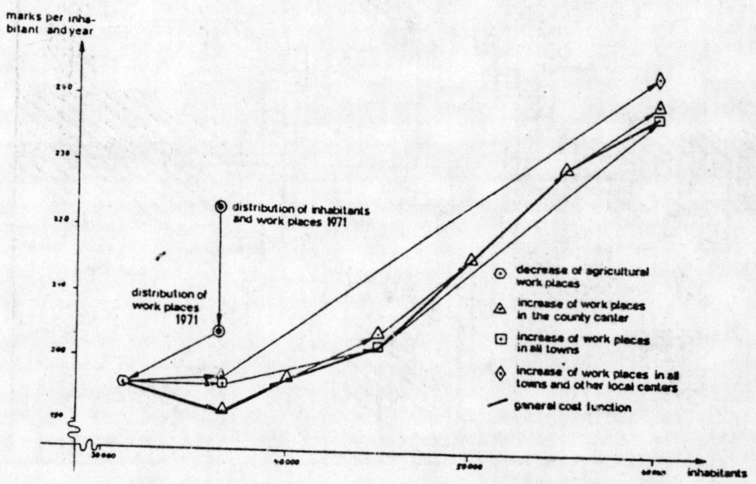

EIGHT

TYPES OF RURAL SETTLEMENTS

RURAL SETTLEMENTS show the reciprocal relationship of human occupance features and environment.[1] Aurousseau has used the expression 'arrangement of rural settlements as geographical entities to express the grouping of dwellings and their inter-relationship'.[2] Essentially, a rural settlement is mainly an agricultural workshop and, as such, it cannot be separated from the land whose use it ensures. Its shape and arrangement are often in strict accord with the kind of work, the agricultural technique and the way the soil is used.[3]

The rural settlement was dominant type of human community for over three millennia and even in future it may be so in most parts of Asia, Africa, and Latin America, as well as in some parts of Europe and North America.

Factors Affecting Settlement Types:

There are two sets of factors which affect settlement types in rural areas. The factors may be called the agglomerating factors and the deglomerating factors. These factors are both physical and cultural and lead to compact and dispersed settlements according to the relative influence of centripetal and centrifugal forces.

Physical Factors:

Agglomerated rural settlements with permanent homesteads are the product of civilized life, which is closely associated with the uniformity of relief, fertility of soil and moderate rainfall. Paul Vidal De La Blache has aptly observed that the clustered village is indigenous in districts where the arable area is continuous, admitting of uniform and extensive exploitation.[4] In Bihar Plain, the fertility of soil is coupled with a rapidly growing population, leading to intensive cultivation which is conducive to the concentration of settlements.[5] Compact settlements are relatively common in the more fertile central and western parts of the study area. Another factor leading to compactness is occasional floods in several areas of the almost flat land of the Bihar Plain. In these areas, elevated sites are few and far between. These are built up into compact settlements. In low-lying areas liable to be inundated, large elevated sites are absent and, hence, settlements are necessarily hamletted. The same is the case in marshy areas and near meandering rivers which change their courses frequently.

The rainfall affects settlement types in two ways. Areas of heavy rainfall are marked by the deglomerating factors of floods and marshy lands. But in areas of moderate rainfall such as Saran, Bhojpur and Gaya districts, surface water accumulates in lakes and ponds. Compact settlements are built around these water-bodies. In areas where the ponds are infrequent, deep masonry wells are constructed for the purpose but being costly to construct the wells are, therefore, also infrequent. But the settlements around these wells are compact. Such settlements are common in Champaran, Muzaffarpur, Darbhanga, Saran and in parts of Patna district where the water table is lower as compared to areas farther east. "The collective building of dams and irrigation channels for the storage and distribution of rain water and the construction of tanks for artificial irrigation have promoted the evolution of compact village'.[6] Physical factors which act as a hindrance to easy living lead to fragmentation of settlements. About this phenomenon Paul Vidal De La Blache observes that 'the scattered manner of grouping suits localities where as a result of the dissection of relief, soil and hydrography, the arable land is itself divided up'.[7] Sprinkled settlements are found on account of adverse physical conditions like the relatively rugged lands near the southern margin of Bihar Plain, the Siwalik hill region in the north, and the Kosi flood plain in the east. There are only a few small sites in the Kosi flood plain which remains above the water during the monsoon. These sites are small in size and can, therefore, accommodate only a small hamlet. Thus large compact settlements are relatively absent here. In the scarp lands and hilly areas, the land is too poor to support large compact settlements, and mixed cropping and pastoral farming leads to fragmented settlements.

Settlements are generally built near water-bodies. If they have to depend upon deep wells or rivers, they are generally compact. However, in areas where the water table is high and wells can be dug easily or where the drainage texture is dense, that is where surface streams and rivulets are numerous, settlements can be built practically all over the region. In such cases, therefore, hamlets, semi-sprinkled or semi-compact settlements are more common than compact settlements. Such areas are found in the Kosi basin and the Panar-Mahananda Valley in the north-eastern part of North Bihar.

Cultural Factors:

Compact settlements are well adapted to the economic conditions of paddy cultivation.[8] This type of agriculture periodically requires a large labour force for transplantation, irrigation and harvesting. Hence, both the farmers and the associated agricultural labourers tend to reside in the same nucleated settlement. Moreover, the village community tends to be self-contained, hence, other non-agricultural activities and cottage industries are also located in the same settlement. These include the village blacksmith, carpenter, potter, weaver, tailor, etc. Due to the lack of transport facilities till very recently, this economic self reliance was a major factor leading to compact settlements.

During the historical times, the need of defence from external lawless elements was of a paramount importance. This requirement could be met only if the settlement was compact. Quite often this led to the establishment of walled villages. Settlements having a fort in the middle or those inhabited by the same clan or tribe also belong to this category. Social relationships and cooperation amongst the villagers have also been important for the generation of centripetal forces. A pond, temple, well, community hall, panchayat house or even a mango orchard in the central part of the village could be utilized by the entire village community on cooperative basis. It, therefore, attracted houses which clustered around it. Social relationships or customs guided and controlled by the village elders have always been important in village life. The panchayat (village council) is one form of this control. Although less important during the British period[9] it is again becoming extremely important.

Superstitions, though less significant than other factors, also have played its role in causing agglomeration. The dih (ancestral site) is considered auspicious and people do not like to shift their buildings from it. Also a settlement does not tend to expand towards the south and the west because these two directions are considered inauspicious.[10] Thus even when the houses have to be rebuilt in course of time due to increase in population or division of the family, they continue to cluster in the same locality. This increases compactness of the settlement.

On the other hand, the same social customs and traditions involving the caste system, particularly in relation to the untouchables has led to the fragmentation of rural community. The lower castes, particularly *harijans*, are forced to build their houses a little away from the main settlement, often towards its south. These hamlets or *tolas* derive their name after the caste inhabiting them, for example, Chamartoli, Mushartoli, Domtoli, etc. In the past, the landlords preferred to settlements of different castes in separate hamlets, allotting to them poor lands. The best land was reserved for the families belonging to the upper castes or their own relatives.

In areas where the physical factors did not prevent dispersal and the land was relatively free from invadors or robbers, small hamlets rather than large clusters came into existence. This factor has been important in the Bihar Plain which has remained relatively more peaceful than other parts of India during the last few centuries. Sometimes, the emergence of a market site around a railway junction or a railway station, a little away from the main settlement, attracts a few residential buildings also. This in turn results in the creation of a separate hamlet. It is possible that during the course of years this hamlet may outgrow the older cluster on account of better economic advantages.

The Scale of Economies and Rural Settlement Types:

We have seen that settlement types is the outcome of the interplay of physical and cultural factors. Of these two, the economies of man have played the most significant role. The economy reflects the physical characteristics of land and the cultural attainment of people who reside in it. In order to understand the differences in settlement types over the globe, we should see the broad classes of economy. Each class presents a different kind of human settlements according to their needs, functional specialization and dimensions of economic development.

1.**Hunting - Fishing and Food Gathering Economies:**

In this type of economy, the inhabitants are completely absorbed in securing food, shelter, and clothing from the local environment in which they live. Adjustments are searched with the available physical environment with little attempt to change that setting. The population supporting capacity of such an economy is limited in any given area. They occupy any area temporarily, lead a mobile life having no fixed place of abode.

On fringe area of the densely settled parts of the world the hunting - fishing and collecting economy is still dominant. In East Indies and Poleward margins of the America and Eurasia, Eskimo, Smenoid and Fini people still lead a primitive life by hunting, fishing, collecting or a combination of all these. Similarly, Bidumbu of Amazon Basin, Baddu of Congo Basin and Bushmen of Kalahari desert in South Africa, still follow a primitive way of living.

2. **Pastoralism:**

The domestication of animals gives a way of living to the human being which is known as pastoralism. Here the main job is to watch animals, manage fodder and water for them and protect them from wild animals. Pastoralism offered support for large human groups and acted as a determinant of a particular kind of settlement pattern.

The Masai pastoralists of Northern Tanzania make Kraal a semi-permanent settlement site on the high but slopy ground after fencing with thorny bushes cut from the scrub of the savanah. They make houses with thin branches of plants and trees and thatching with grass, and plaster it with clay and cow dung in order to make it water proof. Such a hedge guards both people and their cattle from lions at night.

3.Agriculture:

Agricultural economy developed with the domestication of plants and animals. Permanent rural settlement starts with the development of permanent agriculture. Hence no longer necessary to hunt for food or to move continually in search of pasture ground for animals. Agriculture enabled man to select a place of habitation and to live either in groups or in isolation that is either a clustered or scattered settlement patterns.

Manufacturing:

The development of industries by man is a very complex of his economies. This way of living requires not only direct production from the land, but alteration or combination of agricultural and mineral products by processing in the factories. As it demanded living in groups over a small piece of land, hence industrial economy produced significant effect upon the location, siting and functioning of rural settlements.

On the other hand, the increased use of ores in manufacturing necessitated the supply of materials directly from the mines. The forests supply us wood and other products such as timber, fruits, gums, saps, etc. These exploitations of resources have given rise to various types of rural settlements.

Commerce:

In case people are concerned with the transportation, sale and distribution of any products either from land or factories is known as commerce. Both exploitation and commerce are limiting elements in settlement pattern. Mining involves the concentration of human beings where there are ore deposits. Exploitation of the forest may require either large numbers concentrated at one site or very small groups scattered through the forest. Use of the sea requires ports on sea's edge. And commerce demands ties to certain sites at route ends and crossing "points"[11].

Dualism in Rural Settlement Study:

The presence of contrasting patterns of human habitat on the earth surface is known as dualism in relation to rural settlements.

1.Mobile Versus Sedentary Inhabitants:

In some parts of the Globe people move from one place to another without fixed abode. These are nomadic people who move here and there like some of the tribal groups of Asia and Africa. Their living depends upon herds of animals such as sheep, goat, camel and cow. Most commonly, nomads inhabit desert margins as Turkana in northern Kenya and Fulani in Nigeria where rainfall is scanty for agricultural operations. The animals need pasturage and hence it requires constant search of water spot and patches of grassland. Nomads are always ready to move when a word of rainfall in accessible area reaches them, because rainfall means new pasture ground. Although nomads live in groups but their dwellings are purely temporary and are easily moved from one place to another.

There are also nomadic people in the Arctic Tundra e.g. the Lapps of northern Scandinavia. They still depend upon reindeer for their livelihood and move from summer pasturage in the Tundra to winter shelter within the margins of the northern coniferous forest or Taiga. Similarly, in some areas of Tropical forests, some tribal groups depend entirely upon hunting - fishing and collecting the edible plant products of the forest. For a period, they attach themselves to specific locations, building crude dwellings as centres of their functional activities, but with the exhaustion of local resource supply they move to a new area in search of fertile land, food, and animal pasturage.

On the other hand, the majority of world's population are tied with specific places on the surface of the earth. This sedentary or fixed abode provides long - lasting patterns and forms of rural settlements that can readily be observed and compared. An understanding of these contrasting situations is necessary in order to know the cultural phase of the rural settlements.

2.**Disseminated Versus Agglomerated Settlements**:

Among sedentary groups the characteristics of rural settlements vary widely. At one extreme is the isolated dwelling that houses an individual or a family, but at the other dwellings may be so closely packed that no surface is left open even for kitchen garden.

In case dwellings are scattered over the land the settlement pattern is said to be dispersed. When houses are packed close together, the settlement pattern is known as agglomerated. Those terms are used relatively.

3. **Rural Versus Urban Settlements:**

The distinction between rural and urban, like the distinction between the disseminated and agglomerated in the description of settlement pattern, is a relative one. There is no immediately evident sharp line that divides rural folk from urban. A rural population is one predominantly engaged in primary production of the basic necessities of life directly from the land itself. Urban folks are engaged in transporting, manufacturing, buying, and selling the materials for their food, shelter, clothing, and general comfort; or in educating the people, managing the affairs of state, or merely living in town.

Obviously, rural population is more likely to be arranged in disseminated pattern than urban population. Yet rural folk need not necessarily be scattered over the land. In fact, agglomerated rural population is more common and more numerous, for the world as a whole, than is disseminated. Urban population is almost entirely agglomerated. It is estimated that three-fourths of the world's population lives in agglomeration of one type or another.

Despite the huge size of many centres, such as London, New York, and Tokyo, the actual world total of urban population is far less than the total of rural population. Urban settlement characterises the western metropolitan civilization whereas the rural agglomeration is most typically Asian or ancient civilization.

Major Settlement Types:

A cursory glance at the rural landscape or the toposheets of the Bihar Plain reveals a variety of rural settlement types. Broadly speaking, the accumulation of agrarian houses and highways in the countryside, where people lead their life by ranching of cattle and agricultural practices with a few secondary or tertiary occupations, is known as a rural settlement. Primarily rural settlements may be classified into two broad groups or compact and sprinkled types. Compact or agglomerated settlements have narrow lanes and tortuous streets separating the houses. Sprinkled or dispersed settlements exhibit privacy marked by scattered dwellings made by peasants in their respective farms and fields. In between these two extremes, semi-compact and semi-sprinkled types are more numerous and these result 'from physical, social and economic history of the community'[12]. The ratio between compact and sprinkled settlements may vary from place to place and from time to time because human habitations are something dynamic as innate social centrifugal and centripetal forces which are constantly at work within them[13].

The typology of rural settlements has been discussed here on the basis of size and spacing of rural settlements. The settlements, having lower spacing and greater population size, have been declared to be compact settlements. The hamlets, having a higher spacing and lower population size have been classified as dispersed settlements. But the nature of their compactness or dispersion can only be judged after a detailed spatial analysis of the physical and cultural characteristics of settlement patterns.

In other words, a settlement of one hamlet only is called dispersed settlement while a settlement having one large hamlet and one or two smaller sub-hamlets falls in the category of semi-compact settlement. Similarly, a settlement having a number of hamlets and therefore, no recognisable central site is classified as a semi-sprinkled settlement. A settlement built in a secluded place where the hamlet is small and the houses are also comparatively far apart, is called sprinkled or dispersed.

The phenomenon of dispersion under Indian environment is quite different from that of the American prairie where the settlements are raised by individual farmers on their respective farms, as the agriculture is highly mechanised and the size of the farms is also enormous. These factors compel the inhabitants to settle separately from one another because it facilitates agricultural operations. But under Indian conditions, a large peasant family has only one to four hectares of land to support it. This makes people settle close to each other as far as possible because they have to cultivate their fields with manual help from their neighbours and agricultural operation can be successful with this cooperation alone. The isolation, thus, is not inherited but is due to certain compelling physical and cultural conditions.

The first Report of the Commission on Types of Rural Settlements published by the International Geographical Union in 1928 recognised only two types of settlements, compact and dispersed. This classification has been recognised universally by now. Several generalised classifications have been attempted by different authors, but no general laws, covering these generalisations, have been formulated as yet.

Two methods of classification personal observation and statistics, have been predominantly used in determining the types of rural settlements. The most successful methods have been based on personal study of settlement types from topographical maps and a detailed knowledge of their variation. Such maps of settlement types have been constructed for Belgium[14], Netherlands[15], Germany[16], Switzerland[17], Italy[18], the Balkans[19], Romania[20], and Poland. The diverse definitions and the subjective view of the authors, however, make it difficult to use such maps for comparative study either of the whole of Europe or of the region under consideration here.

In 1955 Eric Wolf[21] devised a typology of rural settlements in Latin America and applied the typology to rural settlements in the old world as well as the New World. He started "with the assumption that a useful classification of peasant communities must centre on differences in the way in which the communities are integrated with the outside world, he discriminated two main types: 'closed' or 'corporate' as opposed to 'open'. Closed or corporate communities are marked by a clear structural identity that persists over time, a sharp distinction between members and non-members, a steady-state approach to economic activities, and a number of characteristic cultural traits - a "cult of poverty" extolling hard work and simple living, "institutionalised envy" design to keep any individual from advancing very far ahead of his fellows and a self-conscious maintenance of local distinctiveness in dress, housing pattern, language, custom, etc." Open communities are marked by cash crop cultivation and consequently less standoffish in relation to the outside world. In fact open community is in fairly continuous interaction with the outside world and is marked by greater social heterogeneity, intensive concern with social status, and less attachment to established patterns of equilibrium. Wolf did not argue that these two categories are mutually exclusive and suggested five more in terms of their form of integration with larger socio-cultural systems.

Attempts have also been made to use the rubrics "centripetal" and "centrifugal" forces to express differences in community structure. These are similar in context, although not identical, to the types Wolf has isolated: centripetal villages are those in which social institutions - economic, kinship, political-ritual produce a constant tendency for members to move out beyond the village boundaries into the world of larger society. Centrifugal rural settlements are those in which such institutions tend to hold or draw back members within their boundary. The classification of rural settlements has just begun, and large scale revisions in existing typologies must be expected as a greater knowledge of cross cultural variations in rural community - society relationship accumulates.

In this book a new and simple technique has been devised to study the rural settlements of Bihar Plain. It takes all settlement units into consideration and is based on the ratio between the population size of settlement units and their dispersal. This method can be applied for determining the index of dispersal of rural settlements on the basis of population size of settlement units (hamlets or tolas) of an *anchal* divided by the spacing between them in the same unit area. The settlements are products of socio - economic and physical factors which sometimes harmonise with the clustering of settlements and population but sometimes are at variance with them. The different values of the index of dispersal of settlements, can be grouped according to quartile values. This will give the settlement class at different levels, such as compact, semi - compact, semi - sprinkled and sprinkled types

1.	Index of Dispersal Values	=	Average Population Size of the Tola/ Average Spacing of the Tola
2.	Settlement Form	=	Index of dispersal values grouped according to median and quartile value.

The average population size of the *tola* (hamlet or settlement unit) was calculated by dividing the rural population of the *anchal* (administrative unit) by the number of tolas contained in it. Similarly the average spacing between *tolas* was calculated by dividing the rural area of the *anchal* by the number of *tolas* and then by working out the square root of the figure to arrive at the distance in kilometres between *tolas*. The index of dispersal value is the ratio between the two values and ranges between 2 and 12 for the Bihar Plain.

With the help of this formula, the data for each of the 395 *anchals* in the entire region was calculated and a map has been prepared for settlement types. The map (Fig. 8.1) prepared with the help of above formula reveals four main characteristic types of rural settlements in the Bihar Plain which are as follows:

Compact Settlements (Dispersion Index Over 9)

The fertile plains of Sitamarhi, western half of Darbhanga, central part of Saran, Begusarai district and the Gangetic flood plains of Patna Divisions are areas of compact settlement (Fig.8.1). A small patch also occurs in northern Bhagalpur district. In all these areas, the population size of the settlement varies from 500 to over 1000 persons with a spacing of around one kilometre between each settlement unit. The houses are closely huddled together and over-crowding prevails everywhere.

The part marked by compact settlements in Tirhut Division, is a moist-tract of riverine plains with clayee strip on the surface. Along its northern side, the water of the foothill streams sinks underground in the pebbled plain, then reappears and flows through poorly defined channels. Here the population density rises upto 1171 persons per square kilometre and one village gradually merges into the other through a group of hamlets sprung close together (Fig.8.2).

In the areas free from waterlogging and disease such as malaria, the settlement size may vary from a large hamlet containing 60 to 80 houses to large nucleated villages consisting of hundreds of houses. They are found on the high banks of the rivers where uniformity of relief and soil fertility have enabled a large number of cultivators to live together in compact communities. They were formed by a natural process of agglomeration.

The compact settlements consist of a cluster of buildings with streets which are irregular in width and layout. The houses are irregularly placed with respect to the street frontage. They are surrounded by arable lands, common pastures and orchards. The arable lands are divided into amorphous pattern of plots, many of which may belong to one peasant. There may exist a common pond, a temple or a mosque in the central part of the village. Thus compact villages are distinct and separate organism with its individual life and personality which forms part of the landscape'[22].

There are some contrasts between the settlements of the north-west and those of the south-east in Tirhut division. In the north-west, the compact villages are found in a narrow belt of Terai Region, approximately 32 to 48 kilometres in width. In this zone, the people and the houses seem to be crowded over a smaller piece of land. In the districts of Saran, Siwan, Sitamarhi; Muzaffarpur and Darbhanga, the village nuclei are more marked and are usually larger than in other parts of the Plain. In the east, where larger patches of Bhangar soil are found, big compact villages have been established over larger plots of the land. The bhangar forms typical paddy lands, which are generally conducive to large human settlements. Rice cultivation requires cooperation of the fellow villagers from beginning to end. That is why compact settlements are seen in the typical rice growing tracts which have escaped the influence of disintegrating forces of the cultural setting[23]. The development of compact settlements are due to the higher density of population, fertile soil, frequent floods and also due to the reasons of defence.

The compact settlement zone on the southern bank of the river Ganga has the same advantage of the bhangar soil. This area is also flood affected and settlements have developed on relatively infrequent higher sites. Paddy is the prominent cultivation here which needs joint efforts of the villagers, causing the villages to grow in size. This belt runs 112 kilometres east-west parallel to the Ganga and is nearly 16 kilometres broad from north to south. It is fertile alluvial flood plain of insufficient rainfall (annual 125 centimetres) in most parts of the year which compels the inhabitants to dwell by the side of *ahars*, *pynes*, tanks or other water-bodies for agricultural purposes. Cooperation among villagers is necessary not only in paddy cultivation but also in the construction of irrigation channels a necessary imperative for subsistence.

A small patch in Munger and Bhagalpur districts has a light strip of alluvial soils and receives more than 140 centimetres of annual rainfall. It is also a plain land suited for paddy cultivation. The frequent occurrence of floods in Bihpur and Parbatta *anchals* compelled the villagers to live in compact settlements, as sites with a high elevation are relatively rare. Here the average population size of the rural settlements is over 1000 and the spacing between them is more than one kilometre.

The typical village in many parts of southern Japan consists of a close packed cluster of bamboo and thatch dwellings and sheds, so tightly pressed together as to allow only narrow passage between adjacent buildings. The whole settlement occupies a bit of ground only slightly above the level of the surrounding irrigated rice fields. Seldom are there roads leading to and from the village. Narrow pathways following along the tops of the low dykes that separate the rice fields are the only connecting lines from one village to next. Commonly, the village is encircled by a bushy hedge that stands out prominently because of the absence of trees and bushes elsewhere.

Inhabitants go out from the village early in the morning to work in their fields, returning again at night. A farmer's land is seldom in one continuous piece; it is likely to be in several fragments in scattered locations about the settlement. The whole life of the inhabitants, often members of only one or two large family groups, is a daily pulsing out onto the land and back into the village. The fact that the land holdings are scattered and the cultivation is intensive means that the villagers must devote constant attention to their work. The village is the focal point from which a small portion of the human habitat is made to perform its function.

In south-eastern Austria, for example, villages such as Riegersburg i.e., on mountain slopes are common. The more level land is used for crops and pastures; the steep slopes are occupied mainly by the village, with an ancient castle situated on the highest portion of the hill.

In certain other parts of Europe, as in Hungary, rural agglomerations of several thousand people are not uncommon features. These huge villages cover considerable areas of land, with each dwelling and its associated buildings set on a small plot. But the farm buildings are definitely clustered, arranged along streets as crop collection centres set in open cultivated or pasture land.

On the eastern seaboard regions of the United States, as in new England or the South, agglomerated rural settlement was the early mode. In Colonial New England, farm houses were built close together, usually fronting on a common. The common was originally a pasture area near the farm houses, owned and used collectively by all the inhabitants of the village where it still remains today, it has become the village park. In the south, early establishment of plantations, with their needs for large labour forces and the consequent importation of slaves, developed another kind of rural agglomeration represented by the compact slave quarters.

Some of these examples suggest that there is a great variety in the detail of rural agglomerated settlement. The unifying characteristic is the tie of the population to the agricultural land and livestock rearing.

In the Bihar Plain, isopleth line for dispersion index 8 runs on the side of compact settlement demarcating the zone of semi-compact settlement. This zone comprises East Champaran, eastern Darbhanga and the whole of Saharsa district and the entire Ganga belt south of the river from Bhojpur to Bhagalpur. In these areas the average population size of the settlement unit (hamlet) is varying from 500 to 800 and their average distance is about one kilometre from one another.

The semi-compact settlement is an intermediate type between the zones of compact and sprinkled settlements. The fundamental characteristic is one main settlement with two or more hamlets around the central site. Here the houses or settlements are neither agglomerated nor dispersed in numerous detached hamlets and are closely linked up with the main site by footpaths or cart tracks. The hamlets consist of people of different castes and classes, each forming a separate community with distinctive names such as *Goartoli, Babhanitoli, Chamartoli, Koiritoli*, etc.

In North Bihar, the plains of Saran district and Sadar subdivision of Champaran district have semi-compact settlements which roughly correspond to the zone of Calcareous soil in a narrow strip. The most notable surface materials are *Kankar* or nodular limestone. The water table is relatively high owing to impermeable strata and constitutes one of the powerful forces creating cluster and hamlet type of settlements. A closely allied factor is that the region is normally free from inundation. The distribution of villages is comparatively more uniform than in any other part of region. The cluster and hamlet type of settlement widens the social distance and reduces cultural cohesion.

The semi-compact type of settlement is also found in the eastern part of the Baghmati-Kamla Plain and in the Ganga-Kosi interfluve. Here also, the high water table has been the main reason for the relative fragmentation of settlements. The light yellow soil in south-eastern Bhagalpur district is more fertile and has a comparatively low water-table. Here, the villages are semi-compact because the security from predators in the past was a very important factor. (Fig.8.3).

In South Bihar Plain, semi-compact rural settlements predominate in the region of tank, well and *pyne* irrigation, in a belt parallel to the Ganga but a little bit away from its bank is the zone of wheat, paddy, and potato cultivation with less than 125 centimetres of annual rainfall. The compactness is more marked here than in North Bihar, due to suitability of higher sites. Also, congregation of more dwellings in the central village makes household land more valuable and so the centrifugal forces compel the villagers to seek another site for building their houses. This site is most probably inferior to the earlier central site, but is closer to the fields. The need of agricultural cooperation and construction of *ahars* and *pynes* for irrigation as also occasional flooding in the rainy season are other reasons which induce the villagers to live in semi-detached hamlets.

Semi-Sprinkled Settlements

The settlement having less than 500 population and a spacing of approximately more than one kilometre from each other have a dispersal index between 5 and 7. This type of settlement is the characteristic feature of the whole of Southern Upland Plains, western half of Purnea and Central Champaran districts. In Southern Upland Plains the decreasing fertility of soil towards the south is due to comparatively lower rainfall with a quick run-off which makes the upper layer of the soil leached. This prohibits high density of population and consequent congestion of houses.

Due to the damp climate and water-logging in Purnea district, large tracts of land are not capable of supporting a dense population. This belt is characterised as marshy land with waterlogging in *chaurs*, and is marked by autumn paddy cultivation with flooding in the rainy season. It is the most extensive flood zone of Bihar. Here linear hamletted settlements are found along the banks of rivers and rivulets. The predominant house is built with straw and reeds or bamboo. The availability of water everywhere along rivulets helps the inhabitants to settle anywhere, because except the danger of floods, there is no other handicap (Fig.8.4).

Semi-sprinkled settlements have a small nucleation comparable to that which is found in the cultivated fields of compact settlements. They are characterised by the presence of small hamlets, where one fails to recognise any central site. The number of hamlets ranges from 40 to 50 per revenue village or even more. Still they are regarded as a single unit for the purpose of administration. Sometimes each hamlet is occupied by people of a separate caste but sometimes the whole village is named after numerically the most important caste.

Another belt of this settlement type lies in the south-western part of Champaran district along the riparian tracts of the Gandak river. It is located in the excessive flood zone with thousands of small rivulets which has given rise to hamletted settlements. It is a narrow belt, 128 kilometres in length, and 2 kilometres in width. Nowadays, the construction of numerous canals with flood protection embankments have minimized the occurrence of floods, so that the process of compact settling is in progress over the entire belt, but the process is very slow.

A narrow belt of hamletted type of settlements has developed in the central part of the Gaya district but it seems that its occurrence is mainly due to the poor quality of soil. There are small hamlets here and there in the entire region, along the banks of numerous *pynes*, *ahars* and rivulets rising from the Chotanagpur plateau and flowing down to the Ganga. In this region canal irrigation brings about a considerable change in the settlement pattern. The easy availability of water helps the villagers to settle anywhere along the banks of canals and along roads, as the region is entirely free from floods due to higher elevation. In the drier west, compactness is more marked but their development seems to be suppressed by the poverty, and low fertility of soil. More recently, canal irrigation has made the area surplus in foodgrains.

Sprinkled Settlements

In *anchals* marked by sprinkled settlements the population size of the village ranges from 100 to 300 and the inter-village distance is more than one kilometre. This type is typical of the Chotanagpur Scarp Belt, Southern Upland Plains, Himalayan Foothills in Champàran district and the flood plains of the Panar and the Mahananda river basins in Purnea district. All these areas are poor in agriculture and suffer from physical handicaps. In the districts of Saharsa, Katihar and Purnea the dispersal is partly caused by higher rainfall, damp climate and regular inundation by the rivers. The dissected and broken hill country of north-western Champaran and Chotanagpur Scarp Belt present a similar feature of dispersal but here the causes are different. Irregular relief and occurrence of forests have caused scattering. Settlements are found only in the infrequent cultivable patches along river valleys.

The belt of sprinkled settlements is characterised by the presence of a complete diffusion of homesteads over the entire village area and relatively long distance between dwellings as compared to the congestion seen in settlements of the plain. Even the houses stand separate from each other. In its larger perspective 'everything spells isolation and privacy'[24] is a rule. Such isolated living tends to separate men, psychologically as well as economically[25]. Thus, there is hardly anything like joint village community in the sprinkled settlement area (Fig. 8.5)

In their broader aspects the entire Kaimur Plateau and hilly areas of Gaya, Nawada, and Munger districts have this type of settlement, but at some places in the valleys, semi-compact settlements are also discernible. Contributing causes for such settlements are tribal character of inhabitants, mining camps, fear of carnivorous animals in forest, low fertility of soil and rugged nature of land cut up by a host of minor streams on the scarps. The rugged topography having patchy agricultural fields supports only one or two families at a place, and permits the growth of tiny hamlets only. As the inhabitants cannot derive their livelihood from the limited cultivated fields, such small clearings dotted in the forest, require large areas of pastures and bush lands for the rearing of their cattle and for hunting which supplements their incomes.

In the Panar-Mahananda basin of Purnea district, the soil is a fertile friable loam which is extremely suitable for agriculture. The water table is sufficiently high. Non-masonry wells can be dug easily, bringing centrifugal forces in operation. But most important of all, the substitution of perennial irrigation by regular inundation of the basin renders most of the territory useless for permanent settlement[26]. This shows that the frequency of inundation in the region is a paramount factor causing the dispersal of settlements. The dissected and broken hill zone of north-west Champaran and

Kharagpur hills in Munger district are similar in character to the rugged scarpland zone of Chotanagpur which presents dispersal of rural settlements.

Rural Settlement types in India:

In India about 75% people are living in rural settlements which are either compact or semi-sprinkled type. Dispersed settlement types are found only in small pockets of Rajasthan desert, parts of Siwalik Himalayas, northern parts of Peninsular India e.g. Amarkantak mountain, Chambal valley, Bundelkhand and Baghelkhand plateaus and 'Pat' region of Chotanagpur Plateau. Even in the mountainous areas normally small hamlet with 5 to 25 houses is found rather than a homestead. In the arid west of Thar desert due to lack of water, need of defence, the watch-towers of Pathan villages still dominate the scene. In north eastern states of Nagaland, Manipur, Mizoram, Tripura, Shillong Plateau and Arunachal Pradesh defence is the main factor from neighbouring countries, from floods, from wild beasts and malaria menace in the valleys, and hence villages are found on hill tops or spur even if the communication problem is there.

In the flood plains of Brahamputra in Assam, the Hooghly in West Bengal, the Ganga, the Yamuna, the Ghaghra and the Saryu in Uttar Pradesh, the Sutlej and the Ravi in the Punjab – the rural settlements are necessarily compact in upland plains surrounded by farms and mango gardens ,in areas of rare floods-semi-compact settlements, and in seasonal flood prone areas linear hamleted settlements are found either on higher levees or flood protection embankments.

In northern India, the rural settlements are gradually nucleated and large in population size (500 to 25,000) situated on the neo-tectonic higher mounds in the plains. About the rural settlements of Uttar Pradesh the description of Rahman is as follows:

"These villages form large enceintes (enclosure) of sun-dried brick huts. In the centre one sometimes finds a few masonry houses and the *Pukka Haveli*, a small burnt- brick house belonging to the landlord or moneylender. The huts of the lower castes are found on the outskirts of the village. There are generally two or three entrances to the village, but the absence of main road shows that it is self-sufficing. Each village has one or two temples or shrines, where water is sufficiently abundant. The village pond is surrounded by groves of neem, pipal, and plantains, a splash of green pleasantly breaking the monotony of the grey and drab houses"[27].

Near the Terai regions of southern part of Himalaya and the arid margines of Thar desert in the west the rural settlements are smaller in size but rich enough due to provision of assured irrigation and agricultural development under green revolution in the production of especially wheat, rice and maize. In the more intensively cultivated areas of Bihar, Uttar Pradesh, the Punjab and Haryana there is severe competition for space between fields and houses in the village. (Fig. 8.6).

In the riverine flood plains of Bangladesh the settlement type is distinctively homestead hamleted type not the compact village, but the population density is very high. In some of the reclaimed areas of Sundarban delta close stipple of homesteads are found but never more than 3 to 4 homesteads at one place. Near Comilla amorphous clusters are quite apparent, but near Noakhali close stipple of homesteads with tank is a common feature in the homogeneous environment whereas along the Damodar river of India in West Bengal linear cluster along the river embankment is the common feature of rural settlements in almost all parts of north-eastern India especially in various river basins (Fig. 8.7). In Maharashtra, rural settlements are usually large and compact, but more widely spaced (Fig.8.8) than in the Ganges valley or the east coastal plains of India.

In the Cauvery delta of Tamil Nadu, near Tanjore, there is a tendency of strong nucleation associated with large semi-perennial tanks (Fig. 8.9). Near Mannargudi, the rural settlements are smaller and more scattered. In deltaic condition, there is an usual tendency of the location of settlements along the levees, but some linear patterns are also available across the drainage lines as old beach-ridge settlement.

In Kerala, the rural settlement pattern produces a close stipple of habitations. Due to high density of population (800 persons km^2)

there are no grouped villages except the transitional areas of Cape Comorin, Shencottah, Palghat and the parts of Malabar coastal strip. Here as most of the fruits are grown in house compounds, hence the actual dwelling space reduces too much. "The village is loosely built, and may indeed spill all over the village lands" (Spate, 1964).

All along the "Malabar" coast there is a marked linear tendency of, houses and coconuts on the sandy ridges with their fresh ground water, paddy in the lows. Inland, the lateritic topography exercises a marked effect, settlement being strung out along valley- flanks forming a complete ring around the rises" (Spate, 1964) (Fig.8.10).

In the entire wetter western parts of the state of Karnataka, the basic settlement type is linear dispersion of homesteads isolated in orchard - and - garden patch, aligned along a sand-bar, or along a valley side.[28] In the Malnad, the houses are often concealed within the fringe of forests; the trees are preserved as shade for spices or coffee. So dispersed are the homesteads that there is something approaching the privacy, almost isolation of the individual farm pattern. Associated with this settlement pattern there may be rather greater individual independence and initiative, though to be sure the village unit does function as a whole for taxation purposes, in caste or minor land disputes, and increasingly for welfare and development purposes if the Government is successful in encouraging *Panchayatiraj*, i.e., local government by Village Councils.

On the open plateaus of the east, on the other hand, village settlements are markedly nucleated. In the north there are very tightly packed villages of flat-topped mud or masonry houses, adapted for heat, dust and drought, often arranged in streets, and sometimes still within defensive walls. They give an impression of unity but there is often a quite marked cellular structure of caste and occupational groups within the village[29]. In the tank country of the south, the separation of the mainly thatched outcaste hamlet of the *Harijans*, or untouchables, from the tiled houses of Hindu village which makes the most glaring social cleavage. But there are other caste and faction groups, fluctuating and reforming in almost amoeba-like fashion, absorbing parts of other groups in some circumstances, undergoing fission in others[30].

Rural Settlement types in Ghana:

According to J.B. Wills[31] - in Ghana compounds are circular, built of locally obtained clay, usually in the form of several round hutments joined by an encircling wall, and vary in size according to members in a family. The mud and wattle buildings can be permanent; they are abandoned only when there is more trouble to repair than to re-build. New compounds are usually built in the vicinity of old and the same area of land being subject to cultivation. If a compound farm is moved some distance, it is more frequently to a recently abandoned compound farm than to land at the periphery of the zone not subject to continued cropping. Rural Settlement is thus regarded as permanent from generation to generation.

In Ghana, all permanent rural settlements are nucleated, but vary in type in different parts of the country. Firstly, in the north-east and east, settlements consist of round-houses and round house compounds, scattered irregularly over the area of grazed grassland which is the village site. Secondly, in the north-west, the settlements consist of rectangular houses and compounds, also irregularly scattered over an area of grazed grassland. The third type, which is similar to those found in the forest zone, occurs in both Ashanti and the south-west of Gonja district. It consists of rectangular mud and wattle huts or houses, usually with an interior courtyard, which are clustered along and near the central village path. Settlements associated with shifting cultivation are, of course, temporary, being usually constructed of wattle, mud and thatch.

Types of Rural Settlements in Israel:

Israel showed a strong preference for cooperative organization in its rural areas. Various forms of such organization constitute the basis of the four types of rural settlements found in the country - namely the Kibbutz, the Moshav, the Moshav Shitufi and the Moshava[32].

1. In the *Kibbutz* everything is collectively owned by the members except the land, which is the national property. The basic principle is that every member should give to the community to the best of his abilities, and take the share from it according to his needs. Thus, all

needs of the members - food, clothing, education, entertainment, recreation - are fully met by the community. All meals are served in a communal dining hall while communal laundries, clothing stores and shoe makers provide the needed items according to member's requirements. In general, the largest Kibbutzim have been attained in settlements having a population of 1500 to 2000.

2. The *Moshav* is a small holder's settlement in which, although each settler works on his separate plot of land, lives in his own houschold and draws income from his farm's produce, he is obliged to participate in the joint marketing of produce, joint purchase of farms, household implements, mutual aid and responsibility in case of illness, conscription and so on. Moshav villages range in population from 150 to 900.

3. The *Moshav Shitufi* is a co-operative small holder's village where production is carried out communally as in the Kibbutz but where family life is self-contained as in the Moshav. Most Moshav Shitufi have remained much smaller in population than the average Kibbutz, none of them exceeding 400 inhabitants.

4. The *Moshava* is a village of the regular European type where land, buildings, farming installation and so on are all privately owned and the cooperative organizations are relatively weak. Many moshavot (plural of moshava) pre-date the Israel and because of their laissez-faire basis of organization, they can absorb large number of immigrants and transform into towns and cities of 20,000 to 70,000 people[33].

Rural Settlement Types in Africa:

The majority of people (85%) in the continent of Africa live in rural settlements of small hamlet and permanent nucleated villages. A collection of number of households constitute a village which may be of various sizes. There are some tribes such as Tuareg, Fulani and Masai who lead a nomadic life in temporary settlements.

The compact rural settlement is found throughout Africa from forests and hill slopes to grassland because it helps in traditional block - farming system. Sometimes villages are surrounded by walls of clay for the purpose of defence from wild beasts and enemy. In the marshy areas of the Niger delta, the shores of lake Chad and in the inland delta region of Mali compact rural settlements are found in areas above seasonal flood margin.

In Africa dispersed rural settlements are associated with the Tonga people of Zimbabwe, the Tiv people or Middle Benue valley in Nigeria, the Ibo people of Iboland, Nigeria; the Mossi of Upper Volta and Wolof of Senegal. The available evidence suggests that in all these areas dispersal is a secondary form of settlement resulting from disintegration of nucleated rural settlements. In areas of scarcely available farmland a measure of security is found in individual land ownership, the people have tended to move out to build on one of their farm plots (Udo, 1965).[34] Further, the stabilization of village boundary and the creation of forest reserves resulted in land shortage, and this accelerated the emergence of individual land tenure and the dispersal of rural settlements (Udo, 1966).[35] In this process even nucleated walled villages were relocated on more accessible sites on the nearby plains (Gleave, 1966)[36] as in Shemdam Division of Nigeria.

World Distribution of Rural Settlements:

Rural settlements around farms is the characteristic feature of the greater part of Asia. Except small areas, such as Hokkaido, the northern island of the Japanese group, isolated farmsteads are rare. Throughout the southern islands of Japan, the densely peopled plains of China, Indonesia, Malaysia, India, and Pakistan, close-set compact hamlets and villages are found throughout the intensively cultivated plain lands.

On through the Near East, as in the lowland of the Tigris and Euphrates rivers, and into Africa as in the valley of Nile, the rural agglomeration persists almost exclusively. Most part of Africa is occupied by tribal people, such as the Guinea lands, the Cong , Basin, parts of the East African Plateau, the agglomerated pattern of rural settlement is found e.g. Ujamaa villages in Tanzania.

The hamlet or village is the characteristic settlement unit throughout most of the southern and eastern Europe. Even into the western part of Europe it continues as a prominent form, but the disseminated pattern becoming more and more prominent as one proceeds north westward. Yet even in north- western Europe a thin scattering of rural population fails to cover up the basic nucleated pattern.

The whole of South and Middle America's into Mexico, agglomeration is the rule, but in North America, and especially in the United States, it is virtually absent in favour of isolated rural settlements.

In colonial days, the United States followed the European tradition of rural agglomeration but the need for protection in a wilderness also lent strength to the tradition.

In United States a. land survey system was established for the public lands in the interior and later the same extended throughout the west. This system provided a framework within which a disseminated rural settlement pattern developed. In this regard large farms and roadways helped to bring about a settlement pattern in USA where farm houses and buildings are disseminated rather than agglomerated. As settlement spread into the drier west, larger acreages were allowed for homesteading, so that farms came to be spaced more widely. Mechanization of agriculture and advancement in transportation have likewise tended to increase dispersion.

Canada is an area of scattered rather than clustered rural population. So also are most of Holland, Australia and New Zealand, the areas of European colonization in South and East Africa, and some parts of South America. The pattern of agglomeration has been lost in these areas.

REFERENCES

1. R.L. Singh: "Meaning, Objectives and Scope of Settlement Geography," *The National Geographical Journal of India* Vol.VII, 1961, pp.12-13.
2. M.Aurousseau: "The Arrangement of Rural Population", *Geographical Review,* Vol.10, 1920, p.223.
3. A.V. Perpillou: *Human Geography, Edinburgh, Longman,* 1966, pp. 406-414.
4. Paul Vidal de la Balache: *Principles of Human Geography*, New York, 1962, p. 316.

5. E. Ahmad: "Rural Settlement Types in Uttar Pradesh,"*Annals of the Association of American Geographers,* Vol.XLII; 1952, p. 230.
6. R.K. Mukerjee: *Man and Habitation*, London, 1940, pp. 63 64.
7. Paul Vidal de la Blache: *Op. cit.,* p. 316.
8. R.B. Hall: "Some Rural Settlement Forms in Japan," *Geographical Review,* Vol. XXI, 1931, p. 98.
9. O.H.K. Spate: "The Indian Village." *Geography,* Vol. 37, 1952, p. 148.
10. R.L. Singh: "Evolution of Settlements in the Middle Ganga Valley", *The National Geographical Journal of India,* Vol. 1, 1955, p. 104.
11. H.M. Kendall et. al: *Introduction to Geography*; Harcourt, Brace and World Inc., New York, 1967, pp. 378-383.
12. R.E. Dickinson: "Rural Settlements in the German Lands," *Annals of the Association of American Geographers,* Vol. XXXIX, 1949, p. 240.
13. M. Anass: "The Pattern of Rural Settlements in the Sub-Himalayan Region (East); *Geographer,* Vol. VI; 1954, pp. 24-25.
14. M.A. Lefevre: 'L.' *Habitat Rural in Belgique Liege*, 1924.
15. H.J. Kauming: 'L' Habitat Rural aux Pays- bas', *Tudsch Kon. Ned. Aardrs. Gen.* Vol. 55, pp. 644-45.
16. R. Martiny: 'Grundrissgestaltung der dentschen Siedlungen' Petermans Milt, 1928, p. 197.
17. Ch.L. Biermann: *Habitat Rural in Suisse Comptes Rendu,* Union Geographique International, de Paris, Section IV, pp. 17-32.
18. R.Bassauti: *'Richarche Suit tifi degli insediamenti rurali in Italia*, Cemptess Rendu, Union Geographique International de Paris, Section III, pp. 7 - 16.
19. Crijic: *La Geographie Humaine des Balkaniques*.
20. V. Mihaelescu: Une Carte de 'L' *Habitat Rural en Rumania, Comptes Rendu*, Union Geographique International, de Paris, Section III, pp.33-35.
21. Eric Wolf: "Types of Latin American Peasantry: *A Prelimi nary Discussion",American Anthropologist;* New Series, 57, 1955, pp. 452-471.
22. Paul Vidal de la Blache: *Op. cit.*, p. 300.
23. R.L. Singh: *Op. cit.*, p. 102.
24. Paul Vidal de la Blache: *Op. cit.*, p. 301.
25. V.C.Finch and G. Trewartha: *Op. cit.*, p. 544.
26. M.Chisholm: *Rural Settlement and Land Use*, London, 1952, p. 134.
27. O.H.K. Spate: *India and Pakistan*; Methuen & Co.Ltd., London, 1964, p. 507.
28. A.T.A. Learmonth: "Retrospect on a Project in Applied Geography in Mysore State, India", *Geographers and the Tropics:* Liverpool Essays (Edt. R.W. Steel and R.M. Prothero), Longman, 1964, p. 329.
29. O.H.K. Spate and C.D. Despande: "The Indian Village", *Geography,* Vol. 37, 1952, pp. 142 - 152.
30. H. Tinker: "Authority and Community in Village India", *Pacific Affairs,* Vol. 32, pp. 354-375.
31. J. Brian Wills: *Agriculture and Land Use in Ghana;* Oxford University Press, London, 1962, pp. 215-217.
32. Efraim Orni and Elisha Efrat: *Geography of Israel, Jerusalem*, 1964, pp.206-211.
33. A.L. Mabogunje: *The Development Process: A Spatial Perspective*; Hutchinson University Library, London, 1982, pp. 204 -205.
34. R.K. Udo: "Disintegration of Nucleated Settlement in Eastern Nigeria", *Geographical Review,* Vol. 55,1965, pp. 53 - 67.
35. R.K. Udo: "Transformation of Rural Settlement in British Tropical Africa", *Nigerian Geographical Journal,* Vol. 9, No. 2, 1966, pp. 129 - 144.
36. M.B. Gleave: "Hill Settlements and Their Abandonment in Tropical Africa" *Transactions of the Institute of British Geographers;* No. 40, 1966; pp. 39 - 49.

Fig. 8.1

Bihar Plain : Types of Rural Settlements

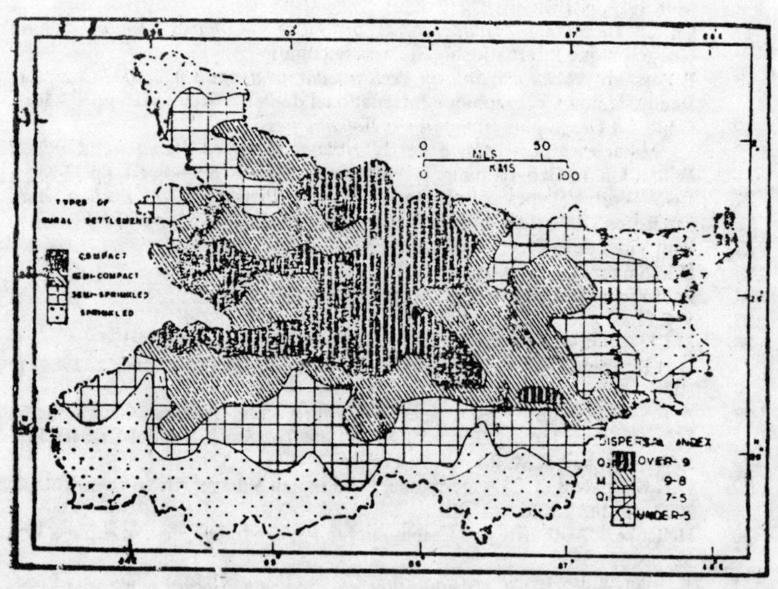

Fig. 8.2

Compact Settlements

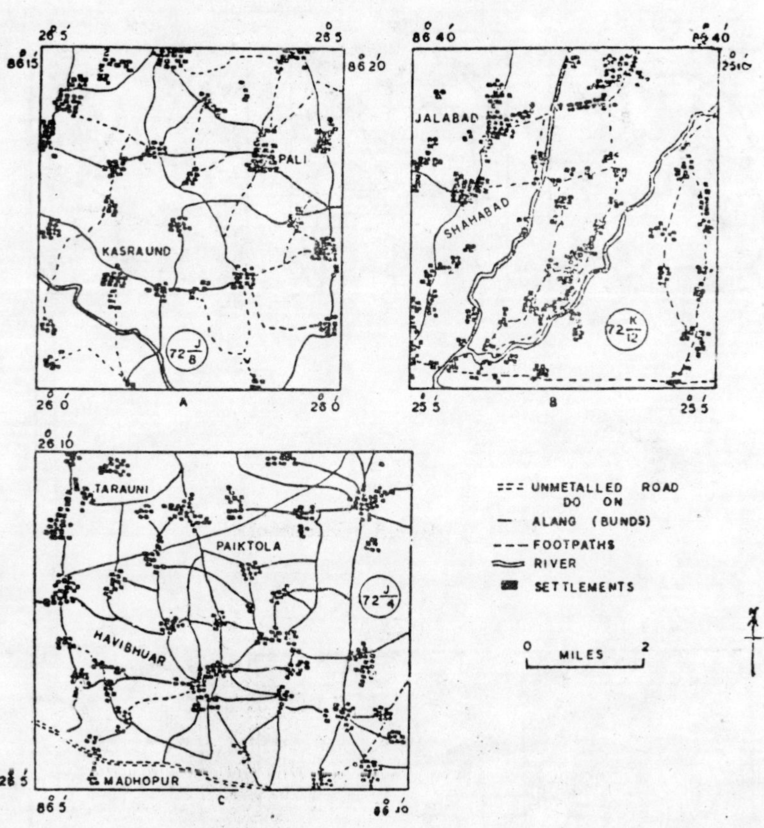

Fig. 8.3

Semi-Compact Settlements

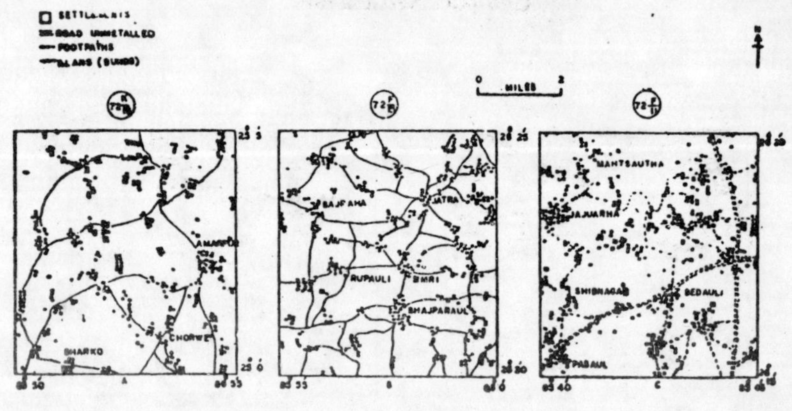

Fig. 8.4

Semi-sprinkled Settlements

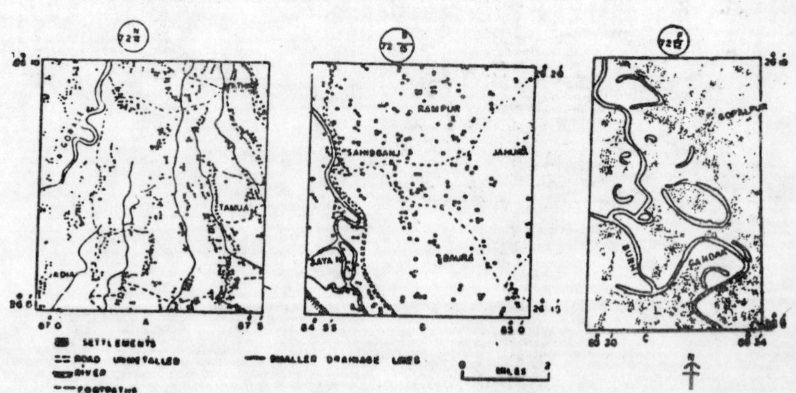

Fig. 8.5

Sprinkled Settlements

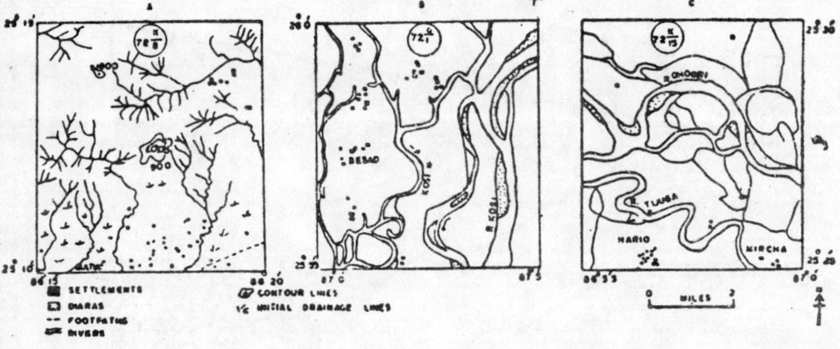

Fig. 8.6

Punjab Village Types

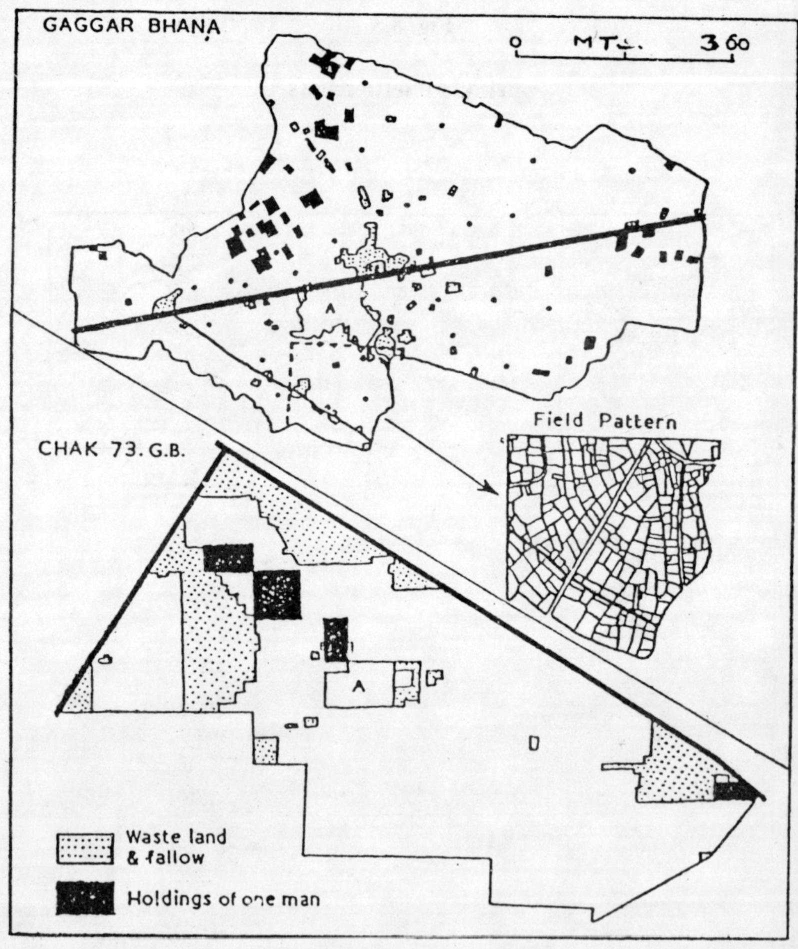

Fig. 8.7

Bengal:Settlement Patterns.

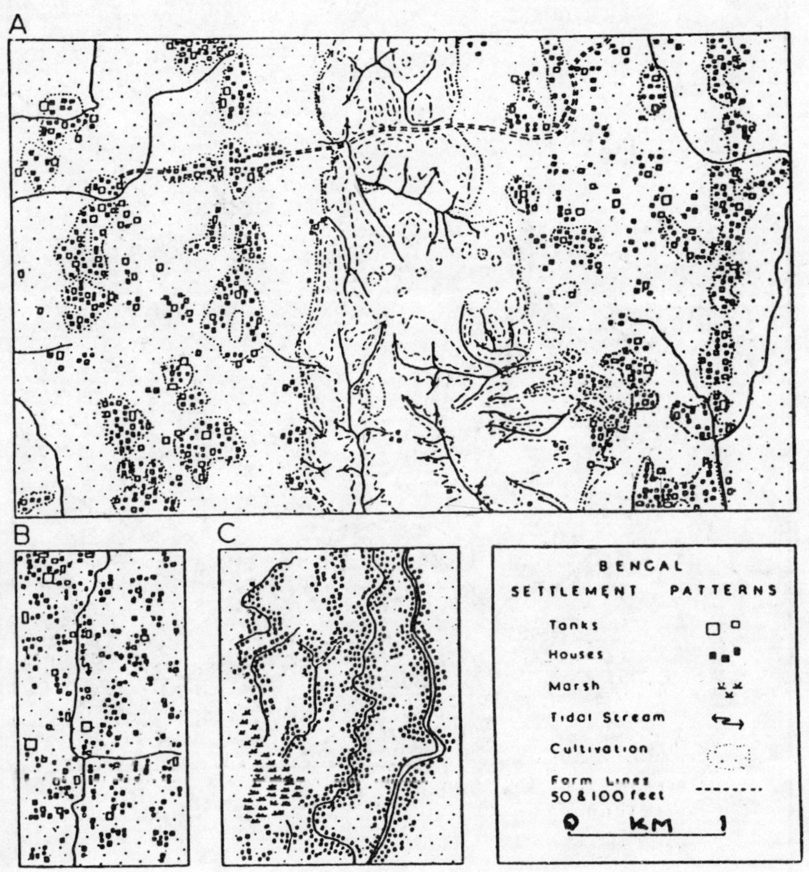

Fig. 8.8

Maharashtra : Settlement on the Lavas

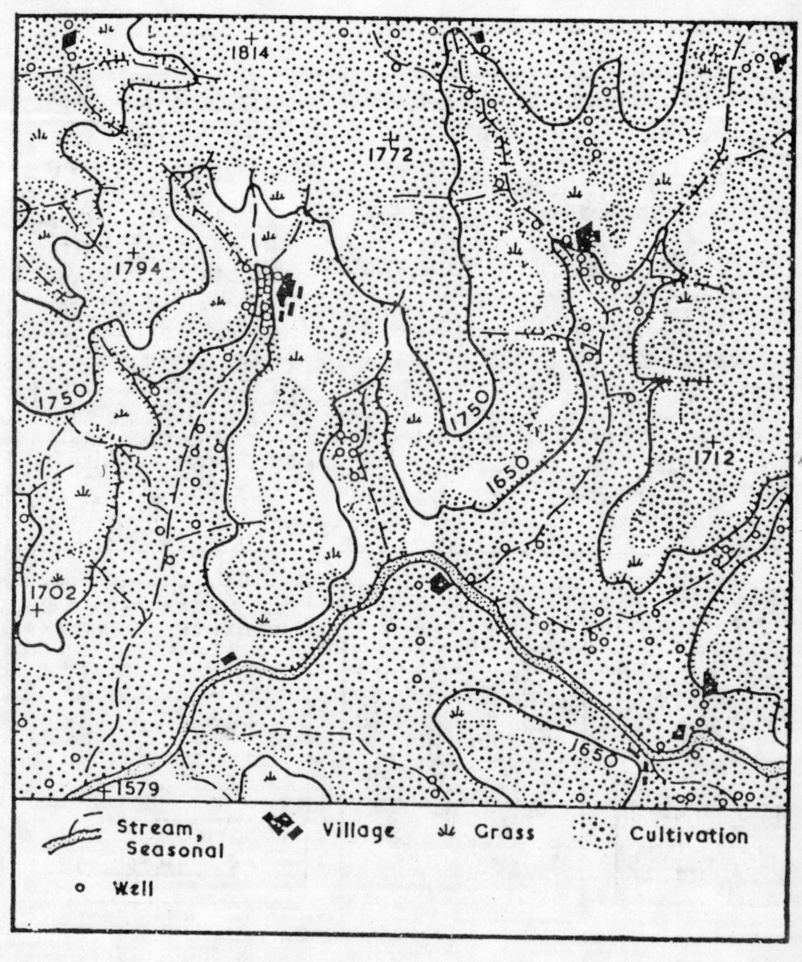

Fig. 8.9

Telangana : Settlement on the Gneisses

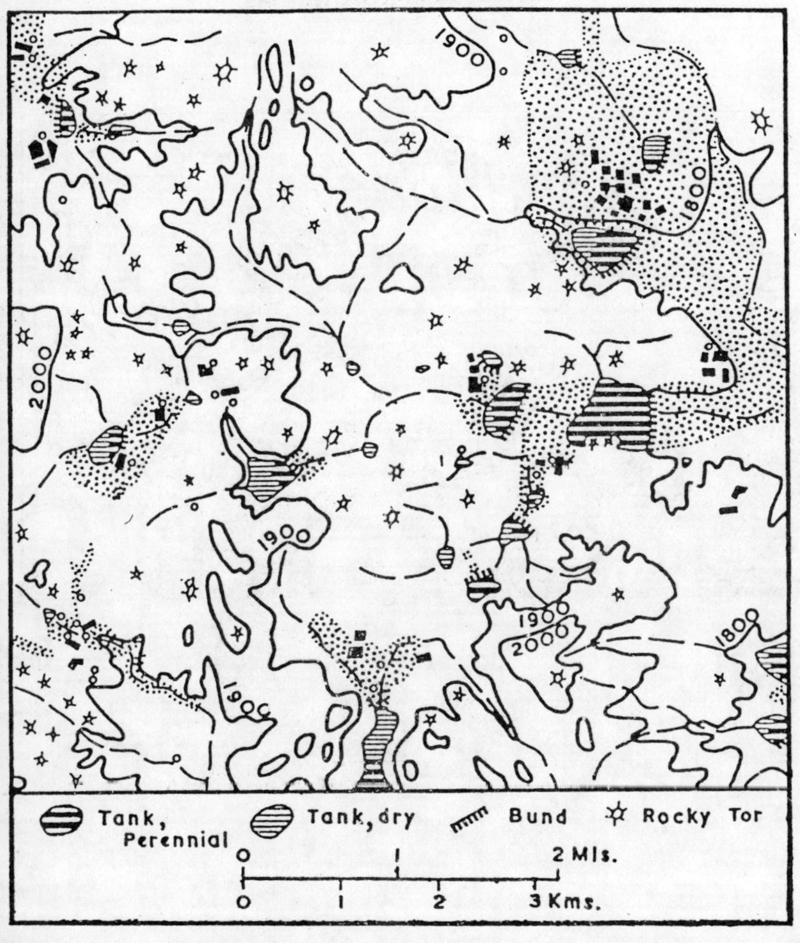

Fig. 8.10

Kerala : Inland Settlements

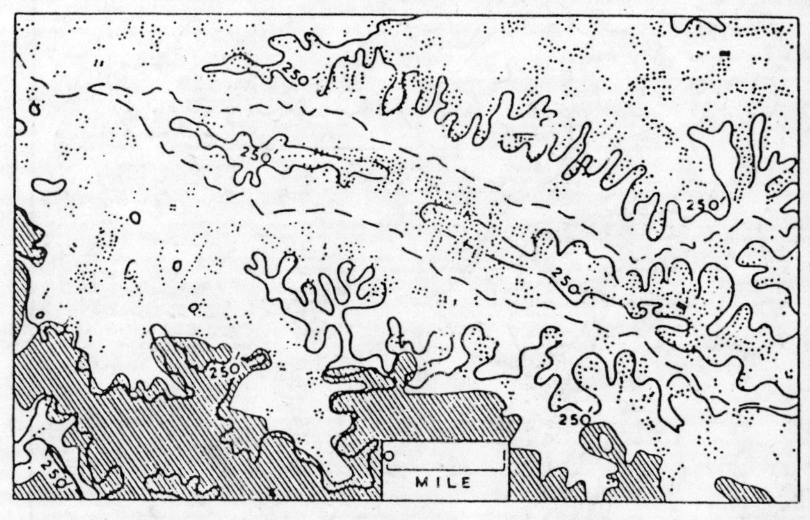

NINE

THE CONCEPT OF SATELLITE VILLAGES

Although the literature available on satellite settlements is scanty, even then a theoretical base of satellite settlements has been considered here as they are vital organs of the settlement hierarchy for rural development. In case the administration is efficient and safety is assured then satellite village is considered essential especially in fertile plain land, because such settlement pattern has greater potentiality for proper utilization of the land resources available in the surroundings intensively, besides saving the time for farming; as in compact villages much time goes waste in travelling from the place of residence of peasants to the place of work in the field (Fig. 9.1)

Generally in satellite settlements very rich people or poor agricultural labourers are residing, because due to cheaper land it is easy to find a housing site in satellite village in relation to the congested central village. In this regard, the satellite village is considered as the reserve of agricultural labourer or the paradise of the poor as well as the rich farmers in disguise.

Satellite rural settlement is a secondary or a subsidiary settlement, maintaining close links with a central settlement, of which the satellite is a part and parcel of. Satellite settlements may either be temporary or permanent. Temporary satellite settlements are common in areas engaged in animal husbandry as a supplement to arable farming. Sometimes pastures are available at several kilometres away from the main settlement site, and hence it is convenient to establish dwellings at strategic points rather than driving the herds over lengthy distances each day which may be very tiring for the livestock. The conditions in which population is increasing, the satellite settlements which are temporarily or seasonally occupied, may come to be permanently occupied, and will posses a complete independent economy, separate from the village from which they originated as the off shoot. The extreme point is when they became permanent settlements and hence succeed in overcoming the distance problem.

The 'hiving off' of excees population into new settlements is not merely a process of historical interest, but this can be witnessed even in the present day. This process is still a priority for solution to the problems of overpopulation and over concentration. In Sudan, it is normal for each village to have its cultivated land within 1.5 to 1.8 kilometres; in case of population increase, instead of expanding the settlement size of that village, a new settlement site is found some 2 to 3 kilometres away usually bearing the same name of the parent village. Thus the establishment of satellite village is the only appropriate solution here. In some cases the process of de-villagization may be the solution as in India, but in Tanzania and Algeria, devillagization would be quite contrary to the country's socio-economic and development objectives.

Logic in Favour of Satellite Rural Settlements

(1) **Production and Distance Relations:-**

The distance is important in relation to the movement of goods and people from the peasants homestead to the agricultural field in the rural sector. Time spent in such a travelling could be put to other uses, which may provide increased production for the costs in overcoming distance. The total time involved in cultivating a field for an additional hour rises with the increasing distance from the homestead or village; as the time consumed in travelling must be added to it. The return from this last hour of actual work done must be greater on the more distant plot than which is near the homestead in order to compensate for the time spent in travelling. The causes for such a long distance travel may be poor land distribution, fragmentation of holdings, too large size of farm plots, and poor access to fertile land.

Chisholm (1973) pointed out that distance should be measured in terms of time taken in travelling; as for example in south-east Nigeria the oil-Palm growers spend about one third of time they devote to farming to travel between their house and their farms.[1]

Lasson[2] obtained some rates of decline for gross and net product of farm with the increasing distance from the homestead. He came to the conclusion that it is the influence of distance, than any other factor. Table 9.1 is derived from his findings which relate to the period 1939-43.

Table 9.1:Sweden : Percentage Production in Output per Hectare for each km increase in Distance from the Farmstead

Size Group of Farms (ha.)	No. of farms	%decrease in output for 1 km increase in distance	
	-	Gross-Produce	Net Produce
10 - 20	95	4	74
20 - 40	85	9	50
over 40	47	26	46
Average	-	13	57

Source: Chisholm, M., P. 51.

The larger farms show a much more rapid decline in per unit land of gross production than small holdings. The owners of smaller farms must extract every bit of income they can from their land, and therefore tend to push production to the maximum level possible on their land. To maintain their level of gross output they must incur increasingly greater costs of inputs as the distance increases.

Ellger, M.G. (1977)[3] comes out with a graph which shows the percentage loss of working time (Fig. 9.2) with increasing distance between the homestead and the field under the assumption that the farmer spends on an average 6 hours daily on the field. Furthermore, it is assumed that the daily maximum loss of working time on the way to the field should not exceed 33%. That would be the equivalent of a 5 km radius around the village centre, covering an area of

78.5 km^2 (7850 ha.). For access to the grazing land a maximum distance of 7 km is assumed. Ellger's graph is remarkably accurate and applicable for Tanzania (Fig. 9.2). The graph clearly depicts the relationship between distance travelled and time lost.

However, there are some adjustments that farmers make to meet the exigencies of distance to reduce the costs that they incur in overcoming distance. Evidence shows that the actual level of labour input diminishes with increasing distance.

Chisholm presents Dutch study based upon observations of the amount of time actually applied to the land; with travelling time omitted. The figures are approximate and obtained from diagrams prepared by Visser (in Chisholm) showing a very marked decline in the actual labour input : (Table 9.2).

Table 9.2 : Netherlands: Man-Hours Per Annum Per Hectare Actually Worked on Plots of Over 15 Hectares:

Distance from Farmstead (kms)	Grassland Plots	Arable Plots
0.5	220	400
1.0	210	360
2.0	180	300
3.0	160	240
4.0	130	190
5.0	110	150

Source : (Chisholm. M., P.53).

It is the diminishing of the actual labour input which underlies the adjustment to distance.

There are three ways in which adjustments to distance may take place. One is that the same product may be cultivated less intensively or there may be a substitution of products towards those which are less demanding of labour.

The second adjustment is the substitution of less demanding products of greater distance; with a consequent change in the type of husbandry. This labour adjustment is more readily visible on the ground.

The third adjustment is the moving away from the village and re-settling nearer to one's field or plot as satellite settlement. The idea behind is to reduce the extreme distance from the homestead to the plots.

There are numerous cases in which the spatial distribution or crops around a village is primarily related to distance in Africa. R.M. Prothero (1953)[4] provides the following examples;

"........ the soba, in Nigeria have four important categories of land use which may be directly distinguished. Within the walls, the dwellings are intermingled with gardens or small plots where vegetable, culinary herbs and the like are grown in great profusion and apparent confusion, with careful inter planting and careful catch cropping. These require frequent visit and receive manure to enable cultivation to proceed year in year out.

Outside these walls the situation is apparently different. The situation depicts the gradual change in the methods of husbandry. The situation is as such,

"........ cropped land extends to a distance of 0.8 to 1.2 kms, fertilized with manure, and droppings of migrant cattle; growing the staple crops of Guinea corn, cotton, tobacco and groundnuts. .... beyond that again is a zone varying in width from 0.8 to 1.6 kms, which is under rotation farming .... fourth comes the heavy bush in which there are small clearings around isolated settlements, these clearings reproducing the sequence described......"[5]

From the account given by Prothero, it is evident that this arrangement arises from the problems posed by distance, coupled with the quality of topography and indeed the soils. The topography modifies the theoretical symmetry.

In Senegal, P. Pelissier[6] provides an example of an area where cotton and millet are found near the village, and fallow land along with groundnuts cultivation are found at a farther distance. The zoning of production around village is more or less in accordance with the principles of Von - Thunen. Such a pattern is influenced by the inherent qualities of the terrain.

Table 9.3 : Average Distance to Plots for Selected Countries

Country	Average Distance (km)
Belgium	0.3 - 1.0 km
Netherlands	0.3 - 1.0
Switzerland	0.3 - 1.0
France	0.3 - 2.0
West Germany	0.3 - 2.0
Bulgaria	2.0
Rumania	0.7 - 2.5
Spain	0.3 - 6.0

(Source: Douring, F. p.41) in Chisholm.

It is interesting to note that Douring, F.(1965)[7] used indirect measure to calculate the average distance for selected countries, on the basis of median village sizes and the average number of plots per person. He found the theoretical average distance to be in kms.

In Tanzania, the theoretical range of distance to agricultural plots could be about 0.5 to 5.0 kilometres. In some of the extreme cases it may be 7 to 8 kilometres or even more.

In China, J.L. Buck, (1937)[8] found that the average distance from homestead to field was 0.6 kilometres. He took a sample of 17000 farms, and perhaps this was before collectivization. It is quite apparent that the problem of distance is sufficiently high in determining the patterns of land use around villages, in all parts of the world as a common phenomenon. The impact of distance upon gross and net production is quite evident. One kilometre may be considered as a turning point beyond which the farmer may not operate efficiently and may experience decline in net returns with increasing distance from his parent village, that is his original homestead. Hence after one kilometre from the homestead the establishment of satellite villages may be beneficial for efficient farm operation.

Table 9.4 : Relationship Between Number of Satellite Settlements with Total Rural Population of the village in North Bihar, India, 1985

Village	No.of Satellite Settlements	Rural Population
Arga	3	.1270
Rambhadrapur	3	1200
Parsa	3	1250
Majrahia	3	1300
Boran	3	1500
Sarhilla	4	1400
Kharsam	4	900
Mahdewa	4	1100
Rajaur	4	1100
Parwana	4	1600
Dumra	4	2000
Karian	5	3000
Hirni	7	4000
Sonar	11	5000

Source: Field work by R.B. Mandal.

In Northern India the satellite settlements are more prominent in flood affected areas and in areas of high population density. In most cases the distance of satellite village from the parent village is one kilometre with slight fluctuating trends.

Fig. 9.3 shows the relationship of number of satellite villages with the population of the whole village in the revenue collection area in Bihar Plain. It has been found that the Pearsonian correlation value is very high r = 0.92228 and the regression value is y = 5.23x - 4.14$\pm$ e. It has been concluded that with the increasing population and decreasing number of satellite settlement the parent village is tending towards more compact whereas either on increasing or decreasing population as the number of satellite settlements is increasing the rural settlement is more and more tending towards sprinkled or dispersed pattern.

Anti-Polar concept of land use and Location of rural settlement:

This concept indicates[9] that the intensity of land use is decreasing in the form of a series of concentric ring from the centre of the village towards the periphery. This is due to the higher input, better irrigation and treble crops around the fertile productive land of the village, while on the other hand, the features on outskirts of the village, are single crop and less productive land. The extensive farming, increased area of cultivable land on outer margin is against the smaller areal extension of pole of the earth. Hence this concept earned the name as anti- polar concept of land use.

For testing the validity of this hypothesis, a village Bhalua in Saran district, Bihar has been considered here as sample study. In this village settlement area and treble cropped land have been considered as intensive land use; double cropped as semi-intensive use; orchard and waterbodies for irrigation as semi-extensive use whereas others have been considered as extensive use, beginning from the centre of the village to the outer periphery (Fig. 9.4).

In modern times, due to 'Green Revolution', the scientific way of cultivation on the outer margins of the village suggests that now this concept is losing its ground. But this proves the validity of the concept that the previous conditions of land use around the village was anti polar type from the centre of the village to the outward and the same is still continuing in traditional rural communities for most of the villages in India. But currently, in some localities the facilities of irrigation, intensive cultivation, deeper harrowing of fields by tractor, use of chemical fertilizer and compost coupled with green manure on marginal fields help in raising multiple crops, and hence the security of crop is necessary. This has given rise to satellite settlements and intensive agricultural experiment cum irrigational centre even near the fringe area of the village, and this trend is universally discernible in most developing countries of the world.

Satellite Settlements in Japan

In Japan the form of sattelite settlements or hamlets varies from tightly nucleated patterns in plains to scattered hamlets in mountainous area. About 50 per cent Japanese rural settlements can be classified as plain village, over 30 per cent as foothill village, and 20 per cent as mountain village. In the plain 'ribbon development' of rural settlements is more prominent while in mountainous areas 'lump-settlement' concentrated in various suitable siting conditions is the rule varying with the physical environment.

"According to the 1960 World Agricultural Census, the average size of Japanese farm settlements was 39 farming households and 25 non-farming households making a total of 64."[10] Hence the average Japanese satellite settlement is very small. It has been revealed, there is much communal unity in Japanese satellite settlements especially in terms of wedding, funeral, cooperation for the construction of buildings, repair of houses and on other special occasions. Their relative isolation and the frequent conflict over water rights and boundaries of common land arose among inhabitants of satellite settlements a strong 'village consciousness'. Due to small size of the satellite settlements, the life span restricted to the narrow confines where the inhabitants come into daily contact with people whom they knew very intimately. Nowadays about 23 per cent satellite settlements have the facilities of agricultural cooperatives, telephone and most of them are electrified for efficient agricultural operations and establishment of household industries. The satellite settlement shows a tight social framework in the lives of Japanese rural settlements which impose an ideal of small settlement unity and harmony.

Need of Satellite Settlements in Tanzania

As a solution to over - concentration of population and lengthy distances to fields, the appropriate and most viable solution, in Tanzania would be the establishment of satellite villages.

Prior to villagization the greater part of the population was living in scattered settlements. Due to weak economic base of the country it was impossible to provide social facilities to inhabitants of every homestead. It was also difficult to communicate effectively with each and every homestead. It was equally difficult to select regional and district crop priorities and targets. Some structural changes were required to enable the planning system to function effectively. So indeed by 1984 Tanzania saw a radical change in its spatial structure and in its spatial reorganization of rural settlements.

Scattered homesteads were reorganised and nucleated settlements were created to facilitate the objectives of rural development.

But villagization is not without problems, where a detail treatment is needed. In Tanzania, objectives of the CCM party and government were realized with the new spatial structure. But these spatial structures were not adequately planned. The assumption was that conditions in the whole country were homogenous. These conditions are climate, communication networks, land tenure system, vegetation, hydrology, topography, agricultural systems and people. But thinking in such a way was a gross mistake, what was required was a balance between the advantages of scattered settlements; or individual homesteads with the advantages of nucleated settlements, and possibly to do away with disadvantages of both. Scattered homesteads have, in many cases, better access to land, depending upon the tenure system. and also to fuelwood. The agricultural system is usually fallow which enables the natural cycling of nutrients to the soils. The soils are "recharged" naturally. But essential medical services, schools and sometimes water supplies are far away for most homesteads. So are shops, roads and market places. These are all available in nucleated settlements, which in turn have the problems of overpopulation, if not well planned, and lengthy distances to fields. It is the central village concept or the satellite village concept which so far strikes a balance. This position makes such settlements, quite necessary especially in view of existing problems of nucleated settlements.

The Central Village Concept

The central village has one or two more subsidiary villages at strategic locations in terms of:

(1) land availability,
(2) water sources,
(3) fuelwood sources, and
(4) distance to services in the central village.

There is a strong interrelationship between the subsidiary villages and the central village and in turn, between the central village and the rural growth centres (Fig.9.5). The subsidiary villages are served by the central village with a dispensary, a school, a shop, a market, a milling machine, a store, a party office, a church and a mosque, also a cemetery and a bus stop. A number of such groups are then served, in turn, with a large trading centre with a wider range of services, industries and trading centres or shops. These in turn are secondary to the district town which is the focus of whole village network. At the top is the regional town.

This structure conforms both to the general notion of decentralization as a whole, at the same time the basic interests of the farmers are given priority.

REFERENCES

1. G.K. Jambiya: The Effects of Establishing Satellite Settlements Upon Agricultural Production: *The Case of Kanyelele Village - Mwanza Region;* Dept. of Geography, University of Dar es Salaam, 1982.
2. M. Chisholm: *Rural Settlement and Land Use*; Hutchinson University Library, London, 1973.
3. M.G. Ellger: *Physical Planning for village Size and Layout in Tanzania*; Dar es Salaam, 1977.
4. R.M. Prothero: "Land Use at Soba, Zaria Province, Northern Nigeria", *Economic Geography,* Vol.33, 1953, pp.72-86.
5. M.P. Collunson: "Guidelines for the Long Term Development of Agriculture in Mwanza Region", *Mwanza Integrated Regional Planning, Project Report,* Vol. II, 1976.
6. M. Chisholm; *op.cit.*
7. *Ibid.*
8. J.L. Buck; *Land Utilization in China*, University of Chicago Press, Chapter VI, 1937.
9. R.B. Mandal: Land Utilization; *Theory and Practice;* Concept, New Delhi, 1982, pp.123-126.
10. T. Fukutake: *Japanese Rural Society*; Oxford University Press, Tokyo, 1967, p.81.

Fig. 9.1.

Conceptual View of Satellite Settlement

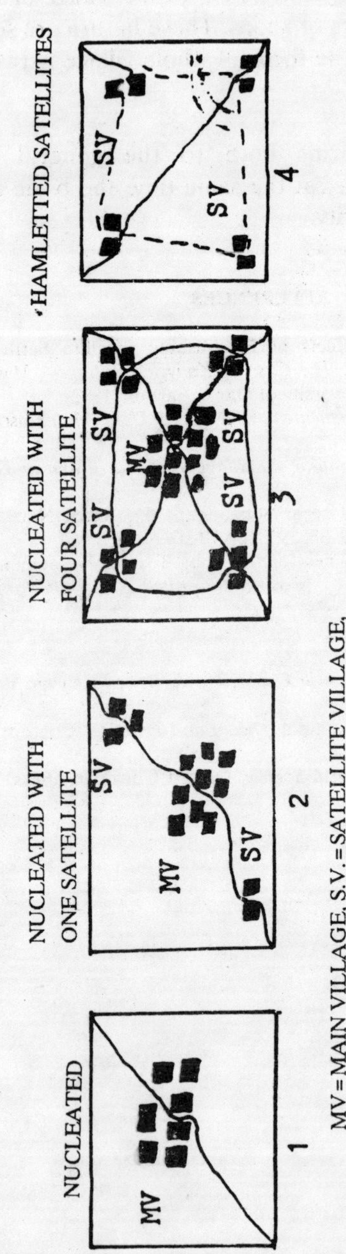

—/— - - ROAD Or FOOTPATH

1. Intensive Use of Land in Nucleated Settlement
2. Medium Use of Land in Semi Nucleated Settlement
3. Semi-Extensive Use of Land in Satellite Settlements
4. Extensive Use of Land in Hamletted Settlements

Fig. 9.2

Percentage Loss of Production in Spatio-Temporal Dimensions

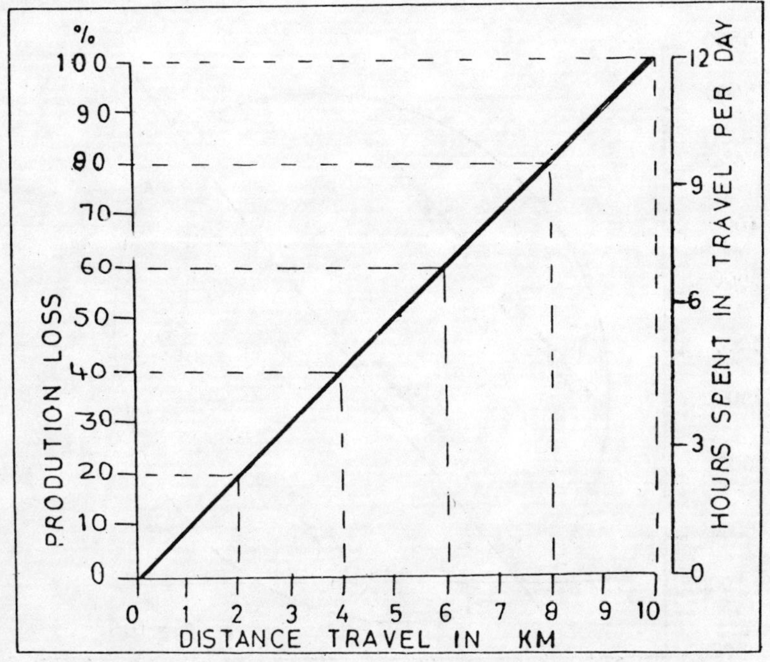

Fig. 9.3

Relationship of Number of Satellite Villages with the Total Population of the Revenue Villages in North Bihar, India

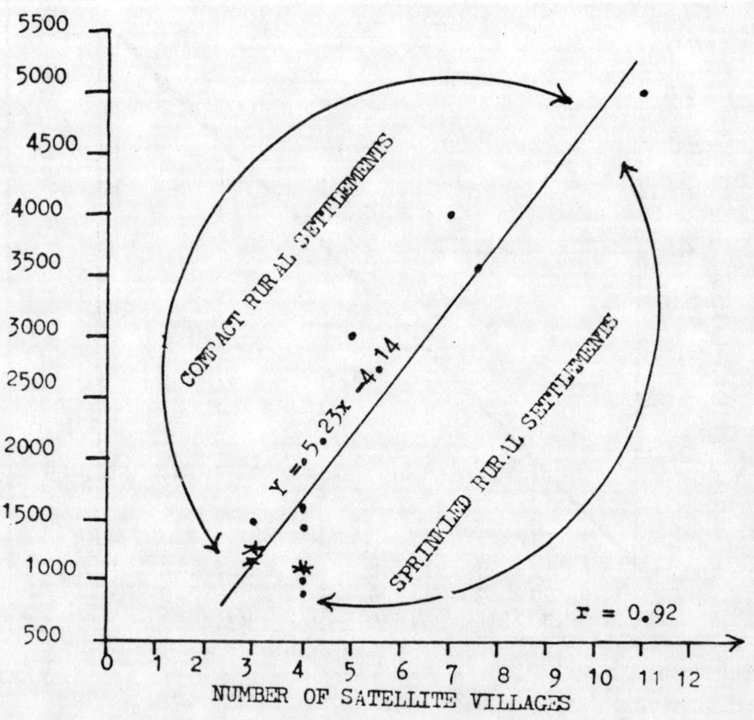

Fig. .4

Anti-polar Concept of Land Use and Location of Rural Settlement

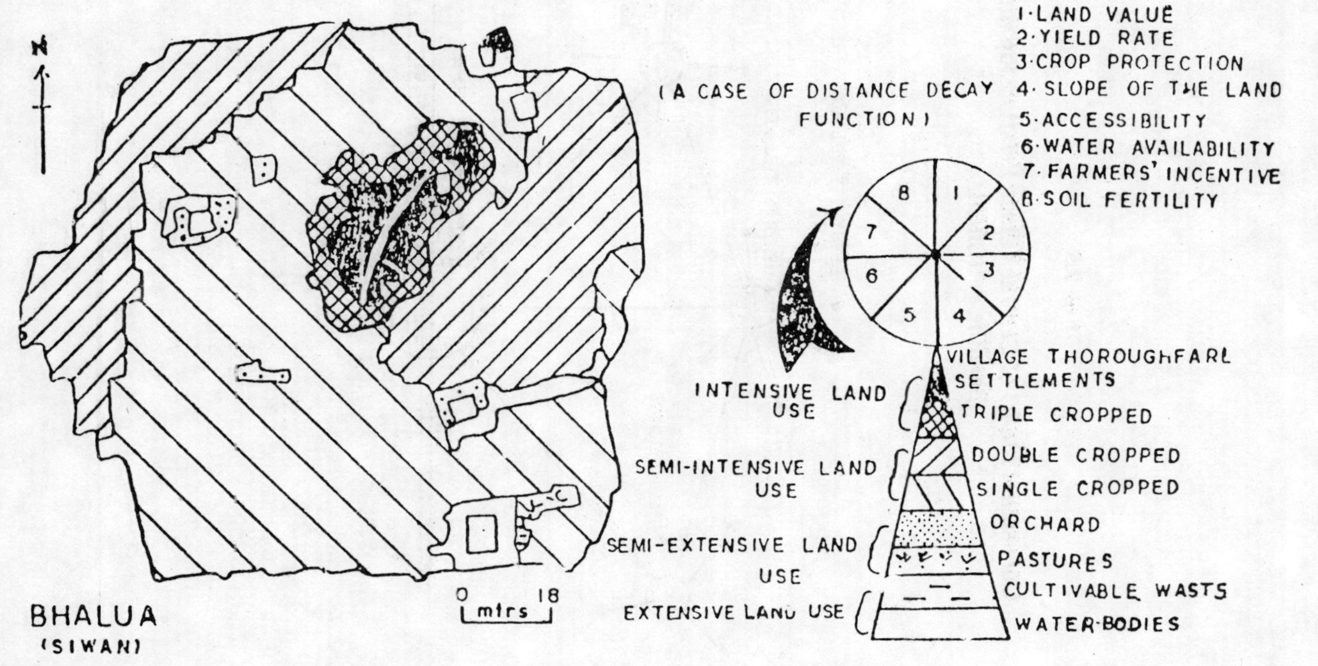

Fig. 9.5

Conceptual Model of Central Village Relationship with Satellite Settements

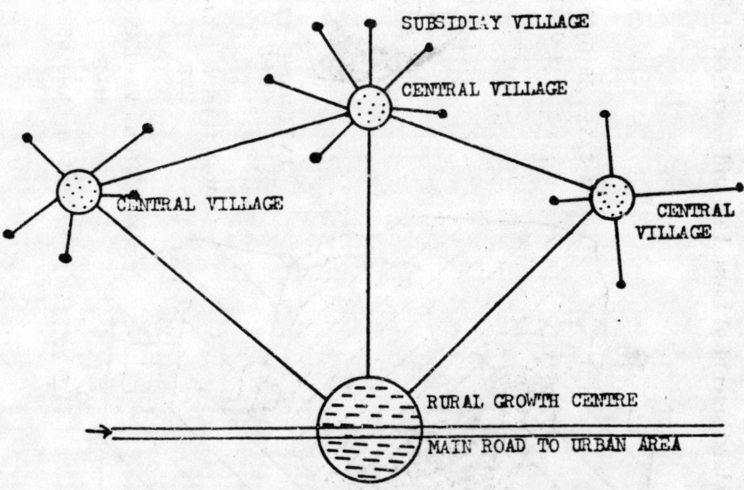

TEN

GROWTH AND DEVELOPMENT OF RURAL SETTLEMENTS IN TANZANIA

Rural settlement is a dominating cultural feature and mainstay of agricultural society in Tanzania. It is formed with the association of houses, highways, availability of water and the organization of functional space in relation to certain group of people over a definite defensible piece of land.

In 1954 Kohn talked about 'settlement ensemble' as "individual buildings and other facilities....in clusters located at focal points in the pattern of roads".[1] In 1954, G. Trewartha used the term 'settlement unit' as "an organised colony of human beings together with their houses and other buildings and the paths and streets over which they travel."[2]

Hence keeping in view the above definitions the following characteristics of rural settlements can be recognised:[3] (a) the economic area at any given time is essentially larger than that demanded by the settlement site; (b) the economic area and settlement site are directly connected with one another. It means the rural settlements of the food gatherer in the forest environment, the fishermen, the hunter and the pastoralists are the same as those of agriculturists and planters. In this way, a study of rural settlements should not include only the distribution of rural population, but a history of the settlements, the settlement function, the number and types of houses, community organization besides the size of the area occupied by settlements, and other infrastructure facilities related to a social group.

Regarding the evolutionary patterns of rural settlements Dikson (1953) has pointed out that "rural settlements of today are clearly the product of a long process of development and change associated with the changing social, economic, political and legal conditions and that their origin and development vary from one region to another".[4]

Regarding the development approach, rural development has emerged as a distinctive field of policy and practice and of research in the 1970's and 1980's especially since the inception of the 'new strategy' for development planning by World Bank and UN Agencies. This strategy came to be formulated as a result of the general disagreement with previous approaches to development planning at national and sectoral levels. It is defined by its concern with equity objectives of various kinds - especially forcing people to live in compact villages for the reduction of inequalities in income and employment, and in access to public goods and services and the alleviation of poverty.

It is this focus on distributional issues which has marked out 'rural development' as a distinct field, because an overwhelming majority of poor people in the Third World Countries and especially in Tanzania live in rural areas. The World Bank, indeed, recently defined rural development as "a strategy designed to improve the economic and social life of a specific group of people - the rural poor".[5]

This chapter aims to investigate the patterns of rural settlements growth and distribution in Tanzania with special reference to villagisation program at national, regional, district and village levels besides delineating in brief the types, patterns and regional characteristics of developed and traditional rural settlements.

According to the compactness of houses the rural settlements are of four types:[6]

(a) compact or nucleated,
(b) semi-compact or semi-nucleated,
(c) semi-sprinkled or hamletted, and
(d) sprinkled or Dispersed.

When the houses in the settlement site are found very close to each other without any satellite settlement, then the same is known as compact settlement. On the northern fringe of Dar es Salaam Matongani village is an example of compact rural settlement.

If the houses in the village are found not so close but having one central nucleation and other one or more satellite settlements then the same is known as semi-compact settlement. South-east of Biharamulo at four kilometres away Rubondo is an example of semi-compact settlement.

In case the houses are distributed in a village in such a fashion that it is not easy to identify the central part of the village, then it is known as semi-sprinkled settlement. The pattern may be linear as Kimwani on lake Victoria or amorphous as Luhama south-east of Biharamulo.

When the settlements are rarely found here and there either due to high slopes, forest environment, semi-desert or desert conditions and the area highly prone to floods thenit experiences dispersed living in Tanzania. Areas infested with *tse-tse* flies and the land having stony waste ground are also less attractive to people, as for example dispersed living of the Miombo woodland of west central Tanzania. An example of dispersed village is Rwangati on the Rwangati mountain slopes near Kabilikiliro bay of Lake Victoria.

Trends of Development

In Tanzania before Independence in 1961 most of the people in rural areas, who did not have a fixed abode from one generation to another as they practised shifting cultivation were living in forests. Hence, it created a tendency of scattered, frequently moving households and not settled village communities. Neither the provision of basic services e.g., health, education, pure water; of economic infrastructure such as roads, godowns, small scale irrigation and forestation, nor of inputs such as improved seeds, extension services and fertilizer could go very far within the limits of household and the shifting residence imposed by the pre-colonial long cycle rotation agricultural system. By this way "we shall be able to develop our land and to raise our standard of living. We shall not be able to use tractors, provide schools for our children, build hospitals, or have clean drinking water. If we do not start living in proper village communities then all our attempts to develop the country will be just so much wasted effort".[7]

After independence, in order to change the aforesaid situations the government of Tanzania started 'village settlement schemes' in the name of 'Ujamaa village' in Five Year Plans. This scheme was a self-help program under which people residing in dispersed settlements and practising shifting cultivation should settle at selected housing site in the form of compact and semi-compact villages. This scheme of rural housing development is more or less the Ghana's roof loan scheme, the Sudan's cooperative and comprehensive rural development projects in al Jezirah ; the rebuilding of villages through self-help in Liberia; Kenya's site and service scheme; India's many projects such as village redevelopment on the model of Shamspur, homesteading and rural housing lots; and Pakistan's recent 'five marlas' scheme of house lots for rural poor. These are only some of the examples that can be cited to substantiate the point about the variety of ongoing programmes in different parts of the world like villagization in Tanzania.

Ujamaa villages: An Integrated Rural Development Approach

In terms of development from below, Ujamaa (familyhood) policy has multipurpose objectives such as political unit, social unit and economic unit. From economic consideration, the "village and ujamaa Act" of 1975 indicated about two types of rural settlements in Tanzania: the traditional African villages and the Ujamaa villages. The latter in some places called "registered Ujamaa Villages" and in others 'permanent', 'planned' or 'development' villages.[8] According to 1975 Act, one village will house at least 250 families within specific boundary. The villagers will organise under a cooperative with self-government by a village council elected by a village assembly of all adult members of the village. The council's duty is to see day-today administration, promote development, encourage cooperation, undertake village planning besides coordinating various activities of the village. In these villages although cooperative communal farming will be encouraged but the council will guide private ownership of production also. The supply of machinery, the development of small-scale industry and other major services e.g. fetching loan through cooperative chain, purchase and supply of inputs and the provision of local shopping/marketing centres will be provided communally.

For the integrated development of Ujamaa Village it is necessary to have sufficient land for cultivation by the peasants so that they can raise both subsistence and cash crops for the next 20 years. Hence after leaving aside the traditional mode of living and agricultural practices, now peasants are adopting modern technological innovations, fertilizers, insecticides and irrigation for good agricultural produce. But the high yield of crops depends on other factors such as seeds, correct methods and timing of planting, weeding and harvesting. All these require the proper analysis of ecological conditions in order to select the variety of seeds, fertilizer besides other factors. Hence, at this juncture farmers require the assistance of agricultural extension workers. As for example Ilonga Research Station experiments with maize, Lyamungo does coffee research, Ukiluguru does work with cotton and Mlingano for sisal. The research stations for animal husbandry are Uyole and Mpwapwa which aim at better animal husbandry.

Like traditional settlement, the success of Ujamaa policy is highly dependent on the availability and supply of water for both agricultural and domestic use. The supply of water is essential in order to utilise women labour force in more productive work than devoting much time in collecting water for domestic use. In different environmental conditions different sources of irrigation should be searched.

The control of vermin and crop is quite essential in rural development process. As the existence of a certain pest follows ecological zones the peasants of those areas will be in a better position to fight against them communally when they live in social groups of Ujamaa.

Recently, the formation of new compact rural settlements become the keynote of Tanzania's agrarian development. The bases of such a consideration are the desire to reduce population pressure from high density areas of the Kilimanjaro, the Pare, the Usambara mountains' and some parts of the southern Highlands by the shifting of some villages in lowland areas. It has been felt essential in order to provide social services and infrastructure facilities cheaply to a large number of people. Secondly, over greater parts of Tanzania the traditional settlement type is of scattered or dispersed type. Hence in order to provide good service facilities in a planned way in 1962 Nyerere noted that:

> 'Before we can bring any benefits of modern development to the farmers of Tanganyika, the very first step is to make it possible for them to start living in village communities'.

It has been felt that "Ujamaa villages have come to pursue not only the path of Ruvuma schemes but also that of all the earlier rural development policies."[9] It can be said that the Ujamaa village conception is a combination of the 'improvement approach', the "transformation approach" and "the cooperative schemes of Ruvuma". The transformation approach for its part has contributed to villagization dimension and in implementation the Ujamaa village has in many cases been seen as a 'resettlement project'.

Luttrell[10] argues that the Uajamaa village policy stresses three interlinked facts:-

(a) new settlements to introduce modern techniques of production;

(b) new permanent compact planned villages to conform to a grid pattern streets, and

(c) ideal social relations of production which are based upon community property holdings. In this way, the Ujamaa Vijijini programme is regarded as a vehicle for socialist rural transformation.

Village Settlement Schemes

In Tanzania, the unsuccessful operation of the 'land development' and 'soil conservation schemes' as well as 'focal point approach' from which only the rich large scale farmers benefitted paved way for the World Bank recommendation in 1962 to transform peasant agriculture through settlement schemes. It would involve a change to mechanized methods and a break with traditional social structures. But the main beneficiaries were spatially concentrated privileged group of farmers who intended to get success through the roads of transformation to modernization.

In Tanzania, some areas have developed Ujamaa living spontaneously by people who adhered to socialist principles. Others old settlement schemes were 'taken over' by the government, and third groups of villages were established under 'Ruvuma Development Association' in southern Tanzania. In many cases old settlement schemes were rebaptised between 1968-1969, such as Upper Kitete and Kerege. In other areas some progressive farmers established cooperative system in agricultural development and marketing of their produce such as in Bukoba, Kilimanjaro, Arusha, Takuyu and Lushoto. In some literature they have been termed 'Kulak-Ujamaa'.[11]

This is because it has been stated that if farmers could not be forced or persuaded, the only alternative is to ignore them altogether and go for mechanized agriculture with the help of outsiders as 'groundnut scheme' and 'settler farms' by Europeans or to take them away from the traditional surroundings to settlement schemes where in return for receiving land they might agree to follow the instructions of the agricultural staff. As with the 'Meru Land Case' when the authorities tried to resettle the landless Meru peasants, the first settlement scheme by the Government of Tanzania was started on the abandoned land cleared for the groundnut scheme at Urambo and Nachingwea. Successively about 23 schemes were started with high capital investment, paid high wages and in order to have close supervision and to learn modern farming practices. Apart from these projects, most of the unofficial settlements were established as cooperative farms by members of TANU Youth League in the spirit of 'building a nation'.[12]

The First Five Year Plan (1964-1969) proposed the establishment of 74 model village settlement schemes of about 250 families. The execution of the program was the concern of the village settlement Agency. In 1965 the Agency was working on 23 settlements, whereby 8 schemes were designed as pilot projects so as to gain experience in planned resettlement and developing modern agricultural techniques. The three Israeli Schemes were located around Mwanza, and seven others by the Tanganyika Agricultural Corporation were distributed in different parts of Tanzania (Fig. 10.1). The Five Year Plan suggested two model layouts for the villages: "either in a single, large village around a service centre or two to three smaller satellite villages grouped around a common service centre".[13]

Growth and Development of Villagization

The decisive impetus to the villagisation movement came from the Arusha Declaration and the ideological foundations laid down in Nyerere's "Socialism and Rural Development" in 1967. Uptil now the progress towards villagisation has been uneven but the recent shift is truly encouraging (Table 10.1).

TABLE 10.1 : Trends of the Growth of Ujamaa Villages in Tanzania

Year	Number of Ujamaa Villages	Population
1967	48	5,000
1969	809	10,000
1970	1,956	531,200
1971	4,644	1,545,240
1972	5,556	1,980,962
1973	5,628	2,028,164
1981	7,750	14,874,522
1983	8,187	15,060,926
1984	8,200	15,869,205

Source: Prime Minister of Tanzania Office, Dodoma, 1975 and 198? 1984 figure is estimated.

The progress in villagisation after 1965 Arusha Declaration was slow, as for example in 1967 the number of Ujamaa villages were only 48 with a total population of 5000. But in 1968 with the call to 'go to Ujamaa' raised the number of villages to 809 in 1969, 5556 in 1972 and 8187 in 1983 representing over 90 percent of the rural population. The average number of residents per village increased from 272 in 197? to 511 in 1974, and 1919 in 1980-81. So far as the regional variation in villagisation is concerned highest number of villages 643 is found in Mwanza Region and the lowest 47 in Dar es Salaam Region due to its urban characteristics (Table 10.2).

TABLE 10.2 : Number of Ujamaa Villages in Tanzania upto December, 1983

Sr.No.	Region	Total Number of villages	Number of Ujamaa villages	% of Total
1.	Arusha	463	457	99
2.	Dar es Salaam	47	47	100
3.	Dodoma	423	423	100
4.	Iringa	593	593	100
5.	Kagera	505	505	100
6.	Kigoma	222	218	99
7.	Kilimanjaro	372	349	94
8.	Lindi	362	362	100
9.	Mara	348	340	97
10.	Mbeya	577	571	99
11.	Morogoro	459	425	93
12.	Mtwara	489	489	100
13.	Mwanza	643	643	100
14.	Pwani	355	352	99
15.	Rukwa	304	304	100
16.	Ruvuma	313	312	99
17.	Shinyanga	628	589	93
18.	Singida	323	311	96
19.	Tabora	375	365	98
20.	Tanga	538	536	99
	Total	8339	8187	98

Source: Principal Secretary, Prime Minister's Office Dodoma, September, 1984.

Table 10.2 shows that 98 per cent rural settlements of Tanzania have already come into the fold of Ujamaa living upto 1983. This also highlights that the progress of villagisation programme is quite satisfactory and there is always hope that slowly and perceptibly the standard of the villages will improve.

In Tanzania, in the last few years emphasis has shifted away from communal production to block farming in which peasants cultivate their own plots within an overall block of land allocated to the village and on individual holdings within a village framework. This should be seen in terms of a sequence of stages eventually leading upto fully cooperative villages. In reality, such a "step-by-step transformation" was explicitly foreseen individuals. Nyerere's 'Socialism and Rural Development' (1967):

"Where necessary then, progress can be made in three stages. The First may be to persuade people to move their houses into a single village, if possible near water, and to plant their next year's food crops within easy reach of the area where the houses will be... For another step is to persuade a group of people perhaps the members of a ten-house cell - to start a small communal plot on which they work cooperatively, sharing the proceeds at harvest time according to the work they each have done...Once these two steps had been effected, the final stage would come when the people have confidence in a community farm, so that they are willing to invest all their effort in it, simply keeping gardens around their own houses for special vegetable, etc. Then the socialist village would be really established and other productive community activities can get underway".[14]

Hence 'almost all the help which government can give in the way of tractors, improved houses, and rural water supplies, will be concentrated on these new village settlement schemes (Smith, 1966, p.361). [15] This means that most of our farming would be done by groups of people who live as a community and work as a community. "They would live together in a village, to cultivate farm together, market together and undertake the provision of local services and small local requirements as a community" (Nyerere, 1968, 351).[16]

Density and Size of Settlements

In Tanzania, the density of rural population per square kilometre varies from 66 in Mwanza region to 6 in Tabora. On the basis of Quartile and Median the country has been divided into four regions. The high population density regions are found around lake Victoria, Kilimanjaro, Central mountains besides Dar es Salaam and Mtwara. Medium high density areas are found around lake regions of Kigoma, Shinyanga, Mara, Coastal region of Tanga, capital region of Dodoma besides the highland of Mbeya.

In all these areas, population density varies from 33 to 16 persons per km^2. Entire central parts of Tanzania except mountainous regions come under low density below 16 persons per km^2. It includes Morogoro, Iringa, Singida, Lindi, Ruvuma, Rukwa and

Tabora. The factors which generally affect the density of population are agricultural and industrial developments, availability of drinking water, suitable landscape available for settlement siting and the salubrious climatic conditions for the growth of plants and providing habitable environment to the people.

In Tanzania, the population progressions (Table 10.3) show that the growth of urban population would be more rapid than rural. This is due to the massive natural growth and increased dimension of rural-urban migration. It means the growth and expansion of urban areas shall continuously reduce the spatial dimensions of rural areas, but on the other hand urban centres may diffuse urban economic and social components to rural areas. Hence the population supporting capacity of the rural area will improve automatically. Hence it should be our motto to enhance the construction of planned rural communities so that in future it may match up with the urban environment without any physical obstruction.

Table 10.3 : Estimated Rural and Urban Population in Tanzania in thousands (1978 - 2000)

Year	Total	Rural	Urban	Urban as % of Total
	17,512.6	15,095.7	2,412.9	13.8
1980	18,178.0	15,413.0	2,763.0	15.2
1981	18,778.0	15,822.0	2,956.0	15.7
1982	19,398.0	16,235.0	3,163.0	16.3
1983	20,038.0	16,654.0	3,384.0	16.9
1984	20,699.0	17,078.0	3,621.0	17.5
1985	21,341.0	17,466.0	3,875.0	18.2
1990	25,114.0	19,680.0	5,434.0	21.6
1995	29,684.0	22,062.0	7,622.0	25.7
2000	34,815.0	24,125.0	10,690.0	30.7

Source: Derived from 1978 Census assuming total population growing at 3.3% per annum and urban population at 7 per cent per annum.

In Tanzania, average population size of rural settlements varies from 2633 the bigger one to 1314 the smaller. The median value is 1736 persons per village. The high population size areas of Mwanza and kigoma regions are flood affected; Kilimanjaro is mountainous whereas Dodoma lies in semi-desert environment. The low population size regions are Lindi, Mtwara, Iringa and Rukwa. Areas having occasional floods and drought may have bigger rural settlements size, whereas the areas having excessive flood and drought are more prone to scattered and lower population size settlements (Fig. 10.2).

Table 10.4 shows that in Tanzania, the majority of villages lie in the size categories of 500 to 5000 population in 1978. The highest number of villages is 3930 lies in the size category of 1000 to 2000 persons per village. The Zanzibar and Pemba islands of Tanzania also denote the same population size distribution of villages. Villages are more evenly scattered in Pemba than on Zanzibar Island. Even in the tiny villages there is a mosque, a school and a shop or two.

In any region, the density of rural settlements is governed by four factors e.g. agricultural development, availability of drinking water in the nearby areas, development of road transport and productive defensible terrain with more equable climatic conditions. On the basis of Quartile and Median, the rural settlements of Tanzania have been divided into four categories: high density areas, medium high density areas, medium low density areas and low density areas. It shows that above median value of .010 rural settlements per square kilometre, the areas are relatively more dense in terms of rural settlements and comprises areas around lake Victoria, Tanga, Kilimanjaro, Dar es Salaam and Mtwara. The road leading to Morogoro-Dodoma, besides the centrally located mountains of Uluguru and Ushambara's are comparatively densely settled due to cooler climate and healthy mountainous environment (Fig. 10.3).

Semi-Pastoralist Rural Settlements of Sukuma People

Sukuma's a dominant tribe lives in Mwanza Region of Tanzania, southern side of lake Victoria. Their main profession is to grow cotton, maize and rearing cow.

In such a situation each homestead in Sukumaland has a thorn hedge surrounding the house. Within the hedge they are making houses for the whole family with a separate boma for the cattle besides grain store. Beyond this area is a little meadow where the calves graze and firewood stored. This is followed by fields for growing crops which are generally separated by either walls of milk-weed or a small fallow/grazing land. Several such homesteads form a village (Fig. 10.4).

Pastoralist: Rural Settlements of Masai People

Masai is a dominant tribe of semi-arid parts of northern Tanzania. They occupy the land between Mount Kilimanjaro on the east and Lake Manyara, and the Rift Valley on the west. One Masai family owns at least 150 to 500 cows. In case 10 to 20 families live together then they are facing problem of getting good pasture ground for their cattle. Masai is making Kraal a semi-permanent settlement site on the high but slopy ground after fencing withthorny bushes cut from the scrub of the Savanah (Fig. 10.5).

Such a hedge guards both people and their cattle from lions at night. They make houses with thin branches of plants and trees collected from savanah thickets. After lassing the thin branches with each other, they are thatching the house with grass and plaster it with clay and cow dung, in order to make it water proof. Thus Masai collects branches of small trees for both thorn fence and for the home, but such a hut is generally constructed by women.

Table 10.5 shows that due to migratory trend the number of pastoral settlements and population of Masai are giving a fluctuating trend Ngorongoro area of Tanzania in between 1957 - 1980. The lowest number of villages (215) was in 1957. Since then it was increasing upto 1977 but later on, the number of villages declines due to instructions of the government to live in big compact Ujamaa villages. In case of pastoral population from 1957 to 1970 it gives a declining trend but from 1974 to 1980 it was constantly increasing due to the effect of villagisation program which almost establishes the transhumans life of the Masai in relatively large permanent settlements (Fig. 10.6).

Table 10.6 shows that in northern Tanzania there are seven pastoral zones but the carrying capacity of population per village is very small 10 to 30 persons. This also shows that the carrying capacity of the land is very small because Masai pastoralist generally rear a big herd of cattle which needs a big area of grazing land besides some cultivation in a semi-arid Masai lands. In such a situation, in order to have a proper sustenance of both livestock and people it is better to have a smaller population size of settlements.

Table 10.4 : Distribution of Villages ++ By Region and Size in Tanzania (1978)

REGION	SIZE CLASS Less than 200	200 to 499	500 to 999	1000 to 1999	2000 to 4999	5000 to 9999	Total
Dodoma	-	4	54	178	184	5	425
Arusha	-	3	48	220	154	2	427
Kilimanjaro	-	3	26	143	192	3	367
Tanga	-	23	135	250	127	-	535
Morogoro	-	16	99	217	128	4	464
Coast	2	21	108	149	51	3	334
Dar es Salaam	1	5	15	27	4	1	53
Lindi	-	2	52	131	85	-	270
Mtwara	-	6	116	263	76	-	461
Ruvuma		-	54	141	96	4	295
Iringa	-	18	138	292	115	-	563
Mbeya	-	3	80	326	166	-	575
Singida	-	3	23	185	92	-	303
Tabora	-	7	61	176	123	3	370
Rukwa	-	5	42	120	47	2	216
Kigoma	-	3	6	53	149	6	217
Shinyanga	-	11	62	270	276	4	623
Mwanza	1	1	30	276	192	2	502
Kagera	-	-	53	320	269	2	644
Mara	-	2	25	193	123	3	346
MAINLAND (TOTAL)	4	136	1227	3930	2649	44	7990
North	-	-	22	16	13	-	51
Central	-	1	31	19	1	-	52
West	-	-	11	9	2	1	23
Pemba North	-	-	1	3	13	6	23
Pemba South	-	-	4	5	12	6	27
ZANZIBAR (TOTAL)	-	1	69	52	41	13	176

Source: Bureau of Statistics

++As defined under the 1975 village Act.

Ilomba Village: A Small holders Rural Settlement

Ilomba village is situated 15 kilometres east of Mbeya town along the main road to Dar es Salaam, one kilometre north-west of Uyole Agricultural Centre. The village has 143 households with a population of 700 in 1979. The crops grown are maize, wheat, peas, potato, pyrethrum, sorghum, millet and variety of vegetables. The villagers rear and keep some livestock also.

Ilomba people are Safwa tribe intermixed with the Nyakyusa and Kinga. The Safwa tribe is indigenous of Mbeya district. They were invaded by the Nyakyusa and forced to occupy the mountain slopes of the Mbeya ranges. The villagers are mostly peasants with barely a few employed by the Uyole Agricultural Centre (Fig. 10.7).

Table 10.5 : Trends of Masai Pastoral Settlements in Ngorongoro, Tanzania

Year	Number of Pastoral Villages	Number of Pastoral Population
1957	215	10,633
1960	220	9,573
1961	216	9,239
1966	300	8,728
1968	384	7,569
1970	600	5,435
1974	722	12,645
1977	791	16,705
1978	700	17,982
1980	690	18,524

Source: N.C.A.A. and estimated.

Table 10.6: Pastoral Zones of Ngorongoro, Tanzania, 1977

Pastoral zones	Pastoral Persons per village
Kakesio	30.8
Endulen	18.4
Olairobi	28.4
Oldoinyo ogol	29.6
Melenda	24.6
Nairobi+	15.9
Kapenjero	10.6

Source: After Kaj Arhem, BRALUP 1981, p. 46.
+ Estimated figure.

In Ilomba village one can observe three types of settlement infrastructure. In the first category are those houses which act as service provision centres. These are staff quarters of TAZARA railway. The second category houses are institutional centres such as school, CCM office and the social centre. In third category comes the residential houses for the villagers. The houses are constructed along the lava plateau. The houses are not evenly distributed. The central and western part of the plateau are densely settled because during 'operation sogeza' people had to look for places that are near to their mountain farm plots.

In the first and second categories of houses the material of wall is brick and the material of roof is corrugated iron sheets. The villagers house on the other hand has materials of wall timber plastered with mud and the roof is thatched with grasses. These building materials are available locally, as every villager has 0.8 hectare of eucalyptus and cypress trees on lava plateau and mountain slopes respectively.

Besides these houses one can notice some wooden cylindrical structures smeered with cow dung outside villagers' house. These are silos in which grain is stored after harvest. In Ilomba it can also be observed that the type of housing reflects the general income of the people. This village is strategically located and has well developed transport network. This is potentially promising for both agricultural and commercial activities.[17]

CHEKERENI: UJAMAA VILLAGE

Chekereni is located 20 kilometres south of Moshi town in Moshi Rural District of the Kilimanjaro Region in Northern Tanzania. It is a part of the Lower Moshi Irrigation Project on the southern rear end slope of Mount Kilimanjaro. The village lies between 3° 26' - 3° 27' latitude south of Equator and between 37° 22' - 37° 24' longitude east of Greenwich. The village is surrounded by Mabogini village in the north, Rau village in the east, Matakuja village in the west, and Kahi village on the south.

The village was established in 1970 with 32 families - under the national policy of Ujamaa and self-reliance as laid down by Arusha Declaration of 1967. Before 1970, the area was covered by bushland. In 1984 the village has a total population of 3100, showing an admix-

ture of 17 tribes which are as follows:
Chagga, Luguru, Kikuyu, Gogo, Taita, Fipa, Nyamwezi, Zigua, Haya, Pare, Sukuma, Makonde, Kamba, Nyiramba, Kurya, Sambaa and Rangi. Some of these tribes have been attracted to this village in order to avoid the high pressure of population on the slopes of Kilimanjaro and others have joined in response to the party's call to form Ujamaa village. Many families anticipated better income and improved life through hardwork in the Ujamaa village. They also thought that it is easier to get assistance from the government if they live and work together in Ujamaa village.

The village government contains five committees such as:

a. finance and planning,
b. works and transport,
c production and marketing,
d defence and security, and
e health and social welfare.

Village Land Use

The total area of Chekereni is about 1400 hectares; which are put under a systematic land use programme, although the programme changes from year to year depending upon villagers objectives. For 1984 the village land use is shown in the following Table 10.7.

Table 10.7: Chekereni Land Use: 1984

Sr. No.	Description	Area in Hectare	%
1.	Collective farm	101.2	7.22
2.	Pasture land	248.1	17.71
3.	Forest area	3.2	0.23
4.	Individual farms	849.9	60.68
5.	Residential area	141.6	10.11
6.	Schools, Churches, shops	16.2	1.15
7.	Reserve area	40.47	2.89

Source: Chekereni Implementation Report; 1984.

It is quite evident that the area under communal farm which is 7.22% of the total area of the village is a relatively small area in comparison with 700 households in the village. For high level productivity it should be at least 50 per cent of the total area.

Settlement Patterns

Chekereni Ujamaa village has plans (Fig. 10.8) of having similar settlement patterns throughout its six wards, that is square pattern. About 75 per cent houses are made of mud and wattle and roofed with corrugated iron sheets. Most of the houses cover an area of 35 square metres with 2 rooms and a small kitchen shade. Windows in the houses are of 30 cm x 50 cm small size and most of the houses contain 4 windows. The height of the houses vary from 2.5 metres to 4 metres. The average number of persons in a household is 5 but it goes up to 15 in some cases.

The village has a programme of improved housing for the villagers. The Tanzania Housing Board agreed to give loan to the villagers and the following housing design (Fig. 10.9) has been approved for construction. There are many water taps in the village, besides each and every house has pit latrine.

Most of the villagers are peasants. Kilimanjaro Agricultural Development Centre (KADC) is an irrigation project which is located in Chekereni village as part of the Regional Integrated Development Programme (RIDEP) which is currently operating in all regions of Tanzania. The KADC is involved in developing agriculture for the command area of Lower Moshi irrigation project. The village needs road development, dispensary and proper credit facilities to the peasants for its proper planning. However, it comes in the list of most developed villages in Tanzania.

Mahembe Village: Sprinkled Settlement to Compact Ujamaa Living

Mahembe is an Ujamma village located on latitude 4° 46'S and longitude 29° 44'E in Kigoma Region of Tanzania. Upto 1962 it was just an ill-organised semi-sprinkled settlement but now with the resettlement scheme on the same old village site houses are relocated and redistributed in a planned way according to the Ujamma principle (Fig. 10.10). According to 1978 census population of the Mahembe village was 2580 with an area of 6 square kilometres. The Kaseke river is flowing east of the village from north to south, and a tributary of the same river is flowing from north to south in western part of the village. In the far west Lake Tanganyika is located, besides one road passes from Kigoma in the south to Kasulu in the north. The neighbouring village in the north is Mashengish which is now an Ujamaa. The eastern side is a slopy ground from the water-divide of central part of Mahembe village upto Kaseke river.

Rural Housing Conditions

According to Household Budget Survey 1977 the average living space per person in rural areas of Tanzania is about 8 to 10 square metres, and the occupancy rate is 1.7 persons per habitable room. In rural areas the average household size has increased from 4.5 to 5.1 persons in between 1967 and 1978. In the long run it has been hoped that with the further development of villagization programme, the qualitative and quantitative growth of houses in rural areas would be accelerated.

According to 1969 Household Budget Survey the rectangular shape of house is commonly found (71%) in the rural areas of Tanzania. Out of this 36% houses had hipped roof, 19% gabled roof and 14% tile roof. About 2.5% houses are of beehive type and 2.5% roof structures without walls. The houses are usually small of one to three roomed having a length and breadth of (2 - 4m). In 75% households the open space is found in front, and surrounding areas of the house. In 1977 survey it has been found that in more than 95% houses floor, foundation, materials of wall and materials of roof were built with the materials available locally.

In the rural areas of Tanzania 45% walls are constructed with mud and pole: 32% with poles, branches, grass, and 16% with mud blocks. In roofs 11% are made of mud whereas one per cent roofs are made of grass and leaves, and 26% with tin roofing sheets. The average life of a house made of locally available materials is 7 years.[18]

With the ongoing villagisation programme the housing components for the socio service such as schools, dispensaries, roads, community centres have improved a lot, but there is still a need for further qualitative improvement of the rural settlement patterns in many respects.

Developed Villages

In Tanzania, Mbeya region has been declared by the CCM party as having the biggest number of villages which have attained the highest level of social-economic development in the country.

The list indicates the number of developed villages in different regions (Table 10.8) of Tanzania (1984).

This categorisation is a basic component in the new system of giving award to the best villages from district to national levels. There are 7430 villages in the country with minimal social and economic development under the categorization: 7266 on the mainland and 164 on the Isles.

Some 852 mainland villages have attained the second stage and 21 on the Isles. 97 mainland villages have attained the third stage and none on the Isles. No village in the country has attained the fourth stage.

The fourth stage implies a developed village with advanced stage of socio-economic development undertaken along socialist lines.

Table 10.8 : Developed Villages in Tanzania

Name of the Regions	Total Villages	Lowest Level	Higher Level	Higher Level	Name of Highest Level
Mbeya	588	469	96	23	Mbuyuni, Ifuko, Matwiga, Luwalaga, Ifumbo Kanga, Kukusya, Lugombo, Ikolo, Iwala, Ifupa, Isansa, itumpi, Songwe, Msangano, Ilembo, Misia, Ibembwa, Wasa, Mbimba, Itapula, Itambule and Ivuna.
Iringa	605	455	136	14	Lulanzi, Magulilwe, Mfyome, Magubike, Sawala, Mtambula,

					Makoga, Utawala, Igongole, Matambwa, Image, Igosi, Ligumbilo and Mapogoro.
Dodoma	441	336	41	14	Bahi, Ikova, Bereko, Masawi, Mlalilyagu, Chamma, Songambele, Kibabwe, Masanga, Chamwino, Handali, Mvumi, Makulu, Makangwa, Barabarani and Kigwe.
Kagera	512	372	134	6	Itera, Ihanda, Bugene, Kishao, Ndama Tukutuku
Arusha	447	375	67	6	Kambi ya Simba, Mareu, Enda, Kisa Upper Kitete Enguiki
Rukwa	488	432	44	12	Malagano, Ulinji, Kasense, Ikozi, Minga, Lyapona, Kalambazita, Mtalamile, Songambele, Azimio, Mtatumbile, Kipiii, Lwega.
Mtwara	481	457	22	2	Mnauya, Idamnole.
Lindi	361	332	38	1	Litama
Ruvuma	313	268	41	4	Ilela, Matetereka, Amani, Makoro and Kigonsera.
Shinyanga	628	624	4	0	
Mwanza	640	624	12	4	Katoro, Sima, Mkule, Mwemwenge.
Mara	344	315	28	1	Butiama
Kilimanjaro	362	317	40	5	Chekereni, Nronga, Mbosho, Marawe, Kyura

Tanga	538	502	35	1	Magamba-Kwalukonge
Zanzibar South	52	50	2	0	
Tabora	367	363	2	2	Mole, Bukama
Singida	323	303	18	2	Nsalembwa and Msange
Dar es Salaam	49	42	7	0	
Coast Region	362	316	46	0	
Morogoro	448	426	22	0	
Kigoma	218	196	21	0	
North Pemba	27	26	1	0	
South Pemba	34	25	9	0	
Zanzibar Urban	21	13	8	0	
Zanzibar North	50	49	1	0	

Source: Daily News; Dar es Salaam, 5.9.1984.

TRADITIONAL REGIONS OF RURAL SETTLEMENTS

(A) Coastal Region

According to Prins (1967)[19] and Altschul (1967)[20] the settlement pattern in the eastern coastal zone of Tanzania is directly influenced by its ecology, history and culture. It is a completely homogeneous region in terms of its proximity to the sea, sandy soil, maritime equable climatic condition besides lagoons, estuary, and beautiful sea beaches.

All these have attracted the foreigners since long, and hence the settlement pattern in the coastal region is governed by these physical and cultural factors. During historic times Tanzania came into the contact of following people.

In Tanzania due to these contacts various cultures emerged e.g. Azania and Swahili which have their definite impact in shaping the settlements. Kiswahili house type is an example of these. Murdock (1959)[21] observes that Azanians brought Neolithic culture in Tanzania with "stone-walled habitation enclosures, pit dwellings, menhirs, stone faced cultivation terraces, irrigation ditches, graded roads with a dominantly north-south orientation, giving evidence of a relatively dense population practising, an intense form of agriculture coupled with animal husbandry".

Year	Earliest contact	Settlement pattern
1500 B.C.	Goddesses of Hindu Religion India (Brahma, Vishnu, Mahesh) God migrated to India through the valley of Nile.	Settlements in Kilimanjaro, Meru, Pare and Lake Victoria Plains.
2000 B.C. to 4th B.C.	Azania	Brought neolithic culture of stone walls, graded roads, agriculture and animal husbandry.
578 -879 A.D.	Persians	On slave trade routes developed settlements of Bagamoya, Sadani and Pangani, etc.
880 - 1500	Arabs	
1500 - 1729 A.D	Portuguese	
1730 - 1856	Oman Arabs	Trade of slave, gold, ivory and Eboni wood
1856 1900	Missionaries and German	Developed settlements in the interior for raw material extraction.
1900 - 1960	British	
1961-onwards	Independent Tanzania	Integrated compact rural settlements growth by Ujamma policy.

Source: Various sources.

In 16th century the coastal settlements developed mainly at strategic points for defence, and at sea beach location for fishing and trade. German and British colonizers have developed some manufacturing and urban (semi-urban) centres with few buildings of mosque, retail shops, fruit vendors and headmans house. In between 16th to 18th centuries Arab Sultans have developed some coastal settlements: the earliest were stone wall structures followed by mud-wall structures, and the later wattle and thatch structures influenced by the trade but made out of locally available raw materials. In the 19th century trade centres have developed at caravan terminals and embarkation points of Arab traders. Indian businessmen constructed stone houses on plantation sites. Africans lived in traditional cluster of Swahili huts. In the coastal areas each settlement had its zone of influence, routes inter-linking the neighbouring settlements besides its own trade relations with the 'clove or spice island' of Zanzibar. Prins classified the rural settlements of the coastal regions in different types, which are as follows: walled villages, closely built villages, dispersed villages and hamlets, but they are mainly guided by the availability of space, resources available and the need for defence and comfort.

The Highland Region

It has been subdivided into three:-

(a) The north-eastern highlands or north-eastern Bantu.
(b) the southern highland cluster of Hehe, Bena and Sangu people, and
(c) the Nyakyusa in the south-west towards Lake Nyasa.

All these areas have adequate rainfall, fertile soil, perennial rivers and the local people were practising shifting cultivation, but now they are living in permanent settlements of Ujamaa Vijijini. Most of these settlements are found along the streams where ditches have been dug to bring water to the surface for domestic use.

At the time of war in the 18th Century most of the settlements were constructed for the purpose of defence during war. The homesteads were common hide-out or modified caves to accommodate cattle, women, children at the time of war. Hence up to the time of independence in highland areas the pattern of settlements were dependent upon historical, physical, cultural and security points of view. Most of the hutments were found scattered over the mountain slopes with enough land for cultivation in the surrounding area.

The Pastoralist and Semi-Pastoralist Settlement Region

It covers the Savanah area of Tanzania right from the north through central Tanzania to the south. This area comes under inadequate rainfall and hence it has a definite impact on people, animals and patterns of settlements. The main tribes living here are Kurya groups, Masai groups, Iraqw, Gogo, Kimbum Nyamwezi and Fipa. Their settlements consist of homesteads with Kinsmen. The young men live as warriors in their own Kraal. The Baraguyu Masai live in a series of relatively small communities called *ikang'itie*. Being nomadic pastoralist Màsai are practising 'transhumance', but they return to the main settlement with the change of season. It corresponds with the economic activities and ecological conditions of the region. As for example in 1940's Gorow people built four wall houses, Iraqw had semi-dug out houses and the Kainum constructed round thatched houses. Due to the fear of the raids of Masai, Sonjo people made clustered houses for security reasons". They grouped themselves in five communal villages of an unusual type. Each contain about one to two hundred families and was surrounded by natural forest with a fortified gate. Inside the village, people carried on agricultural and economic activities using a well developed system of irrigation. These settlements were quite safe from attack by the enemy.[22]

The settlement patterns of semi-pastoralist Kurya people were homesteads arranged in a circular form joined with thorn fence and cattle *boma* in between, so that they can see the cattle through the window. *Tembe* house type is common in central Tanzania among Gogo, Rimi and Rangi. The form of the house is generally rectangular, roofs are made of sticks, thatched, and then covered with soil on the top. It is completely influenced by the ecological condition.

In south-western part of Tanzania, the Kimbu, Nyamwezi and Fipa people prefer to live in concentrated villages with several hundred homesteads. But slowly with the increasing population, the shortage of cultivable land, the fear of witchcraft and the decline in soil fertility have forced many such large villages to decline.

Thus the traditional settlement patterns in Tanzania were the true symbol of ecological adaptation in relation to physical forms and structure of houses. Hence under rural agricultural settlements the following sub-categories may be seen: market centres, traditional peasant houses, unplanned settlements, planned but scattered settlements, planned village settlements and the most latest Ujamaa villages.

The majority of Tanzanians live in their huts and cottages of Ujamma villages, which are in most cases compact and semi-compact planned rural settlements mainly established after relocation from the earlier abode of dispersed living. Hence, after Arusha Declaration in 1965 'to go for Ujamaa' compact village living, the transformation programmes of rural development involves the creation of permanent and concentrated settlements, and the farming systems based on more intensive and permanent use of the land by efficiently run, planned forms of economic size. In the economic field, Ujamaa living is the major instrument of integrated rural development, and the establishment of parastatal organizations for running and developing the other economic sectors such as industry, power, transport and so on. These transformation programmes would have to rely "on securing quicker and higher returns on investment and efforts by suing selected, sparsely populated areas for planned settlement schemes and cattle ranches".

In this way, the planning and implementation of rural development strategies that will be effective in expanding opportunities for productive employment and raising the income of families in the village sector of Tanzania is an extremely demanding task. For rural settlements, the programmes of rural development need to be supplemented by the provision of rural transport services; the construction of crop storage facilities; the development of processing and marketing facilities; the establishment of rural service centres; the organization of wholesale and retail trade; the distribution of farm inputs and implements; the provision of health services, education, training and enhancing the opportunities for cultural activities.

In Tanzania, about 40 per cent of villages have now a clean water supply, 92 per cent have primary school, 35 per cent have dispensary and 74 per cent have shops. However, these achievements are clearly at the expense of the productive sectors, not self-generative. Hence, it may lead the economy to such a pass which may jeopardise the future of these facilities.[23] Anyway, if one wants to see Tanzania self-reliant and prosperous, hardwork in the agricultural activities and the improvement of related settlements and their inhabitants can only make rural sector, the economic, social and political bases of the country.

REFERENCES

1. C.F. Kohn; "Settlement Geography", in James, P.E. and Jones, C.F. (eds.); *American Geography, Inventory and Prospects;* Syracuse University; 1954; pp. 125 - 139.
2. G.J. Trewartha; Japan; *A Physical, Cultural and Regional Geography*; Madson, 1954.
3. C.K. Omari and E.A. Lukwaro; "Settlement Patterns and Ujamaa", *Tanzania Notes and Records,* No. 83
4. Dickson, R.E.; Germany: *A General and Regional Geography*; Doulton, New York, 1953.
5. John Harris (Edt.); *'Rural Development Theories of Peasant Economy and Agrarian Change'*, Hutchinson University Library, London, 1982, p. 1.
6. R.B. Mandal; *Introduction to Rural Settlements*; Concept Publishing Company, New Delhi, 1979.
7. J.K. Nyerere; *Freedom and Unity*: A Selection from Writings and Speeches 1952 - 1965; Oxford Press, Dar es Salaam, 1966, p. 183.
8. C.K. Omari; "Ujamaa Cooperative Farming the Way Ahead", *Journal of Rural Cooperation;* Vol. V; No. 1; 1977; pp. 25 - 26.
9. Henry Mapolu; *The Social and Economic Organization of Ujamaa Villages*; M.A. Thesis, University of Dar es Salaam, 1973.
10. William Luttrell; "Villagisation, Cooperative Production and Rural Cadres: Strategies and Tactics in Tanzanian Socialism Development", Economic Research Bureau; University of Dar es Salaam, 1971.
11. P.L. Raikes; "Village Planning for Ujamma", Economic Research Bureau; University of Dar es Salaam; 1972.
12. U. Schuler; *Rural Development Strategies and Land Use and Settlement Planning in Tanzania*; Ardhi Institute, Dar es Salaam, Part I, 1984, p. 77.
13. N. Newigor; "Village Settlement Schemes" (H. Ruthenber, Edt.); Smallholder Farming and Smallholder Development in Tanzania, Munchen; 1968.
14. J.K. Nyerere; *Socialism and Rural Development*, Dar es Salaam; 1967.
15. H.E. Smith; *Readings on Economic Development and Administration in Tanzania*; Oxford University Press, London 1966, p. 361.
16. J.K. Nyerere; *Freedom and Socialism*, A Selection from Writings and Speeches 1965 - 1967; Oxford University Press; Dar es Sallam, 1968, p. 351.

17. H.M. Mushala (Edt.); *Ilomba Village Report*; Department of Geography, University of Dar es Salaam; 1980, p. 10.
18. Rune Karlson; "Housing Conditions in Tanzania", *Bulletin of Research and Information;* Vol. 1, No. 4 December 1981, p. 5.
19. A .J.H. Prins; *Swahili Speaking Peoples*, London, 1967.
20. D.R. Altschul; *The Arrangement and Dimensions of Rural Settlements of the Northern Coastal Zone of Tanganyika:* Pangani District; Department of Geography, University of Illinois; Urbana, Technical Report No. 3; 1967, p. 200.
21. G.P. Murdock; *Africa, Its People and their Cultural History*; McGraw Hill: New York, 1959.
22. J. Mckay; "A Review of Rural Settlement Studies for Tanzania"; *East African Geographical Review;* No. 6; April 1968, pp. 37 - 49.
23. *Africa South of Sahara*, 1983 - 1984; 13th edition; Europa Publications Ltd.; London, 1983, p. 836.

Fig. 10.1

Village Resettlement Schemes in Tanzania

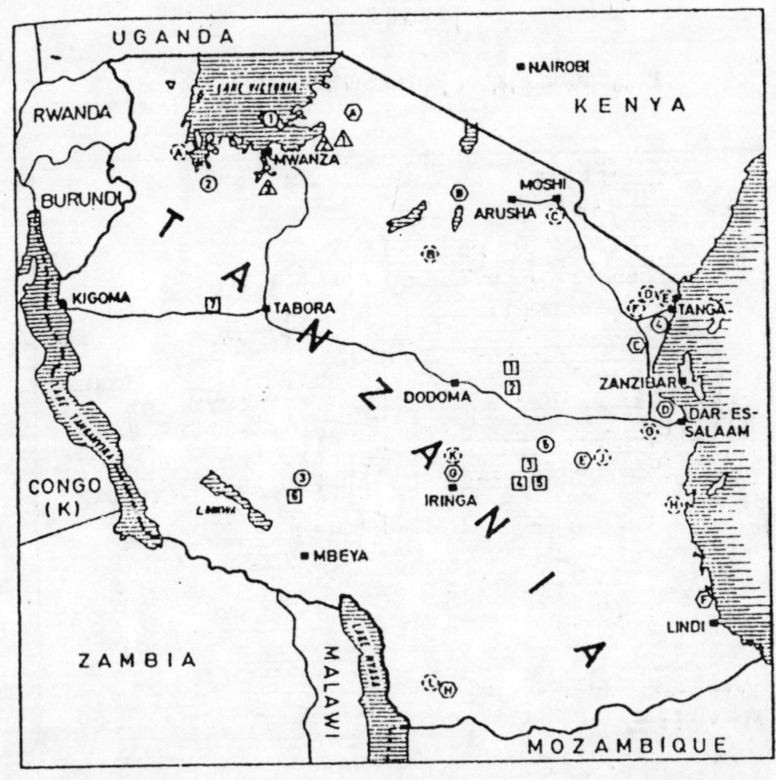

△ ISRAELI SCHEMES
1 KALAMERA
2 NYATWALI
3 MBARIKA

○ ASSISTED SCHEMES
1 GALU
2 BUYOMBE
3 KIPEMBAWE
4 AMANI
5 MKATA

□ EX-TANGANYIKA AGRICULTURAL CORPORATION SCHEMES
1 MATANGORO
2 KONGWA
3 KICHANGANI
4 JCHONDE
5 SONJO
6 LUPATINGATINGA
7 URAMBO

⬡ PILOT VILLAGE SCHEMES
A RWAMKOMA
B UPPER KITETE
C KABUKU
D KEREGE
E BWAKIRA CHINI
F KINGORONGUNDWA
G KIWERE
H MLALE

PROPOSED SCHEMES
A BWANGA
B BASHANET
C URUCHINI
D BAMBA
E MARAMBA
F KIWANDA
G KWALA
H RUFIJI
J DUTUMI
K ISMANI
L LITENYA

Fig. 10.2

Population Size of Rural Settlements (1978)

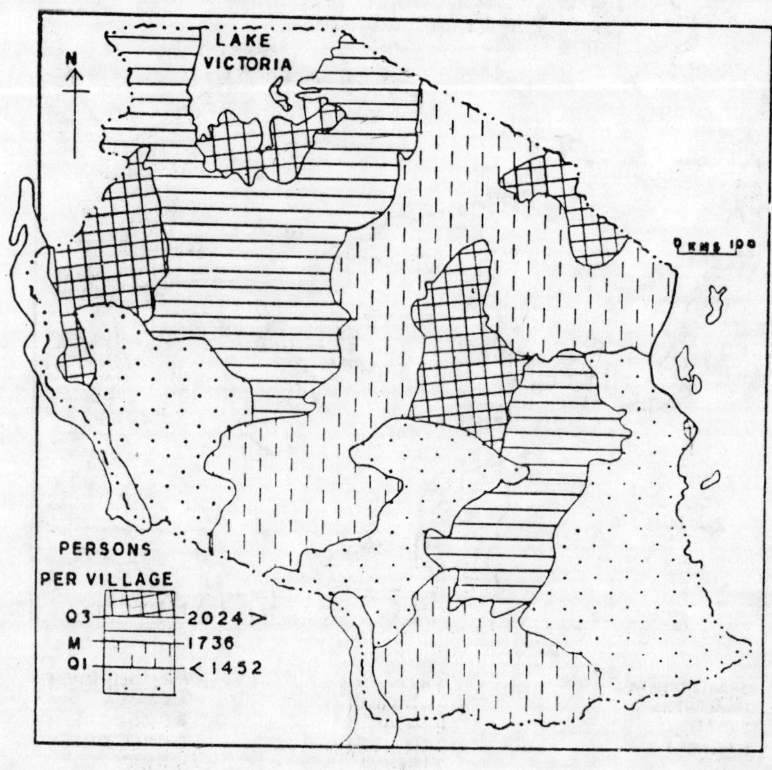

Fig. 10.3

Density of Rural Settlements (1981)

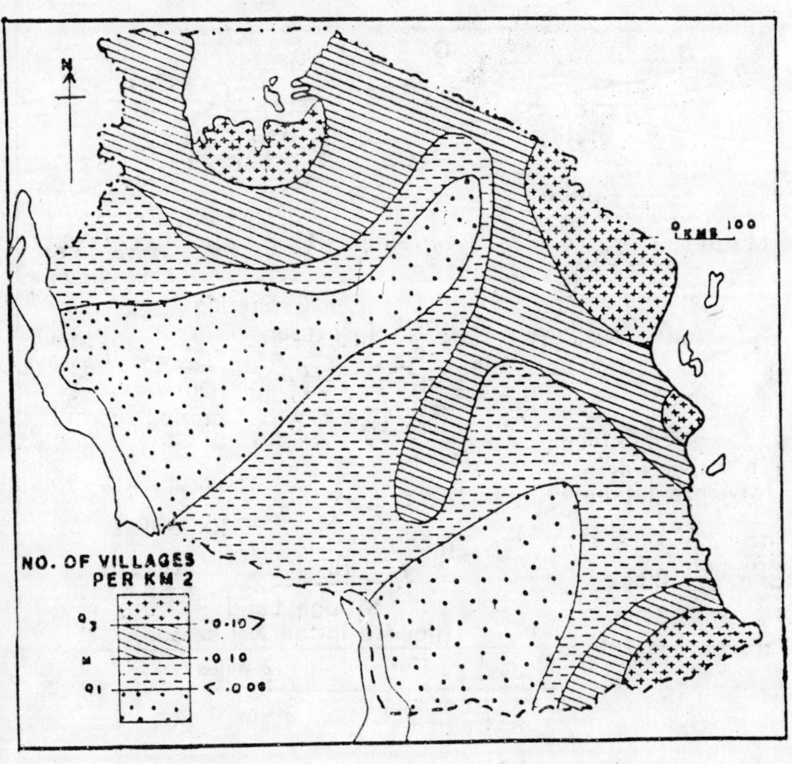

Fig. 10.4

Patterns of Homesteads Location in Sukumaland Tanzania (After-Hickman, Dickins and Wood, 1975)

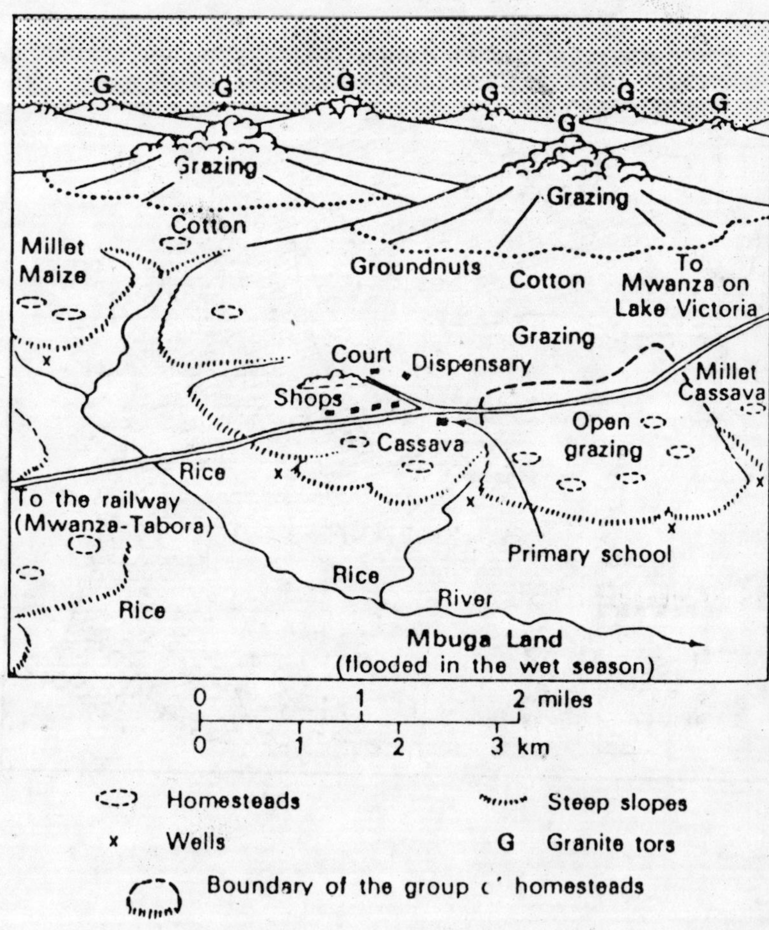

Fig. 10.5

A Traditional Masai Settlement Pattern (P. 90)

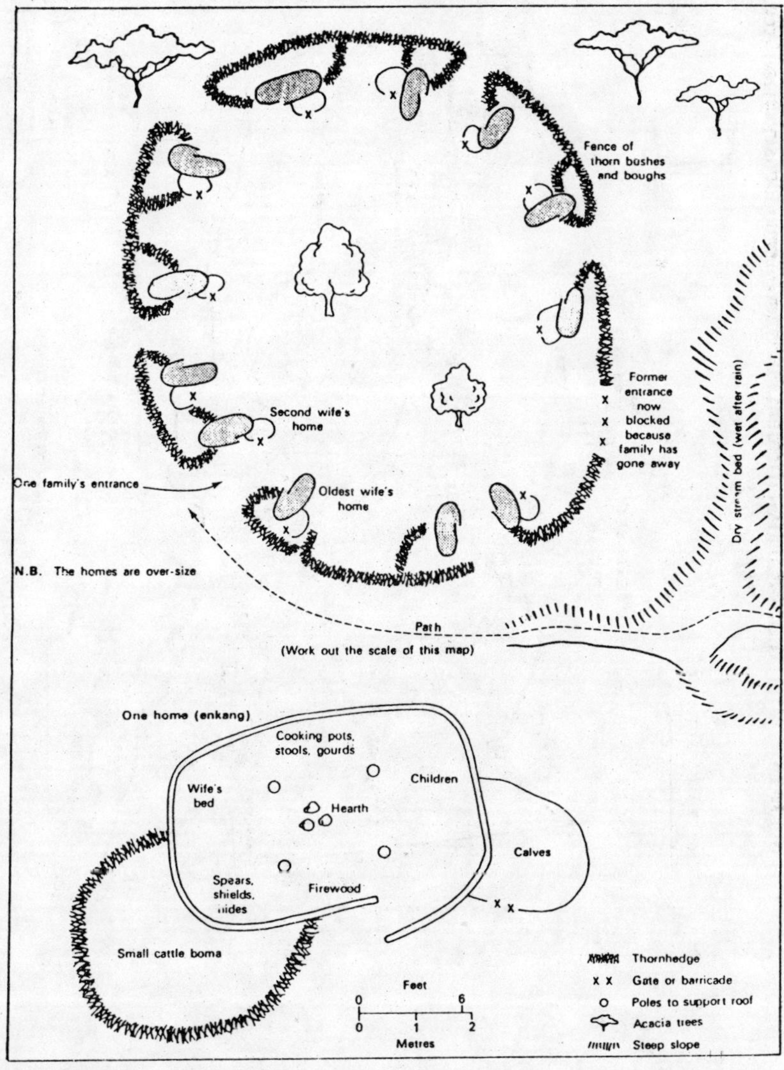

Fig. 10.6 Masai Rural Settlements in Ngorongoro Conservation Area

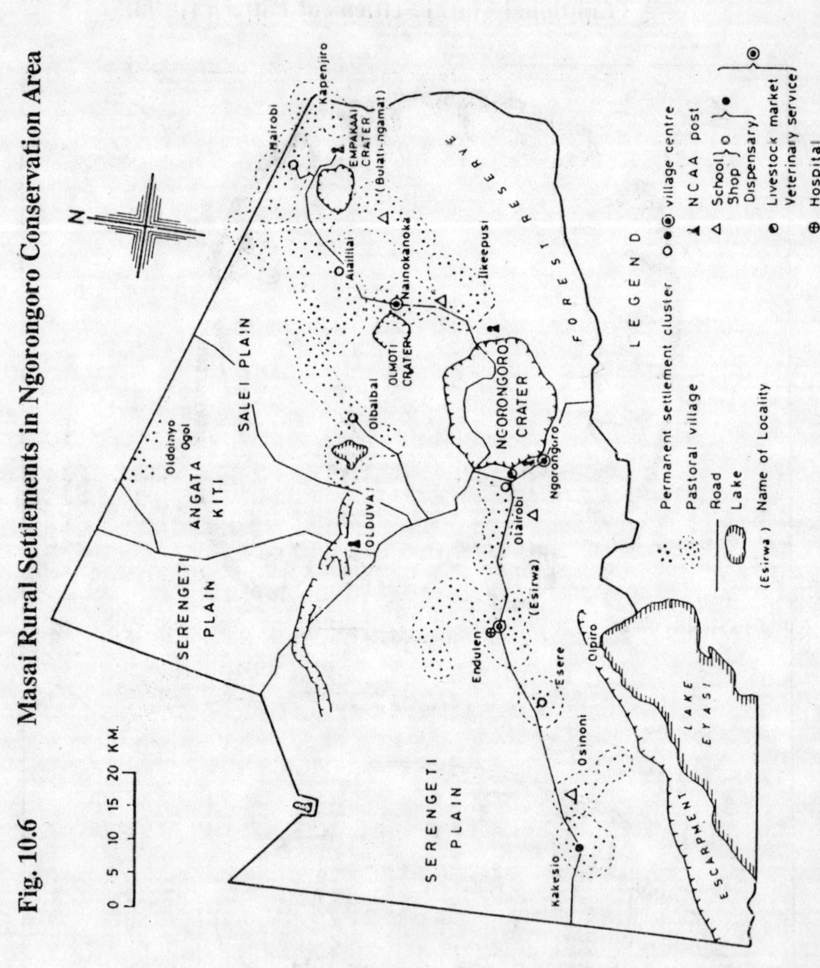

Fig. 10.7

Ilomba Village Location, Siting and Settlement Pattern in Mbeya Region, Tanzania

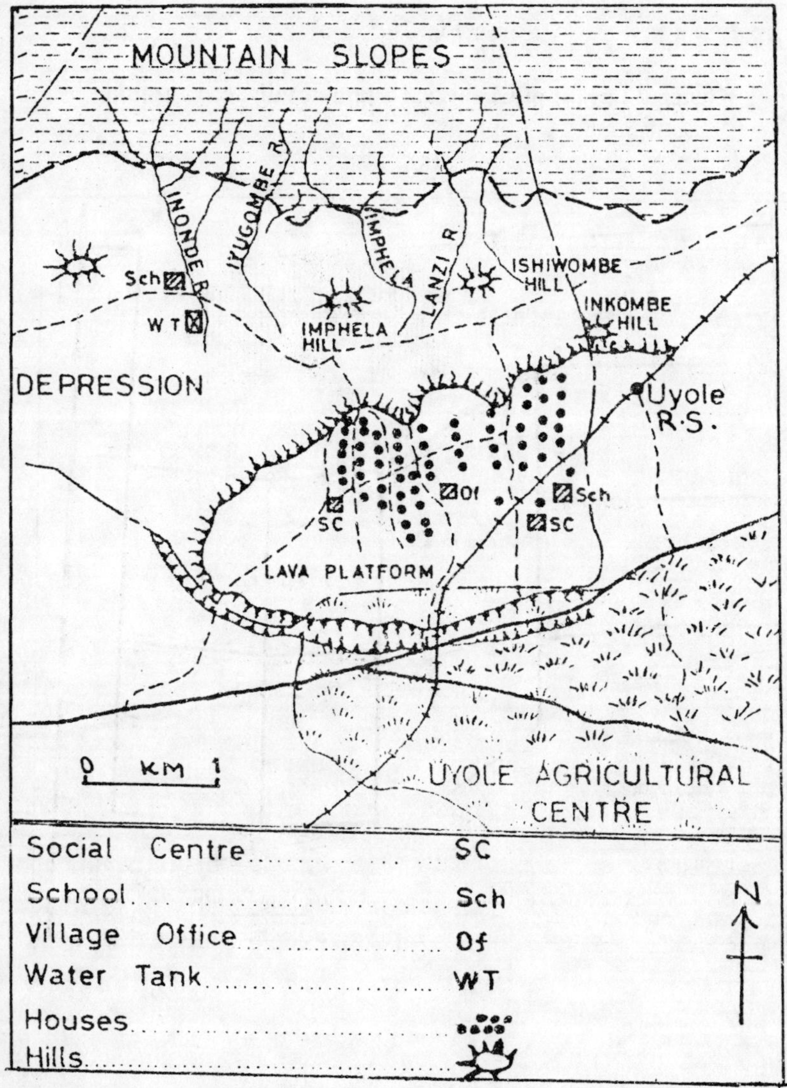

Fig. 10.8

General Layout of Chekereni Ujamaa Village, Tanzania

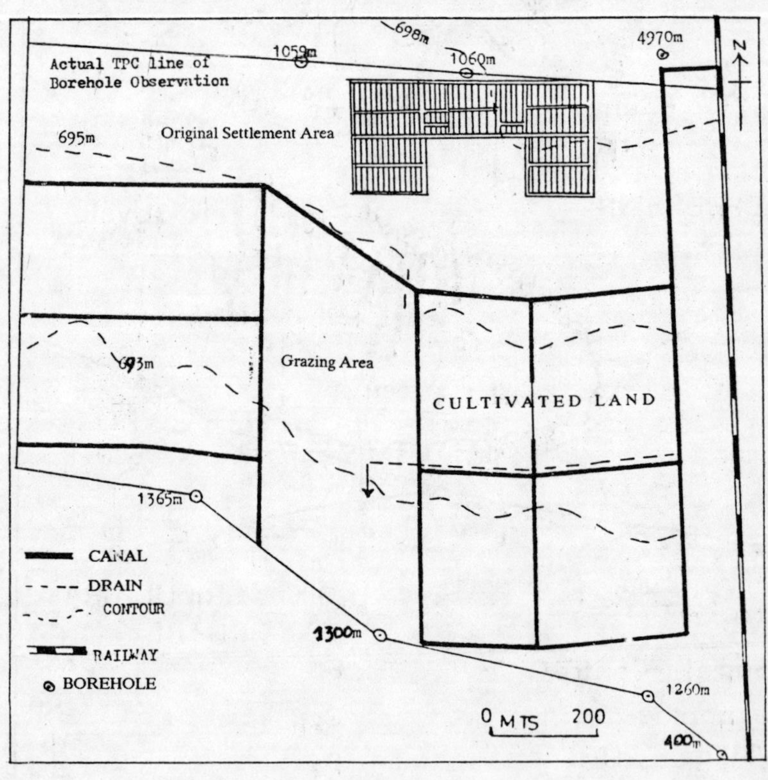

Fig. 10.9

Model House Plan of Chekereni Ujamaa Village, Tanzania

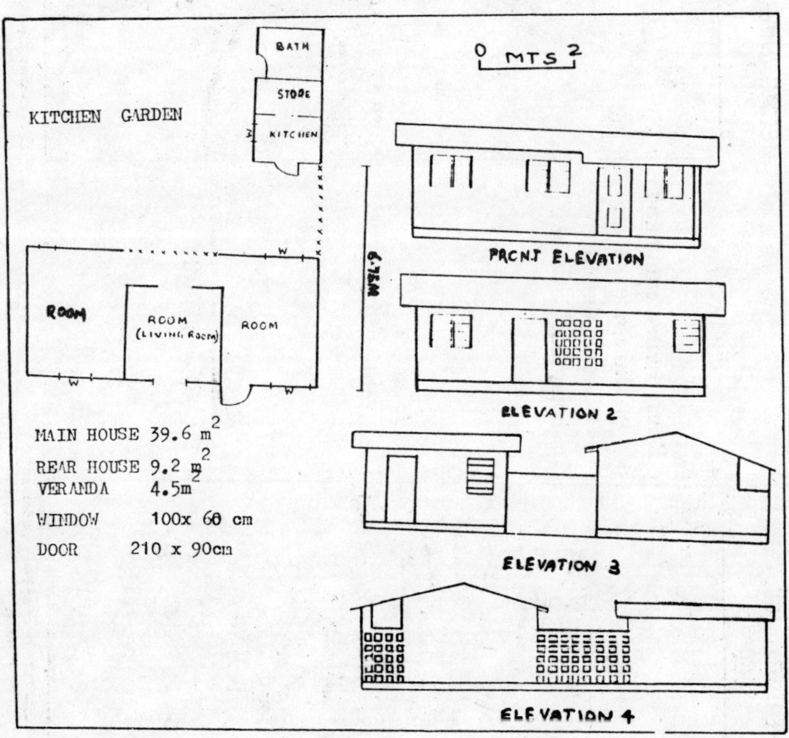

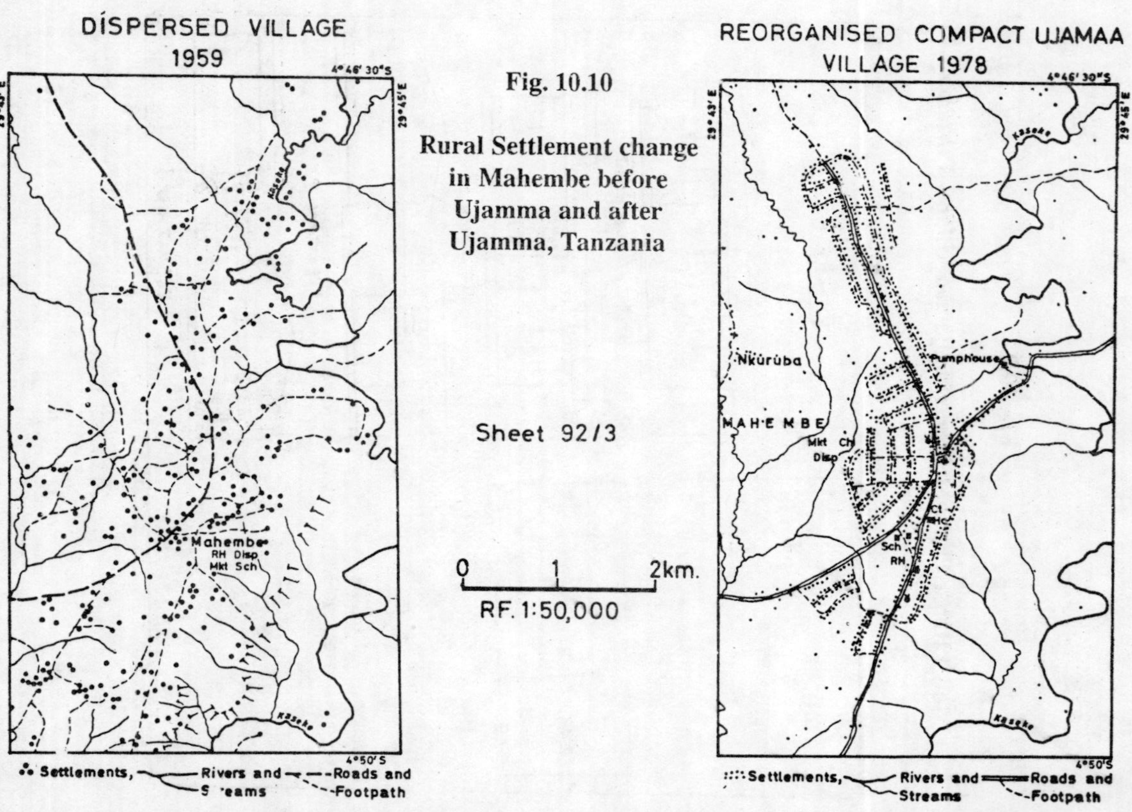

Fig. 10.10

Rural Settlement change in Mahembe before Ujamma and after Ujamma, Tanzania

ELEVEN

VILLAGE PATTERNS AND STRUCTURE

The Morphology of rural settlement is its anatomy governed by physical and cultural factors and manifests in the physical form and structure including the layout of streets and spacing of buildings. The layout means external and internal[1] form of settlements which in turn depend upon the physical and cultural[2] conditions of the landscape and the society[3]. Even a cursory observation of one inch topographical sheets of the survey of India and 16 inches to 1 mile cadastral maps of rural settlements would reveal that nowhere settlements have grown in true geometrical form. They have rather, flourished in an easily discernible haphazard form which is the result of natural growth.

The form of the village is guided by its site, as for example, settlements in valleys tend to have string shape whereas settlements on slopes of the mountain are likely to have streets and houses arranged which conform closely to the contours of the slope.

Similarly, a small rural settlement in the Terai area of Northern India or Japan is usually oriented to the rice fields, but it is also closely related with the neighbouring hill slopes. In these areas, the fertile rice land is very valuable for intensive subsistence farming, and the rural settlement is tightly pressed into a very small space on upland near the mountain in terraced fields where rice, tea, onion, wheat and other crops are grown.

The outer shape and inner structure of a village are governed by several factors such as physical (e.g. location and siting with respect to relief, rivers and forest), social (e.g. caste, clan groups, religious affinity), historical (e.g. the early need for defence) and economic (e.g. the system of farming, road, industrial location). In case of indigenous growth of villages the farms have been governed by various forces whereas in case of planned settlements it may be the outcome of conscious efforts of the planner.

The physical factors affecting the form of the rural settlements are the configuration of site, water bodies like rivers, wells and ponds, slope and elevation of land such as plains, uplands or valleys, water table, water-logged areas, etc. All these are of paramount importance in the growth of village patterns under effects of natural environment. Among cultural factors historical events, planned geometrical patterns of roads and lanes. field pattern, religious institutions like mosques and temples, etc. are intimately related to the structure of the village. The state of insecurity in the past and the present social make-up of the village are other significant factors in the development of village patterns. But the growth of most of the villages in the Bihar Plain has been so haphazard with narrow, turning and twisting lanes and irregularly piled buildings that no pattern is distinguishable.

The village cart tracks and streets form the skeleton of the internal layout of the village. The buildings determine the form and shape as does the flesh in human body. The nucleus of the village develops at the most accessible place from where the surrounding land can be easily observed[4]. The study of morphology of villages refers chiefly to the clustered settlements, as only the congregation of a number of dwellings and arrangement of associated lanes can give to different village patterns. Thus village patterns involve the study of only those villages which have a compact or roughly compact settlement. Villages with semi-sprinkled and sprinkled settlements cannot be classified and only a rough analysis of their pattern can be made.

The region has a long history since Prehistoric times. With varied physical and cultural conditions, it is marked by several patterns of villages. In each physiographic region the physical elements have differently affected the village forms, and so is the case with cultural and social elements too. Recent archaeological excavations of a few ancient sites in the region have made valuable contributions to this branch of settlement geography. It has been found that the villages of the early times were guided by the ancestral plan as suggested by the excavations of Chirand[5] in Saran district and Vaishali[6] in Muzaffarpur district. Definite evidence of Kushan period settlement plan has been discovered for the first time at Chirand. On occupational floor were found remains of post-holes which might have supported thatch roofs. A number of hearths were found on the floor[7].

The village, according to Kautilaya (III;I) is "a group of Sudras and cultivators, numbering from a hundred to five hundred families; distance – one or two *krosa* (3kms) from the next village". But this does not appear to have very outstanding characteristics. Somewhat pedantically the Mansara[8] describes eight types and the Kamikagama[9] as many as fifteen types of settlements in the past. A passage in the *Mahabharata* (V.47) speaks of villages of straw huts, which got burnt easily. Village fortification seem to have been mentioned in ancient texts (Yajnavalkya Smriti ii; 167). The Buddhist literature such as Jatakas[10] has thrown light on the size of the village, such as *gamaka*[11] (small village), *gama*[12] (an ordinary village); *Nigama gama*[13] (a large village), *Duara gama*[14] (sub-urban village) and *Pachchanta gama*[15] (a frontier village such as Sursand and Bel in Sitamarhi district).

Early history also showed that the villages were located on either side of the road[16]. The villages were also connected with one another on the one hand and with administrative centres on the other. These centres have been described as a *fortress* in the centre of 800 villages, a *dronamukha* commanding 400 villages, a *Karvatika* controlling 200 villages and a *Samgrahana* in the midst of a group of ten villages[17].

In ancient times, the inhabited area of the village was fenced on all sides by walls or wooden palisades. The village wall was at a distance of 20 metres from the border houses, so that people coming by the village gate would be seen by the inhabitants from their houses. Even areas inhabited temporarily were fenced with bamboos. The village wall had four large gates facing the main roads. At the main gate of the village there was planted sacred pipal or banyan tree where the presiding diety of the village was supposed to dwell[18]. These historical records also show that in ancient times various grades of village pattern were planned, while at present it is a result of natural growth.

The ideal outer shape of a village would be a circle, and any departure from this can be measured geometrically to determine the distortion. This statement is based on the fact that if each corner of a village has equal importance in a plain land without any physical or cultural obstruction and is built on a favourable site, then the village should develop in a circular pattern around the central nucleus. As has been stated earlier, the nucleus can consist of a tank, a tree, a temple, a community hall, etc. Before arriving at this conclusion thousands of village patterns on topographical sheets were examined. Although it would be possible to find more extreme cases as the visual inspection indicates that there is a considerable variability among settlement patterns. Four villages have been selected here to illustrate the point. These settlements resemble in varying degrees to the three basic types; circular, square and rectangular.

In order to determine the shape, a circle with its circumference touching the two extreme points of a settlement was drawn. Now the pattern seems to be obvious in its geometrical perspective in comparison with the circle. The formula for the measurement of this is [19]

$$MC = \frac{100 \times Aa}{\pi r^2}$$

where MC is the measure of circularity in shape; Aa is the actual area contained in the settlement and πr^2 is the area of the circle of settlement = A. The above measure has been applied to each of the four villages shown in Fig. 11.1 with the results given in Table.11.1.

Table 11.1.Measure of the Degree of Circularity in the Shape of Rural Settlements

Name of Settle ment	Area of Circle in square Metres	Area of Settle ment in square metres	% circularity (MC)	No. of Houses
Gothini	731924	570655	75	742
Sarea	285908	169966	60	112
Kaila	127070	90649	72	116
Lagma	285908	132139	46	105

The MC values are mathematically independent of the size of the entities; and comparisons are also facilitated by the fact that the measure has an absolute maximum value of 100% and for all practical purposes, a fixed minimum of 0.01%. The MC value does not only express the degree of circularity in shape but also provides a clue to the type of geometrical figure which most closely resembles the settlement in question. Although no hard and fast rule can be applied, it appears that as the MC values decrease the settlement tends to resemble first a circular, then star, square, rectangular and in the end an elongated shape, in the order mentioned.

The geometric shape of a village appears to have some-relationship with its compactness. The degree of differentiation in compactness of a village pattern helps in regional planning, because the problems of housing and highways become more acute as we tend to move from compact to amorphous patterns. The hierarchy of the growth of village pattern shows both the shape and the intensity of compactness of scattering of settlements in a region within a definite set of environment.

The poverty of the region and the problems associated with the settlement go on increasing with decline in compactness as indicated by the multiplication factor associated with the number of problems in the last column. The multiplication factor is only approximate and is designed to give relative importance of problems rather than their absolute numbers. Also, different types of settlement patterns are apt to develop under different environmental conditions. These are discussed below:

Table 11.2 : Settlement Pattern and Environmental Conditions

Village Pattern	Settlement Types	Environmental Conditions	Poverty and Problems
Circular/ Star	Compact settlement	1. Any where with favourable conditions 2. Flood with low water-table	N x I
Square / Rectangul-ar/ Semi-	Semi-compact settlement	1. In areas of tank, well and pyne irrigation	N x 2

circular			
		2. Any where in compact and semi-compact settlement depending on site	
Linear	Semi-Sprinkled settlement	Wet and riverine flood plains	N x 3
Amorphous	Sprinked settlement	plateau fringe and highly flooded belts of river Kosi	N x 4

RACTANGULAR PATTERN

The commonest form of nucleated rural settlements in Bihar Plain is the rectangular pattern. It is not only limited to this region, but is also found in other parts of India as well as China and Japan,[20] where the plough culture of alluvial plains is the factor largely responsible for its growth. Village plans of the ancient past also refer to the rectangular development of standard village, in Mansara[21] and Kamikagama[22]. The chief reason for this pattern is the rectangular form of the cultivated fields.

The aggregation of square and rectangular buildings produces rectangular plans for the village. The rectangular alignment of dwellings with their main axis from north to south and east to west are mostly designed to get maximum sunlight and fresh air. In compact settlements the rectangular and square blocks of land give rise to greater concentration of dwellings which produces a rectangular settlement. In an agglomerated settlement, this tendency seems to be of a higher degree, but in semi-sprinkled settlement it is not easy to identify this geometrical pattern. The size of the settlement would depend upon the size and shape of the site as well as the physical limitations on building activities. The pattern may be disturbed in some cases, with the extension of new buildings on the outskirts of the village. The controlling factor of this pattern is the parallel street pattern of the village and the rectangular form of land. Aer in Bhojpur district, Sarea in Saran district and Ghoghaili in Bhagalpur district are good examples of rectangular village pattern.

HOLLOW RECTANGULAR PATTERN

Hollow rectangular pattern is marked by an unbuilt open space in the middle of the village. It is most frequent in zones of strife where the central vacant space was occupied by the old fort of the local chieftains, around which the villagers congregated. In most of the old sites, the ruins of forts are marked by mounds in the centre of the village. As superstition does not allow building houses on ruined sites, the open space remains unoccupied and results in a hollow rectangular pattern. Other features which result in this pattern are temples, mosques, ponds and shady tree in the middle of the village where the peasants assemble, tether their cattle or thrash their crops. In hot weather peasants gather under the trees for relaxation and in winter evenings a fire may be built around which the village folk exchange talks or stories. In most cases, this is a place where the weekly or biweekly markets are held. The village Madhopur Bhual and Kusmaha in the district of Gaya are examples of hollow rectangular pattern.

THE SQUARE VILLAGE

Square pattern and rectangular pattern are always complementary to each other. Due to attractive and restrictive physical forces in the village site the square may turn into a rectangle or vice-versa. This pattern is generally associated with villages lying at the crossing of cart tracks or roads. It is also related to some features restricting the extension of the village outside a square, space such as an old boundary wall. Among the present features thick orchards surrounding the village on all or some sides, tanks and roads seem to have a similar restricting influence. Mixed patterns of 'four squares'[23] might be seen when the village consists of four distinct blocks lying at the crossing of two main lanes or cart tracks. These four square units are sometimes occupied by four distinct types of castes. The best examples of such village pattern are Kaila, Katsa and Santhi lying along the intersections of cart tracks and associated with adjacent lowlands and water-bodies in the districts of Bhagalpur and Saran.

HOLLOW SQUARE VILLAGE

The hollow square pattern is again similar to the square pattern, with a hollow space in the centre of the village. Similar to hollow rectangular settlements, the unbuilt space is caused by the presence of a square tank or a temple or a mosque or a garden or a pasture ground. One of the best examples of hollow square pattern is Ranjodha village in Bhagalpur district. Here the villagers have dug-out the earth from the middle of the village to build the plinth of their houses. This has resulted in a ditch full of water located in the centre of the village.

ELONGATED VILLAGE PATTERN

Elongated village pattern is easily recognised by its simple arrangement of houses along a line or a series of lines. The settlement is prolonged in one direction and restricted in another due to certain physical features. The occurrence of such village pattern is guided by the character of site. The flood affected areas and the proximity of a river lead to the elongation of a village. Whenever the site is a narrow strip between two streams, flowing very close together, the village becomes elongated. Clusters situated on a bank marking the edge of an alluvial terrace also show a similar influence.

Among cultural features roads, either metalled or unmetalled, have greater importance in the elongation of a village. In case the road is recent and the village has no marketing centre, the settlement pattern might be different. But, if there is a market, it is invariably situated along the road, and the settlement is necessarily elongated. Such villages are known as strassendorf (street village). For example Phulwaria in Raghopur Diara of Vaishali district is an elongated village along the river Ganga and only one cart track passes through the village. The village Damgara in Bhagalpur district lying along an unmetalled road also shows elongation, but at some places the pattern has been disturbed by the open spaces and the construction of new buildings by the side of the main site. Still another good example is furnished by the village Mohammadpur in Patna district which has developed elongation being in between the Patna canal and the river Ganga. This street village shows the importance of water siting, which is of greatest value in the development of linear settlements. Majrahia (Fig. 11.2) in Rusera block of Samastipur district is a good example of this pattern along a linear water-body which lies to the east of the settlement.

In areas affected by floods, this pattern occurs along rivers, ox-bow lakes or old channels. Here the linear cluster usually becomes abnormally elongated along the higher banks, e.g. the villages in the Kosi flood plain.

CHESSBOARD PLAN

The chessboard or grid iron pattern denotes a 'right angled mesh of streets with or without a central rectangular market place.'[24] Thus chessboard plan is the feature of some large rectangular and square villages. In such large settlements, two streets corresponding with the four gates of the villages are wide enough to allow the passage of bullock-carts cut each other at right angles. A few other subsidiary lanes run more or less parallel to the main lanes, in order to provide access to other houses of the village. The four walls of the dwellings run in cardinal directions so that the grid plan is rarely disturbed. Generally, the village is divided into *tolas* according to different castes and each grid may be occupied by one caste. This pattern also helps the poor peasants to draw drinking water from a centrally located well. In this case each intersection of lanes may have masonry well and in building the houses one of the primary considerations is accessibility to the nearest sweet water well. Sarea village in the district of Saran is the best example of this pattern. This village is located near the river Gandaki. Another example is furnished by the village Nokha in Bhojpur district whose growth is restricted on two sides by water-bodies and on the other two sides by cultivated lands and railways. These villages have lanes in a grid iron pattern.

CIRCULAR VILLAGE

A circular village may have several variations, which are caused by an attempt to build a maximum number of houses at one site. The houses may be concentrated for the purpose of defence or built around the mansion of the local *zamindars* or around a well. It may also be necessitated by a desire to have a higher site for building purpose. In the Bihar Plain this pattern is not the heritage of the past but is due to natural growth of the village according to the shape of the site. Sometimes a semi-circular plain may develop on the crescent shape of meander. The settlements of 'horse-shoe' pattern develop on the sharp bend of meanders of roads. At some places hollow-circular pattern also develops because of open space in the centre of the village.

The best example of circular pattern is the village Gothini in Saran district which has developed in between the bend of the Gandak river on the west and an unmetalled road on the east. Other examples are village Barawan in Bhojpur district and Pokkra in Saran district. The village Satwa in Saran district is a fine example of semi-circular pattern on the arcuate bend of the Gandaki river. The example of hollow circular pattern is given by the village Babhana in Gaya district. In this village the central space is occupied by a pond and except the higher ground around the pond, the land is not suitable for building purposes, so that the village has developed in a hollow circular pattern.

HERRINGBONE PATTERN

The herringbone pattern is a form of village occurring rarely in the region. This village pattern consists of one main lane and several subsidiary lanes meeting the former at acute angle. It is evidently a result of the unusual importance of the main street indicated by the subsidiary nature of the bye-lanes. An example of such village is Jalalabad is Munger district where cart tracks play an important role. The village has one main road and there are several subsidiary lanes that meet at acute angles.

FAN PATTERN

The fan pattern develops on some focal point and houses are situated on lanes of importance radiating from the centre. This focal point may be a tank, riverside, a road, an orchard, a well or a place of worship. The lanes of the village converge here in such a fashion that they form a fan or cone. This pattern also developed owing to the convergence of tracks more on one side of the village rather than on the other. The village Bhusia in Bhagalpur district presents the best example of a fan pattern.

STRING PATTERN

The string pattern village is common in the districts of Saharsa and Purnea. These large and linear settlements develop in one line along the bank of river, *nala* or *pyne*, or along a road. In this pattern the settlement grows in a single line in order to have an easy approach from the road or the water body. In flooded riverine tracts of Saharsa and Purnea where the river embankments are suitable for settlement, the houses are built in a single profile on the crest. It seems that this pattern is associated with the paddy cultivation region where houses are constructed on artificial *bundhs* or cart tracks. There are two examples like Tamua in the district of Saharsa along a tributary of the river Kosi and Maniakha in the district of Bhagalpur on the bank of the Ghogha river . These two patterns show the characteristic features of their growth. Sometimes a settlement may consists of more than one 'string' depending on the number of channels or distributaries traversing the village.

STAR PATTERN

It is one of the most typical village pattern in the Bihar Plain. When the circular settlement extends in several directions along the footpaths and roads, the village assumes this shape. The development of such settlement is common in the flood zones where elevated sites are rare, or at nodal centres where the newer settlements project along the cart-tracks, which radiate from the central village. There is a clear-cut zone of such settlement in the Terai Region of Sitamarhi and in eastern Champaraņ districts. The occurrence of such settlements also takes place with the construction of new-dwellings on the outskirts of circular and square shaped villages.

IRREGULAR PATTERN

The irregular pattern is the most common village pattern found in the Bihar Plain. It is the more common form in larger villages than amongst average sized compact settlements. In this pattern houses are huddled in an irregular fashion without following any definite plan. The larger villages generally consist of several *tolas* with different forms. When compiled together these do not provide any definite pattern. This pattern is not possible in the dispersed settlements where dwellings are scattered in the whole village without any definite street. Village Araje in Saran district is an example of this pattern. The village is located close to the river Gandak along a cart track, the conflicting influence of the two led to the emergence of irregular pattern for the settlement.

DOUBLE-NUCLEATION

When the settlements of two revenue village develop at a single site, a double village called 'double dorfer'[25] results. From the point of view of revenue and administration, each village has a separate entity but geographically they are always one. In rural areas a minor *nala* is often the cause of such a pattern. Sometimes a mound, a road, a tank or a river may result in the development of twin settlements situated on either side of it. It is also caused by the construction of new shops at the railway station, though the distance may be one or two kms from the parent village. In the Bihar Plain, this village pattern is the most typical on the river banks because in such places there is a struggle for good water frontage and higher site on the levee. The best examples are Khanpur and Narhan in Samastipur district. These settlements have similar sites on the bank of river Purain and the Burhi Gandak respectively.

RADIAL PATTERN

The convergence of lanes in a circular village with fine straight line causes the growth of radial pattern. Their growth also depends upon the concentric growth of dwellings and if the pattern is due to this reason the result is called Cobweb pattern. Sometimes, the influence of a sweet water well or the village shop in the centre of the village also lead to the origin of radial pattern of lanes. Village Baheri in Darbhanga district is a fine example of this pattern and from the central site of this settlement roads are radiating on all directions hence radial pattern results.

A circular village with its houses arranged in a radial pattern on a high mound, well above flood level generally develops for protection. In European countries such village is generally encircled by a wall. Later on with the expansion of settlement site and construction of wall farther away from the centre of the village, the place of original wall after demolition serve the purpose of street. In modern times radial villages are found in newly planned areas of Israel where the central part has been designed for the establishment of shops and recreational activities.

The crossroad village is as divergent of the radial pattern where the settlement is relatively more compact than the street village. The residential houses, stores and markets are located as close to the cross roads as possible in order to take advantage of the traffic going both ways. A modern cross-road settlement may consist of a diesel filling station, a grocery store, and some other sorts of retail store built near the junction of cross-road. Such village tends to develop in an irregular rectangular pattern. It is quite apparent that trade is an important function of such cross-road rural settlements.[26]

L-SHAPED PATTERN

The L-shaped village pattern is the common feature found at several sites where two linear forces meet at right angles to each other. This pattern is a subsidiary of the rectangular or square form. These two forces may be two roads and cart-tracks or a road and a water front meeting at right angles. There are several villages in the region which have grown along the curvature of the rivers or roads. Their arcuate bend leads to the development of L-shape at a later stage. Datiana and Nabkarhi in the districts of Patna and Muzaffarpur respectively are examples of this type. Both these villages have been caused by the meeting of two cart-tracks and the two linear sides of the settlements meet to form the L-shape.

"Green Villages" had their origin from the forest clearing. Since Anglosaxon times green villages help in keeping the cattle nearest to the pastureland in order to safeguard them from plundering hordes of people. The cattle Kraal settlement of Masai semi - nomadic people in Kenya and Tanzania has close affinity with the green villages of England, which provide shelter to the village stock at night within the compound of green bush-fenced kraal where circular houses of tree-branches and leaves are constructed for the safety of cattle ranchers. In 1964 Stamp reported 1475 green villages in England.[27]

In the real world it has been found that some villages do not fit into any of the shapes outlined above. Such villages are indeed formless without any significant background of physical and cultural features. Such pattern is regarded as amorphous.

AMORPHOUS PATTERN

If the village lands are dotted with many hamlets and individual farmsteads, all being very small rectangles linked with the central hamlet by crude paths, no definite pattern can be recognised.[28] Such an irregular pattern may be known as amorphous pattern, which leads to a scattering of houses over the area. The amorphous pattern may be found in the plains of Saran and Champaran districts and the whole of diara belt along the Ganga, but is more common in the Kosi flood affected area in the east and along the southern border of the study area. Excellent examples of such villages are Gaura, Rampur, Jagdishpur and Sahibganj in Vaishali district in diara of the river Ganga.

SOME UNCOMMON PATTERNS

The triangular, parallelogram and sigmatic settlements occur rarely in the region. The triangular settlement is formed by a road or elevated margin of meander loop. The village Kalakund in Bhagalpur district is an example of triangular settlement. The parallelogram shape is similar to rectangular and square patterns with a slight variation. In the region under study, Gaibandhi in Muzaffarpur district is an example of a parallelogram village built along unmetalled road. Its shape is direct result of the alignment of roads and lanes. The external boundary seems to consist of four lines of square but they do no meet at right angle.

When a village grows in a 'S' shape, it is known as a sigmatic settlement. The development of such pattern is mostly due to physical conditions of the landscape, which seems to be rare in the region. Perhuka in Patna district is an example of S-shape where the growth pattern is fully controlled by physical conditions of *pynes* and lowlands of paddy fields surrounding the village. In this village, the burial place of Mohammedans and a tank are placed in such a manner that the villagers have been forced to build their houses in a typical double arcuate form leading to the development of sigmatic pattern.

MORPHOGENESIS OF RURAL SETTLEMENTS CASE STUDY OF VILLAGE KHARSAM IN SAMASTIPUR DISTRICT

In earlier times, settlements originated on suitable water sites, surrounded by the fertile agricultural tracts for the sustenance of inhabitants. Village Kharsam developed in the olden days on these considerations. This fact is supported by the recent excavations in the old settlement centre (*garh*) in 1958 which has resulted in the recovery of earthen jars of fused clay, grinding stones, some beads and other articles. The excavation was in connection with the construction of a dam by the Irrigation Department on the Kareh river.

The *garh* site is situated to the south of the present village. Some parts of this site were eroded by the river Kareh in 1930. The black squares (Fig. 11.3) represent the settlement as surveyed in 1889. Portion with dots represents the development of new settlement up to 1930 and the white squares represent the development of settlement in recent times. The growth of the settlement has mostly taken place towards the southern side of the main village and eastern side of *tola* Lalpur. The erosion of the eastern bank by river Kareh has resulted in the shifting of Lalpur settlement thrice between 1880 and 1960.

During the floods of 1930, the course of the river shifted towards the east and Lalpur settlement also gradually shifted towards the east inside the dam. In 1958 when the dam was constructed in the middle of Lalpur settlement, a new hamlet originated on the side of pre-established village roads. Thus before 1958 the village often suffered from floods but the construction of the irrigational dam has now made it safe from the river. At present most of the houses cling to the roadside. The bye-lanes are in zig-zag fashion and their development is still under progress. The settlement is rectangular in nature surrounded by the irrigation dam on the south, lowlands on the north and orchards on both the east and the west.

This settlement is a typical example showing the shifting of settlements due to floods and the changing course of rivers which are common in North Bihar. Such settlements are numerous in the flood plains of the Gandak, the Burhi Gandak and the Kosi which have great erosive power, and are capable of establishing permanent channels by erosion. The other smaller rivers are no doubt notorious for their floods, but they have poor thrust and do not cause permanent damage to the settlement site which may necessitate the shifting of buildings on a wide scale.

The regional distribution of village patterns proves that the 'massing and the characteristic appearance of the villages vary from region to region and is a function of the activity carried on the natural environment, the time period and the tradition of the people'[29]. In Bihar Plain the regional distribution of village patterns is significant as different patterns predominate in different areas, mainly depending upon the physical characteristics of the landscape and the influence of water-bodies and transport routes.

A detailed study is made to investigate the predominating village patterns in different parts of the Bihar Plain. This study is based upon one inch topographical sheets of the survey of India which show both the physical and the cultural landscapes. There is a profound influence of these factors on the external and internal layout of the village. It may, however, be noted that the patterns that have evolved are largely a result of the physical character of the site itself which has influenced the eventual form from the very inception[30].

The rectangular village which is the prominent type as also its allied patterns are most numerous in the Terai region of Champaran, western part of Saran, northern half of Bhojpur and in the central parts of Munger and Bhagalpur districts. The physical conditions of these regions show that they are relatively elevated plains mostly devoid of floods and waterlogging.

The square pattern or roughly circular pattern villages are found in the districts of Patna and Gaya. This region is mostly devoid of floods. Here canal, tank and well irrigation is prominent. There is another region of square pattern village in the compact settlement area of Bhagalpur district. The square pattern is only a variation of the rectangular pattern and is found in close association with it. Together they cover the largest part of the South Bihar Plain adjacent to the Ganga.

The linear settlements and their variations occupy a large belt in North Bihar, comprising the whole of Saharsa and Purnea districts, except the eastern portion and southern part of Samastipur and Vaishali districts. This pattern has obviously developed in the flood zones of the Bihar Plain, where the siting of village depends on the occurrence of linear embankments and levees of rivers and rivulets.

The star pattern has developed in the higher Terai regions of Sitamarhi and Madhubani districts, where elevated sites and the development of numerous cart-tracts have resulted in large villages of struggling nature whose size is often conspicuous in the entire region.

The circular village which is related to the need of defence occurs in regions most disturbed in the past, as for example Patna, Gaya and Bhojpur districts, where it often degenerates into square or rectangular patterns. Circular form in the larger villages indicates their ancient character. Patterns related to the circular type also occur in the same areas.

The chessboard pattern is characteristic of large villages and is not uncommon in the zones of compact settlements. The fan pattern, sigmatic settlement and horse-shoe patterns are the results of the peculiarities of site and are independent of any regional characteristics.[31] Such villages are very few in the Bihar Plain.

The amorphous pattern is clearly related to the sprinkled and semi-sprinkled settlement regions of the Bihar Plain. The amorphous pattern is concentrated in the eastern parts of Purnea district, parts of the Gandak flood plain in Saran and Champaran districts, and the entire Chotanagpur Scarp Belt in Rohtas, Nawada, Gaya, Munger and Bhagalpur districts. It is also found in the Kosi and the Ganga flood belts occasionally.

STRUCTURE OF INDIAN VILLAGE

The structure of village is the form and general make up of streets and houses with its objective boundaries and subjective feelings for the villagers and its neighbours. The interactions of different kinds of social norms, and availability of resources determine the structure and organization of village communities in India. Kinship, caste and territorial linkages are some of the determinants which shape the spatial and social structure of rural settlements. The collective form of individuals-forms the family which may be simple or compound, and a family may belong to a lineage. These may be grouped together in the form of sub-caste or caste. The group of Muslims in a Hindu village function as separate caste. Hindus are divided into four different categories of Brahmin, Kshatriya, Vaishya and Sudra which are known as different *varnas*. A family belongs to a village, and the village is a multi-caste in its composition. In such a situation the village itself is a part of network of neighbouring villages, the region, and the nation. The structural model of Indian rural settlement as presented in Fig. 11.4 shows that dotted circles are comparatively less effective units of social structure[32]. Non-Hindu groups fit well in this scheme, because they are outside the *varna* organization of Hindu society.

In India a village presents a far more complicated structure and this is reflected in the built structure of the houses of different castes and the existence of streets in between them. Those castes who are always separated from the others are those, whose touch is supposed to pollute the rest which is known as untouchables.

Such a structure to have separate sub-areas for habitation within a larger unit called a village can be explained on different grounds like caste-hierarchy, ideas of impurity and pollution, the need for certain occupations to have room for carrying out different processes needed for their craft. The first reason applies to the distance found between the untouchables houses and the rest, and the third applies to castes like *Kumhar* (potters), weavers (Jullah), dyers, shepherds, etc. It is such because in Indian Culture people are more and more intended to form separate groups, which are known as forming the caste hierarchical structure of rural settlements.

In the rural settlements of Malabar coast " Malayali prefers compounds, at a distance from his neighbours[33]."

The social structure of the village is so wide that it cuts across the boundaries of kin, caste and unites a number of families in an integrated manner ultimately forming a multi-caste community.

"Structurally the village communities can be divided into three main groups: the single settlement village, in which the community shares a common and compact settlement site, the "nucleated village" which has a central settlement as the nucleus around which there are a number of smaller satellite settlements, and the third "dispersed village" community in which the community consists of a series of dispersed boundaries having well-defined ties with one another[34]."

In Maharashtra the nucleated village structure is clearly defined from the surrounding agricultural fields. Such village types are found on high Deccan plateau. In this structure the boundaries of the fields owned by one village gradually merge into another except where the barrier is created by the hills, streams or a highway. The second type of linear rural settlement is found on the Konkan coast along the roads. The houses stand in the compound with fences, fruit trees and coconut gardens. Sometimes the streams divide one village with the other, but where there is no stream it may be difficult to recognise the discontiguity of the village because there is no sharp distinction between the habitation area and the cultivated area.

The third type of village is found in Satpura mountains where the houses are situated in the fields in a group of two to three huts all belonging to a single close kinship group. The other cluster of houses may be located at 100 metres away which depends upon the size of the agricultural plot. Such scattering is also due to habit of the *Bhil* people to change the settlement site even on a smaller pretext. In such a situation it is difficult to distinguish settlement from the cultivated area and one village from another.

Inside the village narrow streets connect one house with the other and sometimes an arterial road passes through the village, giving the village form a ribbon development, and the continuation of these footpaths extends up to the nearby village. Due to wide gap between two clusters of houses, the individual group of cluster is more prominent in space in comparison with the whole settlement form.

In the Northern Plains of India, the villages are quite stable and the same village boundary is continuing since thousands of years. In the villages for a particular caste there may be only one family, whereas for other castes there may be several familics.

REFERENCES

1. E.Ahmad: "Indian village Patterns." *Geographical outlook,* Vol. III, 1962, p.5
2. R.L.Singh "Banaras and Its Umland", in Banaras: *A study in Urban Geography,* The National Geographical Society of India, Varanasi, 1955, P.339.
3. P.W.Bryn: *Man's Adaptation of Nature*, London, 1933, p.23.
4. S.L.Duggal: "Moradabad District: *Settlements in Relation to land Use", Indian Geographer*, Vol. 6, 1961, pp.66-77.
5. Chandrashekhar Singh: *op.cit* p. 26.
6. Anant Prasad Banerji Shastri: *op.cit,* p.96
7. *Indian Nation,* 15th June 1969,p. 3
8. P.K. Acharya: *Mansara Shilpashastra,* Oxford University Press; London, 1933.
9. Renou Louis: *The Civilization of Ancient India,* Calcutta, 1959,p.51
10. E.B.Cowell: *Jatakas Stories*, Luzac, London, 1975.
11. *Vinaya Pitaka* 1: 208, Jataka 119, 253, 107.
12. *Ibid,* 1:109: 110,111; 4L; Jataka 163: 366.
13. *Ibid,* 1:110, 188 Jataka 330.
14. Jataka, 361.
15. Jataka 79:302.
16. L.S.S. O'mally: *Bengal District Gazetteer,* Champaran; Calcutta, 1907 p.85. The imperial road which Budha followed during his march from Rajgriha to Kushinara and several villages on both sides of the road.
17. Nagendra Nath: *op.cit p.* 15.
18. Balbhadra Jha: "Village in Ancient India." *Journal of Bihar Research Society,* Vol. 41, 1955 pp. 68-86.
19. Jack p. Gibbs: *Urban Research Method,* New Delhi, 1966, p.101.
20. L.D. Stamp: *Geography of Asia*, Allahabad, 1962, p.593.
21. A.B.Havel; Ancient and Medieval Architect of India, *Op.cit,* p.7.
22. Renou Louis; *op.cit.*
23. E.Ahmad, *op.cit.*
24. R.E. Dickinson: "The Town Plans of East Anglia," *Geography, March* 1924, P. 74.
25. E.Ahmad; *op.cit,* p.11.
26. R.L. Singh: : Evolution of Settlements in the Middle Ganga Valley," The *National Geographical Journal of India,* Vol. 1, 1955, p. 112.
27. L.D. Stamp: "The Common Lands and Village Greens of England and Wales," *The Geographical Journal*, Vol. 130, 1967.
28. L.R. Singh: The Terai Region of Uttar Pradesh- *A Study in Human Geography,* Allahabad, 1965, p.44.
29. P.W. Bryn: *op.cit,* p.24.
30. Carter V. Bohman; *The English Village, Pelican*, London, 1951, p.99.
31. E. Ahmad: *op.cit,* p. 15.
32. S.C. Dube: Social Structure and Change in Indian Peasant Communities," *Transactions of the Third World Congress of Sociology,* vol.1-11: pp. 259-266.
33. Eric J. Miller "Village structure in North Kerala", *The Economic Weekly, 9th February,* 1952.
34. S.C. Dube. *op.cit,* p. 265.

Fig. 11.1(a)

Village Patterns

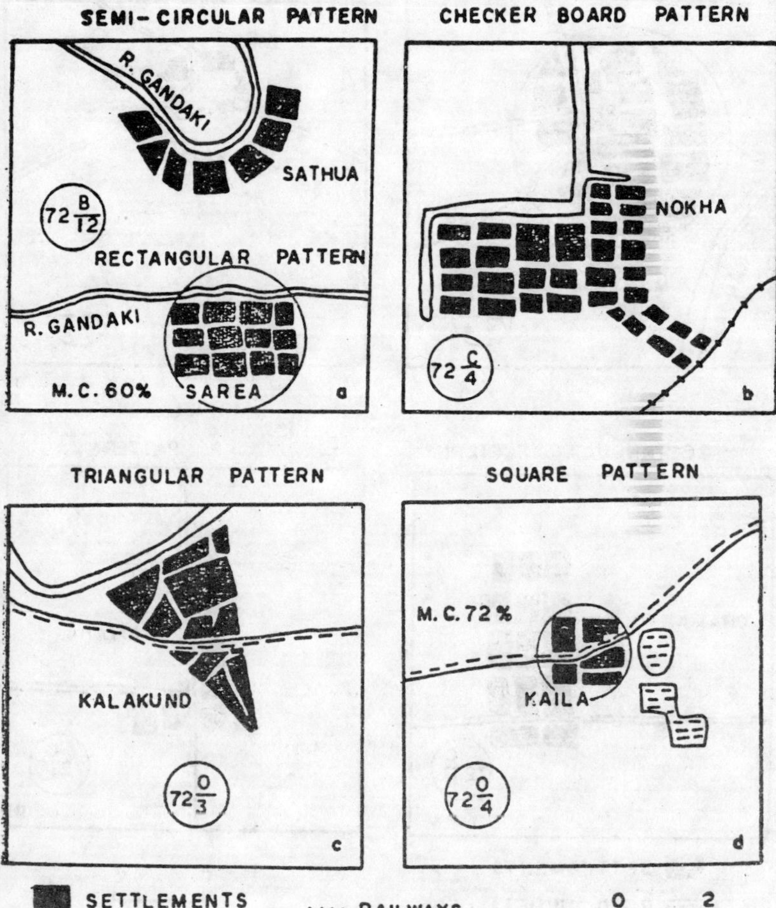

Fig. 11.1 (b)

Village Patterns

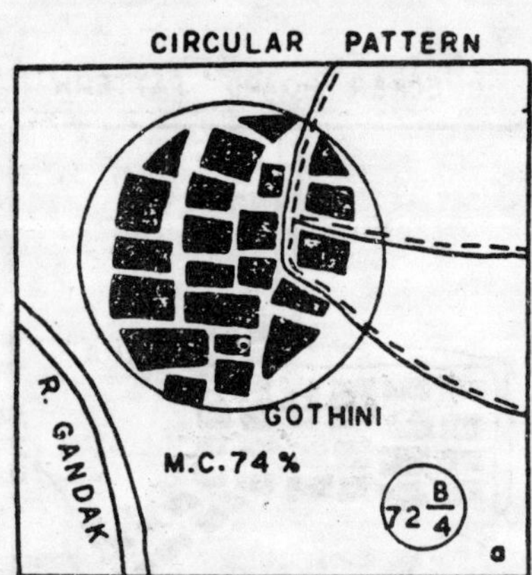

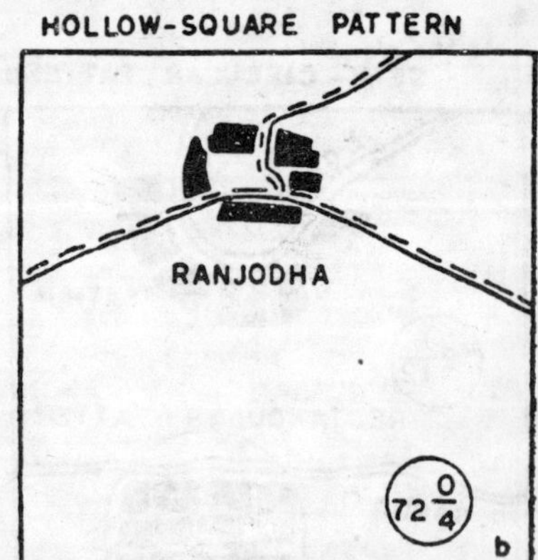

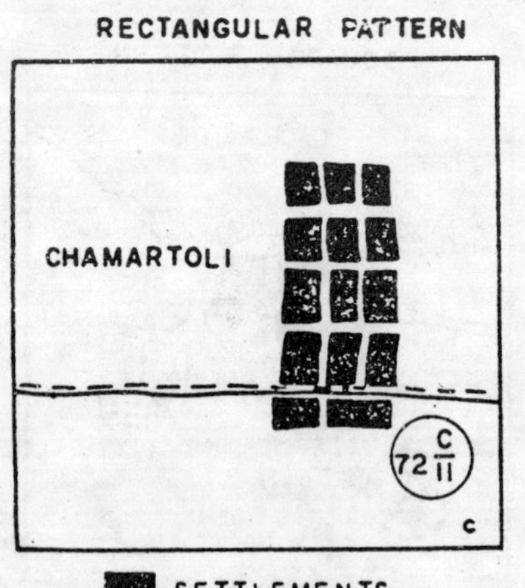

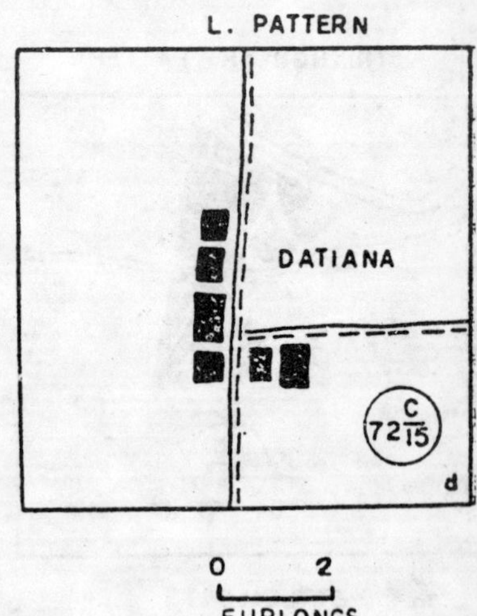

Fig. 11.2

Village-Majhrahia Linear Pattern

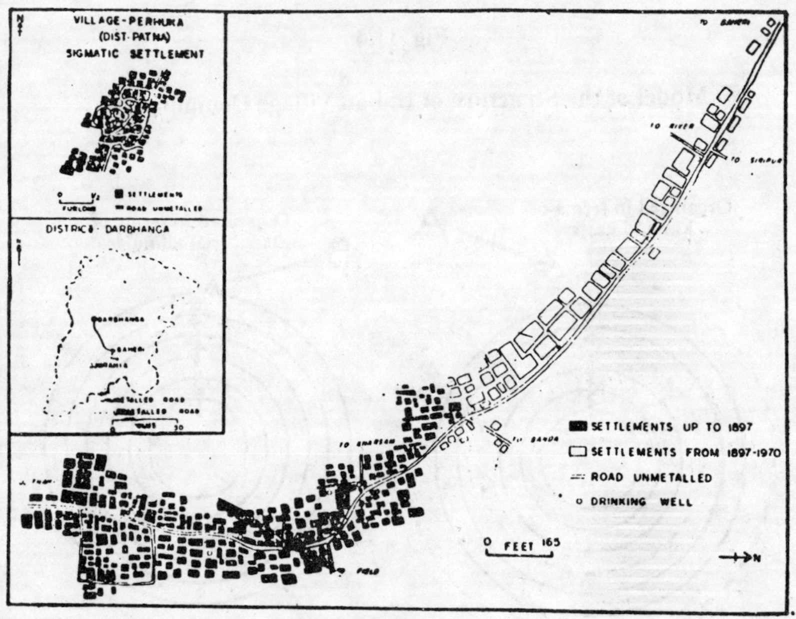

Fig. 11.3

Village-Kharsam

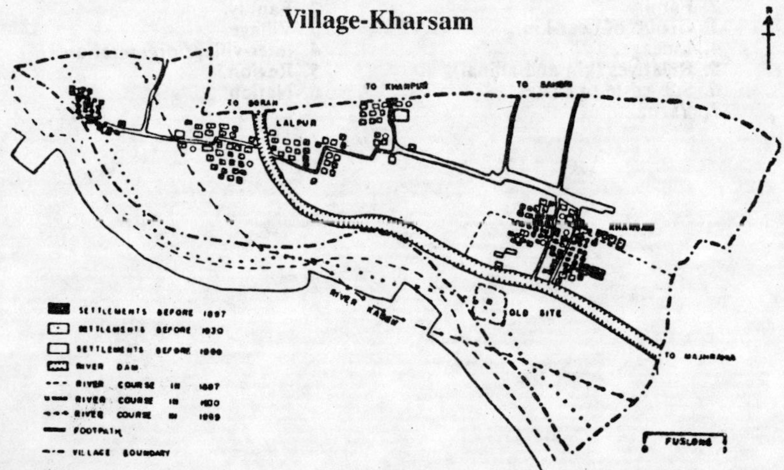

Fig. 11.4

Model of the Structure of Indian Village Communities

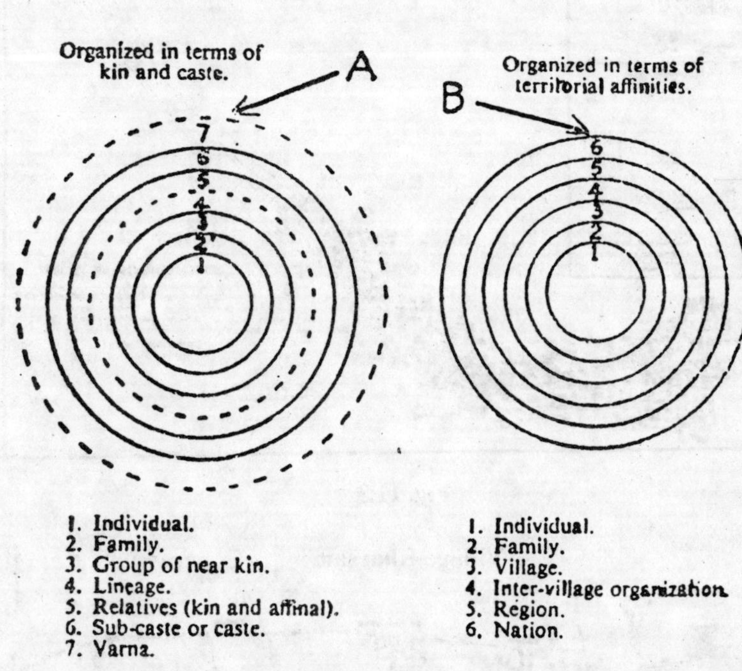

TWELVE

SIZE AND SPACING OF RURAL SETTLEMENTS

J.W. WATSON has identified geography as a discipline in distance[1]. But the study of rural settlements from this angle has so far been virtually non-existent. A study of the type, forms and patterns of rural settlements has engaged geographers to such an extent that they have done little to identify, quantitatively analyse, and express the significance of their size and spacing.

The variation in size and spacing of rural settlements from area to area is a physically established fact due to the variations in ecological conditions. According to Mukerjee[2], the covariance of spacing of rural settlements depends on such fundamental factors as fertility of land, productivity of agriculture, nature of crops, agronomic characteristics, distribution and availability of water, density of rural population, size of rural settlements, types of rural settlements, mode of living, history and stages of land occupancy, relative strengths of tribal population and several other factors. But according to Donglass[3], the spacing of small settlements depends upon three principal items:

(a) The agricultural prosperity,
(b) Surface configuration, and
(c) Historical habits.

He was of the opinion that small settlements are a rural luxury and they are the thickest where there is the greatest agricultural prosperity.

T. Prasad, (1977)[4] described the spatial pattern of rural settlements in Visakhapatnam taluka of Andhra Pradesh. He correlated the spacing of rural settlements with various physico-cultural factors. The closely spaced villages are correlated with the well knit transport arteries, the availability of water and fertile land. The large sized widely spaced villages are correlated with the absence of transport facilities and the presence of swampy ground.

H.H. Singh and Jagdish Singh (1977)[5] made spatial, dispersion and chi-square analyses of rural settlements in Upper Domodar Valley and concluded that the trend of dispersion of rural settlements is approaching towards regularity from randomness and the environmental factors control the spatial distribution of rural settlements.

This chapter aims to identify the regional patterns of spacing of rural settlements in the Bihar Plain and Bagamoyo district of Tanzania in order to evaluate the characteristics of determinants which command the spatial characteristics of settlements in different areas. Spacing is also another expression of density, but it does not imply a geometrical pattern in the arrangement of settlements.

The formula for determining the spacing of rural settlements is based on their density in the rural area. Walenty Winid a Polish geographer derived a formula [6] to determine the frequency of towns in any area. As the settlements are ordinarily placed at the intersection points of a rectangular grid, he assumes that the best figure to use for inter settlement distance is equal to the square-root of the area divided by the number of settlements within that area. The formula is as follows:

$$D = \frac{A}{N}$$

Where D is considered as the average distance between settlements, A is the total area under consideration, and N is the number of settlements within that area. The method applied for size of the rural settlements is as follows:

$$S = \frac{P}{N}$$

Where S is the average size of population per village, P is the rural population of the *anchal* and N is the number of villages in the *anchal*. The data was calculated for all the 395 *anchals* and grouped into four classes of hierarchy on the basis of quartile value. A distribution map was prepared by drawing isopleths which gave a good regional pattern for the analysis of the population size of rural settlements.

In the Bihar Plain, the size and spacing of rural settlements are mainly dependent upon three factors:

(a) Effects of flood,
(b) Natural fertility of soil, and
(c) Surface configuration.

It is a region of destructive floods. Numerous rivers and rivulets draining the Himalayan foothills in the north and Chotanagpur in the south flow towards each other and ultimately discharge their water into the Ganga in the Middle. The effects of recurrent floods in these rivers seem to be most potent on the landscape of the region and guide the size and spacing of rural settlements in their respective commands.

The scatter diagram (Fig. 12.1) which has been prepared on semi-log graph shows that as the size of village population increases in flood affected areas, their spacing also increases. This dual relationship of size and spacing in the flood affected areas suggests that it is the most significant controlling factor for both higher size and greater spacing of rural settlements in the region.

In areas prone to floods, the land is fertile, because of annual inundation by the rivers that bring new alluvial deposits in the field. There is, however, medium density of population in these areas. The relatively higher sites fit for human settlements are somewhat rare in such areas because of the lack of slope. Thus, these areas turn into a vast lake as far as our eyes can see during the rainy season. During this period one has to travel by boat from one settlement to another. Settlements are, therefore, large in size but at greater distances from one-other. In flood affected areas, the spacing of settlement is over 2.40 kilometres from each other and the size of population of the village ranges from 900 to over 3000 persons.

The areas which are not affected by floods have smaller villages and their spacing is also closer. The fertile plains of Saran, Bhojpur, Gaya, Patna and parts of Muzaffarpur and Darbhanga districts have very little effects of flood. Here the settlements are closely spaced within 2 kilometres distance from each other and their size also decreases roughly from 300 to 1000 persons per village.This shows that as the fertility of soil increases, the size and spacing of rural settlement also register a decline to a certain extent.

It may be noted that in spacing of settlements there comes a stage when the land reaches the limit of its capability to support the population. Under such conditions, if the settlements grow larger in size, their spacing may not increase in all cases to maintain the balance of the man-land ratio. In South Bihar Plain-Patna, Gaya, Bhojpur and Rohtas have assured irrigation facilities from canals, *pynes* and *ahars*, and with greater use of fertilizers in the fields they produce larger quantities of foodgrains. Thus they are also aided by the natural fertility of the soil and adequate amount of rainfall. Thus these areas can support larger villages with closer spacing. In North Bihar Plain, Saran and parts of Muzaffarpur and Darbhanga districts also have good fertile soils coupled with sufficient rainfall and relative freedom from floods. They are thus able to support large sized villages with less than two kilometres spacing.

Human habitations are often found in rugged terrain, forest clad mountain slopes and non-cultivable waste lands. Such lands never support a dense population, because the fertility of soil is low. The few inhabitants in such areas depend upon cattle rearing, hunting and also forest products like timber, herbs, etc. for their livelihood. The whole of Dun and Sumeshwar hills in north-west Champaran district and the Chotanagpur Scarp Belt in the South Bihar Plain are devoid of population concentration, except for a few tribal and scheduled caste people. Here factors like the fear of wild animals, the lack of transport facilities and building materials and above all the poverty of land are important as they retard the size and increase the spacing of rural settlements. The conditions are not favourable for human settlement above 150 metres contour line, because such lands have a high slope coupled with over 150 cm of rainfall, which leaches the soil and reduces the fertility to a great extent. These areas are also rugged and covered with dense forests, with the settlements few and far between.

In this regard, it is also noticeable that where the density of road is high, population tends to live in small villages as in Saran, Patna and Gaya districts; and conversely, where the road density is low, and there is greater concentration in large and medium sized villages, as in Saharsa, Purnea and Darbhanga districts.

SPATIAL PATTERN OF RURAL SETTLEMENTS

Six types of settlement areas have been identified with the help of median and quartile analyses of data on spacing of villages (Fig. 12.2). For the purpose of discussion, these six categories were combined and reduced to three groups of areas:

(a) Area of High Spacing (1.82 to 3.50 kilometres),
(b) Areas of Moderate Spacing (1.31 to 1.81 kilometres), and
(c) Areas of close spaçing (0.88 to 1.30 kilometres).

In the flood affected areas of the region where the size of the settlement is also high, the distance between settlements ranges from 1.82 to 3.50 kilometres. This is because higher sites are relatively infrequent and the need of cooperation in paddy cultivation and crop storage makes compact settlements imperative. For example, we can take Maner *anchal* in Patna district where the spacing of rural settlements is 2.02 kms. and the average population size of the villages is 2001 persons. This *anchal* falls in the diara of the Ganga and the Son. In Patna district, Pandarakh, Mokameh, Sarmera and other *anchals* have higher spacing and population size. These are also affected by floods from the Ganga, the Son and the Sakri. It seems that both size and spacing vary according to the intensity of floods. In this respect, Maner ranks first in Patna district. In Gaya district, Kawakole falls in this category because the district is free from floods, except in small areas like Kawakole *anchal* which lies in the flood belt of the river Sakri, the spacing is high because of the effect of floods. The larger size of villages in these areas indicates higher fertility and better land potentiality.

On the other hand, the areas of high spacing coupled with low population suggests that the land is poor in fertility and cannot support a large population. For example, in Rohtas, Nauhatta and Adhaura *anchals* of Shahabad district, the average spacing between villages is 2.76, 2.46 and 2.96 kilometres respectively, while the size of population is 767, 542 and 186 persons per village only. In contrast, Koilwar and Jagdishpur *anchals* in Bhojpur district are liable to floods. Here the size and spacing ranges from 1150 to 1155 persons and 1.95 to 1.82 kilometres respectively. Saran has no area in this category, except for some southern parts because the district devoid of flood problems has good soils.

The district of Champaran is a land of rivers like the Narayani, the Burhi Gandak and a host of minor rivulets. It is a fertile area liable to floods. The size and spacing of settlements, therefore, depend largely upon the intensity of floods. Here, due to a relatively higher gradient of land, floods are not intensive in general, but there are some *anchals* like Madhubani in the lower reaches of the river Narayani and Chiraiya in the basin of the river Burhi Gandak which are marked by a high size of 2884 and 2220 persons and large spacing of 3.50 and 3.07 kilometres respectively.

In Muzaffarpur district, *anchals* like Riga, Nanpur and Raghopur, which lie in the flood belt of the river Baghmati and the river Ganga, have a spacing of 1.82, 3.49 and 2.19 kilometres coupled with a population size of 1865, 1944 and 1532 persons per village respectively.

The eastern zone of the Bihar Plain covers the districts of Darbhanga, Saharsa, Purnea, Bhagalpur and Munger. These are the lands of rivers, *Chaurs*, lakes, *tals* and marshes and all of them present a similar character in the size and spacing of rural settlements. For example, in Bhagalpur district the riverine *anchals* of Bihpur, Naugachhia and Gopalpur have a population size of 2246, 2545 and 2934 persons per village and a spacing of 2.57, 2.64 and 3.49 kilometres respectively.

In the Chotanagpur Scarp Belt of South Bihar Plain villages are situated at relatively greater distances. Siting is selective and related to forest clearings, slope, extent of alluvium, water supply, etc. The distance between villages may be abnormally large if wide patches of forest or difficult terrain such as steep ridges intervene. Except small residuals and rocky exposures, the soil is uniform in thickness and fertility and the land is level in the plains so that the villages are fairly evenly distributed. All the marginal *anchals* of flood affected areas with assured natural irrigation and good fertile soil come under this category. Here the inter-village distance is reduced to some extent and their population size also gets decreased.

Under this category, the rural settlements with a population of 933 and above, and a spacing of 1.31 to 1.81 kilometres are fairly widely distributed over the entire flood plains of the Ganga, the Kosi, the Kamla, the Balan and the Bhuthi rivers, except in the marshy areas of Saharsa and Purnea districts in the north-eastern sector of the plain. The marginal flood plains of the Gandak, the Burhi-Gandak and the Adhwara group of rivers are typical examples of this class of settlements in the west.

In South Bihar Plain, due to relatively more recent development of settlements and an inferior quality of soil, villages have a lower population size coupled with higher spacing. Only agriculturally prosperous *anchals* such as Paliganj, Bikram, Arwal, Karpi, Daudnagar and others come under this category of spacing.

The areas which are fertile and free from floods are included in this category. Here the spacing of rural settlements ranges from 0.88 to 1.30 kilometre. The spacing of rural settlements and the population size of the villages decrease drastically in areas free from floods even though the density of population per square kilometre is high. This means that the availability of water is the main consideration for the development of settlements in such areas. Wherever a well is constructed, some houses are built and a settlement unit is established. In the fertile plains, settlements are very closely spaced because the land capability is high. For example, all the well irrigated tracts of Saran district have a closer spacing of rural settlements coupled with lower population size and higher density of population.

In South Bihar Plain of Patna district, the *anchals* like Phulwari, Dhanarua, Punpun and Naubatpur fall in this category. The area of assured *pyne* and canal irrigation in Gaya district are also in the same group, which includes the whole of Gaya district except some *anchals* in the Chotanagpur Scarp Belt. In Bhojpur and Rohtas districts, the *anchals* of Arrah, Charpokhri, Rajpur, Itarhi, Bikramganj, Karakat, Dinara, Dawath, Kargahar, Kudra and Bhabua are similar in character. In North Bihar Plain, the whole of Saran district and the *anchals* of Hajipur and Sadar Subdivision of Muzaffarpur district as well as a few *anchals* in Champaran, Darbhanga, Munger, Bhagalpur and Purnea districts can be included in this category.

All these are marked by stable agricultural conditions on a fertile but relatively high land which is free from floods. There is no dearth of settlement sites and they can be built close to each other. As the total number of settlement units increases, their spacing and population size naturally decrease, even though the average density of population remains high.

Nearest-Neighbour Analysis of Rural Settlements in Bagamoyo District

Nearest neighbour is generally measured as crow flies distance in between two nearest rural settlements. This concept has been originally devised by Clark and Evans (1954)[7] who were plant ecologists. The measure provides a departure from observed spatial distribution to a theoretical random distribution between agglomerated and uniform patterns (Fig. 12.3). This scaler distribution is known as R scale or nearest neighbour scale and its value can be calculated with the help of the formula.

$$Rn = \frac{\bar{r}A}{\bar{r}E}, \quad Where \quad \bar{r}A = \frac{\sum r}{N}$$

where r is the distance from each point to its nearest-neighbour which is the actual straight line measurement, and the estimated mean distance is

$$\bar{r}E = \frac{1}{2\sqrt{\frac{N}{A}}}$$

where N is the number of rural settlements and A is the area contained by these centres.

The standard error of the expected mean distance is given as:

$$\sigma r E = \frac{0.26126}{\sqrt{N^2 / A}} = \frac{.26126}{\sqrt{36/232}} = .6632$$

If the value of R lies between .99 to 0 it may be known as approaching clustered, 1 is random, and 1.01 to 2.15 as approaching uniform, provided that the value of $\bar{r}$-E is significantly different from $\bar{r}$ A, otherwise, the pattern should be considered as random and the difference between $\bar{r}$ A and $\bar{r}$ E is attributed to the chance factor only. The Z statistic is:

$$Z = \frac{\bar{r}A - \bar{r}E}{\sigma \bar{r}E}$$

is a standard normal variate (the limit of which at 5 per cent and 1 per cent levels of significance 2.58 and 1.96 respectively) and is used to test the significance of difference between $\bar{r}$A and $\bar{r}$E.

The ratio of observed mean distance ($\bar{r}$ A) to expected value ranges from zero (0) on the clustered side to 1.00 random, up to 2.1491 towards uniform pattern signifying maximum dispersal, which is analogous to the hexagonal arrangement of settlements.

Spatial Pattern of rural settlement in Bagamoyo district is very uneven (Fig. 12.4). For example, in the ward of Zinga Kirege the distance from one village to another is 1.50 kilometre which is the lowest figure for the whole district whereas in the wards of Magomeni and Kibindu the inter-village distance is very high 9 kilometres (Table-12.1).

Table 12.1 shows that the approaching cluster pattern of rural settlements is found only in Yombo Ward (.46). In other two wards of Zinga Kirege and Msata the pattern is approaching random (.81 and .84).

The wards having more than random patterns are Kiwangwa, Miono, Kiromo, Vigwaza, Tarawanda, Chalinze and Mbwewe. In all these wards the Rn value ranges from 1.09 in Chalinze to 1.57 in Kiwangwa. The wards approaching uniform distributions are under forest bush cover coupled with badland topography where either the cultivation of land or the development of transportation line for the human settlements are bit difficult. In areas of clustered pattern these difficulties are normally not found.

The upper and lower ranges of random matching (Fig. 12.5) and Table 12.1 for the nearest neighbour at 95 per cent probability level have been measured with the help of a formula:

Table 12.1 : Nearest Neighbour Statistics for Rural Settlements in Bagamoyo District, Tanzania, 1985

Sl. No.	Wards	No. of villages	Area Km^2	Density of Villages per km^2	Mean observed distance in km(rA)	Mean estimated distance in km (rE)	Rn value
1.	Kiwangwa	6	232	.0259	4.90	3.12	1.57
2.	Msata	5	311	.0160	3.50	4.16	.84
3.	Miono	7	132	.0530	2.80	2.18	1.28
4.	Mkange	6	298	.0200	6.37	3.60	1.76
5.	Magomeni	2	158	.0126	9.00	4.54	1.98
7.	Kiromo	2	35	.0571	3.00	2.08	1.44
8.	Zinga Kirege	5	67	.0746	1.50	1.85	.81
9.	Yombo	4	40	.100	2.33	5.00	.46
10.	Vigwaza	5	138	.0362	3.33	2.63	1.27
11.	Tarawanda	3	110	.0272	4.00	3.12	1.28
12.	Chalinze	5	111	.0450	2.60	2.38	1.09
13.	Lugoba	5	78	.0641	3.00	2.00	1.50
14.	UbenaZamozi	4	147	.0272	5.50	3.12	1.76
15.	Mbwewe	6	290	.0209	4.60	3.60	1.28
16.	Kibindu	3	254	.0119	9.00	4.54	1.98

Source: Calculated by the author.

$$1 \pm 2^{\sigma} \frac{rE}{rE}$$

where 1 is for random matching,
2 is for 95% probability,

$\sigma \bar{r}E$ is equal to $\dfrac{0.26126}{\sqrt{N^2/A}}$,

where 0.26126 is some empirical constant,
N is the number of rural settlement,
and A is the areal unit where the settlements are located;
and $\bar{r}E$ is the mean estimated distance.

The calculation with the help of the above formula is as follows:

$$1 \pm 2\frac{\sigma \bar{r} E}{\bar{r} E} = 1 \pm 2\frac{0.026126}{\sqrt{\frac{N^2/A}{\bar{r}E}}} = 1 \pm 2\frac{0.26126}{\sqrt{\frac{6^2/232}{3.12}}}$$

$$1 \pm 2\frac{0.26126}{\sqrt{\frac{.1554}{3.12}}}\; 1 \pm \frac{2 \times .66}{3.12} = \frac{3.12}{3.12} + \frac{1.32}{3.12}$$

$$(Upper) = \frac{3.12 + 1.32}{3.12} = \frac{4.44}{3.12} = 1.425\,(Upper)$$

$$(Lower) = \frac{3.12 - 1.32}{3.12} = \frac{1.80}{3.12} = 0.575\,(Lower).$$

Table 12.2 : The Upper and Lower Ranges of the Random Matching at 95% probability level for the first nearest-neighbour in Bagamoyo District, Tanzania, 1985.

	Wards	$\sigma \bar{r}E$	Maximum range	Minimum Range (2 - Maximum)
1.	Kiwangwa	.6632	1.4250	.5750
2.	Msata	.9215	1.4430	.5570
3.	Miono	.4285	1.3930	.6070
4.	Mkange	.7517	1.4180	.5820
5.	Magomeni	1.6420	1.7230	.2770
6.	Kiromo	.7728	1.7430	.2570

7.	Zinga Kirege	.4277	1.4624	.5376
8.	Yombo	.4131	1.4952	.5048
9.	Vigwza	.6138	1.4668	.5332
10.	Tarawanda	.9134	1.5855	.4145
11.	Chalinze	.5505	1.4626	.5374
12.	Lugoba	.4615	1.4615	.5385
13.	Ubena Zamozi	.7919	1.5076	.4924
14.	Mbwewe	.7415	1.4120	.5880
15.	Kibindu	1.3879	1.6114	.3886

Source : Calculated by the author.

The frequency curve of Rn value shows a normal distribution (Fig. 12.5) which reveals that most of the wards find their location around the line of random distribution and fanning for a fewer observations towards the cluster and uniform patterns of rural settlements in Bagamoyo district.

Table 12.3 Fig. 12.5 show the relationship between size and spacing of rural settlements in Bagamoyo district, Tanzania. The result is that in most cases high population size of settlements are found to be closely spaced while the smaller population size settlements widely spaced. For example, in Chalinze ward the average population size of the settlement is 3135 persons (1978) while the inter-village distance is [illegible].60 kilometres. In Magomeni Ward the average population size is 1098 persons while the inter-village distance is 9 kilometres. For these two sets of data the Pearsonian correlation r is -0.3154 whereas the linear regression of Y on X is; Y = 2016.41 - 76.68 X. This shows that size and spacing of rural settlements are negatively correlated.

Rank-Size Relationship of Rural Settlements in Bagamoyo District

Zipf[8] (1941) devised a theoretical model to express the relationship between observed and empirical regularity in the size of settlements hierarchy. The orderly development of settlements according to their rank and size is the basis for this relationship. Any divergence from the reality of the rule provides an indicator towards an upsetting factor in a socio-economic equilibrium in the region.[9]

Table 12.3 : Population Size and Spacing of Rural Settlements in Bagamoyo District, Tanzania, 1978.

Sl. No.	Wards	Inter-village Distance in Km(x)	Average Population Size (Y)
1.	Kiwangwa	4.90	1317
2.	Msata	3.50	1275
3.	Miono	2.80	1655
4.	Mkange	6.37	1081
5.	Magomeni	9.00	1098
6.	Kiromo	3.00	1588
7.	Zinga Kirege	1.50	1619
8.	Yombo	2.33	1229
9.	Vigwaza	3.33	1589
10.	Tarawanda	4.00	2168
11.	Chalinze	2.60	3135
12.	Lugoba	3.00	1919
13.	Ubena Zamozi	5.50	2451
14.	Mbwewe	4.60	1627
15.	Kibindu	9.00	1478

Source: Calculated by the author.

Under the rank-size rule, the number of settlements should continue to increase as their size decreases so that we should expect not only villages with higher population size, but more smaller sized settlements than villages and more isolated farm-steads than smaller settlements.[10] Haggett has noted that this relationship may not hold true universally, because isolated farmsteads are not everywhere more numerous than hamlets.[11]

The existence of a straight line rank-size curve for settlements in many countries and regions of the world[12] suggests that this is a 'normal condition'[13] even though the reasons of its existence are not yet clear.

This rank-size rule is a regular relationship which often exists between absolute size of a settlement centre (measured by its population, not area) and its rank (the centre with the largest population in the region ranking 1, the next largest 2, and so on to the smallest village). This relationship may be expressed by the simple formula:

$$Pn = \frac{P1}{n}$$

where Pn is the population of the nth rural settlement in denominator, and P1 is the population of the region's largest rural settlement, i.e. the centre which ranks 1 in the list.

Fig. 12.7 and Table 12.4 show the actual rank - size relationship of rural settlements in Bagamoyo district, Tanzania. In Bagamoyo the village having largest population (5407) is Bwilingu in 1978. According to the rank-size rule the second village should have a population of half of the first ranking village that is 2702 but in reality the second village has a population of 4665. Similarly, the last 68th ranking village should have a population of 5404/68 = 79.47, but in reality it has a population of 418. This shows that in rural area due to similar agricultural economy everywhere there is not much variations in the concentration of population. The other thing is that rank-size rule does not hold good in smaller parts of a bigger region.

Although statistically the relationship between rank and population size is obvious, but Pearsonian coefficient of Correlation has been calculated which comes to r = -.09128 which is highly significant, and the regression of Y on X is; Y = 3207.18-44.18 x. The standard error of estimate, sey was not calculated as the rank order is entirely an independent variable but is effected by the change in population size of a place and, therefore, there is no point in carrying out the estimate to a definite mathematical conclusion. This chapter was aimed to demonstrate the relationship that exists between average population size of rural settlements, their rank and spacing not only on national but international scale.

Table 12.4 : Rank and Size of Village in Bagamoyo District, Tanzania (1978)

Village	Village	Rank (x)		Population (Y)	
Bwilingu	Mkange	1	35	5404	1487
Ubena Zamozi	Makurunge	2	36	4665	1474
Lugoba	Mazingara	3	37	3622	1430
Kiwangwa	Kifuleta	4	38	3400	1426
Vigwaga	Diozile	5	39	2967	1413
Malaula	Ruvu Darajani	6	40	2967	1406
Pera	Msoga	7	41	2896	1398
Tarawanda	Yombo	8	42	2801	1374
Msata	Yisezi	9	43	2593	1341
Kibindu	Mapinga	10	44	2519	1274
Miono	Makombe	11	45	2449	1240

Ropongwi	Buyuni	12	46	2440	1223
Kikaro	Mazizi Pogwe	13	47	2425	1186
Mbwewe	Matimbwa	14	48	2423	1148
Msolwa	Kwangandu	15	49	2409	1140
Mlingotini	Masuguru	16	50	2402	1036
Maturi	Kidogozero	17	51	2269	1012
Kiromo	Mataya	18	52	2170	1005
Tukamisasa	Mnuga	19	53	2043	966
Kisanganindukin	Hondogo	20	54	2033	922
Pingo	Pande	21	55	2030	914
Mboga	Visakazi	22	56	1922	826
Zinga	Kongo	23	57	1792	806
Mandera	Msinume	24	58	1782	759
Kirege	Saadani	25	59	1716	733
Matipwili	Kaole	26	60	1705	723
Pongwe Kiona	Masimbani	27	61	1690	610
Malivundo	Kilemera	28	62	1671	605
Fukayosi	Mkenge	29	63	1658	544
Madesa	Mkoko	30	64	1609	529
Kimange	Kweikonje	31	65	1578	520
Chasimba	Kidomole	32	66	1568	508
Kwahurombo	Msungura	33	67	1505	459
Kwamduma	Kwamsanja	34	68	1496	418

Source: Prepared from 1978 Population Census, Vol. II, The United Republic of Tanzania, (1981); pp. 204-208

REFERENCES

1. J.W. Watson: "Geography: A Discipline in Distance", *Scottish Geographical Magazine;* Vol. 71, 1955, pp.1-13.
2. A.B. Mukerjee: "Spacing of rural Settlements in Andhra Pradesh", *Geographical outlook;* Vol. VI; 1969, P.1.
3. G.T. Trewartha: "The Unincorporated Hamlet: The Element of the American settlement Fabric", *Annals of the Association of American Geographers*; Vol. 33, pp. 32 - 81.
4. T.Prasad: "Dispersion and size of Rural settlements in Visakhapatnam Taluka". *Deccan Geographer;* Vol. 1, 1977, pp. 191-197
5. H.H. Singh and Jagdish Singh: "A Quantitative Approach in the Distributional Pattern of Uural Settlements: A Part of Upper Damodar Valley". *Uttar Bharat Bhoogol Patrika;* Vol. XIII; Nos. 1-2; 1977, pp. 128-138.
6. G.T. Trewartha; *Op.cit.*
7. P.J. Clark and P.C. Evans: "Distance to Nearest-Neighbour as a Measure of Spatial Relationships in Populations", *Ecology,* Vol. 1954, pp. 445-453.
8. G.K. Zipf: *National Unity and Disunity*; Principia Press, Bloomington, 1941.
9. R.B. Mandal; "Rank-Size Relationship of Urban Centres in Bihar", *Indian Geographical studies;* R.B. No. 3, September, 1974, pp. 41-49.
10. R.H. Alan Baker: "Reversal of the Rank-Size Rule", *The Professional Geographer,* Vol. XXI, 1969, p. 386.
11. P. Haggett: *Locational Analysis in Human Geography*, Edward Arnold, London, 1965, p.106.
12. F.W. Boal and D.B. Johnson: "The Rank-Size Rule", *Professional Geog-*

rapher, Vol. XVII; 1965, p. 21.

13. B.J.L. Berry and W.L. Garrison: "Alternative Explanations of Urban Rank-Size Relationship", *Annals of the Association of American Geographers*, Vol. 48, 1958, p.83.

Fig.12.1

Size and Spacing of Rural Settlements in Bihar Plain

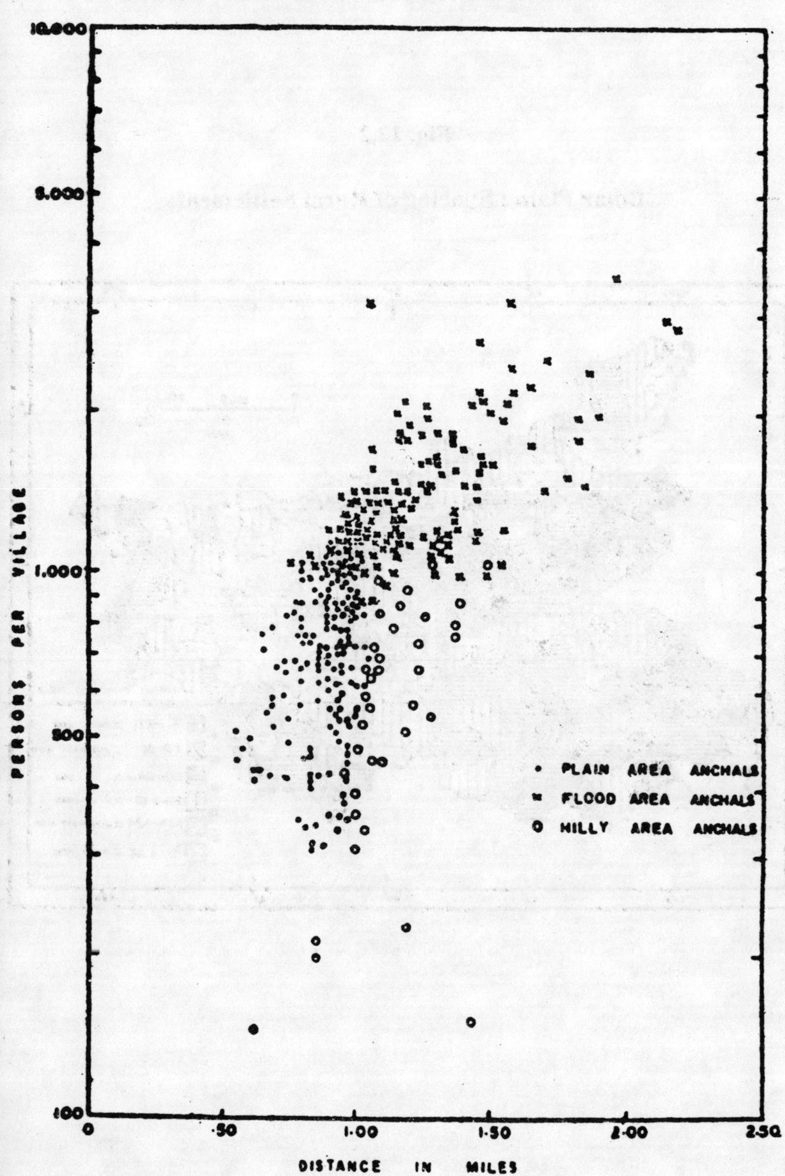

Fig. 12.2

Bihar Plain : Spacing of Rural Settlements

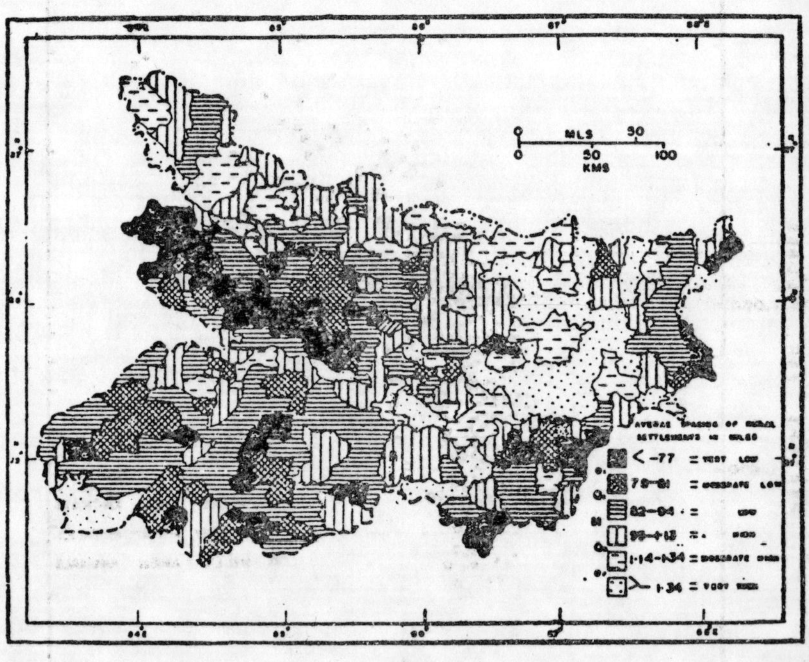

Fig. 12.3

The nearest neighbour, R^n, scale

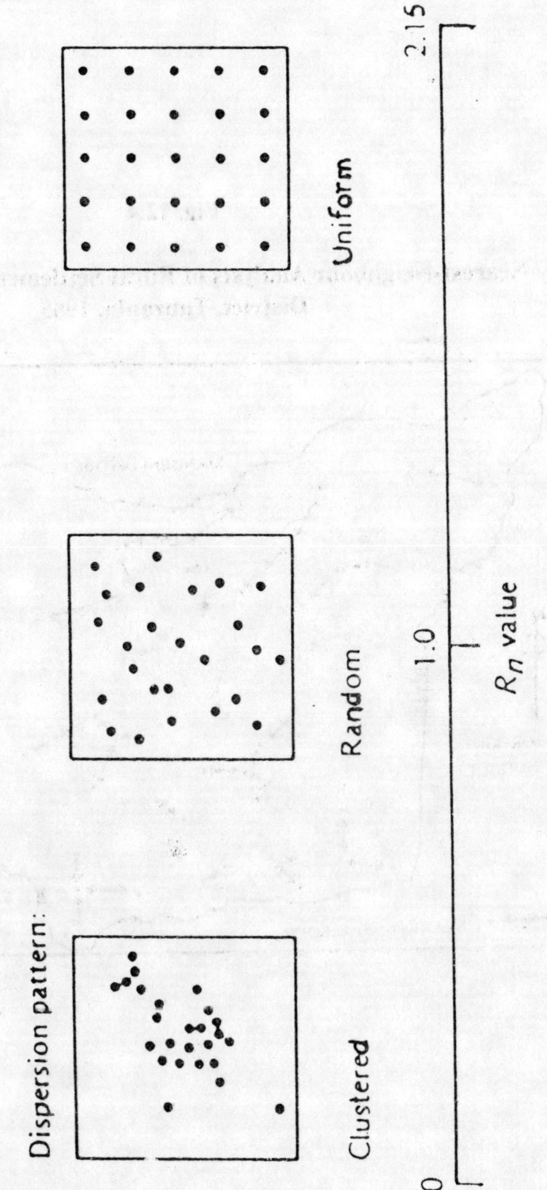

Fig. 12.4

Nearest-Neighbour Analysis of Rural Settlements in Bagamoyo District, Tanzania, 1985

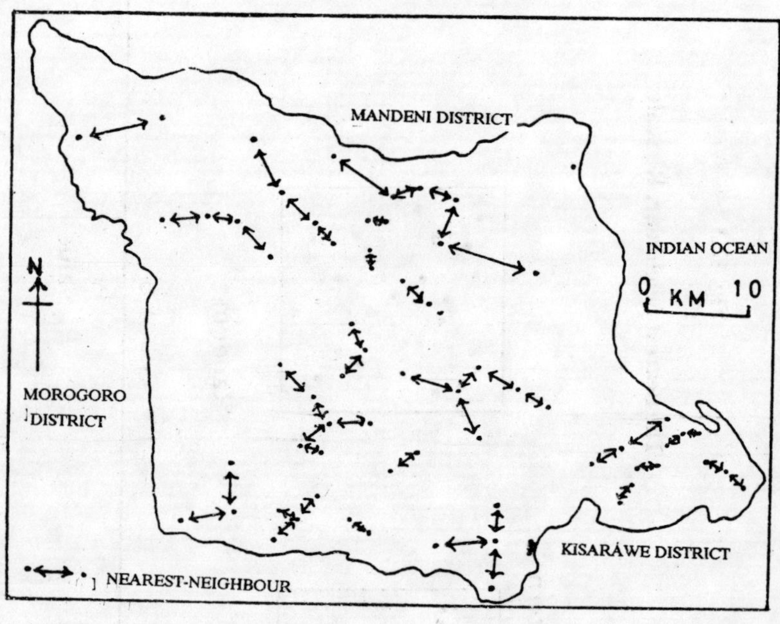

Fig. 12.5

Significance Value for the Rn Statistic, Bagamoyo District, Tanzania

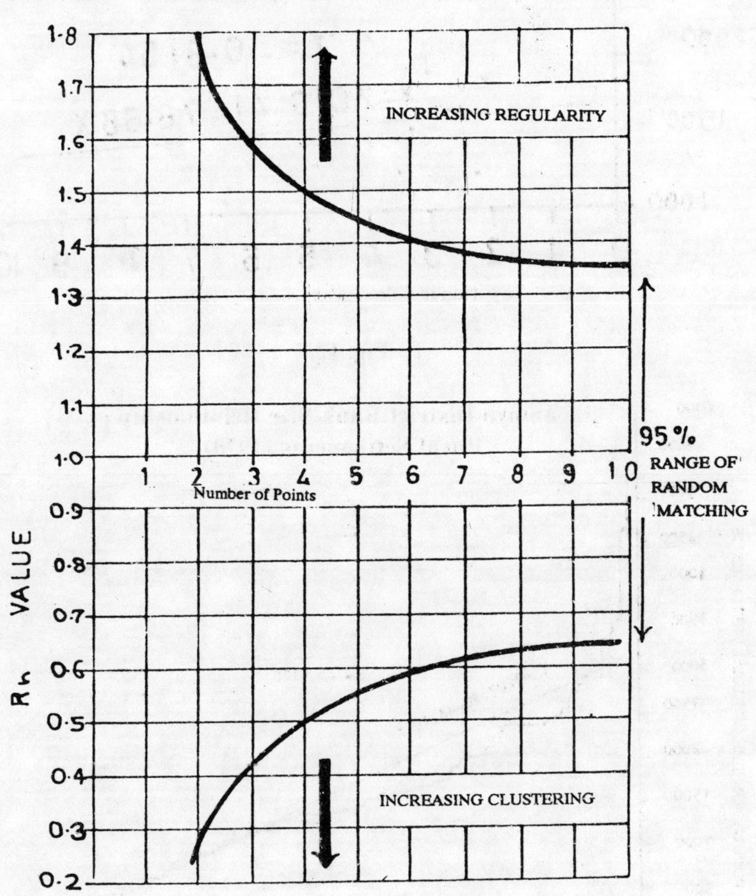

Fig. 12.6

Relationship of Size and Spacing of Rural Settlements in Bgamoyo District, Tanzania

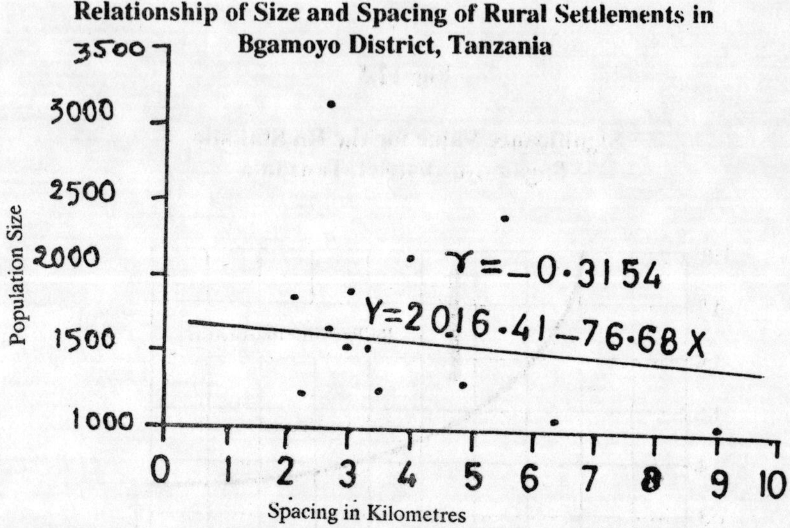

Fig. 12.7

Bagamoyo District:Rank-Size Relationship of Rural Settlements (1978)

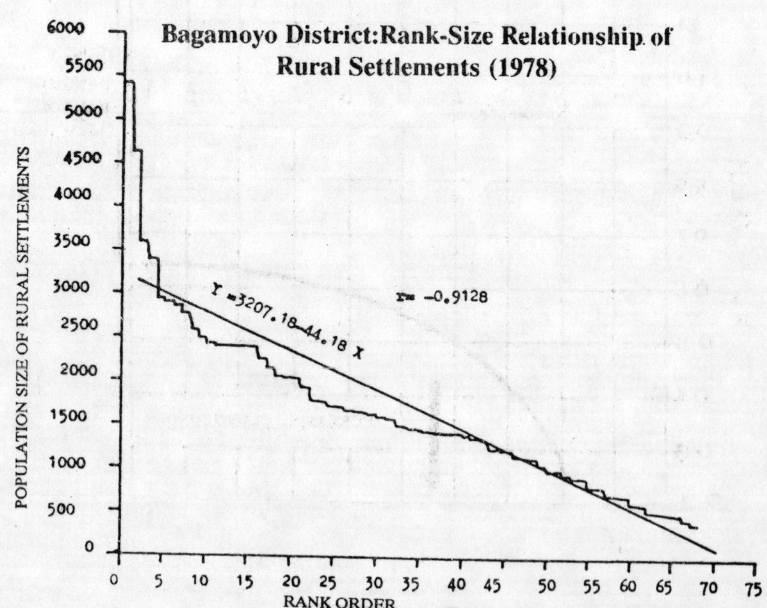

THIRTEEN

RESETTLEMENT SCHEMES FOR RURAL DEVELOPMENT

Resettlement is the relocation of inhabitants housing site in a planned way by some agency or the local government. The causes of such a resettlement my be to alleviate from over-population or the evacuation of areas affected from natural disaster e.g. insect infestation, floods, famine, declining soil fertility, inundation due to construction of large dams, and sometimes sparsely populated areas motivate planning agencies to promote resettlement schemes, so that the land can be put into the productive forces.

Although most of the resettlement schemes have been introduced in order to solve a variety of problems, with special reference to agricultural development and save the inhabitants from the problems of flood. "The rationale is: if traditional cultivators can be grouped together in a new setting where the social and physical constraints of their home territory are not present, and if they can be provided with credit, training programs, and economic incentives, then a flourishing commercial enterprise should emerge from this reordering of human and physical resources".[1]

Settlement schemes should not be considered as local project; but must be planned according to future need in almost all regions of the country and appraised in terms of overall national development. Resettlement schemes are quite often the follow-up of land redistribution and consolidation in order to provide a new setting for the immigrants on land. These are aimed at making the inhabitants more stronger and well prepared to share the responsibilities of citizenship. Such a move to new land is associated with the notion of liberation from scarcity, natural hazards and repression. But sometimes it also means eviction, deprivation and the emergence of misery-ridden communities as in some parts of Latin America. Such a resettlement scheme frequently takes the form of civil war. Sometimes the settlement schemes seem to be a waste of resources as in case of western Nigeria where a few thousand settlers enjoy the most favourable conditions while millions are underprivileged. The new settlement scheme is getting success when there is a good reason to assume that it can be reproduced over the whole country for a longer period of 10 to 15 years.

Nowadays the resettlement scheme only for agricultural development is no longer valid. Any policy of agrarian reform must take into account the agricultural and industrial activities taken together because they are closely linked in rural settlement planning.

Resettlements have been organized for a variety of other reasons such as to minimise population pressure, unemployment, diversification of agriculture, compensate war veterans and strengthen national defence. There may be some motivation for all these experiments, but the basic criterion for rural settlement as part of land reform is to provide a flexible and progressive framework for human activities in relation to man and land. Rural settlements are generally planned with a view to overall national development. But even careful planning must not always anticipate all the desired future trends, which should be adjusted from time to time. As for example in Libya the growth of oil industry jeopardized a scheme for the resettlement of nomads, as the original planned income targets were far above the current income level of the tribes. Long-term settlement projects require the minute observation of income trends through other sectors of the economy and should be adjusted at the earliest possible.

The neglected aspect of settlement planning is how to treat the indigenous population in a new resettlement scheme. This problem was there in the resettlement of Javanese peasants in Sumatra who have not been considered as part of the settlement plan. Advance sociological research is needed to have some sort of adjustment.

Even in some well planned settlement scheme of Gal Oya in Ceylon, clusters of poverty-stricken, and old peasant farms can be found around the prosperous planned settlement area. It is a little bit difficult to devise a formula for the success of resettlement schemes but an independent agency can do the work well with all aspects of large settlement projects even in fragile political condition of a nation.

Table 13.1 : Evacuees Associated with Large Dams in Less-developed Countries

Country	Dam	Year of Completion	Tentative Evacuees
India	Damodar valley (4 Projects)	1953-1959	93000
Zambia/ Rhodesia	Kariba	1958	34000/22000
Egypt/Sudan	Aswan	1964	70000/48000
Ghana	Volta	1964	82000
Pakistan	Mangla	1967	90000
Nigeria	Kainje	1968	44000
Ivory Coast	Kossou	1971	75000
Philippines	Upper Pampanga	1973	14000
Laos	Nam Ngum	1971	3000
Pakistan	Tarbela	1974	86000
Thailand	11 Projects	1963-1977	130000

Source: R.P. Lightfoot: The Journal of Tropical Geography, Vol. 47, 1978, p. 63.

In various parts of the World at least 315 manmade lakes have been built upto 1973 for the purpose of economic development and these dams have displaced a large number of people (Table 13.1) which range from 50 to 100,000. Unless the administrators and planners are safeguarding their interest properly, "the evacuees will inevitably suffer from the experience and moving: their assets, productivity and incomes will be jeopardized, while they will develop an acute sense of uprootedness and discontent".[2] In one way, these dams help in terms of irrigating fields and supplying cheap electric power, at the cost of other man's flooded home and village community.

In most of these resettlement schemes, the settlement sites are badly planned and inadequately financed, and hence the evacuees are permanently worse-off both socially and economically. There are many aspects of resettlement process: (a) the failure of these resettlement projects may account for detail analysis of the total public and private costs of these projects; (b) the need to search alternative planning strategies for reservoir related resettlement in the future. Mainly, the planners input to most resettlement has been a consolidated and organized settlement site. Such settlement sites have been developed with various other provisions for the Kariba, Volta, Kainji, Kossou, Damodar, Kosi, Gandak, Aswan and all the thirteen Thai Projects so far completed: Khiew Lom, Sirikhit, Nam Ngum, Huai Luang, Nam Oon, Lam Pao, Nam Pong, Pa Mong, Bhumiphon, Krasiaw, Kwae Yai, Lam Dom Noi and Lam Takhong; and (c) the large scale construction of planned settlements have not always been attractive to evacuees, and in the past people have preferred to manage their own affairs rather than move to settlements made for them. Quite a larger number from the Volta and Aswan projects either never joined or have since left their settlement areas. This is partly due to the failure of the settlements to provide adequate incomes, but about 20 per cent of the Tarbela evacuees, 70 per cent of all Thai evacuees, and over 90 per cent from the Damodar project opted immediately for some form of privately managed resettlement, without even a trial period in their respective planned settlements. For these reasons, alternatives to large scale planned settlements bear consideration. In future there should be option for settlement plans where some evacuees should be encouraged to purchase or make their own houses out of the government compensation money.

The past resettlement experience were helpful in solving some of the problems of relocation of rural settlement especially related to social and economic needs. The resettlement due to the Gesira irrigation scheme of Sudan has highly favoured the commercial production of cotton for the World Market. In 1924 a small resettlement took place in north central part of Tanzania due to the epidemic of sleeping sickness. It has been controlled by clearing of the bush for resettlement for the inhabitants of affected area. Here the complaint was that the concentrated arrangement of houses on resettlement site was not the answer for the scattered rural settlements which were abandoned. Similarly, the tsetse clearing scheme at Anchau in Nigeria was set in motion, but the authorities concerned had to employ punishment threat so as to complete the resettlement process. In the 1950's at the Zande resettlement scheme of Sudan, the farmers were forced to go on resettlement site in place of the supervision of agricultural activities. But the inhabitants of Zande reacted to this, and the scheme was completely abandoned just within four years of its beginning. In 1953 a similar resettlement scheme was failed in northern Nigeria, because the agricultural fields of farmers and the sources of water supplies were lie very far in comparison with original home and hence this resettlement scheme also failed.

The most ambitious resettlement programme can be observed in case of the composite rural structure of Israel. They created a settlement scheme of four tier central place hierarchy: A level-agricultural villages with 60 to 100 families; B and C level-rural centres located in between 5-6 farm villages with a population of 300 to 400 families; and at the appex is the location of town with a population of 15,000 to 20,000, and these should offer the services of banks, hotels and processing of goods in small-scale industries.

A four tier Israeli model of resettlement scheme has been adopted in case of Volta resettlement program in Ghana where the 739 villages were regrouped at 52 locations established according to central place principle: Agricultural villages (A-level): Satellite villages with less than 5000 population at B-level; service centres with 5000 to 8000 population at C-level; and Central town with 8000 to 10,000 population at D-level. Such a resettlement scheme has not been adopted elsewhere in Africa due to lack of resources.

Most of the resettlement schemes directed for regional economic development encountered with some kind of problem of environment and site hazards, lack of education and health program, and the most important thing is that farmers cannot live away from his farm which is the base of income to the rural people.

In Tanzania due to villagization and resettlement scheme 95% rural population has already been shifted to resettlement sites of about 8200 up to 1984. The justification of this programme is to bring peasants living in dispersed hamlets to compact Ujamaa villages where the facilities like dispensaries, education, pumped water, electricity, post office and bank can easily be operated for planned rural development; through cooperative participation in raising cash crops and increasing crop yields.

In Tanzania, the resettlement of people into Ujamaa villages has brought many changes in village sites and the settling pattern. In reality, there has never been an uniform way of settling people. In some cases no prior preparations were made, but changes of various levels have taken place. Quite often settlements have spread along roads within the limits permitted by topography of the land. An example is given here as a case in point. Fig. 13.1 shows the location of Lugoba village in Bagamoyo district of Tanzania situated on the interfluve of river Ruvu before villagization. Fig. 13.2 illustrates the siting and location of Lugoba village after villagization. The traditional groupings have changed into nucleated ones, giving rise to new boundary extensions, the size of the agricultural plots have changed and scattered houses have now rearranged along roads. Ujamaa villages, therefore, provide the most suitable institutional framework for political and economic organization and mobilization of physical and human resources through equitable distribution of land which has been achieved throughout Tanzania.

Tanzania and Uganda have been supporting refugee resettlement communities for nearly two decades. Some of these refugees have decided to settle permanently, while others have been repatriated. At the independence of Mozambique in 1974, for instance, many refugees who were established in settlements in Southern Tanzania repatriated home, but shortly they re-emigrated back to their resettlement schemes. The main country of origin of these refugees[3] have been shown below in Table 13.2.

Table : 13.2 Refugee Migration and Resettlement in East Africa, 1979

Country of Asylum	Number of Refugees	Main Country of origin
Kenya	6,000	Uganda, Ethiopia
Uganda	112,000	Rwanda, Zaire
Tanzania	167,000	Burundi, Rwanda, Uganda
Sudan	250,000	Ethiopia, Zaire, Uganda
Ethiopia	11,000	Sudan
Somalia	500,000	Ethiopia
Mozambique	100,000	Zimbabwe
Rwanda	7,500	Burundi
Burundi	50,000	Rwanda

Source: UNHCR Bulletin, Spring 1979.

Besides the repatriation of these refugees as one solution, the most productive strategy for them is rural settlement schemes, where refugees can bring their skills as cultivators into play, and become self-sufficient. Wherever such schemes have flourished with the help of international aid, the refugees are reluctant to repatriate despite the declaration of amnesty, such as in north-western Tanzania, the refugee settlement of Ulyankulu and Katumba are viable agricultural settlements and it is unlikely that now the refugees may be repatriated.[4]

In Zambia the Chilimanyama Kombo resettlement area was depopulated in 1928 when the Nsenga Reserve was established and was resettled between 1940 and 1942. The local government then divided the area into blocks, built rectangular network of roads and constructed dams and sank wells to ensure adequate supply of water at chosen places of provisional rural settlement sites. The immigrant inhabitants was apportioned to the various blocks of land according to their carrying capacity, and within the blocks individual village is located with reference to the infrastructure facilities provided. Such a resettlement site and housing pattern clearly reflects a conscious planning with the help of local government[5] (Fig.13.3).

In Kenya, the Mwea resettlement scheme of peasants on white Highlands of Kikuyu reserve was a political move in order to increase agricultural productivity and intensive use of the land. This scheme has earned more criticism because only small number of families benefitting from the scheme does not justify the large sums of public money expended. The execution of this resettlement scheme resulted in a considerable decrease in the number of Africans employed on white farms from 269,000 in 1960 to 194,000 in 1967, and during this period the number of large farms had declined from 3609 to 2745. This scheme has helped in the extension of commercial farming in Africa besides rural development.[6]

In Uganda, the objectives of establishing farm settlements since independence is to introduce modern agricultural techniques in order to check the increasing migration from rural to urban areas. The Nyakashaka farm settlement was established by missionaries for the sole purpose of setting young school-leavers. On irrigated agriculture Mabuku resettlement scheme was started in 1966.

In this way, in Uganda resettlement scheme has frequently been designed to create barriers of settlement as a defence against the reinvasion of the tsetse fly from uncleared areas. Different measures have been adopted for the planning and implementation of such schemes. The cost - benefit appraisal of such schemes may be useful both for the settler themselves, and other peasants as well who are behind the scene. Noticeably, such a project may involve the problem of phasing the settlement scheme to coincide with the tsetse eradication operation, besides coordinating the planning and budgeting.

Vietnamese Refugee Resettlement in U.S.A.

With the onset of Vietnam war in April, 1975-125,000 Vietnamese decided to take shelter in the refugee camp of United States of America. They have been readjusted into the resettlement scheme in California and Texas. The reaction about the resettlement programme was mixed. Some felt it was launched too quickly and haphazardly, while others felt this group of refugees as more American than any previous or subsequent groups. Later on, it was found that upto 1975 about 47 per cent refugees went to the places of their choice. After viewing at education, occupation, resettlement data and demographic factors, it can be concluded that the main determining factor of their staying at a particular resettlement site or decision to move was based on resettlement experience. Well over a third of those who stayed in a resettlement camp longer than a month, later moved from their initial placement point. The biggest influence was the state of first settlement, as those who settled in the state of their choice were the most likely to stay. Besides this the level of education, and the satisfaction with the job helped them stay in the place of resettlement more permanently. But it has been realised that the same loosely structured resettlement process for refugees. still exists with federal, state and local government authorities, which quite often exhibit overlapping priorities. In view of this, the U.S. Government rationalized some of its settlement policies by passing the Refugee Act. The office of Refugee Settlement has also initiated social experiments such as the Cambodian cluster Project, and the Highland Lao initiative, which have been designed to enhance lives of refugee communities.[7]

Laotian Refugee Resettlement in Thailand

The Thai administration has tried to reduce the influx of Laos refugees with a measure of delay in departure in the third resettlement site of the country. In 1981 the government completely banned the departure to resettlement sites for the Laotian Arrivals from Laos fell from 20,000 in 1981 to 5000 in 1982, however blocking the resettlement departure did not totally stop the influx of refugees in the country. The resettlement departure declined from 9300 in 1982 to 7100 in 1983, and again increased to 9078 in 1984 which shows increased reluctance on part of the potential resettlement to accept more Laotian refugees.[8]

THE VOLTA RESETTLEMENT EXPERIENCE. GHANA

The Volta resettlement scheme was developed in order to help people who come under the flood affected area due to the construction of Volta dam with a view to: (a) resettlement may be used to enhance the social, economic and physical conditions of the people; (b) improve the agricultural production especially of cash crops; and (c) locate new settlements in a planned way.

In 1962 after the suggestions of a preparatory commission and consultation with the affected population, the government of Ghana has identified a number of potential sites. At the end of 1962 people had proposed 38, of which 35 were confirmed as suitable rural settlement sites after checking soils, availability of cultivable land, potentiality of getting water, ease of access and ease of constructing houses as well as infrastructure facilities and ultimately 52 sites were chosen (Table 13.3). According to the desire of 6000 people Anlakwae and 3000 people Ntoaboma sites were selected and road connections provided through Togo mountain and Kete Krachi area in case of the first resettlement site and Afram Plains across the Obasum river in case of second (Fig, 13.4).

The break down of 52 selected village sites are as follows:[9]

(1) sites selected by the people and accepted by the Volta Resettlement Authority - 26

(2) sites selected by the Volta Resettlement Authority and readily

accepted by the people - 6

(3) sites selected by the people and forced on the Volta Resettlement Authority - 15

(4) sites selected by the Volta Resettlement Authority and forced on the people - 5

THE KOSI VALLEY RESETTLEMENT EXPERIENCE IN NORTH BIHAR, INDIA

Settlement shift takes place in several conditions, e.g., forced migration due to floods, embankment erosion, famine condition, excessive taxation, social boycott, population explosion and the whim of rulers.[10] In the Kosi basin it is particularly caused by excessive floods and execution of the Kosi project and the only competent authority to rehabilitate is the Government.

(1) **Resettlement Scheme:**

(a) The State Government established its rehabilitation offices in September 1957 at Nirmali and Supaul. According to this scheme, in between the two embankments of the Kosi, each family was to be given a higher site to settle outside the embankments.

(b) For the construction of approach road, school, tank, well and other amenities, each village will be given 40 per cent extra land besides its settlement site.

(c) According to this scheme the government is ready to give compensation for the houses inside the dam so that the residents of riverside may construct their houses outside the embankments on the site allocated while their houses on the riverside are left at the discretion of the residents so that they may be able to keep watch over their agricultural fields.

Table 13.3 : Volta Scheme Households for New Resettlements Sites: 1964

Region	Resettlement Area	Number of Sites	Number of villages involved	To be Affected by the Floods		Opted to move to Resettlement Sites	
				Population	Households	Population	Households
Eastern	A_1 Kwahu	5	174.0	11,433	2,389	9,631	1,984
	A_2 South Afram	6	48.5	11,578	1,815	11,173	1,750
	A_3 Akwamu	5	74.0	6,734	1,400	6,004	1,242
	Total	16	296.5	29,745	5,604	26,808	4,976
Volta	B_1 Ewe-Guan	9	106.5	8,077	1,712	6,520	1,369
	B_2 Buem Akan	4	96.0	4,695	1,061	4,352	989
	B_3 Pai	3	43.5	5,499	1,116	4,947	988
	B_4 Krachi	7	77.0	15,462	2,707	13,276	2,244
	Total	23	323.0	33,733	6,596	29,095	5,600
B/Ahafo	C Brong Ahafo	5	70.5	6,927	1,158	5,843	989
Northern	D Gonja	8	49.0	7,880	1,299	7,503	1,234
	Grand Total	52	739.0	78,285	14,657	69,249	12,799

Source: Robert Chambers; The Volta Resettlement Experience, Pall Mall Press, London, 1970, p. 146.

(2) **Procedure of Resettlement**:

The villages lying inside the embankment should be resettled on sites allocated outside in a planned manner as examples of ideal rural settlements and according to varying siting conditions the plan may vary for each and every village.

In larger villages a high school must be established and the plan should be prepared immediately so that the resettled persons and their children may receive education easily. In the same way, the approach road should be constructed by the government but its repair work should be done regularly by the villagers, because it is not possible to keep rehabilitation organization permanently. Similarly, the repair works of well, tank and community hall are also allotted to the Gram Panchayats.

(3) **Action Taken**:

In between the two embankments of the Kosi, the settlement survey of 297 villages was completed by 1970 out of which the land evaluation assessment of 291 inhabited sites is available. Table 13.4 shows the payment of advance money for house construction to the resettled families.

Table 13.4 gives an idea that at the beginning of this scheme the total number of families who were given resettlement grant was quite high, and this trend continued even after the 1968 flood when thousands of houses were washed away in the Kosi belt.

In between Maina and Koparia rural settlements on several relocated sites as provided by the government, houses with brick and mud walls were constructed where the resettled families deemed to live permanently. According to this scheme all villages should be relocated outside the embankment. This utopian scheme has never been realized and the author regrets to point out the following observations when he visited the area in June, 1975.

Kosi Valley

Table 13.4 : Progress of Resettlement Work on Rehabilitation Sites (1958-1970)

Year	Total Number of Families Received Grant
1958 - 1959	9863
1959 - 1960	9775
1960 - 1961	3075
1961 - 1962	2347
1962 - 1963	975
1963 - 1964	896
1964 - 1965	864
1965 - 1966	1504
1966 - 1967	2616
1967 - 1968	3490
1968 - 1969	5897
1969 - 1970	4418

Source: Department of River Valley Project, Government of Bihar, India.

RESULT OF FIELD OBSERVATIONS

The Kosi lies in a saucer shaped region but its natural leveles are so high that flood waters never rise up to these levels. The two artificial dykes which lie quite apart from the main course of the river command thousands of rivulets branching from the main channel upto dyke during the rainy season. Every year floods of the Kosi cause innumerable miseries to the inhabitants and they live on house tops almost permanently for months between June and September. On each house top permanent *machans* are found on which the entire family resides during floods in the northern half of the basin and the main source of communication then is only a boat.

Even in such conditions no one wants to leave one's house. The people lead a miserable life on these *bamboo - machans*. During high floods every village turns into a ferry village having enormous fishing grounds. Barely few primary schools are found and there is no question of health centres and community hall. The village sites inside the Kosi river cling on higher sites having no approach road and other amenities of life. The settlements are of semi-compact and semi-sprinkled type.

In such a condition they become socially boycotted as no resident outside the Kosi river dykes wants to marry his daughter in such an area. The residents of this belt thus appear to be outcastes or second class citizens.

The government has spent millions of rupees on these rural settlements to rehabilitate the residents outside the flood protective dykes on safer and higher sites but after taking the rehabilitation grant no one seems to have permanently shifted outside the dykes.

In the Kosi belt, the survey of village homestead land has been done to give them the same extent of land which they previously occupied. But in the entire Kosi belt only a dozen villages have been shifted permanently, and even there the shift is partial. This is because the allotted site is not really a highland. During rainy season the new village sites become the abode of neck deep to knee deep water everywhere yearly. The second problem is that the government has not provided land for backyard and kitchen garden to raise vegetables and for tethering cattle. The provision of these facilities besides drinking water, schools, community hall and access path is necessary. Nowhere on lower allotted site, these facilities are available. Again, the agricultural fields mostly lie between the two artificial dykes. The farmers find it difficult to protect their crops after floods, and the crossing of high dykes with cattle is also a problem. The long distance travel to their respective fields is a bigger problem still. This is not so in case of the villages which are near the dyke e.g. Ghibak and Dabhari west of Supaul. But in case of the villages which lie 4 to 5 kilometers away, the problem defies solution. Thus the resettlement plan of the government of Bihar has met a very limited success.

THE NAM PONG PROJECT: THAILAND

The Nam Pong dam in Thailand was ready in 1964. The houses of 5012 households were flooded by the project. A survey showed that upto 1973 about 638 of these households were living in the planned settlement areas, and the rest were scattered over 18 provinces in northeastern, northern and central Thailand[11] (Fig. 13.5).

The resettlement experiences, approaches and measures taken may provide guidelines to others in the similar situations, and also raise issues of strategic importance in planning and implementing resettlement and development programmes.

REFERENCES

1. M.S. Berfein: "Settlement Schemes and Rural Growth", in *Contemporary Africa Geography and Change* (edt. C.G. Knight and J.L. Newman); Prentice Hall, New Jersey, 1976, pp.251 - 252.
2. R.P. Lightfoot: "The Costs of Resettling Reservoir Evacuees in Northeast Thailand", *The Journal of Tropical Geography,* Vol. 47, December, 1978, pp. 63-74.
3. J.R. Rogge: "Refugee Migration and Resettlement", in *Redistribution of Population in Africa* (by J.L. Clarke and L.A. Kosinski (Edt.); Heinemann, London, 1982, p.41.
4. G.W. Amarteifio: "Social Welfare", in Robert Chambers (Edt.): *The Volta Resettlement Experience;* Pall Mall Press, London, 1970, p. 116.
5. George Kay: *A Social Geography of Zambia;* University of London Press Ltd; 1967, p.65.
6. R. Chambers and John Moris (edt.): Mwea: *An Irrigated Rice Settlement in Kenya,* Africa - Studien No. 83, Weltforum Verlag, Munchen, 1973, pp.539.
7. Sandra Woods: "The 1975 Refugees: *Their First Five Years in America",* *Refugees;* No.15, March, 1985, pp. 15-17.
8. Rob Burrows: "Laotian Refugee Numbers Increasing", *Refugee,* No.15, March 1985, pp. 13 - 14.
9. R. Chambers: *The Volta Resettlement Experience;* Pall Mall Press, London, 1970.
10. R.B. Mandal: "Ecology of Rural Settlements in the Kosi Basin", *Indian Geographical Studies,* R.B. No.8; 1977; pp. 45 - 50.
11. R.P. Lightfoot: *Op. cit.*

Fig. 13.1

Centre of Lugoba Village, Tanzania, 1966 (After-Fennia)

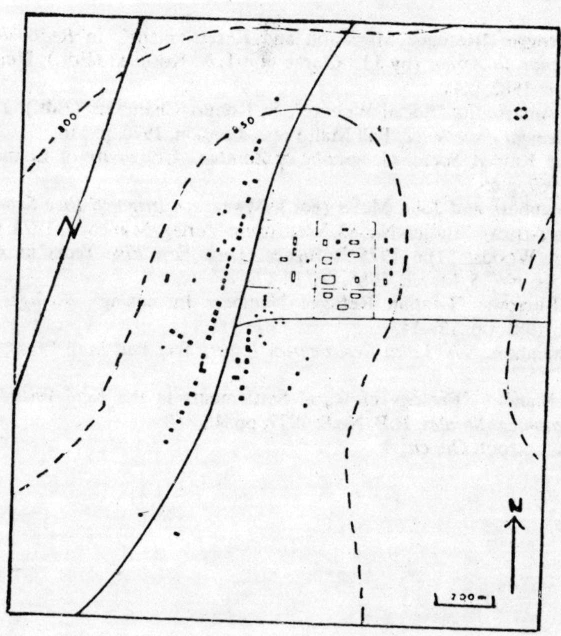

Fig. 13.2

Location of Lugoba in Tanzania, 1977 (After-Fennia

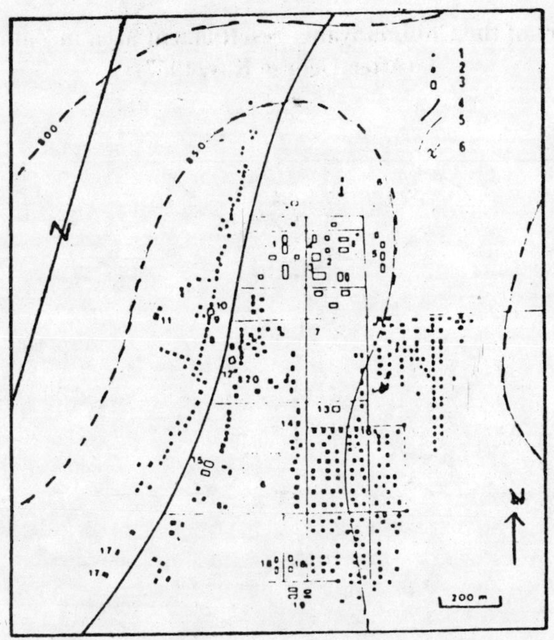

1 = water post, 2 = house, 3 = public building, 4 = tarmac road, 5 = contour line (in ft.), 6 = overhead power lines. Village services (numbered)) school, (2) Roman Catholic mission station,) Roman Catholic church, (4) dispensary, (5) :achers' accomodation, (6) sports field, (7) cemtery, (8) shops, (9) post office, (10) trading place, 1) warehouse, (12) bus stop, (13) market place, 4) cooperative store, (15) administrative buildngs, (16) bar selling beer, (17) grain mills, (18) ccomodation for health centre staff, (19) health entre, (20) mosque.

Fig. 13.3

Part of the Chilimanyama resettlement area in Zambia (After-George Kay, 1967)

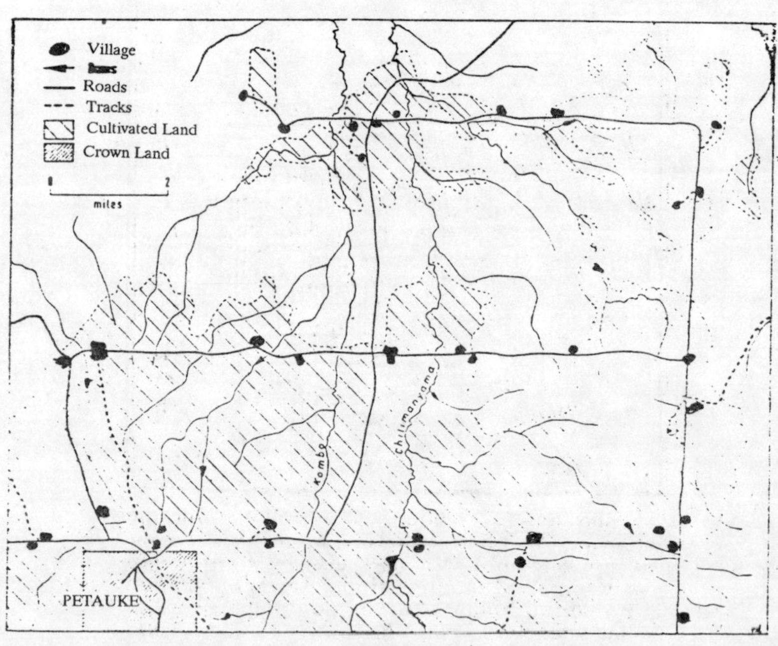

Fig. 13.4

Volta Resettlement Experience, Ghana (After-R. Chambers, 1970

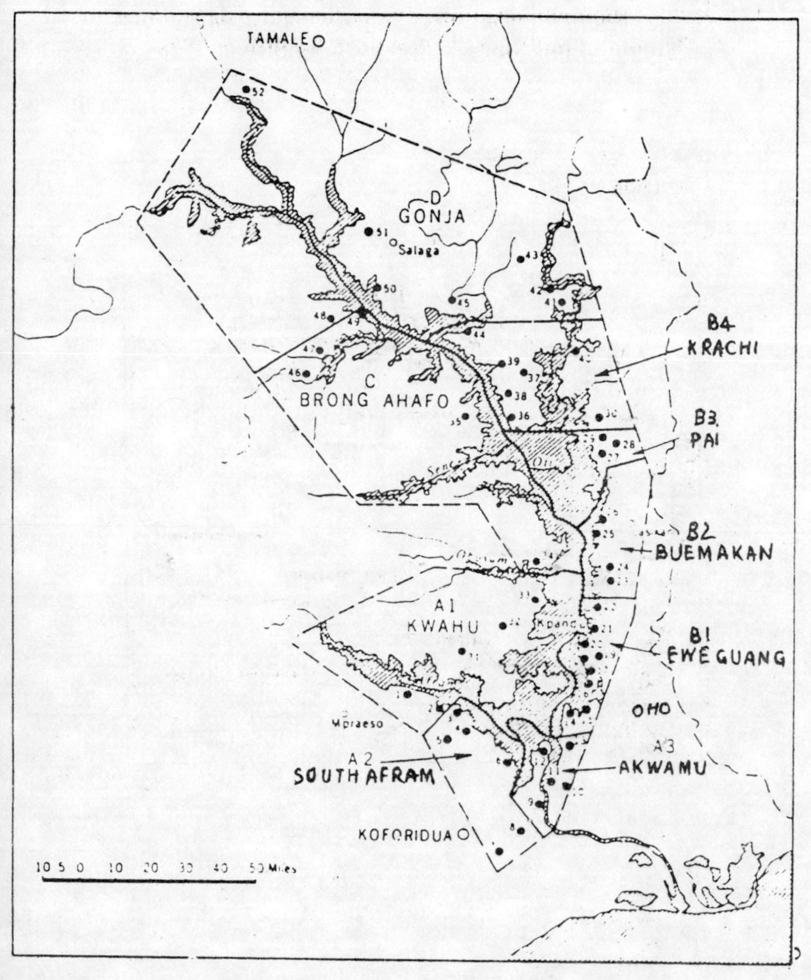

Fig. 13.5

Reservoirs requiring organized resettlement programmes in Thailand and Laos. (After R. P. Lightfoot 1978

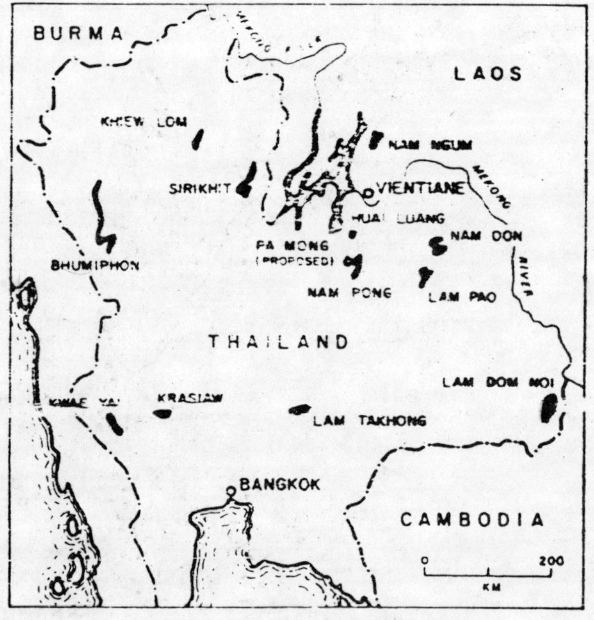

FOURTEEN

REMOTE SENSING AND RURAL SETTLEMENTS

Remote sensing is the process of obtaining synoptic mountain view picture of the earth's surface by means of cameras or other devices which can look down on the ground from above either through aeroplane or satellites. Hence the outcome of remote sensing in the form of aerial photographs and satellite imageries are the well established tools for geographers and the spatial analysis of regional data obtained from photographs.

There is a saying that "you cannot see the forest for the trees."[1] Similarly if you are standing in the centre of the village as an investigator you cannot get the idea of the whole village for two-three houses of the nearby areas. But if you observe the whole village through aeroplane then you can see the shape, size, street pattern, skyline, arrangement of houses in space at a glance, and hence it is useful for the geographers to get up above the village or forest to obtain the "mountain view" of the whole landscape environment.

Development of the Subject:

The beginning of aero-space was made by Montgolfier voyage of balloon near Paris on 21st November 1783.[2] This provided a powerful tool to the geographers for the study of landforms and terrain conditions of all sorts including rural settlements.

So far as the hyper - altitude photographs are concerned they are available from 1946 onwards beginning with Atlas Sounding Rockets

(V - 2, Viking, Aerobec), and thereafter from sub-orbital and orbital flights in the framework of the space programmes of the USA (TIROS, NIMBUS, ESSA, ATS, MERCURY, GEMINI, APPOLLO, LANDSAT, SKYLAB, etc.) and others by ESA (The European Space Agency) and Indian Space Research Organisation (ISRO),Ahmadebad. According to an estimate in January 1985 about 360 satellites were found moving in the sky. Some satellites have a power to scan the same settlement on the ground on every 9th day after moving the entire world, whereas others on the 12th and 18th day. Since orbital photographs are usually taken from high altitude it has a hundred times more power than the most surveys aircraft. It is quite clear that they opened new vistas especially for small scale reconnaissance of terrain, resources, and settlement systems of areas in which we cannot do field-work. As for example - "Philip porter's air - photo and field study told the government of Liberia for the first time how many citizens it governed and just where they lived and what land they used."[3]

Characteristics of Aerial Photographs and Their Utility

Photogrammetry has been defined as the art, science and technology of obtaining reliable information about physical objects and the environment through processes of reading, measuring and interpreting photographic images and patterns. It is highly useful for geographers because:

(1) It gives instant recording of required information,
(2) It gives very detailed information,
(3) the method gives almost objective results,
(4) the information is readily reproducible, and
(5) photographs are the most acceptable substitute for maps.

Definitions of Characteristics

1. **Aerial Photograph**: Aerial Photograph is perspective image that is geometrically related to the type of camera with which it is taken from the air or parts of the terrain.
2. **Types of Photographs**:
   (a) **Vertical Photographs** : - A photograph taken with the optical axis of the camera coinciding with the direction of gravity.
   (b) **Oblique photograph**: A photograph taken with the optical

axis of the camera intentionally tilted from the vertical. High oblique contain horizon at the upper end where as low oblique do not. (Fig. 14.1).

3. **Scale of a Photograph:**

$$\frac{\text{Focal length of the camera}}{\text{Flying Height above datum}} = \frac{f}{H}$$

$$\frac{6''}{24000'} = \frac{1''}{4000' \times 12''} = \text{R.F: } 1{:}48000$$

$$RF = \frac{f}{H} = \frac{0.5''}{50000''} = \frac{0.1''}{1000} = 1{:}\ 10000$$

4. **Image displacement**: Due to differing altitude of the ground horizontal displacement of the objects on the photographs are found which is known as image displacement or parallactic displacement on a truly vertical photographs. This displacement is directly proportional to the relief of the terrain and to the distance from the principal point, and is inversely proportional to the camera altitude. Displacement may also becaused due to (a) photographic deficiencies (b) tilting of the camera lens axis at the instant of exposure, and (c) variations in local relief.
5. **Overlap and Sidelap**: - Along a given flight line, photographs are taken at such frequency as to cause successive photographs to overlap each other by about 55 to 65 per cent. This percentage is referred to as forward overlap. Overlap between the photographs of adjacent flight line is called sidelap. It usually amounts to 15 to 30 per cent.
6. **Vertical Exaggeration:** It is the exaggeration of vertical distances with respect to horizontal distances. This exaggeration makes slopes to appear steeper than they are and objects seem taller than they are.
7. **Photo Interpretation**: It is an act of examining photographic image of objects for the purpose of identifying the objects and deducing their significance by reading, analysing and interpreting

the photo for relevant results of landforms, drainage, settlements, erosional features, etc.

8. **Mosaics:** - A mosaic is a series of overlapping vertical photographs assembled in sequence on mounting board to form one single picture of the terrain.

Types of Mosaics:

1. An assembly of photographs laid in a sequence as to allow the photo number and flight number of each photograph to appear on the finished assembly is called index mosaic or a *photo index*.
2. A mosaic which is assembled from a single strip of photography is called a *strip mosaic*.
3. A mosaic which is assembled without considering any plotted control is called an uncontrolled mosaic.
4. A mosaic assembled to fit control which has been plotted on the mounting board is called a controlled mosaic.

Advantages of Mosaics:

1. It can be compiled more rapidly and economically than conventional maps.
2. It has vast amount of detail in which terrain features can be easily recognised and interpreted.
3. No detail is omitted, and
4. To the layman, mosaic may be more intelligible, because terrain images can be seen as they would actually appear from above.

Application in Settlement Studies

Air photographs provide the means of bringing settlement patterns study upto date, and they are of basic value where cadastral survey is lacking altogether such as in many African countries. The ordnance survey use 1:2,500 scale aerial photographs for revision. They are providing detailed supplementary information about settlements which does not appear on maps, for example, relationship with 'ridge and furrow' to settlement form, relationship of settlement of land-use and land-forms and evidence of the relict feature of ancient settlements.

The use of aerial photographs and remote sensing to archaeological investigation has been well established in many parts of the world, but their utility for the analysis of rural and urban settlements as modern investigation has also been established.[4] Such as Kohn (1951) used both field observation and photo interpretation techniques in the study of rural settlements in Wisconsin dairy area, North-Dakota spring area and Washington irrigated area.[5] Tator (1951) studied about Indian village sites in Mississippi delta areas[6] and remarked " the flatness of the delta terrain, along with the factor of subsidence, make difficult the location of old sites, particularly on the ground. Careful study of large-scale aerial photographs; with detailed analysis of contrasts of tone and shape of soil and vegetation pattern is required."

In this way, remote sensing of the rural environment and rural settlements is an effective tool for the study of human occupance features of the Earth's surface. The method, character and arrangement of facilities men build in the process of occupying an area are easily subjected to study from above.

Mostly the settlement patterns are composed of visible and spatially arranged facilities, more can be learnt of them from remote sensing than any other single source. Kohn (1951)recognised distinct ways in which aerial photographs facilitate the study of rural settlement geography:

1. They provide information concerning the character and aerial distribution of the contemporary elements and types of settlement.

2. They reveal the detailed physical conditions and accurate areal patterns involved in the process of original settlement and the subsequent occupance, thus relating the distribution and spatial orientation of the settlement features to their physical environment.

3. They indicate the inter-relations between settlement features and their surrounding areas.

Roscoe (1960)[7] reported on Kohn's work that the first step in rural settlement photography is a spatially arranged inventory of the various structures and cultural conditions. Items to be interpreted, in general order of the ease which they can recognize, include road nets, villages, hamlets, field patterns, farmsteads, the spacing of farmsteads, road and lane turning, farm lanes, farm boundaries, farm size, individual farm buildings, minor farm facilities, and rural non-farm facilities (e.g. churches, temples, ponds, school, fire service stations). After the completion of inventories, these features can be analysed in terms of their origin, function and the associated elements which could be grouped into recognisable settlement types and regional patterns. The identification of regional settlement pattern in its sequent occupance provides the geographer with information required to demarcate geographical regions. It also helps geographer to advise the regional planner on matters concerning redevelopment of the area or the pioneering development of similar but unoccupied areas.[8]

Principles of Object Recognition in Rural Settlements

It is easy to recognise features on oblique photographs but in vertical photographs the interpreter has to exercise *mental activity* and *visual perception* of the objects besides examining the 1. shape, 2. size, 3. photographic tone, 4. pattern, 5. shadow, 6. topographic location and identification, and 7. texture of the photograph.

A checklist for typical features of settlements is as follows:

Table 14.1 : Coding of the Feature of Rural Settlements for Air Photo Interpretation

Code	Colour	Features
2.00	Black	Houses
2.01	Dark green	Metalled Road
2.02	Brokenline (black)	Footpaths
2.03	Hollow circle (black)	well
2.04	White	Wall
2.05	Broken Pink	Roof
2.06	Broken green	courtyards
2.07	Black Dots	Fallowland
2.08	CF (black)	cultivable Fallow
2.09	Wa (black)	waste land
3.00	W (blue)	water bodies
3.01	Broken line and stroke (black)	Fence
3.02	Double brokenline(black)	Unmetalled road
3.03	Black Mound	Graveyard
3.04	T (Red)	Temples
3.05	M (Red)	Mosque

3.06	C (Red)	Church
3.07	IN (Brown)	Industries
3.08	Sch (Green)	Schools
3.09	Ad (Green Flag)	Administrative c
4.00	PO (Brown)	Post Office
4.01	HOS (Green)	Hospital
4.02	SU (Blue)	Surface well
4.03	Ta (Blue)	Tank

Aerial Photo Interpretation:

It requires photo reading, scientific analysis and interpretation. The aerial photo should be supported with topographical sheet of the area R.F. 1: 63360 or 1:50,000 and census figures if possible, although in settlement analysis the aerial photographs and satellite imageries are not in much use upto now due to smaller areal extent of buildings and even settlement as a whole.

Results From Aerial Photograph of Kipande Village

Location: - Kipande village is located in Kipande ward of Sumbawanga district in Rukwa region of South-Western Tanzania. One metalled road is running through central part of the village from Mpanda in the north to Sumbawanga in the south. It is an Ujamaa village with 1800 persons (1978) situated along both sides of the road in a planned way. Piped water is available in the village (5 points) but ditch in the surrounding area is also serving the purpose. Due to crystalline basal rock and poor amount of rainfall there are many limitations in agricultural development, but according to the 1975 call of Chama Cha Mapinduzi (CCM) party, people have collected and constructed their huts on planned settlement site in order to achieve more collective advantage than dispersed living. The surrounding area of the village seems to be an erosional plain surface with patchy undulations and cultivated land. On northeastern part of the village rainfall stream is following the fracture line in Gondwana rocks, and the similar situation is found in southern part of the village. But in spite of some favourable and some negative points Kipande village is well placed along the main highway of the area (Fig. 14.2).

Features of Kipande Settlement

Kipande is a linear rural settlement along the metalled road. Its northern end is narrow due to lowlying area on both the eastern and western parts of the road. The total number of houses is 250. About 25 footpaths are radiating from the centre of the village to different directions like roots of a tree. These footpaths are connecting the various groups of households with the surrounding villages, agricultural plots and grazing land. The material of wall of the house is either stick plastered with mud or cement bricks. The material of roof is either dried grass or corrugated iron sheets. The average number of windows are four in one Kiswahili house with having four wooden doors. In each house either the kitchen room is found separate or the central corridor is used as kitchen. Kipande village has one post office and one administrative office of village chairman.

Land System of the Kipande Ward in General

Area	652 km^2
Latitude and Longitude	$7^0$52'S 31^0 32'E
Mean annual rainfall	828-950mm
General Morphology	Coarse textured very gently undulating plain (moderately dissected-ruggedness value 0.08)
Rock	Very limited metabasite. Very extensive *Ufipa* schists, gneisses and granite-gneisses
Local relief	40-50m
Altitude	1760-2049 m
Geomorphic process	Peneplanation and valley incision
Dominant land facets	Very gentle convex *interfluve, very gentle concave valley, gentle to low moderate* convex valley, gentle **piedmont.**
Modal slope class	Very gentle
Drainage density class	Low (0.25)
Drainage pattern	Angulate
Geomorphic history	Youthful dissection of Post-Gondwana and African planation surface.

Agriculture	
Suitability for maize	Marginal (moisture and nutrient availability limitations) except for soil-physiographic unit 3.1 which is moderate.
Suitability for cotton	Not suitable (High soil temperature limitation).
Suitability for flue-cured tobacco	Not suitable (High soil temperature cured tobacco limitation).
Suitability for rice	Not suitable (high soil temperature limitation).
Suitability for irrigation	Marginal on soil-physiographic unit 3.2 on slopes less than 8% (moisture holding capacity limitation) and on soil-physiographic unit 3.1 on slopes between 5 and 8%. Not suitable on soil-physiorgraphic unit 3.5 (soil depth limitation) and on slopes greater than 8%. Suitable on soil-physiographic unit 3.1 on interfluves and in very gentle valleys.
Soils	
Soil-physiographic units	Very extensive 3.2 on upper interfluves. 3.5 on lower interfluves and in very gentle valleys. Limited 3.2 and very limited 3.1 in gentle to low moderate valleys. 3.1, 3.2 and 3.5 on piedmonts.
Soil Map of the World units	Very extensive Orthic Ferralsols and very limited ferric Luvisols on upper interfluves. Ferralic Arenosols on lower interfluves end in very gentle valleys. Extensive Lithosols, limited Orthic Ferralsols and very limited Ferric Luvisols in gentle to low moderate valleys. Ferric Luvisols, Orthic Ferralsols and Cambic Arenosols on piedmonts.
Soil Taxonomy System	Very extensive Typic Eutrustox and very limited Typic Haplustalfs on upper interfluves. Ustoxic Quartzipsamments on lower interfluves and in very gentle valleys. Extensive Typic Ustorthents, limited Typic Eutrustox and very limited Typic Haplustalfs in gentle to low moderate valleys. Typic Haplustalfs, Typic Eutrustox and Typic Ustipsamments on Piedmonts.
Vegetation	Very extensive grassland and bushed grassland very limited woodland savana in the east.

This chapter has been organized to highlight the principles of remote sensing employed in settlement studies. Although most of the rural settlement studies based either on aerial photographs or satellite imageries are quite different from each other due to the nature of terrain, spatial organization of rural settlements and the purposes involved of the investigator.

REFERENCES

1. Robert H. Alexander. "Man's New Views of the Earth: the Potential of Remote Sensing," *Problems and Trends in American Geography* (Edt. S. B. Cohen: Basic Book Inc. Publishers, New York, 1967, pp. 239-250.
2. H.T. Verstappen: *Remote Sensing in Geomorphology:* Elsevier Scientific Publishing Company, New York, 1977, P. 1.
3. Philip. W. Porter: *Population Distribution and Land Use in Liberia;* Ph. D dissertation, University of London, 1957.
4. G.A. Storkes: "The Aerial Photograph: A Key to the Cultural Landscape", *Journal of Geography,* Vol. 49, 1950, pp. 32-40.
5. C.F. Kohn: "The Use of Aerial Photographs in the Geographical Analysis of Rural Settlements," *Photogrammetric Engineering:* Vol. 17, 1951, pp. 716-725.
6. B.A. Tator: "Some Applications of Aerial Photographs to Geographic studies in the Coastal Gulf Region," *Photogrammetric Engineering,* Vol. 17, 1951, pp. 716-725.
7. Robert G. Reeves et al (Edt) : *Mannual of Remote Sensing:* American Society of Photogrammetry, Falls Church, Virginia, 1974, p. 2044.
8. *Ibid.*

—

Fig. 14.1

Types of Aerial Photographs

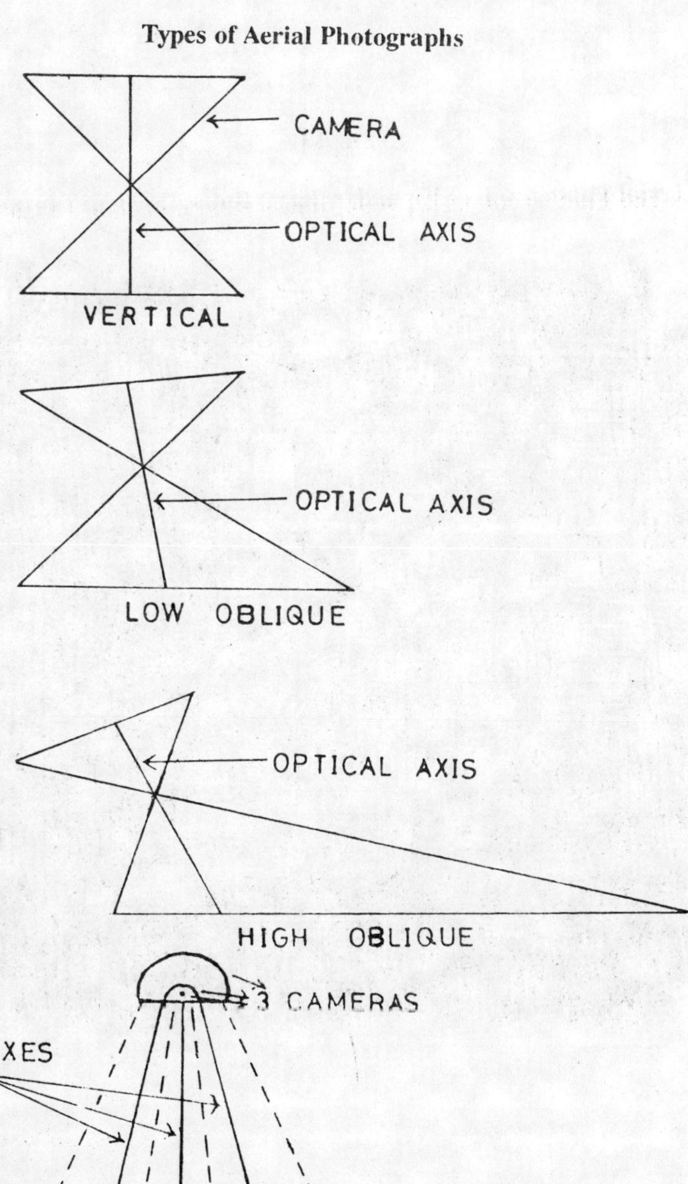

Fig. 14.2

Aerial Photograph of Kipande village, Rukwa Region, Tanzania

Fig. 14.3

Aerial Photo Interpretation of Kipande Village, Tanzania

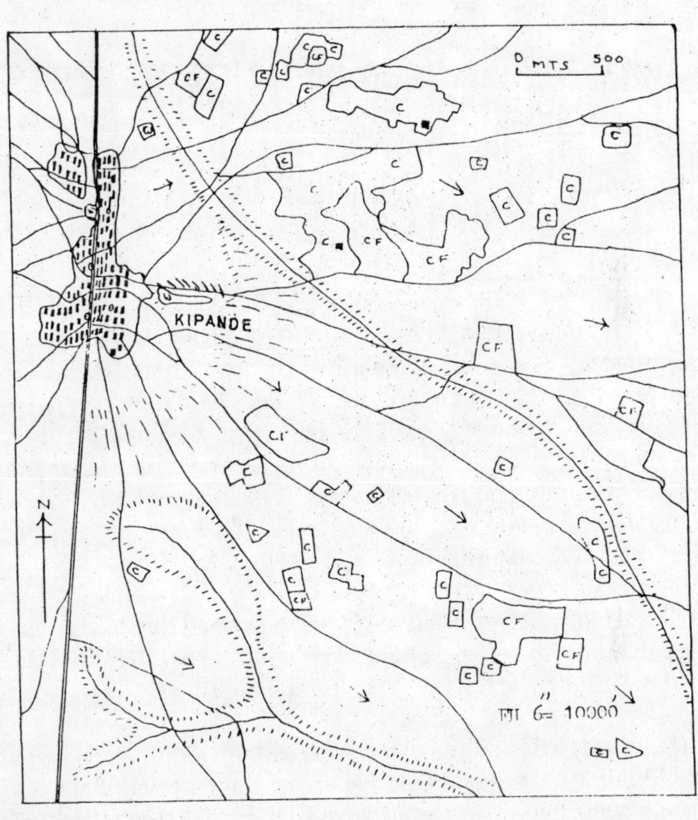

KEY

HOUSEHOLD

FOOTPATH

CULTIVATED LAND

CULTIVATED FALLOW

STREAM

WATER SITE

WATER PIPE

ROAD

DIRECTION OF SLOPE

BUSH FALLOW

FIFTEEN

RURAL DWELLINGS AND HOUSE TYPES

A HOUSE is one of the three basic needs of the mankind. It is being used by man as a safeguard of the body from various natural elements since times immemorial. Though its importance varies in various climatic conditions yet the basic needs remain more or less the same, as it provides shelter and protection from the rigours of climate.[1] Therefore, it is essential to consider the location, architectural style, shape and size, building materials, house plan, cost, classification and occupancy rate of houses.

The significance of housing often overlooked due to the way it is integrated into the environment, its characteristic, organization, the functions it fulfills and its socio-cultural dimensions.

If a study of traditional technologies in housing is genuinely aimed both at restoring a true picture of the past and making a significant contribution to development, it should never depart from that context; inter-regional exchange of the most relevant techniques, and the combining of traditional elements with those derived from popular inventiveness or borrowed from outside constitute one of the most convincing approaches regarding habitation.

The agglomeration of houses marks the origin of settlements and reflects the nature of a region since their character is related to the environment and the cultural heritage of people.[2] This is because the rural houses are of simple structure and designed to provide facility of residence for the family of peasants and for storing of grains and implements.

In prehistoric times, people lived in caves and bushes in the north western Terai region of Champaran district and on the edge of the Chotanagpur Scarp Belt. Evidences have been found in Lomas Rishi cave and Nigope cave[3], 26 kilometres north of Gaya in Barabar hills and some caves of Rajgir hills regarding these settlements. Thus the earliest shelters used by man were caves. Rocks rolled against the entrances kept wild beasts away and gave safety to their occupants. Where there were no caves, man took to erecting piles, on which they placed platforms. On the platforms they built huts of grass, reeds (wattle) and wooden stakes. Sometimes they laced their buildings with the tendous of animals they had killed, sometimes using ropes woven from grasses. Always in these early forms of buildings, the idea of protection from enemies came first, comfort in bad weather being a minor consideration. In general, the housing requirements can be grouped into:

(a) The satisfaction of fundamental physiological needs;
(b) Psychological needs,
(c) Protection against communicable diseases, and
(d) Protection against accidents.

As time passed, people became more civilized and they learnt to lace branches together and to daub structures with clay to make them wind and watertight. Inhabitants of the plains dug the clay in blocks, dried the blocks in the sun, and made houses of these unburnt bricks. This is still done in the Bihar Plain where unburnt brick huts are very common among the peasants.

The archaeological survey of Chirand village in Saran district in 1969 shows an ancient housing plan which dates back to 2000 B.C. On the occupational floor remains of post holes have also been found which must have supported a thatched roof. A number of hearths were also found on the floor.[4]

The early houses of this period, were, generally, simple circular structures of reeds or thatch with a sloping thatch roof supported by bamboo or wooden poles. Gradually, the huts took in oval, rectangular or square floor plan with a symmetrical roof sloping on two sides (Fig. 15.1). The supply of building materials depended upon local available trees, reeds, bamboos or similar vegetation.

The development of two or more buildings in a house surrounding an inner courtyard is a much later development. This was necessitated by an increase in the size of the family coupled with greater skill in construction, also the increase in the affluence of the society. This naturally resulted in the evolution of mud-walls and tile-roofs which are relatively more permanent materials for house construction.

The monasteries and *stupas* built with burnt bricks or stones were predominant features during the Budhist period. Temples were common in the Hindu period but during the Muslim period most of the tombs and mosques were built by demolishing or converting the Hindu temples as is evidenced by their characteristic features even today. The British Period was marked by the construction of *Kothis*, dak-bungalows, churches and buildings for government offices of that time. These are built of burnt bricks cemented with lime or mortar, and are with tile roofs. In recent years, construction of government offices in rural development blocks, hospitals and educational institutions shows *pucca* flat roofs and brick built walls reinforced with cement and concrete. In the rural areas, however, the mud built house continues to be, by and large, the most common dwelling of an average person. Thatch, reeds or wattle are common building materials for the poor people particularly in the eastern parts of the Bihar Plain where rainfall is heavy. Economically better off people refer to have mud-built or brick-built houses with tile-roof as in the central part of Bihar Plain. The more affluent people, are gradually resorting to burnt brick walls with *Pucca* (masonry) roofs. Typical house types of the Bihar Plain can be seen in Fig. 15.1.

Review of Literature

Gopal Krishan[5] in his paper entitled 'impact of population growth on rural housing' examines the kinds of changes and adjustments in housing that have been made to accommodate the fast growing population of the Salamatpur village in the Punjab. The study indicates that the rural population is tackling this situation by adopting a three-fold strategy; internal changes within a house by subdivision, or gradual roofing of available open space; extension into open space adjoining the house; and encroachment upon cultivated land and land reserved for cattle. Some factors, other than population growth, contributing to the aggravation of the rural housing situation have been highlighted. These include the gradual diversification of rural economy, the changing family structure with an increasing tendency towards nuclear families, increasing awareness of the environmental problems of the *abadi's* interior and the advantages of its periphery.

S.B. Singh[6] while delineating about 'rural dwellings in the district of Mirzapur' describes the various types of dwellings and the effects of environment on dwellings. Dwelling includes houses besides all other human structures where people congregate and goods are stored. Various types of houses depending on size, shape and building materials are identified. Some common features of dwellings in the region and the general morphology of the dwellings are also discussed briefly. It is concluded that the form, function and structure of dwellings are governed and affected by the socio-economic conditions of the people on the one hand and physical environment on the other.

S.N. Mishra[7] analyses the pattern of dwellings as affected by various natural and cultural features in the hilly and forested tract lying to the south of river Sone in Mirzapur district of U.P. The evolution of house forms has been traced from sketches dating from stone age caves to the present-day urban house. It is said that courtyard, verandah, the rectangular house plan, the absence of windows, the single storey, ridged roofs with symmetrical slopes and side gables, northerly and easterly house orientation and the presence of a threshing ground are the most common features of the dwellings. An outline of the general morphology of dwellings has also been presented. A threefold classification of house types and their regional distribution has been attempted, taking into account the socio-cultural variations, size and shape of the houses and building materials. The industrial towns of Renukoot, Pipri, Obra, Chopan, Renusagar and Dala exhibit a variety ranging from the labourers slum to larger modern buildings. The soil and natural vegetation provide the cheap building materials, but the various cultural groups have used them differently. Industrialization and other developments after independence have resulted in improvement in morphology and other conditions of housing.

V.N.P. Sinha describes[8] the physical factors concerning the availability of the chief building materials, climatic conditions and the cultural factors governing variations in house-types. In the classification of house types and their regional distribution, three criteria-the size, the building materials and the shape have been considered. In the case of size, the number of rooms, which ranges from one to five, is used as type feature. Besides these rectangular, square and planned types have been distinguished. In listing building materials - wall and roof are both taken into account. These chosen types have been identified all over the region according to their chief characteristics. It has been concluded that in order to make the houses look attractive, it is essential to rationalise their form, standardize components, accelerate construction time and cheapen cost of building materials.

According to K.S. Gopalkrishnan and D.C. Barai[9], the rural dwellings in the Cauvery Delta are well adopted to the local environment. This has not only determined the nature of building materials but influenced the form of the roof as well. House types have been changing with the application of new techniques and architecture. They reflect the cultural heritage of the local people in relation to physical environment of the area. The influence of physical factors like physiography and climate, precipitation, prevailing winds and insulation together with cultural factors are discussed in determining the size, orientation and ground plan of rural dwellings. It also highlighted house types and their distribution, some common features of delta dwellings and general morphology of rural dwellings.

S. Mukerjee[10] studied about the materials of wall and roof in the rural house of Maharashtra in the context of the patterns of their distribution and correlation with climatic factors like temperature, humidity and the amount and intensity of rainfall. It has been concluded that the architecture of rural houses in the region has been influenced by the climatic factors.

U.C. Gupta and Bahari Lal[11] in their study of rural dwellings in Bundelkhand highlighted about the building materials, residential accommodation, regional distribution, classification of house types and the measures of their planning.

J.N. Pandey[12] discussed the settlement history and house types of the village Paras-Rampur. Three sets of house types based on socio-cultural variations, size, shape and building materials have been recognized. The majority of the houses seem to suffer from lack of sanitary facilities, poor ventilation and dampness.

J.P. Sharma[13] highlighted the influence of geographical factors on rural house types and their internal layout for Ravi-Chenab inter-fluve. Plan, shape, size, building material, style of construction and types of roofs of houses, all correspond to the physico-economic and socio-cultural conditions of the region. Altogether four types of rural dwellings have been identified, namely the *Basohli*, the *Bhaderwahi*, *Chambiali* and *Gaddiali* types. The number of storeys and the slopes of roofs distinguish these types.

J.P. Sharma and K. Singh[14] analysed the transition zone of Cis - Siwaliks lying between the Siwalik Hills and the fertile plains of the Gangetic basin in terms of tne growth of variety of house types. A characteristic feature of all types is the predominant use of locally available building material, small size, slopy roofs, simplicity of style and small entrances (to keep off wild animals as well as cold breeze). The economic activities of the residents are reflected in the layout and architectural designs like storage sheds, open spaces for processing of grains, orientation of house fronts and entrances in particular direction and the number of entrances. Altogether five types of houses have been identified in different sub-units of the region.

S.M.S. Hasan[15] while studying house types in the Kumaon region, described the influence of environmental conditions on house types and their internal layout. The analysis has been done on regional basis, which has been demarcated after considering relief and climatic conditions.

S. Singh[16] describes the village layout. house types and the internal layout of houses in five sample villages within the commuter's zone of Varanasi city. It has been investigated that the settlement structure and the roof plan of the houses reflect the physical and social conditions and specify standards of living. Most of the houses conform to the layouts laid down in the religious literature and show adaptations to the geographic environment.

PHYSICAL FACTORS

Man taps resources and builds houses out of local materials.[17] Physiography, drainage, climate and vegetation have profound effects on the rural house types. Due to the difference in these physical factors, particularly, because of the high intensity of rainfall, the districts of Purnea and Saharsa have thatch or wattle (bamboo, reeds, straw, grass or leaves) as the dominant building materials used in the construction of houses. On the other hand, the dwellers of Kaimur plateau in Rohtas district live in houses built of stone pilings. The people of southern upland plains in South Bihar use mud for the walls and tiles on a bamboo frame as the roofing material in their houses. Mixed type of houses predominate in the North Bihar Plains. This distribution attests to the profound influence of physiography and climate. Thus the inhabitants of Saharsa and Purnea districts do not build mud walls because of their destruction by waterlogging during the rainy season as it is a lowlying area and is further subject to a heavy rainfall. Similarly, the inhabitants of Gaya and Rohtas districts cannot use bamboos in their houses simply because bamboos are not cheaply available there, as compared to the North Bihar where they are in plenty of supply. The North Bihar in general has a heavy rainfall of over 150 cm in comparison with 125 cm of rains in the South Bihar Plain.

Climate has a pronounced effect upon various architectural designs and the climatic factors like the amount of rainfall, snowfall, directions of wind and storms, aspects of slopes of sun rays are important. 'The rural interiors are much more stingy of air and light than those of the towns'.[18] The amount of rainfall determines the variation in the construction of roof and the walls. The intensity of slope of the roof depends upon the intensity of storms in summer season, level of temperature and the amount of rainfall. Climate is also the main reason why most of the inhabitants of the region build their houses facing east instead of west. East facing houses are better ventilated, and the sun rays of the early morning are able to enter it while the west facing house is subject to the scorching after-noon sun, as well as westerly dust storms in the summer season. The slope of the roof ranges between 40° and 60° so that rain water may be quickly drained. An open courtyard is an essential part of the rural house because it provides the family with sunshine in winter days and cool and safe sleeping space during the warm summer nights. It is also used for drying grains, tethering cattle and for various household chores.

CULTURAL FACTORS

The socio-economic structure of the region determines the regional variation in dwellings. The cultural factors include the economic conditions of the inhabitants, traditions and social conditions, religious superstitions, administrative laws and the materials used in the construction of houses. There are marked differences between houses of the upper and the lower classes of people. The economically advanced areas of the region such as Patna district and parts of Gaya district have good rural houses, but economically backward areas such as Saharsa and Purnea districts have relatively poor materials used in the construction of houses. These houses also represent the cultural attainment of the past and the survival of the tradition may be seen in their simple architectural features.[19]

In the region under study, the cultural environment becomes more effective in determining rural-house types because of the great diversity in castes and classes, and a wide gap between the rich and poor. In certain localities there are some socially backward and untouchable castes such as *Mushars*, *Doms*, etc. People of these castes practically live away from the main village and have only small thatched hovels indicative of their poverty and backwardness. Inhabitants belonging to the richer classes have better residential buildings built with burnt brick walls and concrete or lime mortar roofs and are located in the best part of the village.

The hamlets of the poor or the backward *harijan* (untouchable) classes are generally built with thatch or wattle walls and thatch roofs. Even amongst them, the extremely poor may use discarded tin sheets, wood scrap and other waste materials in the construction of houses. Such houses are low, generally less than two metres in height and the door ways rarely more than 1.25 metres high. The houses are also single roomed structures, less then 30 square metres in area, and are no better than beggar shacks.

In contrast the upper caste Hindus or the well-to-do peasants prefer to build their houses with mud-walls and tile-roofs. The more affluent amongst them may construct flat *pucca* (masonry) roofs supported by brick built walls. The houses face towards the east or the west, and may contain a number of rooms, a courtyard, and verandahs with separate cattle sheds according to Hindu principles. Their height is also 4 metres or more. Double storey houses, however, are comparatively rare except in urban areas. The less fortunate have to be satisfied with mud-wall houses with thatch roofs, or partly tile and partly thatch roofs. In the eastern parts of the study area, the thatch roof is preferred as it is cheaper and easily renewed every year. Here the heavy rainfall and waterlogging forbid the construction of mud-walls and tile-roofs.

Houses are representative of brief periods of time only, as they last but a comparatively few years of time in the life span of people. They are pulled down or they fall into ruins when new ones are built in their place, so that the types of houses indicate to an extent the stage of civilization and arts attained by a region at a particular age. But wherever the form is preserved through the ages, the cause may be traced to both tradition and utility in the type of houses.[20] Man has the peculiar tendency to respect tradition and keep on to time honoured customs not only when they do not cost anything or interfere with progress, but even when the observance of such traditions and customs is economically unsound, and impedes progress. The traditional house in the Bihar Plain can be divided into two categories: (i) the mud wall and tile roofed structures and (ii) the thatch walled and thatch roofed structure. The other house types are a variation or hybrid form of these two basic types. The former belongs to the west and the south, and the latter to the east and the north within the study region.

Religion and castes also play an important role in determining the plan and architecture of houses. The Muslim houses are generally marked by a closed inner courtyard and lack of windows and are so placed in relation to each-other that the purdah of their woman folk is fully preserved. Hindu prefer to build their houses facing in any direction, except the south which is considered inauspicious. The untouchables are forced to build their houses a little away from the main settlement usually towards the south. Such sites are usually lowlying, dirty and devoid of lanes and drains. These factors continue to be there even today in spite of the laws calling for equality amongst all the citizens.

Finally, we can say that the character of the rural dwellings is normally determined by the nature of building materials available, their abundance and the ease of handling. In relatively developed areas such as Patna district, where transportation is more developed, the effect of urbanization has spread over larger areas. Here the inhabitants may bring building materials, such as wood, brick or stone from distant places for construction purposes. In less advanced areas like the Chotanagpur Scarp Belt and parts of Purnea and Saharasa districts, however, building materials can be brought from outside only at a heavy cost due to poor transport facilities. Here it is inevitable that local materials will be mainly used[21] in the construction of dwellings.

CLASSIFICATION OF HOUSE TYPES AND THEIR REGIONAL DISTRIBUTION

Within the study area, there is considerable diversity in the morphology of traditional peasant dwellings (Fig. 15.1). In order to classify these dwellings and map their distribution, a basic classification system becomes essential.[22] Due to the lack of a scientific and technological approach in the construction of houses, the basic form and type of houses in the area is influenced by the availability of building materials and its use in response to physical and human agencies.[23]

Houses can be classified according to physical factors, build and architecture, accommodation space, sanitation, occupancy rate, density of buildings, etc. Thus in the classification of house-types, their size and shape, building materials used and methods of construction become important, while houses differ in their architectural planning and building materials according to the choice and means of their individual owners. The houses and buildings generally show definite adaptations to physical conditions in different localities. It is interesting to note that the local variations in house types are well recognised by the people as is evident from the large number of terms used to describe different types of housing units and their component structures.

Linguistically, a house is known as *makan* or *ghar* in the Bihar Plain. Local variants of the latter are *grihi* in Gaya and Saran districts; *ghaur* in South-East Tirhut; *ghara* in South Munger and *gharo* in South Bhagalpur.[24] The word *Haveli* is used to denote female apartments in the entire Ganga valley. Local names used for various structures are *Jhopra* or *Jhopri* for a hut, *Khopri* for a temporary thatched shed, and *kutti* for the hut of a hermit. A *machan* is an elevated thatched shed built in the fields to keep vigil over the crops. A *marai* is a thatched hut built in the *khalihan* or granery. A palatial building would be known as *Dharhar*. A transportable hut made of reeds is used by the village circus man or Nut, and is called *Sirki*.

A small hovel or hut is called *Gohiya* north of the Ganga. South of the Ganga in Patna and Gaya it is called *maruka* or *Kurha*, in Shahabad *tati* or *Garhanghar*, and in south Bhagalpur *dhaka* or *Morko*.[25]

Houses built with mud are generally known as *kutcha* or *katcha*, while brick built structures are called *pucca* or *pokhta*. Stone built houses are locally known as *Chandni* in Bhojpur. A dilapidated structure is called *Khandhar*. Straw huts are called *tataughar* in the north, *dochara* in Bhojpur and *Kharoghar* in South Bhagalpur. More commonly, however, they are known as *phus ka ghar*.

Local names are also used for houses of various sizes and plans. Thus while the commonest house is single storeyed the 1st floor is called *kotha* in double storeyed houses. Similarly the treasury house is known as *tahkhana* or *tarhara*, particularly in the south.

Different parts of a house are given characteristic names. A brick built plinth is known as *Kursi* but a mud built platform is called *Dawa*. A sloping roof is known as *Chauni* or *Chhappar*, but a flat roof is known as a *chhat*. Roofs sloping in one direction are called *ekpalia* in the south and *ekchari* or *Palani* in the north, those with two sided slopes are termed *dopalia* in Bhojpur and *dochara* in Tirhut. Roofs sloping to four sides from a point are known as *Chaupar*, which is the meeting place of village elders. Thatched roofs are sometimes built on top of a boundary wall to save the mud from damage in the rains. This is called *parchhatti* or *Chhapri*. The inner courtyard is called *anngan* or *angna*, while the outer courtyard is called *aguara* or *aguari*. The backyard is termed *pichhwara* or *pichhutti*. The outer varandah used for meeting people is called *osara*. A *dalan* is an out house used as a meeting place of men-folk in Tirhut, and the same is known as *Chaupal* in Patna division. A cattle shed is known as *goshala* or *bathan*.

According to housing structure, their functional importance and the economic standard of the people, we can classify the rural houses into four types:[26]

Rudimentary house

One roomed house of the poor peasants come in this category. Such occupants have very few possessions to keep inside the house, because their life is purely based on hand to mouth economy. For them, a house is meant only as a place of cooking food and taking rest.

In such houses, even newly married couple sleep in one corner and the other corners are used by parents and other family members. One corner is occupied by the kitchen and one by the family deity. Water is kept in a pitcher in between the family deity and the kitchen. In courtyard the *Tulsi* plant is necessarily planted in a Hindu family. Some banana trees may also be planted on the backside of the house. Such houses do not have provision of ventilation. They are low in elevation and are, generally, insanitary.

Compact house types

When a house contains two or more than two rooms it comes under this category. There are separate bed rooms for the inhabitants, a kitchen, store room, etc. Such houses belong to middle class families and are generally marked by mud-wall and tile-roofs, an outer verandah and an inner courtyard. This house type is most commonly found all over the Bihar Plain. There may be a large variation in the size and space of such houses depending on the economic level of the owner.

Straggling house types

The house in which man and beasts live together with cooperation can be called the straggling house type. Mostly lower middle class people and poor families, who have little living space, live in such a manner. The milkmen (*goala*) usually belong to this category but the better-off amongst them live in compact houses.

Vertical house types

Double and treble storeyed houses belong to this category. The upper storeys are mainly used as bed rooms and the lower floors are utilised as store-room, kitchen, cattleshed and for business purposes. These houses are built with bricks and masonry and have flat intermediate roofs. Only the rich people can construct such buildings in rural areas. They are common in rural service centres and towns, but are relatively rare in villages.

HOUSE TYPES ACCORDING TO SIZE

A classification of houses according to the number of households they contain furnishes an accurate idea of the economic level of the community.[27] The houses vary in size from a palatial building to a single regular room or hut, showing the abode of the rich and the poor respectively. The size of the house is primarily determined by cultural factors such as the economic conditions and the size of the family. The caste factor plays a prominent role in controlling the size of the dwellings. Most of the houses belonging to the lower castes are small in size, because they are not only poor and socially backward but there is little *purdah* in their families, so that one or two rooms with a verandah is enough for them.

Dwellings having no regular rooms

Such houses usually consist of a fencing wall, a courtyard and a shed or varandah with two or three walls, only. These are better referred to as barracks and not as houses. They are few in number. In the rural areas of the Bihar Plain only 0.1 per cent of the families live in small dwellings having no defined room. The proportion of such houses is relatively higher in Champaran and Munger districts being 0.2%.

One roomed houses

Houses with only one room generally occur in Tirhut and Bhagalpur divisions, such as Saharsa (43.30%), Munger (43%), Purnea (40%) and Darbhanga (39%) districts and the regional average is 31.5 per cent. Such houses are very small in size. 'It presents a rudimentary form of the compact house where human beings and animals find shelter under the same roof'.[28] This type of house is built by the poor people and *harijans* who cannot afford to build larger structures. Such houses are insanitary, unventilated, low roofed and overcrowded as the entire family has to be packed in a single room without consideration of privacy or convenience.

Two roomed houses

Two roomed houses are of importance in the districts of Muzaffarpur (36%), Darbhanga (35%), Saharsa (32%), Purnea and Champaran (31%). This is the general type of housing for middle class peasants, because it is built cheaply. Such houses have generally rectangular ground plan reasonably fit into the field patterns of the region. Except Saran district, the whole of North Bihar shows a concentration of two roomed houses. They constitute only one-fifth of the total number of houses in South Bihar. The regional average is 29.7%. Houses of this group are relatively better built.

Three roomed houses

These medium sized dwellings belong to middle class families. This house-type is more common in Patna, Gaya and Bhojpur districts where more than 18% households live in such houses. In the eastern part of the study region comprising the districts of Bhagalpur division, the percentage is less than 16%. Then, this is essentially an area of small houses. In the region as a whole 16.9% houses belong to this category.

Four roomed houses

Four roomed houses are larger in size and belong to upper

middle class people of the region. 99.5% of the houses in the region are of this type. There are only two or three such houses in each village. Still there is a great regional difference in this house type. The ratio of such dwellings is less in the Kosi-belt where the people are relatively poor because of annual-floods. The percentage in most of the region is less than 10, except in Patna, Gaya, Bhojpur and Champaran districts where it is between 11 to 16% (Table 15.1).

Houses having five or more rooms

This group represents 12.3% of the rural houses in the Bihar Plain. The proportion of households occupying five rooms or more is less than 10% in most of the regions except in the west, where it rises to around 30% in Patna, Gaya and Bhojpur districts. Saran has 13.9% houses in this category. Such houses belong to the rich farmers. They are well constructed with brick and mortar, and often have a high plinth and a flat brick and lime roof, they are well ventilated and clean.

To sum up, the largest number of families live in small sized houses of one to two rooms. The percentage of such houses comes to 61.2% in the Bihar Plain. Locally, such houses abound in the entire North Bihar particularly towards the east. Their ratio rises to two-thirds or more of the total number of houses in the Tirhut and Bhagalpur divisions. In Patna division, however, their ratio is around one-third to one-half only.

Medium sized houses of 3 and 4 rooms are prominent in Patna division where they constitute about one-third of the total number of houses. In Tirhut and Bhagalpur divisions, the figures are around one-fifth only, as compared to the regional average of 26.4%.

Large houses, as is to be expected are concentrated in Patna, Gaya and Bhojpur districts in Patna division where they account for over one-fourth of the total number of houses. Such houses contain five or more rooms and are mostly brick built or *pucca*. Compared to the regional average of 12.3%, their number is less than 10% in all other parts of the Bihar Plain with the exception of Saran district (13.9%).

We may, therefore, safely conclude that the size of houses decreases as we move from west to east and from south to north in the Bihar Plain. The larger houses are to be found in Patna, Gaya and Bhojpur districts and their adjoining areas. In contrast the smaller houses are concentrated in the relatively backward areas of Saharsa district and the five districts of Muzaffarpur, Darbhanga, Munger, Bhagalpur and Purnea which adjoin Saharsa.

MATERIAL OF WALL

Mud is the most important material used for the construction of walls in the rural areas of the entire region. The percentage of walls built with this material ranges between 45.8 and 93.1 in all the districts except in Saharsa and Purnea districts where the figures are 12.1 and 13.1 (Table 15.2) respectively. The figure rises to over 80% in Bhagalpur and Bhojpur and over 90% in Gaya district. These figures may be compared with 66.6% for rural areas of the entire state (Fig. 15.2).

Vegetation material which includes grass, leaves, reeds, bamboo and timber constitutes the second most important building material for walls. The share of this material is significant in Champaran, Mazaffarpur and Darbhanga districts where it is between 35% and 45% and rises to over 80% in the districts of Saharsa and Purnea. In all other areas the figure is above 10% and it is negligible in Patna division.

Brick constitutes the next important material in wall making. Unburnt brick is not so important, but burnt brick accounts for approximately 13 to 20% of the walls in Bhojpur, Rohtas, Munger and Saran districts, rising to 29.3% in Patna district. It is obvious that such walls are common on either side of the river Ganga and form a compact belt. Brick built walls are less than 10% in all other areas including average for the State of Bihar. Since the share of all other building materials taken together is less than 0.5%, they do not need to be considered. These materials include metal sheets, stone, cement, concrete, etc. and are clearly beyond the capacities of persons living outside urban areas.

TABLE 15.1 : SIZES OF RURAL DWELLINGS ACCORDING TO NUMBER OF ROOMS IN THE BIHAR PLAIN

Districts	Total No. of households*	No. defined rooms % of H.H.	1 Room % of H.H.	2 Room % of H.H.	3 Room % of H.H.	4 Room % of H.H.	5 Room % of H.H.
Patna	75711	.1	18.9	23.4	18.0	13.2	26.4
Gaya	112324	.1	16.0	20.5	18.3	15.0	30.1
Shahabad	44010	.1	15.5	21.1	18.8	15.4	19.1
Saran	115896	.1	28.7	29.8	18.8	8.7	13.9
Champaran	104490	.1	27.4	31.1	20.8	10.8	9.7
Muzaffarpur	144246	.1	33.0	36.0	17.6	7.4	5.9
Darbhanga	163869	.1	39.0	35.3	15.2	6.2	4.2
Munger	112351	.2	43.0	29.9	13.0	6.8	7.1
Bhagalpur	56781	.1	41.3	31.0	14.3	7.0	6.3
Saharsa	60312	.1	43.3	32.0	15.3	6.2	3.1
Purnea	107994	.1	40.0	31.2	15.9	7.6	5.2
Bihar Plain	1147994	.1	31.5	29.7	16.9	9.5	12.3

Source: Census of India, 1961, Report on Housing and Establishment: Bihar, Vol. IV, Part IV-A, Table VI-3, p. 432 (Based on 20% Sample).

* Household is a group of persons, who commonly live together and would take their meals from a common kitchen unless the exigencies of work prevented any of these from doing so.

From the above consideration it would appear that mud, and grass leaves and twigs are the two principal building materials used for the construction of walls in the region (Fig. 15.2). They fall in two distinct belts. Mud is the predominating material in Tirhut, Patna and South Bhagalpur division, particularly west of the river Baghmati and south of the river Ganga. Mud walls account for over 80% of the walls in Rohtas, Gaya, Munger and Bhagalpur districts and over 95% walls in the Chotanagpur Scarp Belt. In these areas the intensity of rainfall is low, while due to granular clayee soil and warm temperature the walls harden into strong durable structures.

Walls built with dried hay, bamboo splits and sticks predominate towards the north-east in the districts of Eastern Darbhanga, Saharsa and Purnea. Their share is generally one third of all walls in Tirhut division but rises to over 80% in Purnea and over 95% in central Saharsa district. Another patch of a high concentration of such walls is in extreme northern portion of Champaran district. In both these areas the soil is river alluvium but the rainfall is more than 150cm in the extreme north-east and north west respectively. Due to heavy rainfall, mud-walls are liable to crumble and dissolve in flood affected lowlying areas while bamboo and thatch walls are both cheap and durable.

Brick built walls attain sizeable proportions along the river Ganga and form a compact belt in Saran, Bhojpur, Patna and Munger districts. Their highest concentration, however is around the city of Patna, where they account for more than 40% of all walls. Urban influence coupled with relatively higher incomes and better transport[29] are clearly responsible for this phenomenon.

MATERIAL OF ROOF

The roofs of the rural houses in Bihar Plain are by and large constructed of a bamboo lattice covered with thatch or tiles. The roofs are sloping in character and offer a quick run-off of rain water.

The most prominent roofing material is half-round earthen tiles. The percentage of tiled roofs ranges between 26.2% and 87.8% but there is a wide variation. Tiled roofs are the most common in the districts of Patna, Rohtas, Saran, and Munger where more than two-thirds of the roofs are of this type. In contrast, the percentage falls to 40 or less in Champaran, Muzaffarpur and Darbhanga districts and is almost negligible or less than 10% in the districts of Saharsa and Purnea(Fig. 15.3).

TABLE 15.2 : MATERIAL OF WALL IN RURAL AREAS OF THE BIHAR PLAIN

Districts	% of Grass, Leaves, Reed or Bamboo, Timber	% of Mud Built	% of Bricks	% of others
Patna	0.8	69.0	30.1	0.1
Gaya	0.1	93.1	6.8	0.0
Shahabad	1.3	85.1	13.4	0.2
Saran	10.3	70.1	19.6	0.0
Champaran	45.2	45.8	9.1	0.0
Muzaffarpur	35.7	54.1	10.2	0.0
Darbhanga	40.3	48.5	11.2	0.0
Munger	15.2	69.3	14.7	0.0
Bhagalpur	8.8	83.5	7.7	0.0
Saharsa	83.6	12.1	4.3	0.0
Purnea	84.85	13.1	2.2	0.2
Bihar Plain	33.4	53.8	12.7	0.1
Bihar State (Rural)	22.8	66.3	10.6	0.3

Source: Census of India, 1961 Housing and Establishment Tables, Bihar, Vol. IV, B, Table IV, pp. 471 - 475.

The highest concentration of tile roofs is to be found in the valleys of the Ganga and the Gandak in the districts of Saran, Bhojpur and Patna, as also in Gaya and Munger, where it forms a compact patch. The percentage is low in the Chotanagpur Scarp Belt, Terai areas and in the greater part of Eastern Tirhut and Bhagalpur divisions.

Items of vegetation including grass, leaves, reeds, thatch wood or bamboo are the predominant roofing materials in north eastern Bihar Plain as well as in other parts of Tirhut division and Chotanagpur Scarp Belt. The share of such materials in these areas is around 60% in Champaran, Muzaffarpur and Bhagalpur districts, 80% in Darbhanga and around 90% in Saharsa and Purnea districts. They form a compact belt in Eastern Darbhanga, Saharsa and Purnea where their percentage rises to over 95% of the roofs. Another patch is to be found in extreme north-west Champaran district.

In all these areas, the rainfall is over 150 cm and rises to more than 200 cm per annum towards north-west Champaran and in north-east Purnea respectively. It is clear that heavy rainfall coupled with availability of cheap thatching material is the main reason for the construction of such roofs. In Chotanagpur Scarp Belt the predominance of thatch roof is not the result of rainfall, rather it is because of cheap thatching material available from local forests and the economic backwardness of the inhabitants who cannot afford tiles.

Other roofing materials, such as metal sheets, asbestos sheets, brick and lime, cement, concrete, etc. are almost negligible in the construction of roofs and together constitute less than 3% of all the roofs. Brick and lime are important as a roofing material only in Patna district, and the adjoining belt on either side of the Ganga because of urban influence. Metal sheets are frequently used in northern Saharsa and Purnea districts where due to frequent floods and heavy rainfall they have been widely distributed as aid from the Government.

Table 15.3 : MATERIAL OF ROOF IN RURAL AREAS OF THE BIHAR PLAIN

Districts	% Grass, Leaves, Reeds, Thatch, Wood & Bamboos	% Tiles and Slate	% Asbestos C.I. Sheets and Others	% Brick and concrete
Patna	16.4	79.0	0.1	4.5
Gaya	39.1	59.0	0.0	1.9
Shahabad	8.5	87.8	0.4	3.3
Saran	14.6	82.3	0.1	3.0
Champaran	57.1	40.8	0.2	1.9
Muzaffarpur	59.1	38.8	0.2	1.9
Darbhanga	72.0	26.2	0.2	1.6
Munger	29.9	67.2	9.5	2.4
Bhagalpur	59.3	37.4	0.3	3.0
Saharsa	91.1	6.8	1.2	0.9
Purnea	89.6	2.8	6.5	1.1
Bihar Plain	49.3	48.1	0.3	2.3
Bihar State (Rural)	44.6	52.2	0.9	2.3

Source: Ibid.

HOUSE TYPES ACCORDING TO BUILDING MATERIALS

The availability of local building materials is of primary importance in considering the house-types of the region.[30] The chief amongst them are clay, sand, bamboo, grass, reeds, timber, etc. The clayee soil contains a high percentage of cementing materials and is good for the construction of walls and manufacture of tiles, burnt bricks and unburnt bricks. It causes only a small regional variation in construction, because there are few materials which are universally available in the entire region.

In the Bihar Plain the houses of the peasants are mostly mud-walled huts, built of earth dug up in the vicinity of the settlement, with which broken pottery or straw is mixed to impart solidarity in construction. The roof is mostly made of a bamboo lattice, known as *thaath* and covered with thatch or tiles. Thatch is commonly used by the poor and is more common in the eastern parts of the region. The more affluent cover the *thaath* with tiles, or build *pucca* roofs. Tiles are also more common in the western parts of the region. There is little provision for ventilation, but this does not cause much hardship to the peasants who regard their houses merely as a place for cooking and sleeping.

The riparian tracts of the Bihar Plain are liable to floods. In such walls and thatched roofs, for the soil is often so sandy that mud for the walls cannot be obtained, and even if it is available, the walls are liable to crumble due to waterlogging in the monsoon season. The risk of the houses being washed away which is the chief reason for using cheaper but more durable building materials, usually a 'piece of the natural vegetation'.[31] The houses are, therefore, erected above the level of flood water and are built with bamboo frame-work thickly plastered with clayee soil cover, and the roof is thatched with straw. The poorer members of the society build huts made of reeds, known as *sirki*, which precariously support a thatched roof. Such houses are so light that they can be easily demolished and transported, so as to give rise to the saying 'a man like a snail can carry his house anywhere and raise it anew'.

Mud wall and tile roof zone of the South Bihar Plain

The mud walled and tile roofed houses cover about 70% of total number of houses in the South Bihar Plain and 25% in the three adjoining districts of Muzaffarpur, Darbhanga and Munger. They are generally built by the middle class people. The plains of Gaya, Shahabad, Munger and Bhagalpur have over 80% of the houses built with these materials. The thatched roofs having higher slope are more suitable for the heavy rainfall areas in the north-east.

The mud walls are about 0.5 metre thick and the lower section near the plinth is about one metre thick. On the eaves line the walls are about 2 metres high, while at the crestline they are 2.5 metres high.[32] Such walls effectively keep off the heat during the summer season. If well covered by the roof, they are able to withstand erosion during the rains and are as durable as brick walls. Tile roofs are more durable than thatch since the latter are damaged by the rains and require frequent change. For tile roofs the fear of fire is also much less during the summer season as compared to the thatch ones. The plan and size of the buildings are variable according to economic conditions of the owner.

The zone of maximum concentration of this type is the whole of Rohtas, Bhojpur, Saran and also parts of Patna, Gaya and Munger districts. In these areas almost 90% of the houses are of this type. In the Garkha *anchal* of Chapra Sadar Subdivision and Arrah *anchal* of Bhojpur district the figure rises to over 95%. The ratio of such houses gradually decreases towards east and north, and in Saharsa and Purnea districts, they are almost totally absent.

Houses built with vegetation matter

Houses built with reeds, bamboo, thatch, etc. are predominant in the districts of Purnea, Saharsa and Eastern Darbhanga as also north-western part of Champaran district. Such houses are generally smaller in size than tile roof structures. The length ranges from 8 metres and width 3 to 4 metres only. The walls are made of bamboo splits covered with straw or sometimes plastered over with clay. They are usually 2 to 2.5 metres high, with a 3 to 4 metres crest. The house is mostly surrounded by a courtyard or *angan* having huts on the four sides, the intervening space between them being confined by walls formed of the same materials. Outside the compound an open-cow-shed may be found. The roof consists of a bamboo frame supported by wooden poles and covered with straw. The share of such houses is over 95% of all houses in central Saharsa and adjoining parts of Purnea and Darbhanga districts. Such houses also account for about one-half of all houses in Tirhut division except in Saran district.

The lower class of inhabitants like landless labourers (*banihars*) build their houses with a bamboo framework covered with reeds or straw and thatched with straw or grass. Such houses consist of a single room being 2.5 to 3 metres in length and 2 to 2.5 metres in width, with a thatched roof sloping on two sides called *du-chapra*. The structures have no windows, and the only means of entrance is a doorway closed by a loose mat formed of grass and secured with splits of bamboo. The inside walls are plastered with clay.

Houses built with mud walls and thatched roofs

Houses belonging to this class are predominantly found in the districts of Champaran, Muzaffarpur and Darbhanga north of the Ganga, and Gaya and Bhagalpur south of it. They are also predominant in the entire Chotanagpur Scarp Belt in the south. The building materials are locally available mud and the roofing material is grass or paddy straw. Such dwellings are rectangular in plan but the roofs are generally gabled in form. Over 70% of the houses in Muzaffarpur, Darbhanga and Bhagalpur districts have thatch roofs, while over 80% of the houses in Gaya and Bhagalpur have mud walls. The walls vary between 2 to 2.5 metres in height near the doorway, but rise to 3 to 4 metres at the crest of the roof. The size of the building is variable depending upon the economic condition of the owner. The chief advantage of such dwellings is its lesser cost and suitability for the regional climatic conditions.

Brick built houses

The upper class affluent inhabitants of the region prefer to use bricks in the construction of walls. Brick built roofs, however, are few and belong only to the rich. In Patna, Saran and Muzaffarpur districts on either side of the river Ganga, brick built houses are found to be concentrated. There are generally single storeyed structures with brick walls and tile roofs. The height of the building is between 3 to 4 metres, while the plan is rectangular in shape and variable in size. Such houses usually contain an inner courtyard (*angan*) and an outer verandah with two or more rooms. In the Bihar Plain as a whole, the place of such house-type is insignificant but it is important in the district of Patna, especially in Patna Rural 'B" *anchal*, where it accounts for 73.2% of the total number of houses, presumably because of urban influence. Such houses are comparatively durable and impermeable to excessive moisture. They are indicative of the general prosperity of the region. Another reason is that areas like Patna district which have better communication and transport facilities are also favoured by an easy availability of coal which is necessary for the manufacture of bricks.

Other types

Other building materials such as unburnt (sun dried) bricks, wood, stone or cement concrete are relatively less used in the rural houses of the Bihar Plain. Houses built with corrugated iron sheets are, however, frequently encountered in Kishanganj subdivision of Purnea district. The walls are usually built with mud or bricks, but the roof is of corrugated iron sheets. This material is favoured because of heavy rainfall in the area and the Government has distributed corrugated iron sheets as aid to the flood affected people.

HOUSE TYPE ACCORDING TO SHAPE

Local availability of building materials, their cost, ease of handling, the needs of peasants, climatic conditions, the economic position of the peasants and the cultural heritage of the rural housing design are the chief determinants of the shape of houses in the Bihar Plain. The shape is generally guided more by the ancestral pattern than the recent technological developments. According to shape, houses may be classified into rectangular and square patterns. Besides these two broad classifications, L shaped, T shaped, U shaped and circular house types are also to be occasionally found in the region.

The rectangular house

The rectangular house type is one of the most commonly accepted designs of rural dwellings in the region, and the overwhelming majority are of this shape.[33]

Most of the rural houses in the region including institutions such as schools, hostels, etc. as well as residential buildings are built in linear fashion and consist of several rooms in a row with a courtyard in front of the structure. Most of the houses contain verandahs which are used as kitchen, cow-shed, or for general household work. The rectangular houses have a rectangular ground plan which varies in size and area according to the needs of the inhabitants.

The square house

There is no distinction between square and rectangular houses. It depends mostly upon the needs of the cultivators, and the size of the plot. Such houses are widely distributed over the whole of the Bihar Plain with certain exceptions. There is a prejudice in some part of the region against square houses, and people believe that a house should be oblong and the two longer sides should run north and south.[34]

The square house may contain one or more rooms with a courtyard or *angan*.[35] The door of each room opens to the courtyard whose size varies according to the size of the house. The rural houses usually contain small windows opening outwards, while the verandah faces inwards towards the inner courtyard.

Other house types

L shaped houses consist of two limbs with the space enclosed between them bounded by two boundary walls forming a courtyard. If the rooms are on three sides of the courtyard, the plan is U shaped. T shaped houses are rarely found.

The circular houses are not strictly circular, but are square with round corners or are oval in shape. These are occasionally found only in the forested areas of the north west or the south. The roofs of such houses are usually thatch, while the walls are of timber or reeds. The plan and architecture of most of the houses are very simple having only one main door with partitions separating the main room of the house into two compartments. In front part of the house, a small verandah is commonly found, which is used for meeting the outsiders. The houses are generally dark, poorly ventilated and have low roof.

REGIONAL GROWTH OF RESIDENTIAL HOUSES

The region shows a growth of rural dwellings from 4.04 millions in 1911 to 8.03 millions in 1981 but the increase has not been uniform and there was a decline during 1911-21 particularly in Saran, Muzaffarpur, Darbhanga and Saharsa districts. This was due to heavy floods which washed away thousands of houses, while thousands were badly damaged. From Table 15.4 given below it would appear that the increase from 1931 to 1941 was normal but from 1941 to 1951 it has been accelerated presumably because of higher population growth. Thus to cope with the rise in population an increase in the number of dwellings became essential.

Table 15.4 : REGIONAL GROWTH OF HOUSES IN RURAL AREAS
(Figures in 00000)

Districts	1911	1921	1931	1941	1951	1961	1971*	1981*
Patna	2.6	2.6	2.8	3.2	3.2	4.2	5.3	6.7
Gaya	4.0	3.9	4.2	4.2	4.5	6.8	7.9	8.5
Shahabad	3.5	3.4	3.5	3.8	3.9	5.6	6.2	7.4
Saran	4.9	4.3	4.5	4.6	4.3	5.8	6.9	7.7
Champaran	3.4	3.5	3.8	4.1	4.0	6.2	7.8	8.9
Muzaffarpur	5.0	5.2	5.4	5.7	5.6	6.9	6.6	8.7
Darbhanga	5.8	5.5	5.8	6.5	6.8	7.2	8.3	9.5
Munger	3.7	3.8	4.0	4.3	4.5	4.9	5.2	6.8
Bhagalpur					2.2	2.6	3.3	4.0
Saharsa	3.9	3.3	3.9	4.4	2.7	3.2	3.4	4.5
Purnea	3.6	3.7	3.9	5.1	5.4	5.4	6.4	7.6
Bihar Plain	40.4	39.2	41.8	46.0	49.2	59.2	68.8	80.3

Source: Based on housing tables of different Census Years.

Assuming that one house is sufficient for a family having five persons, there was only 3.68% shortage of houses in 1911, but with the increase of population, this percentage has risen to 9.5% in 1951.

With Five Year Plans starting afte: 1951, the conditions improved to 8.26% because the Housing Department had taken some steps for the removal of housing shortage in rural areas. (Table 15.5).

The shortage of rural houses is particularly marked in the district of Saharsa and the adjoining parts of South Muzaffarpur, South Darbhanga, North Munger and Purnea districts. These areas are flood affected and economically backward. On the other hand, the number of houses is more or less adequate in the districts of Patna, Gaya and Shahabad where people are more affluent.

DENSITY OF RURAL HOUSES

In calculating the density of rural houses per square kilometre, vast tracts of agricultural lands, orchards, etc., have to be included, as the separate built-up area of each settlement in the entire revenue village or *mauza* is not available. In most of the villages, the main settlement sites are actually located in a number of small hamlets. These are the real clusters of houses. Fields and orchards surrounding them are entities quite distinct from them. Therefore, the density should preferably be worked out on the area figures for settlement sites only. The village settlements are often more congested than many urban centres, but since the data is not available the intensity of congestion cannot be calculated.

Table 15.5 : HOUSING SHORTAGE IN RURAL AREAS OF THE BIHAR PLAIN

Years	Actual No. of Houses	Houses required on the basis of Five persons per family	% of Housing shortage
1911	4035382	4189547	3.68
1921	3915418	4131947	5.23
1931	4182270	4515226	7.37
1941	4607552	4976156	7.40
1951	4924731	5444604	9.54
1961	5920692	6453709	8.26
1971	6880000	7856431	9.87
1981	8030000	8432153	10.63

Source: Ibid.

The density map of houses (Fig. 15.4) shows that the districts of Darbhanga, Muzaffarpur, Saran and the city and Sadar subdivisions of Patna district have the highest density of houses in the Bihar Plain. Here the number of houses ranges between 62 and 106 per square kilometre. In the zone of the highest density Patna Rural 'B' with 14.4 houses, Bairgania with 94 (Sitamarhi district) Samastipur with 63, Pusa with 104, Manigachhi with 103 and Pandaul with 62 (both in Darbhanga district) have the highest density of houses in rural areas of the region.

In other parts of Tirhut division and the adjoining parts of North Shahabad, North Gaya and Patna districts, the density of houses ranges between 47 to 58 per square kilometre. The density is much lower in Bhagalpur division towards the east and Chotanagpur Scarp Belt towards the south, as also in north-west Champaran. In Bhagalpur division there are 35 to 58 houses per square kilometre with small patches rising to 77. In Chotanagpur Scarp Belt and north-west Champaran there are only 11 to 47 houses per square kilometre. The lowest density is to be found in Nauhatta and Rohtas *anchals* of Rohtas district, Dumaria and Rajauli *anchals* of Gaya district, Chakai *anchal* of Munger district and Katoria *anchal* of Bagalpur district, where there are less than 19 houses per square kilometre. This belt is least settled on account of rocky and forested character of the land and lack of agricultural land.

THE RESIDENTIAL FUNCTION OF RURAL HOUSES

The most important use of the rural house is for residence. Naturally, if an area is culturally developed, many houses would be used for shops, factories, public utility services and other non-residential uses. On the other hand, if an area is economically and culturally backward, the majority of the houses would be used for residential purposes only. High incidence of residential use also suggests that the region is less urbanised and is extremely dependent on agriculture.

From the point of view of percentage of houses used as dwellings in rural areas (Fig. 15.5) we can divide the region into three zones. The zone of highest percentage of residential units (80-100) is found in the east, spread over the districts of Purnea, Saharsa, Bhagalpur and Munger. This area is amongst the poorest parts of the Bihar Plain and also suffers from lack of transport and urbanisation. The second zone accounting for 60 to 80% of dwellings and this is found in the districts of Tirhut division in North Bihar, except Samastipur subdivision of Darbhanga. The third zone of 50 to 70% houses is spread over the greater part of Bhojpur and Patna districts and northern Gaya district. This area has a developed transport network and a high degree of urbanization, leading to several rurban service centres. Thus many of the houses are used for the purpose of business, industries, educational institutions, government offices, transport offices, warehouses etc. in this belt.

An interesting study can be made by considering the average number of houses per village and classifying the villages in an area according to the number of houses they contain. It is obvious that in flood affected areas where the size of revenue village is larger, the number of residential houses would also be high. In the rugged and infertile areas, since the density of population is low, the number of houses per village would also be low.

This can be seen in Fig. 15.6 which suggests that the area under study can be divided into four zones. This map has been prepared by drawing isopleths for the median and quartile values of average number of houses per village on the basis of *anchal* level data. The highest figures of over Q 3 value, that is over 176 houses per village are to be found in the flood affected areas of the region from Madhubani Block-West Champaran district in the west to the southern part of Katihar district in the east. Due to the higher siting of village and high density of population the size of the village is large in this belt.

The zone of above mean, that is, 131 to 176 houses per village covers the semi-flood affected zone of the Bihar Plain, covering parts of Muzaffarpur and Darbhanga districts and the entire flood plains of the Ganga, the Chandan, the Chir, the Sakri, the Kiul and the Son in South Bihar Plain.

The third zone of 130 to 91 houses, that is below mean covers the entire district of Saran and Southern Upland plains of Rohtas, Patna, Munger and Bhagalpur districts. This is the most fertile and flood free area of the Bihar Plain.

The zone of under Q1 or less than 91 houses per village comprises the entire Chotanagpur Scarp Belt, and three-fourth of Rohtas district. It also includes the peripheral areas of Purnea, western Saran and north-western Champaran districts. These areas are marked by low fertility, dense forest cover and economic backwardness. The population density is also low, hence the size of the village is small.

We have seen that the majority of people in the Bihar Plain live in small houses containing less than two rooms each. Since an average family consists of five persons it is obvious that this condition would lead to shortage of living space which leads to overcrowding in the rural houses. This can be clearly visualized by considering the average number of persons per room in the rural areas of the study region.

For the Bihar State as a whole the occupancy rate per room comes to 2.29. In the study area also the median value is close to this figure. However, there is a great regional imbalance and in Saharsa district the figure is 2.84, while in several other districts of Tirhut and Bhagalpur divisions it is above the regional average. In contrast, the rate is substantially below 1.75 in all districts of Patna division. It seems that Saharsa has top position in the list because it is the most rural and economically backward area in the entire region, while the districts to the west are relatively better-off in this respect. It may further be pointed out that the number of one room and two room houses taken together (small houses) account for over 75% of the houses in Saharsa. This is indicative of the poverty and resultant overcrowding in Bihar Plain

We may distinguish three distinct belts of relative occupancy rates in the Bihar Plain (Fig. 15.7).

The first zone with figures above Q_3 i.e. over 2.71 persons per room is to be found in an elongated belt in Vaisali, Samastipur, Begusari, Saharsa and Purnea districts. This area is marked by recurrent floods and marshy lands and has a high density of residential houses.

The second zone ranging from Q_1 to Q_3, i.e. on either side of the median from 1.87 to 2.71 is to be found both to the north and south of the first zone. The belt, is more extensive in the north and covers the rest of the North Bihar Plain, as also Munger and Bhagalpur districts of the South Bihar. In this area, the density of population is high and the economy is purely agricultural. In many ways, it is the most representative part of the entire study area.

The third zone shows values below Q_1, that is, less than 1.87 persons per room. This zone is entirely confined to the districts of Bhojpur, Patna and Gaya in Patna Division. Here the density of population continues to be high except in the Chotanagpur Scarp Belt. This area is culturally advanced and economically better part of the Bihar Plain. It also has better transport facilities and exhibits a higher number of large houses containing more than five rooms. In the Chotanagpur Scarp Belt, the reason for low occupancy rate is not economic well being rather it is the low density of population in the area.

RURAL HOUSE TYPES IN INDIA

Rural house shows a close dependence on the physical and cultural factors. Climatic conditions, landform features, physical features, drainage lines and soil types have their differential impact on the house types, in terms of construction materials, their size, shape, location and comfort. It means house types and environmental conditions are closely correlated. A house may be a small hut of wattle and daub in the equatorial forests of Congo basin or it may be a multi-storeyed building like New York and Tokyo. The house denotes all human structures whether they are meant to live in, work in or store things in. The brownish colour of mud wall, reddish colour of brick walls, various colours of wall painting in religious and administrative houses show the various sentiments of mankind. On the other hand, in the Plains of Rhyne and Danube in Europe and the plains of the Ganga river in India, the houses are found very close together in rural areas whereas in the plateau of Peninsular India and Scotland, the houses of peasants are found a bit farther apart due to undulating land, and difficult to get sustenance in compact dwellings.

In any study of rural areas the investigation about peasant dwellings is very important because it is the centre of combined living, functional space and social status in the society. In this way, "rural house type is the true indicators of its environmental conditions and the living standard of the people". Although from the point of view of architectural style it is very simple but it is important from geographical point of view. In most cases the houses are of rectangular or square in shape which contain one verandah in front. The courtyard is square in shape, surrounded by small rooms in all directions. In rural areas the houses are generally of one storey which either lacks window or if it is found, its location must be in upper part of the backside wall having small in size.

Among the physical factors house type is mostly affected by the insulation, direction of prevailing wind and the amount of rainfall. In areas of extreme climatic conditions, the houses are constructed in such a way so that they keep the interior cool during the summer and warm during the winter. In such a situation thick mud wall is needed but window is not at all considered essential for cross ventilation. In rainfed areas the roof is generally constructed gable shape but with the decreasing amount of rainfall the roof also tends towards flat. In different regions of India the impact of geographical conditions can clearly be observed on house types which are as follows:

In Karnataka the walls of the houses are constructed very thick of mud and the roof is covered either thatch made of grass leaves or tile. In northern Karnataka single roomed circular house with domal roof is more prominent. The main gate of the house has a length of one metre and breadth half metre. The houses are constructed very close together in a beehive shape. In southern side of the Pennar river hut looks like egg in shape with conical roof tops.

In Malabar and Konkan coast of Western India, mud wall and roof tops covered with coconut leaves are the most prominent features found in rural houses. In areas of Travancore and Cochin the lower part of the roof is very artistically made to curved towards up. In Periyar region the house of Urali people is found as semi-circular hut constructed out of bamboo splits. Mala Arya people of Kottayam division make their huts on tree branches with the help of bamboo and grass. On the slopes of Cardamom hills – Mulawan people live in square shaped huts.

In Tamilnadu the houses are generally made of brick walls and tile roofs. On Nilgiri mountain – Toda people live in semi-circular houses. The height of such house is 6 metres and ground with 3 metres. For sleeping, Toda people make one rectangular earthen platform inside the house. For houses lying in one row – the roof is constructed jointly. In areas of Deccan Lava Plateau – the houses having flat roofs are very common due to semi-arid climatic condition. On Malwa plateau stone houses are commonly found.

In Rajasthan, the Punjab, Haryana and Uttar Pradesh houses having flat roof are very common due to dry climatic conditions. In such houses protection is the prime motto in order to save the property from thieves. On the interfluve areas of the Ganga and the Yamuna rivers houses of the landlords are generally made of cement and concrete, whereas houses of poor peasants are made of mud wall and tile roof.

In Orissa thatch and tile roof houses are more prominent. Here double storey mud wall houses are also found. Bhuiya people live along the roads in double-row houses. In the coastal plains of Andhra Pradesh the poor man's house is generally circular in shape but its variant is rectangular or square shape in the west. In Madhya Pradesh, Gond people are making parallel linear houses on both sides of the road. In most cases Kitchen garden is found in backside of the house.

In West Bengal for the construction of houses, the soil is dug out of the tank lying very close to the house. It is essential in order to make the plinth of the house a bit higher from the level of flood plain. Due to higher amount of rainfall the roof is generally made gable except cement and concrete houses.

In West Bengal, "the homestead never consists of a single hut-even the poorest families always have a separate kitchen... A prosperous family build larger huts and more of them",[36] up to a dozen grouped near the tank for bathing and domestic water supply. Generally sleeping, living, cooking, and reception houses are under separate roofs, although any of them may be used as a store or sleeping place, and mostly the peasants family lead their life in open space or verandah. In the house storage bins for grains, cots, fishing nets and gear are prominently found.

In the Chakrata area, on southern slope of Himalaya, the houses are found on different terraced contour interval in cluster and linear in shape. The material of wall is either stone or wood, and the roof is either concrete, tile or grasses available locally. Most of the houses are made of double storey, whose lower portion is meant for live-stock, the middle portion for kitchen and sleeping, and the third top one for the store of food grains and fuel wood. In the valley of Kangra the houses are found very far apart. The wall may be of wood or stone but the roof is generally made of flat slate. The same type of house is found in the valley of Kashmir but due to lack of space houses are also found on boats in the lakes of Dall, Ulur and others.

Thus in India, "the geography of the house often reflects age-old religious and magical traditions: the round huts of some lower castes in Telangana, with bold vertical strips of white and rusty red are clearly culturally rather than geographically influenced. At the other extreme from the rude massive huts of Bundelkhand,...the elaborate courtyard house of the richer Uttar Pradesh farmer, and the carved timber of Kumaon"(Fig 15.8).[37]

The Conditions of Housing in India

In India the housing conditions of the poor and the less privileged, continue to cause grave concern. The task of providing a roof over every head is therefore formidable and would require sustained effort over a long period. In rural area, the problem is of access to even the most rudimentary level of huts.

Housing shortage in India has been estimated to be about 20.7 million - 16.1 in rural and 4.6 million in urban areas. This is only a rough estimate and does not take into account semi-permanent and temporary structures which serve the needs of a large section of our population. However, the figures do give us a broad idea of the extent of housing shortage in our country. The shortage is more marked amongst the economically weaker sections of the society and the low income groups, but the gap is quite substantial in case of the middle income group. The *Economically Weaker Sections (EWS)* are those who have a total family income of upto Rs. 330 per month; LIG are those with a family income of upto Rs. 600/- per month. The corresponding amount for the MIG is upto Rs. 1500/- per month and for HIG above Rs. 1500/- per month. In the formulation and implementation of housing development schemes in the public sector, the target groups are mainly the EWS and LIG and to some extent the MIG which are the weakest sections of the society. (LIG-low income group, MIG-middle income group, and HIG-high income group).

Housing in Sixth Plan:

The Sixth Plan has identified, that the public sector has a *'marginal though promotion'* role to play in respect of housing and has mentioned that the emphasis of the public sector will be on the 'absolutely shelterless'. In rural housing the primary target group is the landless families and the plan objective is to provide developed house sites to cover each one of the rural landless families. The total number of eligible families has been estimated to be 14.5 million by 1985. The scheme of provision of house sites to the rural landless which was in operation since 1970 had provided house sites to 7.7 million families before the commencement of the sixth plan. The Plan target is to provide house sites to the remaining 6.8 million. The programme component is such that it adopts a low cost solution using locally available building materials as far as possible and the beneficiaries are expected to play a positive role by providing their own labour as a major input. The total provision in the State Plans for house sites and construction assistance is about Rs. 3540 millions. (1985-86).

In case of slums the stress is on providing a package of essential services like potable water supply, paved pathways for access, street lighting facilities and sanitary latrines in place of manually cleaned privies. The components of the programme will show that the major thrust of the scheme is to concentrate on general improvement of the environment and public health and hygiene. The approach is in preference to the less cost effective programme of slum relocation and rehousing of slum dwellers. There is no doubt that the quality of housing in slum is very poor but they do serve the basic need of shelter and in the context of overall shortage more practical and pragmatic approach is to make the existing houses in the slum areas more liveable by eliminating squalor, filth, improving the environment and providing the basic sanitary facilities and water supply, rather than going for a large scale rehabilitation programme.

Further on international scale the attention given to the subject of providing appropriate shelter has been inadequate. Two significant events marked the growing interest of the international community to the deficiencies of shelter and infrastructure services. One was the Vancouver Habitat Conference of 1976 and the other was the Mar-Del Plata Water Conference of 1977. The Vancouver Resolution for the first time identified the problem of housing on international level. Human settlements as a separate subject area as distinct from other activities and for the first time recognized the need for considering human settlement development programmes not merely in welfare terms but as positive instruments for national development. The Mar-Del Plata resolution decided to launch an international water supply decade from 1981 to 1990 where the global programme of safe drinking water to cover the entire world population was drawn up. Both these are momentous decisions and call for comprehensive action programmes.

So far as human settlement is concerned the historic Vancouver declaration was also followed by the important 'Manila Communique' of 1981 which expresses grave concern about the deteriorating conditions of the shelter for the poor and urged the countries to draw up positive action programmes for meeting the challenge. An important development in respect of human settlement improvement programme is the resolution passed in the 36th Session of the U.N. General Assembly proclaiming 1987 as *"the International Year of Shelter for the Homeless"*. The recently concluded 5th session of the U.N. Commission on Human Settlement in Nairobi has decided to proclaim 1987 as "the International Year of Shelter for the Homeless". Indeed it has an ambitious goal. It is to provide shelter and neighbourhood to all the poor by the year 2000.

Happily India is one of the very few countries which in its internal planning has been acting on these principles for some years. India's National Plan Strategy is based on the principle of direct attack on poverty. It has a well articulated national action programme to improve the physical quality of life of the people. The multi-point Minimum Needs Programme most of which is incorporated in the new 20 Economic Point Programme includes rural house sites, rural health, rural education, rural electrification, rural roads, rural water supply and slum improvement in urban areas which show the awareness and commitment of our country to the programmes involving the improvement of living conditions. Our objective is to provide by the end of the Sixth Plan period, house sites to all the rural landless and at least one source of potable water supply to each of the 2.31 lakh problem villages and cover 10 million slum dwellers through the slum improvement programmes.

Considering the magnitude and complexities of the problem in a country of the size of India it will be idle to presume that the task is a simple one. While one can say confidently that the progress of the different schemes is quite encouraging and there can be no room for complacency and long and sustained efforts will be necessary to reach our goal. The International Declaration will only help us to rededicate ourselves to our task.[38]

RURAL HOUSING IN EUROPE

There is a substantial difference from one region to another as regards dispersal of dwellings in Europe, i.e., whether on isolated farms or grouped together in hamlets or villages. As for example in France 40 per cent of the houses are grouped in villages, 45 per cent in hamlets and 15 per cent isolated dwellings. There are quite a large number of hamlets in the northern Alps and villages in the southern Alps.[39] However, the study of housing must also be considered according to altitude; the higher one goes, the more isolated are the farms and hamlets, while in the valleys one finds villages. In the narrow valley at the place of safety requirements where roads in the mountain passes make it essential for the houses to be grouped together. These factors are less important as one goes higher into the mountains. The problem of water supply is not sufficient explanation for the grouping of houses, except in certain areas with calcareous rock. In Italy 54 per cent houses are hamlets, while 10.5

per cent are isolated dwellings. In Switzerland 25.5 per cent of the communes are villages and 74.5 per cent are hamlets and isolated houses. The situation is more or less the same in Austria.

COOPERATIVE HOUSING PROJECT IN LA TRINIDAD

In 1979 the Cooperative Housing Association of Aachen, Federal Republic of Germany spent $20,000 in a housing project La Trinidad, which has now completed. The 44 families which took part in the project have been selected on the basis of their income (not more than $125 per month), the number of their children and willingness to take part in the project.

In this project each and every family was obliged to work from 1400 to 1700 hours and on Sundays from 800 to 1100 hours. Architects and engineers cooperated in their spare time. The major difficulties were: organization of the working group, participation of individual family in the project and finding solution to individual problems. The social worker looks after "assistance in self-help concerning health, education, food and community organization". The national organization SENA provides guidelines for wood and metal working, and women's club was established to do needle work on clothes.

The building materials were arranged locally, and the back walls and the partition walls of each house were made of burnt brick by the group. For the covering of roof, tiles were also made by people of the project group.

"The total cost of a house, including land comes to about $1750, an amount paid by the families in full in instalments of 20 per cent of their monthly income. This is less than they had been paying for the shacks they have been living in before. The money-which flows back into a revolving fund - is being used either to finance a new housing project or to construct small workshops in order to create jobs. Both because of the low costs achieved by a high degree of self help and the method of full participation by the group members, La Trinidad is considered by its initiators to be a model for other similar projects".[40]

REFERENCES

1. V.N.P. Sinha: "Houses and House Types of the Chotanagpur Plateau", *Geographical Knowledge,* Vol. 2, 1969, p. 91.
2. S.N. Dickens and F.R. Pitts: *Introduction to Human Geography,* New York, 1963, p. 199.
3. G. Cunningham: *Archaeological Report,* London, 1861-62, p. 47.
4. Indian Nation, 15th June 1969, p. 3.
5. Gopal Krishan; "Impact of Population Growth on Rural Housing", *Geographical Review of India,* Vol. XL; No. 2, 1978, pp. 138-143.
6. S.B. Singh; 'Rural Dwellings in the District of Sultanpur', *Indian Journal of Geography;* Vol. XI-XII; No. 1, 1976-77, pp. 11-18.
7. S.N. Mishra; "Human Dwellings in Sonpar Region (U.P.): A Geographical Analysis"; *The National Geographical Journal of India;* Vol. XVI; ;NO. 1, 1969, pp. 8-23.
8. V.N.P. Sinha; "Houses and House Types of Chotanagpur Plateau', *Geographical Knowledge;* Vol. 2; No. 2, 1969.
9. K.S. Gopalakrishnan and D.C. Barai 'Rural Dwellings in the Cauvery Delta', *The National Geographical Journal of India;* Vol. XVII; No. 4; 1971, pp. 197-206.
10. S. Mukerjee; 'The Influence of the Architecture of Rural Houses in Maharashtra', *Indian Geographical Journal,* Vol. XLVI; Nos. 1 & 2; 1971, pp. 42-48.
11. V.C. Gupta and Behari Lal, 'Typical Rural Dwellings in the Bundelkhand region', *Geographical Review of India,* Vol. XXXVII; No. 2, 1975, pp. 189-195.
12. J.N. Pandey; 'Rural House Types in the Middle Ganga Plain; A Case Study of Paras Rampur', *The National Geographical Journal of India;* Vol. XXI; No. 1; 1975, pp. 47-52.
13. J.P. Sharma & K. Singh; 'Rural House Types in the Cis Siwalik Zone', *Deccan Geographer;* Vol. XII; No. 2, 1974, pp. 85-95.
14. J.P. Sharma; "Rural Dwelling and House Types in the Himalayan Ravi Chenab Interfluve', *Geographical Review of India:* Voi. XXXVII; No. 1; 1975, pp. 30-41.
15. S.M. Shahidi Hasan; 'Regional Variations in the House Types in Kumaon', *The Geographer,* Vol. XXII; No. 1975, pp. 56-61.
16. Surendranath Singh; 'Morphology of Rural Houses in the Commuters Zone of Varanasi', *Uttar Bharat Bhoogol Patrika;* Vol. IX; No. 2, 1973, pp. 47-59.
17. L.R. Singh: The Terai Region of U.P.: A Study in Human Geography, Allahabad, 1965, p. 37.
18. Victor Olgyay: *Design with Climate* Princeton Press, 1963, p.3.
19. R.L. Singh: "Typical Rural Dwellings in the Umland of Banaras". *The National Geographical Journal of India,* Vol. III, 1957, p. 52.
20. K.M. Subrahamanyam: "Four Main House Types in South India", *Journal of Madras Geographical Association,* Vol. XIII, 1938, p. 168.
21. M.L. Fuller and F.G. Clapp: "Rural Dwellings of Shensi, China", *Geographical Review,* Vol. 14, 1924, p. 215.
22. W.A. Noble: "Approaches Towards an Understanding of Traditional South-Asian Peasant Dwelling", *Professional Geographer,* Vol. 21, 1969.
23. R.C. Sharma: "Western Rajasthan: A Study of House Types", *National Geographer,* Vol. III, 1964, p. 48.
24. G.A. Grierson: "The Native House", in *Bihar Peasant Life,* Patna, 1926, pp. 333-344.

25. *Ibid.*
26. S.L. Duggal and K. Gaur: "Rural House Types", in *Human Geography,* Meerut, 1958, p. 259.
27. V.N.P. Sinha: *op. cit;* p. 93.
28. L.R. Singh: *op. cit.,* p. 40
29. S.N. Mishra: "Human Dwellings in Sonpar Region (U.P.)", *The National Geographical Journal of India,* Vol. XV, 1969, p. 2.
30. Paul Vidal de la Blache: *Principle of Human Geography,* New York, 1962, p. 238.
31. J. Brunhes: *Human Geography,* New York, p. 76.
32. E. Ahmad: "Rural House Types", *Bihar, Physical, Economic and Regional Geography,* Ranchi University, 1965, p. 278.
33. K.H. Buschman: "Settlements and Habitations in India", *Geographical Review of India,* Vol. XVI, 1954, p. 19.
34. S.D. Prasad: *Report on Housing and Establishments in Gazetteer of India,* Bihar; Vol. VI, Part IV A, 1961, p. 498.
35. Ashok Mitra: 'House Types in India", *Illustrated Weekly of India,* November, 1968, p. 26.
36. J.C. Jack: *The Economic Life of a Bengal District;* Oxford, 1961, p. 21.
37. E. Ahmad: *Settlement in the United Provinces;* Unpublished Ph. D. Thesis, London University, 1948, in O.H.K. Spate, India and Pakistan, 1964, p. 177.
38. M.K. Mukherji; "A Roof Over Every Head", *Akashvani,* August 15, 1982, pp. 5-7.
39. M.O. Cepede & E.S. Abensour: "Rural Problems in the Alpine Region", *FAO of the UNO,* Rome, 1961, p. 146.
40. *NGO News on Human Settlements,* No. 3, 1982, p. 2.

Fig. 15.1

Bihar Plain : House Type

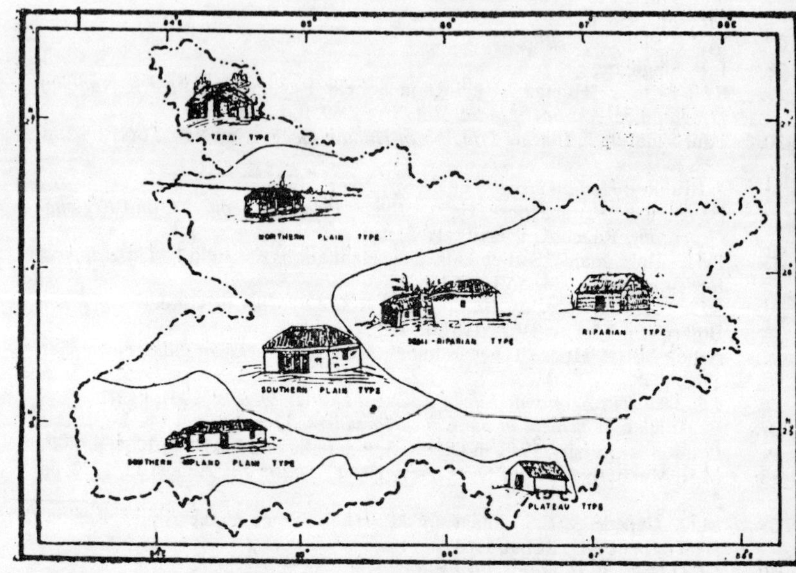

Fig. 15.2

Bihar Plain : Material of Wall (Rural Areas)

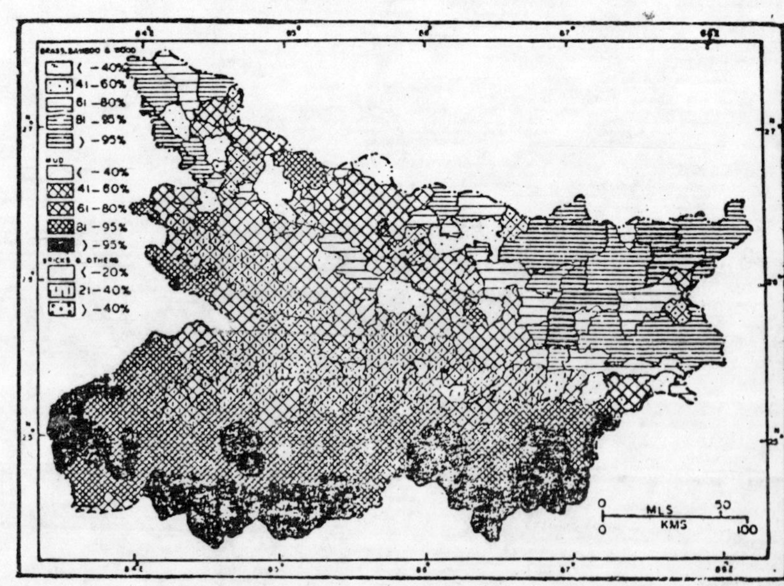

Fig. 15.3
Bihar Plain : Material of Roof (Rural Areas)

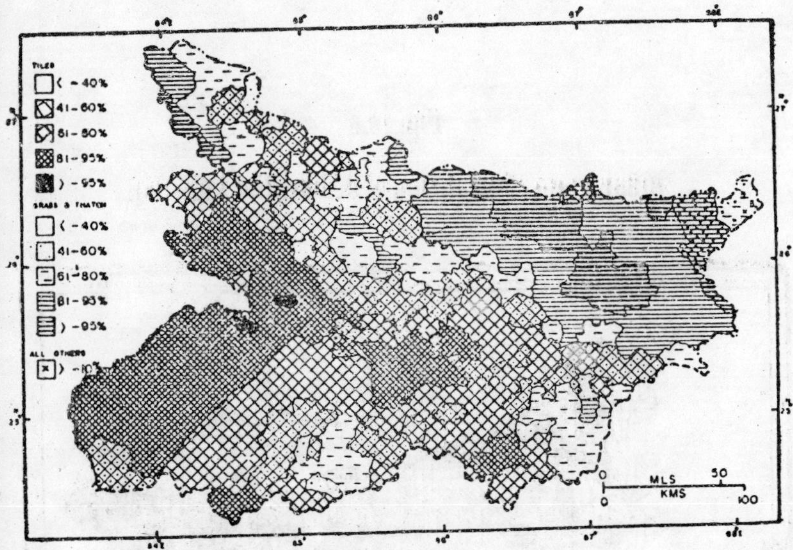

Fig. 15.4
Bihar Plain : Density of Rural Houses

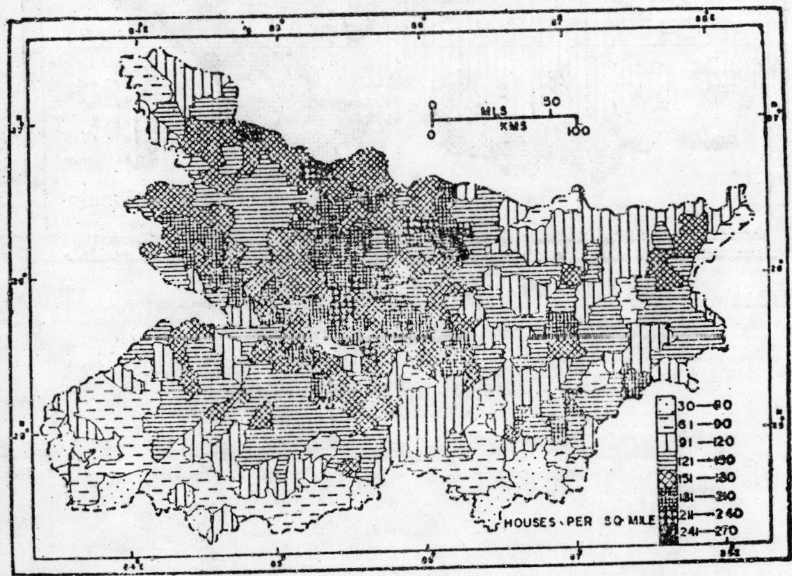

Fig. 15.5

Bihar Plain : Rural House Residential Function

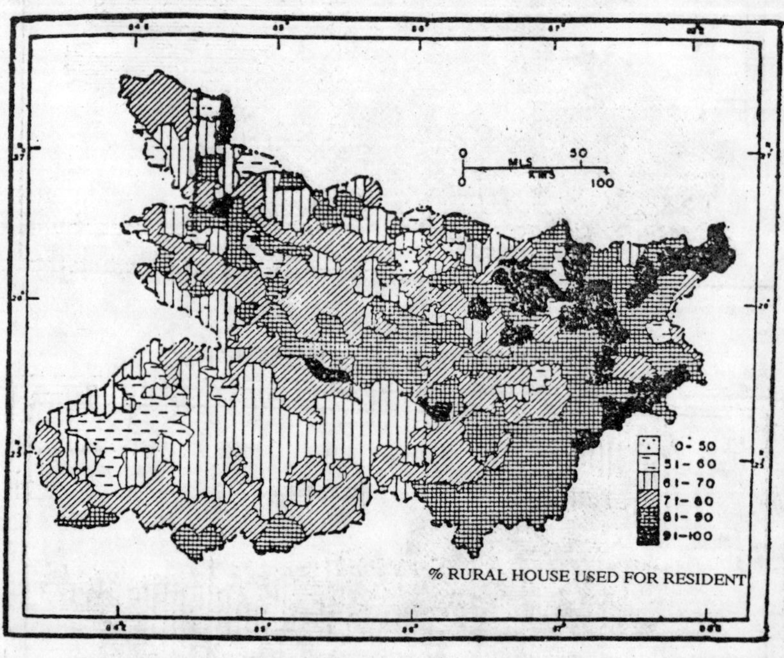

Fig. 15.6

Bihar Plain : Intensity of Residential Houses (Per Village)

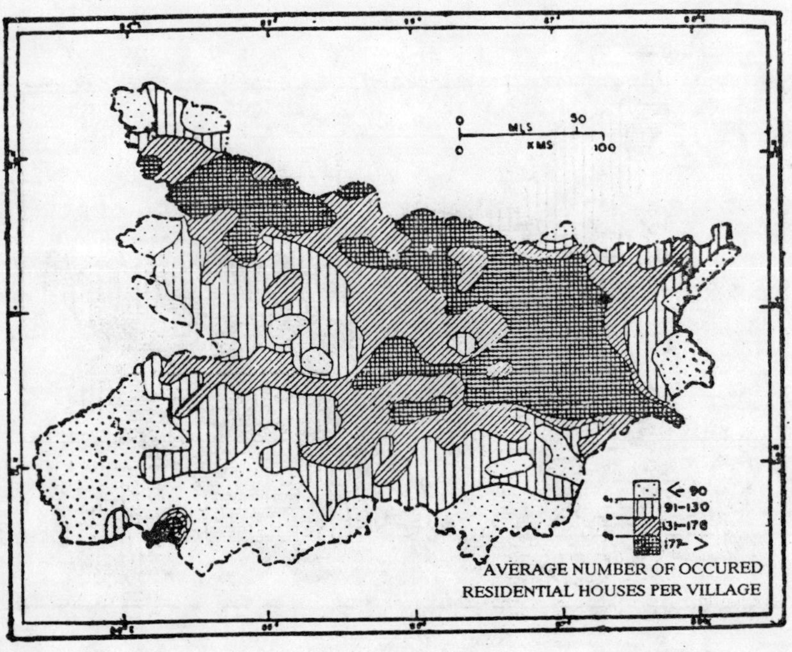

Fig. 15.7

Bihar Plain : Occupancy Rate per Room

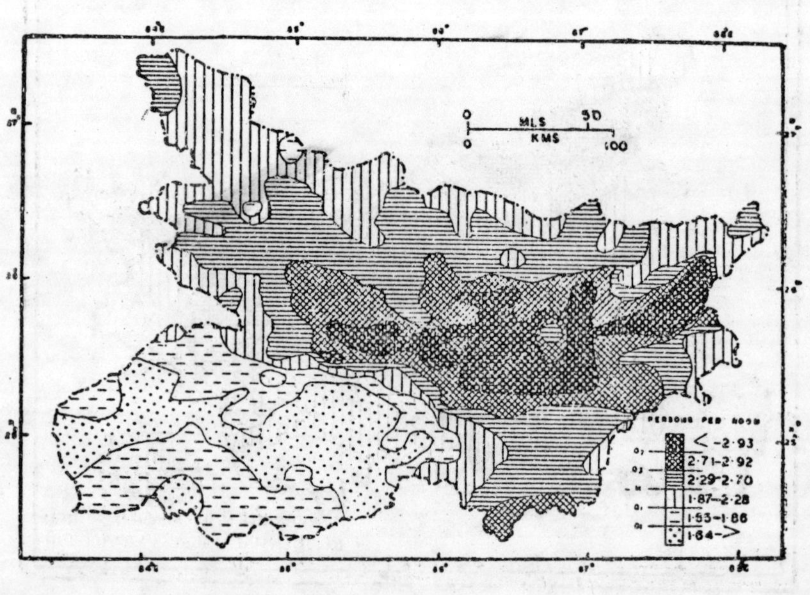

Fig. 15.8
Some N Indian House Types. Redrawn Fowler from Illustrations in these by E. Ahmad and B. Mukerjee (see Bibliographical Note)

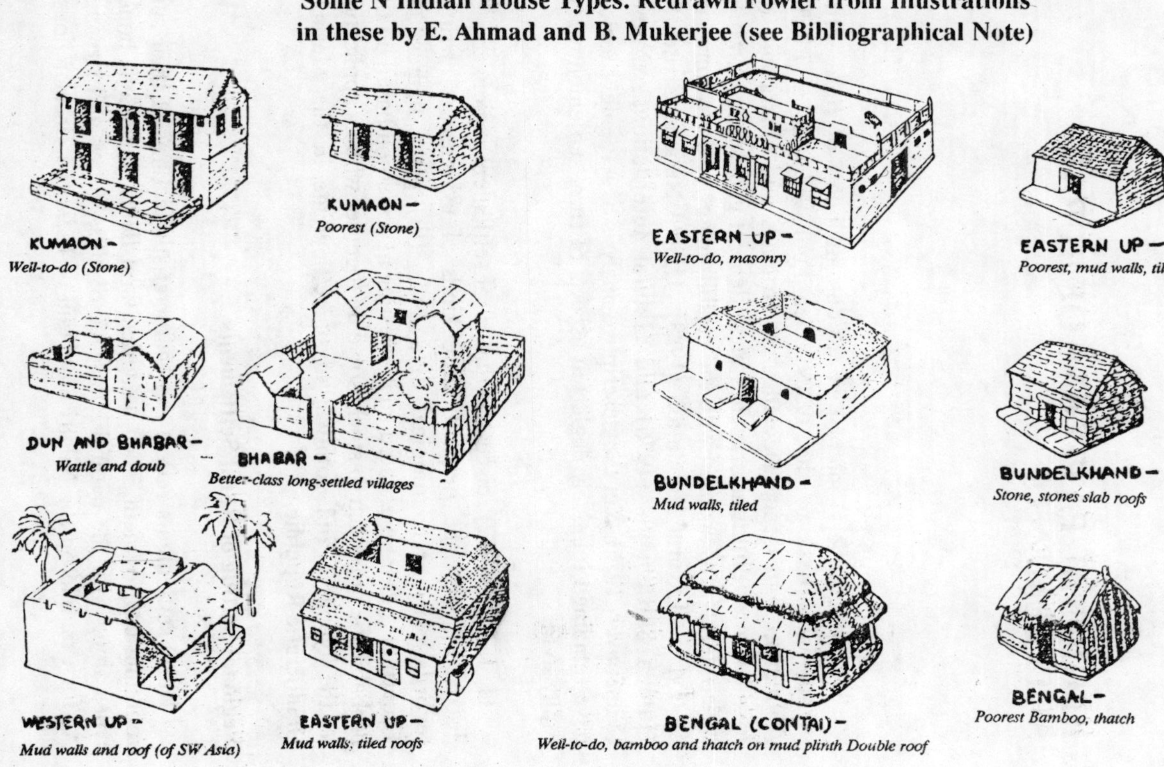

SIXTEEN

REGIONAL PATTERNS OF RURAL SETTLEMENTS

The geographers' interest in various attributes of rural settlements dates back to the 1920s when Paul Vidal de la Blache, Ahlmann, Aurosseau, Demangeon, Brunhes and others laid the foundation of different branches of settlement geography. A worldwide interest was aroused with the establishment of the commission on Types of Rural Habitation (1928), United Nations Centre for Human Settlements (1976) and Habitat International Council (Vancouver, 1976). Yet the descriptive analysis of settlement regions have remained relatively neglected aspects of rural settlement geography so far.

H. J. Nitz (1972)[1] discussed that rural settlement regions can be discovered with the help of three kinds of evidence (i) written records; (ii) archaeological data and, (iii) place names. R. Thuermer[2] (1983) presented an interesting new method based on the probabilistic approach to stochastic data together with its application to the typology and zonification of settlements in the German Democratic Republic.

Regional Setting of Rural Settlements

Rural settlements reflect the characteristic features of their surrounding environment, such as agricultural fields, highways, house types along with the natural landscape of hills, valleys and streams. As for example on the Nilgiri mountain of India the circular house types of Toda people on the hills in forest environment has different characteristics in comparison with the gabled roof, rectangular house of rainfed plain of West Bengal. Hence according to regional characteristics settlements may be typically recognized, as 'Indian', 'Chinese', 'Persian' and 'Swiss' which represent mostly their environment and cultural activities of inhabitants.

Rural Settlements of Yangtze Delta : China

It is a plain land made of various streams. The density of population is more than 1,000 persons per square kilometre who live in small villages distributed evenly throughout the countryside. Travel by boat is convenient and hence houses lie alongside streams and rural settlements have developed near the confluence point of streams. Locally available bamboo, wattle and grasses are the main building materials used in the construction of house.

Light wooden bridges across the streams connect the neighbouring villages and farmlands[3]. Most of the agricultural products collected by the neighbouring small town which serves the villages in the respective hinterland besides distributing city oriented manufactured goods to them.

Rural Settlements in the Loess Lands of Northern China

In the arid north-western Kansu Province of China, the stone and mud-walled shelter is quite different from Yangtze delta. In winter this region is completely under cold winds, and remains very hot during the summer. Here the nucleated settlements are always protected with the surrounding walls against both flood water and robbery which are harassing the villager near the northern frontier zones. In terraced fields on the mountain slopes the crops which mainly grow are wheat, beans and millet.

Turkish Rural Settlements

For the rural settlements of Southern Turkey in the Plateau of Anatolia, Brice[4] used the name "Anatolian village". Here rural settlements are located in the Jullab valley in between the Kurdish Hills and the uplands of northern Syria. The villages are found to be clustered near drinking water well or near remains of the mounds of older settlements. In each there should be 500 inhabitants. The materials of wall is burnt brick and the material of flat roof is mud resting on wooden beams.

In areas of the lack of timber, the roofs are made with corbelled cupolas. Every household has its well protected compound wall, within which the sheep, goat and livestocks are kept during the night. Each village contains two wells-one for drinking water and the other for washing and for the use of farm animals. In the surrounding area of the village are located "the small family worked plots including a few cotton fields, irrigated by the river Jullab, and the grazing ground"[5].

Rural Settlements in Zambia

In Barotse Province of Zambia ecological factors are more dominant in deciding the regional patterns of rural settlements. In Zambia flood plains and the Luena flats villages are sited on commanding landscape, but most of them have to be vacated during flood. Nowadays, the dry edge of the plain is the centre of the life of Lozi people. The productive agricultural lands are found in seepage zones at the foot of the sandy scarps, where water is readily available. Besides this, rural settlements at the edge of the plain have ready access to the resources of both the plain and the plateau. The plain is the main source of grazing and fish, besides housing materials of bamboos, reeds, grasses and clay. On the other hand, the upland plateau is only useful during flood times for grazing and the land is so poor that only cassava can be grown. The houses are generally circular and rectangular type, especially *dambos* houses of Luena flats away from the Zambezi Valley.[6]

Rural Settlements in Liberia

In Liberia[7], West Africa the regional pattern of rural settlements is largely governed by the intensity of agricultural land use. In many areas shifting cultivation still prevails, and the size of the village varies according to the availability of cultivable land. The rural settlement consists of an irregular arrangement of household compound, shifting cultivation, woodland and palm forest and the highways connecting one village with the other. The kitchen garden is meant for growing vegetable and fruits and the agricultural lands are cultivated on a rotational basis for producing food and cash crops. Nucleated settlement is the main feature but elongation starts with the construction of road. The land adjoining the road is considered as very valuable.

Rural Settlements on Malabar Coast, India

'Mayur' on the Malabar coast of Peninsular India is a narrow coastal settlement, bordered by brackish lagoons and the sea. It is a typical example of Indian rural settlements, having an area of 12032 square kilometre and a population of about 4,000 in 1981. Here coconut sticks and leaves are used as building materials of houses which are square to rectangular in shape. Due to high population density it is difficult to maintain even the current low standard of housing. "Most of the land not used for housing is devoted to coconut palms for which sandy soil and climate are well suited"[8]. Most of the inhabitants are landless, and great prestige is attached to land-owning, and quarrels over a small piece of land is very bitter. Fishing is another main occupation of inhabitants.

Here in the Bihar Plain, India an empirical approach to regionalisation on the basis of various attributes of settlements has been suggested. The regional analysis of rural settlement pattern goes to show the condition of settlements in different areas depending upon settlement types, their density, distribution, architectural styles and material of construction as the chief elements of rural settlements. These are the result of environmental conditions, agricultural prosperity of the land, history of land occupancy and cultural background.

Most of the above phenomena, however, are inter-related and affect the distribution pattern of settlements. A synoptic model (Table 16.1) has been suggested in which a score of 1 to 4 matrix of coefficient of correlation (Table 16.2) has been prepared to show the relationship between elements of settlements in the region and also to help in finding out the problem of settlement areas.

TABLE 16.1 : **Sunoptic Model for Weighing the Variables of Rural Settlements**

Weighting value	Types of settlements of settlement	Density	Density of houses	Village patterns	Materials of wall	Materials of roof Popula	Density of Rural tion
	X1	X2	X3	X4	X5	X6	X7
1	Sprinkled	Very low	Very low	Amorphous	95 to 60% Mud & Grass	95 to 60% Grass	Very low
2	Semi-Sprin -kled	Low	Low	Linear	60 to 40% Mud & Grass	60 to 40% Grass	Low
3	Semi-Compact	Medium	Medium	Rectangular	Mixed	60 to 40% tile	Medium
4	Compact	High	High	Square Circular Star	Brick and others	95 to 60% tile	High

Source : Compiled from Survey of India one inch toposheets, Census of India, Population Table, District Census Hand Book, Housing and Establishment Table and Reports of Bihar, 1961 and 1971.

On the basis of weighting of different elements of settlement (Table 16.1) a matrix of coefficient of correlation has been prepared. From the Table 16.2 below it is quite apparent that all the seven elements of settlements show a good relationship amongst each other but the highest relationship (0.96) is with the density of houses and population density in rural areas. The lowest but still significant relationship exists (0.79) between the village pattern, material of wall and the density of settlements.

TABLE 16.2 COEFFICIENT OF CORRELATION MATRIX

	X1	X2	X3	X4	X5	X6	X7
X1	1.000	-	-	-	-	-	-
X2	0.826	1.000	-	-	-	-	-
X3	0.954	0.922	1.000	-	-	-	-
X4	0.894	0.885	0.863	1.000	-	-	-
X5	0.844	0.796	0.871	0.795	1.000	-	-
X6	0.850	0.881	0.851	0.847	0.815	1.000	-
X7	0.916	0.893	0.961	0.890	0.846	0.842	1.000

Thus, map of settlement types, density of villages, building materials and density of houses and rural population show a marked similarity in their spatial distribution patterns and exhibit close association with each other. Figs. 16.1 and 16.2 have been drawn by applying sieve technique[9] to the above distribution maps relating to settlements.

The sub-regions distinguished on various maps[10] of house types, building materials, etc., are formal so far as the element considered is concerned. Their borders, however, are not precise as they are based primarily on isopleths, which are lines of generalisation and not of differentiation. The correspondence of isopleths lines is nevertheless an inherent principle behind the sieve method and if the heterogeneity is well marked, the method is quite successful. Applying this technique to the sub-regional maps it is possible to distinguish geographical areas of more or less homogeneous characteristics as discussed below.

According to this, the Bihar Plain can be divided into four broad settlement regions which can be further subdivided on the basis of minor elements (Fig. 16.1):

(i) Compact Settlements
(a) High Density (b) Medium Density,
(ii) Semi-Compact Settlements
(a) Medium Density (b) Low Density,
(iii) Semi-Sprinkled Settlements
(a) Medium Density (b) Low Density,
(iv) Sprinkled Settlements
(a) Low Density (b) Very Low Density.

Compact settlements are found in the districts of Saran and Muzaffarpur and parts of Bhojpur, Patna and Darbhanga. Thus compact settlements are characteristics of the riparian tracts of the river Ganga, the Baghmati-Kamla Plain and the flood free zone of Saran district. Here the population density is extremely high and the villages are large in size. As the *tolas* or hamlets are also large, there is a lack of distinction between the two, and the region appears to be uniformly settled. Their size may vary from a larger hamlet comprising 30 to 40 dwellings to a large cluster consisting of three to four hundred houses. They are found on the high banks of the rivers where uniformity of relief and soil fertility have enabled a large number of cultivators to live together in compact habitation. Thus the areas of higher density are free from floods and have good agricultural potentiality due to better irrigation facilities and fertile soil. The Settlements date back to prehistoric times and have had a steady growth and evolution.

The compact settlement zone can be divided into two parts (a) high density and (b) medium density. The high density zone is in the west, falling in the basin of the river Gandak and includes almost the entire district of Saran. Here the density of villages is more than two per sq. km. Medium density area adjoins it on the east and south in the districts of Muzaffarpur, Darbhanga, Patna and Bhojpur. In these areas, the density of population continues to be high but owing to frequent floods in the Baghmati and the Gandak belts the settlement density falls to around 1.55 per sq. km.

Semi-compact settlements cover the eastern half of Champaran district, Eastern Darbhanga and the whole of Saharsa district, and the entire Ganga belt south of the river from Bhojpur to Bhagalpur. The northern plains are belts of excessive floods which harass the people of the region every year. Settlements, therefore, have to be built slightly away from the river banks and are, therefore, necessarily semi-compact in nature. The size of the parent cluster decreases, while the number of hamlets increases in these areas. In South Bihar Plain also it covers the *Tal* area and riverine plains of Patna and Bhojpur districts where the floods are frequent.

The semi-compact settlement zone can be divided into two groups (a) medium density and (b) low density. Settlements with medium density are found in two areas, the valley of the Gandak in Champaran and Saran districts and the valley of the river Ganga in north Bhojpur, Patna and Munger districts. In these areas the fertility of soil is high and consequently the population density is also high leading to settlement density of around 1.24 villages per sq. km. In eastern Darbhanga, Saharsa and North Bhagalpur districts, however, the density of semi-compact settlements is low. This area falls in the flood zone of the river Kosi and the lower Ganga. The land is sandy and relatively less fertile, while uplands, are rare. Settlements are, therefore, clustered on these uplands but are found at large distances. The average density is less than 1.9 settlements per sq. km.

Semi-sprinkled settlements are found in the whole of southern upland plains, western half of Purnea and central Champaran districts. In the southern upland plains, the decreasing fertility of soil towards the south and comparatively low rainfall and quick run-off makes the upper layer of the soil leached, which prohibits a high density of population. In Purnea district large tracts of land are not in a position to support a dense population due to the damp climate and waterlogging. Each hamlet has to be built on higher land. There is poor development of agriculture and the small patches of cultivated land are hardly able to support upto ten families in a single hamlet. In central Champaran district the coarse, sandy and less fertile soil can support only a few settlements lying at great distances and, therefore, the compactness of the settlements is reduced.

Broadly speaking, the density of semi-sprinkled settlements range from 1.55 (medium density) to 1.0 (low density) per sq. km. The southern upland plains from Bhojpur to Bhagalpur district and central Champaran in the north-west are areas of medium density.

Northern Saharsa and western Purnea districts, on the other hand, are areas of low density even amongst the semi-sprinkled settlements because of extreme poverty of agriculture and frequent floods.

Sprinkled settlements by their very nature have developed in the regions having rugged terrain covered with forests. The low fertility of soil and fear of wild animals make the people confined to only a few hamlets scattered in such areas. Thus dispersed settlements are typical of the Himalayan foothills in north-west Champaran, the flood plains of the Panar-Mahananda basin in Purnea, and the entire Chotanagpur Scarp Belt and adjoining southern upland plains in the South Bihar. In districts of Saharsa and Purnea, dispersal is partly caused by high rainfall, damping effects of the climate and regular inundation by the rivers. The dissected and broken hill country of north-western Champaran and Chotanagpur Scarp Belt Present a similar feature of dispersal but here the causes are different. Irregular relief and occurrence of forests have helped scattering and the settlements are seen only in the midst of relatively infrequent cultivable patches in the valleys.

As is to be expected, the zones of sprinkled settlements are areas of low to very low density. In almost the entire sprinkled settlement zone, the density of settlements is less than 1.0 per sq. km. in the Rohtas Plateau which is a high and rugged table land with a dense forest cover. Here the density falls to less than 0.31 per sq. km and the area appears to be almost devoid of human occupance.

SUB-REGIONS ACCORDING TO HOUSE TYPES AND BUILDING MATERIALS

House types according to building materials and density of houses per square kilometre present a very clear picture of zonal variation in rural settlements of the Bihar Plain. Since there is a marked difference in building materials it has been found possible to identify three housing regions (Fig. 16.2) with subdivisions as given below:

1. Grass Built Houses
   (i) High density,
   (ii) Medium density,
   (iii) Low density,

2. Mud and Tile Houses
   (i)High density,
   (ii) Medium density,
3. Mixed Building Materials
   (i)High density, predominantly grass roofs,
   (ii)High density, predominantly tile roofs,
   (iii)Medium density, predominantly mud walls,
   (iv) Low density, predominantly mud walls,

Grass Built Houses

Grass built houses are predominant in the western half of Champaran district, and the whole of Purnea, Saharsa and north-eastern Darbhanga districts. In these regions the predominant building material are grass, bamboo, wood, reeds, willows, etc. used both for walls and for roofs. These materials are cheaply available in the locality. Owing to annual inundation and heavy rainfall, waterlogging is a normal occurrence which prohibits the construction of mud-built houses because they would not be durable. The density is normally medium, except in the central Kosi belt. Here the density of houses increases on either side of the river Kosi, because as we go away from the river banks, the relatively higher ground permits a higher settlement density.

Mud and Tile Houses

Mud and tile houses are found in the Gangetic belt and the southern upland plains from Bhojpur to Munger as well as in western Saran. Here the predominating material of wall is mud, because of its property to keep the houses cool. Mud built walls in these areas are durable because rainfall is low and waterlogging is rare. Another reason is the high cost of bamboos for construction purposes. In these areas the walls are very thick, because the locally available soils have less adhesive power, and hence thin walls would not be strong. However, these soils can be turned into good tile, and thus tile is commonly used as a roofing material. The tile is laid on a bamboo thatch structure, which has to be frequently repaired to avoid leaking. The density of houses is generally medium in the South Bihar Plains, except in Begusarai district.

Mixed Building Materials

Houses with mixed building materials are found in two broad zones. In the north, there is a zone consisting of the whole of Muzaffarpur district and the greater part of Saran, Champaran and Patna districts. Here the density of houses is high in the entire area. On the basis of construction material, however, it can be divided into two parts. In the northern part, the walls are built with mud and the roofs usually with the grass or the thatch. In the southern part, however, mud or brick built houses with tile roofs are the rule. This part is the most prosperous area in the Bihar Plain and consists of the districts of Saran and Patna and their adjoining areas. It is also the only area where bricks attain some importance as a building material.

The second zone of mixed houses is to be found in the south covering areas of southern upland plain and Chotanagpur Scarp Belt. This zone has predominantly mud built walls but with a medium to low density of houses. The roofing material is partly tiles and partly grass and thatch. Except in a small patch in central Munger and Bhagalpur districts, where the density of houses is medium, the entire zone has a low density of houses.

SUB-REGIONS OF RURAL SETTLEMENTS

On the basis of the preceding discussion we may identify a number of rural settlement regions in the Bihar Plain. These regions are marked by distinct characteristics of housing and settlement type and serve to determine the overall settlement pattern in the entire study area.

The Zone of North-Western Champaran

This is the area of the Himalayan Foothills, where the Dun Valley and the imposing Siwalik ranges clad with forests and wildlife restrict human habitation. The settlements are of dispersed type and the density is around 0.62 village per square kilometre. The houses are almost invariably built with glass-leaves and bomboo splits.

The Eastern Zone of Saharsa and Purnea

This region is marked by dispersed and semi-sprinkled type of settlements, lying in a linear fashion along the banks of the old river beds and on higher ground. The swamps and marshy lands restrict human habitations. Rivers, lakes and smaller tributary channels abound in the area and prohibit large clustered village. As the region is a low-land, the occurrence of floods, is common. As a result, the density of rural settlements is less than 1.0 village per sq. km. The overwhelming majority of houses are built with grass-leaves and bamboo splits.

Southern Zone of Chotanagpur Scarp Belt and Upland Plains

This zone extends from southern Bhagalpur in the east to Rohtas in the west. The hills of Kharagpur in Munger, Rajgir in Patna, Barabar ranges in Gaya and Kaimur Plateau in Rohtas districts are areas of rugged topography and forest cover. The soils of the Chotanagpur Scarp Belt are poor in fertility. The population density is, therefore, low. Settlement density is only 0.31 village per sq. km. in Kaimur Plateau and about 1.0 village per sq. km in rest of the area. In this zone the predominant material of wall is mud and the material of roof is tile or grass or thatch. Settlements are sprinkled and semi-sprinkled in nature, lying in an amorphous and rectangular pattern over the Chota Nagpur Scarp Belt and Southern Upland Plains respectively.

The Riverine Belt of North Bihar

This is a fertile area covering the greater proportion of Purnea, Champaran, Muzaffarpur and Darbhanga districts. It is drained by the Gandak, the Burhi Gandak and the Baghmati rivers. The region has a high density of population rising even upto 1800 persons per sq. km in rural area. The rainfall is medium to high but floods are not as devastating as in the eastern zone. The settlements are compact to semi-compact, lying in a rectangular pattern. But in some places linear and amorphous patterns are also found. The density of rural settlements is between 1.04 to 1.86 villages per sq. km. The houses are built with both mud and grass or bamboo walls but the roofing material is predominantly grass or thatch.

The Central Gangetic Belt

Although there are a host of minor and major streams in this belt, the predominating channel is the river Ganga with its tributaries, the Son and the Gandak. The region is marked by fertile upland soils which extend over Saran, Patna, Bhojpur and Munger districts. The area is economically more developed than the rest of the Bihar Plain. Consequently, it has a high density of population and is marked by considerable urbanization. It also has good transport facilities and is relatively free from floods. This entire region has, therefore, compact and semi-compact settlements lying in a rectangular, square or star patterns. The density of rural settlements ranges from 2.00 in Munger to 4.00 in Saran.

The majority of houses, here, are built with mud walls and tile roofs. However, as Saran and Patna districts have a lower rainfall coupled with higher prosperity and are also a zone of transition between the grass built houses of the north and the mud built houses of the south, they have a considerable proportion of buildings constructed with mixed building materials. Due to urban influence, brick built houses and flat roofs constructed with bricks or concrete also attain significant proportions.

VILLAGE KHARSAM IN SAMASTIPUR DISTRICT : A CASE STUDY

The village Kharsam is located in Rusera *anchal* of Samastipur district, on the bank of the river Kareh. It is centrally situated in a large rural pocket being 29 kilometres south-east of the city of Darbhanga, 25 kilometres north-east of its district headquarter Samastipur and 19 kilometres north of Ruseraghat railway station. It contains two *tolas* namely, Kharsam proper and Lalpur, which are connected with each other by a good kutcha road. The population of the village was found to be 900 persons living in 417 houses in 1985.

This settlement is rectangular in shape. It is surrounded by an embankment on the south, three ditches on the north and orchards on the east and the west. The houses are generally placed along the village streets which run in a zig-zag fashion. The main roads are 3

Mts wide but the bye-lanes are hardly 1 Mt wide. The Central part of the settlement is occupied by a bamboo grove and a ditch. The spacing between houses is not more than 3 Mts.. Thus it is an overcrowded and semi-compact settlement. The bye-lanes meet the main road almost at right angle, but there are exceptions also. The outer shape of the main settlement is rectangular while that of Lalpur *tola* is amorphous. The condition of houses belonging to the poor, particularly the *harijan*, is deplorable.

According to four housing plans examined on purposive sample basis (Fig. 16.3), the average living space is 25 sq. Mts per person, out of a built up space of 175 sq. Mts. Only 5 persons live in one room and the height of the building is about 3 Mts. An inner courtyard for women and an outer verandah or *dalan* for the men are common features in each and every house. Cattleshed is often located adjacent to the main house, but in some cases it may be a separate structure. Each house has some banana trees at the back. The material of wall is mostly mud, but houses of the poor are built of grass and thatch, while a few upper class houses are built with burnt brick. Both tile and thatch are prominent as roofing materials. Wooden windows 1/2 x 1/2 mt. size are common. A primary school, a temple of the goddess, a temple dedicated to village deity are the public and religious establishments.

The expansion of houses has mostly taken place towards the southern side in case of Kharsam and towards the eastern side in case of satellite settlement of Lalpur. The erosion along the eastern bank of the river Kareh has caused a shift in the location of satellite settlement Lalpur three times. This has been indicated clearly in the map (Fig. 21). Before 1958, this village used to suffer from floods chronically but the construction of a flood protective embankment has made it safe from the floods of the river Kareh after 1958.

Geographers have as yet shown little interest with the study of regional patterns of rural settlements. In this Chapter on the basis of various attributes of rural settlements a matrix of correlation of coefficient has been prepared and it has been investigated that the elements of settlements have profound relationship with each other.

On the basis of this relationship, sieve technique has been

adopted to find out the combination of different elements and its effect on the compactness and regional distribution of settlements. The sub-regional boundaries are clear enough but are not final, for there is considerable overlapping of boundaries depending upon the number of parameters considered.

At the end, a case study of village Kharsam is given here which shows the regional character of rural settlements in its totality.

REFERENCES

1. H. J. Nitz: "Objectives and Methods of Geographical Research in the Evaluation of Rural Settlement Regions", *National Geographer;* Vol. VII, 1972, pp. 1 - 12.
2. R. Thuermer: "The Socio-Economic Regionalization of the German Democratic Republic, " *Wissenschaftliche Mitteilungen,* Leipzig, 1983, pp. 181 - 192.
3. D .C. Money: *Introduction to Human Geography;* University Tutorial Press, London, 1964.
4. W.C. Brice: "The Anatolian Village", *Geography,* Vol. 40, 1955.
5. F. S. Hudson: *A Geography of Settlements,* Macdonald and Evans Ltd, London, 1970, p. 58.
6. George Kay: *A Social Geography of Zambia;* University of London Press Ltd, London, 1967, pp. 62 -64.
7. S. V. Gnielinski: *Liberia in Maps;* University of London Press Ltd, London, 1972, p. 56.
8. J. M. Halpern: *The Changing Village Community;* Prentice-Hall, Inc. Englewood Cliffs, N. J., 1967, p. 68.
9. L. N. Ram: "Cartographic Analysis of Central Functions", *Indian Geographical Studies,* Research Bulletin No. 1, 1973, pp. 82 - 92.
10. G. E. S. Robinson: "The Geographical Region: Form and Function" *Scottish Geographical Magazine,* Vol. 69, 1953 p. 50.

Fig. 16. 1

Bihar Plain : Settlement Regions

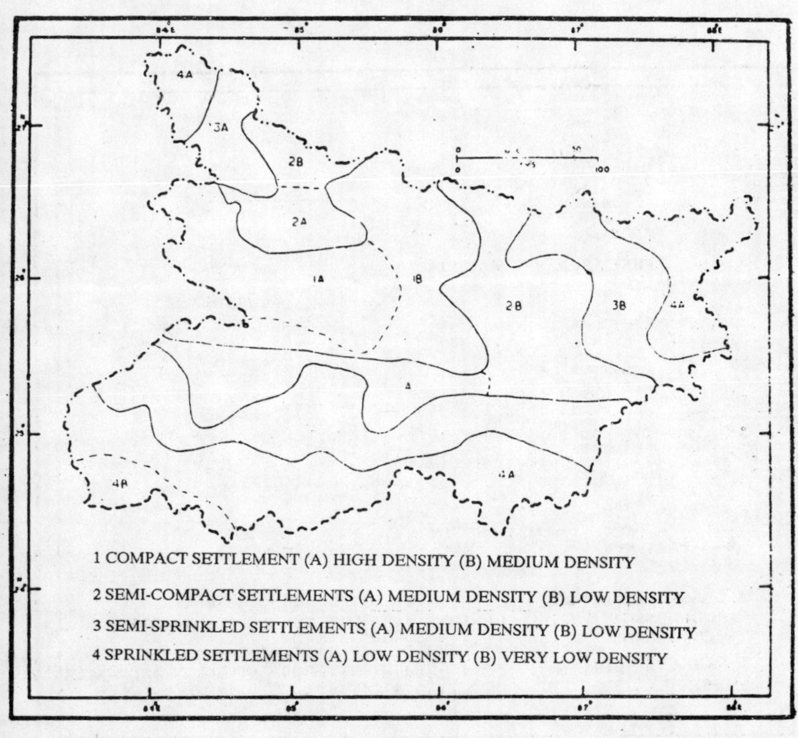

Fig. 16.2

Bihar Plain : Housing Regions

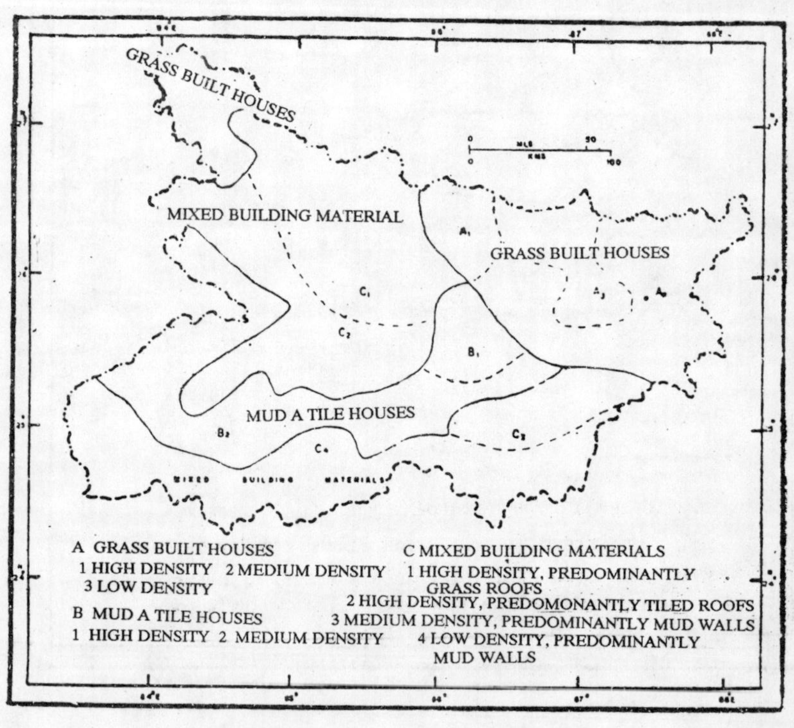

Fig. 16. 3

House Plans : Village-Kharsam (Dist. Samastipur)

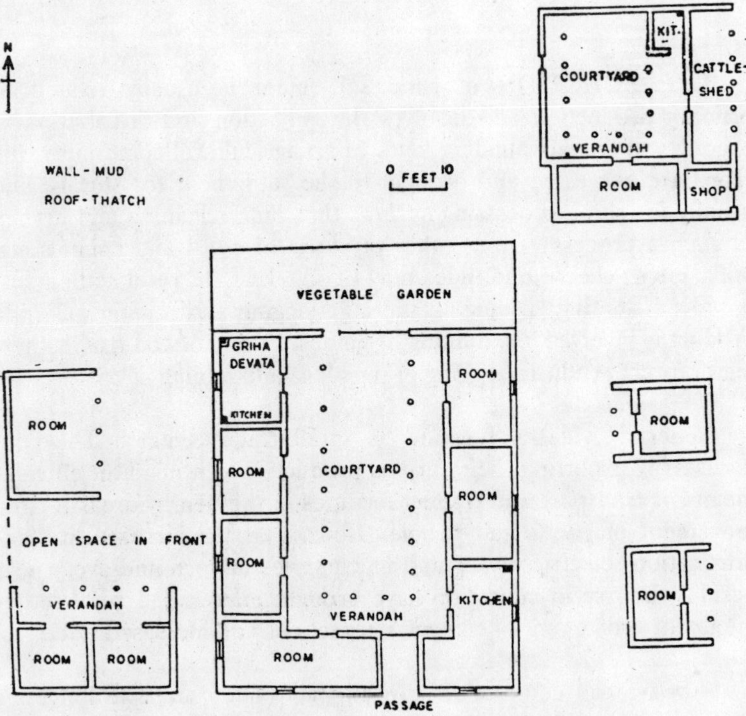

SEVENTEEN

FUNCTIONS OF RURAL SETTLEMENTS

THE FUNCTION of rural settlement is usually related to primary production and involves the collection and distribution of products of the surrounding land. In an agricultural community, the crops are harvested and brought to the settlement for storage and usually for some processing such as threshing, cleaning and drying. In such a process various other products of crops and animals e.g. milk, meat, cheese and hides may be involved. In rural settlements based on hunting, fishing, gathering, logging and mining only one product is involved e.g. hunting of games, fishing of cod fish, gathering of forest products, logging of pine logs and mining of coal.

Generally villages function as small trade centers. They are necessarily exporting their surplus products which need an efficient means of transport and trading facilities in the nearby areas for the movement of goods and people. Nowadays, the increase in communication, electric power and machineries in each and every field besides the rise in education have brought many small rural settlements for greater social contact, interactions and increased trade.

Now we can consider an overall view of the multiple functions performed by the rural settlements as a whole. In rural settlement subsistence is obtained from the surroundings. This is in itself an aspect of productive activity besides the place where reproduction of the human community and social life is regulated. In this way, housing can be viewed from many angles. Firstly, they perform biological function, because houses are the place where meals are prepared, a good part of one's life is spent, and where people born's and die's. On the other hand, house functions as the store place, rearing of livestock, bathing, installation of water closests and place for defection.

As the immediate surrounding is instrumental in agricultural production, hence the settlements function as the linking thread in between inhabitants and the fields, water site, natural environment, gardens, markets, neighbouring villages, and in combination together give a milieu of ethnic and professional groups.

The house as a human settlement is a place of social exchange and sometimes spending liesure hours. In rural areas, the courtyard has multiple use and functions on different occasions of festivals, ceremonials and even in day-today life.

Hence the house is a place of rest, discussion and for receiving visitors. It is also the privileged space of family and social cohesion. The habitation is also a place of greater or lesser convenience, providing for example - running water, lighting, smoke outlet, elimination of mosquitoes and other insects, etc. Such considerations are probably as important as kinds of materials used or the interior arrangement, which does not imply that the disposition of one room to another, or of the house in relation to its outbuilding is unimportant. To the contrary difficult or pleasant living conditions for each family member depends to a great extent on the respective disposition of various rooms, their purposes and use. Depending on where one does or does not crowd others, the serenity of family life is more or less ensured. Such an arrangement reflects, on the one hand, the degree of intimacy desired by the various household members, as well as that of the entire family in relation to their neighbours, and finally the couples intimacy. A last point generally left aside is that the village dwellings and its surroundings are the expression of a way of living and possibly a way of viewing the world, that is peculiar to certain human groups and which differs from one region to another and sometimes from one village to another.

Human settlements also perform a pedagogic function. First of all, the village and habitation are for many people miniature reproductions of what a given group considers as an ideal environment. Through an assortment of interactions, they provide the setting where the groups religious and social life is taught.

More directly, the forms chosen in building the inhabited area or the dwellings themselves contribute to perpetuating a certain life style. How one lives in the habitation and the use made of its various spaces cannot be dissociated from the collective behaviour taught to the youth, i.e., rules of conduct, prohibitions, hygiene, courtesy, etc.

Thus, through the rural habitation we can grasp the *esthetic and cultural manifestation* of rural inhabitants.

RURAL SERVICE CENTRES

This part of the study is concerned with the relationship among rural centres wherein activities other than agriculture assume significant proportions. Such places have been referred to as 'service centres' because the facilities such as retail shopping, entertainment, cultural, professional and similar services provided from these, are sought by people from the surrounding areas.[1] The range of importance of these centres varies from places of a very limited local significance to those with considerable regional importance. The less important a centre is, the great is its dependence upon other more important service centres. Hence it is more convenient to think of them as being organised into successive orders of hierarchy, such as primary, secondary and tertiary service centres, though the proposed divisions may not always be well defined.

Rise of the Service Centers

It has been felt that with the break down of the jajmani system in the larger villages, in the developing countries, non-agricultural functions or services dominate such places and hence leading to rise of service centres. Slowly and slowly at the service centre a concentration of artisans will take place, with the technological and socioeconomic advancement. These objectives can be achieved in a better way with the industrial extension and training, the provision of service facilities for the common masses, supply of electric power, bulk purchase of agricultural produce in grain mandies, provision of credit, standardization of product and efficient marketing can be provided in a better way in service centres in comparison with villages located in dispersed pattern in the countryside. Besides this, an innovation could easily be introduced in service center rather than villages where stagnation is imposed by the jajmani system. Hence due to modern aspects of development, the service centers will supply the large and increasing range of new goods to meet the demands of modern agriculture and high standard of living. After modernization of agriculture, the items which required in bulk quantities were: improved seed, fertilizers, pesticides, improved implements, plant protection aids, steel, cement, diesel oil, tractors and pumping sets. The supply of above mentioned items and repairing service can easily be arranged in rural service centres efficiently in comparison with villages or large urban centres.

In such a development of the service centres, rural society will have two major constituents of settlements: (a) a large number of villages, hamlets or homesteads and (b) a much smaller number of service centres. The villages will, therefore, be predominantly agricultural, with much less social distance between the castes in comparison with mixed pattern of service centres.[2]

Settlement structure is a relatively complex yet stable form of spatial organization. The totality of individual settlements in their geographic distribution, interaction and interdependence comprises the settlement structure of a country.[3]

The functional interaction and interdependence of a settlement structure serve in a socialist country, the satisfaction of peoples' needs.[4] The peoples' need are grouped in three major categories namely, the productive needs of society at large, the general political - administrative activities and the requirements of individual human beings.[5] Facilities necessary to satisfy these needs are located within as well as between the settlements. While these facilities are primarily fixed at definite locations, people possess areal mobility. Service centres gain importance from their primary character as locations of industrial production, administrative centres and as concentration points of facilities for satisfying the individual requirements of people.

To achieve sound development it becomes imperative to establish the facility, types and their capacities in each service centre and then rank these centres in order of achievement. This forms the basis for assessment of the level of development of a settlement system as a whole and is often utilized in formulating a planned hierarchy of service centres in a country.[6] The Bihar plain was chosen as a case study because the socio-economic structure and dynamics of settlement change in Bihar can be regarded as representative of the situation obtaining in India, and the other Third World countries.

FACTORS OF CENTRALITY

The centrality of a service centre, or its importance in the provision of goods and services to the surrounding hinterland population, is indicated by the number of services it provides and by the proportion of these services supported solely by the tributary population.[7] According to Davies[8] there are four techniques of measuring the centrality of service centre:

(i) Direct Measurement Method,
(ii) Indirect Measurement Method,
(iii) Sophisticated Measurement Method, and
(iv) Indices of Potential Functional Status.

The direct measurement method involves a simple addition of all the functions that are found in any service centre. The indirect measurement involves the measurement of the attractive power of centres by determining the dominance of the centre of its link with the countryside. Bracey[9] used this method by considering a parish as the basic frame of reference but selected very few samples to draw his conclusions. The sophisticated measurements make use of the statistical techniques to group various functions. Berry and Garrison[10] have considered a number of functions for each service centre and have examined both the variates and the attributes so as to determine the threshold population of service centres at different hierarchical levels. The indices of potential functional status are found by determining the potential of individual centre in relation to the potential of the region as a whole, so as to classify the centres according to their relative importance. Very little work has been done along these lines.

The direct and the sophisticated techniques have been used in the present study to determine the hierarchical order of different functional classes of rural settlements. Particular care has been taken to consider all the relevant factors objectively before applying advanced statistical techniques. Instead of a few key criteria, a larger number of functions have been considered and they have been given proper weight according to their importance so as to give reasonably objective results. Guha[11] has recently examined the rural service centres in a district of India but this study is limited only to three service units as the basis of classification.

To find out the centrality of a particular village direct measurement technique[12] has been adopted. Medical services, communication facilities, transport facilities, educational services and commercial institutions or markets have been considered as the key criteria for the purpose. In each group, a number of basic functional units were listed. These units were graded, according to their relative importance, into primary, secondary and tertiary orders. The relative importance of a settlement has been determined according to the hierarchy of these basic units present in it. If four or more key functions are present in any settlement, it has been declared to be a service centre. The hierarchy of the centre would depend upon the hierarchy of basic function within the key criteria present. On this basis, only primary and secondary centres have been distinguished in the rural settlements. The tertiary order of basic functions have been found to be concentrated in urban centres only. Nowhere in rural areas, four or more tertiary functions have been found to be located in one centre, although one or two tertiary functions may be found in some of the larger villages. The classification of functions is given below:

According to the above criterion, the absence of any one of the basic functions of one order does not necessarily disqualify a place from being a service centre, if that function is present in the next higher order. This means if three basic functions are available in a centre is primary in order, and the fourth is secondary. The place would be classified as a primary service centre because each higher order function necessarily includes the function of the lower order.

There are 38,520 inhabited villages distributed in eleven districts in the Bihar Plain. The data for basic functions for each of these villages relating to medical, communication, educational services and cooperative societies were compiled from the Census of India 1981. The lists of bus stations, railway stations and metalled roads were collected from various Government offices and the Department of Transport. Information regarding markets was made available by Marketing Departments in different districts.

TABLE 17.1 : Hieararchy of Basic Functions within the Key Criteria

	Basic Functions		
Key Criteria	I Primary Services	II Secondary Services	III Tertiary Services
(a)Medical	I. Rural Health Centres	Dispensary	Hospital
(b) Communication	Post Office	Post and Telegraph Office	I. Telephone Exchange II.Public Call Office
(c) Transport	Bus station (Metalled road within 1 km of centre)	Railway Station (within 2 km of centre)	I. Railway Junction II. Aerodrome
(d) Educational	Middle School	High School	College
(e) Commercial	I.Cooperative Society II. Retail Market	I. Bank II. Wholesale Market	I.Bank and Insurance co. II. Daily Market

METHODOLOGY APPLIED

{Presence of any four functions from
{Primary group (Column I)- Rural

Service Centre {Presence of any four functions from
{Secondary group (Column II)- Rurban

{Presence of any four functions from
{Tertiary group (Column III)- Urban

Applying the aforesaid method 554 rural service centres were distinguished on the basis of Key criteria locally available. Of these 508 are primary service centres and 46 are secondary service centres. There is no rural centre having tertiary service facilities. The regional distribution is given in Table 17.2.

From this table it would appear that the number of primary centres is between 50 and 60 in eight districts. But it is between 22 and 36 in the eastern districts of Saharsa, Purnea, and Bhagalpur. No such pattern is visible in the distribution of secondary centres except that in the above mentioned three districts, there are very few secondary service centres.

TABLE 17.2 : Districtwise Primary Service Centres and Secondary Service Centres

Districts	No. of Primary Service Centres	No. of Secondary Service Centres.
Patna	51	5
Gaya	57	2
Shahabad	50	9
Saran	53	7
Champaran	43	2
Muzaffarpur	44	5
Darbhanga	61	9
Munger	52	4
Bhagalpur	22	2
Saharsa	36	0
Purnea	34	1
Bihar Plain	508	46

Source: Based on Field Work and District Census Handbooks, 1961.

Fig. 17.1 shows the distribution of primary and secondary service centres. It will be seen from this map that areas generally deficient in rural service centres are north-west Champaran, eastern Purnea and the entire Chotanagpur Scarp Belt in the south from Bhojpur to Bhagalpur. These areas have very few primary service centres while secondary centres are totally absent. The maximum concentration of both primary and secondary centres is on either side of the river Ganga and in Madhubani district. In the Gangetic belt some 40% of the secondary centres and 30% of primary centres of the entire Bihar Plain are found to be concentrated. This is also the most urbanised zone in the region and has good transport routes.

It would appear from the table below that there is a close relationship between the density of rural service centres and the density of population. Broadly speaking, the spacing between centres decreases as the density of population increases. Thus in the more crowded areas along the Ganga, where the density of population is generally over 390 persons per sq. km the average spacing of service centres is less than 10.40 kilometre. With a few exceptions, the spacing in the adjoining belt, particularly, in Tirhut and Patna divisions is between 10.40 and 16 kilometre. The third belt containing the least number of service centres includes the Chotanagpur Scarp Belt, hilly Munger district and eastern Purnea district. Here the average spacing between service centres rises to more than 48 kilometre. Thus,there is a clear break in the spacing between this belt and the rest of the study area. It may be noted that in all areas where the spacing is around 16 kilometres or more the density of population is less than 390 persons per sq. km.

Another relationship between rural service centres and urban centres may also be seen from the above table. Broadly speaking, the ratio between these two is more than 10:1 in the belt around the Ganga. In the second zone this ratio falls to around 6:1. In the third zone, the ratio is around 4:1. Thus while the number of towns is more or less constant at one to four in every sub-division, the number of rural service centres changes enormously. This shows that the density of population does not have as great influence on urban centres as it has on rural service centres. One reason for this may be that the lack of transport development precludes the growth of towns.

The rural service centres serve the primary needs of villages, and the distribution of these centres has followed a natural and spontaneous pattern. These centres perform some centralised services for their immediate surroundings.[13] The influence of transport routes and urbanisation have a dominant impact over the development of rural service centres. As a rule, most of the centres have grown like satellites, surrounding the district headquarters and the larger towns. They have also grown along the arteries of roads and railways and at nodal points.

TABLE 17.3 : Relationship between Rural Service Centres and Density of Population

Sub Divisions	No. of Rural Service Centres	Density of Rural population	Average spacing in kms	No. of urban Centres
1	2	3	4	5
Patna City	2	494	5.42	City Regional
Patna Sadar	10	493	8.49	Capital
Begusarai	25	507	8.51	3
Siwan	23	540	8.91	2
Biharsharif	22	482	9.40	2
Chapra Sadar	23	549	8.65	2
Dinapur	12	534	8.68	3
Madhubani	36	464	10.11	2
Buxar	15	399	10.24	2
Jehanabad	14	439	10.46	1
Madhepura	15	363	11.77	2
Bhagalpur Sadar	20	430	11.77	4
Khagaria	16	363	10.96	1
Arrah	18	453	11.20	2
Motihari	28	427	11.76	5
Samastipur	20	513	11.78	3
Hajipur	14	410	11.85	3
Barh	10	563	12.00	4
Muzaffarpur	21	561	12.13	1
Darbhanga Sadar	14	555	12.59	1
Supaul	14	281	12.85	3
Saharsa Sadar	7	354	12.90	1
Aurangabad	19	250	13.68	2
Sitamarhi	14	533	13.60	2
Sasaram	19	268	14.06	4
Gopalganj	9	464	14.83	2
Nawada	11	300	14.86	3
Araria	11	281	15.73	3
Bettiah	17	301	15.93	4
Purnea Sadar	12	293	50.85	3
Gaya Sadar	15	29	56.14	4
Katihar	9	305	57.46	1
Munger Sadar	8	366	60.08	7
Jamui	7	191	68.62	2
Bhabua	7	151	68.81	1
Kishanganj	3	239	79.20	1
Banka	4	230	86.16	1
Bihar Plain	554	352	12.85	87

TABLE 17.4 : Grouping of Functions

Primary Centres	Frequency	Secondary Centres	Frequency
abde	405	abed	32
bcde	34	abde	9
abcd	31	abcde	2
abce	22	bcde	1
abcde	9	acde	1
acde	7	abce	1
Total	508		46

Note:The symbols a, b, c, d and e are the same as in Table 12.1.

An interesting pattern is revealed when we examine the composition of basic functions in both the primary and the secondary service centres. In the primary group, more than 80% of the centres have four functions namely (a) Health Centre or Doctor, (b) Post-Office, (c) Bus Stations, (d) Middle School, and (e) Cooperative Society. The other combinations of basic functions account for around 5% each of the total number of centres. The most uncommon group of functions is that which does not include a post-office, while next to it is the one which includes all the five primary functions.

Amongst secondary service centres two-thirds of the centres have the following combination (a) Dispensary, (b) Post and Telegraph Office, (c) Railway Station and High School. Other combinations of functions are much less important and only two centres have all the five basic functions.

It has been found during the course of field work that the villages near to a service centre will use it most frequently and for most services, while those on the outskirts of the service area will use it least often and for fewest services. This does not represent a gradual decrease in influence outward from the service centre. Around any sizeable centre there is an area throughout which it experiences little or no competition from neighbouring centres.[14] It is only in the marginal areas that the villagers tend to make a choice between two alternative service centres available to them.

According to the criteria set in Table 17.1, there are 554 rural service centres in the Bihar Plain. These centres are not equally distributed among the 395 *anchals* covered by this study. In Manjhi *anchal* of Saran district, there are as many as 7 rural service centres, whereas in Rohtas, Gaya, Jamui-Banka sub-divisions, Eastern Purnea and North-western Champaran districts, there are almost none. This variation is dependent on several factors such as density of population, length of roads and railways and urban influence. An attempt is made here to examine each of the above factors separately.

Service Centres in Relation to Population

The population of service centres in various areas varies from 15000 to 1000 persons. But when the number of service centres and the density of population per sq. km is considered, it is found that the areas of the highest population density, i.e., Patna, North Bhojpur, Muzaffarpur, Saran and Darbhanga districts have a larger number of service centres. The Chotanagpur Scarp Belt and Eastern Purnea, marked by low population density, have very few centres.

Service Centres in Relation to the Length of Roads

It has been found that the growth of service centres have a profound relationship with the development of road communication. The total length of metalled roads in each subdivision was calculated and the correlation between the number of service centres and the length of transport routes was determined by calculating Spearman's rank correlation coefficient. The formula is given below:[15]

$$P = 1 - \frac{6 \times \sum D^2}{N(N^2 - 1)}$$

where 6 = common factor,

P = coefficient of correlation from rank differences

ΣD^2 = sum of the squares of differences in rank

N = number of subdivisions (37)

$$Therefore, \quad P = -\frac{6 \times 3706.0}{37(37 \times 37 - 1)}$$

$$= 1 - 0.43 = 0.57$$

The correlation between service centres and the length of roads was found to be significant at even 2% level. Since $P^2 = .32$, the role of transport routes in the development of service centres is clearly established, as roughly one third of the variation in the number of centres is dependent upon the variation in the frequency of roads.

Rural Service Centres in Relation to Urban Centres

It seems that rural service centres have developed most prominently around the larger towns in the countryside. Since large distances between towns make the distribution of consumer goods difficult, small-rural centres develop around the larger towns as satellite service centres. This pattern is also dependent upon good transportation and communication lines. Thus, the towns act as distribution centres of finished goods for the rural centres, while they also draw upon the rural centres for the agricultural produce of the region. These agricultural goods come from the fertile alluvial fields around the rural service centres. Thus where the density of villages is high, the number of rural service centres attached to each town is also greater.

RURAL SERVICE CENTRES MARKED BY A HIGH EMPLOYMENT IN TERTIARY SERVICES

Uptill now we have considered only the basic functional units which distinguish a service centre. Another possible approach would be to analyse the figures of workers engaged in various occupations in different villages so as to find out the relative concentration of non-agricultural workers in them and thus distinguish the service centres.

'Service occupations in themselves seldom give rise to a settlement'. But where the employment in the three tertiary occupations, viz., trade and commerce, transport and communications and other services including professional and administrative services, is high, the character of settlement is necessarily different. Also there are settlements which may have evolved only due to the tertiary functions such as at nodal points of cross-roads or near railway stations. For example in Bholagurhi, Jorabganj, Mahisampur and Mohabatpur in Purnea district 100% of villages developed on cross roads. In Khusropur of Patna district 79% of the workers are engaged in tertiary services. This village also has developed due to good road and railway communication. In the following discussion, all villages having more than 25% of their workers employed in tertiary services have been considered. This figure may be compared with 9.82% for the total rural workers in the region under study.

Fig. 17.2 shows the regional distribution of such service centres. They are widely distributed over the entire plain. Here also three belts may be distinguished:
(a) The Ganga Belt,
(b) Champaran and Saharsa-Purnea Belts in North Bihar, and
(c) Chotanagpur Scarp Belt.

The tertiary service centres are highly concentrated in the first belt, whereas their distribution is sparse in the other two belts. The pattern shows that most of the centres have developed around certain town groups, whose impact is revealed clearly in this map. One reason for this is the high commuting population, whereby the artisans and other workers of these towns use the tertiary service villages as dormitory and satellite settlements. The map also reveals the zone where vast urbanization belts may occur in future. Two such zones may be mentioned (i) the belt from Buxar to Patna and (ii) Munger - Barauni where the concentration of such centres is extremely high.

Another zone is found around Bhagalpur town group, where 29 centres are located close together. There are also a number of smaller groups in different parts of the Bihar Plain, e.g., Arwal, Arwal group, Bhabhua group, Bikramganj group, Maner group, Fatwah group, Sonepur group, Purnea group, etc. On the basis of percentage of tertiary workers, the centres can be classified into three groups:

(i) Centres where over 75% workers are engaged in tertiary functions,
(ii) Centres in which 51 to 75% workers are engaged in tertiary services,
(iii) Centres in which 25 to 50% workers are engaged in tertiary services.

TABLE 17.5: Regional Distribution of Service Centres Having Marked Employment in Tertiary Services

Name of Districts	No. of centres with % workers engaged in Tertiary Services		
	25 to 50%	51 to 75%	Above 75%
Patna	41	11	3
Gaya	43	15	0
Shahabad	98	20	2
Saran	57	12	5
Champaran	7	0	1
Muzaffarpur	35	6	2
Darbhanga	29	3	1
Munger	79	29	12
Bhagalpur	30	10	9
Saharsa	3	4	0
Purnea	37	6	6
Bihar Plain	459	116	41
Regional Total 616			

Source: Census of India 1981 (District Census Handbook).

These centres are typically distributed around the larger towns of the region, such as Bhagalpur, Munger, Begusarai, Purnea, Patna, Hajipur, etc. Their development is dependent on the transport nodes on either side of the Ganga. The centres decrease in number both towards the Nepal Terai in the north and the Chotanagpur Scarp Belt in the South, with a resultant increase in the spacing between them. This is due to the lack of transport facilities as well as lack of urbanisation in these areas. The centres with less than 25% of their workers engaged in tertiary services have not been considered here as they do not have significant specialisation in location.

Out of 616 service centres of this type, 459 or about 75% have an employment ranging from 25% to 50% in tertiary services. Their number generally ranges between 30 and 50 in a district, but is less than 10 in Champaran and Saharsa and as high as 79 and 98 in Munger and Bhojpur respectively. Here again the number is high in the Gangetic belt. The centres having 51 to 75% employment in tertiary services are 116 in number. They are less than 10 in all districts north of the Ganga except in Saran. Similarly, the number of centres having more than 75% employment is 41 and they are almost insignificant in the district north of the Ganga. In all the three groups the district of Munger has the highest number of service centres of this type, located on either side of the Ganga.

Table 17.5 points to the fact that service centres of different sizes are fairly and evenly spaced over the region. Certain basic causes have resulted in such distribution, because the human services depend upon direct contact with the consumer. These are the nodes of personal services such as those provided by medical or educational institutions; or the services of a doctor, barber, tobacconist or small general stores which are in greater demand in the more enlightened villages around the towns as compared to the interior area.

REFERENCES

1. Ian Caruthers: "A Classification of Service Centres in England and Wales", *Geographical Journal,* Vol. CXXIV, 1958, p. 371.
2. V. Nath., "The Village and the Community" in *India's Urban Future* (edt. Roy Turner), University of California Press; 1962, pp. 151-153.
3. J. G. Feigin: "Die Standortverteilungder Produktion in Kapitalismus und Sozialismus", *Verlag Die Westschaft;* Berlin, 1956.
4. R. Bonisch; G. Mohs Und W. Otswald "Zur Planning der Seidlungsstruktur", in *Territorial Planung 2 Auflage;* Verlag Die Wirtschaft, Berlin, 1980.
5. H.G. Barnum: *Market Centres and Hinterlands in Badenewjrtenberg;* Department of Geography, University of Chicago, Research Paper No. 103, 1966.
6. F. Grimm: *The Settlement System of the G.D.R.,* Leipzig, May, 1979.
7. R.J. Johnston: "Central places and the Settlement Patterns", *Annals of the Association of American Geographers,* Vol. 56, 1966, pp. 541-549.
8. W.K.D. Davies: "The Ranking of Service Centres: A Critical Review", *Transactions and Papers*, Institute of British Geographers, No.40, 1966, p.52.
9. H.E. Bracy: "Towns As Rural Service Centres", *Transactions and Papers*, Institute of British Geographers, No. 18-19, 1952, pp. 98-99.
10. B.J.L. Berry and W.L. Garrison: "The Functional Bases of the Central Place Hierarchy", *Economic Geography,* Vol. 34, 1958, pp. 145-154.
11. Bandana Guha: "The Rural Service Centres of Hooghly District", *Geographical Review of India,* Vol. XXIX, 1967, P.47.
12. W.K.D. Davies : *Op. cit.*
13. Bandana Guha: *Op. cit.*
14. H. E. Bracy: *op. Cit.*
15. H.E. Garret: *Statistics in Psychology and Education,* Bombay, 1969, (Reprint Edition), p. 372.

Fig. 17.1
Bihar Plain : Rural Service Centres Secondary and Primary (Now-Agri). Services

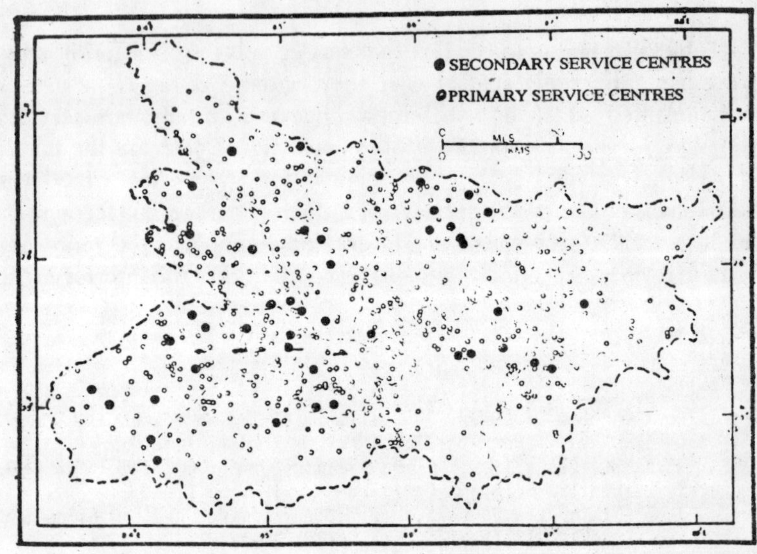

Fig. 17.2
Bihar Plain : Rural Tertiary Services

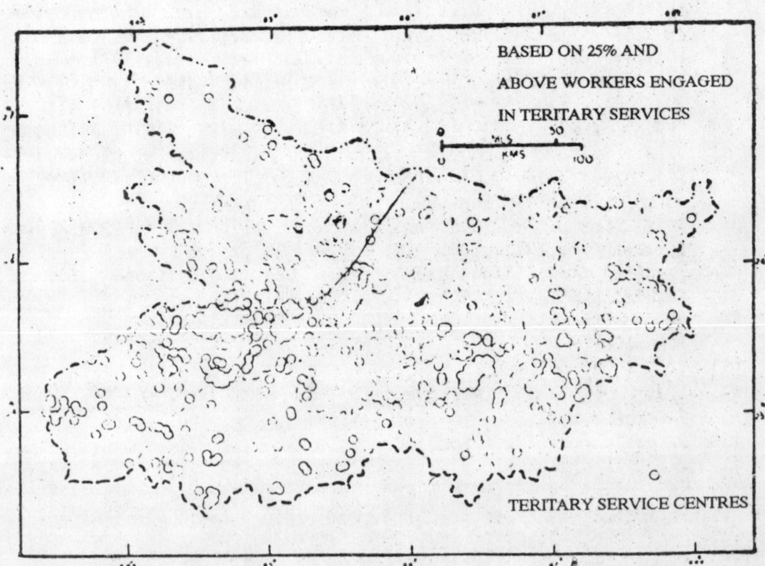

EIGHTEEN

RURBAN CENTRES

Large rural settlements, and small towns are known as rurban centres. On such centres, the concentration of service facilities for surrounding hinterland and business proficiency are of overwhelming importance as they serve a lever of regional development. The concept of rurban centre is a new ramification in settlement geography, where physical landscape is mostly set in a right direction by social behaviour [1] and cultural landscape of the society. Economic prosperity plays an important role in the growth and development of rurban centres. Such small town or small city is essentially equivalent to what Brush has included in his threefold classification of hamlets, villages, and town[2]. The study of rurban centres is of academic interest because it presents the lower end of central place continuum. Any generalizations, theories or laws developed for central place should hold good not only for large urban places but also for all the hierarchic levels including rurban centres. This chapter seeks to identify the factor responsible for the spatial distribution of smaller urban settlements and large villages and their role in maintaining the ecological balance with the rural settlements.

Meaning and scope of the Study

Rurban centres[3] have been variously described as 'rurban settlements' by R.L. Singh[4], 'rurban community' by Galpin[5], 'urban villages' by Dickinson[6] and 'sub-towns' by Smailes[7]. Recent geographic literature contains some important studies of rurban centres[8]. Among the commendable ones are Berry and Garrison's Snohomish county, Washington Studies[9]; King's comparative study of the Canterbury Provincial District, New Zealand[10], and Thomas's study of the functional bases for small Iowa towns[11].

Monkhouse has used the term 'rurban' similar to that of 'rural-urban fringe' and 'rural - urban continuum', and this is better use of the term 'rurban'. Rurban centre is also a small urban centre or larger overgrown village having some importance of secondary and tertiary functions. On the other hand, rural urban fringe is a zone of transition around a town in which urban functions, land use and other activities are mixed with agricultural one's. This zone separates the area exclusively devoted to urban use from that exclusively devoted to agricultural use[12].

The rurban centres have a distinctive feature of their own. Most of the smaller centres are overgrown villages and still retain their rural character. They show a combination of economic, social and educational functions[13]. Most of the towns have a city region around them, the small towns function as the economic and social capitals of their surrounding essentially agricultural areas. By virtue of its intermediate location and the nature of evolution, the small town has certain advantages and offers unique opportunities in the general scheme of rural-urban and agricultural-industrial continuum[14]. Hence the study of smaller urban settlements is highly important as they represent the 'basic connection between the dispersed agricultural population and the agglomerated urban population'[15].

There are several characteristic features which separate rurban centres from the list of rural settlements and urban centres as they are urban islands in the vast sea of rurality[16]. The overwhelming growth of population, laissez-faire growth of rural service centres and inadequacy of service facilities in rural areas are highly in need of rurban centres study. The problem of social disorder in rurban centres necessitates the need for planning and at present this should be in the fore-front of research in geography as this provides the levers of regional development and planning.

Rurban centres may be a commercial, administrative, transportational, industrial or religious node, but their locational force has telling effects on the surrounding zone of influence for maintaining the 'ecological balance'. In general within settlements, the aim of balanced development is equally critical. The aim is the combining of social growth, occupations, enterprises, types of housing and common services that are still to be found in provincial cities and 'urban villages'.

The International Institute for Environment and Development and its associated institutions are completing the first phase of their research into the present and potential role of small towns and intermediate settlements in the development process. Regional studies have been completed in two regions of India and one each in Sudan, Argentina and Nigeria. These studies are aimed at establishing closer links between each regions's settlement pattern and economic base, and to see their impact on the current social structure. They also examine housing and environmental problems in some settlementts.

In March 1983 the International Union of Local Authorities and the All India Institute of Local-Self-Government discussed very broadly on small towns related to the problems and prospects of alternative growth centres. Finally the participants came to the following conclusions:

1. The present problems of the primate cities in which often half or more of the population live under abject circumstances in slums and squatter settlements, can be solved only if they are attacked at the national scale together with those of the rural areas and small towns.

2. Within such a national policy, the development of small and intermediate towns as alternative growth centres can help, both to take some of the pressure off the primate cities and to serve the rural hinterland in its regional setting thus narrowing the gap between standards of living in different parts of the country.

3. As development of the surrounding region is a condition for the promotion of growth centres, the planning and implementation of both have to be closely co-ordinated. Expansion has to be made in the fields of agriculture, horticulture, animal husbandry, fisheries, dairy farming, mining and irrigation, besides the establishment of

co-operative and agriculture credit banks, the improvement of transportation and market facilities. Its implementation will result in a higher productivity in the region, which will lead to an increased capacity to pay of the rural population. The growth centres will profit from this larger spending power and at the same time stimulate further growth of the region and the service which they provide, thus contributing to a general upgrading of the standard of living[17].

The Economic and Social Council of the United Nations has emphasized that in order to hasten the process of rural development and strengthening the regional growth pole, generally the role of rurban centres is getting overlooked. It can be observed that in European, Japanese, North American and Indian agricultural development, the better structural linkage of intermediate centres with the rural areas have helped a lot in diffusing innovations. Such centres provided farms the highly needed repair services, tools and equipment, marketing facilities, consumer goods to support the farm family and transportation facilities. This elaborate structure of settlements is an integral part of agricultural development. The development of rurban centres is thus closely related with the development of agriculture, but it is equally true that the productivity of agriculture depends in no small part on its articulation with the rest of the world through rurban centres. Therefore, one should reasonably except that any increase in rural income would have earliest impact on the growth potential of rurban centres. Nowadays rurban centres would seem to be the critical points of contact between the regional growth pole and hinterlands.

In developing countries the rurban centres are not so well equipped to fulfill the regional demands and tend to be neglected in the distribution of public services. They serve as a place to stop on way to the big city, poorly equipped to respond to the changing agricultural conditions,and serve as weak links in the transmission of development opportunities.

It is due to the inadequacy of rurban centres (small towns), which provide the link between larger towns and tiny villages. In 1981 there were only 2200 small towns in India. Due to their maldistribution and functionally weak regimentation, they are unable to offer the necessary services for village development. The villages are very small to support these services individually. In comparison with India in developed parts of the world, the rural-urban ratio is better which can be seen in Table 18.1.

Table 18.1 : Ratio of Village and Urban Centres

Country	Village Per Urban centre
Indonesia	355
Iran	270
India	190
Egypt	110
Chile	75
Italy	25
Sweden	12
France	10
Switzerland	5

Source: UN Statistical Year Book, 1967: New York 1968.

But in India, the rurban communities are considered as the focal points in the process of modernizing the rural society and economic growth. The expansion of rurban centres' economic activities, serving the region's agriculture, will automatically expand the demand for labour and so help to absorb the out-migration of agricultural labourer before it invades the primate centres. In such a situation rurban centres should be converted into true 'ports-of-entry' from the rural areas into the urban centres. They should be the centre for a nation wide system of employment offices and job information, besides agricultural training and extension of agricultural supporting services. Wherever in the settlement hierarchy the rurban centre is inadequate to fulfill these functions "new towns well-designed and endowed specifically to fit these developmental needs - may be planned and constructed as an integral part of the development strategy"[18].

Such intermediate urban centres for marketing, cooperatives, services and industrics scrving agriculture must be strengthened. Dispersed and desolate rural settlements need to be brought together. Such a policy offers some hope of lessening the pressures of large scale migrations out of agriculture directly into the biggest cities. This may also provide alternative settlement systems designed to achieve more balanced regional development.

Rurban units are marked by the growth of certain significant urban functions. In fact, they are foci of a number of market villages. Such centres often have significant retail and wholesale marketing facilities. Post and telegraph facilities, market, a dispensary, a veterinary hospital, rural professional services, a high school and community block development offices are other characteristic functional units found located in them. Sometimes these centres are trade centres for the surrounding rural area, or administrative centres due to their being the headquarters of the local administration. On account of their distinct commercial, cultural and administrative elements, such units are characterized by a greater number and variety of services, which are rarely present in a village. Many other functions are attracted to such centres by virtue of their being the seat of local administration.

Many services are found only rarely in rural areas, such as cinemas, hospitals, libraries, etc. These are today available only in towns, as they are too costly to be operated in open country locations or in very small towns. Some of these services may be located in the country at the edge of a town but this is basically a town location for all practical purposes. Transportation with the help of bus service and the metalled road have enormously lifted the horizons of rural families as far as the accessibility to these services is concerned, yet costs in time and money are still prohibitive. As a result, most rural families use less of these services than they would, if they live in a town and belong to the same income group.

Rurban centres are special type of towns based on services of those involving governmental services of all kinds. Federal and State agencies of various kinds have their offices in rurban centres often in the 'country-seat town'. These include the Block Development Offices and the circle offices of the government. The former will have occasion to visit such offices as part of his business operations, and to a greater extent the rural family will visit them for various aspects of family living. 'Thus the small towns are quite often seen as the 'bridge' between the urban and the rural universe, as the kind of settlement which can offer the best, and none of the worst of both worlds'. Obviously a study of rurban centres would form as much a necessary part of rural settlement geography, as the study of the larger villages themselves.

The city level centres have distinct advantages over rurban centres in industrial development. But it is difficult, if not impossible to carry out a systematic review of the role of small towns. Although one might conceive of industrialization of the country mainly through large cities, undoubtedly rurban centres would play an important part in providing the levers of development as well as ancillary services, such as educational and health facilities which are essential for economic growth.

In the hinterland of a rurban centre, the thorough-fares of most of the rural settlements have been oriented towards it. This is due to the intimate business and consumer relationship of that market with the surrounding rural settlements. This may be generalized into a law for the location of rural settlements and rurban communities. In this way, the location of a rurban centre guides not only the location of rural settlements but also their transport linkages. This is a new tool with the geographers to study the 'law of rural settlement morphology and rurban centres location'.

RURBAN CENTRES: A REVIEW OF SOCIAL CHANGE

It is useful to make an inventory of the functions of rurban centres of various types in different locations so that their implications for planned economic development could be reviewed. Two of the functions, actual and potential of the rurban centres are particularly significant. First, rurban centres can act as channels for mobilizing savings and skills which are not available or not easily tapped in large towns. These might be the places, where some portions of income derived from agriculture are invested in industrial establishments such as household industry or small and medium scale units. Secondly, rurban centres might also in certain circumstances, be especially suitable as centres of formal education and specialized medical services. Rurban centres may be:

(i) Religious, transportation and administrative towns,
(ii) New industrial or power project towns such as Barauni and Birpur,
(iii) Regional or sub-regional centres of services like school, college, hospital, etc.,
(iv) Agriculture market towns or wholesale and retail trade centres,

and

(v) Existing small towns in the vicinity of large cities.

These and other types of rurban centres can fulfill specific functions in economic development. Their costs of providing services and maintaining overheads are relatively small. They, thus, offer several advantages over the larger towns for regional development. They perform useful functions and have obvious potentialities of growth of Community Development. Schemes are at times more effectively carried out in rurban centres. On the other hand, the age group of 34 and above show a net migration from rurban centres. Similar trends have been observed in Indonesia and the Philippines[19], where too, the educational centres draw young people away from the rural areas.

In such centres the occupational structures are certainly varied. Agriculture is invariably the major source of livelihood in a village but it may be negligible in rurban centres. This difference, however, is not necessarily reflected in the social structure. In the rurban centres of Bihar Plain nearly 80% of the people live in areas occupied largely by their own caste or religious groups. The urban character of the settlement has not removed the cultural walls between the groups, instead the urban housing pattern has been modelled upon rural customs and traditions. The study has revealed that rurban centres do not differ much from villages in terms of the proportion of joint households and of various types of kinship units. Moreover, the migrants always move to the quasi-urban areas, and thus form strong urban pockets in the rural landscape.

EVOLUTION OF RURBAN CENTRES

There are several parameters which act as 'carriers and barriers' of rurban centre development, but population migration from rural settlements to rurban centres and the orientation of main thoroughfares of rural communities towards the nearest rurban centres are some of the forces which have highly contributed in the growth and development of rurban communities.

In any region, the development of rurban centres has been dependent upon minor points of focus that initially were not associated with retail trade. Cross roads, flour mills, post offices, railway stations and police stations were there which provided a meeting place for the peasants. Enterprising businessmen took advantage of these facilities to open retail shops at such centres. This, in turn, led to the establishment of grain collecting centres, electric lines, telephones and other similar facilities, and the combination of these elements led to the greater concentration at some of the places, while competition between the growing centres created the hierarchy of rurban communities.

The smallest rurban community is a rural settlement with basic public utility services such as an allopathic doctor, middle school, post-office and a metalled road connection. Rural settlements of this category are closely spaced and may or may not have a retail marketing centre. They do, however, have a weekly or bi-weekly market known as hat.

Rurban centres, generally, provide services like a high school, telegraph office, dispensary, retail market, block development office and a bus stop or a railway station. Such centres are located on the main transport routes between bigger urban centres and are, therefore, interspersed between towns and tiny rural settlements.

Further development of these facilities and the addition of a telephone exchange, bank, cinema, wholesale market, etc. led to the final growth of urban centres. Rural settlements which have grown into rurban centres are potential towns. A rise in their population coupled with population segregation in land utilization and increase in employment in tertiary services would make them eligible for classification as towns. It would appear that the evolution and spacing of rurban centres location for a particular period of time and space largely depend on economic prosperity and transport facilities.

SYSTEMS OF RURBAN CENTRES

In the system of rurban centres two sets of variables have deterministic influence on the proper functioning of the centre. The first set of variables include those having predominance in rural areas and operate through larger villages controlling the satellite hamlets. The nearness of smaller villages to larger village or rurban centre attracts a large number of visitors. The higher density of population provides the market for local produce, while lack of population in the sphere of influence always restricts the development of any rurban centre. The second aspect in rural areas is that of topographic condition of the region. Highlands with stony wastes prevent the development of rurban centres, riverine productive plains become conducive to their development while lowlands liable to flood obstruct the movement of transport vehicles. The third group is that of soil characteristic, economic situation and social and cultural factors each of which have impact upon the development of the centre.

On the urban side three tertiary functions are important for regulating the rurban system. The number of shops, types of shops, utility services and other tertiary services are the main activities of the rurban centre. The other group of factors are nodes of transport. The centre may be situated on the roadside, railway side or have a riverine location while in some cases three variables may converge at a particular centre and give added impetus to all functions of the rurban system. Still another set of factors is wholesale market control. This regulates the capital investment and is related to the productivity of the hinterland as well as the incentive provided to the businessmen. They together determine the market turnover and the hierarchy of rurban centres.

When all these factors assemble at one place they give rise to a central place system. Here the decision about the production, distribution and consumption of goods is taken through the system of exchange, the process of distribution, the supplies from producers and the demand of the consumers. Thus a centre is created where the social, economic and cultural functions are performed for the surrounding hinterland. When this centre ranks between the purely urban and the rural sectors, it forms part of the rurban group. Further, development of this system leads to the development of major trade and urban centres as well as subdivisional and district administrative headquarters. Again these three together help in the development and proper functioning of city level centres reaching ultimately to the regional capital (Fig. 18.1). This indicates that rurban centre is part and parcel of central place system as envisaged by Christaller and Losch.

METHOD FOR WEIGHTING AND CLASSIFICATION OF RURBAN CENTRES

For this purpose the Bihar Plain has been considered as a region, where the location of large rural settlements and small town function as the rurban centres. A rurban centre is essentially a local focus of activities and is marked by commercial, industrial, administrative and cultural institutions. It is, however, difficult to differentiate on functional basis between the large village and smaller town, and a combined list of criteria has to be developed. The measurement of functional indices, particularly in a developing region such as Bihar Plain, must be based on the variety and type of nodal functions other than those available in most of the villages. The nodal functions considered in this study have, therefore, been classified by giving adequate weighting as shown in Table 18.2 below:

Table 18.2 : Weighting and Classification of Rurban Centres for the Purpose of Obtaining Values of Rurban Index

Sl. No.	Nodal Functions	Class I 15 points	Class II 10 points	Class III 5 points
1.	Education	College	High School	x
2.	Medical	x	Hospital	x
3.	Communication	x	Telephone Exchange	x
4.	Finance	Bank	x	x
5.	Transport	x	Railways	Highways
6.	Administration	Sub-divisional office	Block Development office	X
7.	Trade	x	Wholesale Market	x
8.	Recreation	Cinema	x	x
9.	% of total workers engaged in tertiary occupations	x	over 15%	25 to 50%
10.	Diversity Index	9 Nodal functions available	7 to 8 Nodal functions available	5 to 6 Nodal functions available

Centres having at least three nodal functions given in the above Table 18.2 have been considered as rurban centres. Classification of rurban centres on the above basis from the list of villages is easy, but a problem arises in the selection of rurban centres from the list of towns. Both the towns and cities have functions of higher order as compared to the rural, which creates confusion. Thus for the selection of rurban centres from the list of towns, the following method was devised:

$$RI = Pc \frac{tw}{TW} \times 100$$

Where

RI= Rurban index

Pc= Total population of the centre

Tw= Workers engaged in tertiary occupations in that centre, and

T W= Total number of workers in that centre.

After calculating the value of RI by the above method for all towns, the mean was determined, and accepting the mean as the line of demarcation, all towns having an RI value less than mean were classified as rurban centres. Further a detailed list of villages selected as rurban centres on the basis of Table 18.2 was prepared. The two combined lists of rurban villages and rurban towns were given proper weight as per the Table 18.2 to identify 396 rurban centres in the Bihar Plain. The rurban index values were put to statistical analysis for determining hierarchy and functional character (Table 18.3).

FUNCTIONAL HIERARCHY OF RURBAN CENTRES

One great difficulty in determining the hierarchy of rurban centres in the region under study is lack of relevant data. The services are inadequately distributed, and little published material is available. The author had, therefore, to fall back upon the information contained in the Census of India 1981, and supplemented by field work.

The RI values were found to range between 20 and 150, with mean 52.93 and a standard deviation of 32.46. Taking standard deviation as the factor of gradation, 4 groups were recognised. The values were rounded off to the nearest multiple of 5 since the RI values increase in steps of 5 only. These groups are as follows:

Table 18.3

Group	RI Value	Description	No. of Rurban centres
I	120 to 150	Above Mean-2	29
II	90 to 115	Above Mean-1	21
III	55 to 85	Above Mean	77
IV	20 to 50	Below Mean	269

Thus out of 396 rurban centres, 269 of the centres have a value below mean, and may be said to be non-specialised, and therefore, rural in character. Of the balance, 29 have a high RI value, 21 have a medium value and 77 have a low value. A detailed list is given below and all 127 centres have been shown in Fig. 18.2.

R.I VALUES OF RURBAN CENTRES

Group I : Centres (RI value 150 to 120)

Aurangabad T, Jehanabad T, Nawadah T, Buxer T, Siwan T, Gopalganj T, Sitamarhi T, Begusarai T, Khagaria T. Madhepura T, Saharsa T, Jamui T, Madhubani T, Dinapur Nizamat T, Bhabhua T, Banka T, Barh T, Araria T, Sultanganj T, Forbesganj T, Supaul T, Khagaul T, Naugachhia T, Rusera T, Jainagar T, Raxaul T, Dumaraon T, Fatwah T, Bikramganj T.

Group II: Centres (RI value 115 to 90)

Seikhpura T, Lakhisarai T, Murliganj T, Banmankhi T, Bakhtiarpur T, Chakia T, Shikarpur T, Bagaha T, Barbigha T, Colgong T, Jogbani T, Teghra T, Maharajganj T, Mirganj T, Chanpatia T, Barauni T, Birpur T, Dalsinghsarai T, Dinapur cantt T, Daudnagar T, Warsaliganj T.

Group III Centres (RI value 85 to 55)

Hilsa, Mohania, Behea, Mairwa, Ramnagar, Jhajha T, Nirmali T, Kasba T, Barahiya T, Bakhtiarpur, Jhanjharpur, Bel, Mahnar T, Nokha, Piro, Ramgarhwa, Sakra, Balia, Maheshkhunt, Kharagpur T, Jagdishpur, Rafiganj, Bahadurganj, Bihariganj, Bihpur, Mahiuddinnagar, Dumra T, Bargaon, Kanti, Haripur, Dighwara, Musaurhi, Bihta, Phulwari, Rajgir T, Bodh Gaya T, Bikram, Nabinagar, Sugauli T, Manihari, Lalgunj T, Nasriganj T, Itarhi, Jagdishpur T, Koilwar, Sonepur, Mashrakh, Paliganj, Arwal, Hisua, Tilauthu, Kudra, Lauthaha T, Revelganj T, Wazirganj, Tekari T, Sherghatti T, Khusropur, Islampur, Naubatpur, Silao, Barun, Obra, Deo, Belaganj, Khidirsarai, Chenari, Sasamusa, Ghorasahan, Lauriya, Bidupur, Sursand, Bariarpur, Sahebpur Kamal, Singhwara, Barari, Dalan.

N.B.: 'T' denotes Town.

It is interesting to note that all centres in the first two groups are towns, that is, urban settlements. They are mostly small towns, but population is no criterion for determining the RI values. Thus Barh and Dumraon with population over 18000 have RI values of 135 and 120 only, while Madhepura and Bhabua with a population below 12000 have RI values of 150 and 140 respectively. In the third group of 77 centres, 18 are towns and the rest are villages. It is these villages which have the highest potentiality of growing into towns, particularly if their populations are high. The number of such rurban villages is large in areas where there are fewer towns.

Centres in the first group are mostly subdivisional headquarters of administration because they have daily retail market, wholesale market, S.D.O. (Sub-Divisional officer) court of revenue and criminal cases, often a civil court, banks, telephone exchange, college, cinema and goods transportation facilities which combine to put them in the highest rank. All these centres are full-fledged towns with a higher percentage of workers engaged in tertiary functions, as compared to those in primary services. It is interesting to note that this list does not contain a single district headquarter except Saharsa. All the district headquarters and five other subdivisional headquarters have marked urban character.

The other towns included in this group are Sultanganj, Forbesganj, Khagaul, Naugachhia, Rusera, Jainagar, Raxaul, Dumraon, Fatwah and Bikramganj. All these towns have excellent transport connections and are leading market centres of their region. Forbesganj, Raxaul and Jainagar are on the Indo-Nepal border and, therefore important 'break-o-bulk towns'. Khagaul is a centre of the railways. The others are grain collection and distribution centres. The service area of these rurban centres roughly extends to a radius of 16 kilometres, though in most cases it is strictly a matter of terrain conditions and transport facilities.

The centres of the highest order having RI values between 150 and 120 provide such basic amenities as education upto college stage, medical facilities, bus or railway transport, telephone exchange, wholesale market, etc. but may not always encompass such urban facilities as banking, cinema and subdivisional court. Their population usually ranges from 10,000 to 30,000 and the employment in tertiary services is over 50% of total workers. There is usually a marked tendency for a distinct business core to develop in such centres which is conspicuous by its absence in the lower order centres, that is, in rural villages within the same population group.

The second group includes settlements in which the functional index ranges from 90 to 115. These centres generally have a population of 5,000 to 15,000. They have functions and services of the same type as found in the first group, though of a lower degree. The occupational structure of the population also reveals that usually between 35% and 50% of the working force are employed in tertiary services. But the higher order centres of this group are distinguishable by greater nodality and more pronounced urban character.

The centres of third group with RI values above mean i.e., 55 to 85, are 77 in number. These include 18 towns and 59 villages. Their population generally ranges from 2,000 to 15,000 and the employment in tertiary services is close to 25% of the total workers. These centres have been greatly benefited by the development of transport and communication and thus have acquired the status of regional collecting and marketing centres. They services and functions of an urban centre. They are usually found in clusters around the larger cities. This effect is well marked in all cases and is discernible as a node in the overall fabric of rural settlements, though the percentage of non-agricultural population is not always high.

Table 18.4 : MATRIX OF CORRELATION COEFFICIENT FOR RURBAN CENTRES IN THE BIHAR PLAIN

Rurban functions	X1	X2	X3	X4	X5	X6	X7	X8	X9	X10	X11	X12	X13
X1	1.00												
X2	0.138	1.000											
X3	0.049	0.067	1.000										
X4	0.632	0.909	0.532	1.000									
X5	0.228	0.248	0.268	0.192	1.000								
X6	0.050	0.066	0.980	0.542	0.268	1.000							
X7	0.898	0.303	0.553	0.640	0.175	0.549	1.000						
X8	0.581	0.682	0.961	0.527	0.171	0.952	0.563	1.000					
X9	0.916	0.304	0.374	0.662	0.148	0.400	0.633	0.388	1.000				
X10	0.999	0.671	0.976	0.173	0.336	0.983	0.175	0.298	0.126	1.000			
X11	0.150	0.216	0.569	0.144	0.752	0.267	0.163	0.259	0.125	0.832	1.000		
X12	0.354	0.700	0.951	0.550	0.261	0.951	0.557	0.925	0.264	0.297	0.253	1.000	
X13	0.731	0.252	0.254	0.174	0.115	0.021	0.183	0.076	0.133	0.036	0.584	0.080	1.000
	Tertiary workers%	Bank	Hospital or Dispensary	Cinema	Telephone Exchange	High school	College	B.D.O.	S.D.O	Road	Railway	Wholesale market	Diversity Index

The centres below mean number 269, wherein the agriculture constitutes directly or indirectly the occupation of more than 75% of total workers. The centres of this category are large in size and diversified in nature but are mostly confined to primary activities. They have, therefore, not been considered while preparing the matrix of correlation coefficients. This matrix has been prepared by calculating the pearsonian correlation coefficient between each of the 13 nodal functions mentioned in Table 18.2 above.

It is clear from the matrix (Table 18.4) that the Block Development Office, wholesale market, hospital and high school are found in close association with each other. These are the primary services available in rurban centres of even the lowest order. Closely associated with hospitals and high schools are road transport facilities, because practically all Block Development Offices today have been connected by metalled roads. The correlation between these services is seen to range from +0.92 to +0.98.

The relationship between the distribution of highways and railways and that between railway stations and telephone exchange are equally high and are close to 0.80. Services of a higher order such as banks, cinemas and colleges, however, show a low relationship with the services of the lower order. There is a high correlation between the distribution of banks and cinemas and that between cinemas and subdivisional courts. These are located usually in towns rather than in purely rural centres. This is also indicated by the high correlation coefficient of 0.90 between tertiary workers and the distribution of colleges or subdivisional courts. The tertiary services however, have a very low correlation with the distribution of hospitals and high schools. Banks which have a high relationship with wholesale markets, show a low correlation with the distribution of high schools, hospitals and roads. The correlation coefficient in each of the above cases is less than 0.10.

It is apparent that there is a clear division between rurban centres of low order containing Block Development Office, hospital, high school and wholesale market and those of the higher order containing subdivisional court, college, bank, cinema and a high percentage of tertiary workers. The centres of the higher order which contain most of the places mentioned in group I above, contain all services of the lower order and are, therefore, marked by greater diversity. This is apparent from the matrix when we consider that the correlation coefficient between high school, Block Development Office, wholesale market and roads on the one hand and diversity index on the other hand is less than 0.10. Diversity index is highest where the percentage of tertiary workers is also high. This fully justifies the hierarchy groups suggested earlier.

SPACING OF RURBAN CENTRES

The spatial distribution of rurban centres presents several aspects of geographical interests. The dispersed nature of the centres falling above Mean $+2\sigma$ category are quite evident from Fig. 18.2. The presence of a twin rurban centre in Dinapur cantonment and Dinapur Nizamat is noteworthy in the entire plain. Normally, the spacing of such settlements in the Bihar Plain is irregular mainly due to topographical and other factors affecting their historical evolution. This implies that each centre possesses its own specific sphere of influence within which it dominates over the surrounding villages. The delimitation of actual configuration of each sphere of influence would entail a detailed study of consumer behaviour in the area which is outside the scope of this Chapter. Nevertheless, certain generalisation can be made from the pattern obtaining here.

Table 18.5 : SPACING OF RURBAN CENTRES IN THE BIHAR PLAIN

Districts	Number of centres	Spacing in kilometres	Average population size, 1976
Patna	17	19.26	9,579
Gaya	18	27.88	7,683
Shahabad	15	29.32	8,066
Saran	10	27.96	9,343
Champaran	12	24.97	7,853
Muzaffarpur	10	29.72	8,585
Darbhanga	6	40.40	12,194
Bhagalpur	6	32.50	8,475
Saharsa	8	27.40	9,225
Purnea	9	37.42	8,918
Munger North	6	26.88	19,770
Munger South	10	26.91	14,423
Bihar Plain	127	26.08	10,343

$D = 1.07\sqrt{A/N}$

The North Bihar Plain shows the highest spacing of rurban centres e.g. 40.40 kilometres in Darbhanga and 37.42 kilometres in Purnea districts. Here urbanisation is very slow, because of underdeveloped resources and annual inundation by the rivers. In contrast, rurban centres are closely spaced in the South Bihar Plain, the average spacing being 24 kms with a low of 19.26 kms in Patna District. This shows that the number and spacing of rurban centres is directly related to the level of regional development.

FUNCTIONAL MAGNITUDE OF RURBAN CENTRES

Fig.18.3 illustrates the functional magnitude of 127 settlements in the Bihar Plain. The functional magnitude can be defined as a measure of the importance of a settlement in terms of all the nodal functions considered. The usefulness of this quantitative index in the study of service centres rests on its capacity to reveal at a glance the relative importance of the settlement under study area in terms of all the nodal functions they perform. In Fig. 18.3, eleven major rurban centres in the region with RI values of 150 attain prominence. The overwhelming importance of these 11 centres is as expected because centres with almost identical functional magnitude should come within the same order in any hierarchical classification. In contrast to these are the lower order rurban centres with RI values of 55 to 65 which occupy the troughs in the graph.

To conclude, there is a distinct class of settlements in the Bihar Plain which may be termed rurban settlements. 127 rurban settlements have been identified of which 68 are towns and 59 are villages. Broadly speaking, they are divisible into three groups on the basis of statistical analysis. The centres of higher order are marked by specialised services like subdivisional courts, banks and cinemas, while centres of the lower order are marked by Block Development Offices, hospitals, high schools and wholesale markets. The chief distinguishing feature is the high percentage of workers engaged in tertiary services in these centres although broadly speaking the centres of the higher order also have a higher population.

The concept of the rurban centre is useful because it serves to distinguish rural settlements with a bias towards public utility services, commercial services and non-agricultural population. Similarly, there are full-fledged towns which lack basic urban character and yet cannot be termed as rural settlement. The geography of rural settlements in the Bihar Plain would be incomplete without identifying such hybrid settlements, which have a high potentiality of urban growth. By definition the rurban centres are partly rural and partly urban and have therefore to be viewed as part of the broad settlement geography. In this way, rurban centres will work as 'economic and social capitals' for the neighbouring villages.

REFERENCES

1. R.B. Mandal: "Rurban Centres in Bihar Plain," *Indian Geographical Studies, Research Bulletin,* No. 1,1973, pp. 12-23.
2. J.E. Brush: "The Hierarchy of Central Places in South-Western Wisconsin," *Geographical Review,* Vol. 43, 1953, pp. 380-402.
3. R.B. Mandal: "Law of Village Anatomy and Rurban Centres Location on Loschian Landscape," in *Proceedings of Small Towns, Varanasi,* 1978.
4. R.L. Singh and S.M. Singh: "Mungra Badshahpur: A Rurban Settlement in the Ganga-Ghaghra Doab West,"*The National Geographical Journal of India,* Vol. VI,1960 pp 1991-206.
5. C.J. Galpin: *The Social Anatomy of Agricultural Community,* University of Wisconsin, Agricultural Experiment Station, Research Bulletin No. 34, 1915.
6. R.E. Dickinson: "The Distribution and Function of the Smaller Urban Settlements of East Anglia," *Geography,* Vol XVII, 1932, pp. 20-30.
7. A.E. Smailes: "The Urban Hierarchy in England and Wales," *Geography,* Vol. XXIX, 1944, pp. 41-45
8. A. Gloward and Jr. Stafford. "The Functional Basis of Small Towns," *Economic Geography,* pp. 165-175.
9. B.J.L. Berry and W.L. Garrison: "The Functional Bases of the Central Place Hierarchy," *Economic Geography,* Vol. 34, 1958, pp. 145-154.
10. L.J. King: "The Functional Role of Small Towns in Canterbury," in *Proceedings of 3rd New Zealand Geographical Conference, Palmerrston North,* 1962.
11. E,N. Thomas: " Some Comments on the Functional Bases for Small Iowa Towns," *Iowa Business Digest,* 1960, p. 10.
12. F.J. Monkhouse: *A Dictionary of Geography,* London, Edward Arnold, 1972, p. 302.
13. R.L. Singh and S.M. Singh : *op. cit,* p. 199.
14. K.N. singh:" Small Towns as Rural Development Centres in Uttar Pradesh," in *Abstracts of Proceedings of Fifty-Fourth Session, Indian Science Congress Association,* p. 11.
15. E.N. Thomas : *op. cit.*
16. Kingsley Davis: "Urban Research and Significance," in Gibbs, J.P.(Ed): *Urban Research Method,* New Delhi, 1966, p. xi.
17. Non - Governmental Organization (N.G.O.) *News on Human Settlements,* No. 3, 1983, P.2.
18. *Design for a Worldwide Study of Regional Development,* Resource for the Future - INC, Washington, 1967, pp. 37 - 41.
19. *Urban Rural Differences in Southern Asia:* Report on Regional Seminar, Delhi, 1962; London, 1964, p.3.

Fig. 18.1

Model for the System of Rurban Centres

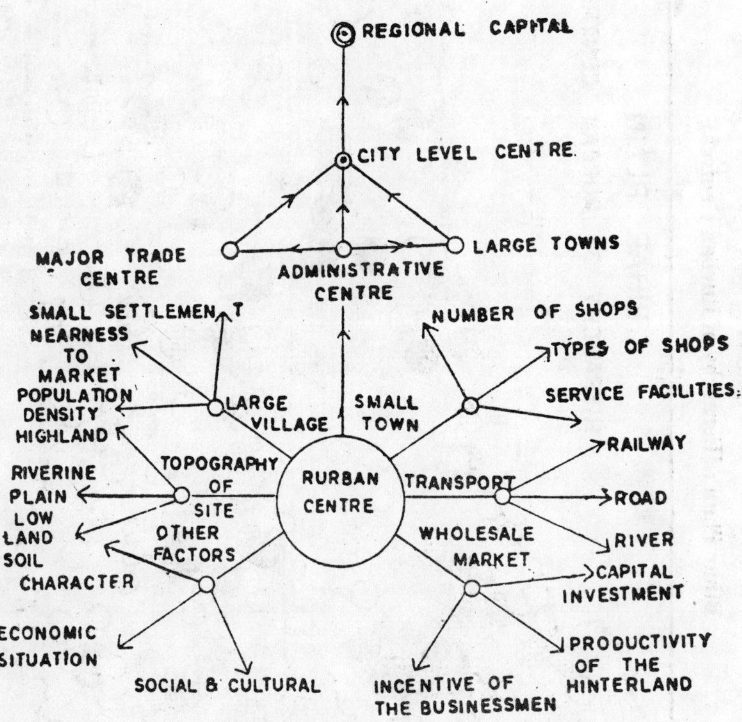

Fig. 18.2

Bihar Plain : Hierarchy of Rurban Centres

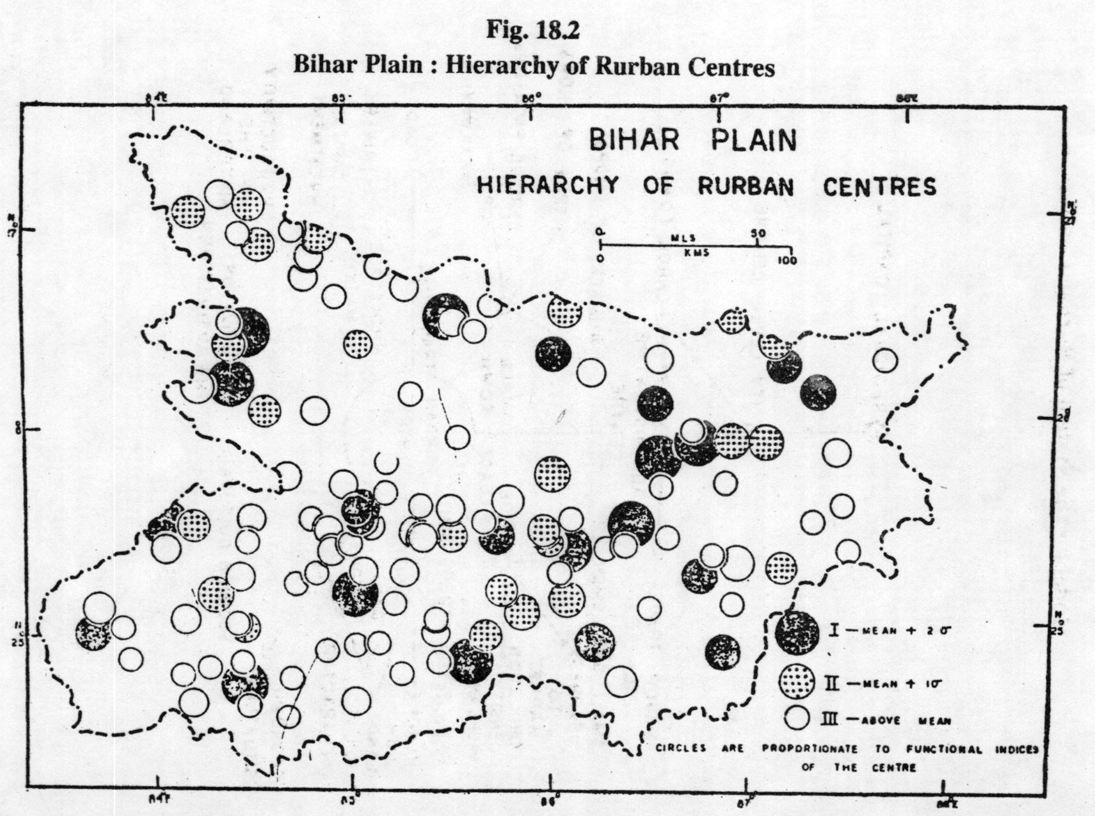

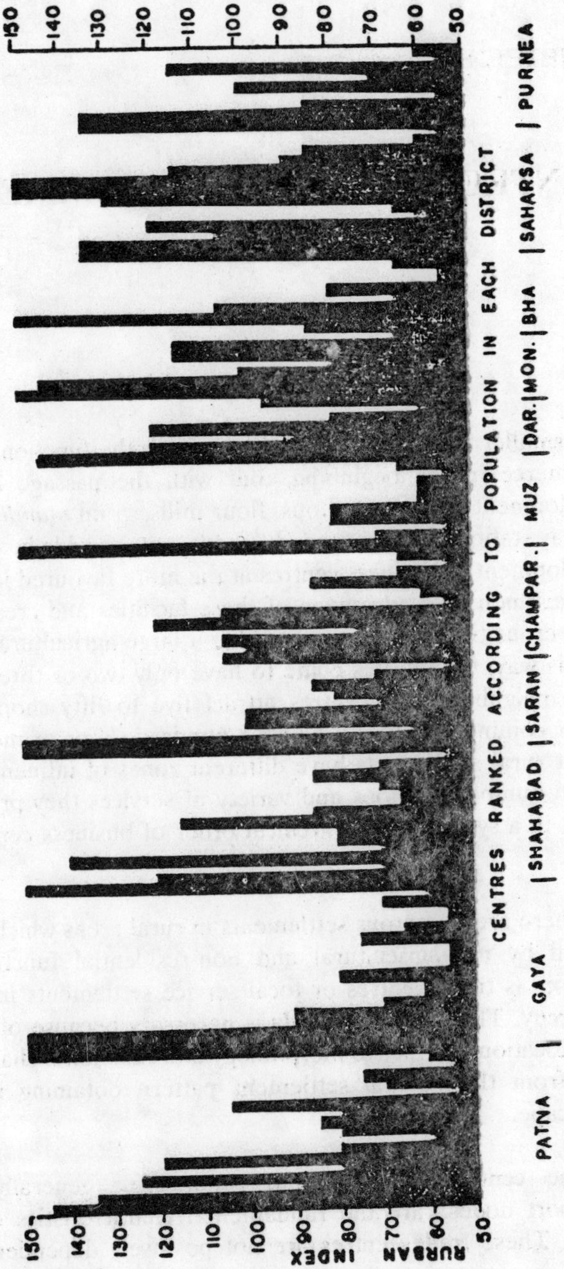

Fig. 18.3

Bihar Plain : Functional Magnitude of Rurban Centres
(Centre : Having R. L. Values above mean)

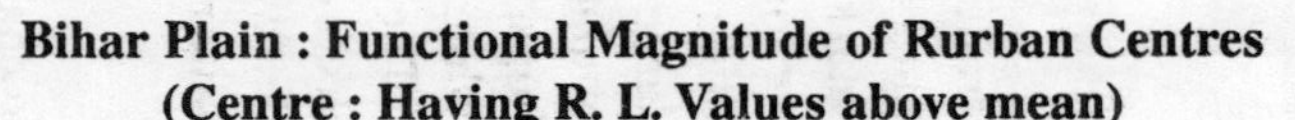

NINETEEN

CENTRES OF TRADE AND COMMERCE

The smaller rural settlements do not have the function of trade and commerce in the beginning, but with the passage of time, the development of grocery shops, flour mills, grain *mandies* (markets), railway stations and cross roads, shops, etc., provide incentive for the development of business centres at the more favoured localities. The businessmen take advantage of these facilities and create large and prosperous business centres, serving a large agricultural population. In this way, the villages come to have only two or three shops, and some neighbourhood centres attract five to fifty shops, while the larger community centres house a hundred shops or more. The different rural settlements have different zones of influence according to the number of shops and variety of services they provide, which result in a systematic hierarchical order of business centres in rural areas.

There are numerous settlements in rural areas which are characterised by non-agricultural and non-residential functions. These develop as trade centres or focal service settlements in the market hierarchy. Their separate study is necessary because of their cross-road location, distinctive morphology and functional character which vary from the general settlement pattern obtaining in the rural landscape.

The centres of trade and commerce, generally occupying transport nodes, are the fundamental characteristics of a central place. These trade centres are not positively dependent upon any basic raw material. They have a tendency to develop wherever there is the slightest opportunity for export and import. They exhibit, therefore, a greater sporadic distribution in the rural environment, than towns or other functions.[1] There is usually, however, a central location of trade centres within a productive hinterland.

The overwhelming importance of towns as centres of trade and commerce is to be expected and is natural in the region. The map showing the distribution of these places is a geographic expression of many facets of the social and economic organisation of today. But it is also in part a legacy from earlier years. Modern transportation has severely twisted the organisational pattern inherited from the past, and the changes have not yet run their course. The urban centres are marked by rapid growth of population and a concentration of business and public utility services. In general, trade has grown rapidly at these centres.

Small business is generally replaced by larger shops in the towns, while the towns grow in their peripheral and rural areas. This reflects the centrality of the larger places in the local highway network and also helps to serve the large population of consumer immediately at hand.

The trade areas of the principal urban centres are becoming complex integrated systems, each with a major diversified centre and numerous smaller, more specialised and slower growing nodes at the outskirts. As the rural people over a wide area travel greater distances to reach the larger food, drugs, clothing or other specialised stores or the complete shopping centre, they have the choice of travelling greater distances in other directions, to smaller or less diversified centres, as clients of a particular seed dealer, appliance service, workshops, etc.[2]

The hierarchy of market centres may be determined by calculating the total area as well as the total population served. If these data are plotted along the X axis and Y axis respectively, we get the typical scatter diagram shown in Fig. 19.1. The diagram has a logarithmic scale on both axes so that straight lines drawn upward towards right at 45° angle mark out equal population densities.

This map shows a remarkable distribution of the centres of trade and commerce on either side of the line corresponding to a population density of 1000 persons in 2.56 sq. km. This is close to the level of rural population density in the Bihar Plain. The distribution of these centres has been classified into villages, towns and cities. The villages are confined to a service area of less than 256 sq. kms and a service population of 1 lakh persons, while the towns generally serve areas of more than 512 sq. kms and a population of over 2 lakhs. Both the villages and the towns are found mixed in the marginal zone with a service area of 256 to 512 sq. kms and 1 lakh to 2 lakh persons served. This mixed zone is mostly occupied by rurban centres.

The service zone of towns extends to 2048 sq. kms and a population of 6 lakhs. Above this is the service zone of cities and larger town groups. There are very few exceptions. It is to be noted that since the density of population is more or less constant over the greater part of the study area, little change has been found in the size of trade area with change in population densities as suggested by Berry.[3] In fact the trade areas increase with increase in the population size and rank of centre. Thus, the trade area of villages ranges between 51 and 512 sq. kms that of towns between 256 and 2048 sq. km, and that of cities between 768 and 2560 sq. kms. Since the density is more or less constant, this results in corresponding ranges of population served from 20,000 to 2 lakhs, 1 lakh to 6 lakhs and 4 lakhs to 12 lakhs respectively.

We have seen above that as the population of a centre grows, the area and the population under its regional influence also grow. The population of the centre, however, is related to the number of retail functions it provides. Thus, we are led to believe that the population of centres is dependent upon the number of different kinds of business that they provide to their market areas.[4]

It will be seen from the scatter diagram (Fig. 19.1) that the threshold value of centres of trade and commerce lies close to a population of 1000 persons and to about 25 business types. The scattering is wide in the population group below 10,000 persons but the trend becomes remarkably clear in the centres of a higher population group. The city of Patna stands out by itself because its high population is largely the result of administrative and other specialised functions that commensurate with its function as a regional capital. In contrast, smaller centres having a population of less than 10,000 cluster on either side of the regression line with a range of 25 to 85 business types.

In order to prepare Fig. 19.1 all villages and towns having more than 100 shops to their credit were listed. Field survey and interrogation of a large number of persons elicited the information regarding the types of shops in each of these centres. Out of 218 centres listed, 87 were found to be towns and 131 villages. The population of these towns ranges from 4500 to 364000, while that of the village ranges from 1500 to 16000. The majority of the villages, however, have a population between 2000 and 6000. All villages have less than 70 functional types, the majority having between 30 and 60 functions. In contrast towns generally have 64 to 110 business types with the highest figure at 156. A detailed table of business types listed is given at the end of this chapter.

Another close relationship is found between the number of shops or functional units and the population of the centre. It appears that the total number of retail and service establishments is a function of the centre's population. With the growth in population, the number of retail establishments tends to multiply. The rate of growth is proportionate to the rate of growth of the centre's population. This can be seen in Fig. 19.2 which is a scatter diagram of the same 218 centres on a double logarithmic graph. The trend of growth along a straight line (which is a line of constant rate) is unmistakable. The cluster of centres in the lower portion of the graph indicates the grouping of villages. The number of shops in them generally varies between 100 and 200 with few exceptions. In contrast, the number of functional units or shops in towns varies between 300 and 1000 and rises to over 2000 in towns with a population more than 50,000. The city of Patna again stands out with more than 800,000 population and over 8000 shops (1981).

A close study of three maps (Fig. 19.1, 19.2., 19.3) would show that there is a distinct hierarchy of centres ranging from cities and towns to rurban centres and villages. The relationship of functional units and functional types with the population of the centre suggests that the larger the centre, the larger the number of both functional units and types of functions.

This is again reflected in the service area of various trade centres, whereby the larger the centre, the larger the area and the population served by it. Since the population of a centre is directly dependent upon the number of central functions, and the number of shops is proportional to the population of the centre, it follows that central functions would determine the hierarchy of the centres of trade and commerce.

Berry[5] has suggested a general expression for the progression of business types at different levels of hierarchy in lowa and South Dakota by the formula $d2^{w-1}$. Here 'w' is the order of the hierarchy and 'd' is a number that varies from area to area. In Iowa and South Dakota, both of which are areas of much lower densities than the Bihar Plain, the value of 'd' was found to be 24 and 15 respectively. The bifurcation ratio 2 is applicable to these areas because their settlement pattern is rectilinear or rhomboidal. In its most general form the formula should be dK^{w-1} since the bifurcation ratio K is also a factor which may vary from place to place.

In the Bihar Plain the above formula has been tested with ample satisfactory results (Fig. 19.3). Here the progression of functional types has been found to be of the order of 50, 75, 113, and 171. This can be written as $75 \times (1.5)^{-1}$, $75x(1.5)^{0}$, $75x(1.5)^{1}$ and $75x\ (1.5)^{2}$. It will thus be seen that the value of d which depends upon density of population in the region is 75 while the bifurcation ratio K is 1.5 for the trade centres of the Bihar Plain. Admittedly, this leads to a complex settlement pattern. This is but natural in such an old but undeveloped and densely settled part of the world. The scatter diagram (Fig. 19.4) shows that settlements at each hierarchical level are distinguishable as villages, rurban centres, towns and cities respectively with overlaps.

LAW OF RETAIL GRAVITATION

In case the population and the number of functional types for each centre are known we can calculate the market area around that centre with reference to other central places in the neighbourhood.

This can be done by applying the laws of retail gravitation developed by Reilly.[6] However, we can arrive at practically the same conclusion by considering the number of shops in a centre since there is a very close correlation between number of business types and the number of shops at a centre. In fact the use of number of shops gives better results. Whereas slight discrepancies and chance location of a business type at a centre may distort the result, the number of shops being dependent upon a number of factors is likely to give a better evaluation of the centre's importance in terms of market gravitation. Reilly himself used population as an index of size, while Berry has preferred business type as the fundamental measure of the attractiveness of a centre. In the present study, it has been found appropriate to consider number of shops as the basic measure of the importance of retail trade at any given place.

According to the break point equation of retail gravitation, the trade area boundary between two centres A and B is, in kilometres from B, equal to:

$$\frac{KMS\ Between\ A \text{ and } B}{1 + \sqrt{\frac{Size of\ A}{Size of\ B}}}$$

where A and B are two trade centres and their relative size is determined by the number of shops, that is, retail outlets that they possess. Berry has pointed out, however, that this equation cannot be applied indiscriminately.[7] He suggests that it must be applied to cities and larger regional centres first to determine, market areas for goods of city order. Smaller centres may then be added to derive market areas for the lower order of goods. This process has been applied in the present study, first to distinguish the market areas for cities and district headquarters; then smaller towns, rurban centres and other trade centres were included to determine their market areas for goods of a less specialised nature available in them.

Thus for Patna and Muzaffarpur which are cities selling goods of a higher order the break point is determined as follows:
Distance between A and B = 61 kilometres
Size of A = 9,273 shops
Size of B = 3,554 shops

The distance from Muzaffarpur (B) to the break point of market area is:

$$\frac{61}{1+\sqrt{\frac{9273}{3554}}} = 23.12 \ Kilometres$$

Similarly for goods of lower order the break point between say Hilsa and Islampur was found as follows:

Distance between A and B = 16 kilometres

Size of A = 298 shops
Size of B = 180 shops
The distance from Islampur (B) to the break point of market area is:

$$\frac{16}{1+\sqrt{\frac{298}{180}}} = 7.01 \ Kilometres$$

The result of this study has been incorporated in Fig. 19.5. It has been found that the cities and district headquarters form large retail market zones, which very broadly attest to their regional importance as we know. On the other hand, for goods of a lower order, their influence gets somewhat restricted because of the right of smaller towns, rurban centres and market villages which surround them. This is obvious, because if alternatives are the same, the consumers tend to select the closest centre even though it is much lower in the retail hierarchy. There is, however, a tendency for the breaking point at outer margins to be deflected towards the less attractive of the alternate centres.

On the other hand, the smaller centres tend to restrict the market zones of the larger centres in respect of goods of a lower order, their own market zones are squeezed by the overwhelming influence of a larger centre nearby. In rural areas, the distance to be travelled has a major impact on the choice of marketing centre because of the time and cost involved in travelling. Hence, the influence of any market centre seems to vary directly according to the number of shops in any centre and inversely according to the square of the distance between them.

This is most noticeable in case of the smaller trade centres in peripheral areas of the Bihar Plain. Bhabua, Sherghati, Jhajha, Banka, Kishanganj and Ramnagar each have much larger trade areas than is warranted by their size. This has happened because the larger and more important centres such as Arrah, Gaya, Bhagalpur, Purnea and Motihari are at great distances from these centres and, therefore, exert little influence over their trade areas.

On the other hand, much larger centres like Patna, Gaya and Bhagalpur have relatively small trade zones for goods of lower order because of the presence of smaller centres around them. It will be noticed that in areas where transport facilities are poor, fewer trade centres have developed and, therefore, the retail marketing area is relatively large. This can be seen in the Chotanagpur Scarp Belt and in Saharsa and Purnea districts. In comparison with this, trade centres are located close together and have, consequently, much smaller retail trade areas on eitherside of the river Ganga. Most of the rurban and rural trade centres fall in this category (Fig. 19.5).

From the point of view of zone of influence, we can divide the centres of trade and commerce into three categories for goods of a lower order:

(i) Centres of the hilly tracts,
(ii) Large sized centres of Plains, and
(iii) Small sized centres of Plains.

The hilly areas are mostly forested and prohibit human habitation and development of communication lines. Here the centres serve relatively larger areas, but a smaller number of people. The inhabitants of such lands are poor and have little to sell in the market, because their land is not fertile and the economy is undeveloped.

TABLE 19.1: Population and Area Served by Centre of the Hilly Tracts

Centres	Population served,1961	Area served in sq. kilometres
Bhabua	489,887	3561
Jamui	231,299	950
Banka	342,386	1597
Jhajha	439,876	2624
Ramnagar	198,032	1088
Sherghatti	383,989	1882
Kudra	83,402	404

The bigger market areas around cities and towns of the region indicate that they have better transport connections. Thus all centres of the plains, which have better communication and transport facilities have attracted large market areas and serve a large population. The table given below brings this out clearly.

TABLE 19.2 : Population and Area Served by Larger Centres in the Plains

Centres	Population served 1961	Area served in sq. kilometres
Arrah	771,383	1659
Muzaffarpur	1,461,734	2557
Darbhanga	1,078,993	1820
Chapra	1,198,172	2220
Gopalganj	425,412	893
Rusera	501,778	1055
Gaya	386,747	755
Biharsharif	728,541	1467
Bhagalpur	657,827	1272

The shrinking zone of influence of trade centres and the increasing number of markets are also related to the number of streams intersecting the region. It is quite obvious that in the entire belt of the Kosi, the Ganga, the Gandak, the Sone, etc., the trade centres have very small market areas. In these areas the streams are great barriers in the movement of freight, and where there are a number of streams to be crossed to reach a market the range of cart travel is particularly restricted.

So far as goods of a higher order are concerned, the cities and the larger regional centres occupy a different position. They serve much larger areas and population and their trade zones are not restricted by the smaller centres, rural or urban.

HIERARCHY OF MARKET CENTRES

The hierarchy of market centres consists of several smaller places, overlaid by successively smaller number of larger places and culminating with the city of Patna. The higher an urban area stands in this pyramidal structure, the more numerous and diversified are its business establishments and the more complex its relationship with other places in the system. The principal trade centres in the Bihar Plain are normally the headquarter towns of all districts. These are served by a network of subsidiary trade centres represented by the subdivisional headquarter towns or other towns of similar size, down to rurban villages and market villages.

To measure the hierarchy of market centres, the number of central functions at a centre seems to be the most suitable criterion. A detailed field work was undertaken in September-November, 1970 and the number of central functions at each trade centre was tabulated. The list of functional types identified is given at the end of this chapter.

We may divide the trade centres into four classes of hierarchy, viz., cities, towns, rurban centres and market villages containing at least 100 shops. The number of centres which have less than 100 shops are innumerable and their identification and classification is both tedious and without justification.

Patna is the regional capital of the Bihar Plain having 156 types of functions. It thus has an influence over the whole State of Bihar. The other six cities are Muzaffarpur, Darbhanga, Gaya, Bhagalpur, Munger and Biharsharif, while Arrah and Chapra are also near this mark and discharge similar trade functions. All these are district headquarters. Other district headquarters, like Motihari, Saharsa and Purnea are lower in the hierarchy of market centres. At these places, retail shops of almost all the commodities are found. Retail business of specialised nature such as embroidery, fishing equipment, steel furniture, toys, glass and porcelain, etc. are not available in the smaller towns, but are found in cities only.

The towns are in the next lower order of specialisation. Here the types of functions vary from 75 to 113 in number. Towns have shops like those of dry cleaners, bedding stores, watches, rubber stamps and seals, newspaper vendors, radios, boxes, trunk, suitcases, etc., which are not found in the rurban centres. Rurban centres, whose specialisation consists of wholesale grain markets, cement shops, fertilizer stores, book-stall, medical stores, etc., are centres of the next order. Due to their smaller trade area such centres specialise in selling goods which are locally consumed and do not attract people from larger distances. Villages, the lowest order centres, contain shops like grocer, halwai (restaurant), pan (betel), bidi (leaf cigarettes), cloth, lac, bangles, flour-mills, etc.

Amongst the retail trade shops in the Bihar Plain, the grocery group is most important. Such shops sell cereals and pulses, spices, jaggery, oil, ghee, condiments, tea, coffee, indigenous drugs, dry fruits, saffron, tinned goods, foodstuffs, cigarettes and a number of other miscellaneous articles. The retail shop-keepers get their stock from the local wholesale dealers either on cash or credit and get a good margin of profit at the lower order centres. Rural settlements as centres of trade and commerce and containing shops of this group are widely and fairly distributed over the region.

THE ROLE OF TRANSPORT IN THE LOCATION AND DEVELOPMENT OF COMMERCIAL CENTRES

Though different modes of transport play an important role in trade,[8] railways are the leading carrier of goods because of their capacity of bulk transport. Next in importance is the road transport. The most important routes are furnished by the National Highways and the State Highways which connect all the important trade centres of the Bihar Plain.

The development of means of transport has made a great impact on market centres in the region. The larger centres have good connection of rail, road and waterways. In Saran, Champaran and Muzaffarpur districts, all the important trade centres are well connected by the railways and metalled roads. In Darbhanga district, Samastipur was connected by a broad gauge line from Barauni in 1962, providing the only area where broad gauge line is found in

North Bihar. Elsewhere, broad gauge railways are found only in South Bihar Plain, while metre gauge lines are the rule in North Bihar. With the development of modern transport, the traditional bullock carts have not been eliminated, rather their number has enormously increased. Trade through water has, however, declined. Darbhanga, Muzaffarpur and Champaran are now directly connected with Nepal both by railways and roads via Jainagar, Sitamarhi and Raxaul facilitating international trade.

In Champaran and Saran districts there are a number of trade centres. In these areas transport lines are well established. Railways are more important in Champaran, while both roads and railways play an equal role in Saran district. In Muzaffarpur and Darbhanga, development of transport has taken place along narrow belts due to numerous parallel rivers. Consequently, there are few trade centres and most of them are located along the railway lines.

It has already been observed that free movement of land produce and other goods from different areas was hampered due to the lack of proper transport facilities in the districts of Saharsa and Purnea. This condition still persists. The roads are extremely few, while railway communications are lacking in the Kosi Belt. In this area, therefore, most market centres are small. For example, Nirmali, a very important trade centre in Saharsa district, has very little to do with adjoining centres of Saharsa, Madhepura or Supaul. This is entirely due to poor communications. Lack of market centres has resulted in larger trade zones which is misleading and cannot be compared to conditions in other parts of the Bihar Plain.

In the western part of Bhojpur district, markets have a marginal location.[9] Buxar, Dumraon, Arrah and Behea are located on the northern margin along the railway line. These are old established markets. Mohania, Kudra, Sasaram and Dehri lie on the southern margin along the Grand Chord railway line and the Grand Trunk Road. Sasaram is the most important amongst them. The markets of Nokha, Bikramganj and Piro are aligned along the Arrah-Sasaram Light Railway and its parallel road. Only one small centre namely, Kochas lies in the interior.

In the central part of South Bihar Plain, there is a close mesh of metalled roads and railway lines, so that market centres are more uniformly distributed. Generally, the catchment areas of the market centres became smaller and the number of markets increases from west to east. In the western part of Patna and Gaya districts, Bihta, Daudnagar, Aurangabad and Paliganj have trade zones elongated from north to south along the road. Further east, Masaurhi, Jehanabad, Tekari and Rafiganj have market areas elongated from east to west.

In eastern South Bihar Plain, Munger is favourably situated for trade both by rail and river. The most important river marts are Munger, Simaria and Gogri on the Ganga and Khagaria on the Burhi Gandak. Munger, Barahiya, Lakhisarai, Jamalpur, Sheikhpura and Bariarpur are the chief centres of trade connected by the railways. In Bhagalpur district the largest centre is Bhagalpur, followed by Sultanganj, Barahat and Banka.

While trade areas are relatively small in a zone near the Ganga on account of better transport facilities, they are much larger in the south along the Scarp Belt. Here the lack of transport facilities makes collection and distribution of goods localised in only a few centres, resulting in large than normal trade zones. Bhabua, Sherghatti, Jhajha and Banka are centres of this type and have flourished on account of a lack of rivals in their vicinity.

TABLE 19.3 : FUNCTIONAL TYPES OF SHOPS

A. *Food, Drinks and Intoxicants*: Grocer, Grain Retail, Grain wholesale, Hotel, Toddy, Halwai (Sweet meats), Cooperative store, Vegetables, Fish, Meat, Bakery, Confectionary, Poultry and Eggs, Tobacco leafs, Bidi(Leaf cigarette), *pan*, Tea stall, Ice cream, Milk, Banana, Fruits, Wine and Bar, Coffee House, Residential Hotel, Opium and *Ganja* (Marijuana), Curd, Dry fruits and nuts, Parched Grain, Tobacco *(Hookah)*, Butter and Ghee, *Sattu* (parched grain flour), Cold Drinks, Tea Wholesale, Flour Mills, Rice Mills.

B. *Textiles*: Embroidery, Drycleaner, Cloth Wholesale, Cloth Retail, Laundry, Caps, Wool, Ready-made Clothes for Adults, Ready-made Clothes for Children, Ready-made

Clothes for Gents, Lady's Tailors, Gent's Tailor, Children's Tailor, Khadi Cloth (Hand Spun), Handloom Cloth, Dyer, Cotton. Woollens, Hosiery.

C. *Wood and Wood Materials*: Saw Mill, Wooden Furniture, Timber.

D. *Steel Machinery, Vehicles and Electricals*: Steel structurals, Radio, General Machinery, Cycles and Cycle parts and repairing, Steel Furniture, Automobiles, Motor parts and Repairing Motor Cycles and Scooters, Motor Cycle Repairing, Electrical goods, Utensils, Steel Grills, Agricultural Equipments, Fodder Cutting Machines, Electrical Repairing, Hardware, Sewing Machine, Steel Trunks, and Boxes, Stainless Steel Utensils, Electric Fans, Aluminium Utensils, Printing Press, Typewriters, Cement Grills, Guns.

E. *Leather*: Gents' Shoes, Shoe-repairing, Lady's Shoes, *Chappals* (Sandals), Leather wares, Shoe-making.

F. *General Merchandise*: Book Stall, Metal Engineering, Jewellery, Lac goods. Barber Saloons, Bangles, Wholesale, Bangles Retail, Stationery, Crockery, Glassware, Consumers Cooperative Store, Envelopes, Rubber Stamps. Watches and Clocks, Watch Repairing, Photographic Studio. Lantern. Fountainpen, Scientific Equipment, Newspaper, Rope and String, Party Decorators, Earthen Ware, Carpets, Handicraft from Leaf and Bamboo, Lottery Tickets, Blood Bank, Bedding and Up-holestry, Commercial Institutions, Fishing Lines and Nets, Seeds, Book Binding, Optician, Tyre, Batteries, Plastic Goods, Cooking Gas, *Pooja* Articles, Magazines, Paper Flowers, Crockery and Furniture Hiring.

G. *Chemicals and Pharmaceuticals*: Medicine, Fertilizers, Homeo Medicine, Surgical Instrument, Ayurvedic Medicine, Unani Medicine.

H. *General Repairing*: Blacksmith, Utensil Repairs, Picture Frames, Gold Smith, Fan Repairing.

I. *Fuel*: Coal Depot, Kerosene Oil Wholesale, Petrol Pump, Fire Wood.

J. *Recreation*: Cinema Hall, Musical Store, Sport Goods, Toys, Dancing Girls, Musical Bands, Gramophone Records.

K. *Building Material*: Cement, Bomboos, Burnt Bricks, Sand, Quick Lime, Paints.

REFERENCES

1. E. Ullman: "A Theory of Location of Cities," *American Journal of Sociology*, Vol. XLVI, May, 1941, p. 855.
2. John R. Borchert: *Upper Midwest Urban Change in the 1960's*, Minneapolis, June, 1968.
3. B.J.L. Berry : "Systematic Variations of the Hierarchy," In *Geography of Market Centres and Retail Distribution*, New Jersey, Prentice Hall, 1965, p. 32.
4. *Ibid.*, p. 35.
5. *Ibid.*, pp. 38-39.
6. W.J.Reilly: "The Law of Retail Gravitations, New York, 1931,"Quoted by B.J.L. Berry: *Geography of Market Centres and Retail Distribution*, op. cit., p. 40.
7. *Ibid.*, p. 41.
8. E. Ahmad: *Bihar: A physical, Economic and Regional Geography*, Ranchi, 1965, p. 192.
9. Jagdish Singh : *Transport Geography of South Bihar*, Banaras Hindu University, 1964, p. 198.

Fig. 19.1.

Centres of Trade and Commerce : Area and Population Served

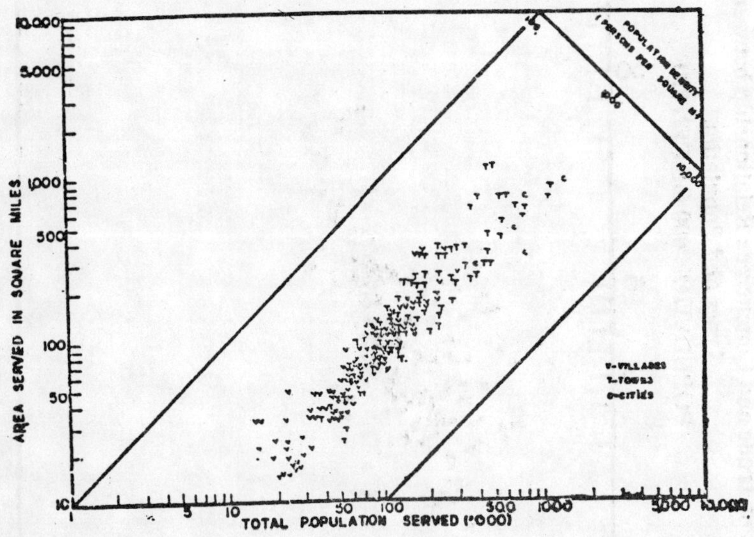

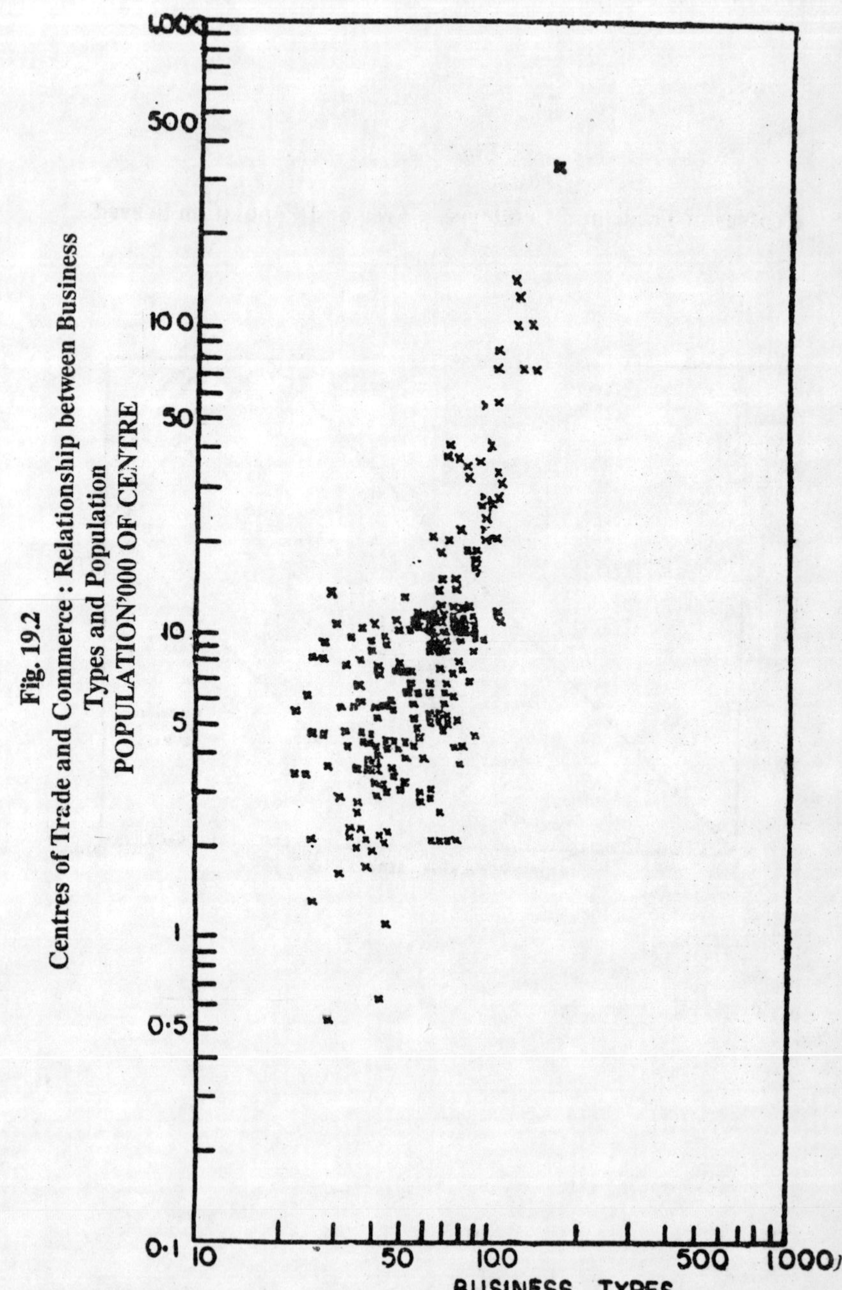

Fig. 19.2
Centres of Trade and Commerce : Relationship between Business Types and Population

Fig. 19.3.

Centres of Trade and Commerce: Relationship between Population and Functional Units

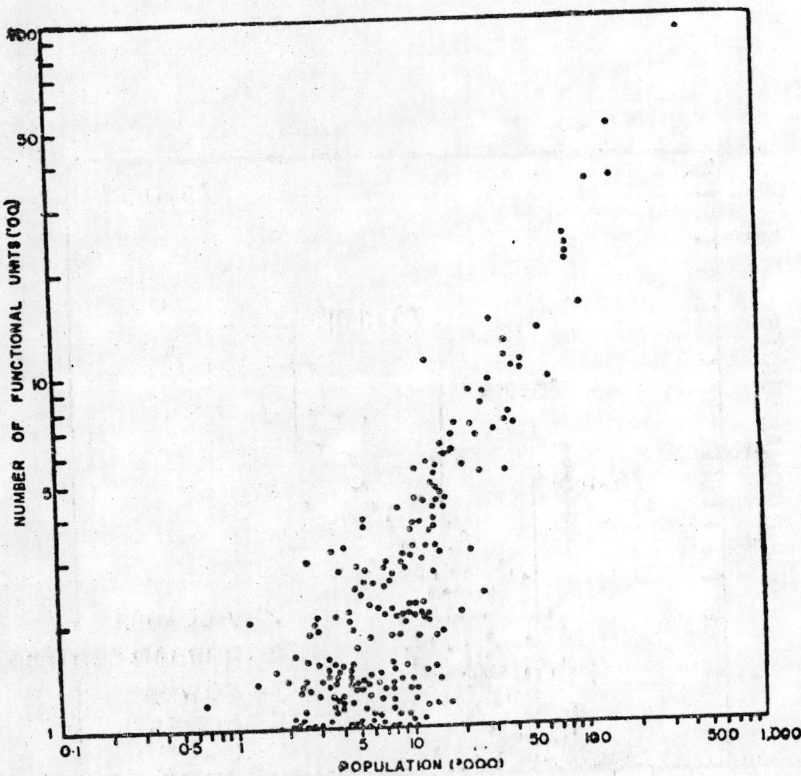

Fig. 19.4

Centres of Trade and Commerce Hierarchy and Functional Relationships

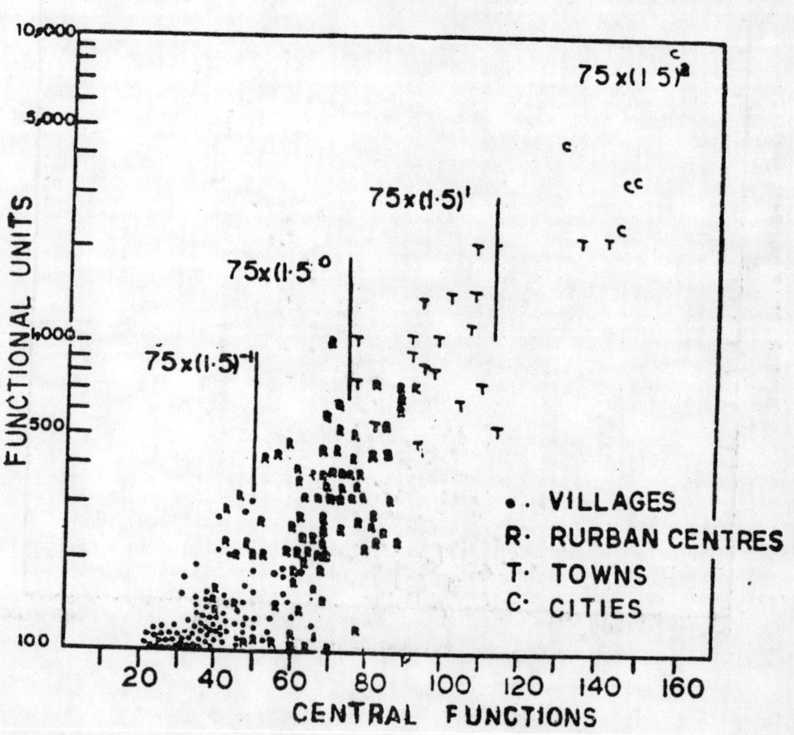

Fig. 19.5

Bihar Plain: Retail Trade Zones

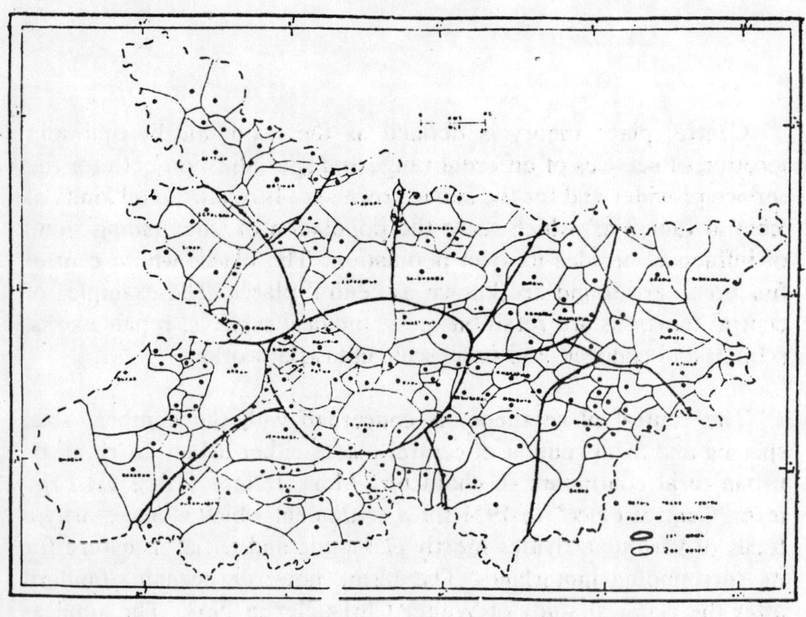

TWENTY

CENTRAL PLACE HIERARCHY

Central place theory is defined as the economically optimum location of services of different range and specialization both for the service provider and for the service receiver[1]. It relates to all kinds of 'central functions' which serve the population of surrounding 'zone of influence' besides its own population. The places where central functions are found are known as central places. The examples of central functions are retail business, medical services, repair works, schools and colleges, and small scale industrial works.

The central place theory is concerned with the number, size, spacing and arrangement of central places either urban[2] or rural[3] or urban-rural continuum in character. Mark Jefferson first used the term 'Central Place'[4] in 1931 for a settlement which is necessarily a focus of various activities mostly economic and social in nature for its surrounding hinterland. The term, however became standard after the classical study of Walter Christaller in 1953[5]. The application of various theories and studies on central places has increased rapidly since World War II. Christaller's hypothesis on the degree of 'centrality' of a place was based on the number of telephone connections at a place as the prime criterion for the respective importance of the centre. As it has turned out, this is only one of the possibilities for determination of centrality of places and the categorising of their functional importance[6], and many other parametres can be suggested for the purpose.

Much of the work relating to central place theory has been concerned with the identification of hierarchies of settlements as central places. These hierarchies were determined through the employment of a variety of criteria. But there remained the problem of a common measure of all functions. The centrality of a place, as Christaller pointed out, cannot be determined simply by the sum of its central functions[7]. He, therefore, considered the population of a place, in relation to an index calculated from the number of telephone connections in that place. But according to Ullman[8] such a measure would not seem to be valid for a country where telephones are used extensively for non-central functions. In India, where telephone connections are mostly confined to larger towns, such a study becomes particularly meaningless.

Another method would be to group the settlements in terms of the 'scale of their equipment'[9]. This measure either examines the overall facilities found within a settlement[10]; or makes use of indicator functions[11]. These methods again are largely applicable to the urban centres and it is difficult to determine their importance or their extent of impact upon the surrounding countryside. Hence a realistic method of market area definition is based upon consumer behaviour data collected in rural areas.[12] The more complex market centres are classified on the basis of these data. Overlapping areas, and the relationships between market area characteristics and the central place hierarchy are considered.

Classical Central Place Theory

The work done by Christaller and Losch regarding the spatial structure of economic development through nucleated settlements come under classical central place theory. Christaller pointed out that the number of retail establishments and total population give only the aggregate importance of a central place. According to Preston[13] "the term nodality stands for the aggregate importance of a placc as a providcr of central goods and services both for its own residents and for the consumers, and the term centrality will stand for the importance of a place as a provider of central goods and services in excess of the needs of its own residents". Christaller's each order of central places would be uniformly spaced in a hexagonal pattern. In marketing principle of central places (k = 3 network) the frequency of occurrence of different levels of market areas follows the geometric progression of 1, 3, 9, 27, 81, 243, ..., n, at successively lower levels of hierarchy; in transport principle of (k = 4 network) the progression of occurrence of market areas is 1, 4, 16, 64, 256, ..., n; but in administrative principle of k = 7 network the frequency of the occurrence of market areas is 1, 7, 49, 343, 2401, ..., n (Fig.20.1).

Central place theory is a deductive model from abstract to reality. It gives the regional planner normative construct against which the reality can be compared. The model can be constructed on the basis of hexagonal hierarchical lattice and spacing of central places, and comparison could be made with the real world situations, so that the alternative choices adopted or the gap may be filled for the future provision of service facilities, and the optimum location of central places on the principle of least-cost effort. The basic assumptions of Christaller's (1933) central place model are as follows:

1. the landscape is an isotropic plain, having equal geographical conditions throughout the region,
2. that people and their demand for goods and services are equally distributed,
3. the accessibility to all places is the same,
4. the central places are service centres which depend entirely upon the trade of their zone of influence,
5. all functions found in the lower-order central places are also found in the higher order central places; and
6. that the sellers and buyers act as service optimizers.

The last point shows that the principle of least-cost effort underlies in the central place theory. In such a situation consumers are moving to the higher order central places only for higher order goods. This facilitates the lucrative businessmen that in which place the location of a particular firm may be profitable.

In 1954, Losch used the same hexagonal lattices for his theoretical landscape but he did not consider fixed K system (k = 3, k = 4, and k = 7) as Christaller. He developed a more sophisticated form of *economic landscape* by superimposing the various hexagonal systems. By superimposing all the lattices on one point, and rotating them he achieved six 'city rich sectors', and six city poor sectors.

In his first step Losch derived a spatial demand cone in order to prove why Christaller's triangular-hexagonal spatial patterns were the most efficient. Later on he discovered that Christaller's K = 3, K = 4 and K = 7 networks were the first three cases in an entire progression of market area sequences in which the spacing of centres or order could be calculated by the equation of

$$dn = dn - 1 \sqrt{K}$$

where K is the hierarchy ratio and dn-1 is the spacing of the next lower order of centres. The market area patterns of central places found out by Losch are shown in Fig.20.2. Centres are located with respect to the hexagons in three possible ways: on apex K = 3 and K = 12; on the middle of the edge K = 4,9, 16 and 25 and within the hexagon as K = 7, 13, 19 and 21.

Losch devised an integrated hierarchy of central places incorporating all these possible arrangements of hexagons; so that it may reflect the complexities of real world. He made his economic landscape around a single metropolitan centre using all the ten hexagonal lattices of market areas. Hence in Losch network each place has one common place i.e., the metropolis. Then he rotates the separate patterns of network around the metropolis until the maximum coincidence of central places is achieved. The result is a division of the region into six city rich and six city-poor sectors (Fig.20.3). City-rich sectors show the functional specialization and a well developed connection of transportation routes.

Thus the contribution of Losch is mainly regarding the market areas, because his K values are variable. In making the central place hierarchy he considered the bottom-top approach. Losch also hypothesized that individual demand decreases as the distance of the consumer increases from the point where the goods are offered.

Modern Central Place Theory

Berry and Garrison[14] emphasized that retail establishments and consumer services should be the focus of central place study. They relaxed the assumption of isotropic plain surface of Christaller by introducing the concept of range of goods and demand cone. Dacey[15] analyses the spatial aspects of central places and uses the regional method to compare the observed pattern with three expected distributions: (a) hexagonal distribution, (b) random distribution, and (c) the clustered distribution.

Recently it has been considered that the central place theory as formulated by Christaller gives a picture of particular time period although settlement evolved through a longer period of time, hence Curry[16] emphasized the need to develop a dynamic central place theory and highlighted that the time factor in central place activities is the key to the understanding of geography.

From the Abstract to the Real World

Hexagonal service areas have been observed in Southern Germany by Christaller (1933), in East Anglia, Great Britain (Berry, 1967), and in parts of China before the 1950's (Skinner, 1954)[17]. However, it is only in old, established and stable human landscapes where central places are predominantly found. Although both trade areas and hierarchies of central functions can be distinguished in the real world, they rarely display the regular patterns described above in the real world with respect to the theoretical landscape. The reason for this is that the real world is much more complex than the theoretical landscape. The distortions of the model in the real world are caused by:

(a) the uneven distribution of population,
(b) variations in purchasing power and spending patterns,
(c) the unequal travelling facility to different directions,
(d) the failure of consumers to act as optimizers,
(e) the non-service function of many urban settlements, and
(f) central places of different ages provide varying technological and organizational influence.

Maximum and Minimum Trade Areas

For each central function, be it a commodity sold or service provided, there is a 'threshold'. This refers to the number of customers necessary for the central function to be viable, i.e. for the shopkeeper to make sufficient profit, or for a government service to serve sufficient people that the service providers regard their activity as worthwhile.

Suppose in planning a primary school there is a rule that the school should have at least 100 pupils to be worth the expense of construction and the provision of textbooks and teachers. This threshold of 100 pupils can be translated into a population threshold if the age structure of the surrounding population is known. For instance, 25% of the total population might be between 7 to 14 years old, the primary school going age. It means to obtain 100 potential pupils there needs to be a population of 400. Using the population density figure for the area, the threshold population of 400 can be converted into a threshold area which can be drawn as a circle. If the population density of the area is 10 persons per km^2 then the threshold area should be 40 Km^2. Using the formula for the area of a circle (πr^2) the radius of the threshold area or minimum trade area is found to be just over 3.5 Kms.

$$\text{area of circle} = \pi \text{ radius}^2$$

$$40 = 3.14 \times r^2$$

$$r^2 = 40/3.4$$

$$r^2 = 12.4$$

$$r = 3.52 \text{ Km.}$$

In the simplified, theoretical landscape these will be circular but when 'packed' to ensure that all parts of an area are served they will become hexagonal in shape (Fig. 20.4). When the assumptions are relaxed and the complexities of the real world allowed to enter the model, these hexagons may become distorted.

In sparsely populated areas where the purchasing power is low, in order to accumulate sufficient demand for a commodity to make it profitable a large threshold area would have to be served because the people in such a rural or peripheral areas are beyond the range of the service. It means in order to have a profit from the sale the minimum trade area exceeds maximum trade area.

In such a situation generally the street hawkers or the suppliers of goods and services move in their trade area. This increases the service area and fulfilling the threshold demand. Throughout India such patterns have been now regularised in the form of periodic markets. Even then the hawkers are serving the area in the gap of two periodic markets especially in the off days. In this way, they move around in a cyclical way to different periodic markets in the area, and coming back to the same place once in a week. In the state of Bihar, India, the distance of one periodic market from another is hardly 5 Kilometres which could easily be covered on foot. For rural townships in Zambia, the radius of the area served is about 9 Kms and for the market town approximately 22 Kms (Fig. 20.5). It means that the distance between villages and rural townships is about 5 Kms.; between rural townships and market towns about 16 Kms; and from village to market town not more than 22 Kms.[18]

Functional Hierarchy of Central Places

Any study of central places has necessarily to include both the urban and the rural settlements, as in any scheme of hierarchy, towns, perform more central functions than villages. However, in the transitional cases consisting of rurban centres, villages may sometimes be central places of a high order than the smaller towns. The purpose of determining the hierarchy of central places would be defeated if we confine our study to rural settlements only. In the following pages, therefore, both towns and villages have been examined together to determine their centrality. The villages alone form the basis for further studies.

Most of the settlements have acquired their urban status due to their achievement in special socio-economic functions. They have grown to be the chief centres of an area because such functions are retail shops, wholesale, warehouses, banks, garages and offices have developed to me[illegible] the requirements not merely of the town's own population but c[illegible] that of the surrounding area. W. Christaller explained market areas in terms of the provision of services, constructed a theory with the help of smallest units of settlements which developed in areas of uniformity. He favoured that the most efficient system of clearly defining market areas should be based upon a hexagonal lattice. This geometrical form approaches close similarity of the circle, but a circular lattice suffers from the disadvantage of allowing unsupplied or overlapping areas (Fig. 20.4).

As 'the chief profession of a town is to be central to its rural surroundings' then the centre of the hexagon is the location of the 'central place'. Christaller clearly indicated that there should be mutual dependence between the central place and the supply region. In plain areas the equal spacing of settlements results in competition developing between them in the provision of services. Village shops, for example, usually stock a limited range of goods and thus villages are lower - order central places with small market area, whereas towns provide a wider range of services for a larger area and hence they are higher order central places. In case higher order and lower-order centres are considered to be equally spaced then the hexagonal market area of higher-order is larger than that of lower-order central places and the latter areas and functions must be contained or present in the former. Hence in this model, a hierarchy of central places is conceived, ranging from small hamlets to large towns.

In Christaller's hexagonal lattice, each hamlet is located at the meeting point of three uniform market areas and hence with equal number of people having equal ease of movement and equal purchasing power, one-third of the hamlets' trade will be with each central village. Hence the total hexagonal trade area is 2 around a village (one-third of six hexagon) plus one of its own market. Christaller used the term 'K value' to refer to the total number of settlements served by each central place. Hence in this case K = 3. He also assumed that in one region the K value would be fixed ranging from hamlets, villages, small towns and so on.

In case of the establishment of third-order (K = 3) centres the number of units of trade of the central place is 27 (Fig. 20.6) and the calculations are as follows:

(a) Six centres are located at the vertices of the hexagon each share their trade between 3 centres and therefore the central place A has $\frac{1}{3}$ = 2 units of trade.
(b) The other 12 peripheral settlements each share their trade between 2 centres and therefore A's share is $\frac{12}{2}$ = 6.

(c) Inside the hexagon is 18 other centres whose entire trade is directed towards A and therefore a further 18 units are added.

(d) The entire trade of A is conducted in that centre which provides 1 unit.

In this way, the total trade of A is found by summing up the above parts: i.e.,

$$2 + 6 + 18 + 1 = 27$$

As the hierarchy of the settlements is established so the trade of each central place develops as follows:

1, 3, 9, 27, 81, ...

i.e., $1, 3, 3^2, 3^3, 3^4$ ... (K = 3)

This model of central place suggests that it is possible that the function of such places controls their size of the supplying area, besides it offers a partial explanation that why settlements are scattered in the region differ in size. K = 3 hierarchy of central places in Southern Germany is as follows (Table 20.1).

Table 20.1 : Christaller's' Central Place Hierarchy in Southern Germany

(K = 3 network)

Class	Average Radius of Supplying Area in Km.	Typical Population Size
Market town	4.0	1,000
Central township	6.9	2,000
Country town	12.0	4,000
District city	20.7	10,000
State Capital	36.0	30,000
Provincial Capital	62.1	100,000
Regional capital	108.0	500,000

Source: W. Christaller; The Central Places in Southern Germany, English translation by C.W. Baskin, 1966.

CENTRALITY

Determination of central place importance is a universal problem in studies of space economies, and the only satisfactory model for its solution developed so far is the one offered by Christaller in 1933. His approach requires clarification both in operational definition of the concept of 'centrality' and its systematic measurement. Thus the areal distribution of the central place function was established in this study by applying the following modification of Christaller's model to places with 2500 or more inhabitants in 1960 and that appeared in the U.S. Census of Business for 1963 and 1972.[19]

$$C = R + S - \delta MF$$

where C = centrality, R = total sales in retail establishments, S = total sales in selected service establishments, δ = average percentage of median family income for a central place spent on retail and service goods, M = median family income in a central place, and F = the total number of families in central place. In this model R + S provides an estimate of total retail and service activity in a town, or its "nodality", while δMF provides an estimate of local consumption. The difference is an index of the volume of extra-local trade, or centrality. The results of this procedure were used to establish the magnitude of the central place function for places.

Table 20.2 : Weighing and Classification of Central Functions

	Functional indicators	I 20 points	II 15 points	III 10 points	IV 5 points
1.	Education	University	College	High School	X
2.	Medical	Medical College	X	Hospital	X
3.	Communicattion	X	X	Telephone Exchange	X
4.	Finance	X	Bank	X	X
5.	Transport	Airport	Railway Junction	Railway Station	Highways
6.	Administration	District Court	Sub-Divisional Office	Block Development Office	X
7.	Trade	X	X	Wholesale Market	X
8.	Recreation	X	Cinema	X	X
9.	% of total workers engaged in tertiary occupation	X	X	Over 50%	25 to 50%
10.	Diversity Index	X	9 functional indicators available	7 to 8 functional indicators available	5 to 6 functional indicators available

The author has investigated the central place system of the Bihar Plain by means of functional indicators covering the categories of education, medical facilities, trade, administration, communication, transport and employment in tertiary services. Each category is represented by one type of central function and most of the types have been sub-divided according to their position in the functional hierarchy. A score has been allotted to each of the central functions, irrespective of the number of occurrences (units) of that particular function as shown in Table 20.2.

The following criteria was adopted for selecting central places:

1. Only those centres are listed where at least three of the above functional indicators were present, irrespective of the functional units.
2. After the index had been calculated, weighting for functional diversification was added according to the scale given below:

Number of functional indicators present	Weighting for diversification
3 to 4	zero
5 to 6	5
7 to 8	10
8 & over	15

The central places distinguished on the above basis are mostly service centres and their centrality index depends entirely upon the hierarchy of the services located in them. However, in order to have an adequate influence upon the surrounding countryside as also to justify its nomenclature, a central place must also have a retail trade function which has not been considered above. For this purpose a ranking technique based on localisation coefficient of the retail trade units was applied[20]. This method is commonly used in industrial geography and gives a high value for centres having a large number of outlets for retail trade. The location coefficient is based on the number of shops located at a particular place in relation to the total number of shops in the area for centres of the same group, and is therefore, a measurement of centrality or degree of focality. The formula used is:

$$LC = \frac{t}{T} \times 100$$

where LC = the location coefficient of shops in the town or village,

t = number of shops in that centre, and
T = total number of shops in the entire urban area or rural area of the Bihar Plain.

The total number of shops in the urban areas of the Bihar Plain were found to be 71,073 and that in rural areas, 24,184. The location coefficient values for urban centres range from 13.04 for Patna and 0.02 for Lauthaha. In rural areas, the values are generally from 1.86 to 0.01. Multiplying the relevant location coefficient by the centrality index gave the final degree of centrality which is considered here as centrality value:

CV = C1 x LC,
where CV = centrality value,
C1 = centrality index for services,
LC = Location coefficient for retail trade.

The final list of all central places in the Bihar Plain shows a total of 414 centres including 87 towns and 327 villages. A closer examination of the figures of centrality value which range from 2,999 to 1, reveals that the data has a very wide range. There is a large concentration of units near the lower values with a rapid progression towards the highest values. Various statistical techniques such as Mean and Standard Deviation, Median and Percentile, Arithmetic progression, etc. were applied to determine the natural breaks in the progression of values. It was found, however, that the data is most amenable to the order of geometrical progression and this alone is able to give the true picture of hierarchy and natural groupings. To find out the geometrical progression, logarithms were used to determine the break points. The following breaks in centrality values emerged:

3.47697, 2.98026, 2.48355, 1.98684, 1.49013, 0.99342, and 0.49671.

The result is given in Table 20.3.

TABLE 20.3 : **Hierarchy of Central Places in the Bihar Plain**

Order of Central Places	Range of centrality values	Actual No.of centres	Theoreticall progression of centres accor ding to K=3	No. of towns	No. of villages
I	2,999 & over	1	1	1	-
II	2,998 to 955.4	3	2	3	-
III	955.3 to 304.4	7	6	7	-
IV	304.3 to 97.0	32	18	27	5
V	96.9 to 30.9	62	54	33	29
VI(a)	30.8 to 9.8	125	162	15	110
VI(b)	9.7 to 3.1	108			
	3.0 & below	76	486	1	183

According to K = 3 network used by Christaller, the number of centres in each size class should progress as 1, 2, 6, 18, 54,.... and the progression of market areas of each level should be 1, 3, 9, 27, 81, ... It will be seen that the actual distribution closely corresponds with the theoretical distribution for higher levels, and fails only in the lowest order centres[21]. On the basis of the above groupings of centrality values in Table 20.3 a map of central place hierarchy in the Bihar Plain has been prepared, which gives a clear idea of K = 3 network of central place in the region. A comparative map showing the theoretical model is shown in Fig.20.7 which closely corresponds with the actual hierarchy observed.

Fig. 20.7 shows that there is a group of central places on both banks of the river Ganga. This is clearly suggestive of the potential impact of a well developed communication system on the evolution of central places.

The highest rank is that of Patna, with Arrah, Muzaffarpur, Darbhanga, Munger, Nawada and Gaya forming a well defined hexagon of second order. This is the only complete hexagon formed in the region under study. Other hexagons of the same order are incomplete and in the theoretical model are centred around Siwan, Saharsa, Sasaram and Banka. None of these centres are central places of the same magnitude as Patna. Saharsa is very small but divisional headquarter while the other three are subdivisional centres. It is interesting to note that Sasaram and Siwan have higher centrality values than that of Saharsa, while Banka is a centre of the

5th order. (Fig.20.8).

Both Sasaram and Siwan are under the profound metropolitan influence of Varanasi, which is less than 125 kms away and inhibits their growth. Banka is located in hilly tract with poor transport facilities and has little scope of development. Saharsa, although a divisional headquarter is located in an area which is economically backward due to ravages of the river Kosi. It thus exhibits primitive urban development and can never be placed in the same rank as Patna.

It is obvious that the observed pattern does not fit in with the theoretical pattern because of administrative, transport and economic limitations as also the influence of centres lying out-side the study area. It is only in the region around Patna where the transport network is adequate for a logical evolution of the central place that the hierarchy corresponds with the theoretical pattern.

As is to be expected the towns generally occupy a higher place in the hierarchy of central place than the villages (Fig.20.8). All central places in the first three groups are towns or cities. In the fourth group, out of 31 central places only four are rural settlements. In the fifth group 33 are towns and the rest 29 are villages. On the other hand, 293 centres of the sixth order are rural settlements. The five rural settlements belonging to central places of the fourth order are Hilsa in Nalanda District, Bel in Sitamarhi, Ramnagar in West Champaran, Mairwa in Siwan and Balia Lakhminian in Bagusarai district respectively. These central places are important rurban development.

According to the theoretical hierarchy, there should be 162 central places of the order VIA and 486 of the order VIB. In the observed pattern, however, the corresponding figures are 125 and 184 respectively. A lower number of smaller centres indicates that there has been a lack of development of central functions in the rural areas of Bihar Plain. Due to economic backwardness, over-dependence on subsistence agriculture and lack of transport facilities, many centres with a potential location as central places have refused to grow. Christaller's theory was proposed as a rational scheme of general economic theory or the most favourable state[22]. It was not considered applicable fully to a backward area like the Bihar Plain even by Christaller himself.

If we consider the pattern of network rather than the absolute centrality values calculated, it would appear that the hierarchy of central places is well established and closely corresponds with theoretical model. The actual location of central places on the map shows a close correspondence with each other, and considering the distortion affected by transport routes (Fig. 20.9) and rivers, no closer correspondence can be expected.

In the vast agricultural plains of Bihar the development of central place is dependent upon minor points of focus that initially were not associated with retail trade. Cross-roads, flour mills, post-offices, railway stations and police stations were some of these. They provided a meeting place for the farmers. Enterprising businessmen took advantage of these facilities to open retail shops at such centres. This, in turn, led to the establishment of grain collecting centres, electric lines, telephones and other similar facilities. Combination of these elements led to greater centrality for some of the places, while competition between the growing centres created the pattern of a central place hierarchy.

The smallest central place in the study area is a village with basic public utility services such as an allopathic doctor, middle school, post-office and a metalled road connection. Villages of this category are closely spaced and may or may not have a retail marketing centre. They do, however, have a weekly or bi-weekly market known as *hat*.

Rural central places of a higher order generally provide services like a high school, telegraph office, dispensary, retail market, block development office and a bus stop or railway station. Such centres are located on the main transport routes between towns and are, therefore, interspersed between towns and rurban centres.

Further development of these facilities and the addition of a telephone exchange, bank, cinema, wholesale market, etc. led to the evolution of a rurban centre. We have discussed earlier the characteristics of rurban centres which include both smaller towns and larger villages. Villages which have grown into rurban centres are potential towns. A rise in their population coupled with functional segregation in land uses and increase in employment in tertiary services would make them eligible for classification as towns.

It would appear that the evolution and spacing of rural central places largely depends upon economic prosperity and transport facilities. Fig. 20.9 shows that there is a large concentration of central places on either side of the river Ganga, but their number decreases as we proceed towards the Himalayas or towards Chotanagpur Plateau. Also, the density and grade of central places decrease while the relative distance between them increases. This pattern fits in the economic prosperity of the two areas.

The Contributions of Central Place Study in Regional Planning

1. It guides the planner in identifying the existing hinterlands of localized or mobile services.
2. It helps in identifying the planner that which areas and which people are out of the reach of individual service or service centres.
3. It shows the planner that which centres are stronger in terms of available services and so could cater either for an increased local demand or for a demand in a larger hinterland.
4. It helps the regional planner to reorganise the central places in such a way so that they can combine hinterlands covering all people in that area.
5. It requires from the planner to keep up-to-date information for each district level systems of central places on the following headlines:

   (a) Population distribution,
   (b) Location of all government and private services,
   (c) Threshold values for individual service under different forms of management as for example mobile versus fixed businessmen, part-time versus full-time health worker, and
   (d) The real trade areas of various services demarcated on the basis of consumer behaviour pattern as against the assumed ones demarcated on the basis of gravity potential model.

The Values of Central Place Theory

1. It enables a comparative analysis of regional centres to be made.
2. It shows the interdependence of town and region.
3. A hierarchy of functions and settlements is devised.
4. The idea of competition between centres is stressed.
5. The intensity and spacing of centres suggests further investigation as to how these service centres have evolved and are changing their character at present.
6. On the basis of a theoretical structure it is possible to make a number of predictions about the pattern of future settlement location.

Criticisms of Central Place Theory

1. Christaller's Central Place Theory is concerned only with one central place activity, that of the servicing functions for the hinterland. Other aspects such as places of residence or industrial centres are not considered besides the sites of: availability of mineral resources, favourable climate, strategic position, growth of a port, railway expansion and urban 'overspill' requirements.
2. Central place theory may have played a significant part in the development of a settlement in an agricultural area, but works less well in industrial areas.
3. There may be planned delay in establishing full services in 'New Towns' until they increased their populations.
4. The theory does not work well in areas where the industries are expanding or retarding.

REFERENCES

1. L.M. Vanden Berg: *Central Place Theory and the Planning of Rural Service Centres in Africa;* Zambia Geographical Association: Occasional Study No. 11, 1981, p. 1.
2. W.A.V. Clark: "Consumer Travel Patterns and the Concept of Range", *Annals of the Association of American Geographers,* Vol. 58, June 1968, p. 386.
3. Om Prakash Singh: "Functions and Functional Classes of Central Places in Uttar Pradesh", *The National Geographical Journal of India,* Vol. XIV; 1968,pp. 1-2.
4. M.Jefferson: "The Distribution of World's City's Folks", *Geographical Review;* Vol.XXI; 1931,p. 453.
5. Walter Christaller: *Central Places in Southern Germany* (translated by C.W.

Baskin); Prentice Hall, New Jersey, 1966.

6. G. Kuluczka: "Central Places and Their Functional Areas in the Federal Republic of Germany" Paper read at the 21st International Geographical Congress, India, 1968 (unpublished).
7. Scot Peter: "The Hierarchy of Central Places in Tasmania", *The Australian Geographer,* 1968, p. 135.
8. E. Ullman: "A Theory of Location for Cities", *American Journal of Sociology,* Vol.6, 1940-41, p. 858.
9. H.E.Bracy: "Towns as Rural Service Centres", *Transactions and Papers, Institute of British Geographers,* Vol. 49, 1953, pp. 95-105.
10. H.E.Bracy: English Central Places, Identification, Distribution and Functions", in *Lund Symposium on Problems of Urban Geography,* 19th International Geographical Congress, 1960.
11. A.E. Smailes: "The Urban Hierarchy in England and Wales", *Geography,* Vol. 29, 1944, pp. 51-55.
12. G.Rowley: "Central Places in Rural Wales", *Annals of the Association of American Geographers,* Vol. 61, No. 3, 1971, pp. 537-550
13. R.E. Preston: "Two Centrality Models", *Yearbook Association of Pacific Coast Geographers;* Vol. 32,1970, p. 62.
14. B.J.L. Berry and W.L. Garrison: "Recent Developments of Central Place Theory", *Papers and Proceedings of Regional Science Association;* No. 4, 1958, p. 107.
15. M.F.Dacey: "Analysis of Central Place and Point Patterns by a Nearest Neighbour Method", *Lund Studies in Geography, Service B, Human Geography,* Vol. 24, 1962, pp. 55-75.
16. L.Curry: "A Classical Approach to Central Place Dynamics", *Geographical Analysis,* Vol. 1, 1969, pp. 272-282.
17. G.W. Skinner: "Marketing and Social Structure in Rural China", *Journal of Asian Studies,* Vol. 24, 1954, pp. 3 - 43.
18. Doxiadis Associates: *Consultants on Development and Ekistics;* Rural Townships in Zambia, General Report, Athens, 1967, p. 51.
19. R.E. Preston, *op. cit.*
20. W.K.D. Davies: "Centrality and the Central Place Hierarchy", *Urban Studies,* Vol. 4, 1967, p. 65.
21. B.J.L. Berry: *Geography of Market Centres and Retail Distribution;* Prentice Hall, New Jersey; 1967, p. 65.
22. W.K.D. Davies; *op. cit.,* p. 77.

Fig. 20.1

Hamlets, Villages and Towns in Fixed K Hierarchy of Christaller

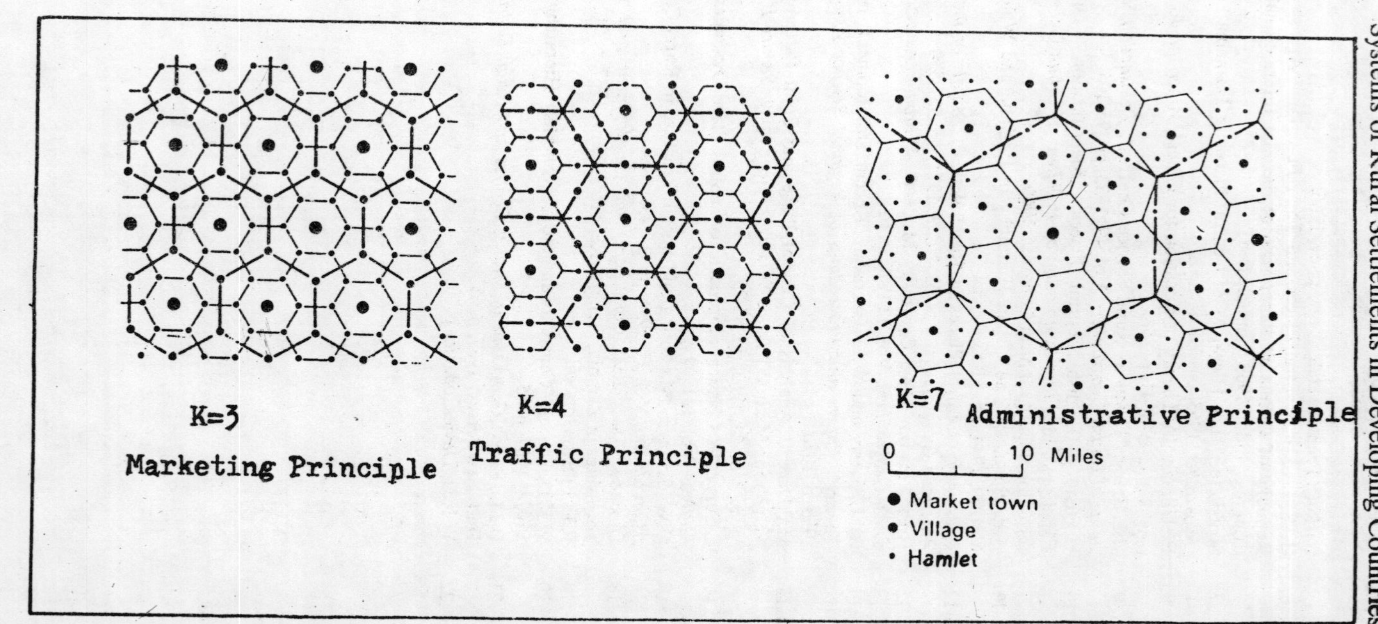

Fig. 20.2

The Nine Smallest Market Areas in Losch's

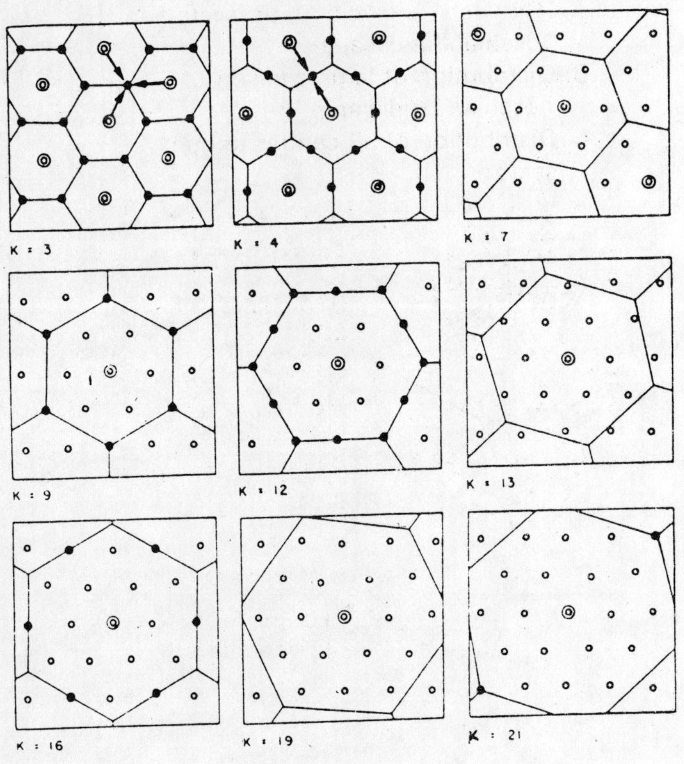

Fig. 20.3

Loschian Economic Landscape (After P. Haggett, 1965)

A. 'City rich' and 'city poor' sectors in Löschian landscape
B. Distribution of large cities in Löschian landscape
C. Distribution of all centres in one sector

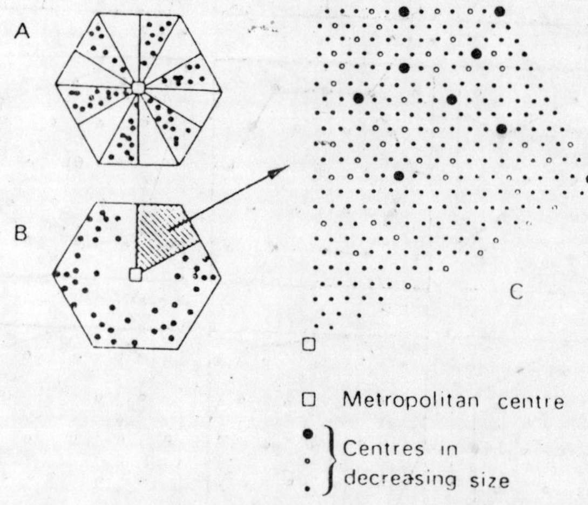

Fig. 20.4

The Packing of Trade Areas of Central Places

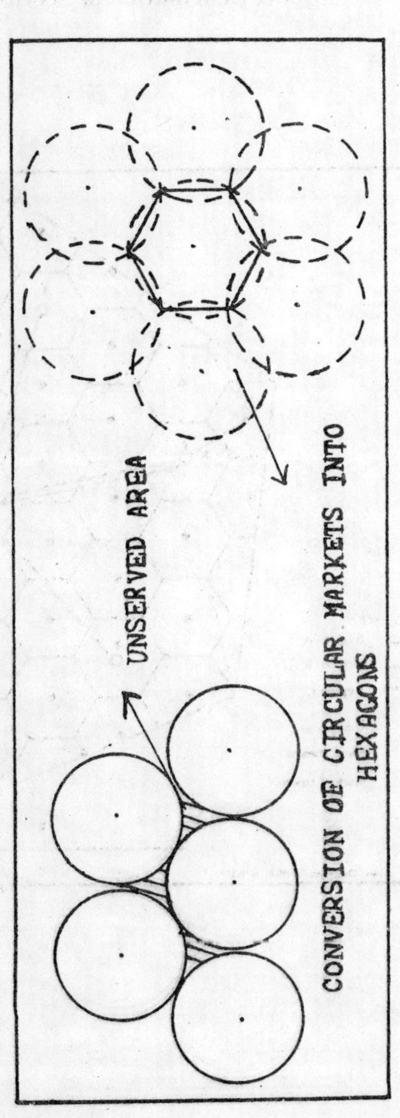

Fig. 20.5

Model Distribution of Service Centres in Zambia

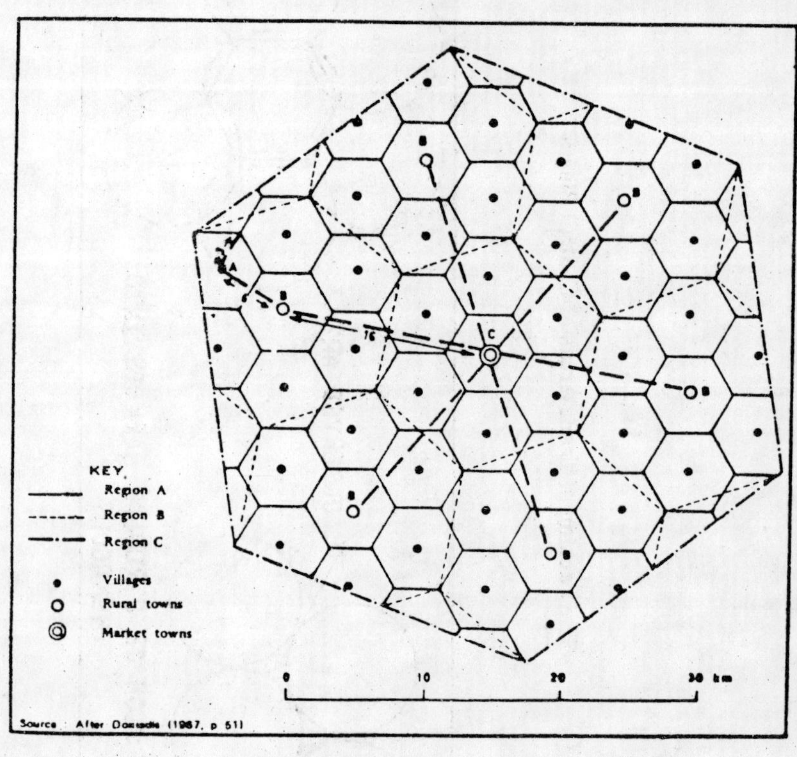

Fig. 20.6

Trade in a Third-order Hexagonal Area of Central PLaces

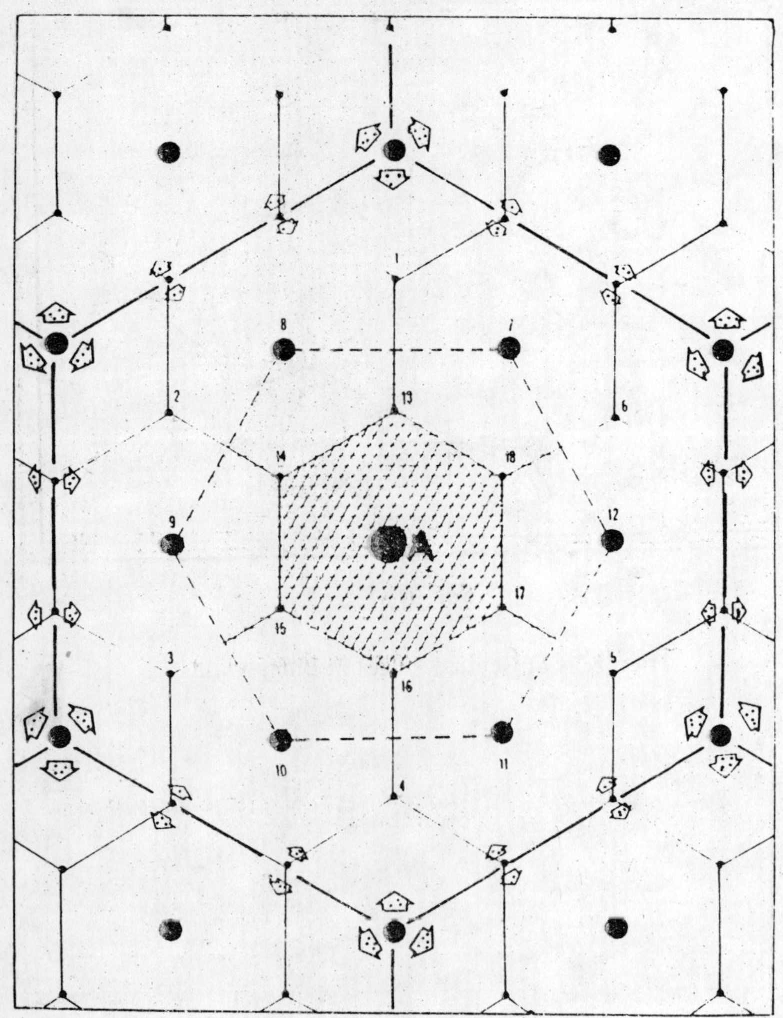

Fig.20.7

Bihar Plain : Central Place Hierarchy (Actual Pattern)

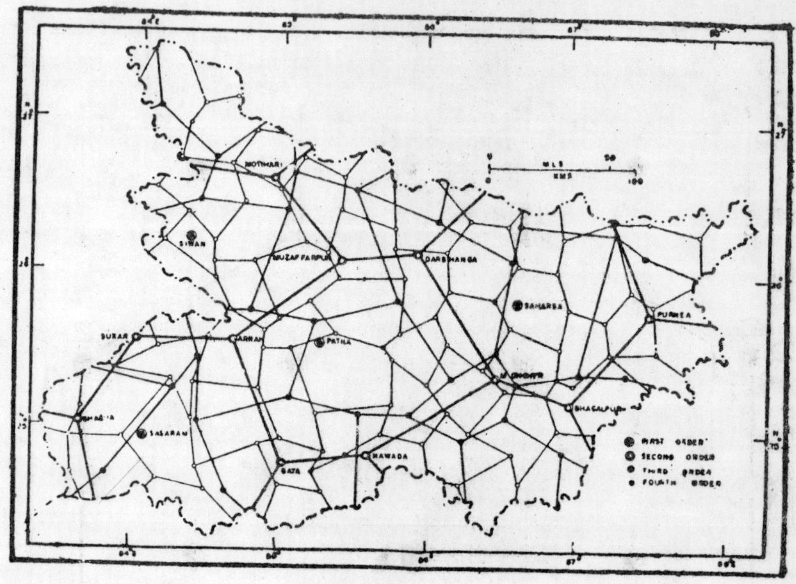

Fig. 20.8

Hierarchy of Central Places in Bihar Plain

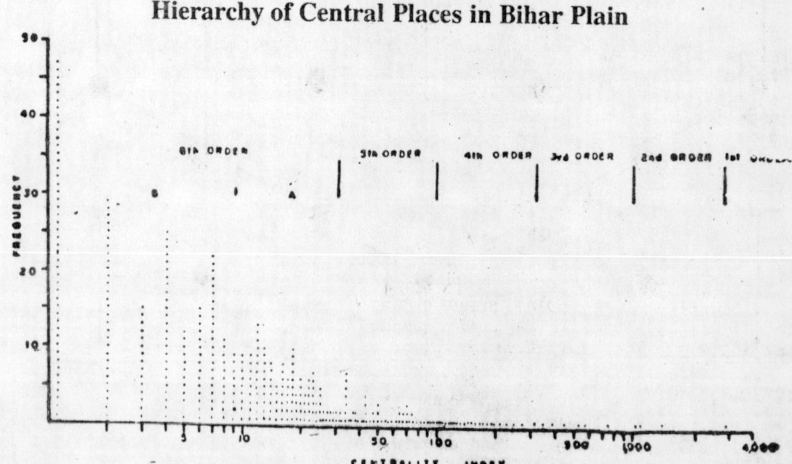

Fig. 20.9

Bihar Plain : State Bus Transport (Origin points and Destination

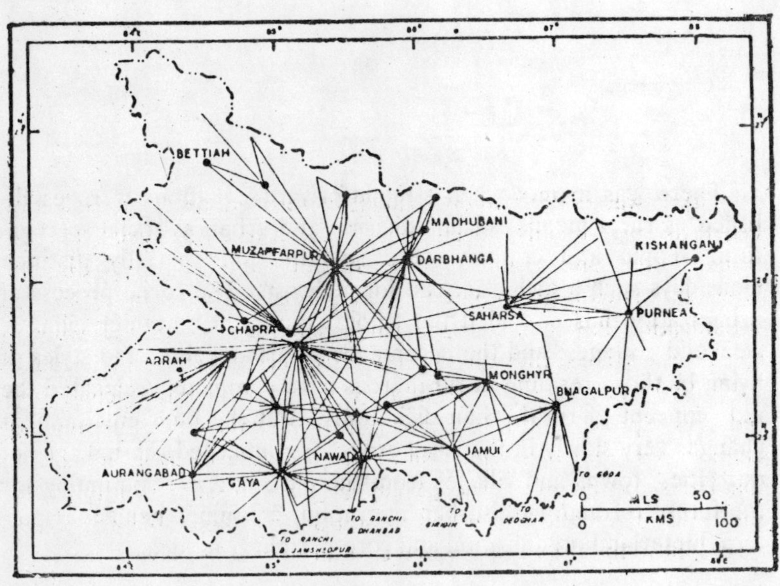

TWENTY ONE

RURAL-URBAN LINK

There was a time when straightforward equations were established as rural means, social cohesion and urban as social segregation. Town and country were socially and spatially distinct. Nowadays such a dichotomy no longer exists. The social process of urbanization has pervaded the whole country. Commuter villages, weekend cottages, and the acceptance of urban values and styles of living by those residing in rural areas have completely relegated the old concept of rural-urban dichotomy.[1] But the built environment changes very slowly in the rural areas. We inherited the linkages of our cities, towns and villages from the past, and are continuing for the future through rural-urban migration, consumer behaviour pattern, hinterland organization and core-periphery models.

Rural living is not very different from urban living, and with the universal availability of radio, newspaper and automobiles, the two rural and urban settlements have become a continuum rather than a dichotomy.[2] Further, the distinction between the two is not often clear-cut, specially in conditions of housing, facilities of shopping, manufacturing, transport, education, and the manner of living. For example, in the Bihar Plain, Noorsarai, Silao, Baheri, Kusheswarsthan and Baghopur are all designated as rural settlements in 1981 census but they are little different from the small towns in the area. Thus the line drawn between rural and urban for statistical or census purposes is necessarily arbitrary. The functions of the urban settlements constitute the main unifying bond between the people of the town and the zone of influence.[3] By virtue of such a distinct location and layout, the urban centres form a socio-economic hub for the whole, disseminating cultural influence, and acting as collecting and distributing centres of regional produce. The commuter relations between the urban places as centres of employment and the rural areas as a residence of the employees is another link between urban centres and their hinterland. A third form of inter-relation is provided by outdoor recreation. This interdependence may establish a community of interest among the people of a zone of urban influence.[4]

The rural activities are accommodated in villages and agricultural land connected with primary and secondary occupations, while urban activities are accommodated in shops, workshops, offices, warehouses and public buildings. The natural link between the two is provided by transport routes. The characteristics of rural settlements, their size, functions, spacing, layout and build vary regionally with the physical environment, density of population and with the character of human economies and culture.[5]

The close inter-relationship between rural and urban areas is provided by the daily quick delivery of perishable goods like milk and vegetables to the town dwellers. Such close tie-up depends upon the facilities of transport. Cities like Patna, Muzaffarpur, Bhagalpur, Gaya, Munger, Biharsharif and Darbhanga in India are easily accessible from their rural areas which form large city regions. On the other hand, the smaller towns with very poor accessibility have very small hinterlands. For example, Barbigha and Barahia in Munger; Murliganj and Birpur in Saharsa, Chakia in Champaran and Revelganj in Saran district, in India, are small towns with very small hinterlands.

Urban centres as regional administrative headquarters constitute another reason for the link between the town and the country.[6] The urban centres have a strong impact upon the rural settlements of the surrounding city region due to the expansion of urban built up land for residence, commerce, industry, transport, recreation and market gardening. Thus they affect both the character and structure of rural settlements, especially placing of rural dwellings.

It is, therefore, apparent that both towns and villages are interdependent and cannot be studied in isolation. It is true that they each have their own characteristics and to this extent may be said to have an independent location and functional structure. But where characteristics such as utility services, trade and commerce, administrative and other nodal functions, etc. have to be examined, the two must be studied together as part of the same continuum. The best example of this link is provided by the urban centres which include both towns and villages.

It can be readily seen that in all the studies of rural service centres, the towns occupy a higher position than that of the villages as centres of cultural activity. In this, the general hierarchy of cities, towns, rurban centres and rural settlements has a common application over the whole area. In area where urban centres are lacking or where smaller towns do not surround the parent city, some villages have emerged as major service centres, such as Koilwar in Bhojpur district Dalan in Katihar district, Sasamusa in Saran district and Dhaka in Champaran district. These villages are, therefore, most significant in the study region and have the highest potentiality of growth due to independent hinterlands of their own.

Urban centres are conspicuous by virtue of the services, they perform for the rural inhabitants. Centres of the highest ranks are Patna, Muzaffarpur, Gaya, Darbhanga, Arrah, Saharsa, Purnea, Biharsharif, Motihari, Barauni and others to name a few. It is apparent that the areas in their hinterlands would depend upon and, in turn, be served by these centres. In this connection G.K. Mishra[7] while delineating the 'rural-urban continuum' highlighted the spatial interaction at various levels of functional hierarchy of Central Places in Raichur district, India. He applied the principle of 'minimum aggregate travel distance' for making inter-regional adjustments in identifying the existing central places within the hinterland. All the central places are considered as growth foci which will develop into small towns of Raichur rural-urban continuum, bridging the existing gap between towns and rural settlements in Raichur district.

Review of Past Literature

Cities act as catalysts in introducing new innovations in rural areas, perhaps more slowly but nonetheless inevitably. Many rural settlements at the fringe of urban centres are rural or urban just because the municipal limit does not or does include them.

Besides these in India, the social structure is such that the separate grouping of urban centres as contrasted with rural areas is less efficient for the purpose of social analysis. This is because even those economic activities which are normally considered to be urban activities-textile manufacture, metal work, construction, the manufacture of chemicals and fertilizer, electric machinery and supplies, cement wholesale and retail trade, weaving apparel and food processing have segments of their labour force in rural areas.[8]

The social elements such as the prevalence of joint families have in some cities showed little differentiation from the age old rural tradition, and the prevalence of the same in an unanticipated manner in cities.[9]. Moreover, some of the studies of neighbourhoods of Indian cities have found much in common with rural social patterns.[10] As for example, in the entire area around the Asansol industrial complex, villages as well as towns might well be considered as one unified urban area as rapid urbanization turned the hinterland of each large factory into dormitory settlements for its workers.[11]

R.E. Pahl[12] (1966) in his book *Urbs in Rure* in London's rural-urban fringe of Hertfordshire found that 'a housewife who lives in a rural area, but who does all her shopping in a neighbouring town, may be participating in urban life as much as another housewife living in a peripheral urban estate'. This sharing of urban provisions-work, services, entertainment and so on-by people living in and believing themselves are parts of a village community. Ruth Crichton (1964) in her *Commuter' village* found that 'recent changes in the size and shape of her village have discouraged integrations with the Reading town'.

Rural communities can be isolated as separate systems for the purpose of academic study but this is an increasingly unreal exercise. In fact, many areas commonly referred to as rural are more urban than rural in all the more important aspects which go to make up the way of life of the individuals who comprise its resident population.[13]

Opler[14] in his study of "the extensions of Indian village" pointed out the common origin of villages and towns and descent shared with a cluster of surrounding villages; village exogamy creating kinship ties with other villages; caste assemblies cutting across village lines; customary work obligations of practical and ritual services in another rural community; pilgrimage to distant shrines and religious centres in towns, connections in towns, connections with market towns and with courts, land registration and records office, official of the government and agricultural-implement stores, and temporary out-migration for higher education in urban areas.

Besides, there are some examples that many artisans and small manufacturers of the former villages are becoming urbanized and hence the villagers must either go into the towns to get carpentry done or hire urban specialists to come to the village to perform the required job.

D.N. Majumdar reports "that one of the most important continuing contacts with the city is in the marketing of village surpluses, fruits, milk, grain and animal products. For this purpose, each individual may own or hire his own bullock cart, or he may deal with one or more of the middlemen who gather the material in the village and sell it in the city."[15] The villagers like to sell their product in markets nearest the city or proceed direct into the city to fetch higher price. The "initial effect of the extension of transportation into the rural areas was to permit urbanites to set up rural markets rather than to encourage the villagers to come into the cities."[16]

THE ROLE OF URBANIZATION IN REGIONAL DEVELOPMENT

Urbanization is the increase of population in urban areas. In most cases it has been observed that urbanization is a component of regional economic development because urban centres provide, inter-aliaa variety of centralized services for the surrounding zone of influence, e.g., marketing of agricultural surplus, products of cottage industries, the supply of fertilizer, engineering goods, pumping set, medicines and specialized skills in a wide variety of situations which are necessary for regional development.

All over the world cities truly function as the centres of modernization and economic change, because there lie the seats of government, centre for higher learning, finance and industrial centres. Cities are also the foci of political and economic activities. Hence, urbanization has a number of meaning attributed to it in terms of regional economic development. (1) One meaning is "improved possibility of using information and facilities inexpensively and without time-lag in any part of society, polity or economy". (2) Urbanization may also be taken to stand for relatively greater development of non-agricultural production and greater movement of urban used goods and services to rural areas. (3) Urbanization also means a change from farm process to an instrument of the process of change. Thus we can look upon urbanization both as an instrument of change and a criterion for regional development. (4) Urbanization of sub-urban areas has a strategic role to play as they provide a nuclei for external economies, because urbanization may be a source of such industrial development as characterised in Japan and China, some parts manufactured in rural areas of dispersed locations and assembled in urban areas.[17]

The transformation of rural service centres in both time and space, due to concentration of commerce, transportation, and professional services gives rise to the development of urban centres. All these are helping in continuous change in entire rural-urban continuum. At the same time, the dynamics of regional economies, population growth, increasing employment in the tertiary sector, and the continuation of these processes for longer period of time and over increasing dimensions of space are signs of regional development. Thus urbanization is a polarization process of various economic forces which has been widely adopted for regional development.

Urbanization usually brings with it regional prosperity as the provision of infrastructure facilities, stimulate the development of locally available resources, increasing regional income and employment levels. Hence urbanization and regional development are closely correlated. However, the general pattern of urbanization brings regional prosperity abound. On the other hand, urban slums are areas of regional, economic, cultural, political and social deprivation, because they have not reaped the rewards of urbanization and regional development.

Urbanization provides new economic opportunities through providing employment in new industries, including the provision of several other infrastructure facilities, e.g. electricity, irrigation, provision of higher education, transport and communication lines and better opportunities of employment in urban areas. Besides this, urban area also provides the facility of new political features of urban, state and national levels, marketing of produce, diversification of occupations, commercialization of agriculture and change in consumption pattern. The problem of urbanization and regional economic development are basic issues of investigation all over the world. Almost all countries, developed and developing, continue to witness the process of urban development, with its specialization of services, industrialization, multifarious nodes and modes of transportation linkages, and allied functions. Urban development of course, is in different stages of development in different countries.

The process of urbanization includes the change of economy which may be from forest to agriculture, agriculture to manufacturing oriented production centres and centres of exchange of goods. During ancient period urbanization was the basic way of life in the valley of Nile, Greece and Indus Valley, especially at Mohanjodaro and Harrappa. After industrial revolution a worldwide preferment of urbanization was quite noticeable when most of the lower order production centres have developed into urban centres. Besides, this has also engulfed the productive *bariland*, of the countryside, which favours the concentration of industries and opens a new vista of employment opportunities at urban centres. This gave a great impetus to the growth of urban population. Later on, with the establishment of government offices, the opening of higher educational institutions and nodes of transportation, nowadays urbanism becomes the focus of civilization, because most of the administrative, political, educational, religious and policy decisions are centred in the urban areas in each and every part of the Globe. Hence urban aggregations have become focal points in the modern world. City dwellers now control most of the large scale institutions that dominate the economic life and welfare operations generated from the offices located in the cities.

Due to urbanization, the development of a region takes place in the following way:-

1. Urbanization has raised the level of rural-urban migration in each and every part of the Globe. This is due to the changing social order as set forth by the people of various castes and classes, such as in India-Brahmins migrated to the urban centres partially for maintaining the traditional occupation, inclusive of secured jobs in different departments of the government. In this way, only a certain group of people have dominance in urban areas. Proportionately the other dominant residents of urban areas are businessmen and industrial labourers.

2. Urbanization helps in the change of traditional social order which could be observed mostly in the commuting population to urban areas who works in the industrial establishments located at urban centres.

3. In rural areas higher social prestige is attached with the people who have a job in urban areas. Further, the city in which an emigrant is employed and the nature of his job become additional criticism of status differentiation of household in the village.

CONCEPTS OF URBAN-REGIONAL DEVELOPMENT GROWTH FOCI

According to R.P. Misra there are four tiers of the concept of 'growth foci' which help in urbanization and regional economic development in India.[18]

1. Service Centres at the Local Level:

Such centres are larger villages of lowest rank in urban development having a population of 5000 to 10,000 persons concentrated at one nucleated settlement or detached into a number of tiny hamlets. The service centres of this category have the functional units of grocery stores, general merchant shops, minor repair facilities, tailor shops, barber shops, restaurants, primary and middle schools, a sub-post office, cooperatives, community centre and other necessary infrastructure facilities.

2. **Growth Points:**

These form the second higher category of service centres in any region. For the sake of regional economic development growth points will serve at least ten to twenty smaller service centres. The population of such centres will range from 50,000 to 100,000. It is just like a major urban centre in Tanzania.

3. **Growth Centres:**

In the hierarchy of growth foci, the third level centres are called growth centres. Growth centres are necessarily production centres and manufacturing is the chief function. In this way, it is a centre of marked secondary and tertiary functions. They will serve a population of 100,000 to 200,000 having a wider zone of influence, e.g. Mwanza in Tanzania.

4. **Growth Poles:**

At highest level of the growth foci hierarchy lies the growth poles. Such centres may have a population of 500,000 to 2,500,000. In growth poles tertiary population have higher share in comparison with secondary and primary services. They are the focal points of regional economic development having predominance of financial, educational, technological and industrial functions. In Tanzania - Dar es Salaam is the example of growth pole.

The Theory of Development Poles:

It was first propounded by Francois Perroux. He considered that growth is concentrated in various spatial foci as well as in leading industrial functional zones useful in analysing the various consequences of alternative choice of location. According to Perroux,[19] "growth does not appear everywhere at the same time, it shows itself in poles with variable intensities, which spreads by different channels and with variable effects for the economy as a whole". Perroux interpreted it essentially in economic and functional sense.

Friedman's Core-Periphery Model

The core periphery model was initially put forward in a study of Venezuelan regional development policy by Friedman.[20] Development takes place from small number of "centres of change" located at the point of highest potential interaction within a communication field. Innovations diffuse from these centres to areas of lower potential interaction. Such 'core regions' are major centres of innovative change, while all other territory consists of 'peripheral regions', which are dependent on core regions for development. It is happening due to the weakening of the periphery by resource transfer to the core, and besides production increased scale of agglomeration of economies at the core[21].

Fig. 21.1 shows that the peripheral areas send labourers and consumers, food and raw materials to the core regions or urban areas whereas core regions supply industrial products, finance and innovative information for economic development to the peripheral regions. Lampard[22] also favours this point that the specialization of a business which generated in the urban centres later diffused to the countryside. Further, Kolb[23] stressed the need for a universalist - achievement of value structure for the rationalization of production and hence industrialization, because urban environment provides a necessary condition for the evolution of such values in terms of rural development. These interactions are found because the economy of rural areas is primitive whereas in core regions it is fully developed due to leadership in business, industrial production, nucleation of transportation lines and political favour.

IMPACT OF URBAN CENTRES ON COUNTRYSIDE IN THE BIHAR PLAIN

In the process of urbanization, slow but noticeable changes are taking place in the Bihar Plain. These changes are more in Munger and Patna districts and comparatively less in Darbhanga and Muzaffarpur districts. Existing cities are heading towards a higher level of urbanization. The variety and amount of nodal services are increasing and becoming more complex. The processing and manufacturing activities are being added to rural areas where they did not exist before. They are expanding where they had already been in existence. All these changes are not confined to cities only. The impulses which these changes generate, are not only restricted to towns only but are carried into the countryside as well. Thus towns and cities as the centres of present day civilization and services, greatly affect the rural settlements in their spheres of influence. Their impact is to be seen on practically all spheres of activity and in every walk of life.

Commercial impact of towns provides an initiative to the rural folk to construct their houses on the road side. Such settlement develops a number of business establishments, particularly on cross-roads. Urban centres also provide the facilities of electricity and telephone to the settlements in their vicinity. Thus in areas around Patna, Gaya and Biharsharif good electric and telephone exchange facilities are available to many rural settlements. An impact as recreational facilities is also evident in the hinterland of a town. People living close to the towns have ready access to cinema hall, and in such areas there is a gradual decline of folk art and drama. But perhaps the greatest impact of towns is upon the occupational structure in rural areas. Most of the rural settlements on the urban fringe have a greater percentage of workers engaged in tertiary services.

REFERENCES

1. J. Eyles: 'Inhabitants Image of Highgate Village', Department of Geography, London School of Economics, Discussion Paper 15; 1967.
2. M. Aurousseau: "The Distribution of Population". *Geographical Review,* Vol, XI; 1921, p. 567.
3. United Nations Population Studies; No. 8, 1950, p.2; Quoted by A.E. Smailes: *The Geography of Towns,* London, 1966, pp. 32 - 33.
4. Hans Carol: "The City Centred Region", *Terra;* Vol.81, 1969, pp. 117-122.
5. Harold M. Mayer and Clyde F. Kohn: "Rural-Urban Link", in *Readings in Urban Geography,* Chapter IX; Allahabad, 1967, p.27.
6. R.E. Dickinson: The Regional Relations of the City; in *City Region and Regionalism;* 1960, p. 167.
7. G.K. Mishra: 'Rural-Urban Continuum', *Indian Journal of Regional Science;* Vol. IX; No. 1, 1977, pp. 36 - 44.
8. R.D. Lambert: "The Impact of Urban Society Upon Village Life" in *India's Urban Future* (edt. Roy Turner), University of California Press, Berkeley, 1962, p.118.
9. K.M. Kapadia: "Rural Family Patterns", *Sociological Bulletin,* Bombay, Vol. V; 1956, pp.111-126.
10. A Bopegamage: "Neighbourhood Relations in Indian Cities, Delhi", *Sociological Bulletin,* Bombay, Vol.VI, No.1, 1977, pp.34-42.

11. Vithal Babu: *Report on a Preliminary Industry on the Growth of Steel Towns in India;* UNESCO Research Centre, Calcutta, 1959.
12. R.E. Pahl: "The Rural-Urban continuum", *Sociologia Ruralis,* Vol.6, Nos.3-4, 1966, p.316.
13. H.E. Bracy: "People and the Countryside", Routledge & Kegan Paul; London, 1972, p.139.
14. Morris Opler: "The Extensions of an Indian Village", *Journal of the Asian Studies;* Vol. XVI; November, 1956, pp. 5-10.
15. D.N. Majumdar: *Caste and Communication in an Indian Village;* Asia Publishing House, Bombay, 1958, p. 329.
16. *Ibid.*
17. B.F. Hoselitz; "The Role of Urbanization in Economic Development: Some International Comparisons", in the *City in the Third World* (Edt. D.J. Dwyer), MacMillan, London, 1974, pp. 169 - 190.
18. R.P. Misra: *Growth Poles and Growth Centres in Urban and Regional Planning in India;* Institute of Development Studies, University of Mysore; 1971.
19. Tormed Hermansen; "Development Poles and Related Theories: A Synoptic Review", in *Growth Centres in Regional Economic Development,* (Edt Hansen) Macmillan, New York, 1972, pp. 160-203.
20. John Friedmann; Regional Development Policy, *A Case Study of Venezuela,* Cambridge: M.I.T. Press, 1966.
21. R.B. Mandal and G.L. Peters, (Edt.); *Urbanization and Regional Development;* Concept Publishing Company, New Delhi, 1982, pp. 1-10.
22. E.E. Lampard; "The History of Cities in Economically Advanced Areas"; *Economic Development and Cultural Change,* Vol. 3; 1955.
23. W.L. Kolb; "The Social Structure and Functions of Cities", *Economic Development and Cultural Change;* Vol. 3; 1955.

Fig. 21.1

Core Periphery Model and the Process of Feedback Mechanism

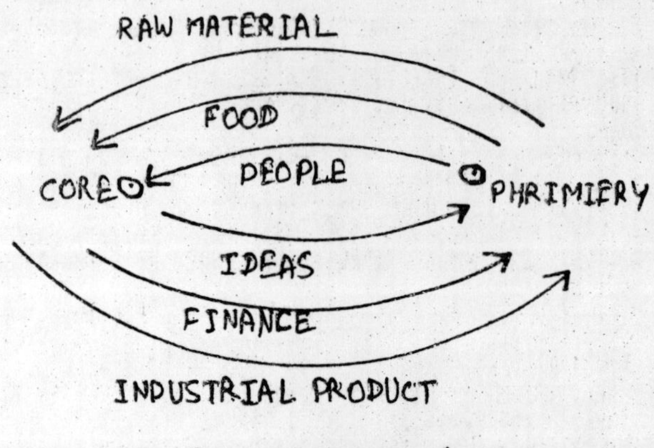

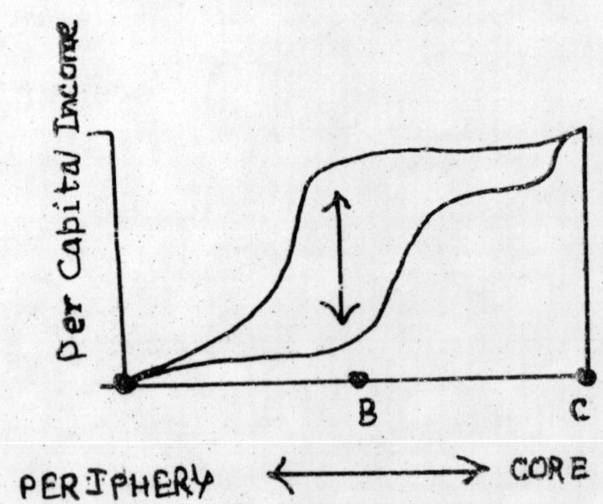

TWENTY TWO

PROBLEMS AND TRENDS OF RURAL SETTLEMENTS

Shelter is the basic right to each and every person in the society. The arrangement of adequate shelter for the entire rural population is the most pressing problem nowadays in all parts of the globe. In most countries of 'The Third World, the lack of minimum standard shelter-service has assumed staggering dimensions. In the last two decades of 20th century the world population will increase from 5 to 8 billion. In Africa the increase will be from 460 to 815 million'.[1]

Housing has got low priority in the programmes of most governments, because it is considered that housing is not contributing to the national economic growth. But it is quite apparent that inadequate shelter affects the health of the population, the occurrence of social tensions, juvenile delinquency, etc. in terms of social costs of the society. In such circumstances, the focusing of attention on problems of shelter in the United Nations Habitat Conference in Vancouver (1976), and the subsequent goading by the United Nations Centre for Human Settlements (Nairobi), the national governments now tend to attach greater importance to housing and related issues.

The problem of rural housing is different from that in urban areas. The problems in urban areas are that of slums and overcrowding due to scarcity of land and high cost of construction, but problems in rural areas are of cheaper and simpler construction with some amenities and good sanitation. The problem of rural area is vast as 75 per cent population of India lives in villages. The financial resources of the states are limited, therefore, stress is to be laid on low-cost houses with maximum amenities. A large proportion of about 54 million houses is to be rebuilt or substantially improved.

The problem is to improve the standards of rural housing: (1) by demonstrating improved standards through model houses built in selected areas; and (2) by assisting the villager to build better type of houses within his means and with the resources readily available through methods of aided self help. The emphasis is to be laid on the use of local material to avoid high cost. These houses should provide adequate ventilation, remove the proximity of cattle or other animals, and provide manure pits, sanitary latrines and other simple and essential amenities which are necessary for decent living. All these steps can go a long way in making the houses cheaper with the help of local materials. The experience has shown that a house built with the villager's own labour is not likely to cost more than $ 1000 to 2000/- per unit.

A Vicious Circle of Poverty and Ill Health of Rural Settlements

In rural areas due to poverty people are making small rudimentary and congested houses in limited space. Although flood damage for such houses may be little, but for the poor even slightest damage counts much. During summer season such houses are heavily prone to the break-out of fire which sometimes damages the entire village; but for the poor agricultural labourers and peasants there is no option at all to improve their living abode. Recently due to increase in population, the lack of residential houses, lack of adequate supply of drinking water in all seasons and insanitary village roads are common features. Further, it has been observed that in rural areas the number of livestock is increasing, but due to expansion in agricultural sector the grazing land is decreasing. Hence, there is a shortage of food, fodder and fuel. In rural areas the leaking of roof and wall rusting are common problems, besides the lack of transport, poor supply of diesel and kerosine oil, sugar and fertilizer. Nowadays in Northern India due to 'green revolution' the lack of agricultural labourer is felt everywhere. Hence on the hands of the vicious circle of poverty the rural houses and settlements in totality give a poor look of insanitary living, but whom to blame, rural people are living in such a condition throughout the world since millennium; and it is hopeless to hope from the government regarding the revolutionary development of rural social, political, economic and settlement sectors.

The desire of United Nations Centre for Human Settlements (Nairobi) to observe 1987 as the International Year of Shelter for the homeless aimed at meeting the basic needs of those below the poverty line by directly improving their shelter or neighbourhood through projects that would be replicable within the economic and institutional framework of developing countries. UNCHS further hoped that such projects would address issues "as improving the basic shelter units, generating employment in the formal sector, facilitating access to land, water, and to sanitary, health and educational facilities, developing administrative and financial measures to benefit the poor and diavantaged; promoting indigenous building materials and construction techniques; fostering community participation in settlement planning, development and management; and promotion of enterpreneurial and cooperative action for the poor and disadvantaged for their own benefit."[2]

Habitat and Water

The United Nations Conference on Human Settlement; Habitat in Vancouver, Canada (1976) considered the need for a global approach to safe water supply and the provision of sanitary facilities as part of human settlements programme. Upto 1986 only 27 per cent of those in rural communities were getting safe drinking water. With regard to sanitation only 13 per cent of the rural population were served. These statistics on water supply and sanitation prepared by the Economic and Social Council, the World Health Organisation clearly show the extent of the problem and the consequences are communicable diseases, (Fig 22.1) and high proportion of early deaths in developing countries. One of the 64th recommendations made by the Vancouver Conference regarding water supply and sanitation is as follows:[3]

"Safe water supply and hygienic waste disposal should receive priority with a view to achieving measurable qualitative and quantitative targets serving all the population by a certain date; targets should be established by all nations and should be considered by the forthcoming United Nations Conference on Water".

Another conference was held in Mar del Plata, Argentina in 1977, and designated the period 1981-1990 as the International Drinking Water Supply and Sanitation Decade[9]. In the light of this each country should set its own goals. The fulfillment of these goals is an enormous task, which requires a vast amount or resources-financial, technical and human. It may be difficult for national governments to meet the target alone and hence United Nations development system has recognized the intensity of the problem and evolved strategies to fulfill it. (Table 22.1).

Problems of Natural Disaster

The tropical and sub-tropical areas of Africa, Asia, Latin America and the Carribean seem to be more prone to natural disasters. "Severe earthquakes, volcanic eruptions, drought, floods and hurricanes cause heavy destruction and inhibit economic growth and development. It has been estimated that the total toll of natural disasters in the period between 1900 and 1976 amounted to approximately 4.6 million persons killed and over 230 million left homeless. It has been estimated that no less than 45 million dwellings have been damaged, and this represents three years of all the world's housing development programmes at the present rate of implementation."[4] (Fig 22.2.).

Problems and Trends in the Bihar Plain

The rural settlements of the Bihar Plain have certain specific problems of their own as this region differs from many other parts of India in its physical characteristics, cultural heritage and traditions, and economic backwardness. The heavy precipitation in the area causes soil erosion and the havoc of floods has destroyed human life, crops and numerous settlements and created difficulties in the construction of houses. These have profoundly affected the historical development of settlements and transport routes and have also contributed to economic backwardness in the region.

TABLE 22.1 South-East Asia: Access to Drinking Water and Sanitary Facilities

	1970	1980	1990
Total Population	1644 million	2068 million	2482 million
Access to Safe Drinking water			
Urban	74 million (49%)	154 million (66%)	247 million (91%)
Rural	49 million (71%)	244 million (31%)	845 million (87%)
Adequate Sanitary Facilities	112 million	166 million	203 million
Urban (28%)	((75%)	7 1	%
Rural	27 million (4%)	53 million (7%)	274 million (28%)

This Table includes the following countries :
Bangladesh, Burma, India, Indonesia, Maldives, Nepal, Srilanka & Thailand.

Source : WHO/SFARO/
Decade Watch, Vol.3, No.2, September, 1984, p.1.

The concentration of a considerable number of people is dependent upon relatively restricted agricultural land which has given rise to problems of food supply, uneconomic holdings and consequent poverty in the region. In areas which have a primitive and backward economy accompanied with illiteracy and poor cultural growth, settlements are marked by poor structures and lack of civic amenities. Such areas demand, close attention from the government and local authorities.

In the hill top settlements of Kharagpur, Chotanagpur Scarp Belt and even in some plain areas, people face the problem of drinking water during summer season, as the wells go dry. On the other hand, the riparian tracts of the North Bihar Plain face the problem of floods during the south-western monsoon. These settlements urgently require transport and communication facilities, educational institutions and medical facilities.

About 90% people of the region live in rural areas, consisting of

38,520 inhabited villages in 1981. Still the village has been largely neglected by the planning bodies resulting in slum like conditions. Therefore, it may be truly said that India lives in her huts and cottages of olden days.[5] The rise of urbanisation in phatches[6] has not been conducive to rural development. Rather, it has contributed to the decay of rural settlements in the Bihar Plain and in most developing countries of the world.

During ancient period, the neglect of villages by the king and in the modern time by the educated youth is quite discernible. It is indicative of the sad fate of the village communities. Here is an example from the Mughal period. At that time 'the villages were neglected and despised and the village life was dreaded by them as a punishment. No doubt, the villages were the places from where their food and income came, but that was their only connection with them. Life in a village was as intolerable to Moghals as residence on the 'Getic and Sarmation shores' away from the seat of empire and of God, was to a cultured poet of imperial Rome'.[7] The condition has not changed much as today.

The problem of housing in the village is vast. Nearly all the villages have ill-ventilated houses in unhealthy environment due to a lack of proper sanitation, water supply and open spaces. The streets and access paths are very narrow and so badly arranged that in the rainy season, they turn into open drains.

In the Bihar Plain, the present housing problems are made up of three elements:

a. houses needed to remove the existing housing shortage or deficit,
b. houses needed to replace the larger quantity of substandard housing now occupied, and
c. houses needed because of the additional population increase in rural areas.

Housing problems are closely linked with many other factors, such as the impact of history on present living conditions, the consequences of continually expanding populations, and the conditions that exist as a result of the present economic, social and political systems besides lower levels of education and even the influence of religion. Broadly speaking, the poor economic situation is more responsible for the present housing situation than any other single factor.

There are number of factors which impede housing schemes in rural areas. The most important is the increase in construction cost. Poverty among the rural folk prohibits them from using even locally available materials. This fact has created great disparity between the houses of the poor and the middle class people, and has retarded the development of rural settlement in various forms. Due to poverty, the rural inhabitants construct a limited number of houses on a limited piece of land, with low bamboo or mud walls and cheap thatching materials like sugarcane leaves, straw or dry grass. Such houses are often unventilated, insanitary and with a short life. Congestion of such houses within small areas leads to slum like conditions. Very few villagers use burnt brick or concrete in the construction of houses. A few persons use burnt bricks for walls and tiles for roofs, other build mud walls and tile roofed houses. But the majority of houses are built with thatch as the roofing material covering mud walls or bamboo-straw walls.

It is fortunate that climatic conditions in the North Bihar are favourable for the peasants. A person can sleep outside for the greater part of the year and also spend many days outdoors. So the house has come to mean only as a shelter during the winter or the rains and a place for preparation and consumption of food.

The forest environment in Southern Gaya, South Munger and Bhagalpur districts, parts of Himalayan fringe in west Champaran district, the northern edge of the Kaimur Plateau in Rohtas district and the northern Kosi region are comparatively sparsely populated. Extensive forest areas in Champaran and Kaimur plateau are protected and are not open for settlement. Also, one of the main reasons for the persistence of forests is the physical character of the land as they occupy scarps, residual hills, badly dissected plateaus and ravines. Here ploughing of the land is difficult, run-off is quick. It is difficult to tap the underground water because of the rocky substratum, surface water bodies are practically non-existent, and the streams are dry for most parts of the year. Wild animals make life insecure and insects abound. Naturally such conditions are not conducive to settlement growth.

The population distribution reflects the habitat.[8] On Dun hills villages are farther apart than in the plains. Here siting is selective, related to slope, forest clearing, extent of alluvium and water supply. The distance between villages may be abnormally great if wide patches of forest or difficult terrain or steep ridges intervene.

The behaviour of the river Kosi during the last three decades has led to a deterioration of the settlements in the Kosi Plain of the North Bihar. It is one of the wildest and most uncertain Indian river. Within the last two centuries its course has shifted 114.56 km[9] from east to west converting about eight thousand sq. kms of fertile rice lands into sandy flats and grassy marshes, and seriously disrupting the rural settlements of the region.

During the rainy season of 1969, the floods affected 2203 villages with a population of 28.21 lakhs in an area of over 5691 sq. km in the study region. The districts worst affected by the floods are given in Table 22.2.

Table 22.2 : SETTLEMENTS AFFECTED BY FLOODS IN THE BIHAR PLAIN (1969)

Districts	No. of villages affected from flood	Area Estimated in sq. km	Affected Population
Patna	168	356	195,000
Shahabad	250	781	204,000
Saran	78	220	100,000
Muzaffarpur	309	553	201,000
Darbhanga	188	412	193,000
Munger	523	1544	52,6000
Purnea	68	220	67,000
Saharsa	200	545	1,022,000
Bhagalpur	162	481	182,633
Champaran	57	579	130,972
Total	2,003	5,691	2,821,605

Source: Indian Nation, Patna, September 2, 1969.

We may consider a few examples to illustrate how floods affect the villages in the region under study. On September 3, 1969, many villages in Gopalpur Block were completely submerged under the water of the Ganga and the Kosi. In most of the villages only house tops were visible. Eighty to ninety houses in Chapter and Khatharia villages collapsed. Similarly in Mokameh during August, 1969, thousands of hectares of land in Gangapur, Vijaygarh, Bodhpur Kasba, Mekhra, Tajpur, Sherpur, Dumra and the surroundings of some other villages of Diara area were submerged. The Ganga started croding its bank towards the south. About 600 families were rendered homeless and took shelter in tents and school buildings. In 1987 the entire Bihar Plain was covered with knee deep to neck deep water during rainy season.

During the flood season, large areas remain surrounded by water which also enters the houses. Under such conditions the majority of the people are faced with scarcity of fuel, food articles and other necessities of life. Arrangement for drinking water is non-existent in most of the villages. This may be followed by epidemics. Development of settlements under such conditions is almost impossible. In the months of May and June, the cyclonic storms and breakout of fire create problems of same magnitude for rural settlements. Each year the cyclone blews off a large number of thatched roofs, uproots several hundred trees and caused considerable damage to standing summer paddy crops and vegetables in the Bihar Plain from March to June.

The small hamlets of low caste people in the vicinity of main settlements are marked by additional problems. The entire region gives an impression of complete scattering of settlements in this regard, because of the form of caste control.[10] Dispersal is heightened by the fact that the higher castes who are owners of land but are not necessarily its cultivators, live in the central site. The satellite hamlets are occupied by the lower castes such as dom, chamar, paswan and pasi who constitute the very necessary agricultural labour force. These appendage habitations known as *tolas*, are located within 100 to 200 metres of the principal habitation, as the orthodox upper castes cannot tolerate the untouchables living near them. Thus a sort of social segregation has taken place. Since the lower castes are also generally the poorer class, their hamlets or *tolas* are marked by low unventilated and bamboo built thatch houses with thatch roofs. The hamlets are insanitary and rarely have even a drinking water well. There are no roads or drains, and they are practically unfit for human occupance.

It is unfortunate that these lower castes, whose labour is needed not only for agricultural operations but also for many other odd errands are made to live in such hovels. The untouchables and the depressed in spite of their numerical superiority and indispensability have been made to live a sub-human life of poverty, misery and squalor destined by religious and age old traditions. Their plight is an over-whelming and burning problem which must be eradicated with the advancement of time in the new and scientifically advanced world.

It is essential to throw some light on the attitude of the government regarding the problems of rural administration with new awareness of their importance. The government has often put forward specific proposals for new settlements, but these have remained largely unexecuted, and there has been practically no development of village houses and street patterns. The government has also paid little attention towards the development of sanitation, drinking water supply, widening of roads and lanes and provision of drainage.

The defective planning of the State Government and a perpetual shortage of funds are great handicaps in the development of rural areas. The arrangement of medical and educational facilities for the people are also insufficient. These are quite frustrating for the rural folk who seem resigned to fate for all their woes.

The growth of villages has been a steady process until very recent times, when internal decay began to set in and eat up their vitality. The new forces of transport and commerce have contributed to the 'decay of villages, chief of which is the rise of towns'.[11] In accordance with the socio-economic development, the rural settlement is in a process of continuous change in response to the historical circumstances, physical factors and the more dynamic changes brought about in land tenure and growth in the population size of rural settlements. The land reforms, development of transport routes and the community development programmes of the post independence period have fostered some remarkable changes in the morphological aspects, typological characteristics, distributional patterns and functional organization of the rural habitat. The greater need of irrigation and intensive cultivation have resulted in a tendency towards loosening out of the rural agglomeration. This is already in process because the farmers prefer to build their houses, even if temporarily on their own farms for a more efficient and intensive utilisation of land.

The growth of population will require more housing facilities. The growth and expansion of the existing village site is natural because the rural-urban migration cannot very much reduce the natural increase of rural population. Therefore, a number of new hamlets are found to be established and the older ones are forced to grow in size. The establishment of the law and order and the problem of flood in most of the areas, which were overwhelmed by large populations in the past, especially in the riparian tracts of North Bihar Plain, are now greatly controlled. This has also led to a gradual dispersal of settlements.

The evolution of settlements during early historical times led to the origin of small hamlets with narrow lanes. With the growth of population these became more and more congested due to the construction of additional houses in the limited area available, particularly in plain areas. But the newer settlements of Chotanagpur Scarp Belt do not have such congestion of dwellings, firstly because the population density is low, and secondly because enough waste - lands are available for expansion of housing units. In plain areas the congestion of dwellings is steadily increasing and if it is not checked, the villages may turn into slums so common in the present day urban sprawls.

In many settlements, the physical character of land leads to the problem of congestion. In the case of high priced agricultural *barilands*, the newer dwellings are constructed in the smaller hamlets, which lie close to the larger settlements. The already overcrowded older settlements do not expand because this would mean encroaching upon the valuable *barilands*. These factors also lead to the dispersal of settlements.

The progress of block development schemes and cooperative societies have facilitated the construction of a number of schools, hospitals, community and *panchyat* halls, libraries, opening of roads, highways, etc. These are rapidly changing the cultural aspects of rural settlements in the Bihar Plain. New service centres are coming up, and the older and larger rural settlements are turning into rurban centres.

In the olden times, the settlements were smaller having only 5 to 50 dwellings. But now with the growth of population and increase in cultural contact, the rural community has developed enormously giving rise to complex settlements. This has led to a hierarchy of settlements both as regards their commercial function as well as other functions. Their number and size have also increased drastically over the years.

With the change in number and size, the types of rural settlements have also changed from dispersed of the historic times to the compact and clustered types of the present. A few decades ago Chotanagpur Scarp Belt in the South Bihar Plain and north-western hilly and forested tracts of Champaran district were totally devoid of settlements for the fear of wild animals but now they are dotted with dispersed settlements. This may be a step towards compact settlements in future.

In coming days, the socio-economic, administrative, recreational and cultural services[12] will have a tendency to concentrate in character. the tightly nucleated villages and hamlets will themselves be expanding and tend to become central villages. The highway orientation of urban sprawl and the development of industrial complexes around Patna, Arrah, Munger, Barauni, Jamalpur, Muzaffarpur and Bhagalpur are transforming the rural landscape rapidly. Over the Chotanagpur Scarp Belt, where the cultivable land is in small patches the tendency of dispersion has already been checked. The existing trends as already visible will change the fundamental basis of social organisation of the rural communities and the physical structure of the villages.

Some Future Trends

In India, the change in the settlement pattern and social organization of villages has brought a substantial structural anomalies in the size and composition especially in recent past, and the situation may be explosive in the near future. It has been anticipated that rural settlements will undoubtedly remain the dominant place of abode for peasants in India, but there will be important changes in the physical layout and socio-economic composition. The physical change may be well-marked in compact settlements. In most of such nucleated settlements there is acute congestion and shortage of housing, and hence the rural settlements are under heavy pressure to expand. "This pressure is increasing rapidly, because with population growth the demand for houses is increasing and with a rise in standard of living people wish to have better, more spacious, and more comfortable houses. The pressure will mount steadily, and there might be an explosion of villages similar to that which we are seeing today in the case of metropolitan area like Delhi. This explosion would create a serious land use situation in many areas. Expansion of villages in most cases can take place only at the expense of cultivated lands. In most fertile areas there is already intense pressure of population upon cultivated land and any large scale diversion of these for house building purposes will aggravate the population pressure still further. Careful land use planning will, therefore, be necessary."[13]

The growth of village means continuously expanding size of the habitation site. Sometimes it presents serious difficulties, because the land near the settlement is quite often considered highly potential for agricultural development, and only rarely topographic factors make such expansion difficult, and for these reasons sometimes satellite settlement develops very close to the parent existing settlement. In areas of assured irrigation farmers like to live on irrigation site in order to protect the establishment or for enjoying the open environment, and cultivating the land intensively with the hope of producing high value crops such as fruits and vegetables. Hence the rural settlements are expanding both in a nucleated and dispersed fashion according to the demand set by the inhabitants for a particular type of land use.

REFERENCES

1. The Basic Right to Shelter", *NGO News on Human Settlements,* No.2, 1984, p.1.
2. "ECOSOC Approves International Year of Shelter for the Homeless", UN-CHS, Nairobi, 1983, p.10.
3. "Habitat and Water", *Habitat, UNCHS,* Nairobi, 1983, p.5.
4. "Natural Disaster", from Fifth Session of the United Nations Commission on Human Settlements, Nairobi, 26 April - 7th May, 1982.
5. N. Subrahmanyam: "The Geographical Personality of India", *Journal of Madras Geographical Association,* Vol. XIV; 1939, pp.20-21.
6. K.K. Sinha: "The Growth of Towns Along the Ganga in Bihar"; *Transactions of the Indian Council of Geographers,* Vol.V; 1968, pp.147-155.
7. M. Ghosh: *The Patliputra,* Patna, 1919, p.5.
8. E. Ahmad: "The Rural Population of Bihar", *Geographical Review,* Vol. 51, 1961, pp.253-276.
9. K.N. Das: "Westward Drift in the Courses of the Kosi", *The National Geographical Journal of India,* Vol.XIV, 1968, pp.23-31.
10. A.N. Bhattacharya: "Effects of Tribal and Caste Factor on Rural Settlement in Uttar Pradesh", *Indian Geographical Journal,* Vol.22, 1956-57, pp.94-101.
11. Jadunath Sarkar: *The Mughal Administration,* Patna, 1920, p.40.
12. V. Nath: "The Village and the Community", in *India's Urban Future* (ed. Roy Turner), University of California Press, Berkeley 1962, pp.151-153.
13. Ibid.

Fig. 22.1

Impacts of Clean Water and Adequate Sanitation

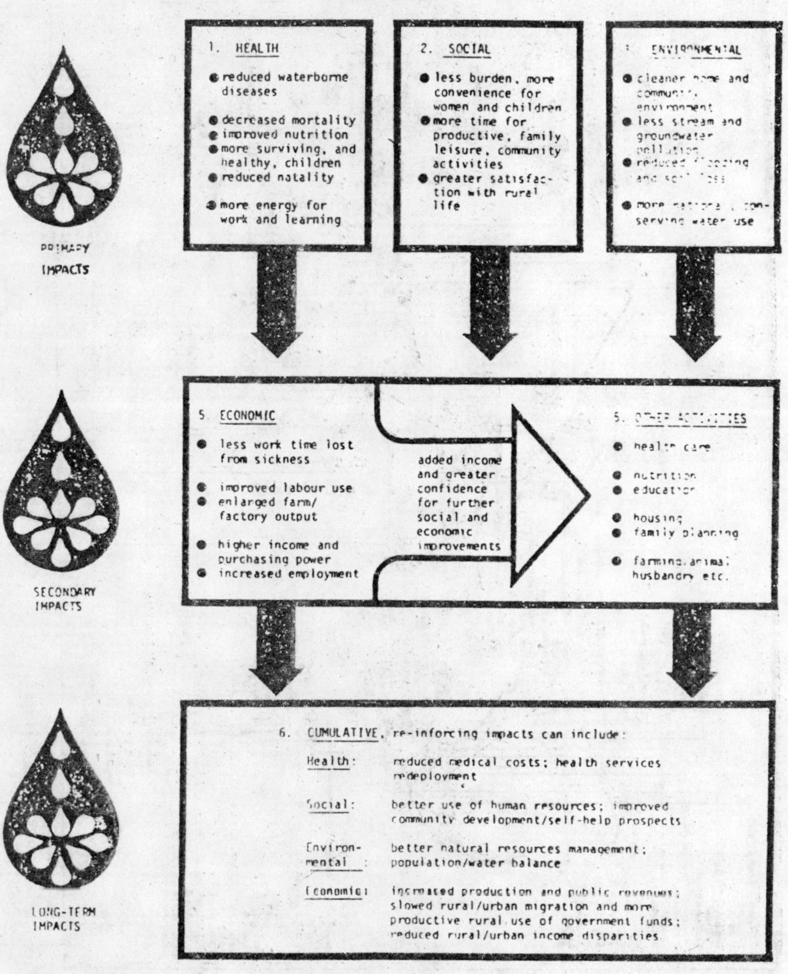

Source : International Drinking Water Supply and Sanitation Decade 1981-1990. "Impact of Community Water Supply and Sanitation Programmes in Developing Countries".

Fig. 22.2

Victims of Natural Disasters 1970-80

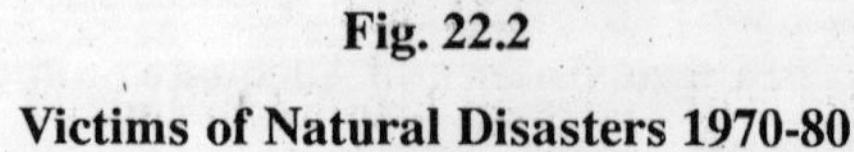

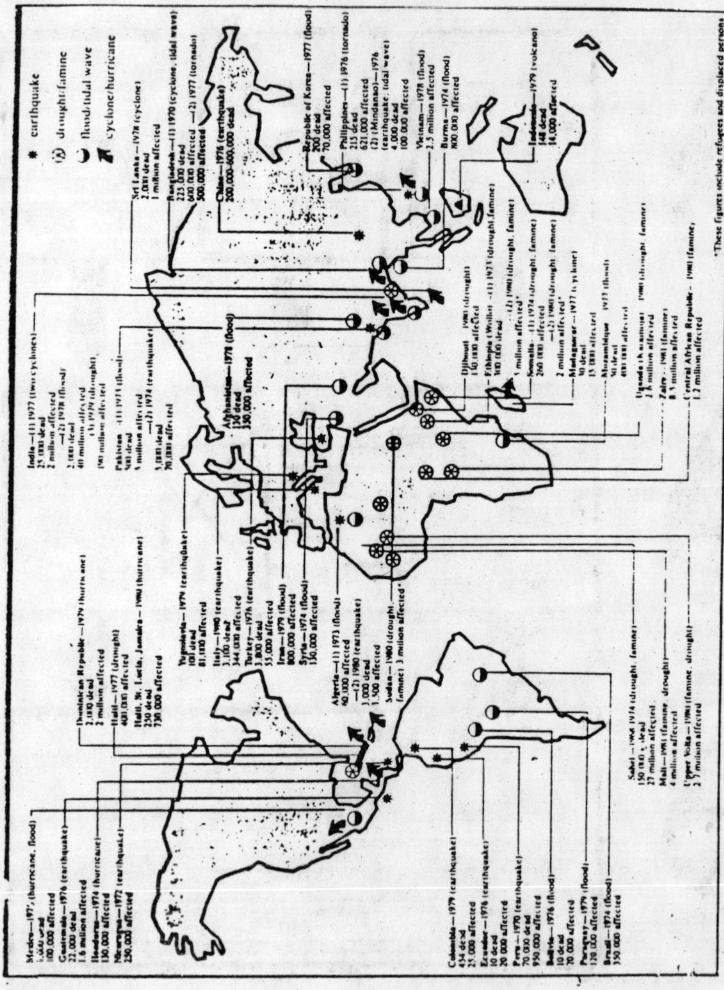

Source : Unicef News Issue 109/1981/2.

TWENTY THREE

ENVIRONMENTAL POLLUTION AND THE HUMAN SETTLEMENTS

In the last quarter of 1984 the leakage of cyanide poisonous gas from a pesticide factory in the city of Bhopal, India killed 2500 people and made blind 50,000. Near about the same time in Mexico city, Mexico - 350 people died with the break out of fire in a gas depot. All these are the 'frightening tragedies' whose insane effect is not limited to our urban environment only but it has affected the rural environment too.

It shows that the conflict between man and nature has reached a disastrous proportion in many places but the pace of development is just making adjustment with the local environment. In almost all countries of the world the consequences of environmental pollution are leading to death, deprivation, desertification, drought and destruction of human settlements and natural environment.

The dumping grounds of pollutant waste materials either in solid or gaseous form are Abiotic Environment (lithosphere), water (hydrosphere), and air (atmosphere). But their combined harmful effect is revealed on the Biotic Environment or biosphere (living world) (Fig 23.1). These indicate the enormous pollution of air, water, soil as the natural landscape and resources useful for mankind. Currently, the rapid urbanization is beyond our control, which is resulting into overcrowding, shortage of food, energy crisis, social conflicts and economic drudgery. Under such circumstances it has been pointed out that by the year 2000 AD most countries of the world will face an acute ecological crisis if some urgent improvement measures are not taken.

Hazardous Waste

It has been indicated that 5 million chemical substances have been identified for the benefit of human society but they brought a new danger through the generation of hazardous waste in the process of manufacturing. These waste materials have bad consequences of causing cancer, delayed nervous damage, malformation in unborn children, and mutagenic changes (Table 23.1). Uptil now many hazardous wastes were disposed of without proper evaluation of the environmental consequences such as fire, explosions, air and land pollution: contamination of food and drinking water; damage to people's health; harm to plants, animals, birds and fishes.

TABLE 23.1 : KILLER CHEMICALS

Pesticides that are tightly controlled in the United States and other industrialised nations are freely sold in the Third World. A number of these toxic chemicals have been linked to serious health hazards. Examples:-

Pesticide	Suspected Health Hazards	Approximate Lethal Dose
Aldrin	Cancer, damage to foetus, nervous disorders	Teaspoon
BHC	Cancer	Teaspoon
Chlordane	Cancer	Teaspoon to a tablespoon
DBCP	Cancer, male sterility	Teaspoon to a tablespoon
DDT	Cancer, nervous disorders	Teaspoon to a tablespoon
Heptachlor	Cancer	Teaspoon to a tablespoon
Kepone	Cancer, Nervous disorders	Teaspoon to a tablespoon
Parathion	Damage to foetus, nervous disorders	A few drops
Parquat	Damage to foetus, and respiratory system	Teaspoon to a tablespoon
Nitrofen	Cancer, birth defects, female sterility	one-half pint
Toxaphane	Cancer	Teaspoon
2.4'.5T	Cancer, birth defects	1 Ounce

Source: Toxcology Branch of the Centery for Environment and Health, US Center for Disease Control Credit: Pesticide Digest, No. 1; 1983.

Hazardous Waste

The most worst incident happened was that of the "Minamata Disease" in Japan and Indonesia (1950's) where the discharge of methyl mercury to the sea caused the contamination of fish in Djakarta Bay, which caused high fever, mental disorders to 2000 people out of which 400 died. Similarly in Northern India (1981 -82) about 3000 people died with the outbreak of Minamata (encephalitis). In USA an area of about 65 square kilometres was contaminated with wastes from manufacture of defoliants, pesticides and chemical warfare agents, causing crops to get dry and livestock drinking from the well to perish.

Now the same condition is prevailing in other developing countries where water bodies are so polluted by factory waste and chemicals that they become sources of mass epidemic diseases. In this way, developing countries are the first victim through oceans, into which industrialized western countries continue to dump waste of household and industries. Due to technologically inadequate methods of oil extraction on the continental shelf, and of oil refining and transportation annually up to 10 million tons of oil gets into oceans and seas. This crisis of environmental pollution between man and the biosphere is getting increased day by day, because the big corporations of the Western World, intensively transfer ecologically harmful industrial goods which highly pollute the environment in developing countries.

Acid Rain:- Acid rain is polluting the environment due to the burning of fossil fuel-in power stations, factories and motor vehicles which bring down dilute sulphuric and nitric acid. This has the great power to kill fish and other creatures living in water, besides corroding buildings and ancient monuments of the world. It is also damaging forests, crops and poses a substantial threat to human health. In American and European countries due to tall chimneys in the factories they got success in warding off the problem of pollutants in the nearby areas but the sulphur and nitrogen compounds emitted by burning fossil fuels can be blown thousands of kilometres by the winds, to cause acid rain in countries far from their points of origin.[1] According to an estimate about 284 million tons of sulphur oxide and 90 million tons of nitrogen oxide the world is getting yearly which have already caused environmental pollution on regional scale in industrialised countries. The "dry deposits" of sulphur and nitrogen oxides pollute the environment just near the source but the longer the gases stay in the air, they are going into complex changes and the repurcussions are disastrous for human being, fish, animal and vegetation upto far away places. Each and every country is generating such pollutants and sending some parts of it through winds to the neighbouring countries. In this way, there are both 'net exporter' and 'net importer' of air pollutants.

Lakes and rivers are the first victims of acid rain. According to an estimate in Southern Norway out of 5000 lakes - 1750 have lost their fish and others 900 are seriously affected. Similarly near Shahadra in Delhi, India the nearby ditches are so much polluted that vegetation dried off, fishes died and it is quite unfit either for animal or man to touch and how much dangerous it may be through acid fall and breathing of such a polluted air which is beyond estimate. In 1982 in the Federal Republic of Germany about 7.7 per cent forest is reported to be damaged.

It has been estimated that the opening of a large metal smelter in northern Mexico in the last quarter of 1985 may export acid rain en-bulk to USA parts of Rocky Mountain as nowadays the USA is doing for the Canada.

Damage by the acid rain in Canada and eastern United States of America is well documented, but the risk of acid rain damage to the fragile Rockey Mountain ecosystem is a relatively new development. Recent research has revealed that many of the 10,000 mountain lakes above 2900 metres (9500 feet) are highly sensitive to acid pollution because the rock lacks the alkaline soils that neutralize acid. The existing industries in the central and northern Rockies of USA have already caused an enormous problem with the acid rain measured at two sites in Wyoming and Colorado was found to be 10 times as acidic as polluted rain water. In some mountain lakes of Colorado no trout have hatched since two years. But now the problem may be more vigorous as the new Mexican smelter - at Nacozari, 100 kilometres from the US border opened in 1985. It will become the second largest emitter of sulphur in North America after the Canadian Sudbury complex in Ontario. Gaseous sulphur and nitrogen oxides are the destructive constituents of acid rain[2] (Fig. 23.2).

Energy Farms

The world has enormous amount of biomass, but its regional distribution is quite uneven. In some regions the reserves are being dissipated because they are burning fast than they can be replaced by growth. It has been seen by experience that all energy productions present environmental problems even if it is attractive. Some plants have been discovered which may be the alternative source of our energy requirements. But such energy crops could impoverish the productive capacity of the soil and may destroy wildlife habitats. It is said that managing the forest with fertilizers and pest control from cutting the wood and converting it to energy as fuel and disposing of its burnt wastes are all dangerous for a good environment. Soil erosion and leaching are also harmful because they make the soil poorer, loss of nutrients and productivity declines. Regaining of natural fertility takes a long time.

The production of ethanol in sugar factory has also great power of polluting the environment in case it is discharged without treatment into inland or coastal waters. Under energy farms, many countries are planting trees for industry, fuelwood, charcoal besides soil protection and reducing the flood problem. Such plantations cover 2.7 million hectares in Indonesia, 2.6 million in India, 400,000 in Bangladesh; 300,000 in the Philippines and over 200,000 in Thailand, but we should keep a watch as deforestation may not aggravate further because it may pollute more our already polluted environment.

Alarming Antibiotic Resistance

Nowadays lot of reports are coming about the increased ineffectiveness of a range of antibiotics which have prompted World Health Organization to identify the main factors contributing to antimicrobial resistance. It has been found that the misuse of antibiotics in hospitals and private practice, and unwise self-treatment have contributed much to the problem of resistance. The use of antibiotic drugs on animals and food-stuffs constitute another part of the problem (Fig. 23.3).

It has been investigated that the antibiotic resistance is now passing from one bactorial species to another by genetic particles. Further discovery is that species previously found to be vulnerable to antibiotics are now showing resistance such as mosquitoes in the house even after Tik-20 spray, and pests eating maize even after pesticides spray.

Environment and Development

We are concerned both with the economic development and making a better environment for the well being of the entire world communities moving on one ship. If one is going to be affected others may not be spared or one person's success should not diminish chance of others. The sustainable development - applicable to all - is not possible without constant attention to environmental concerns. Indeed with having constrained environment we may be able to achieve development cheaper and sooner. But for the well being of human society good environment and development are just the two sides of the same coin. Adjustments have to be found instead of getting a crisis. It has been observed that "in Jordan experiments done with the help of the World Food Programme which demonstrate that an environmentally sound management of low rainfall grazing areas will also produce more fodder and support more sheep".[3] Thus the world is in need of a balance and appropriate environment in which civilization flourishes and each individual gets the right to equal participation in the society. It is hoped that development and environment with our conscious efforts are going well together with some adjustments (Fig. 23.4).

Environmental Change

Environments change people just as people change environment. Environment affect our health, behaviour and feelings, and they express society's dominant values and the values of dominant group. Unfortunately, our polluted environment from spaces to place, often gives dissatisfaction to the people while simultaneously supporting social inequalities. If we want a better society we have to consider the environment's role; to make meaningful change and we must also enter the process of social change. Current social change, family - composition, ethnic make up of communities, and the automation of work, for example - are also demanding that we think about environment in new ways.

Problems Related to the Environment of the Settlements

The growth and expansion of settlements on the earth surface determine the use categories of land and the resulting environmental problems. These are the major problems of environmental pollution in relation to human settlements:

(a) Extreme population densities - both high and low, because the resulting environment will be uncontrolled of the land,
(b) Overcrowding, congestion of houses and sub-standard inadequate dwellings,
(c) Scarce supply of infrastructure facilities and service to a community,
(d) Water pollution,
(e) Air pollution,
(f) Noise Pollution, and
(g) Continuing Deterioration of the natural landscape - ecological hazards.

The high density of population in urban areas and the lowest density in dispersed living environment are time consuming for the accessibility to jobs, provision of houses and service facilities. Hence in order to avoid congestion in slums people are buying land having low values in the fringe areas which are liable to flooding, places of garbage dumping, along with all kinds of vices of the under worlds. In such areas the houses are also of sub-standard due to lack of funds.

Due to limitations of public investment on infrastructure facilities, the situation is now getting bad to worse regarding the proper availability of service facilities to the toiling masses, both in urban and rural areas. The problems are acute especially in terms of water supply, sewerage services, housing shortage; inadequacy in transport services, bad affairs of the roads; etc. In most of the developing countries barely half of the total population is served by piped water and only 10% is supplied with sewerage services. The water derived from lagoons, irrigation channels and rivers are quite often polluted either due to connection with the drains of industrial waste or direct link with the sewage lines. Such sewage and dumping of garbage also contaminates the sub-surface reservoirs of water. In some cases these pollutants are directly thrown into rivers, tanks and lagoons. It also pollutes air besides attracting rodents and insects.

The congested high density areas of houses receives little or no sunlight and suffer the pollutant effects of traffic jam, produced by motor cars, besides high occupancy rate.

In most cases inappropriate location of industrial plants without the control of the government are generally hazardous for the low income group people and contaminating air, water and land in the nearby areas. In Brazil, Japan and India the uncontrolled growth of industries have immensely damaged the surrounding environment and hence creating serious health problem for the local people.

Environmental Relations with Human Settlements

Human beings obtain their food, clothing and settlements by their ingenuity from the nature. They work under natural environment and use natural resources to get a certain type of food, shelter and clothing. Hence shelter has a dominant impact on the built environment, while at the same time its characteristics are influenced by the natural environment. Human settlements can influence the environment by the following ways,[4] by consumption of natural resources, by adding physical objects to the environment and by acting as an intermediary between human being and the nature.

The form of human settlements is generally determined by social requirements and the physical environment. Settlement is an intermediary linkage between human social organization and the nature. It may be a place of refuge, privacy, safeguards against climatic hazards, prestige and status symbol of a person in the society, besides reflecting the technological, economic and social conditions. On the one hand, the origin of settlements starts depleting natural resources, on the other, its metabolic processes pollute the land, air and water at the same time, because all these are related with the process of feed-back mechanism. Hence the productivity of land and labour, and metabolic processes of the settlement determine the environmental condition for human comfort. Production processes include the use of timber, stone, mud, water and minerals for creating a congenial environment for human living. In order to satisfy the demands set by the people, the selection of accessible and defensible site along with the provision of infrastructure facilities for the network of settlements are necessary. Such a grouping of houses on a particular location may guide the functions in a positive or negative way but that certainly pollutes the environment by noise, congestion of houses, movement of people, atmospheric and water pollution besides the degradation of social norms. The intensity of environmental pollution may be varying in different physical and social conditions. It has been realised that the modification of environmental pollution is possible by way of judicious use, preservation and protection of resources, increase in renewable resources i.e. afforestation and recycling with the growth of population the current situation may deteriorate further but in order to save the environment from such a deteriorating situation the local government should frame some laws or rules of human behaviour in relation to settlement, society, production programmes and the environment.

REFERENCES

1. "The State of the Environment Report", Prepared by the Environment Liaison Centre, Nairobi on World Environment Day, 5th June, 1983.
2. John McCormick: "Mexico's Acid Rain Exports", Daily News, Dar es Salaam, 7th April, 1985.
3. J.C. Wheeler: "Dawning Challenges Ahead", *ECOFORUM,* Vol.8, No.6, 1983, pp. 13 - 14.
4. A.L. Mabogunje et.al: *Shelter Provision in Developing Countries;* John Wiley and Sons; New York, 1978, p. 4.

Fig. 23.1

Taxonomy of the Environment

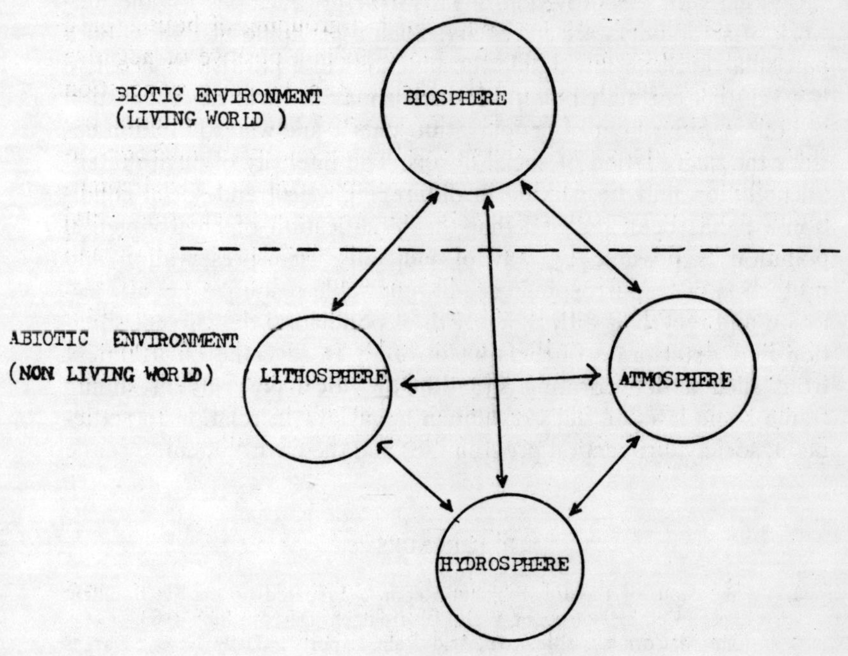

Fig. 23.2

Mexico's Acid Rain Export in the Rocky Environment of United States of America

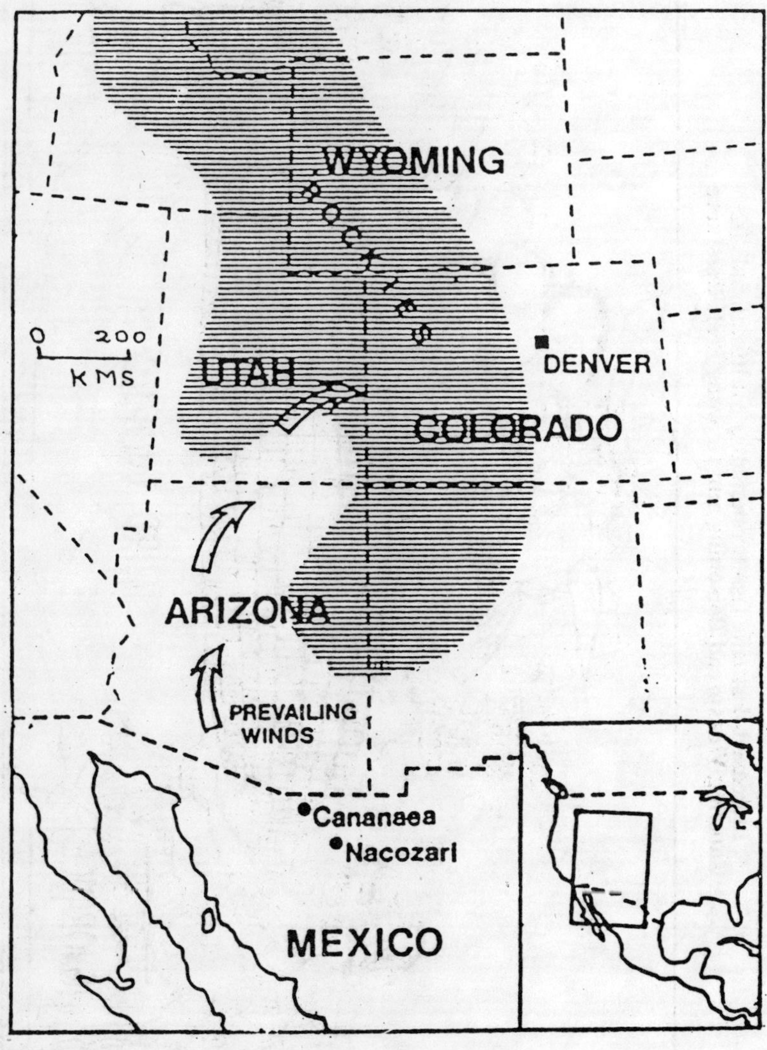

Source : John McCormick, 1985

Fig. 23.3

Increased Pesticide Use Promoted by Multinationals is Causing Widespread Poisoning and Growing Pest Resistance

Fig. 23.4

Adjustment Between Development and Environment

"Resolution of development conflict requires that unity be restored."

Credit: Development Forum

TWENTY FOUR

VILLAGE VIABILITY ASSESSMENT

Planning in Existing Villages

In Tanzania since the villagization programme was implemented in 1974 the village has become the focus of efforts to increase agricultural production and the village level planning is seen as an essential pre-requsite of achievement of this aim. However, due to speedy development of villagization programme, villages have been established without any attempt being made to assess whether the resource base available to the village is sufficient to support its population. Due to this, it has been proposed that an essential preliminary stage in the land use planning of existing villages is an assessment of the village viability. This is to check that the essential conditions in the form of adequate water, fuelwood, arable and grazing land-exist or not for successful village development and also to identify what problems exist in the field.

Village viability Surveys

It aims at determining that the physical resources available to a village are sufficient or insufficient for its inhabitants to achieve a specified standard of living and to absorb natural increase in population. First of all we have to decide a specified level of standard of living.

In order to have flexibility in planning two standards have been identified:[1]

(a) A minimum requirement level for every family must be: sufficient land to fulfill subsistence needs such as shelter, clothes, food, water supply, salt, soap, medicine, children's education and casual entertainment. A survey of income and expenditure of sample villages may provide a clue for these minimum needs.

(b) A high standard of living may be determined according to the national objectives of raising the standard of living of the peasants at par with urban wage earning labourers in terms of good food, clothes, children's education, etc. At present, this would amount to an annual income of Rs. 12000/= in India and T.Sh. 50,000/= in Tanzania (1985).

Village viability may be assessed on the basis of following resource assessment in each sampled village:

1. **Domestic Water Supply**

The arrangement of adequate water supply is quite essential in order to have a viable rural settlement. For a piped water supply, the Water Development Department suggests a minimum daily flow of 35 litres per head. For a viable rural settlement it is necessary to have a source of drinking water supply upto a distance of one kilometre or half an hour walk in one way. In case one member of a family is spending his all time in running for drinking water, such a house site or village should be considered non-viable, and hence such sites should not be selected for future extension of colony or rural settlement planning.

2. **Fuelwood Supplies**:

The fuelwood requirements for village viability will be assessed on the basis of following assumptions:

(a) the annual domestic consumption of fuelwood including char coal is 1.5 m^3 of solid wood per head.

(b) 64 m^3 of solid wood is required to cure one hectare of tobacco according to Tanzanian estimate.

(c) one hectare of *miombo* woodland produces 53 m^3 of solid wood for fuel over a minimum requirement period of 30 years in Tanzania.

(d) The annual yield of eucalyptus plantations is 10-15 m^3 per hectare of solid wood, with a felling cycle of eight years.

(e) In India farmer in rural areas has no dearth of fuel wood because they are using waste of sugarcane sticks after preparing jaggery, sticks of Tur pulse after harvesting, sticks of Maize after harvesting, twigs of trees after trimming each year, besides dried cow dung and about 40,000 biogas plants throughout India in 1987. Hence in India in terms of fuelwood supply rural settlements cannot be considered non-viable except those areas which are in Thar desert or in flood affected areas.

In terms of fuel, recently a study has been conducted in rural areas of India where bio-gas plants were being tested. The rural inhabitants - "*Harijans*", the depressed or scheduled classes were asked about their problems. Their main anxiety is the appearance of these bio-gas plants. The rich people in the village communities are collecting all the cow dung for the bio-gas plants, leaving nothing for the domestic use of the poor inhabitants of the village. It requires the care and foresight when planning the development of an area - as one group of people often has to pay more heavily than others for steps that have been taken[2].

3. **Village Population:**

For a small group of people it is difficult to get various types of service facilities and hence in order to provide services to a large number of inhabitants the growth and development of planned rural settlements is essential. Both in India and Tanzania village formed the basic element of the enumeration areas of population in various censuses and hence there are accurate figures for total population, number of households, age-sex ratio, especially in 1978 census in Tanzania, and 1981 census in India. Therefore, in order to judge the village viability in migration and outmigration of population, future population estimate according to the resources and a knowledge of the growth rate of population are necessary. India and Tanzania are countries with predominance of rural population, and that solutions had to be found to the problems of a rural society.

4. Population and Their Requirements

This is the first step of village resource assessment which will take into consideration the following components:

(a) number of people and households in that village;
(b) the number of families and persons depending on agriculture for their livelihood;
(c) the consumption of food in calories per person of different age group/household;
(d) production of food per hectare and per family;
(e) the amount of water needed per person/per family/per day.
(f) the amount of fuel consumption per family (firewood);
(g) population projection for 5 to 10 years.

5. Calculation of Subsistence/Food Requirements

The amount of calories required by an individual per year can be calculated. This can be computed into number of calories required per family per year from the food crop in question (Kg x Cal.). In case the amount of Kilograms of food required per family per year is X_1.

$$X_1 = \frac{\text{Calories required per family in a year}}{\text{Calories from 1 Kg staple food}} = [\text{Kg}]$$

If area of the land required is X_2

$$X_2 = \frac{\text{Yield of the crop required (Kg)}}{\text{Actual yield of the crop per land unit(Kg 1 ha)}} = [\text{ha}]$$

Therefore, the land required for production of food crop is estimated.

6. Cash Target:

Fix a target for the whole village in Rupees and that will require to achieve by the village as cash income. Determine the amount of (Kgs) cash crop that will be required to achieve the set target of income, i.e.;

$$Y_1 = \frac{\text{Target income (Rs)}}{\text{Producer prices of the cash crop (Rs 1 Kg)}} = [\text{Kg}]$$

This will determine the amount of land required to produce the required number of Kg (Y_2).

$$Y_2 = \frac{\text{Required yield of the crop (Kg)}}{\text{Actual yield per land unit (Kg/ha)}} = [\text{ha}]$$

In this way, we can get the number of hectares of land required for the production of cash crop to meet the cash income target.

7. **Calculation of Carrying Capacity of the Land (K)**

It is known as the number of people or families supportive capacity of the land.

$$K = \frac{\text{Land area available (ha)}}{\text{Land required per family } (X_2 + Y_2) \text{ (ha/family)}} = [\text{ha}]$$

In case the land required is less than land available than the village is viable, and if the land required is greater than the land available then the village is non-viable.

8. **Land and Natural Resource Surveys**

It is necessary to identify the land uses of the village to get the real total amount of land available for cultivation. Land survey will comprise making the prismatic compass traverse and plain tabling of the village as to demarcate the actual boundaries of the village. In the land survey, it is also possible to map soil types, direction of slope, various uses of the land, vegetation, areas of soil erosion, settlement site, communal land, grazing land, marshy areas, and cultivated land. In this way, the topographical map of the area can be prepared depicting different topographical levels in percentage (Fig. 24.1).

9. Demarcation of Village Boundaries

In India, for almost all villages the boundaries are well marked, and it is well known that how much land is available for cultivation. But in Tanzania, it is necessary to demarcate the village boundary accurately for both agricultural and administrative purposes in close contact with the officials of neighbouring villages so that dispute may not arise in future. Aerial photographs and satellite imageries should be the base for preparing such maps. The work done by Ardhi Institute in Dar es Salaam is a good attempt in this direction which provides a useful check on the information collected in the village.

10. Net Sown Area Available to the Villages

Generally, the village land is classified into different categories at the time of settlement survey and land revenue assessment. In villages, the land may be divided into net sown area (sown once), gross sown area (sown more than once), fallow land, pasture land, land under water bodies, settlement, highways, gardens and waste land. But so far as the net sown area is concerned different types of cultivated land requires different management practices in terms of fallowing, use of fertilizer, need of irrigation and the selection of crops. The cultivated land lying more than 5 kilometres away from the settlement should be considered unavailable for all practical purposes.

Information should be collected regarding the cultivated land available to the villagers besides the land engaged in staple food crops, fruits, vegetables and cash crops. Input and output in per hectare of land should be assessed, because it will be a good measure of viability or non-viability of the village. In case, the current production level is not sufficient than the difference between the minimum area of stable crops that a family feels it must cultivate to satisfy its annual food requirements and the area of land each family uses for the generation of cash should be increased or scientific cultivation should be adopted. The land cultivated by the farmers either through hand hoe. ox, ox driven plough or tractor should clearly be stated.

11. Requirement of Fallow Land

The requirements of fallow land of a village should be known in advance in order to determine the amount of land to be required in the cultivation cycle. The length of fallow should also be known in relation to soils and land units, and it is recommended that observations should be started on crop rotations and fallowing. Initially village survey, should be conducted in order to know the cultivation history of specific fields in different classes of land.

12. Transport Facilities and Accessibility

Transportation lines are considered as life blood for the growth and development of villages. Those villages which have either road or railway facility, the dimension of growth and areal expansion is found to be much accelerated in comparison with others. This is because transportation facility gives way to fast movement of goods and people. For this fact, most of the ports and urban places are nodal points of development. In terms of village viability assessment the investigator should see whether the village has the facility of railway, metalled road, unmetalled road, water channel or footpath. It is necessary because for different levels of population concentration different modes of transportation lines are required and that may be one of the criteria for judging the viability of a village.

13. Provision of Education and Literacy

For sound economic growth the provision of at least primary education is necessary in villages. Literate person can give sustenance to so many persons of a family but illiterate cannot. Hence literate persons are more valuable resource of a village. In this way, the level of literacy should be one of the important criteria in judging the viability of a village.

14. Yield and Price of Main Crops Grown

On regional level the Bureau or Directorate of Statistics has been entrusted with task of collecting the information about yield and price of goods sold in the market for both moist and drier parts of the region. Estimates of yield obtained in the village will be made both from farmer's and marketed surpluses with the acreage under cultivation.

15. **Occupancy Rate**

In a settlement, the number of persons living per room is known as occupancy rate. In areas where the population is high in comparison with the number of houses the persons per room is coming high. In such a situation a large number of people are sharing the limited facilities available in a village. Hence low occupancy rate may be a sign of viable village and high occupancy rate as non - viable village.

16. **Number of Livestock and Availability of Pastureland**

The total number of livestock in the village should be ascertained because it is a wealth to the peasants according to the ecological conditions. The number of families that own livestock, and the number and type of animals each family owns should also be determined as accurately as possible. The amount of grazing land of a village includes pastureland and fallow land within 2 kilometres of the settlement centre. According to the amount of grazing land and the number of animals, livestock carrying capacity of each type of grazing land will be assessed so that the carrying capacity of livestock in the village may be obtained.

17. **Contribution of Livestock to the village Economy**

Livestock contributes the food supply and cash income in three ways:-

(a) Livestock sales provide cash,
(b) Livestock slaughtering provide meat, and
(c) Cows and buffalos provide milk.

The size of families according to the number of livestock should be determined. The income from livestock may be compared with the income of food crops sale, so that the grade of subsistence of the village may be assessed for judging its viability.

18. Viable and Non - Viable Villages

When the information collected has been analysed it will be possible to classify each village, according to its viability into one of the following:-

(a) villages that are viable,
(b) villages that are non - viable because of inadequate water supplies,
(c) villages that are non - viable due to inadequate fuelwood supplies,
(d) villages that are non - viable with respect to food supply
(e) villages that are non - viable with respect to cash income levels.

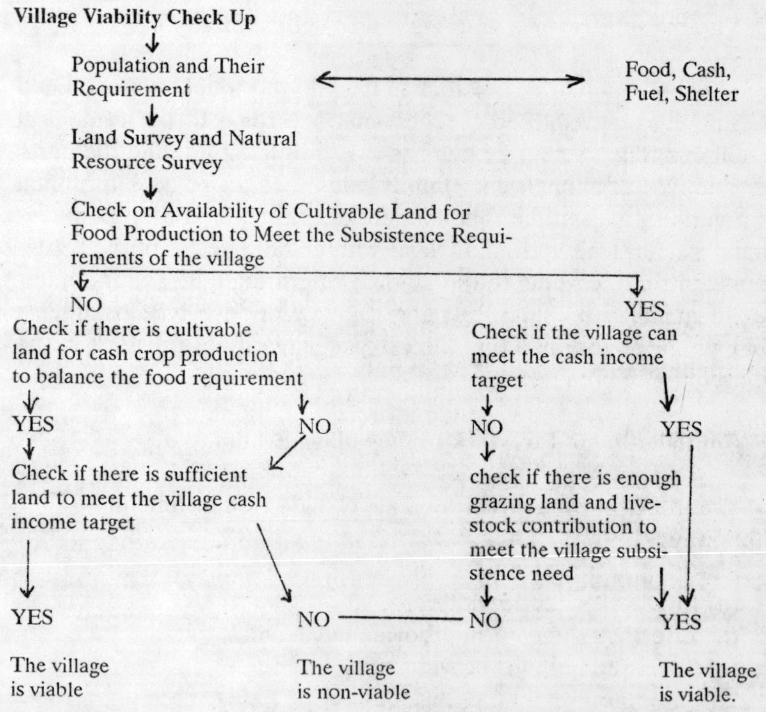

SOLUTIONS TO NON-VIABILITY

Solutions to the problems described above can be considered under the following headings:-

1. Technological improvements
2. Reduction of the number of families in a village
3. Relocation of the village centre
4. Creation of satellite settlements around the village centre
5. Provision for a two house-system with temporary houses in distant cultivated areas
6. Reduction of the number of livestock in a village

VILLAGE PLANNING PROCEDURES

The procedures discussed below are designed to assist the villager in drawing up and implementing plans to enable them to overcome problems of viability where necessary and to achieve their development aims, while maintaining or improving the long-term productivity of the land. The planning process can be divided into the following stages:-

1. A review with village representatives of their development plans.
2. The formulation of alternative strategies for achieving village development objectives.
3. Discussion and agreement on a specific development strategy
4. Production of a detailed development plan.
5. Assistance with implementation of the plan.

PLANNING IN NEW AREAS

Although population movement is a last resort when selecting the most appropriate solutions to the problem of non - viability, it is clear that a certain amount must occur if only to accommodate natural population increases.

When a village population exceeds the officially proposed maximum of 600 families a proportion of the families may have to be moved. Villages that the viability survey has shown to be capable of absorbing a considerable increase in population represent the obvious new locations for people displaced from non - viable villages.

In the long term, however, entirely new village locations will have to be sought. The planning of future settlement sites provides an opportunity to learn from the mistakes of the past when village sites were selected on the basis of existing infrastructure only. All relevant criteria must be considered when deciding on new settlement sites. The existence of roads and other infrastructure forms a useful starting point to the selection process but the primary importance of the physical resource base must be recognized when final locational decisions are made.

The factors that will be considered when selecting new village sites will be:

1. Water Resources,
2. Fuel-wood reserves,
3. The carrying capacity of the land, and
4. Existing roads and other infrastructure.

When a proposed village area has been defined and mapped and the number of families it can support, is established, it will be possible to draw up a settlement plan for the village. The plan will consist of a map accompanied by a written report. The map will show the following-

(a) Proposed sites for the village centre and possible satellites,
(b) The location of all water sources, both existing and proposed,
(c) Proposed sites and areas for block farming activities,
(d) The location and extent of all areas of grazing land,
(e) The location and extent of areas suitable for exploitation for fuelwood,
(f) Proposed sites for any necessary fuelwood plantations conside. ed necessary,
(g) Suitable alignments for village roads.

The accompanying report will contain a description of the topography, soils and vegetation of the village lands, an assessment of their potential for both crop and livestock production and an indication of the type of cultivation practices that will be necessary on the block farms of erosion is to be minimised.

REFERENCES

1. Tanzania, Tabora Rural Integrated Development Project, Land Use Component, Project Report 87, 1980, Land Resource Development Centre, Survey, England; pp. 150 - 165.
2. M.G.K. Menon: "Development of Technology in and for India", Institute Fur All Gemeine Uberseeforschung, Weltforum Verlag; Munchen, 1976, p.88.

Fig. 24.1

Land Available in Each Topographical Level

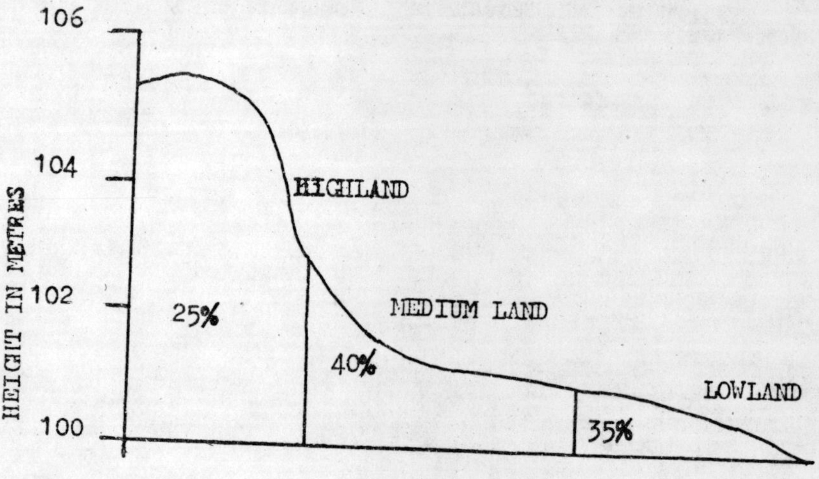

TWENTY FIVE

BASICS OF RURAL SETTLEMENT PLANNING

Planning is concerned with deliberately achieving some objective, and it proceeds by assembling action into some orderly sequence[1]. Rural settlement planning refers to a science and art of ordering land use, settlement siting, buildings and communication network in rural areas to secure maximum practicable economic growth, convenience, and safeguarding the beauty of cultural and natural environments.

Firstly, there may be questions why to plan? for whom to plan? and how to plan?

Secondly, the plan may be fresh one, may need partial modification and sometimes requires complete relocation. Thirdly, the plan may be financed by the government, foreign agencies, cooperative organization and private agencies. Fourthly, the plan may be for short term or long term perspective and rolling plan for long time to come (15 to years or so).

Fifth point is the participants of the plan, which may be the government, people in general, private or foreign agencies, emergency plan, slow dose of the plan, and sometimes it may be a forced plan.

The question what to plan in a settlement? may get the answer that:

(a) planning for site, servicc and sanitation,
(b) planning for residential houses,
(c) planning to increase employment opportunities,
(d) planning for irrigation, agriculture and livestock development,
(e) planning for improving the transport and communication.

The seventh requirement is that rural settlement plan should be integrated with the regional and national plans. All plans are designed for the people, on a particular landscape under certain land use and environmental constraints. Thus the information about physical conditions, current land utilization and population growth is essential for rural settlement planning.

The planning process starts with; resource assessment, village viability assessment, setting the objectives, strategy, evaluation, implementation and monitoring the whole planning process from time to time, so that new ideas can be introduced, alternative strategy can be formulated, and people's choice may be included in the plan.

Review of Literature on settlement Planning

Aspects of human settlement planning edited by Habitat conference secretariat (1978)[2] is a collection of United Nations studies on various aspects of human settlement planning including the elements of health, social services and climate besides examining the role of land use studies, transport networks, public utility services and local administration.

Friedmann and Connell (1983)[3] highlighted multi-disciplinary approach to the general development planning and its goal, and advocate a balance between territory and function in a "communalistic society". Further the authors' look at the disadvantages of the advent of the transnational corporation, which is seen as exploitative in its search for source of cheap labour, besides giving a critical account of rural development strategies.

The Economic Bulletin for Europe (1983)[4] argues that human settlements from the essential physical framework for most other activities of society. Settlement planning should therefore be the basic reference point for all other development planning. Further it suggests that since human settlement entails an adaptation of the environment, the planning of such adaptation to promote development can most successfully be undertaken through action at national and regional levels.

United Nations Centre for Human Settlements (1982)[5] discusses value of remote sensing for human settlement planning. This is true because the applications of remote sensing give us information about land use and its change; providing information on change in the environment and monitoring; contributing knowledge about natural disaster and prediction about floods, drought besides cartographic information.

United Nations Centre for Human Settlements (1981)[6] focuses attention on the question of rural settlements and rural growth centres in relation to rural development policy in developing countries where mostly poor people live in rural ares. Emphasis has been made on agricultural and industrial development, besides rural development in terms of transport, communication, marketing and social services.

Brebner and Briggs (1982)[7] compared the Tanzanian and Algerian policies of creating nucleated village communities with a communal mode of production, highlight differences in planning and building. In both cases the villagization facilitated the provision of services, and the agricultural production is not upto mark due to newer environment and the continuance of drought.

Planning process

In case a planner wishes to know the cause of changes taking place within the planning area, process studies help in explaining the magnitude and direction of changes taking place in terms of other components of the system, which are external to the ecosystem such as economic market forces.

The resource ecosystems are complex which consist of many plant species, animal species and abiotic factors. They also include human population and infrastructure facilities. But the types and methods of process studies should be kept limited to the items included in the analytical survey and inventory unless some excluded components have significant impact in the plan designed. The main objective of process studies is to describe cause and effect relationships using a suitable equation and to measure the coefficients of the equation. The resource system may be explained with classical exponential population growth model. In case of small population, and weather conditions, require probabilistic models. For behavioural process such as population migration and selection of nomadic settlement sites are some of the examples of activities which are difficult to describe through mathematical equations because all these are stochastic processes.

Modern planning theory is based on the notion that all sorts of planning constitute a distinct type of human activity, concerned with controlling a settlement system. It gives an idea that all planning is a continuous process where planner devises appropriate ways of controlling the system concerned, and then by monitoring the effect to see how far the controls have been effective or how far they need subsequent modification.

In Modern Planning, more and more emphasis is given on tracing the possible consequences of alternative policies, and then evaluating them against the objectives in order to choose a preferred course of action. This process should continuously be repeated as the monitoring process throws up divergence views of planner's and the real state of the system.

The modern concept of planning is derived from cybernetics identified in 1948 by Norbert Wiener an American scientist. Cybernetics is essentially a new way of organising existing scientific knowledge about a wide range of phenomena. Through cybernetics many phenomena such as social, economic, biological and physical can be viewed as complex interacting system. By introducing appropriate control mechanisms, the behaviours of the system can be altered in specific ways, to achieve certain objectives on part of the planners. The basic idea is that it is necessary to understand the operation of the system as a whole in order to control it effectively for successful planning.

With this background, now it is possible to present the schematic summaries of planning process set out by three leading British exponents of the systematic planning approach i.e., Brian Mcloughlin, George Chadwick and Alan Wilson. McLoughlin proceeds through a sequence of processes (Fig.25.1)[8] which constantly reiterated through a return loop. After taking a decision for planning, a planner formulates broad goals for a particular system and identifies objective target dates from goals. After these, the planner generally follows the possible course of action, with the help of models which simplify the operation of the system. Further he evaluates the alternatives in relation to his objectives and the resources available. Then he takes action through controls on investment in order to implement the preferred alternative. After sometime the planner again reviews the state of the system to see the progress of the plan, and to start the further course of action.

Chadwick's description of the process is relatively more complex account of the planning sequence (Fig. 25.2). He has made a distinction between the observation of the system under control (right hand side) and the planner's action in devising and testing his control measure (left hand side). Consequently, there are return loops on both sides of the diagram, indicating that the entire process is cyclical. At each stage of the process, the planner has to interrelate his observations of the system with the development of the control measures he intends to apply.

According to Wilson (Fig. 25.2) there are two sides of the planning process which interact, but he presented three levels vertically. The most basic level is called "understanding" or prediction, which is concerned with devising the working tools, in the form of techniques and models, which are necessary for the analysis of the system under control. The second level is related with analysing the problems and synthesizing alternatives. The third level is related with the positive actions which the planner adopts to regulate the system, goal formulation, evaluation of alternatives and actual implementation of the preferred alternative plan.

All these descriptive accounts are quite helpful in understanding the planning process.

Management Units

After defining the decision making process, management units must be selected which lies within the jurisdiction of management authority (states, districts, sub-division, *anchal, Panchayat*, village). Map is an essential element to show the boundaries of various regional units. Generally the selection of management unit requires the consideration of so many factors, such as the facilities of transportation lines, homogeneity of terrain, resources, human population, socio-ethnic homogeneity and diversity[9].

Inventories: Before rural settlement planning the survey of physical, natural and human resources in detail for each management unit is essential. Some data may be more stable whereas others can temporarily be collected from the land. As for example, some settlements are permanent, whereas settlements of nomadic pastoralists are transitory in nature.

Secondly, the inventory data may be classified according to the method of collection. The degree of remoteness of the survey of resource e.g. satellite imageries interpretation, aerial photograph interpretation and land survey largely determines the cost, the time, and the accuracy of making a survey. The survey from remote sensing covers large area but the accuracy will be great. The ground survey is less expensive and hence the accuracy is less in comparison with photo images. It has been realised that a combination of methods may prove to be most cost-effective.

Thirdly, the total ground survey will not have any error but increased precision always involves increased costs. Fourthly, the resources may be measured directly or indirectly. There is little economic justification for very detailed inventories on foreign funding as most of the extensive survey use relatively inaccurate, imprecise and unrepeatable methods.

The rural population values the environmental factor, or the natural endowment of the surroundings of the village, more and more. This trend could be utilized more purposefully to motivate people to stay in rural areas rather than to migrate to towns. Some aspects of these phenomena vary markedly from place to place and thus they fall within the field of geographical research. As is true of other countries, it is not to be expected that generally valid formulas can be found for the dialectic of concentration and dispersion (Cloke, 1982) of rural settlements[10].

Monitoring: Monitoring is a repeated set of inventories. The planners when measure the trends of the quantity and quality of resources, plus their spatial distribution over time, need monitored inventories. These repeated measurements help in correlations and test of significance between these measurements. Monitoring can deal with the questions as:

- Is the number of houses increasing with the increase of population or decreasing?
- Is soil erosion correlated with the distribution of human settlements?
- Whether clustering process is going on in the settlement or the migration of families from the central site leads to fragmentation?
- Are human settlements changing their location and siting?

Such relationships show just the amount of correlation, but they can often give insights into possible causes of change taking place in the structure of settlements. It is necessary to process monitored data quickly either manually or computer or with the help of mathematical models.

Goals, Objectives and Targets:

The steps in planning process include goal formulation, identification of objectives and target setting. Goals are highly abstract and tend to fall into broad categories such as social, economic and aesthetic, and they include qualities of the planning process such as flexibility. On the other hand, objectives are rather more specific and defined in terms of actual programmes capable of being carried into action, with the expenditure of resources and generate an element of competition of scarce resources. Thus in a settlement, movement is the general goal, the resulting objectives might include: a reduction of travel time in the journey to work, an improvement in the quality of public transport, or a programme of village road construction to keep pace with increasing agricultural activities. Finally in third step *targets* represent specific programmes in which criteria of performance are set against target dates. Thus the detailed targets developed from the above objectives might include: the construction of a flood protective embankment around rural settlements within five years or so. "Targets by their nature tend to be very specific and particular; one problem that emerges from the whole goals - objectives target process, therefore is that of integrating rather disparate individual programmes into a coherent plan" (Hall, 1975)[11].

Planning and managing rural settlements presupposes the existence of goals to be achieved. The information about goals is the primary requirements of decision-makers. With respect to rural settlements, there are different levels of decision making, namely, the individual, family, local, regional and national levels. In most cases the goals of these different levels do not agree, besides any given level of decision making, there may be various decision makers, each of them trying to manipulate the same resources and population for conflicting purposes. Proper planning requires that the goals of different levels and sectors be reconciled, and a single multi-sectoral planning agency may be the best way to eliminate inter-sectoral conflict. After recognising the clear cut objectives, the structure of the decision making process must be defined in order to facilitate detailed allocation of decision to appropriate levels and to formalize the information required for each levels.

Simulation: Simulation is a mathematical tool designed to predict the future state of a system. In simulation, the planner is required to apply mathematical equations to describe expected changes in the resource and ecological system. Such predictions are usually a set of differential equations which consitute a hypothesis about future conditions. Each equation may be an outcome of individual process study. Hence, the study of process is quite essential for successful prediction of future state of settlements.

Optimal Choice: With the help of optimal choice, the planner gets the idea of best management decisions. The set of statistical or mathematical techniques which facilitate the choice of options is known as operations research or the science of management.

Linear programming is a mathematical tool for optimum assumption of any problem by minimizing and maximizing the objective function under certain constraints.

Example 1: The problem concerns the selection of a suitable site for seed farm which requires 30 male labourers and 20 female labourers. There are two families living 40 kms apart from which the male and female labourers can be obtained. Family X can supply 1 male and 1 female labourers daily whereas family Y can supply 3 male and 2/3 female labourer. The problem is to find out the best site for the seed farm so that there is no surplus male or female labourers.

Now:-

X can supply 1 male and 1 female labourers
Y can supply 3 male and 2/3 female labourers.
X and Y are two families living 40 Kms apart.

Requirements = 30 male labourers
20 female labourers

(a) Location of seed farm by supply of labour is objective function

(b) $1X + 3Y = 30$

$1X + \frac{2}{3}Y = 20$ Constraints

(C) $X \geq 0, \; Y \geq 0$ Non-negativity constraints.

Mathematical Solution of the Constraints:

$$1X + 3Y = 30$$

$$\underline{1X + \frac{2}{3}Y = 20}$$

$$0 + \frac{2}{3}Y = 30 - 20$$

$$(3 - \frac{2}{3})Y = 10$$

$$\left(\frac{9 - 2}{3}\right)Y = 10$$

$$\frac{7}{3}Y = 10, \therefore 7Y = 30$$

$$Y = \frac{30}{7}$$

$$Y = 4.3$$

$$X + 3Y = 30$$

$$X + 3 \times \frac{30}{7} = 30$$

$$X + \frac{90}{7} = 30 ; X = 30 - \frac{90}{7} X = \frac{210 - 90}{7}$$

$$X = \frac{120}{7} = 17.1$$

Graphical solution

$$1X + 3Y = 30$$

$$Then\, if\ X = 0, Y = \frac{30}{3} = 10 (10.0)$$

if $\frac{2}{3}Y$ is = 0 then X = 30

$$Similarly: 1X + \frac{2}{3}Y = 20$$

$$if\ X = 0\ then\ \frac{2}{3}Y = \frac{20}{1}$$

$$Y = \frac{20}{1} X \frac{3}{2} = 30$$

if $\frac{2}{3}Y$ is 0 then X is 20

(30, 0)

(0, 20)

X = 17.7

Solution point value.

Y = 4.4

Now when X family supplies 17 male and 17 female labourers then
X = 34 (17+17) X1 : Y1

For Y family supplies

3 x 4.4 = 13 male
2/3 x 4.4 = 3 female

Y = 16
34 + 16 = 50

30 + 20 = 50

Male Female

If a is the distance from X family

and b is the distance from Y family

Now we want to equate the load kilometres of labourers to establish a seed farm.

In case two labourers are coming on one load kms. Then load km from family X is $\frac{34a}{2} = 17a$.

Loads kms from family Y = $\frac{16b}{2} = 8b$

$\therefore$ 17a = 8b.

As the families are 40 kms. apart, therefore a + b = 40.

Therefore we required to solve

$$17a = 8b \quad \text{I}$$
$$a + b = 40 \quad \text{II}$$

From II inference B = 40 - a

Substituting in I 17a = 8(40 - a)

$$17a = 320 - 8a$$
$$17a + 8a = 320$$

$$25a = 320$$
$$a = \frac{320}{25} = 12.8$$

Kilometres from family X.

b = 40 - 12.8

= 27.2 Kilometres from Y.

Plan Design and Evaluation:

The design of the rural settlement plan essentially consists of two elements. Firstly, the choice of system models to represent the main elements which the design should incorporate, and it should give a coherent and realistic picture of the future state of the system in temporal dimension. Secondly, the process of evaluation gives a preferred or optimum solution. At this stage, the goals and objectives which the planner has formulated are applied directly to the alternative simulations of the future state of the system. In a nutshell, evaluation consists of any process which seeks preferences among the various orders of the system. It is little concerned with benefit-cost analysis or economic evaluation.

Implementing the Plan: After systematic evaluation of alternatives, the planner can select a more desired course of action for implementation. In the planning process, the whole exercise of modeling, evaluation and selection are continuously repeated under the control of monitoring system. It is necessary to control the progress of the system which responds flexibility and sensitivity to the information conveyed by the monitoring system.

The monitoring system tests the correspondence between the real world situation and the model designed for such a plan.

Policies on Habitat Planning

In most of the developed and developing countries of the world, the local governments have formulated various policies for the planned development of settlements. Those are as follows: Direct construction of houses on developed site, habitat site development, provision of cheap roof and wall materials, financing for new house construction and repair, and the last is standard setting.

Direct Construction of Houses:

Many countries faced with the problem of housing shortage and hence either internally or with the help of foreign or international agencies, the local governments have embarked on the direct construction of house and the development of residential estates. Such houses are mostly occupied by the middle income group people under the programme of providing low cost housing. It is really a gigantic-task for most of the national governments, however the governments are constructing houses and subletting on subsidised rate, because it is beyond the capacity of urban residents to purchase land and build such nice houses.

Site Development: In site development the government provides the infrastructure of roads, water supply, electricity, drains and sewerage, and the layout of plots which are purchased by the people at cheaper cost through cooperative society.

In urban areas site development brings orderly development especially for the middle and upper income group people. It has slight difference with the site-service provision in the low income residential districts, whose main aim is to enhance environmental conditions in accordance with the magnitude of problem.

Provision of Building Materials

Some governments e.g. Tanzania, Zambia and Kenya in Africa have policies to help low income group people by providing subsidized building material for the construction of houses. Such a provision may improve living conditions in the existing environment, but such help should be arranged with locally available building materials rather than importing on higher costs.

Financing For the purposes of house construction, the availability of finance is a big problem in almost all continents whether it is Latin America, Africa, and Asia. Mainly Life Insurance Corporations Loan, Provident Fund loan against fixed deposit and in some places housing loan by the government are serving the purpose especially in urban areas, but for the rural people the situation is truly alarming.

Standard Setting: Nowadays this is a job of municipality and corporation engineers to pass the housing design of a householder. Illegal construction is generally, not permitted. Such provision is essential in order to maintain the habitable environments. For poor migrants it may be a problem.

Rural Settlement Planning in India

Rural development has assumed a new dimension in Indian planning especially after independence (1947). Villages, Development Blocks and Districts are considered as spatial units for micro-level planning in the context of integrated multi-level planning. This hierarchy of spatial units relates mainly to the development of rural areas. According to a committee on Block Level Planning in India, the national objectives are as follows:

(1) Optimum utilization of potential resources to increase income and employment, (2) Ensuring the benefits accrued from the development programme to the weaker sections of the population in particular, (3) Realistic formulation of the minimum needs programme and creation of social and economic infrastructure to achieve the above objectives, (4) Re-orientation of the institutional set up and building up of appropriate organizational frame to protect the rights and privileges of the poor with progressive promotion of an egalitarian structure of ownership of national assets and utilization of the basic resource at every area level.

In order to achieve the above objectives, it is required to start development work at lowest level everywhere simultaneously so that, ultimately each area and village communities will be involved in the task of rural settlement planning and upliftment of the rural economy.

In India near about 75 per cent people live in villages and still our villages are neglected, despised and altogether giving a look of rural slum due to lack of proper drains, muddy ditches, inter-village narrow unmetalled roads, rudimentary houses, insanitary condition, zig zag lanes, illiterate people and subsistence agricultural economy. Although during prehistoric to historic times "the village Republics of India had been celebrated for their remarkable vitality, organized life and tough tenacity in planned and ordered self-sufficiency", but now with the increase of population manifold, ravages of droughts, floods, and war have dismantled the village life to a begging bowl from centuries. Hence in order to improve the material conditions of our villages Albert Mayer's (1946)[12] "Preliminary outline for village Planning and Reconstruction" proposed one basic pilot project as to establish some "model villages" which would emphasize good housing, sanitation, and sound community structure which have been considered here.

In order to evolve a real programme that can be carried out successfully we may call them purely physical and functional phase, the following items will enter:

1. Better housing in physical space, their arrangement, quality and permanency.
2. Intercommunicating system of simple but all-weather roads to some center for regular reliable disposal of produce.
3. Sanitation–personal hygiene, sewage disposal, drainage.
4. Water supply and distribution.
5. Maximum local irrigation obtainable, and tie-in with any larger schemes, either existing being developed or proposed.
6. Dispensary, clinics and hospital facilities should be arranged.
7. Mosquito and Malaria control.
8. Schools, colleges and training centres arranged.
9. Community house and recreation centre.
10. Meeting house for local council (*panchayat*) or other local governmental or administrative unit (may occupy some physical space as community house).

11. Warehouse if required, and
12. Possibly small building for small machines, looms and so on, which may be justified by local cottage industries; possibly also for central storage of cooperatively used farm implements.

Preliminary Outline for Village Planning and Reconstruction

The objective is essentially the physical and social reconstruction of the village, so planned and carried out that its result will be sought, valued and retained by the villager.

The plan is flexible at this stage, and subject to change and adjustable.

The Three Steps

The first approach is economic, in terms of more or better product and income in agriculture, animal husbandry, irrigation, marketing, roads, consolidation of holdings, cooperative farming, fish culture, local industry - not all of these at any one place, especially at the start, but choosing as a spearhead including the accomplishment of various other objectives. At this stage or village level there should be no propaganda for planning, and the villager should not even be aware that we are working on a certain plan.

Secondly, attempt has been made to capitalize the recognized benefit to gain the villager's goodwill and confidence, to pave the way for acceptance of, and demand for, ultimate all-round benefits, less readily understood should be the friend of farmers who help them in needs and uses educational methods in order to prepare them further.

In the third phase, the general improvement of the quality of village life, health, sanitation, housing, and community facilities not only should be acceptable to villagers, but should be demanded by them. By this time the work and the attitude should be self-continuing and self-propagating, so that the improvement does not disappear when our main pressure is removed. Village participation and finally village initiative on the broadest front should have emerged.

Although these three phases have been delineated separately, but in practice they are not entirely separate, but will overlap and intermingle. The actual sequence and rate of speed will vary in each locality, both because we will try different methods and rates of application, and because reactions will differ in different localities. Where our work proceeds most successfully it is hoped to reach objective in three or four years; in other cases it will take longer time. This does not mean that the reconstruction job will have been completed then. No matter how rapid the rate of diffusion of our ideas and subsequent demand, completion of the physical program by the villagers alone would be far beyond the economic and financial possibilities. But in some instances it should be completed to generate guideline for others.

Scope: The work should be done on a scale that will be neither so small as to be meaningless, nor so large that personal observation and check are not adequate. It is proposed to select one *anchal* in each district, so that work should proceed over 100 to 150 villages in each district at a time.

The reason for preferring this method as compared with concentration on all villages in a district is because we intend to use methods to provoke curiosity and demand from neighbouring villages where the plan is progressing, so that the number of interested villages should increase of their own volition. This will be one of the tests of the success of our work.

Methods

1. **Village and Group Level**: At this level, village level worker (VLW) is the representative and he becomes the funnel through which the help of all the development departments will become available to the villager. Besides this Agricultural Department's, rural development organizer, and other department's representatives will be constantly available and working in the village.

The rural development organizer will also handle ordinary matters of public health and sanitation. He will be able to command a high level advice in place of the present multi low-level people. For farm management, the expert and the villager need the help of each other.

2. *Anchal* **organization**: At this level Block Development officer acts as planner-cum-administrator who will be one of the members of the district committee. The planning should be decentralized; initiative should come from the bottom up, and the field in.

3. **District Plans**: Each of the development department has certain plans for districts in the state. The central planning committee will examine the district plans and coordinate them in time and space with the local plans.

4. **Physical Plans: Community Facilities**

The aim is to reorganize the physical frame and rebuild it - and hence the social life of the village may also be organized automatically. The physical work will have to be done essentially *in situ*. The present village layout is typically uneconomical with excessive winding roads and lanes, and insanitary open areas clustered with ruined walls and malaria - breeding depressions. If we do not reorganize physically, the first cost and maintenance cost of drainage, sanitation, and rubbish control will be excessive if not impossible.

5. **Housing and Village Replanning**

There is considerable interest on the part of some individuals in improving their houses or rebuilding. Some villagers are considering to start a new. The severe shortage of brick, cement, and corrugated sheet and iron made it necessary that new methods be found for which materials are available to the villagers. This problem can be met to some extent by demonstrating stabilized earth construction methods. The new town of Mahewa - while small at present, is developing into a market center. A new market is desired, and considerable interest has been shown on the part of some in putting up new shops, clearing the village lanes, and making a more or less model village of this center. Besides existing resources some stimulating subsidy should be given to such village for organizing the leadership of the village, draining stagnant pools, or grading village lanes. Technical assistance should be given to those individuals who wish to rebuild or repair their own houses. To effectuate plans and ideas, there must be an agreed and detailed frame work.

New framework of relationships must be provided in new kinds of nation-building effort, if the degree of devotion, the sustained efforts, the enthusiasm, and the thoroughness that have been the major factors in the successful Etawah pattern are to survive there or elsewhere.

Housing in Gorakhpur

A second example of successful fostered self-help comes from Gorakhpur, where, in addition to road-building work and local flood control, a housing project was carried through, both to take care of urgent needs and as a demonstration of a way to handle other future needs.

While the mud houses that are the village homes of all but a very few families are certainly primitive, both as physical shelter and with respect to any sanitation, the landless labourers of the lowest castes (Harijans) live in hovels that are indescribably poor.

"The roofs were very low and had no tile. A man could hardly pass in through the door, and he could hardly stand erect in the room. The size of one of these huts in which several families managed to live, was generally about 2m x 3m.. In these huts too they somehow had to store grain, and to keep their few other belongings as well".[13]

Ultimately, India may be able to afford good housing, but for a long time, at least, it is the kind of improved housing we have described that has an important part to play, and it is technological improvement at this level that is badly needed.

Model houses whose construction has been advocated in the Five-Year Plans have been constructed at many places to serve as a guide for the villagers. Such model houses built with local materials and having all the modern amenities should be constructed at the headquarter of each village level worker and should serve the purpose of his residence.

The result of the construction work

"Every family now has its own home, each with two rooms and a verandah. There is no doubling up now. The front verandah measures 3m x 7m. There is no courtyard at present, but the place left behind each house for the courtyard and kitchen garden is 4m x 8m. The people will add these later when they find time. They have more rooms, more space, and good surroundings which look better in their opinion, too. Every family member can share the rays of the sun which they could not get previously" (Mayer, 1959).[14]

6. Principles of Realistic Planning

Once the activities comprising a development program are determined, the quantity, timing, and distribution of those activities must be decided, and their results studied. The several elements must, in other words, be organized into a specific plan. From experience in the Uttar Pradesh pilot project there begins to emerge a distinctive theory of realistic planning. Discussions of the principles of targeting, scheduling, and self-checking are reproduced below from newsletters written by Mayer to co-workers and interested friends.

There are two main enemies of realistic planning for rural development :

First is orders coming out from headquarters, where some highly placed person has suddenly had a bright idea and glibly drawn up schemes, each one of which makes a brave showing on paper and quite satisfies the makers, but which just cannot be done thoroughly and lastingly on any such scale as visualized, or in any such number and variety.

The other is people in the field who have not been previously consulted and who don't want to stick their necks out by saying they cannot do it, taking the risk of being the only one's to do so.

Rural settlement planning must be realistic and operational in nature following the situation and data analysis of a particular area in question, and must be oriented towards the needs of people of that area. Also planners require to create an atmosphere which allows people's participation, and must make sure that all organs and government parastatals who are supposed to implement must be coordinated in all sections of the plan.

Hence planning always involves conflict of values, clash of organized pressure groups, defence of vested interests, and the confusions may arise with the interrelationship of complex decisions, at different levels, at different scales and in different point of time. The use of cybernetics is a great help to the planner, in coming to a particular decision, but its decision may not always be a rational one for the villagers. Because the village is a place of face to face relationship and self expression, the planner should maintain this character in rural settlement planning for development.

REFERENCES

1. Peter Hall: *Urban and Regional Planning;* Penguin Books, Hamondsworth, 1975, pp. 1-2.
2. *Aspects of Human Settlement Planning,* Edited by Habitat Conference Secretariat, New York, Pergamon, 1978, p. 288.
3. J. Friedmann, T. Wheelwright, J. Connell; "Development Strategies in the Eighties". University of Sydney, 1980, p. 121.
4. "Human Settlements: Key Factor" in *Economic and Social Development,* Oxford: Pergamon Press, 1983, p. 158.
5. Remote Sensing for Human Settlements: Contribution of the United Nations Centre for Human Settlements; *Habitat*; 1982, p. 20.
6. "Development of Rural Settlements and Growth Areas, Nairobi, Kenya", *Habitat,* 1981, p. 48.
7. P. Brebner and J. Briggs; Rural Settlement Planning in Algeria and Tanzania: A Comparative Study; *Habitat International*, Vol. 6, No. 516, 1982, pp. 621-628.
8. Peter Hall, *op. cit.,* pp. 272-274.
9. D.G. Peden; *Arid Land Settlements:* "Satisfying Information Needs for Planning with Mathematical Models and Computer Technology", UNCHS (HABITAT) Technical Notes, 7 June, 1983.
10. P.J. Cloke; "Rethinking Rural Settlement Planning", *Institute Tejdscher Voor economics in Social geografy,* Vol. 73, No. 5, 1982, pp. 280-285.
11. Peter Hall, *op. cit.*, p. 275.
12. Albert Mayer et al.; *The Story of Rural Development at Etawah Uttar Pradesh:* Pilot Project, India, University of California Press, Berkeley, 1959.
13. *Ibid.*
14. *Ibid.*

Fig. 25.1

Model of Plan Implementation Process by Mcloughlin (After-P. Hall, 1975)

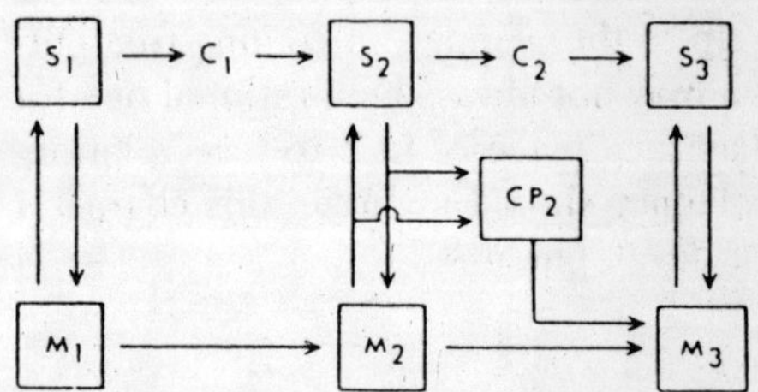

S - Surveys of the real world
C - Control mechanisms
M - Models, forecasts and plans
CP - Comparative analyses of models versus the real world

The plan implementation process, according to Brian McLoughlin. This formulation, in which models interact with surveys of the real world through comparative analyses, and in which control processes are then applied to the real-world situation, draws heavily on analogies and insights from the science of cybernetics.

Fig. 25.2

Model of planning process by McLoughlin, Chadwick and Wilson

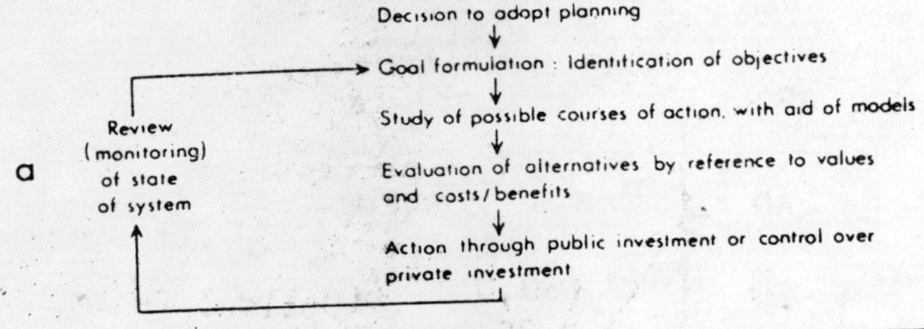

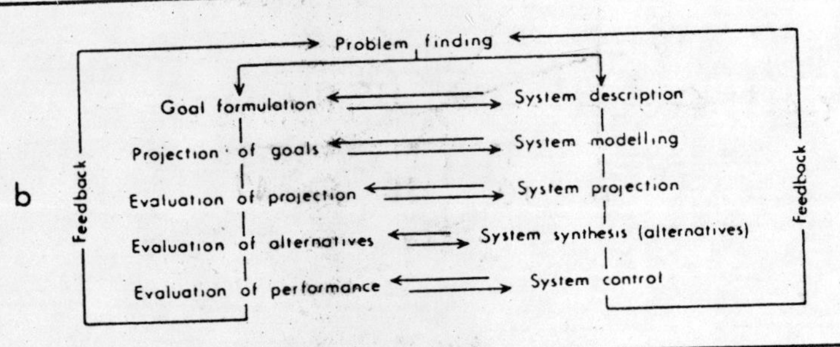

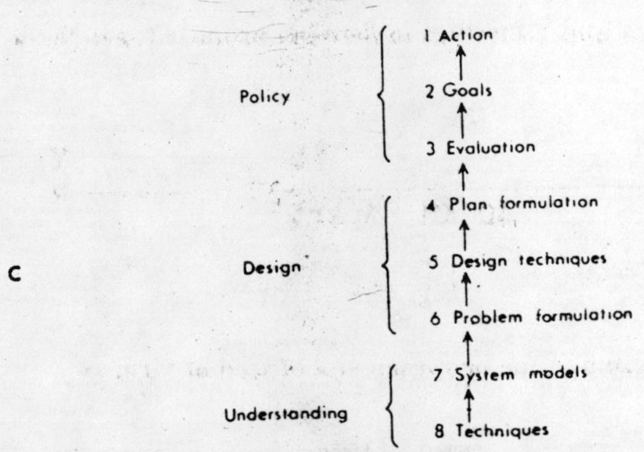

Three concepts of the planning process: (a) Brian McLoughlin; (b) George Chadwick; (c) Alan Wilson. During the 1960s interest developed in systematizing the process of planning, with a new stress on modelling and evaluating alternative designs or courses of actions. These formulations drew heavily from the new sciences of cybernetics and systems analysis.

Fig. 25.3

Use of linear programming in rural settlement planning

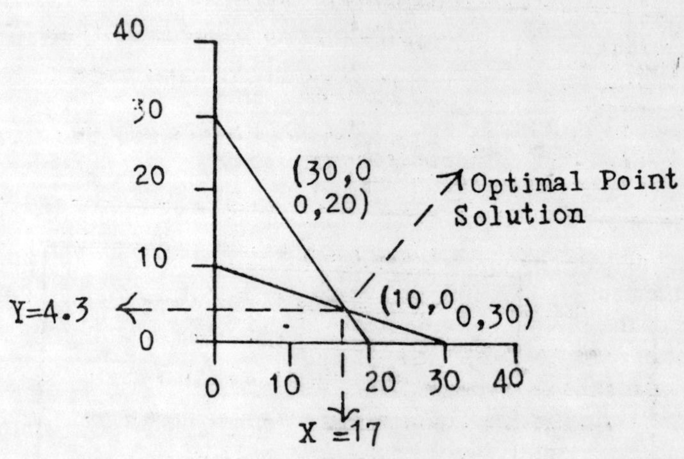

Fig. 25.4

Location of X and Y families in between proposed seed farm

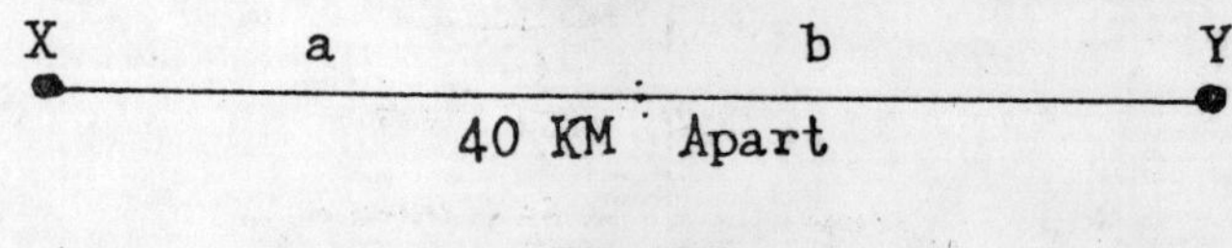

Fig. 25.5

Selection of the proposed site of seed of farm

SEED FARM
12.8 KM
X
Y
27.2 KM

TWENTY SIX

CONCLUSIONS

Settlement Geography which developed in the twentieth century, is one of the recent branches of human geography. Settlement is a symbol of man's occupance of land, and serves as the link between the man and the environment. Since the greater part of the region is rural and agricultural in character, a study of rural settlements of the region is important.

The region has an ancient civilization. The nomadic and semi-nomadic people of early history led an unsettled life, based upon hunting, fishing and gathering. Permanent settlements came into existence with the introduction of agriculture in the region in Vedic times. Today the region is densely settled on account of fertile soil and a warm humid climate, though there are variations on account of the diversities in physical, economic and cultural environment in different parts of the area. The geographical analysis of the settlement patterns, processes, types, hierarchy and mutual relationships through size and spacing in the Bihar Plain in relation to other parts of the World forms the subject matter of this study.

Some common concepts, approaches and principles have been evolved for the study and location of rural settlements. The concepts of settlement geography are found to be changing in time. Similarly, the approaches of the study are also changing from descriptive to quantitative. The location of rural settlement is determined by the ecological balance of different factors available in the region. In different environmental conditions the factors of location of rural settlements are varied in nature which invite geographers to formulate different models and hypotheses with the help of ideographic and nomothetic approaches of study. An attempt has been made here to deal with all these aspects of rural settlement geography.

The evolution of rural settlement has been traced during different historical periods, from prehistoric times to the post independence period. The region was inhabited even during the prehistoric times long before the Aryan occupance, and gradually it became the meeting ground of different cultures. Later, the Mediterranean Armenoids and the Munda speaking Proto-Indices came into contact with each other. The contact between the Aryans and the non-Aryans brought significant changes in the ethnic character. This was followed by the growth of Budhist culture. Its impact in prevailing upon Hindu culture was profound. In the medieval period the Hindus and the Muslims came into contact with each other, resulting in the evolution of a new society. The Mughals organised the area into one unit, while the British further consolidated it. After independence, multi-faced developments such as exploitation of resources, rise in agricultural production, control of flood by terrain taming and development of transport routes have accelerated the pace of urbanization in the region.

Location guides the function and significance of a rural settlement, whereas morphology is the direct product of the ground upon which settlement stands. This study classifies the locational and siting conditions of rural settlements besides examining *the interfluve settlement site theory* and need for the upgradation of rural settlement sites.

The national settlement system spatially encompasses from village level centres upto the highest order settlement of a nation in terms of linkages, interactions, spatial arrangement, hierarchy and functional relations. The present settlement system of most of the developing countries reflects the cultural heritage, colonization patterns, local resource development, and the present socio-economic and demographic policies of the government.

The salient features of distribution and density of rural settlements and their types and patterns in the Bihar Plain have been examined in detail, besides the general conditions obtaining in India, Israel, Ghana, Africa and the World. The density is found to depend upon agricultural prosperity of the region, while the settlement type appears to be closely associated with it. Four types of rural settlements have been distinguished by calculating the dispersal index, whose distribution is dependent upon physiography, soil fertility, water supply, agricultural production, and recurrence of floods. In other words, they are the direct results of geographical environment under which the region has been settled. Settlement patterns on the other hand are a product of historical evolution and cultural environment. Most villages are unplanned, and hence a large number of patterns can be distinguished, the common ones are basically the same. They are distinct from the pattern obtaining in western countries.

Satellite settlement is a secondary or a subsidiary settlement, maintaining close links with the central settlement. Although under agricultural economy where the land is either marginally poor or under intensive use, satellite settlement is considered as essential in order to save the travel time, but in India the satellite settlements are occupied by the lower castes such as *dom*, *chamar*, *paswan* and *Pasi* who constitute the indispensable agricultural labour force. These appendage habitations known as *tolas* are located within a kilometre of the principal habitation, as the orthodox upper castes cannot tolerate the untouchables living near them. Thus a sort of social segregation has taken place. On the other hand, in Tanzania and Algeria the government has impressed people to come to central ujamaa villages by leaving the satellite dispersed hamlet in order to reap the rewards of cooperation, government assistance and planned living through socialism and self-reliance.

The growth and development of rural settlements in Tanzania is quite novel in its characteristics of self-reliance and socialistic pattern. It has been found that the majority of Tanzanians live in their huts and cottages of ujamaa villages which are in most cases compact and semi-compact planned rural settlements mainly established after relocation from the earlier abode of dispersed living in forests. Hence, nowadays ujamaa living is the major instrument of integrated rural development. Here investigations have been made about the patterns of rural settlement growth and distribution in Tanzania with special reference to villagization program at national, regional, district and village levels besides delineating types, patterns, regional characteristics of development of traditional rural settlements.

The average spacing between settlements depends upon fertility of land and floods, the villages being relatively smaller in size and closely set together as the fertility increases and the danger of floods removed. The number of large villages is, however, small and villages of small population size are relatively much greater in number both in the Bihar Plain and Bagamoyo district of Tanzania.

Resettlement schemes have been found in different parts of the world especially in areas of flood, drought, famine, war and by special legislation of the government as in Tanzania and Algeria. Although in each resettlement scheme there is a lot of expense but their success is everywhere in tranquillity due to unsettled mind of such resettlers whose cultivated land is either too away from the resettlement site or due to multiple problems of new environment on resettlement site.

In aerial photographs and satellite imageries due to immense scale reductions they have limited use in rural settlement study. But, nowadays, they are considered as scientific tools of settlement study with the help of stereoscope and some other precision instruments. The device is so developed that the number of storeys of houses, number of cattle grazing in the field, diseased crops and plants, movement of armies and artillery or any other items spatially distributed and their changing character can be analysed through satellite imageries of various times in a day, month and year.

The character of houses depends on two factors: type of building materials available locally, and the economic conditions of the house owners. Thus they are the product of physical and economic environment, with cultural factors being of secondary importance. Houses in the moist and flood affected north-eastern parts are generally built with arboreal matter, while mud and tiles predominate in the drier south-east. Different cultural groups, however, have used these materials differently. At the same time, the size and plan of houses are profoundly affected by economic conditions, so that in all areas the houses of the poor are small, one roomed structure, built mainly with bamboos and grasses while the rich prefer mud, tiles, bricks and RCC.

An attempt has been made to put the above conclusions on a scientific footing by applying statistical techniques in distinguishing density zones, house types, settlement types and spacing. It is believed that these techniques and the general laws resulting therefrom are capable of application in other areas under Indian conditions. The author has also tried to coin a few new terms like 'social and economic capitals' and 'central villages' which seem to better describe the conditions obtaining in the region. Based on the fixed geometric form of village pattern, a new method has been developed for the determination of settlement patterns and this would be marked by compact settlements, while those having amorphous patterns would be marked by sprinkled settlements. Such statistical analyses tend to describe the subject scientifically and logically, as distinguished from mere descriptive geography.

The analyses of functional hierarchy of settlements are based upon similar statistical techniques. This has been attempted at four levels by determining the number and character of:

(a) Rural service centres;
(b) Rurban centres;
(c) Centres of trade and commerce; and
(d) Central places.

The distribution of rural service centres has been analysed to distinguish service zones, and has been correlated with density of transport routes. In case of rurban centres, a new method has been devised to distinguish them from both rural and urban settlements and a composite list of towns and villages has been prepared depending upon certain statistical formulae suggested. The hierarchy of rurban centres is based upon their rurban index values, while a correlation matrix of thirteen nodal functions illustrates the interrelationship of these functions and their role in rurban centres.

The study of commercial centres is based upon extensive field work and statistical analyses of data. Of necessity, the list of such centres is a combination of both towns and villages, since both fall in a continuous hierarchy so far as this function is concerned. The analysis has revealed that there is a direct correlation between the population of a centre, the functional types of functional units, and the hierarchy is determined by nodal functions available in the centre.

The central place theory is similarly concerned with both urban and rural settlements as they form part of the same continuum. A number of parameters were considered and the nodality values and functional indices were calculated, and finally grouped into a hierarchical pattern. They seem to fall into K = 3 network suggested by Christaller, but differ slightly from the theoretical model postulated. It is concluded that this deviation is due to the economic backwardness of the region and lack of transport routes due to which the pattern has not been able to develop fully.

The author has also summarized the broad findings of statistical analyses and case study into five settlement regions which are based on physical conditions, housing conditions, settlement density, types and patterns. These are:

(a) The zone of North-western Champaran;
(b) The Eastern zone of Saharsa and Purnea;
(c) The Southern zone of Chotanagpur Scarp Belt;
(d) The Riverine Belt of North Bihar; and
(e) The Central Ganga Belt.

An attempt has also been made to determine the rural-urban link, the impact of town on their countryside, and the problems of rural settlements. Analyses of growth centres and growth Poles have been made in terms of service potentialities, which may assist in regional planning in the area.

It has been realised, nowadays, that the conflict between man and nature has reached a disastrous proportion in many places. Hence in almost all countries of the world the consequences are leading to death from a new type of disease besides deprivation, desertification, drought and destruction of human settlements and natural environment. It has been observed that the modification of environmental pollution is possible by way of judicious use, preservation and protection of resources and the natural environment.

In any area the planning of rural settlements requires the assessment of resources available in the surrounding area of that site, so that in future the village may prosper and the inhabitants will be getting a proper sustenance for leading a happy life.

Through processes of investigation, plan formulation, monitoring and evaluation in time the success of rural settlement planning may be achieved, but it should be realistic and operational in nature following the situation and data analysis of a particular area in question, and must be oriented according to the needs of that area. The planners should also be required to create an atmosphere which allows people's participation, and must make sure that all organs and government parastatals who are supposed to implement must be coordinated in all sections of the plan.

Practically all conclusions and statistical analysis have been depicted here with the help of maps and diagrams which fully illustrate the broad findings of this study.

INDEX